Lossberg's War

Foreign Military Studies

History is replete with examples of notable military campaigns and exceptional military leaders and theorists. Military professionals and students of the art and science of war cannot afford to ignore these sources of knowledge or limit their studies to the history of the U.S. armed forces. This series features original works, translations, and reprints of classics outside the American canon that promote a deeper understanding of international military theory and practice.

Series Editor: Roger Cirillo

An AUSA Book

Lossberg's War

The World War I Memoirs of a German Chief of Staff

Fritz von Lossberg

Edited and Translated by
Major General David T. Zabecki, USA (Ret.), and
Lieutenant Colonel Dieter J. Biedekarken, USA (Ret.)

Foreword by Holger H. Herwig

The original German edition of this book was published as *Meine Tätigkeit im Weltkriege 1914–1918* (Berlin: Mittler und Sohn, 1939).

Scholarly publisher for the Commonwealth,
serving Bellarmine University, Berea College, Centre College of Kentucky, Eastern Kentucky University, The Filson Historical Society, Georgetown College, Kentucky Historical Society, Kentucky State University, Morehead State University, Murray State University, Northern Kentucky University, Transylvania University, University of Kentucky, University of Louisville, and Western Kentucky University.

Editorial and Sales Offices: The University Press of Kentucky
663 South Limestone Street, Lexington, Kentucky 40508-4008
www.kentuckypress.com

Library of Congress Cataloging-in-Publication Data

Names: Lossberg, Fritz von, 1868-1942, author. | Zabecki, David T., translator. | Biedekarken, Dieter J., translator.
Title: Lossberg's war : the World War I memoirs of a German Chief of Staff / Fritz von Lossberg ; edited and translated by Major General David T. Zabecki, USA (Ret.), and Lieutenant Colonel Dieter J. Biedekarken, USA (Ret.) ; Foreword by Holger H. Herwig.
Other titles: Meine Tätigkeit im Weltkriege 1914-1918. German | World War I memoirs of a German Chief of Staff
Description: Lexington, Kentucky : University Press of Kentucky, [2017] | Series: Foreign military studies | Originally published: Meine Tätigkeit Weltkriege 1914-1918. Berlin : Mittler und Sohn, 1939. | "Lossberg's 1939 prologue" — Chief of Staff of the XIII Army Corps — Division Chief of the General Staff of the Supreme Command of the Field Army (OHL) — Chief of the General Staff of the Third Army (Champagne, 1915) — Chief of the General Staff of the Second Army (The Somme, 1916) — Chief of the General Staff of the First Army (The Somme, 1916) — Chief of the General Staff of the Sixth Army (Arras, 1917) — Chief of the General Staff of the Fourth Army (Flanders, 1917) — Chief of the General Staff of Army Group Boehn — Chief of the General Staff of Army Group Duke Albrecht of Württemberg — After the War — Appendix A. Lossberg's Chronology — Appendix B. Lossberg's Medals and Decorations — Appendix C. The Prussian/German staff system, 1806-1918." | Includes bibliographical references and index.
Identifiers: LCCN 2017032725| ISBN 9780813169804 (hardcover : alk. paper) | ISBN 9780813169811 (pdf) | ISBN 9780813169828 (epub)
Subjects: LCSH: Lossberg, Fritz von, 1868-1942. | World War, 1914-1918—Personal narratives, German. | World War, 1914-1918—Campaigns—Western Front. | Generals—Germany—Biography. | Defensive (Military science) | World War, 1914-1918—Germany.
Classification: LCC D531 .L65 2017 | DDC 940.4/1343092 [B] —dc23
LC record available at https://lccn.loc.gov/2017032725

This book is printed on acid-free paper meeting the requirements of the American National Standard for Permanence in Paper for Printed Library Materials.

Manufactured in the United States of America.

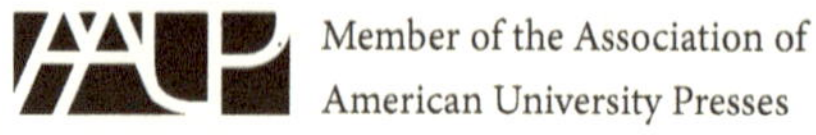

In memory of *Gefreiter* Hans-Werner Biedekarken,
23rd Reserve Field Artillery Regiment,
23rd (Royal Saxon) Reserve Division,
who died in action at the age of nineteen on 1 January 1918.

Contents

Maps

Foreword

Fritz von Lossberg: Lion of the Defensive or Rigoletto?

In the preface to his book, Lossberg casually states: "During the Great War I served as the chief of staff of German combat formations nine times in an uninterrupted sequence." Those assignments included, in succession, the XIII Württemberg Corps; German Fifth, Sixth and Ninth Armies; division chief in the Army Supreme Command (OHL); chief of staff of Third, Second, First, Sixth, and Fourth Armies; and finally chief of staff of Army Group Boehn and Army Group Duke Albrecht of Württemberg. He was the fireman of the German armies in the West. Wherever a breakthrough occurred, Lossberg was hastily dispatched to put out the fire. Not surprisingly, his role was controversial. To his supporters, he was the "lion of the defensive" (*Abwehrlöwe*); to his detractors, he was Rigoletto, the court jester of Giuseppe Verdi's opera by the same name.

Born into a military family from Electoral Hesse, Lossberg joined the Prussian Army in 1886 and experienced the customary rotation of line and General Staff assignments before 1914. He entered the war in the rank of lieutenant colonel with the XIII Corps. Lossberg was a fervent devotee of the Schlieffen Plan and blamed the Younger Moltke for the failure to execute the plan, by allowing the reckless advance of Seventh Army into Lorraine, by sending two corps to the East on the eve of the Battle of the Marne, and by remaining far behind the fighting front at Luxembourg. Lossberg's transfer into OHL as deputy chief of operations in January 1915 was unfortunate: he was constantly at odds with Moltke's chief of operations, Colonel Gerhard Tappen, who vetoed Lossberg's transfer of junior staff officers to the front to gain combat experience.

With regard to the war of attrition raging in the West, Lossberg stood firm with Moltke's successor, Erich von Falkenhayn: every inch of territory was to be held regardless of cost. Thus, when Lossberg, only recently promoted to the grade of colonel, was dispatched to the Champagne in September 1915 to shore up the crumbling front of the Third Army, he immediately commanded that the frontline trace be held at all costs. The Lossberg command style was simple and consistent: upon arriving at any new position, he toured the front, interviewed all division commanders and their chiefs of staff, and insisted on open and frequent communication between front and headquarters. Only then did he report to his superior—to demand the right to make decisions on the spot (*Vollmacht*) and without the consent of his army commander. Over time, Lossberg developed such confidence in his frontline battalion commanders that he allowed them total control over their sectors. After all, they had superior knowledge of the terrain, manpower, and materiel. By 1917 he had introduced that same decentralized control system at the divisional command level as well.

When he was transferred to the Second Army in July 1916, Lossberg brought with him the Falkenhayn dictum that no square inch of hard-won land be abandoned. His new superior, General Fritz von Below, concurred: "The enemy will be able to advance only over corpses."

But the horrendous Somme slaughter constituted a learning curve for Lossberg, now chief of staff of the First Army. He listened to fellow junior officers, such as Max Bauer and Hermann Geyer, who argued for a more flexible defense fought behind the front line. From his headquarters at Bourlon, he ordered that the leading trenches no longer be packed with infantry, that second and third lines of defense be sited on reverse slopes wherever possible, and that these troops be schooled to counterattack the advancing enemy. Daily, Lossberg and his commander toured the front.

Whatever reservations Lossberg still harbored about the elastic defense in depth developed by Bauer and Geyer in December 1916 evaporated as the British drove in the German Sixth Army at Vimy, north of Arras. On 11 April, General Erich Ludendorff asked Lossberg to take the post of chief of staff for the Sixth Army. In many ways, this proved to be Lossberg's finest hour. He, a mere colonel, asked for and received Vollmacht from Ludendorff, who passed this information on to the commander and chief of staff of Army Group Crown Prince Rupprecht of Bavaria as well as to the commander of the Sixth Army. Lossberg next visited the Arras front. He interviewed divisional commanders and their chiefs of staff. He recognized at once that British control of Vimy Ridge made any rigid forward defense impossible. Within forty-eight hours of his arrival at the Sixth Army, he had in place fifteen divisions in a flexible defense ten miles in depth. And when the British VII Corps mounted a new assault at 0530 on 14 April, they were hurled back into their starting positions by 0800. The irony of the moment could hardly have escaped Lossberg: he, one of the staunchest opponents of the elastic defense in depth, had used it to great advantage.

In June 1917 OHL sent Lossberg to establish the Fourth Army's defensive line during the Battle of Passchendaele, which earned from Ludendorff's chief of operations, Colonel Georg Wetzell, the biting comment that Lossberg seemed to be the only German staff officer who could conduct a defensive battle! The Fourth Army did not play a major role in the last roll of the dice of the German

Army, Operation MICHAEL, in the spring and summer of 1918. Lossberg, fearless of authority as ever, criticized Ludendorff's handling of the operation: he failed to concentrate his forces, he advanced into the morass of the 1916 Somme battlefields, he sharply attacked his field commanders, and he failed to recognize that the game had been lost by mid-July at the Second Battle of the Marne. Not 8 August 1918—what Ludendorff called the "black day" of the German Army—but 18 July 1918 had constituted "the decisive turning point of the campaign."

Lossberg was no Rigoletto. He was a professional soldier. He believed that General Staff officers needed frontline combat experience. He was not afraid to issue orders on his own authority to four-star generals. He opened channels of communication with, and delegated authority to, commanders down to the battalion level. He respected authority and the chain of command, but he was never afraid to express contrary opinions even to a chief of the General Staff. OHL's after action report on the Battle of Arras in 1917 perhaps best summed up Fritz von Lossberg's standing in the German Army: the "prodigious creative mental energy of this exceptional man" had shored up the crumbling fronts of German field armies in the West. Truly, the Lion of the Defensive.

Holger H. Herwig
University of Calgary

Translators' Introduction

Few officers in the twentieth century have had as much influence on the development of modern tactics as Friedrich ("Fritz") Karl von Lossberg. Known in the German Army of World War I as *der Abwehrlöwe*—the Lion of the Defensive—he played a key role in developing and proving on the battlefield many of the principles and techniques modern armies to this day apply during the conduct of defensive operations. As the chief of staff of five different field armies, he directed most of the major German defensive battles on the Western Front from the autumn of 1915 until the end of 1917.

Lossberg is mentioned in many of the World War I general histories, as well as in the memoirs of many of the senior German commanders. Any detail, however, of what he did and how he did it is largely missing. In 1939 he published his memoirs under the title *Meine Tätigkeit im Weltkriege 1914–1918*. The book was never translated into English, but it nonetheless remains one of the most important of the German battlefield-level World War I first-hand accounts. Perhaps the primary reason that Lossberg's memoirs were never translated is that his book was published just before the outbreak of World War II. As the storm clouds of war were gathering over Europe for the second time in a generation, the focus of both the general public and the professional military readership shifted to the war that was to come, and away from the war that had been.

During the first year of World War II, however, British military historian Graeme Wynne seriously studied Lossberg's memoirs immediately after they came out. Published in London in 1940, Wynne's influential book, *If Germany Attacks: The Battle in Depth in the West,* drew heavily from Lossberg. Despite the reference to "Attacks" in the book's title, Wynne provided a good overview of Lossberg's career and an excellent synopsis of his role in the development of German defensive tactics.

After 1945, World War I was completely overshadowed by World War II. The grim reality of the battlefields of trench warfare in France and Flanders no longer seemed to have any relevance to the study of military matters, especially when compared to the more recent experiences of fast-moving armored and airborne divisions. Forgotten in the process, however, was the critical fact that World War II was fought with the tactics and operational principles that were so painfully developed and learned between 1914 and 1918.

Approximately thirty-five years ago, military historians again started devoting serious study to the period 1914–1918 as the birth of modern warfare.[1] That interest intensified as the hundredth anniversary of the Great War approached. Wynne's book was a major source for the U.S. Army Combat Studies Institute monograph, *The Dynamics of Doctrine: Changes in German Tactical Doctrine During the First World War,* written by Timothy Lupfer and published in 1981. For many years, however, Wynne and Lupfer were the standard English language references on Lossberg. In 2008 Lossberg was the subject of a chapter in the book *Chief of Staff: The Principal Officers Behind History's Great Commanders,* published by the Naval Institute Press in association with the Association of the United States Army.[2]

Lossberg's memoir offers fascinating insights to the inner workings of the staff at the German Army High Command (*Oberste Heeresleitung,* or OHL), as well as the interrelationships between OHL and the field army headquarters managing the battles on the front lines. In addition to his significant contributions as a tactician, Lossberg was an archetypical example of a German chief of staff. Although almost all modern military staff systems are based on the model pioneered by the Germans, a German chief of staff had significantly more responsibility than his counterparts in the American, British, French, or Russian armies.

Following Prussia's defeat by Napoleon at Jena in 1806, the military reformer David Gerhard von Scharnhorst reorganized the Prussian Army and its entire command and staff structure. Scharnhorst established the first professionally trained General Staff Corps. Since the higher nobility in Germany had the reserved right to hold senior military commands without necessarily having any real military competence, Scharnhorst's system gave the dilettante commanders highly professional staffs headed by a strong and capable chief of staff. Poorly qualified noblemen held high command in the German Army up through the end of World War I, and over that period the German chief of staff evolved into something approaching an unofficial but very real co-commander. Crown Prince Wilhelm of Prussia, the son of the Kaiser, was one of those aristocratic amateur soldiers. Crown Prince Rupprecht of Bavaria was a significant exception to the rule. He was a genuine professional soldier, and a competent and highly respected commander. Up through the end of World War I, whenever a unit failed in combat it usually was the chief of staff rather than the commander who was relieved first.

Characteristic of the German Army up through 1945, and even of the *Bundeswehr* today to an extent, the chief of staff in any other army had no such authority, but a German chief of staff was no ordinary staff officer—he was a German General Staff officer. And the very idea of a specialized and career-managed General Staff Corps was something pioneered by the Germans. Other General Staff officers at the corps level and up included the operations officer

(Ia), the logistics officer (Ib), and the intelligence officer (Ic). There were many other officers on the staff, of course, but they were not General Staff officers. At the divisional level, the only General Staff officer was the Ia, who functioned as both the chief of staff and the operations officer.

Lossberg during World War I never commanded anything. Yet as a chief of staff of various units throughout the war, he had a more direct influence on the outcome of many critical battles than did the commanders of those units. This comes out quite clearly in Lossberg's memoirs, as he describes his almost daily trips into the front lines to assess the situation personally. While his counterparts in other armies hardly ever moved from their respective command posts, Lossberg and the other German chiefs of staff typically moved back and forth, fully trusting the General Staff officers who remained in the headquarters to keep the entire command and control system operating quickly and efficiently.

Vollmacht is another concept that was unique to the German staff system. In the civilian context the word is translated as power of attorney, but there is no real English equivalent term for the military application. Through the end of World War I a senior General Staff officer given Vollmacht had the specific authority in emergency situations to issue direct orders to subordinate commanders in the name of the senior commander. It was used very sparingly, but as the war progressed Lossberg was entrusted with Vollmacht on many occasions.

Fritz von Lossberg was born on 30 April 1868 at Bad Homberg to an old Thuringian military family. In 1886 he joined the elite 2nd Foot Guards Regiment as an officer candidate (*Fahnenjunker*). Commissioned in 1887, Lossberg entered the Prussian War Academy (*Kriegsakademie*) in 1894 while still a second lieutenant. He graduated three years later. After successfully completing his period of probationary service, he achieved full qualification as a General Staff officer in 1900. His career then followed the standard pattern, alternating between General Staff and line assignments, including company and battalion command. Lossberg returned to the Kriegsakademie as an instructor between 1907 and 1910.

Lossberg's memoirs start in October 1913, when he was assigned to the XIII Army Corps as the chief of staff. The XIII Army Corps fought at the First Battle of Ypres in 1914, and then redeployed to the Eastern Front. In January 1915 Lossberg was reassigned to OHL as the deputy chief of the Operations Division. Lossberg was not at all happy with his new assignment. He had a major personality conflict with his direct boss, Colonel Gerhard Tappen—although the chief of OHL at the time, General of Infantry Erich von Falkenhayn, placed a great deal of confidence in Lossberg. Naturally, that did nothing to mitigate Lossberg's shaky relations with Tappen. Lossberg's account of his eight months at OHL in 1915 provides some fascinating insights into the internal politics and intrigues within the German supreme command.

Lossberg hated being at OHL. He hated having to function as a "second banana," and he hated being far removed from the troops on the front lines. When the French launched a major offensive in Champagne in September 1915, the German Third Army immediately requested permission to pull back. Lossberg was critical of that proposed course of action; neither did Falkenhayn approve. Falkenhayn reacted by relieving the Third Army's chief of staff, but significantly not its commanding general. He then reassigned Lossberg as the Third Army's chief of staff, with specific orders to restore the tactical situation. Although he was only a newly promoted colonel, Lossberg asked for and received Vollmacht. The campaign in Champagne quickly cemented Lossberg's reputation as a talented defensive tactician.

On 1 July 1916 the British and French launched their great offensive on the Somme. Two days later Falkenhayn reassigned Lossberg to the Second Army as its chief of staff, again with orders to restore the situation. Shortly thereafter, OHL on 19 July split General Fritz von Below's Second Army into the First and Second Armies. Lossberg and Below went with the half that became the First Army, which primarily fought against the British. The Battle of the Somme is remembered today largely for the massive numbers of casualties suffered by the British Expeditionary Force (BEF), which on 1 July 1916, the first day of the battle, suffered 57,470 casualties, including 19,240 dead and 2,152 missing. The German Army also suffered horrendous casualties during the battle, which lasted until 14 November, but they managed to prevent the Allies from reaching any operationally significant objectives. On 21 September 1916 Lossberg was awarded the prestigious *Pour le Mérite.*

While Lossberg was on the Somme, he determined that it took anywhere between eight and ten hours for a message to travel one way in either direction between a divisional headquarters and the front line. (Most communication wires were cut as soon as the artillery fire started.) The tactical situation usually changed drastically during the time that it took for information to flow up the chain of command and for the corresponding orders to flow back down. Lossberg concluded that the best way to speed up tactical responsiveness was to give the frontline battalion commanders total control of their own sectors. That meant that the higher headquarters would have to support the decisions of the frontline commanders, who knew the terrain and the situation better than anyone else. Thus, the frontline battalion commander also would have operational control of any reinforcements committed to his sector, regardless of the size of the reinforcing unit or its commander's rank. This approach ensured continuity of command and exploited the frontline battalion commander's superior knowledge.[3] A frontline battalion commander now had the authority to withdraw from forward positions under pressure as he saw fit. More importantly, he had the authority to order the remaining battalions of his regiment (positioned to his rear) into the counterattack when he judged the timing right.

On the Somme the three battalions of a regiment typically were deployed in column. The Forward Battalion (*Kampfbataillon*) held the first defensive position—actually a series of usually three or more roughly parallel and mutually supporting trench lines. The second defensive position was held by the Immediate Reserve Battalion (*Bereitschaftsbataillon*). Farther to the rear, and generally beyond the range of the enemy's artillery, was the Deep Reserve Battalion (*Ruhebataillon*). Lossberg's system effectively shortened the chain of command. The regimental commander, then, became the manager of the logistical support of the frontline battalions, as well as the commitment of reinforcements. At the next higher echelon, the role of the divisional commanders replicated that of the frontline battalion commanders. The divisions controlled everything in their sectors without having to wait for specific orders from the corps. When a reinforcing division was committed to a given sector, it came under the operational control of the commander of the reinforced division.[4]

Although initially a proponent of rigid, forward defense, Lossberg by the end of 1916 was experimenting with working models of the concepts of defense in depth, flexible defense, and reverse-slope defense. The idea was to trade—where necessary—space for both time and especially enemy lives. The forwardmost ground was held by fire, not by men. Once the enemy attack culminated, the attacker would be subjected to an almost immediate counterattack before he could set his defense or bring his supporting elements forward.

Falkenhayn was sacked as chief of the General Staff in July 1916. He was replaced by Field Marshal Paul von Hindenburg, with General of Infantry Erich Ludendorff as his first quartermaster general.[5] Ludendorff almost immediately initiated an extensive reform of tactical doctrine on the Western Front. As part of those reforms, the German Army adopted many of Lossberg's defensive innovations and incorporated them into a new doctrinal manual, published by OHL on 1 December 1916. *Principles of Command in the Defensive Battle in Position Warfare* was written primarily by OHL General Staff officers Colonel Max Bauer and Captain Hermann Geyer.[6] The new doctrine was based on three primary principles: flexibility, decentralized control, and counterattack. On the Allied side, the command and control of attacks and counterattacks became increasingly centralized at ever-higher levels as the war progressed. Meanwhile, the German commanders gained an impressive degree of initiative and autonomy.

Despite his own contributions to the new concepts, Lossberg believed that the *Principles* went too far in allowing frontline unit commanders to yield ground in the face of a strong attack. He still believed that a ridged forward defense was the best defensive tactic whenever possible, with the flexible defense in depth allowed in crisis situations only. Lossberg wrote an analysis entitled *Experiences of the First Army in the Somme Battles,* rebutting a considerable amount of what was in the new *Principles.* Military historians in general have been highly critical of Ludendorff's performance on the Western Front, especially at the operational and strategic levels of warfare. On the tactical level, however, Ludendorff must be given credit for encouraging healthy professional debate over tactical doctrine in the best traditions of the German General Staff. Ludendorff had OHL reprint and widely distribute Lossberg's pamphlet. The British later captured a copy, translated it, and distributed twenty-eight hundred copies to their commanders.[7]

On 9 April 1917 the British launched a major attack at Arras, in the German Sixth Army's sector. The Sixth Army was supposed to be operating under the new principles of flexible defense, but they committed their reserves too late. That allowed the British to break into the German front on a wide sector, capture the commanding high ground of Vimy Ridge, and push the German lines back significantly. The Germans were facing a disaster in the making. Two days later Ludendorff telephoned Lossberg to tell him he was being transferred immediately to the Sixth Army as its chief of staff.

The first thing Lossberg did was to ask Ludendorff for Vollmacht. That was a significant departure from accepted practice, whereupon a chief of staff received Vollmacht from his immediate commander. In asking Ludendorff directly, Lossberg essentially bypassed both the commander of the Sixth Army, Colonel General Ludwig von Falkenhausen, and the commander of the army group, Crown Prince Rupprecht of Bavaria. Lossberg, who was still only a colonel, was asking for what amounted to de facto command of the Sixth Army. He still did not completely trust the efficacy of the new flexible defense doctrine, and he believed that he needed almost unlimited command authority to rescue the situation. Ludendorff approved Vollmacht without hesitation, and then informed the army and army group headquarters while Lossberg was en route.[8] When Rupprecht's chief of staff, General of Infantry Hermann von Kuhl, got the word, he remarked, "If anyone can straighten out this tangle, he will."[9]

Despite Lossberg's serious reservations about the new defensive doctrine, Ludendorff had complete confidence that he would be able to do whatever it took to stabilize the situation. Before Lossberg even reported to the Sixth Army headquarters, he went directly to the front lines, talked with the commanders on the spot, and developed his own estimate of the situation. He immediately recognized that because the British now held Vimy Ridge, the enemy had an overwhelming advantage in artillery observation that made a German rigid forward defense completely impossible. Doing what he had to, Lossberg started to establish a flexible defense in depth with lightly manned forward positions. Lossberg estimated that it would take the British at least three days to move their artillery forward over the ground they recently had captured. Until then, the British guns would not have the range necessary to support any continued attacks.

Lossberg used that time to reorganize and reinforce the Sixth Army's new rearward main position and establish a flexible defensive zone eighteen miles long and ten miles deep, manned by 150,000 troops in fifteen divisions. When the British renewed the offensive on 14 April, their intent was to conduct a limited objective attack to expand the salients they had pushed into the German lines five days earlier. According the late British military historian Richard Holmes: "When a more formal attack went in on the 14th it was very roughly handled. The long ridges and shallow valleys enabled the Germans to employ elastic defense at its best, giving ground before the attack."[10] The British troops crossed their line of departure at 0530 hours, but the deeper they penetrated into the German position, the more they encountered unforeseen resistance. By 0800 hours most of the attackers were back in their own trenches, having taken up to 60 percent casualties in their lead units.[11]

Thus, at Arras, one of the German Army's strongest critics of the widespread use of flexible defense in depth became the first to make it work in a large-scale battle.[12] Lossberg later admitted that his defensive system at the Sixth Army ran counter to almost everything he had written in his *Experiences* pamphlet. Ironically, the heavy German casualties on the first day at Arras had caused Ludendorff and others at OHL to doubt the efficacy of the new doctrine. Once Lossberg had made it work, it became obvious that the tactics were sound but that errors in their application had been the initial problem.[13] In January 1918 OHL issued its official after action analysis of the Battle of Arras. Citing Lossberg's contribution, the report credited the outcome to "the prodigious creative mental energy of this exceptional man."[14] On 24 April 1917 Lossberg was decorated with the *Pour le Mérite mit Eichenlaub,* awarded only 122 times during World War I.

In early June 1917 German intelligence had collected strong indicators pointing to an imminent major British attack in the Ypres sector. Once again, Ludendorff sent Lossberg to the threatened sector of the Fourth Army, to take over as chief of staff. That was the first time Lossberg had the opportunity to organize a defense before the start of a battle. The British attacked on 31 July. The Third Battle of Ypres, more commonly known as "Bloody Passchendaele," raged on until 20 November. By the time it was over the British had managed to capture the key Passchendaele Ridge, but they had little besides some three hundred thousand casualties to show for it.

Lossberg played no direct role in Operation MICHAEL (21 March–4 April 1918), the first of the five great "Ludendorff Offensives" of 1918. During the follow-on Operation GEORGETTE (9–29 April 1918), Lossberg's Fourth Army attacked the British in support of the German Sixth Army and captured Mont Kemmel on 25 April. The Fourth Army played no role in the three subsequent German offensives, BLÜCHER (27 May–5 June 1918), GNEISENAU (9–13 June 1918), and MARNESCHUTZ-REIMS (15–18 July 1918). Following MARNESCHUTZ-REIMS, which was a feint toward Paris to draw French reserves away from the British in Flanders, the Fourth Army was supposed to follow through with the long-planned and frequently postponed Operation HAGEN, the final blow against the Allies intended to push the British off the Continent. The plan called for the Fourth Army to deliver the main effort with five corps consisting of twenty-nine divisions, supported on the left by the Sixth Army with two corps consisting of seven divisions.[15]

The HAGEN attack date was set for 1 August, but MARNESCHUTZ-REIMS failed and the Allies launched a robust counterattack into the German positions west of Reims on 18 July. On 19 July, Lossberg strongly recommended to Ludendorff that the Germans withdraw immediately to the Siegfried Position, their starting line for the offensives in March. A dispirited Ludendorff refused to consider it, blaming all the past failures on his operations chief, Lieutenant Colonel Georg Wetzell.[16] On 20 July, Ludendorff summoned Lossberg to OHL. His nerves shattered, Ludendorff talked about resigning. Lossberg recommended that he not resign, but later he came to the conclusion that he should have told Ludendorff it would have been best for him to resign. Ludendorff then sent the German Army's defensive expert to the Soissons sector to assess the situation. Lossberg left under the mistaken belief that Ludendorff would act on his operational recommendations. By the time Lossberg returned to OHL on 25 July, the overall situation had deteriorated further, and he was shocked to find that Ludendorff had not yet acted on any of his recommendations.[17]

In August 1918 Lossberg became the chief of staff of Army Group Boehn. He ended the war as the chief of staff of Army Group Duke Albrecht of Württemberg. The main body of Lossberg's memoirs ends with the inactivation of that army group on 23 December 1918, although he does devote an additional page and a half to a very brief summary of the remaining eight years of his military career.

Following the war, Lossberg remained in the new *Reichswehr* and contributed to the tactical and organizational reforms of General Hans von Seeckt. In late August 1919 Lossberg was assigned as the chief of staff of General Kommando II, one of only two corps-level formations in the one hundred thousand-man Reichswehr. One of his subordinate staff officers was a young Captain Erich von Manstein, who during the Battle of the Somme in July 1916 had served under Lossberg as the Ib of the First Army. Manstein, of course, would go on to become a field marshal and the *Wehrmacht*'s greatest general of World War II. Lossberg reached the rank of general of infantry shortly before his retirement on 31 January 1927. He died in Lübeck on 14 May 1942. During World War II, his son, Bernhard, served as a major general on the Wehrmacht's command staff (*Führungsstab*).

During the interwar years there was a great deal of debate within first the Reichswehr and then the Wehrmacht over the tactical and operational lessons of World War I. Since at least the days of Moltke the Elder the offensive had been the overriding mantra of the German Army. It was ironic, then, that the Germans proved to be the most effective defenders of World War I. In the 1920s and 1930s many German officers argued that trench warfare conditions of 1915–1918 had been an anomaly, and pushed for a return to an overwhelming emphasis on the attack. Not all, however, agreed. In his influential 1938 book, *Die Abwehr* (The Defense), General of Artillery (later Field Marshal) Wilhelm Ritter von Leeb warned against any overly doctrinaire and exclusive focus on offensive operations. In his discussion of the historical background of German defensive operations, he reviewed the major Western Front battles between 1915 and 1917, in which Lossberg played so significant a role.[18]

Leeb argued that Germany's geographic position in central Europe, surrounded by potential enemies on all sides, combined with its comparative industrial and economic inferiority, made it essential that Germany master defensive as well as offensive operations. Pursuing a directly opposite tack to many of the operational theorists of the day, Leeb argued that the dramatic improvements in mobility and weapons effects since 1918 made defensive capabilities even more necessary, and at the same time opened up new operational and tactical opportunities for combat operations, both defensive and offensive. A pure defense, of course, could never produce decisive results in war, but offensive operations had to be focused on a concentrated objective, and an effective defense, therefore, was essential in all other sectors to facilitate massing the required forces for the attack. Leeb advocated defensive zones in great depth, and he built on the mobile defense concept of World War I by integrating tanks.[19]

To this day, the Wehrmacht is remembered primarily for its many stunningly successful offensive operations of World War II. Nonetheless, some German commanders during that war also conducted effective defensive operations against overwhelming numerical odds. Among them were: Field Marshal Albert Kesselring in Italy, Field Marshal Erich von Manstein and General of

Panzer Troops Hermann Balck on the Eastern Front; and Field Marshal Walther Model on both fronts.

German and English are related tongues, but they employ very different notions of style and expression. As author Richard Simpkin once noted, when translating from German to English, "one has to dissect out the underlying thought and express it in a radically different way."[20] In carrying out this translation, then, we have used the principle of dynamic equivalence rather than a word-for-word translation. There are, however, a number of tactical and organizational concepts peculiar to World War I and the German Army during the period 1914–1918 that bear some explaining.

The two basic components of combat power at the tactical level are fire and maneuver. During the more than forty years between the end of the Franco-Prussian War and the start of World War I, technological advances greatly increased the volume and lethality of firepower. But by 1914 mobility technology lagged far behind. Thus, firepower temporarily gained the upper hand over maneuver. That would change during the years following World War I, when greater applications of the internal combustion engine resulted in vast improvements in battlefield mobility, and hence more effective maneuver. Thus, in World War I offensive operations there was a crucial difference between making a break-in (*Einbruch*) and a break-through (*Durchbruch*). Once both sides began to echelon their defenses in greater depth, the attacker with sufficient force and manpower could almost always make a break-in to the defender's positions. But neither side had sufficient mobility to achieve a real breakthrough, which then could lead to an exploitation and a decisive victory. The problem was that the attacker's tactical mobility was always less than the defender's operational mobility, which meant that the defender contained the break-in eventually. Neither side ever achieved a real breakthrough on the Western Front, although the Germans came close in March 1918.

German doctrine recognized two basic types of counterattack. The *Gegenstoss* and the *Gegenangriff* are best translated into English as hasty counterattack and deliberate counterattack. Whenever possible, a German force pushed out of its defensive positions was expected to launch a hasty counterattack immediately, before the enemy could consolidate his defense or bring up enough forces to continue the attack. But in those cases where the attacking force was just too strong, or was too well supported by its own artillery or air cover, such a hasty counterattack would only lead to more casualties. The commander of the forward battalion was given a wide degree of latitude in deciding whether or not a hasty counterattack was feasible. If not, then the standard procedure was to prepare to launch a deliberate counterattack, based on careful planning and the commitment of sufficient reinforcements and fire support. In this translation we have been very careful to distinguish between the Gegenstoss and the Gegenangriff.

The literal English translations of the German general officer rank titles do not line up with their British and American equivalents. The lowest German general officer was a *Generalmajor,* who typically commanded a brigade. The Germans did not have a rank called brigadier general, which in the American and British armies commanded brigades. (In the early 1920s the British changed the rank title to simply brigadier, which it remains today.) Allied divisions were commanded by major generals, while in the German Army divisional commanders typically held the rank of *Generalleutnant.* The German equivalent of the Allied lieutenant general held the rank title of a general of a specific branch of arms—for example, *General der Infantrie, General der Artillerie, General der Kavallerie,* etc. At the level of an Allied four-star full general, the German equivalent was *Generaloberst,* literally colonel general. The Americans in 1918 did not have a five-star equivalent rank. The senior-most British rank was field marshal, The German equivalent was formally called *Generalfeldmarschall,* or general field marshal. For the sake of simplicity, we use just field marshal in this translation.

Throughout Lossberg's memoirs there are many references to officers of relatively junior rank holding senior positions and being in charge of other officers who may have outranked them. While such a situation was (and still is) unthinkable in the British and American armies, it was by no means unusual in the German Army, which operated on the principle that position (or function) took precedence over rank or pay grade. Falkenhayn became chief of the General Staff while he was only a lieutenant general. And although Paul von Hindenburg was a field marshal when he became chief of the German General Staff in 1916, his deputy, Erich Ludendorff was only a general of infantry. Yet, throughout the remainder of the war Ludendorff routinely issued direct orders to field army and army group commanders who nominally outranked him. Even today, the modern German Bundeswehr operates on the principle that position takes precedence over rank, although not necessarily with the same great disparities between the two that existed during World War I.

Although first Helmuth von Moltke the Younger, and then Falkenhayn, and finally Hindenburg were officially the chiefs of the German General Staff, or more precisely the chiefs of the General Staff of the German Field Army, they were nonetheless the de facto commanders in chief of the German Army during their tenures. Constitutionally, the Kaiser was the commander in chief, the *Oberster Kriegsherr* (Supreme War Lord); but Kaiser Wilhelm II was little more than a figurehead from the start, and he became increasingly irrelevant as the war progressed. From mid-1916 on, Ludendorff's official position title was first quartermaster general of the German Army. Sometimes English language readers find that title confusing, because in most armies a quartermaster is a logistics officer. In the pre-1918 German Army, however, a *Generalquartiermeister* (quartermaster general) was a senior department chief on the Great General Staff. The best translation of Ludendorff's title, then, would be vice chief of the General Staff of the German Army. And although he technically was only a staff officer, his command authority was very real and second only to Hindenburg's.

Another point that may be confusing to modern readers is what might appear to be the rather inconsistent manner in which Lossberg refers to corps. There were four basic types of corps in the German Army of World War I: army corps, reserve corps, guards corps, and cavalry corps. As in other armies, German corps were designated by Roman numerals. The same number could be used for each of the different types of corps: for example, II Army Corps; II Reserve Corps; II Guards Corps; II Cavalry Corps. But German corps alternatively were referred to by the names of their commanders. Hence, the XIII Army Corps, commanded by General of Infantry Max von Fabeck, also was called Corps Fabeck. Lossberg used both formats, and we generally have followed his usage in this translation.

During 1915 through 1916 the German Army for the most part stood on the defensive on the Western Front—with the notable exception of the attack on Verdun. German corps-level commanders and staffs (*Generalkommando*, or GKdo) from 1916 on tended to remain in their respective sectors of the front for long periods of time, while the frontline divisions rotated in and out. The idea was that each commander and his GKdo became experts in their particular sectors and provided continuity of command. Such long-term, frontline command structures came to be called groups, identified by the name of the commanding general of the GKdo. When a group commander and his staff were replaced in the line, the group was redesignated with the name of the incoming commander. Such groups commanded no fewer than two divisions, and quite often more. During periods of intense defensive combat they even commanded other corps (which kept their original numerical designations.) The groups and the separate corps, of course, came under the direct command of the numbered field army responsible for the entire sector. In the latter part of his memoirs, Lossberg, as the chief of staff of several different field armies, refers to such groups quite frequently.

The reader will notice that the chapter formatting changes as Lossberg's memoirs progress. The long first chapter devoted to Lossberg's time as the chief of staff of the XIII Army Corps is divided into three major sections, one for each of the three different field armies that the XIII Army Corps operated under. Within each section there are a number of subsections. None of the following chapters are organized into sections, and from chapter 2 on, Lossberg makes decreasing use of subsections. This somewhat quirky organizational format is in the German original, and we have retained it in this translation.

Finally, Lossberg's memoirs at times provide a great deal of tactical and especially order of battle information—which units were in the front lines at any given time, and which units replaced them as the battle progressed. Much of this detail may exceed the interest level of the general reader, but we have retained it all in this translation because it contributes to a more complete picture of exactly how the Germans managed their massive defensive battles on the Western Front in 1915–1917, and how they handled the continuous problems of reinforcements, replacements, reconstitution, logistics, and troop movements while simultaneously fighting the battle. Specialists, too, should find detailed information on the units useful—information that in some cases may not be available in other English-language sources.

David T. Zabecki
Freiburg, Germany

Dieter J. Biedekarken
Imperial Beach, California

Lossberg's War

Lossberg's 1939 Prologue

After twelve years of troop assignments in the 2nd Foot Guards Regiment, I served in General Staff assignments at all echelons prior to the start the war. This General Staff time was only interrupted by my assignments as a company commander, an instructor at the Prussian War Academy, and a battalion commander.

During the Great War I served as the chief of staff of German combat formations nine times in an uninterrupted sequence. I deployed to France in August 1914 as the chief of staff of the XIII (Württemberg) Army Corps, which served under the Fifth, Sixth, and Ninth Armies, whose commanding generals I frequently advised. In January 1915, I became the deputy chief of the Operations Division at *Oberste Heeresleitung* under General Erich von Falkenhayn. During the defensive battles on the Western Front from September 1915 on I was successively the chief of the General Staff of the Third, Second, First, Sixth, and Fourth Armies and of Army Groups Boehn and Duke Albrecht of Württemberg. In all of my assignments as chief of staff I had a close professional relationship with my commanding generals.

In this book I have described my responsibilities and actions during the World War. Whenever I felt that my experience would be of value to today's young General Staff officers I added more detail to my narrative. I candidly comment on the major operational decisions at the highest echelons. I acknowledge here with a full sense of gratitude the special level of trust that General Erich Ludendorff had in me, even though during the last year of the war our opinions about the overall situation diverged.

This book is dedicated to the magnificent German Army. It failed to achieve victory because the political leadership of the German Fatherland failed. As an old soldier I watch with great excitement the rise of the Wehrmacht of the Third Reich.[1]

von Lossberg
General of Infantry (Retired)
Lübeck, April 1939

1

Chief of Staff of the XIII Army Corps

The XIII Army Corps with the Fifth Army

War Breaks Out

On 1 October 1913, I was assigned as the chief of the General Staff of the XIII (Royal Württemberg) Army Corps, commanded by General of the Infantry Hermann Gustav Karl Max von Fabeck. The corps consisted of the 26th Division, commanded by Lieutenant General Wilhelm Karl Florestan Gero Crescentius, Herzog von Urach, Graf von Württemberg, and the 27th Division, commanded by Lieutenant General Friedrich Woldemar Franz, Graf von Pfeil und Klein-Ellguth. In the course of the nine months of peacetime before the war broke out I had adjusted quite well to the commanding general and to the corps General Staff. The entire staff was bound together by complete trust. Inspection trips during the winter and spring, during which I accompanied the commanding general, almost always showed a broad picture of first-class and—above all—wartime-appropriate training of all the troops and their leaders. The Württembergers are born soldiers. Differences between city and country folk are hardly noticeable. Large industrial centers in which socialist tendencies could grow were almost nonexistent in Württemberg. The entire population has a strong work ethic and is intelligent, physically tough, and productive. Class differences are not evident. Every well-educated person speaks the Swabian dialect, which is quite common among the people and which generates a bond to the Homeland and a feeling of togetherness for those from every town, no matter how small. Recognizing this characteristic in the entire population, the Württemberg Ministry of War acted wisely in reorganizing the military districts so that each division received its replacements from a specific region. That was done in anticipation of the large engagements in which the Württemberg divisions engaged. Thus, officers, noncommissioned officers, and enlisted soldiers largely knew each other from their hometowns and saw each other as comrades, which they often had been since youth. From this firm bond of camaraderie and based on my many wartime experiences with the Württembergers I concluded that among all the Germanic tribes they were the best soldiers. Not a single Württemberg unit failed during the war.

I can attest from my own experience that the war broke out as a surprise to Germany and that we did not want it. On 20 July 1914, I was granted a three-week leave, which I intended to spend with my two oldest children on the estate in Holstein that I managed for my wife's parents. Shortly before my departure I received news of my oldest brother's acute illness. I rushed to Berlin and soon after my arrival there I had to say farewell to him forever. Meanwhile, the news in the papers prompted me on 27 July to inquire at the Great General Staff[1] as well as at the Ministry of War whether I should return to my duty station in Stuttgart. At both offices no one believed that war was imminent. Nevertheless, I also made the same inquiry to my commanding general and received instructions to continue my leave. I continued on to Holstein, but there on 29 July I received a telegram instructing me to return to Stuttgart immediately. This experience indicates to me that Germany did not want this war, but that it was forced into it by our enemies.[2]

Because of major delays in the rail network I did not arrive in Stuttgart until the night of 30 July. In the meantime, the corps headquarters had received orders recalling to their garrisons all troops away on exercises. The corps sent two anti-balloon guns to Friedrichshafen to protect the Zeppelin factory there. The railroad security units were already reinforced, and the railroad employees had been issued arms.

On 30 July at 1345 hours the corps headquarters received the "Imminent War Warning" order from Berlin, declaring the existence of a state of war. The order also activated the railroad security units and the replacement commands for the regional commands. In accordance with the prepared plans, the mobile units of the 53rd Infantry Brigade, which included the 1st Squadron, 19th Lancer Regiment, and the 2nd Battalion, 29th Field Artillery Regiment, called up their reservists for an exercise and proceeded to purchase horses. All the other troop units also initiated their preparations for mobilization.

On 1 August 1914 at 1808 hours the corps headquarters received the mobilization order and distributed it immediately.

On 2 August 1914 (1st mobilization day) the reinforced 53rd Infantry Brigade under the command of Major General Otto von Moser was transported to Thionville.[3] The brigade consisted of the 123rd Grenadier Regiment; 124th Infantry Regiment; 2nd Squadron, 19th Lancer Regiment; and 2nd Battalion, 29th Field Artillery Regiment.

Planned and organized by the General Staff officers of the XIII Army Corps, Major Reinhardt the Ia[4] and Captain von Brandenstein the Ib,[5] the mobilization proceeded with no hitches. On its own initiative the corps headquarters ordered every infantry regiment and every infantry battalion to mount two to six soldiers on horseback as internal messengers. The establishment of these elements produced distinct advantages for communications and the transmission of orders within the infantry units in the environment of mobile warfare. A peculiar recommendation came in from a General Staff officer with the 27th Division in Ulm. On his own initiative, and without the knowledge of his divisional commander, he hand-carried the written recommendation to Stuttgart proposing that the additional horses acquired by the cavalry units would first have to be trained for the attack on the squadron level, and therefore the cavalry units should deploy ten to fourteen days later. After receiving a very strong counseling, the officer was sent back to his post.

The widely rumored "gold car" that was supposed to be carrying large amounts of gold from France to Russia through Germany kept the people of Württemberg in a state of great agitation. At many locations the home defense troops shot at ordinary civilian cars if they did not stop immediately upon being challenged. In Stuttgart this unfortunately resulted in the death of a brave one-year volunteer who was on his way to say farewell to his parents in Canstatt. He was shot and killed in a taxi that did not stop immediately after having been challenged.

Rumors of espionage generated unnecessary excitement among the population. At around noon on 4 August a great commotion arose right in front of my office window. When I demanded silence, I was told that just a few minutes earlier a spy who had been cutting the telegraph lines on top of the nearby main post office had been shot and killed. An officer we sent there to investigate reported back to me that everything was fine at the main post office, nobody had been on the rooftop, and not a single shot had been fired.

Transport and Deployment of the XIII Army Corps

On 6 August 1914 the transportation movements of the XIII Army Corps to Thionville began as planned. From our advance party the 1st Battalion, 124th Infantry Regiment, was sent forward to reinforce the IV Cavalry Corps (*Höheres Kavallerie-Kommando* 4), consisting of the 3rd and the 6th Cavalry Divisions and already in position west of the town. The lead detachment of the corps headquarters left Stuttgart on 7 August, arrived in Thionville about 1900 hours on 8 August, and went into quarters. By 11 August all the XIII Army Corps troops had unloaded in the vicinity of Thionville and were billeted according to plan. On 8 August the 13th Engineer Battalion built a bridge across the Moselle River to replace the ferry, and in the following days the unit built another bridge capable of carrying all weapons systems, including heavy artillery. All the routes to be used for the advance were reconnoitered in detail. The entire billeting was organized based on the assumption that the advance movements would proceed toward the west and northwest, but possibly also through Metz toward the south.

The XIII Army Corps along with the IV Cavalry Corps was assigned to the Fifth Army, which was positioned far forward northwest of Thionville.[6] Initially we found only weak enemy forces at the border, and they evaded any serious contact. A French cavalry division also evaded contact. By the morning of 10 August the IV Cavalry Corps had identified on its wide front line the French 4th and 9th Cavalry Divisions and apparently two additional French corps-level cavalry regiments eastward of the Othain sector. That sector itself appeared to be occupied by infantry and artillery units. Reportedly Fortress Montmédy was occupied by infantry and possibly artillery. At the fortress at Longwy there were supposed to be two infantry regiments and horse artillery units. Ordered by Fifth Army headquarters to develop quickly a clear picture of the enemy situation beyond the front line, the IV Cavalry Corps on 10 August conducted a forced reconnaissance against the Othain sector, with the 3rd Cavalry Division to the north and the 6th Cavalry Division to the south. During the early hours of 11 August a General Staff officer from the IV Cavalry Corps arrived in Thionville and reported that the forced reconnaissance had failed, with the 6th Cavalry Division having suffered heavy losses in its *Jäger* battalion and its mounted artillery. The Othain sector was occupied by strong enemy infantry supported by strong field artillery and heavy artillery. The IV Cavalry Corps had been forced to withdraw, but the enemy had not pursued. The morale of the IV Cavalry Corps was low because of their failure.

In my opinion the advance elements of the IV Cavalry Corps had done their duty and had accomplished their mission of clarifying the enemy situation. I passed that opinion on to the chief of staff of the Fifth Army, Lieutenant General Konstantin Heinrich Schmidt von Knobelsdorf, whom I called immediately. After some back and forth discussion, the Fifth Army headquarters gave us permission to send a XIII Army Corps officer to the IV Cavalry Corps in order to pass on the commendation of the Fifth Army headquarters for the courageous conduct of the mission. A senior officer of the corps staff with the appropriate instructions then drove immediately to the commander of the IV Cavalry Corps, to whom he skillfully conveyed the praise. That action quickly changed the despondent morale of the IV Cavalry Corps' leadership into one of confidence, which in turn led to the initiation of forceful action. In the evening of 12 August our staff officer returned with very encouraging—and as it later developed—accurate reports from the IV Cavalry Corps.

Those reports were also augmented with telegraphic reports from the IV

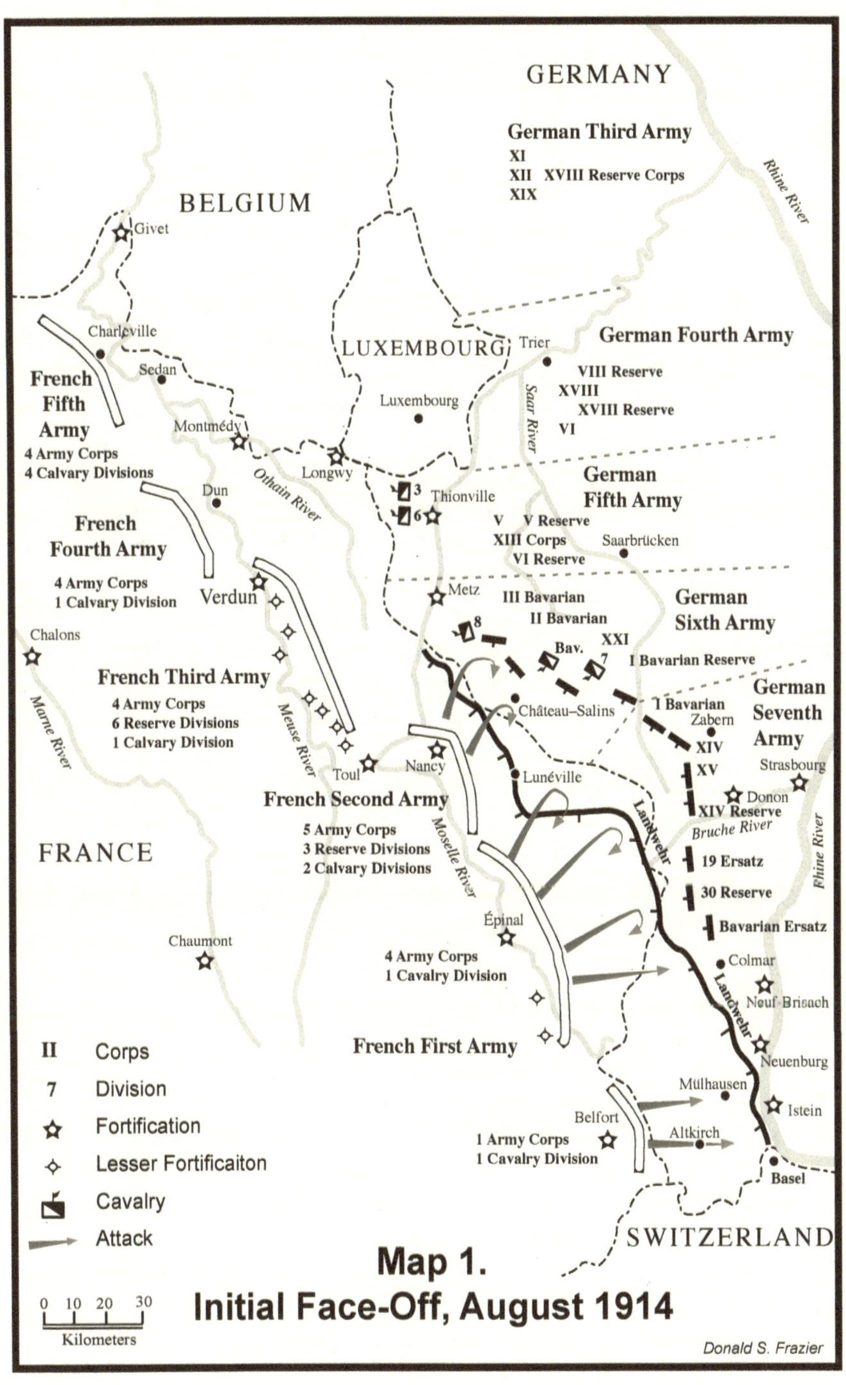

Map 1.
Initial Face-Off, August 1914

Cavalry Corps. The composite reports and the reconnaissance results of the next few days gave the Fifth Army headquarters a clear picture of the opposing enemy positioned to the west. Aerial reconnaissance also provided information about the enemy's deployments in depth. The overall picture was confirmed when the IV Cavalry Corps captured a message indicating that the entire width of the IV Cavalry Corps' front was held by the French II Army Corps, along with the 52nd Reserve Division and elements of French VI Army Corps. The fortresses at Verdun, Longwy, and Montmédy were garrisoned and reinforced. On 14 August aerial reconnaissance reported the movement in a northwesterly direction of two enemy army corps west of Fortress Verdun. Finally, Fifth Army intelligence officers attached to the adjacent Fourth Army on our northern flank received copies of the order of battle and plans of that headquarters and its left-wing corps, which were then transmitted to the XIII Army Corps and the IV Cavalry Corps.

On 14 August at 2200 hours the Fifth Army alerted us by telephone that during the night an order would be issued for the displacement of the corps by 0800 hours on 15 August. We immediately initiated all the preparatory actions. At approximately 0300 hours that morning the order arrived, directing the strong concentration of the XIII Army Corps around Thionville, with the option of advancing either toward the west or toward the south (through Metz). We executed the order immediately. Because of the water shortages in the summer heat, the mounted troops and all of the convoys and trains were bivouacked close to the Moselle River. In the evening of 15 August a strong but short thunderstorm burst, cooling everything down.

On 16 August the troops were billeted in the town, since no order to advance had been received. That evening the commanding general of the Fifth Army, Crown Prince Wilhelm of Prussia, arrived in Thionville for a briefing, along with his chief of staff.

Composition, Situation, and Missions of the Fifth Army on 16 August 1914

The XVI Army Corps was positioned facing west within the extended fortifications zone of Metz, and in such a manner that it was capable of deploying toward the south on both sides of the Moselle River, or to the north.

North of the XVI Army Corps the XIII Army Corps' reinforced 53rd Infantry Brigade had been moved forward to provide border security. To its front the IV Cavalry Corps was reconnoitering to the west. The main body of the XIII Army Corps was located around Thionville, with marching routes available to the south through Metz, or to the west.

The V Army Corps was positioned with its combat units on both sides of the Moselle. It was linked to its right with the Fourth Army's VI Army Corps.

The V Reserve Corps was positioned behind the V Army Corps.

The VI Reserve Corps was positioned behind the XIII Army Corps.

On 16 August, the Fifth Army began displacing its headquarters forward from Saarbrücken to Thionville. The tight deployment of the Fifth Army, which was completed by 16 August, secured the options of initiating attacks to the south, the west, or the northwest. Advancing south, the XVI Army Corps, XIII Army Corps, and VI Reserve Corps proceeded as the first wave, followed by the V Army Corps and the V Reserve Corps in the second wave. An advance to the west or northwest could proceed with the V Army Corps, XIII Army Corps, and XVI Army Corps in the first wave, followed in the second wave by V Reserve Corps and VI Reserve Corps.

Until 15 August the German High Command (*Oberste Heeresleitung*—OHL) assessed that the main body of the French Army, with sixteen army corps, six cavalry divisions, and the associated reserve division groupings—approximately 60 percent of the total French force—was positioning for a major offensive between Metz and the Vosges Mountains, in order to force a decision in the campaign. To ensure unified planning of the German counteroffensive, all German forces in the Imperial Territories of Alsace and Lorraine (*Reichsländer*)[7] were initially under the command of Crown Prince Rupprecht of Bavaria, commanding general of the Sixth Army. By pulling the Sixth Army back behind the Saar River, OHL planned to draw the French from Metz along the Nied River and the Saar to the Vosges Mountains, into an arch. Then we would press ahead with superior forces against both French flanks, with the Fifth Army from the north through Metz and via the Nied Position, which had been reinforced and manned with five *Landwehr* brigades,[8] and with the mass of the Seventh Army from the east out of the Vosges Mountains. The plan also called for committing elements of the Fourth Army and reinforcing the attack front with the IX Reserve Corps, which was then located in the *Nordmark*,[9] and including six and a half *Ersatz* (replacement) divisions and four Landwehr brigades.

On 16 August OHL came to the erroneous conclusion that the French main forces were no longer in Lorraine. Unfortunately, OHL then abandoned its plan for a double envelopment of the strong French forces that had been rushing into Lorraine since 14 September. If that plan had been executed, it undoubtedly would have produced a great operational victory, resulting in the destruction of major elements of the French First and Second Armies. By foregoing the operation in Lorraine by the Fourth and Fifth Armies, OHL decided to force the decision of the war by the wide envelopment through Belgium with the First through Fifth Armies, which only appeared to be opposed by inferior forces. Regrettably, the six and a half Ersatz divisions already heading toward Lorraine were not rerouted toward the German right wing.

On the German left wing the Sixth and Seventh Armies and the III Cavalry Corps were all under Crown Prince Rupprecht, who had been given the mission of securing the overall left flank of the German Army in the west. The execution of that mission was left to the crown prince's discretion. On 16 August he ordered the start of an evasive movement by his Sixth Army, which was then in close contact with the enemy at the border. The Sixth Army was to move in the direction of the Saar River line and Saarbrücken, and then south of there in such a manner that at any time they could shift back to an offensive posture.

Considering OHL's decision based on the events as they unfolded, it is quite clear that the operational actions of the Sixth and Seventh Armies should have been controlled by OHL on a situational basis. Only OHL could have seen clearly in the context of the overall situation how the security of the left flank of the attack front could have been executed in the most efficient manner. (The advance of the First through Fifth Armies did not start until 18 August.) Thus, for example, strong enemy pressure between the Swiss border and Metz might have resulted in the operational necessity of limiting the defense of the Nied and Saar lines and linking it into the south by holding the line Molsheim (Fortification Kaiser Wilhelm II)–Bruche River Position–Strasbourg–Neuf-Brisach–the right bank of the Rhine. Such a decision only could have been made by OHL. The ordering of other evasive actions, the establishment of new front lines from those actions, and the designation of an operational main effort for a counterattack should have been synchronized with the five attacking armies advancing in Belgium. Furthermore, a key element of OHL's operational freedom in Lorraine was the easily available OHL reserve located there, with the six and a half Ersatz divisions. OHL also could have used that reserve initially as a follow-on force for the Fifth Army's second echelon V Reserve Corps and VI Reserve Corps. If the V, XIII and XIV Army Corps in the lead echelon of the Fifth Army had been attacked from the south while advancing to the Meuse north of Verdun, the Fifth Army could have bent back its southern wing and then could have flanked the French attack with the V Reserve Corps and VI Reserve Corps, in conjunction with the Metz Main Reserve launching a surprise attack from the Metz fortifications.

The truth of the matter is that prior to every major decision the commander of the Sixth Army, who had been given an incredible responsibility, correctly contacted OHL, but he never received clear answers. Quite the contrary, the written and oral estimations of officers at OHL, including those by the chief of operations and the assistant chief of staff, were so far apart that the accomplishment of Crown Prince Rupprecht's mission was not made any easier—in fact it was made extremely more difficult.

Thus, Rupprecht soon gave up on his decision to divert his movement toward the Saar, under the assumption that the French wanted to tie him down with numerically inferior forces. Intending to force a resolution of the situation, he decided on the evening of 19 August to attack. It was a frontal assault against numerically superior enemy forces, and even through it ended in a tactical victory, it cost a great deal of blood. It would have been possible to achieve an operational victory that could have destroyed the enemy only if the French had been allowed initially to move deeply into German-held territory. At that point an attack massing on both wings could have choked them off. After such a victory, which would have had to have been launched based on clear orders from OHL, the Sixth and Seventh Armies could have detached strong reserves, which then could have been made available to OHL to follow the overall right wing of the army. If necessary, elements of those forces also could have been redeployed to the Eastern Front to reinforce the German forces there against the Russians.

My comments here are not based merely on after-the-fact analysis of OHL's decisions. These opinions were recorded in discussions I had in Thionville with members of my staff in August 1914. The XIII Army Corps at that time, as part of Fifth Army, received the directive to be prepared to deploy also toward the south through Metz. The execution of such a move indicated the planned use of a great fortified zone to achieve a large, destructive victory in Lorraine. Unfortunately, that opportunity was missed because OHL failed to recognize it.

In my opinion OHL should have acted as follows: The Sixth Army would evade deliberately behind the Nied–Saar Position, while leaving strong rear elements in contact with the enemy, reinforcing the position, and establishing main efforts on both wings in the counterattack. Based on guidance from the Sixth Army, the Seventh Army would make all its available forces ready for the counterattack. The Fifth Army would conduct night marches to stage the XVI Army Corps, XIII Army Corps, and VI Reserve Corps in the southern sector of the Metz fortified zone, in line to attack southward. The V Army Corps would be held in the rear, possibly in Metz itself. That corps would have to be ready either to follow as the second echelon of the three forward army corps, or to advance in coordination with the main reserve in Metz, the 33rd Reserve Division, to the west to attack the flank of a French force breaking out to the north from the Toul fortified zone. The Fifth Army's remaining V Reserve Corps would hold itself ready behind the right wing of the Nied Position, south of Thionville, in such a posture that it could attack either to the south or to the west between Thionville and Metz.

On 18 August the First through Fourth Armies would then start their advance through Belgium and Luxembourg toward the west. The Fourth Army would have to echelon strongly to the left and to the rear, in order to be ready to repel an expected French attack from the direction of Verdun and the north.

It is hardly doubtful that the French First and Second Armies would have continued their attack toward Lorraine if the German Sixth Army had conducted that evasive action. The French army group then could have been destroyed decisively by the Sixth and Seventh Armies and at least three corps of the Fifth Army. After achieving such great operational victory, the entire Fifth Army could have followed the Fourth Army echeloned left. It would then have been best positioned on both sides of Verdun for an attack to the west. Its northern group of approximately three corps then would cross the Meuse together with the Fourth Army. The Fifth Army's southern group of approximately two army corps, the Metz Main Reserve, and the IV Cavalry Corps, would secure the area north of Toul with the relatively weak 33rd Reserve Division, and then attack with the main body across the Meuse, south of Verdun. After an operational victory of annihilation in Lorraine, all the freed-up forces of the Sixth and Seventh Armies would have then been available to OHL for other missions.

The XIII Army Corps' Advance into France

During the Fifth Army's advance to the northwest the enemy situation had for the most part been identified by the IV Cavalry Corps and the aviation reconnaissance elements. Enemy units of all branches were in reinforced positions behind the Othain sector. The rearward position had been identified in the Loison sector, south of Fortress Montmédy. There were only enemy border security elements opposite Metz. Farther north it appeared that strong enemy forces were assembling between Charleville[10] and Montmédy.

According to OHL directives, the Fifth Army on 18 August was to advance with its right wing via Mamer (Luxembourg)–Arlon (Belgium). That required a sharp sideward movement, a shift on line from the depth of the present deployment formation, and then bypassing the small French citadel at Longwy, which had to be taken quickly.

The decision of the Fifth Army was to move the V and XIII Army Corps north, with the XVI Army Corps south of Longwy, and to let the VI Reserve Corps and V Reserve Corps initially follow the right group. The XIII Army Corps' direction of advance was toward Kuntzig, which it had to reach on 19 August. Simultaneously, the V Army Corps on the right was to reach Arlon, and the XVI Army Corps on the left, Ottange. In the second echelon, the V Reserve Corps was to advance by 19 August to Bettembourg and the VI Reserve Corps to Kayl, east of Esch-sur-Alzette, Luxembourg.

Based on the Fifth Army order received at 2150 hours on 17 August, the written corps order was sent to the divisions at 2345 hours, following an earlier telephonic warning order. Since the VI Reserve Corps was to advance ini-

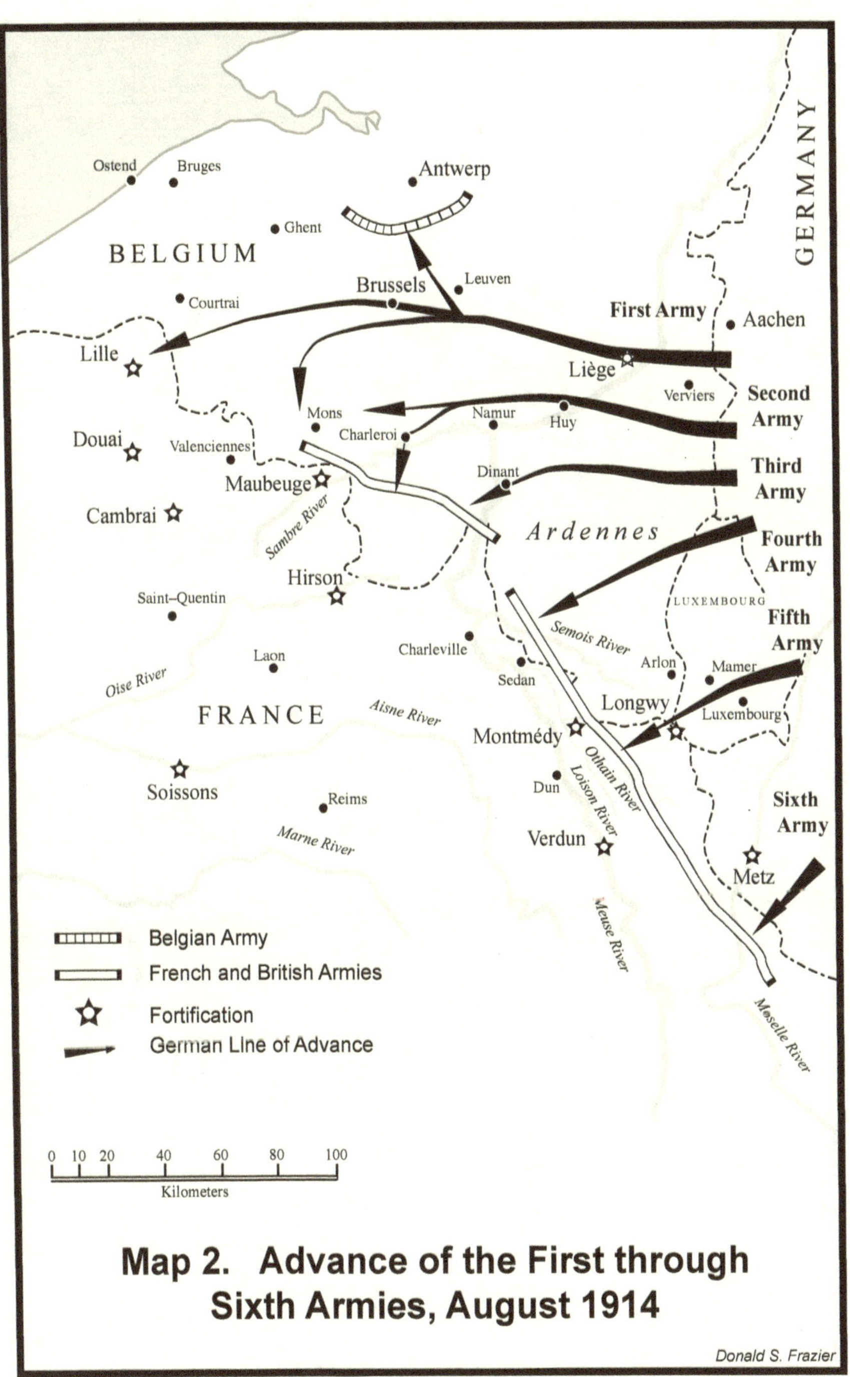

Map 2. Advance of the First through Sixth Armies, August 1914

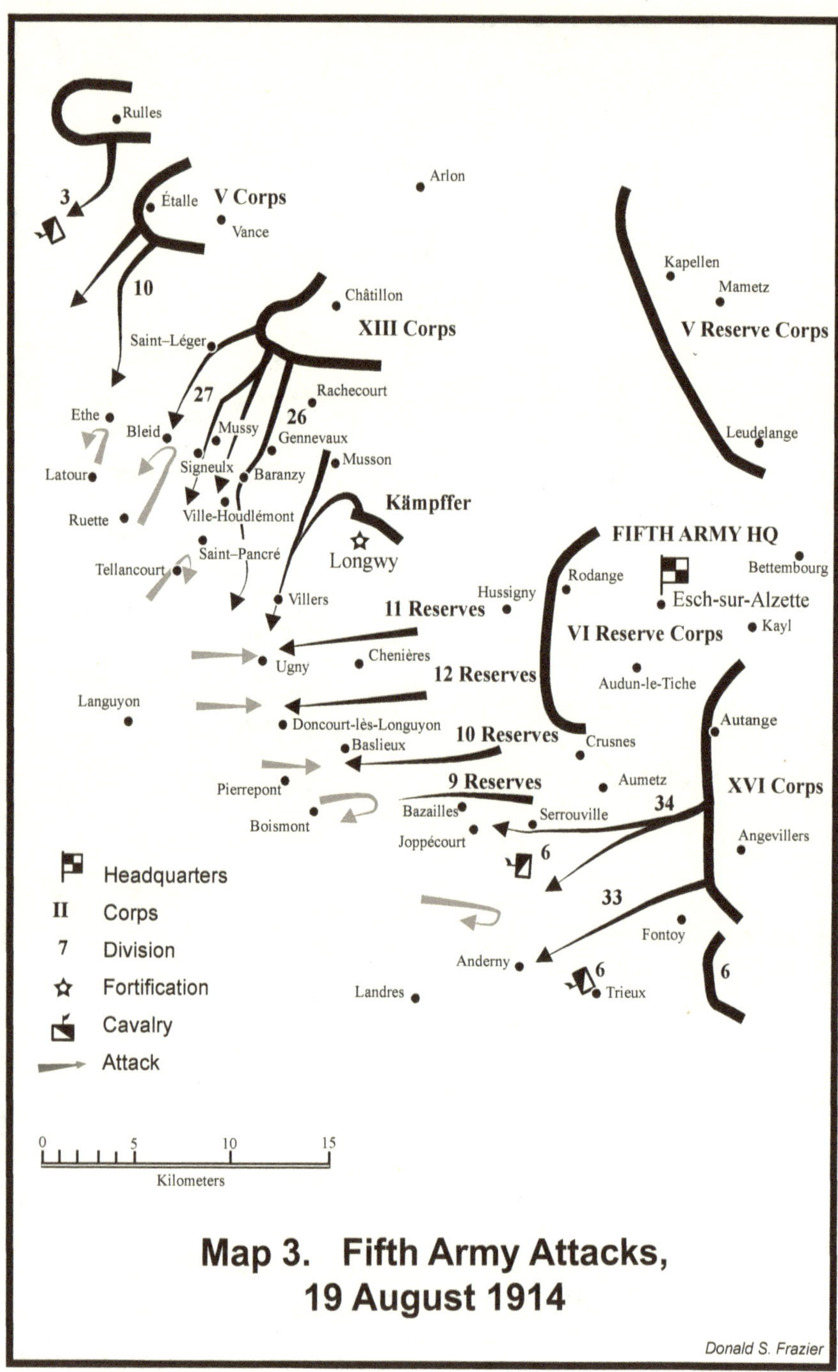

Map 3. Fifth Army Attacks, 19 August 1914

tially on the same road behind the XIII Army Corps, our start was scheduled for very early on 18 August. A rest period during the march was scheduled in such a way that it did not interfere with the movement of the VI Reserve Corps. The corps commanding general observed the entire leading 27th Division and the majority of the following 26th Division as they marched past him. Then the corps headquarters staff rode at a gallop along the march route, first to the head of the 26th Division, and then past elements of the 27th Division. Since the troops were on their first combat march and the replacement troops after a long period as reservists were on their first long foot march, there were fluctuations in the march order and in the attitude of the troops. It was hot and the often inferior roads were dusty, requiring the corps commander to intervene personally. During the entire time there was not a word of encouragement from the commanding general, but only coarse and insulting remarks to the troops and their leaders. On the inside I was very angry about this conduct by my superior, and I was not surprised when both divisional commanders who had been ordered to report to the corps headquarters during the rest period told me in confidence that they felt compelled to complain to me about the commanding general. I promised to straighten out everything without a formal complaint. I knew from experience the difficult temperament of my commanding general, but also his ability to be agreeable to encouragement. I went to General von Fabeck and told him: "Your Excellency has really alienated the troops and their leaders today with your constant sharp criticism and loud voice. Let us assume for a moment that if our army commander, the crown prince of Prussia, had ridden along the march columns of XIII Army Corps today together with your Excellency, and he scolded the troops in the same manner. What would your Excellency have done then?" Fabeck's promptly answered, "I would have lodged a complaint." Then I told him, "Both divisional commanders want to do just that against Your Excellency, and Your Excellency's answer to my question proves that the divisional commanders are not wrong." Fabeck initially looked at me with rolling eyes, turned away, and paced back and forth angrily. Suddenly he came back to me and said, "Lossberg you are right. Fetch the two divisional commanders immediately." When they arrived he very openly asked them to forgive his temper and extend the same regrets to their subordinate leaders. He then asked both divisional commanders to shake hands as a sign that all was forgotten. Both division commanders happily did so, as they were good soldiers. That ended this incident in a fast and smooth manner, which pleased both me and the divisional commanders.

General von Fabeck was a very good soldier overall, but his innate roughness often got the better of him. He rarely uttered heartfelt praise. Even when the troops had conducted a difficult attack he could not find the praise and the fiery words. Even with those troops he usually only criticized such things as an incorrect position of the helmet and other uniform deficiencies. Whenever possible I tried to keep him away from direct contact with troops.[11] That was not so easy because the corps headquarters always positioned its command post far forward, and during the periods of combat it frequently was under heavy fire. In such situations the commanding general was wonderfully courageous and composed, providing a glowing example to the troops. He also was quite amenable to insightful proposals that ran counter to his opinion. Once the order was issued, he also had the gift of always sticking with the decision. In the inevitable crisis situations, he showed that he was a courageous soldier. I had to fight my way through many disagreements with my commanding general, but there still remained an overall and unconditional bond of trust between us regarding the welfare of the troops. We both believed in taking care of them.

The movements on 18 and 19 August, which reached Kuntzig on 19 August, were very exhausting in the extreme heat. The often poor roads caused delays that as always grew longer toward the rear of the column. On both days the troops did not get to rest until late. The people of Luxembourg, through whose southern territory the XIII Army Corps was marching, were very accommodating and openly showed their happiness that they were protected from a French invasion by the German advances. In the towns of Luxembourg, the population willingly made water available for the marching troops. In the billeting towns the troops almost always received free meals. This pleasant attitude in the conduct of the people changed immediately when we entered French territory. We faced strong hostility everywhere. The population also allowed themselves to get carried away by committing violent acts. In some areas they were even armed and fired on us. Energetic action restored order. Armed civilians were executed.[12]

Contact with the enemy did not occur on 18 and 19 August. The 3rd Cavalry Division secured the front of the right march order, while the 6th Cavalry Division operated in front of the army's left wing. Fifth Army headquarters initially remained in Thionville, but was preparing its new headquarters in Esch-sur-Alzette. The advance of the Fourth Army on our right flank reached about the same line. A French forward movement in a northwesterly direction that had been detected on 18 August north of Montmédy appeared to have reached the vicinity southwest of Bulles on 19 August. To evade that force the 3rd Cavalry Division skirted the area around Bulles.

On 20 August the XIII Army Corps marched from Kuntzig to Châtillon, Belgium, while the V Army Corps reached Étalle from Arlon, both in Belgium. The XVI Army Corps that day stopped northwest of Thionville, near Angevillers. The VI Reserve Corps was inserted on its right, and later reached the line Rodange–Audun-le-Tiche. The V Reserve Corps was brought up behind the

Fifth Army right wing to Capellen–Leudelange in Luxembourg. The 3rd Cavalry Division was positioned near Bulles; the 6th Cavalry Division remained on the army's left wing.

Lieutenant General Max Kämpffer, the Fifth Army general of engineers, was given the mission of quickly seizing the citadel at Longwy. The units attached to him for that mission included the XIII Army Corps' reinforced 52nd Infantry Brigade, a *Mörser*[13] regiment, two heavy field howitzer battalions, and the 20th Engineer Regiment. The Longwy garrison of some three thousand troops and forty to fifty guns remained passive, even though German infantry moved close to the citadel from the northeast on the afternoon of 20 August. The reinforcements attached to the 52nd Infantry Brigade included the 2nd Battalion, 65th Field Artillery Regiment, with a light ammunition column; the 8th Artillery Ammunition Column; the 13th Foot Artillery Regiment with a light ammunition column; the 3rd Company, 13th Engineer Battalion; one search light platoon; and the 3rd Medical Company.

The Fifth Army headquarters ordered a halt to the advance on 21 August. The one-day pause was intended to allow the combat forces to close up for a later resumption of the march in such a manner that the V and XIII Army Corps could advance to attack Longwy from the north and the VI Reserve Corps from the south. The XVI Army Corps was to prepare to intervene via a flanking movement. The V Reserve Corps remained in reserve behind the center of the army.

Attack Group (*Angriffsgruppe*) Kämpffer encircled the Longwy citadel from the east and northeast on 21 August, positioned the artillery behind the infantry screening positions, and opened fire that afternoon. The 3rd Cavalry Division was attached to the V Army Corps and ordered to advance toward the west. It encountered strong enemy infantry forces, and before it could attack the division lost contact. Under cover provided by a follow-on battalion from the V Army Corps, the 3rd Cavalry Division withdrew to Bulles. On the army's left wing the 6th Cavalry Division also made contact with advancing enemy elements, and broke contact after a short engagement.

We received reports of the successful conclusion of the battle for Lorraine, which eased the Fifth Army's concern about its left flank. I told my commanding general with confidence that strong forces from the Sixth and Seventh Armies would be redeployed to reinforce the main effort of the German attack at the operationally decisive point.

On 21 August the XIII Army Corps sent its own cavalry and infantry to reconnoiter toward the southwest. A General Staff officer also was sent off in the afternoon to reconnoiter the terrain near Bleid as a possible initial battlefield for the corps. In the course of 21 August aerial intelligence reports indicated that the opposing enemy was advancing against the whole front of the Fifth Army, and apparently echeloned in depth. Since these reports seemed to point toward an enemy attack, possibly to relieve the citadel at Longwy, the Fifth Army headquarters in the afternoon of 21 August decided to move the entire force into more favorable terrain for launching an attack. It held to that course of action, even though OHL in a telephone conversation maintained that the defense was the better course of action within the framework of overall operations, especially considering that the Fourth Army was still lagging behind. OHL finally acquiesced to the Fifth Army's decision. With the battle appearing imminent, all the subordinate corps commanders were ordered to report to the army headquarters in Esch-sur-Alzette for an orders briefing. During that briefing my Ia reported to me via telephone from corps headquarters that in the late afternoon our aviators had observed enemy columns advancing from the west between Ruette and Tellancourt. The corps commander alerted the corps and ordered the 27th Division to assume a position in readiness along the line Saint-Léger–Mousson. He also ordered the 26th Division to assemble near Rachecourt-sur-Marne. I immediately rushed back to the corps headquarters by car, armed with the general intent of the Fifth Army for 22 August. According to that intent, the V Army Corps with the attached 3rd Cavalry Division was to advance with its left wing at Latour-en-Woëvre, and then remain south of the town with security forces on its northern flank. The XIII Army Corps was to attack west of and past Longwy, with the right wing via Ruette, and with its left wing to Longwy. The VI Reserve Corps was to advance south of and past Longwy, with its right wing toward Longuyon and its left toward Pierrepont. The XVI Army Corps would advance with its right wing toward Joppécourt, but without crossing the line Joppécourt–Anderny initially. The 6th Cavalry Division, attached to the XVI Army Corps, was given the mission of screening the army's left flank. The V Reserve Corps was to fill the gap between the VI Reserve Corps and the XVI Army Corps via Crusnes and Aumetz.

The Fifth Army's scheme of maneuver was very bold and went far beyond the intended attack objectives that had been reported to OHL. The result would be a twenty-kilometer gap with the Fourth Army that the combat power of the 3rd Cavalry Division was not sufficient to cover. Thus, the Fifth Army's right flank would be very vulnerable. The chief of staff of the V Army Corps pointed this out during the orders briefing in Esch-sur-Alzette, and he also recommended that the Fifth Army headquarters coordinate with the Fourth Army to initiate the advance of their left wing VI Army Corps. He was told to communicate directly with the VI Army Corps, but that did not happen until 0300 hours on 22 August. After coordination with the Fourth Army headquarters, the order finally went out at 0400 hours for the VI Army Corps to jump off toward the south at 0600 hours. The Fifth Army headquarters was duly informed. In the meantime, the V Army Corps also put its troops on alert. The 9th Division was put on ready status southwest of Étalle, and the 10th Division was pulled into the area between Étalle and Vance.

The Battle of Longwy, 22 August 1914

The situation under which the XIII Army Corps entered into its first offensive battle against an also advancing enemy was extremely favorable. When the corps had been alerted on the evening of 21 August it already had approximately twenty hours of rest. During the hours of darkness, the corps' units assumed the ready positions for the advance, undetected by the enemy, and still had several hours of rest time in the nice warm weather. Assuming that the enemy would continue to advance on 22 August, he had to make contact while still in march columns, while the XIII Army Corps would already be deployed on line. Our own infantry and divisional artillery units were well forward, screening the corps' overall deployment. The assessments we had made from intently studying the terrain on the map were confirmed by the accurate reports of the General Staff officer we had sent forward on 21 August. Time and space were thoroughly calculated for the forward movement of both sides, and formed a firm basis later for developing the battle and the execution of the attack.

The corps order was issued at 2200 hours on 21 August. Starting at 0600 hours the following units were to come on line: the 27th Division initially toward Bleid and Signeulx, and the 26th Division, which initially had only the 51st Infantry Brigade available, with its right wing toward Ville-Houdlémont. The corps order was also delivered to Lieutenant General Kämpffer, who then released the heavy howitzers of the 1st Battalion, 13th Field Artillery, which arrived in the rear of the 26th Division at 0700 hours on 22 August.

At dawn on 22 August there was a heavy fog, which initially prevented any artillery support for the infantry. The divisions, therefore, were ordered to push their artillery forward as soon as their infantry made any contact with the enemy, and to launch a decisive attack only after the fog had lifted. According to the reports coming in, the enemy had occupied the heights northwest of Bleid on a line running to Mussy-la-Ville, and from there to Baranzy. The corps headquarters initially positioned its command post on a hill just south of Rachecourt-sur-Marne, which provided good oversight visibility. Both divisions were connected by telephone line. In the meantime, the entire artillery had occupied firing positions. At 0900 hours the fog lifted quickly and the visibility was good. Our entire artillery immediately started firing at the enemy artillery to the west of Bleid and south of Ville-Houdlémont. They were still mostly in marching columns and suffered heavy losses—as did the enemy's infantry.

On our right wing the 27th Division almost without a fight reached the hills east of Bleid with the 53rd Infantry Brigade. It then pulled up its artillery and seized the town of Bleid at about noon. The forest west of Bleid was taken from the east. On the left the 27th Division's 54th Infantry Brigade quickly made contact with the enemy positioned on the hills southwest of Mussy-la-Ville. After pulling up its artillery, the assault there started overrunning the enemy by 1100 hours. The brigade then advanced to Signeulx.

The 26th Division advanced with three battalions on line—and initially only with its right wing—approximately four hundred meters toward the village of Baranzy, which was occupied by the enemy. After moving the artillery forward, they assaulted and in quick succession threw the enemy out of Baranzy. Farther to the east, the 26th Division took strong fire from armed civilians on approaching Musson. They made short work of the resistance.

The attack resumed after the artillery moved forward. At 0935 hours the heavy howitzers of the 1st Battalion, 13th Field Artillery Regiment, along with the 2nd Battalion, 121st Infantry Regiment, and 3rd Battalion, 122nd Infantry Regiment, were attached to the 26th Division, since those units were no longer needed for the fight for the Longwy citadel.

By approximately 1300 hours the 27th Division's 54th Infantry Brigade and the 26th Division (minus four battalions) had completely destroyed the forces opposing them, inflicting very heavy losses on the enemy infantry. Their artillery, both as it came up and as it withdrew, suffered serious damage from our prepositioned batteries. The 27th Division's 53rd Infantry Brigade moved to secure the flank to the west and advanced as far as Saint-Léger to support the heavily engaged left wing of the V Army Corps. Originally only the 2nd Company, 13th Engineers, had been positioned there as flank security. By resisting stubbornly they held Saint-Léger until reinforcements from the 53rd Brigade arrived. As the fight continued, the 53rd Infantry Brigade reinforced with artillery and cavalry was no longer available to the XIII Army Corps. The courageous conduct of the 53rd had, however, greatly relieved the pressure on the V Army Corps' 10th Division.

The situation forward of the front line and especially on the XIII Army Corps' right flank was still unclear. The corps headquarters ordered a brief halt at 1300 hours to take on rations and ammunition and to conduct a reconnaissance of the terrain for the upcoming fighting. It also was necessary to reestablish contact with the adjacent corps. The attack was scheduled to resume at 1545 hours.

While riding forward the corps staff took heavy fire from armed citizens in Mussy-la-Ville. My helmet rim was dented by a grazing shot, but I did not notice it until a few days later because it was obscured by my helmet cover.[14] The staff's security force cleaned Mussy-la-Ville up thoroughly, and the staff suffered no casualties.

As the new enemy positions were identified gradually during the pause in fighting, the attack scheduled for 1545 hours was thoroughly prepared by the fire of the entire artillery force, including the 1st Battalion, 13th Foot Artillery Regiment. Following the preparation fire, the attack advanced very quickly, and the enemy evaded for the most part.

At 1845 hours the corps headquarters issued orders designating the objectives that still had to be secured on 22 August. The orders also designated a rest period starting at the onset of darkness. Saint-Pancré was designated as the corps' new command post, but the town itself was on fire, so the command post remained at a farm close to the road, co-located with the staff of the 27th Division.

During the night we lost contact with the staff of the 26th Division. Only in the early morning did we learn that the division had advanced with its left wing to Villers-la-Chèvre. We had no clear picture of the enemy situation at that point. Information about the outcome of the V and VI Army Corps' fights was unavailable. But since an enemy counterattack was possible for 23 August, the corps was only alerted for the resumption of the attack.

23 August 1914

Even though there was by the end of 22 August a general feeling of a battle won throughout all the units of the XIII Army Corps, the actual scale of our success did not become apparent until the morning of 23 August. The enemy had disappeared. The battlefield and the withdrawal routes were littered with discarded musette bags, broken weapons, and abandoned ammunition carriages. We had taken approximately two thousand prisoners. Nonetheless, we at the corps headquarters thought that the Fifth Army order that arrived at 0920 hours reporting the enemy's panic-stricken withdrawal was strongly exaggerated. That order also listed the XIII Army Corps' attack objectives for 23 August. Those rather ambitious objectives were for the right wing to advance via Charency[15] to Marville, and the left wing to Rupt-sur-Othain. That required us to seize the Othain Position, which reconnaissance indicated had been reinforced.

As soon as the corps had been assembled in several columns north of Tellancourt we were hit by French artillery. The corps headquarters, which was deployed far forward, also came under fire. Two horses were injured, but none of the members of the staff were hit. The commanding general himself rode up to a fleeing driver who had unyoked his horses and was galloping toward the rear and brought the man back to his senses. More of our artillery, including the

1st Battalion, 13th Foot Artillery, was deployed north of Tellancourt to cover the 27th Division—minus the reinforced 53rd Infantry Brigade, now designated Detachment Moser. That division attacked west of the Tellancourt–Longuyon road and with its right column in the direction of Charenzy, and pushed back enemy forces that apparently were only rear guards. Heavy and apparently long-range enemy artillery fire prevented the 27th Division from moving beyond Alondrelle-la-Malmaison and the ground to the south. Heavy enemy artillery fire also forced the 26th Division to advance slowly toward Longuyon. Since the troops were rather worn out from the previous fighting, the corps headquarters ordered a pause when we reached our positions in the late afternoon. Before receiving that order, however, the 26th Division's 51st Infantry Brigade reached the Chiers River and occupied Longuyon, from which the enemy had withdrawn.

While riding back to the corps headquarters in Tellancourt, members of the corps staff observed gunfire hitting the road and coming from the church steeple of that town. Eight armed citizens, including a priest, were captured, summarily court-martialed, and quickly executed. During the next few days this treacherous type of fighting was used by bypassed French soldiers in civilian clothes, who from the woods fired mostly at supply trains and other rear element columns. Finally, we felt that our only option was to burn down any houses from which such fire was received. This strong response resolved the problem. As we learned later, the French leadership had given their soldiers instructions to commit such acts. We even found civilian clothes in the backpacks of prisoners of war. The infamy of such orders, which were a slap in the face of all international law![16] On 23 August we captured 250 French prisoners, who for the most part had been captured in the forested parts of the battlefield. Many of them had been hiding in the high trees.

24 August 1914

The Fifth Army headquarters had limited itself on 23 August to only short telephonic instructions that kept to the framework of the attack order issued to the corps on the evening of 21 August. For the XIII Army Corps the implied tactical task was to take the Chiers sector completely, and then prepare for and execute the crossing of the Othain and advance into the sector beyond the river. Since the troops were quite exhausted from the previous two days and the enemy situation was not completely clear, the corps headquarters in the evening of 23 August issued only a general directive to further prepare for the attack and to conduct the appropriate staging of the artillery and infantry. After clarifying the situation with the adjacent corps, and primarily to give the infantry a much needed break, the corps headquarters did not issue the attack order to cross the Chiers and advance into the Chiers sector until 0920 hours on 24 August.

The assessment by the corps headquarters that the fighting would be conducted not as a hasty pursuit but as a deliberate attack proved to be correct. French infantry supported by strong artillery opposed the 27th Division along the entire Chiers sector. Opposite the 26th Division, whose 51st Brigade, supported by artillery, had already seized the hills just west of Longuyon, the enemy initiated an attack that was only repelled through the exemplary courage of the troops. Elements of the reinforced 53rd Infantry Brigade rejoined the 27th Division. The remainder of that brigade constituted the corps reserve. In the course of the day, one of its battalions was cross-attached to the 26th Division. The 27th Division advanced slowly in a deliberate attack, with the infantry advancing in waves across terrain that was well covered by the enemy. When, however, the serious situation of the 26th Division was recognized, the 27th Division increased its attack tempo. Meanwhile, the V Army Corps was no longer capable of executing the flank security mission that had been assigned to it by the Fifth Army headquarters. That corps reported that it had to pause until 1600 hours in vicinity of Ruette because its troops were exhausted.

Positioned on top of a hill with good observation, the XIII Army Corps command post recognized through periscope binoculars enemy withdrawal movements, and accordingly ordered an increase in the 27th Division's attack tempo. By evening that division was able to report that it had crossed the Chiers and had reached its attack objective for the day.

In front of the 26th Division the enemy broke off his attack and withdrew toward the west, covered by his very strong artillery. In order to ensure that the division was able to organize its units and to ensure some rest for its troops, the corps headquarters attached the entire corps reserve to it, directing that those elements would be used as an outpost guard. Those forward elements extended the 27th Division's front line to the south, so that by the evening of 24 August the 27th Division held the corps' frontline trace, with the 26th Division deployed close behind the left wing.

On 24 August the adjacent V Army Corps on our right had probed its way forward with only minimal forces into the Chiers sector. The adjacent VI Reserve Corps on our left ran into an enemy counterattack as it was advancing with its right wing division east of Longuyon. After a lengthy fight the VI Reserve Corps finally gained the upper hand, and by the evening they had managed to link up along the Longuyon–Rouvrois-sur-Meuse road with the unit on their left.

Toward the evening the corps commander and I went to the 26th Division. On the trip there and back we had a hard time getting through the burning city of Longuyon. Later that evening we received from the Fifth Army the order for the following day, which required us to attack following the V Army Corps and to cross the Villers-le-Rond–Petit Xivry–Longuyon line.

25 August 1914

The reports coming in throughout the night showed that the enemy had withdrawn to behind the Othain sector. At 0500 hours the corps headquarters arrived at its new command post west of Longuyon. Once there, I dictated the draft of the corps order for our subordinate units, based on what reports we had received. The 27th Division was tasked to advance toward the Othain, supported by the 26th Division's artillery and the corps' heavy artillery, and then force the enemy to expose his true strength. Because there was quite a gap between us and the V Army Corps, the 27th Division was given specific instructions not to let itself under any circumstances be pushed to the right and outside of its designated attack sector. The 26th Division, which had suffered heavily on 24 August, remained initially in its current assembly area as the corps reserve.

It soon became clear from the developing noise of battle that the enemy still had troops located on this side of the Othain. The rather far forward corps command post also took artillery and machine gun fire, but without sustaining any damage. An artillery battalion that was approaching at a gallop right in front of us took some losses. Bolting horses still hooked up to limbers charged toward the corps staff, but we caught them. An administrative staff officer attached to the corps headquarters distinguished himself particularly in this action, despite his relative youth. He was the second son of Duke Albrecht, the commanding general of the Fourth Army, and he was an all-around competent officer.

Toward 1100 hours the 27th Division reported that it had taken Grand-Failly in the Othain sector. Petit-Failly, situated farther north, was free of the enemy. Later during the day it turned out that the enemy was conducting a planned withdrawal under cover of strong artillery toward the Loison sector. The corps staff rode ahead and soon developed the assessment that the enemy also was continuing his withdrawal beyond the Loison. Shortly after 1300 hours I reported to the Fifth Army commander by telephone the situation at the XIII Army Corps and the follow-on units that were still lagging on both sides. I also reported that the XIII Army Corps was continuing the advance to the Loison sector, which elements of our advance guard reached that day. In the evening the 27th Division bivouacked around Rupt-sur-Othain, the 26th Division farther to the east. The XIII Corps headquarters repositioned the IV Cavalry Corps from Tellancourt to Grand-Failly. Aviation reconnaissance showed that the enemy in front of the Fifth Army was withdrawing, partly west toward the Meuse and partly southwest in the direction of Verdun. The adjacent V Army Corps on our right reached Marville with its lead elements; the VI Reserve Corps on the left reached the line Saint-Laurent-sur-Othain–Pillon. The VI Reserve Corps and the V Reserve Corps to its south had only been able to throw the enemy back from the Othain sector after a lengthy fight. On 25 August consistently stronger enemy activity from the south became evident, directed against the XVI Army Corps, which was on the Fifth Army's left wing. That made it necessary to swing the whole XVI Army Corps and also the left wing division of the V Reserve Corps to face the south and southwest. In some areas it became necessary to conduct evasive actions against the enemy attacking with superior forces. Relief, however, arrived in the form of German units from Fortress Metz advancing into the enemy's flank. With the 3rd Cavalry Division moving from the Fifth Army's left wing to its right, it became necessary to reinforce against the threat to the southern flank. The Fifth Army's plan to attack and destroy the enemy east of the Meuse by enveloping him on both of his wings, with the V Army Corps attacking from the right and the XVI Army Corps from the left, thus collapsed. In the evening of 25 August the XVI Army Corps dug in along the line Spincourt–Landres.

In the afternoon of 25 August the garrison of the citadel at Longwy capitulated. More than three thousand prisoners (including twenty-nine officers), fifty guns, and large quantities of equipment were captured by Attack Group Kämpffer, which was dissolved on 27 August.

The Fifth Army headquarters determined that its next task was to pursue the beaten enemy toward the Meuse and, while ensuring security against Verdun, to force the crossing of the Meuse in coordination with the Fourth Army.

26 August 1914

The Fifth Army order issued in the evening of 25 August directed only the V and XIII Army Corps on the right wing to pursue the enemy, which was conducting evasive action toward the Meuse. The other corps generally were to remain in their positions. The IV Cavalry Corps was attached to the XVI Army Corps and ordered to move to the Orne sector in advance of the corps front. As march objectives the V Army Corps was assigned Vittarville, and the XIII Army Corps the line Dombras–Merles-sur-Loison, and to the southeast.

Based on the reports coming in during the night of 25–26 August, the XIII Army Corps headquarters initially estimated that the Loison sector could only be taken with a fight. It soon became clear, however, that the enemy had withdrawn. The order was then issued immediately to cross the Loison, and the corps reported to the Fifth Army that it would advance with the 27th Division to Dombras and with the 26th Division to the line Dombras–Merles-sur-Loison–Villers-lès-Mangiennes. The corps would then dig in there and prepare to advance on either Damvillers or Mangiennes at any time. The Fifth Army headquarters in return reported that the march direction toward Mangiennes was assigned to the VI Reserve Corps, and the V Army Corps was to remain in its current positions near Delut–Marville.

Incoming intelligence reports confirmed that the enemy was withdrawing across the Meuse River. The Fifth Army headquarters decided to advance with freshly assembled covering forces against Verdun and against the enemy's defended Meuse sector. The rest day of 27 August was to be used to reestablish order in the units, replace materiel, and organize the movements of the rear echelons and columns. The assault forces that had been assembled for the attack against Longwy for the most part returned to their parent units. The 13th, 43rd, and 45th Landwehr Brigades directly under the Fifth Army headquarters were disbanded and the troops were reassigned to the rear area command to provide security for the supply lines. The artillery of those brigades was reassigned to the still existing 53rd and 9th Bavarian Landwehr Brigades. The 27th Landwehr Regiment and half a squadron of the 13th Landwehr Brigade were attached to the XIII Army Corps to secure our rearward lines. In the evening of 26 August, the Fifth Army headquarters received an order to pull the V Army Corps out of the front line and to initiate its movement toward Thionville, to make it available to OHL.

27 August 1914 (Rest Day)

An incident occurred in the early morning hours close to the corps headquarters in Grand-Failly, which at the time was secured by forward guard elements. The headquarters commandant of the IV Cavalry Corps conducted a mounted muster, and then he had the horses exercised without saddles on the ground east of the town. Suddenly, the horses were hit by fire from a large group of French stragglers that had left their hiding positions in the forest and were trying to make their way to the Meuse. Many of the horses tore away from their leads and stormed off in wild disarray toward their stables in Grand-Failly. Several horses were hit and rendered unusable. The alerted troops in Grand-Failly later captured the scattered French troops after a short fight. The headquarters commandant received the appropriate admonition for his actions, which were far too peacetime-oriented.

In conversations with my commanding general I developed my ideas on how it would now be necessary to act along the front line of the middle group—Fourth and Fifth Armies—of the German Army. All I knew about the fighting of the northern group—First, Second, and Third Armies—was only that they had beaten the enemy several times during their rapid advance, and were pursuing in the direction of Paris. Of the southern group—Sixth and Seventh Armies—I only knew about the successful outcome of their battle at Château-Salins. Because of that victory I considered that the German Army's overall left flank was secured in such a manner that large elements of the southern group could be assigned to new missions. I assumed that units from the southern group would be redeployed to the Eastern Front, and that several army corps and the III Cavalry Corps would be redeployed north to the overall right wing. Since the southern group had received all of its allocated replacement divisions, I also assumed that two corps would still be available in the south for other missions. From my many General Staff assignments during peacetime I was well acquainted with the strength of the Meuse Position, as well as the significance of the fortification line Verdun–Toul–Épinal and the defensive system existing along the Lorraine border. I also was aware of the minimal strength of the small barrier forts (*Sperrforts*) between Verdun and Toul. From the situation as I saw it on 27 August, it was clear to me that the enemy defending the Meuse line north of Verdun had to hold the river line long enough so that the French and British armies farther north could complete their withdrawal movement and then could assume a front line oriented more toward the north. That meant the enemy initially holding the Meuse line north of Verdun at all costs, and thus very heavy and time-consuming fighting for the Fifth Army units attacking along that front. The Fifth Army had to advance its attack continuously, even after breaking through the Meuse line, keeping Fortress Verdun in its left flank and at an appropriate distance because of its long-range guns. Furthermore, as long as the French had the forces available south of Metz, a French counterattack could be anticipated from the line of fortresses from Verdun to Toul. Such a counterattack could threaten the victorious Fifth Army even after it had advanced across the Meuse and then had pivoted toward the southwest. Executing such a maneuver, elements of the Fifth Army would have to be pulled back across the Meuse to provide security in the area east of Verdun.

Considering the difficulties of crossing the Meuse against a likely equal opponent and the dangers for the left flank that could develop from French counterattacks from the Verdun–Toul line, I thought it would be best to deploy the Fifth Army for an attack toward the west on both sides of Verdun, with the V Army Corps (whose detachment I only learned about later), XIII Army Corps, and VI Reserve Corps advancing north past Verdun, and the V Reserve Corps, XVI Army Corps, IV Cavalry Corps, and two army corps from the Sixth Army advancing south past Verdun. The gap between the two attacking forces would have to be covered by the available Landwehr brigades.

The southern group of armies had been ordered to conduct a crossing of the

Meuse near Saint-Mihiel, at approximately its center of advance, and then to advance in a generally westerly direction. Such a maneuver would interdict the French use of the railroads west of Toul–Verdun, which would severely restrict the resupply of the French combat elements fighting north of Verdun along the Meuse. The success of the attack would automatically force the withdrawal of the French from the Meuse line north of Verdun, and also isolate Fortress Verdun itself. If the enemy were to commit stronger elements against the German attack south of Verdun, they would be unavailable to support the fight against the German Army's overall right wing in the north.

My commanding general, who himself had spent many years in the General Staff, and who therefore, like me, was operationally schooled, agreed fully with my thoughts. One can imagine our surprise when we learned much later that after the Battle of Château-Salins all the units of the Sixth and Seventh Armies were committed to the pursuit in the direction of Épinal, and later for the breakthrough between Toul and Épinal. We also were surprised that the XI Army Corps and the Guards Reserve Corps were detached from the army's overall right wing and had redeployed to the Eastern Front. We had expected that two or three corps from the left wing would have been shifted to reinforce the right wing, thus guaranteeing operational victory.

OHL made a grave mistake when it staged the Sixth and Seventh Armies for a breakthrough between Toul and Épinal. Among the older General Staff officers who had been schooled during peacetime and were quite familiar with the existing French fortification network, we knew that such an attack could only succeed if it was conducted as a siege operation, which of course would have been a lengthy and time-consuming process. Committing strong German forces without the necessary heavy and super-heavy artillery at a point that was not operationally decisive, and for the purpose of gaining a tactical advantage in a long and drawn out fight, robbed the German Army of an operational victory during the World War's first large-scale battle of decision.

In the afternoon of 27 August the corps commanders met at the Fifth Army headquarters in Esch-sur-Alzette and were given a broad-brush briefing of the Fifth Army's intentions. The army order issued that evening directed the detachment of the V Army Corps for its commitment to other missions. The VI Army Corps, the left wing corps of the Fourth Army, was reassigned to the Fifth Army. The IV Cavalry Corps, which up to this point had been on the Fifth Army's left wing, was ordered to reach on 28 August the area near the Meuse line from Dun-sur-Meuse to Sivry-sur-Meuse. The XIII Army Corps was assigned the route of advance Grand-Failly–Marville–Jametz–Louppy-sur-Loison–Dun-sur-Meuse, crossing the Meuse at that point. One engineer regiment and a foot artillery regiment, which until then had been part of the V Army Corps, remained in position opposite Fortress Montmédy. The weather on 27 August was poor for visibility, and we had no aerial reconnaissance. The XIII Army Corps' cavalry units had detected enemy in position on the western bank of the Meuse in the vicinity of Dannevoux–Forges-sur-Meuse, with more troop movements to their rear.

28 August 1914

Moving toward the northwest from its previous positions, the XIII Army Corps advanced along its assigned march route with two mixed battalions forward to secure the move to the west. Simultaneously, those two battalions provided support to the IV Cavalry Corps, which had to conduct a long and hard march on 28 August from the Fifth Army's left flank. The XIII Army Corps' advance was conducted with the 27th Division in the lead and the 26th Division trailing. Upon receiving reports that the VI Army Corps, which had already crossed the Meuse at Stenay, was facing superior enemy forces and had been forced back with its left wing on to the right bank of the Meuse, the 27th Division's 19th Ulan Regiment[17] was sent out toward Mouzon to secure the corps' right flank and to maintain contact with the VI Army Corps south of Stenay. The IV Cavalry Corps was requested to move forward close to the Meuse, in the vicinity and north of Dun-sur-Meuse. That move would later facilitate an early advance of the XIII Corps' artillery on to the dominating hills there.

In the evening the 27th Division reached Louppy-sur-Loison, Jametz, and Marville. The 26th Division, after receiving reattachment of the 52nd Infantry Brigade after its release from operations in the vicinity of Longwy, reached the region north of Rupt-sur-Othain–Grand-Failly. Security forces that moved forward toward Montmédy were able to get close to the fortress in the face of only weak enemy resistance. The 53rd and 9th Bavarian Landwehr Brigades designated to capture the fortress only reached the area in the vicinity of Tellancourt with their right wing, because their march route crossed that of the V Army Corps, which was advancing toward the east in the direction of Thionville. On the left of the XIII Army Corps the VI Reserve Corps reached Vittarville with its lead elements. In the south the XVI Army Corps advanced toward the Meuse, with its lead elements reaching the Mangiennes area. Farther to the west the V Reserve Corps, assigned the mission of screening against Fortress Verdun, concentrated its units around Gibercy. Both aerial and ground reconnaissance reported that the Meuse bridges had been destroyed at Sassey-sur-Meuse and Sivry-sur-Meuse. On the left bank of the Meuse opposite the XIII Army Corps the enemy was digging in west of Sassey-sur-Meuse and Dun-sur-Meuse. Enemy artillery on the left bank of the Meuse fired on anything, even if it was just German patrols.

The Fifth Army order for 29 August, which assumed only weak enemy resistance at the Meuse, ordered the continuation of the advance. XIII Army Corps was to reach the Meuse at 1000 hours via Murvaux, with its lead elements at Sassey-sur-Meuse and Dun-sur-Meuse. After crossing the Meuse at Mont-devant-Sassey and south of it, the corps would then advance in a northwesterly direction to support the Fourth Army. The IV Cavalry Corps was to cross only under the cover of the infantry forces already across, and later, after passing to the left of the XIII Army Corps, was to thrust into the flank and the rear of the enemy forces opposing the Fourth Amy.

29 August 1914

XIII Army Corps initially jumped off in column, with the 27th Division in the lead marching with its main body through Louppy-sur-Loison, Murvaux, and Dun-sur-Meuse. Right flank security was provided by two battalions of the 123rd Infantry Regiment, covering from Louppy-sur-Loison through the forest that lies north of the main route of march. Engineers and bridging units were positioned far forward in order to be in place to support a crossing. The 26th Division followed the main column of the 27th Division. In order to facilitate the passage of the XIII Army Corps, the IV Cavalry Corps assembled in the vicinity and north of Bréhéville, which was south of and close to the XIII Army Corps' route of advance.

An incredible heat set in during the early morning hours of 29 August. I have rarely experienced so much dust as there was on the route of march. It was especially hard on the troops advancing through the forests, and it limited greatly their range of observation. We suffered numerous march casualties because of the heat and the lack of water, and we had to halt for several rest stops. The corps staff rode at the point of the main body of the 27th Division's advance guard. During a rest stop in the forest north of Bréhéville I personally rode ahead to the advance guard. When I arrived I heard surprisingly strong infantry and machine gun fire coming from behind me. I ordered the rear elements of the advance guard battalion to turn around immediately and set them moving toward the sound of the battle. It turned out that the entire two thousand- to three thousand-man garrison of Fortress Montmédy had evacuated the position on order of the French High Command, and while trying to fight their way through south toward Verdun happened to march right through the gap between the 27th Division's resting advance guard and the main body. The point of the French force made contact with the 3rd Cavalry Division's northernmost 24th Dragoon Regiment.[18] Intense fighting erupted, during which the dragoons regiment and elements of the advance guard and the right flank security of the

27th Division suffered considerable losses. For the most part the French territorial troops fought back bravely, but they were overcome quickly by a concentrated encircling attack by the German troops. In some cases the French troops acted treacherously, throwing down their weapons and then picking them up and firing as the German troops approached. We naturally punished such infamous conduct with summary executions. The hopeless fight cost the French 300 dead and 535 prisoners, including seven officers captured. The rest fled into the forests south of our march route and were almost all captured later by the IV Cavalry Corps and the VI Reserve Corps linked in to the south. Major Reinhardt, the commandant of Montmédy, was among the officers we captured. When our Ia, who spoke French fluently, interrogated Reinhardt, he asked him why he had abandoned the position he was responsible for. Maintaining his good bearing, the French major reached into his map case and pulled out an order signed by the French commander in chief, General Joseph Jacques Césaire Joffre, which stated approximately "after Fortress Montmédy has fulfilled its purpose, the garrison personnel will withdraw toward Verdun." In German military thinking such an order was incomprehensible. We considered that every fortification should be defended to the last man, and thus tie down enemy forces, above all enemy artillery. Even if one considered it impossible to hold the totally antiquated Montmédy fortress for long, and then surrendered it deliberately, the withdrawing garrison personnel should not have been ordered to the south toward Verdun, but rather to the southwest toward the Meuse. It must have been clear to the French even at the time that from there the garrison would have been able to escape across the river without a fight. When we told the commandant that, he clearly became very embarrassed, but still maintained his good military bearing. We sent him on to the Fifth Army headquarters for further interrogation. With the surrender of Montmédy, the units committed to taking that fort became available for other missions.

I soon rode ahead to Murvaux. In that densely built-up town I found a hodgepodge of combat units and vehicles and elements of bridging units. By intervening energetically, I gradually was able to establish some order there, making sure that the follow-on units would come on line outside of the town.

Since the enemy situation on the other side of the Meuse was uncertain, our own forward infantry elements were ordered to advance to the Meuse quickly, in order to cover the artillery advance. At 1000 hours the corps headquarters pulled forward the heavy guns of the 1st Battalion, 13th Foot Artillery. At 1115 hours the heavy howitzer battalion moved out from its positions situated behind Hill 350 lying north of Murvaux and moved into the zone of the enemy's artillery fire near Mont-devant-Sassey. The bridging units were ordered forward at 1140 hours. At the same time the 27th Division deployed its forward unit, the

53rd Infantry Brigade commanded by General von Moser, toward the Meuse on both sides of Dun-sur-Meuse, and positioned it behind the divisional artillery brigade, which opened fire at 1400 hours. Aerial reconnaissance verified that the enemy was not responding, from which we concluded that they had abandoned the west bank of the Meuse. As our infantry was advancing at 1530 hours, strong enemy artillery abruptly opened fire on to the forested area southeast of Dun-sur-Meuse. In the meantime the 27th Division's artillery had moved forward to the east of Dun-sur-Meuse. An artillery duel ensued, with the guns on both sides handicapped by inaccurate observation.

At 1700 hours we received from the VI Reserve Corps intelligence based on aerial observation indicating that the enemy was deployed in corps strength west of Brieulles-sur-Meuse–Nantillois. The observers had detected entrenching activities on the western bank of the Meuse. Under such circumstances, both the VI Reserve Corps and the XVI Army Corps could not consider crossing the Meuse that day.

With a similar assessment of the situation, the XIII Army Corps also had to forego crossing the river on 29 August. The 26th Division to the north of the 27th Division had advanced through Milly-sur-Bradon to Sassey-sur-Meuse, but only reached the Meuse with its forward elements around 1800 hours.

By 1900 hours we established telephone contact with the Fifth Army headquarters. At about the same time the officer who had escorted the commandant of Fortress Montmédy to the Fifth Army headquarters came back in his staff car and reported that based on aerial reconnaissance the Fifth Army headquarters had assessed that the enemy was holding the left bank of the Meuse with only weak forces, while he was deployed in strongly reinforced positions between Villers-en-Argonne and north of Montfaucon-d'Argonne. Soon thereafter we received the following order from the Fifth Army by telephone: "Tie down the enemy to the front, with the XVI Army Corps and VI Reserve Corps conducting a penetration of the enemy west of the Meuse in coordination with the Fourth Army." Consequently, the XIII Army Corps issued an order to cross the Meuse with the 26th Division at Sassey-sur-Meuse in the direction of Montigny-devant-Sassey, and with half of the 27th Division at Dun-sur-Meuse in the direction toward Doulcon. The remaining forces would be the corps reserve initially.

Soon after moving out of the forests east and southeast of Dun-sur-Meuse, the 27th Division took strong enemy artillery fire, including from large-caliber guns, and decided correctly to conduct the crossing only after making an extensive reconnaissance at the onset of darkness. At 1800 hours the forward elements of the 26th Division reached the riverbank under the cover of its artillery positioned northeast of Milly-sur-Bradon. They had not encountered any enemy resistance. The stone bridge at Sassey-sur-Meuse was so completely destroyed that it would have taken a long time to rebuild it. Thus, during the night a military bridge was constructed under infantry cover close to the southern edge of Sassey-sur-Meuse.

The IV Cavalry Corps remained for the night north of Bréhéville. The VI Army Corps remained with its northern division positioned near Fontaines[19] and only put out advance guards to probe toward the Meuse. The situation of our adjacent VI Army Corps on the right was not entirely clear, but it appeared that the corps had managed to put its left wing back on the western side of the Meuse. The Fifth Army headquarters was still at Esch-sur-Alzette, but a forward command post had advanced to Beuveille—six kilometers east of Longuyon—from which the army commander and his primary staff operated.

30 August 1914

At 0200 hours the 26th Division's 51st Infantry Brigade started crossing the Meuse on pontoons. By 0500 hours the replacement bridge near the destroyed bridge at Sassey-sur-Meuse was completed. The 26th Division's 52nd Infantry Brigade started crossing immediately, followed by the divisional artillery and then the 27th Division's 54th Infantry Brigade. By 0930 hours the 26th Division was completely across, except for one field artillery battalion that remained in position on the eastern bank. The troops that had crossed initially occupied and reinforced a bridgehead position east of the line Montigny-devant-Sassey–Mont-devant-Sassey. Even though that position could be over-watched by the enemy, the XIII Army Corps could not attack until the VI Army Corps had arrived. During 29 August that unit had gained the left bank of the Meuse along the entire front behind the enemy, who was withdrawing from the Meuse in general. The XIII Army Corps was now in the process of advancing initially in a westerly direction. But some time was still required before the VI Army Corps could execute its portion of the Fifth Army order to advance in a direct southerly direction toward Villers-devant-Dun. The Fifth Army's heavy howitzer regiment was attached to the XIII Army Corps after the surrender of Montmédy, but it had not yet moved up close enough to go into battery. The IV Cavalry Corps, which on its own initiative was marching toward Stenay, was still quite a distance away.

Thus, on 30 August the 26th Division initially had to remain in its positions because enemy forces of divisional strength had been observed in the vicinity of Nouart and could hit the northern flank of our attack, which was oriented toward the southwest. To the front the enemy was deploying infantry against the bridgehead, and also opened up with artillery fire, but did not go into the attack. In the late afternoon the 2nd Battalion, 6th Mörser Regiment, was in position north of Murvaux. In the 26th Division's area of operations the fighting was limited to artillery duels.

The 27th Division opened fire with artillery again at daybreak. The 127th Infantry Regiment took Dun-sur-Meuse without a fight that morning and repaired the Meuse bridge, enabling the infantry to cross in columns. One infantry company advanced toward Doulcon. Infantry patrols were out. At 0745 hours the 27th Division received the order from the corps headquarters to repair the bridge at Dun-sur-Meuse so that it could be crossed by all units of all the arms, and then to move forward the 1st Battalion, 13th Foot Artillery Regiment, to the east of Dun-sur-Meuse. The remainder of the 6th Mörser Regiment then assumed their firing positions.

The 123rd Infantry Regiment, on its own initiative and contrary to orders from the corps headquarters, followed the one infantry company that had already crossed at Dun-sur-Meuse. It was attacked by superior enemy forces supported by artillery, and was pushed to the north against the western bank of the Meuse, with heavy losses. The 123rd Infantry Regiment was then relieved in place by another regiment of the 27th Division that had crossed at Sassey-sur-Meuse, and the 123rd went into corps reserve.

During the course of the afternoon aerial reconnaissance reported that two enemy corps were advancing from the south, and at around 1500 had reached Barricourt and Buzancy with their point elements. This intelligence imposed temporary restraint on our own attack plans.

The IV Cavalry Corps, which had crossed the Meuse on a foot bridge at Stenay, did not comply with the XIII Army Corps' request to advance south; rather, it remained for the day northwest and west of Stenay. Meanwhile, work on an auxiliary bridge was started at Stenay. In the late evening several engineer companies of Attack Group Montmédy arrived.

At the request of the XIII Army Corps, the VI Army Corps at 1700 hours went on alert and advanced from Beaumont-en-Argonne, with its eastern wing toward Nouart. Only at 2130 hours did the XIII Army Corps receive a Fifth Army order that actually directed the VI Army Corps to go forward. At 2230 hours the XIII Army Corps transmitted the army order to the IV Cavalry Corps, ordering that unit to advance in a southerly direction in support of the XIII Army Corps.

The VI Reserve Corps and XVI Army Corps had, in fact, initiated the crossing of the Meuse, but the crossing failed owing to strong defensive fires from the enemy's artillery. At the request of the XIII Army Corps, the VI Reserve Corps on the morning of 31 August sent a reinforced infantry brigade toward Dun-sur-Meuse in order to provide support for the XIII Army Corps in the event of an emergency.

On 30 August at 1930 hours the Fifth Army headquarters issued the order for the VI Army Corps to advance in a southerly direction with its left wing via Nouart, supporting the advance of the XIII Army Corps against enemy forces in prepared positions in the vicinity of Villers-devant-Dun–Dannevoux. The IV Cavalry Corps was also ordered to resume advancing on 31 August, with two mixed Landwehr brigades moving into Stenay.

In the evening of 30 August, the Fifth Army headquarters reassumed control of the V Army Corps, which had become available again after the victorious Battle of Tannenberg in the east. The Fifth Army planned to commit that corps on its northern wing, and issued the corresponding marching orders.

31 August 1914

Trusting that the corps' right flank was secured by the adjacent IV Cavalry Corps and VI Army Corps, which had been ordered to move out toward the south by the Fifth Army headquarters, the commanding general of the XIII Army Corps decided to go on the attack. The corps order that went out at 0914 hours directed the 26th Division to advance via Halles-sous-les-Côtes–Nouart. The 27th Division was to advance across the line Montigny-devant-Sassey–Mont-devant-Sassey–and attack the hills southeast of Mont-devant-Sassey in the direction toward Villers-devant-Dun. The elements of the 27th Division that were still positioned in the vicinity of Dun-sur-Meuse, including the 1st Battalion, 13th Foot Artillery, were to support the advance of the adjacent 11th Reserve Division on our right. Initially our attacks got off to a slow start because of heavy enemy artillery fire targeting the 26th Division and the 27th Division's 54th Infantry Brigade from the early morning on. The artillery fire was followed by intense if not fully coordinated enemy infantry attacks. The anticipated support from the IV Cavalry Corps and VI Army Corps also failed to materialize. Shortly after crossing the line of departure the 12th Division of the VI Army Corps was attacked by strong enemy forces in the vicinity of the Vaux-devant-Damloup hills, and had a hard time maintaining the upper hand. The 11th Division that was moving up to the west of the 12th Division was also engaged in heavy fighting. Consequently, any kind of support from the VI Army Corps became impossible. In the morning of 31 August the IV Cavalry Corps ordered its northern 3rd Cavalry Division to attack the enemy in the vicinity of Beaufort-en-Argonne, and then to continue to advance toward Montigny-devant-Sassey. The 6th Cavalry Division was to screen directly the right flank of the XIII Army Corps by advancing toward Halles-sous-les-Côtes. The attack of the 3rd Cavalry Division was not successful. During the course of the day that division moved back toward the northwest of Stenay in order to conduct horseshoe maintenance. Its Jäger battalion[20] linked up with the 6th Cavalry Division. During the division's advance it had ordered an attached engineer company and the Jäger battalion to attack Beauclair, with elements also advancing toward Beaufort-en-Argonne. The enemy in that position withdrew, however. The division refrained from attacking Beauclair because of increased enemy artillery fire from the direction of Montigny-devant-Sassey, which threatened the divisional left flank. That afternoon the commander of the IV Cavalry Corps ordered the 6th Cavalry Division to withdraw across the military bridge south of Mouzon that had been built by the XIII Army Corps and to then assume positions on the right bank of the Meuse north of Mouzon. The cavalry's withdrawal did not exactly impress us, because the XIII Army Corps was very attack oriented. Our commanding general had established his forward command post near the front line, and the withdrawal took place just at the time when the 26th Division jumped off in the attack. We immediately sent a liaison officer to the commander of the 6th Cavalry Division, who insisted that they leave at least one mounted battalion in position, and that the engineer company attached to the cavalry division be reattached to the 26th Division. The 53rd Landwehr Brigade assumed the mission of the IV Cavalry Corps. At noon the brigade together with the engineer company advanced from Stenay and attacked Beauclair that evening. The 9th Landwehr Brigade, also advancing from Stenay, reached Beaufort-en-Argonne that evening, but the enemy had abandoned the position.

As the arrival of the two Landwehr brigades gave at least some protection to the XIII Army Corps' right wing, the 51st Infantry Brigade deployed to the left initially and on its own initiative attacked Montigny-devant-Sassay. Shortly before the assault I relayed the corps order by telephone to the commander of the Mörser regiment to soften up Montigny-devant-Sassey with a concentrated barrage. I had just completed my telephone call when the signal came from the forward line to "March ahead quickly!" Thank God the officers of the Mörser regiment were paying attention, and they shifted their fire from Montigny-devant-Sassey toward the enemy artillery. In Montigny-devant-Sassey heavy fighting ensued house-to-house and for the barricades. In the bloody melee the brave Württembergers maintained the upper hand and advanced from the town and to the forest to the south and all the way to the Montigny-devant-Sassey–Villers-devant-Dun road. More than three hundred prisoners were taken in the process. The 52nd Infantry Brigade also moved forward, courageously attacking and seizing the town of Halles-sous-les-Côtes by 1900 hours. To the left of the 26th Division, the 27th Division also attacked. During a bloody fight its forward-deployed 54th Infantry Brigade overcame stubborn enemy resistance in the thick of the forest on both sides of the Mont-devant-Sassey to Villers-devant-Dun road. The remaining elements of the 27th Division had to be committed to repel an enemy attack against the left wing of the 54th Infantry Brigade, and to close a gap that had developed between the 26th and the 27th Divisions. In the evening the corps headquarters ordered the troops to dig in and hold at the positions they had reached.

During the course of the morning the 11th Reserve Division of the adjacent VI Reserve Corps on our left forced a crossing at Dun-sur-Meuse and consolidated their position. After the VI Reserve Corps relinquished control of the crossing site at Vilosnes to the XVI Army Corps, the 12th Reserve Division consolidated at Fontaines, southeast of Dun-sur-Meuse. Strong enemy artillery fire, however, prevented the 11th Reserve Division from attacking. After the river crossing the 11th Reserve Division freed up the left wing of the 27th Division, and its elements reached the southern edge of the forest south of Mont-devant-Sassey.

The XVI Army Corps advanced its 34th Division, which up to that point had been held back, to the crossing point at Vilosnes and prepared to cross the Meuse there and at Sivry-sur-Marne with its 33rd Division. The XIII Army Corps headquarters spent the night of 31 August–1 September at a farm north of Sassey-sur-Meuse. We received reports from the VI Army Corps indicating that the enemy opposing them was starting to crumble, and that they would attack on 1 September.

1 September 1914

The reconnaissance reports we received during the night and the early morning hours of 1 September indicated that the enemy was dug into a reinforced position west of Aincreville. There were still considerable elements of the 27th Divisions' artillery positioned east of Dun-sur-Meuse that could deliver flanking fire ahead of the division's lead units, and also provide support for the 11th Reserve Division. Therefore, only the 1st Battalion, 13th Foot Artillery, was pulled ahead across the Meuse at Sassey-sur-Meuse. The 26th Division was ordered to seize the hills south of Barricourt that day, and the 27th Division was to remain in its current position and prepare to attack. The 26th Division reached its assigned objective without any serious fighting, and at Barricourt it linked up with the left wing of the VI Army Corps. The enemy forces that had been in Barricourt had withdrawn.

From a captured French document we learned the details of the improved enemy defenses west of Aincreville. The corps commander decided to attack that position only after a thorough preparation by the corps artillery, which was not yet completely in battery. Landwehr Division Francke,[21] under the command of Lieutenant General Adolf Francke, consisted of the 53rd and the 9th Bavarian Landwehr Brigades. It remained in its current position at Beaufort-en-

Argonne and Stenay as the corps reserve. By that evening indicators suggested that the enemy opposite our front line was withdrawing his major forces under the cover of his heavy artillery deployed in reinforced positions to his rear.

The adjacent VI Reserve Corps on our left occupied the Villers-devant-Dun–Doulcon road with its 11th Reserve Division after the latter town was taken by the 12th Reserve Division, which had crossed the river at Dun-sur-Meuse. The enemy was withdrawing in a southwesterly direction.

While heavily engaged, the XVI Army Corps on 1 September executed a forced crossing of the Meuse in the vicinity of Vilosnes. The corps advanced its 34th Division, which then turned south, but only got a little farther than Dannevoux. Meanwhile, the crossing of the 33rd Division at Sivry-sur-Meuse was impossible because of heavy counterfire. The 33rd Division then was rerouted, passed through a second bridge that was constructed at Vilosnes, and then was sent forward echeloned left and close to the Meuse toward the 34th Division. The right wing of the XVI Army Corps reached Dannevoux in the evening of 1 September, but then encountered very strong enemy resistance. After heavy fighting, the 33rd Division that evening reached the area north of Gercourt.[22] The XVI Army Corps' flank security elements, which had been left behind on the right bank of the Meuse, were attacked from Consenvoye, but German artillery fire defeated the thrust.

The Fifth Army's assessment of the situation concluded that everything now counted on recklessly pursuing the beaten enemy. That assessment was based on intelligence reports and reports from prisoners indicating that the enemy in front of the Fourth Army was withdrawing and dissolving. At 1715 hours the XIII Army Corps was ordered to advance east of the Bayonville–Grandpré road. The objective was the Remoiville–Landres–Saint-Juvin road. During the advance the corps was to take the towns along the route. Landwehr Division Francke was to remain northeast of Beaufort-en-Argonne. The VI Army Corps was to advance on the right of the XIII Army Corps, and the VI Reserve Corps on the left. The IV Cavalry Corps was ordered to reach the Buzancy–Grandpré line and mop up the ground in front of the Fourth and Fifth Armies, and then reconnoiter the whereabouts of the enemy. That order was based on a rather optimistic assessment of the situation by the Fifth Army headquarters. The Fifth Army repositioned its headquarters to Stenay. The V Army Corps remained west of Longuyon in OHL reserve in order to prevent an enemy attack from the Toul–Verdun line.

2 September 1914

By the morning of 2 September the enemy had conducted a planned and apparently orderly withdrawal from the front of the XIII Army Corps. That morning the corps formed into a column, with the 26th Division in the lead and the 27th Division following, and then started marching via Landres toward Saint-Juvin. The 26th Division reached Saint-Juvin without serious enemy resistance, moved advance troops toward Marcq, and then ordered a rest halt. About that time the 26th Division received the order to turn the 119th Grenadier Regiment and the 1st Battalion, 29th Foot Artillery, from Landres toward Sommerance, because the VI Reserve Corps reported enemy in the vicinity of Romagne-sous-Montfaucon withdrawing to the west. At the XIII Army Corps headquarters we still hoped to catch that enemy force.

At 1330 hours an order from the Fifth Army assigned the XIII Army Corps to the Remonville–Bantheville–Romagne-sous-Montfaucon–Charpentry–Véry road for its march movement. The adjacent VI Army Corps on our right was assigned the Buzancy–Verpel–Saint-Juvin–Varennes road. The VI Reserve Corps initially had to remain in the vicinity Brieulles-sur-Meuse–Cierges-sous-Montfaucon as the second echelon of the march movement.

While dictating the order for the corps' left turn movement we received more intelligence that shifted the XIII Army Corps in a new direction. The VI Reserve Corps and XVI Army Corps were reported to be engaged in heavy fighting against a strongly reinforced enemy position in the vicinity of Montfaucon-d'Argonne, Cierges-sous-Montfaucon, and Gesnes-en-Argonne. The XIII Army Corps was ordered to intervene in that fight. The corps commander, therefore, immediately ordered the 27th Division to swing to the left on a wide front to reach the area of Gesnes-en-Argonne by the shortest route, while the 26th Division was to advance toward Épinonville, orienting toward the south with its left wing.

As we later learned, the VI Reserve Corps had pushed back the withdrawing enemy force to its front, and then pushed it off the hills north of Cierges-sous-Montfaucon with the 12th Reserve Division, which was advancing via Cunel. But then very strong enemy artillery fire forced the corps to order a pause and a reconsolidation for further attack, which required waiting for the 11th Reserve Division to engage on the right of the 12th Reserve Division. Advancing via Romagne-sous-Montfaucon, the 11th Reserve Division took Gesnes-en-Argonne soon after midday. Just after 1800 hours the French started their counterattack against the entire VI Reserve Corps. They failed against the 12th Division, but the 11th Reserve Division was forced to yield to enemy pressure, and only escaped complete defeat by the timely intervention of the XIII Army Corps.

The 26th Division could not execute its ordered advance from Saint-Juvin in the Aire River Valley because strong enemy artillery fire blocked the route. In order to support the VI Reserve Corps as rapidly as possible, the division then advanced via Sommerance. Meanwhile, the VI Reserve Corps at the request of the XIII Army Corps turned its 11th Division toward Chatel[23] in order to relieve the pressure on the 26th Division's right flank. The 11th Division reached Chatel on the evening of 2 September. That day the XIII Army Corps broke off toward the southeast and advanced in three columns, with the main body of the 26th Division moving from Saint-Juvin toward Sommerance. The reinforced 119th Grenadier Regiment moved from Landres to Sommerance, and the 27th Division turned its lead elements toward the south to reach the area north of Landres.

The reinforced 119th Grenadier Regiment was the first to enter the fight. Its attached artillery battalion in the vicinity of Sommerance made contact with enemy artillery northwest of Exermont. One battery was attacked by French cavalry, but that attack collapsed in the face of well-placed artillery fire. That was the only French attack that I experienced during the World War.[24] To the right of the reinforced 119th Grenadier Regiment, the main body of the 26th Division developed the situation, but its advance was difficult against the fire of well-concealed enemy batteries. Nonetheless, the 26th Division was able to seize Exermont by that evening.

After breaking off its advance toward Gesnes-en-Argonne, the 27th Division had to march through very thick forested terrain. On its left the infantry units of the 53rd Brigade were able to reach the forest north of Gesnes-en-Argonne with great effort. The brigade's own left wing reinforced the right wing of the 11th Reserve Division, which was withdrawing from a strong French offensive thrust. Only the timely intervention of the 27th Division's infantry elements prevented the defeat of the 11th Reserve Division. Because the artillery could not move through the forest, the 54th Infantry Brigade with most of the artillery moved around the forest in a southerly sweep. By the onset of darkness, the 27th Division was staged along the edges of the forests west and north of Gesnes.

Both divisions maintained contact with the enemy during the night and received orders to continue the attack at daybreak. On the right of the XIII Army Corps, the VI Army Corps' lead elements reached the area north of Chatel. To the right of the VI Army Corps, the IV Cavalry Corps tried to advance via Grandpré, but failed in the face of heavy enemy artillery fire. The corps remained overnight to the north of the VI Army Corps. The pursuit to which the Fifth Army had committed its corps had turned into a heavy engagement, with the enemy even attacking in some sectors.

The Fifth Army redeployed its headquarters to Stenay on 2 September and issued no new orders for 3 September. That evening the XIII Army Corps reported its intent to continue the attack the following day. As I learned later, the Fifth Army in the evening of 2 September received an order from OHL to seize the barrier forts at Troyon, Les Paroches, and Camp des Romains, which were located farther south at the Meuse. It had to accomplish that mission while still maintaining the blocking positions around the Verdun fortresses. Yet, OHL also pointed out that it would be easier to seize those barrier forts from the west. To do that, however, the front of the entire Fifth Army would have had to advance deeply to the south, skirting Verdun on its western side. For the execution of that mission OHL attached to the Fifth Army the Metz Main Reserve force, consisting of five heavy foot artillery battalions. But those units were only capable of attacking from the eastern bank of the Meuse. It was my hope, therefore, that if they could seize quickly the barrier forts south of Verdun from the eastern bank, the advance of the Fifth Army's units west of the Meuse would be strongly supported and the Verdun fortresses could be cut off quickly. As the events played out, unfortunately, that hope was in vain, even though the V Army Corps that later became available again to the Fifth Army was committed on the eastern bank of the Meuse. In my opinion, the Fifth Army headquarters did not recognize the advantages of such an action early enough, and had not acted accordingly.

3 September 1914

The enemy along the XIII Army Corps' front line offered only weak resistance on 3 September. We recognized that his major forces had been pulled out the night before. That afternoon the 26th Division reached the hills northwest of Charpentry and then moved advance guards forward to Véry. The 27th Division closed up behind the 26th Division as far as Épinonville–Gesnes-en-Argonne.

On the right of the XIII Army Corps the forward elements of the VI Army Corps reached Varennes after having engaged enemy rear guards. To the left of the XIII Army Corps the XVI Army Corps remained in the vicinity of Montfaucon-d'Argonne. The VI Reserve Corps reassembled and occupied a bivouac position north of Cierges-sous-Montfaucon. The corps' follow-on mission was to cut off Verdun on the western side.

The advance of the IV Cavalry Corps toward the south via Grandpré ran into strong interference from the troops of the Fourth Army's left wing XVIII Reserve Corps. The 3rd Cavalry Division only reached the vicinity of Binarville that afternoon, while the 6th Cavalry Division remained behind the VI Army Corps. With the inner wings of Fourth and Fifth Armies tightly linked together and with very strong artillery fire supporting the French rear guard elements that were fighting skillfully, there was no viable mission for the IV Cavalry Corps, either west or east of the Argonne. Nonetheless, the Fifth Army headquarters relentlessly pushed the IV Cavalry Corps forward to add weight to the pursuit. In the process the IV Cavalry Corps was hit by the enemy's far superior artillery fire, and it also ran into the same sort of resistance that previously had forced it to make wide sweeping movements. Ultimately, then, the IV Cavalry Corps had to wait for the advance guards of our infantry divisions, and in the process became engaged in their fights. That evening the cavalry finally went into quarters relatively far to the rear of our most forward front line. Then, after only a few hours' rest, it again went forward, only to repeat the scenario of the previous day.

In my opinion the IV Cavalry Corps had been deployed in the wrong place, because it had no freedom of movement in front of the inner wings of the Fourth and Fifth Armies, and it therefore was forced to waste its strength during the long morning advances and evening retreats without adding anything significant to the daily fight. In my mind the IV Cavalry Corps would have been more valuable, perhaps even playing a decisive role, if it had been deployed right from the start on the eastern side of the Meuse, initially covering against the south and Toul. Then, during the advancing attack of the VI, XIII, and XVI Army Corps on the western bank of the Meuse, the IV Cavalry Corps could have been committed against the eastern flank and the rear of the opposing enemy units. Then it could have advanced toward the Meuse, and even crossed it. If such a course of action was infeasible, then it would have been better for OHL to withdraw the IV Cavalry Corps early and redeploy it on the overall right wing of the Germany Army. There it could have played a significant role in the Battle of the Marne.[25]

In the event, there was no viable field of action for the IV Cavalry Corps during the purely frontal fighting of the Fifth and Fourth Armies west of the Meuse. The corps' troopers only added to the burden of the already strained billeting space in the area, and the XIII Army Corps was further burdened by having to use its limited motor trucks to transport forward the oats for the IV Cavalry Corps. At the start of operations, the XIII Army Corps had issued the order for the troops to forage for the oats directly from the crops that were still standing in the fields. The horses liked the freshly cut oats, and if they consumed them immediately after cutting, including the straw, they developed a tolerance for fresh oats. The IV Cavalry Corps, however, insisted on feeding the horses old oats, which had to be transported forward. The complaints about the cavalry coming from the line units resulted in a cynical parody of the HKK4 (*Höhere Kavallerie Kommando* 4) initials of the headquarters element of the IV Cavalry Corps: *Hier kann keiner führen* (Here Nobody Can Lead). The joke was clever, but it had no basis in fact. The IV Cavalry Corps went forward courageously every day, but it could accomplish nothing because it was in the wrong place, where it did not have the freedom of maneuver it needed as cavalry.

The Fifth Army order assigned the following march routes for 4 September: VI Army Corps to Varennes, through the Argonne Forest via Vienne-la-Ville, toward Sainte-Menehould; XIII Army Corps from Épinonville via Neuvilly-en-Argonne toward Clermont-en-Argonne; and XVI Army Corps from Montfaucon-d'Argonne via Avocourt toward Aubérive and Parois. The VI Reserve Corps was supposed to halt in place initially, and then advance behind the XVI Army Corps to the west of Forges-sur-Meuse in order later to secure the southerly advance of the other corps on the eastern flank against Verdun. Landwehr Division Francke was ordered to follow the VI Reserve Corps.

4 September 1914

The lead units of the VI Army Corps reached Sainte-Menehould almost without a fight. The XIII Army Corps had to fight its way forward almost constantly against enemy rear guards, which maintained strong artillery fire from very cleverly concealed positions. That forced many halts. Only after dark did the 26th Division reach Clermont-en-Argonne, which the enemy did not abandon until just before the scheduled assault. The XIII Army Corps headquarters that day had been well forward during the advance. North of Neuvilly-en-Argonne, a patrol leader from the 6th Cavalry Division, First Lieutenant Graf von Holck of the 9th Dragoon Regiment, came up to the staff and gave us a very valuable report. French troops of all units were withdrawing along the road from Le Four de Paris to Les Islettes.

We got a lucky break in Clermont-en-Argonne. The main body of the advance guard of the 26th Division had assembled on the village road with its point element right at the crossing where the road from Les Islettes in the west ended at the main street of the village. A bicyclist coming from Les Islettes rode right into one of our stacked rifle pyramids. The troops that were close by jumped forward and grabbed a French General Staff officer who had just delivered the order to withdraw to the French unit positioned at Les Islettes, and was now trying to deliver the same order to the unit in Clermont-en-Argonne. From that order the intent of the opposing French units became apparent, and that gave us and the Fifth Army headquarters a solid basis on which to plan our actions for 5 September.

According to the captured order the French V and VI Army Corps were to make a stand on 5 September, with the main effort along the line Laheycourt–Villotte-sur-Aire–Rembercourt-aux-Pots, leaving screening forces in the vicinity of Belval-en-Argonne–Triaucourt-en-Argonne–Beauzée-sur-Aire. Instead of staging the 26th Division via Les Islettes as originally ordered, the division now was ordered to advance directly south toward Froidos. The follow-on 27th

Division moved toward Les Islettes, which was free of the enemy, and from there headed south. Thus, we could deploy with two spearheads out of the Argonne Forest. To the left of the XIII Army Corps, the XVI Army Corps reached the area of Aubérive–Parois after heavy fighting with enemy rear guards. At that point our assessment was that the enemy had withdrawn according to plan and in good order.

5 September 1914

The Fifth Army order directed the VI Army Corps and the XIII Army Corps to move out toward the south at 0600 hours. The VI Army Corps was to advance from Sainte-Menehould via Villers-en-Argonne to the L'Aisne sector Les Charmontois to Senard. The XIII Army Corps was to move between the road from Les Islettes to Brizeaux and the Aire River. The corps was to be ready to support the XVI Army Corps in case of an enemy attack from Verdun. The XVI Army Corps was to remain battle ready behind the Jubécourt–Parois sector and cover the movements through the Argonne Forest.

The Fifth Army orders were adjusted to the current situation, and as a result, of all the army's subordinate units,[26] only the VI Army Corps, XIII Army Corps, and IV Cavalry Corps were to follow the retreating enemy. All the other units were tied down initially at Fortress Verdun. What was the cause of this rather unfortunate use of the Fifth Army? It certainly was not the result of any decisions at the Fifth Army headquarters, because the Fifth Army had been forced on to its current march route in the vicinity of Verdun by the march direction that OHL had assigned to the Fourth Army. But the Fourth Army, which was linked into our right flank, had deviated from its initial southwesterly march direction into a southerly and then a more southeasterly direction, less from its own mistakes than as the result of erroneous interference from OHL. Had the Fourth Army been deployed more to the west, there would have been more space for the VI, XIII, and XVI Army Corps of the Fifth Army to pass the Argonne Forest to the west. That automatically would have resulted in a strengthening of the positions of the Fourth, Third, Second, and First Armies on the overall German right wing.

If those forces did not have enough space to march past Paris to the east, the resulting reduction of the corps in the front line would have resulted in an echeloning in depth by the corps of the second line. Only such an echelonment in depth would guarantee the operational freedom of maneuver necessary to respond to any situation. I believe that had such an action been taken, the Battle of the Marne would have ended with a decisive German victory. That would have been the result even accounting for the two major and irreversible mistakes OHL committed. The first was the redeployment of two army corps from the overall right wing to the Eastern Front[27]; the second was to let the Sixth and Seventh Armies in Lorraine run up against the French fortification system. As the situation had now developed, it was no longer possible to fight in depth. Now any of the engaged army corps that were all deployed in the front line could only be redeployed for other tasks by extracting them while in contact with the enemy.

The right wing of the Fifth Army's attack could only have had any advantageous effect if the three good active army corps, the VI, XIII, and XVI, could disengage from Fortress Verdun as far as possible toward the west by advancing west of the Argonne, leaving the security mission against the fortress to the reserve and Landwehr units and the V Army Corps, which still had to advance sharply along the line of the barrier forts south of Verdun. In my opinion, OHL had commanded very poorly at the operational level. It should not have allowed the individual field armies to act more or less independently. Rather, OHL should have done everything possible to keep the overall right wing of the army as strong as possible and to maintain depth at all times. Here alone was where the decision lay.

A French order captured late in the evening of 4 September gave the Fifth Army headquarters reason to order the VI and XIII Army Corps to attack against the enemy's main position on 5 September, and to stage the IV Cavalry Corps in an envelopment of the enemy's western wing and against their flank. The Fourth Army was requested to support.

On 5 September the XIII Army Corps' right-wing 27th Division, advancing via Les Islettes, reached the southern rim of the Argonne north of Brizeaux without enemy resistance. The area was occupied by weak enemy forces, apparently only cavalry, which withdrew before the division's advance guard could engage. The division followed and reached the hills north of Èvres toward the evening. To its left the 26th Division had several scuffles with enemy rear guards during its advance from Clermont-en-Argonne via Froidos and Fleury-devant-Douaumont. The 26th Division remained linked with 27th Division through its forward posts in the vicinity of Fleury-devant-Douaumont. Early in the morning of 5 September the 26th Division's Detachment Teichmann staged from Neuvilly-en-Argonne via Le Claon and toward Les Islettes, following the 27th Division, and remained in corps reserve that evening in the vicinity of Beaulieu-en-Argonne.

To the right of the XIII Army Corps, the VI Army Corps reached the line Les Charmontois–Senard–Triaucourt-en-Argonne after engaging with enemy rear guards. To the left of the XIII Army Corps, the XVI Army Corps initiated movement to the south, and the lead elements of its 34th Division reached Autrécourtsur-Aire that evening. Facing east, the 33rd Division at Ippécourt continued to maintain the screen against Verdun. To the north the VI Reserve Corps tied into the screen against Verdun along the line Parois–Aubérive–Avocourt and to the east with the 11th Reserve Division and 12th Reserve Division.

On 5 September late in the evening the Fifth Army command post at Varennes issued the order for the attack on 6 September. The VI Army Corps was to advance from Les Charmontois and Triaucourt-en-Argonne toward Laheycourt and Villotte-sur-Aire, and then take control of the bridges across the Rhine-Marne Canal at Revigny-sur-Ornain and Neuville-sur-Ornain. The XIII Army Corps was to advance from the eastern sector of Triaucourt-en-Argonne and Èvres via Lisle-en-Barrois and Rembercourt-aux-Pots[28] in order to gain control of the bridges east of Neuville-sur-Ornain. The XVI Army Corps to the east of the XIII Army Corps was to advance in a southerly direction.

The mission of security against Verdun and the Meuse line south of the fortress was given to the VI Reserve Corps with Landwehr Division Francke. The left wing of the Fourth Army would support the XVIII Reserve Corps in the Fifth Army's fight. The IV Cavalry Corps was committed against the western flank of the enemy forces opposing the Fifth Army.

6 September 1914

At the XIII Army Corps headquarters we considered the thrust of the attack and the Rhine-Marne Canal deep objectives of the Fifth Army only possible to achieve if the enemy deliberately withdrew from his known positions along the line Laheycourt–Villotte-sur-Aire–Rembercourt-aux-Pots. That, however, was unlikely. Therefore, the corps' two divisions were to attack initially only the forwardmost known enemy position at Triaucourt-en-Argonne–Èvres.

While advancing, the 27th Division initially met only weak enemy resistance, reaching its assigned objective around 1130 hours. The 26th Division, in contrast, found the hills south of Èvres heavily manned and observed very strong enemy artillery positioned along the hills north of Sommaisne. Only after deploying its own artillery and the attached 1st Battalion, 13th Foot Artillery, along the hills north of the road Èvres–Nubécourt did the 26th Division initiate its attack, which owing to strong enemy resistance progressed slowly. That afternoon the 26th Division finally managed with its right wing to take the hills southeast of Èvres, thereby establishing a link-in with the 27th Division's right wing, which had advanced to Vaubecourt. The 27th Division's left wing was still dragging in the vicinity of Nubécourt and had not linked up with the XVI Army Corps.

The VI Army Corps did not advance with its left wing toward Villotte-sur-

Aire, as ordered by the Fifth Army, but rather toward Laheycourt. Thus, a rather wide gap formed between the XIII and VI Army Corps. Weak enemy forces thrust into this gap by using forested areas for cover, and then moved against the flank and rear of the 27th Division. The ensuing forest fighting slowed down the 27th Division considerably, preventing it from attacking as ordered by the corps headquarters against the enemy on the flank of the 26th Division. By that evening, then, the XIII Army Corps had only managed to reach the line Vaubecourt–Beauzée-sur-Aire–Nubécourt. Unfortunately, the fighting primarily involving the 26th Division resulted in quite heavy losses from the enemy's strong artillery fire.

The XIII Army Corps maintained it position on the night of 7 September. During the course of that day the VI Army Corps on our right was heavily engaged with its right-wing 11th Division, but had advanced to the area south of Laheycourt. North of Laheycourt, however, the corps' left wing was lagging behind quite a ways and had to reorient its front toward the east in order to fend off strong enemy counterattacks.

During its advance the XVI Army Corps encountered strong enemy forces that occupied the hills along the line south of Nubécourt–Saint-André-en-Barrois–Souilly. The attack of the 34th Division advanced only some five hundred meters toward the enemy position by that evening. The 33rd Division that was echeloned to the left was attacked from the east while advancing in the vicinity of Ippécourt. At times it was under a great deal of pressure. Relief only came toward the evening when the VI Reserve Corps' 12th Reserve Division closed in on the battlefield. Since the enemy maintained close contact, the 33rd Division was for now unavailable for the attack that was oriented toward the south. Aerial reconnaissance gave no indication that the enemy was preparing to evade. After analyzing the day's fighting, it seemed that the enemy was determined to seek a decision immediately.

7 September 1914

On the evening of 6 September, the Fifth Army ordered the XIII Army Corps to attack from the line Vaubecourt–north of Beauzée-sur-Aire toward Rembercourt-aux-Pots and Sommaisne. To the right of the XIII Army Corps, the VI Army Corps was to advance to Louppy-sur-Loison and toward Lisle-en-Barrois. The attack of the VI Army Cops was to be supported by the XVIII Reserve Corps, which was fighting on the left wing of the Fourth Army. The 25th Reserve Division, on the XVIII Reserve Corps' left, was to attack from Revigny-sur-Ornain via Laimont toward Chardogne. To the right of the XVIII Reserve Corps, the IV Cavalry Corps was to advance south of the Rhine-Marne Canal. To the left of the XIII Army Corps, the XVI Army Corps' 34th Division was to attack toward Courcelles-sur-Aire. On that corps' left the 33rd Division, which was fighting with its front oriented east, was to follow after it was relieved in place by the VI Reserve Corps.

The fighting on 7 September consisted the entire day of arduously advancing infantry units taking heavy losses from very effective enemy artillery fire. The French artillery was deployed completely under cover, and its fire was directed by several aircraft. We tried to neutralize the enemy batteries based on our own aerial reports and using map spotting, but we apparently had little success. The enemy kept the area through which our infantry was advancing under the most intense shrapnel and shell fire. In spite of this, our courageous infantry managed to take the hills south of the line Sommaisne–Beauzée-sur-Aire. The troops dug in there on 7 September and fended off several enemy attacks during that night. The enemy artillery that day fired with large-caliber guns, leading us to suspect that they were using guns they had pulled out of the Verdun forts.

On both wings of the corps we did not receive the flanking support against the enemy we had hoped for. The VI Army Corps itself was forced to survive heavy fighting, and after making small initial ground gains, it fended off the enemy's deliberate counterattacks. The XVI Army Corps as well advanced only very little with its right 34th Division, while its 33rd Division was forced to remain in its current position and could only be relieved in the evening of 7 September by elements of the VI Reserve Corps' 12th Reserve Division. Along the entire front line of the Fifth Army, oriented toward the south and southeast, we took very heavy artillery fire throughout that night.

On 7 September the XIII Army Corps staff estimated that the enemy intended to maintain at all cost the link between its forces in the field and the Verdun forts. Opposing the enemy, the Fifth Army's VI, XIII, and XVI Army Corps, VI Reserve Corps, and Landwehr Division Francke were stuck in the tight space between the Argonne and Verdun. Those four corps could only regain their operational freedom by attacking the French field army and cutting it off from Verdun. Such an attack would result in heavy losses from the strongly superior enemy artillery, unless a thrust into the enemy's rear could be made by an attack toward and north of Saint-Mihiel. At that time, I told the corps commander once again how much better it would have been if strong elements of the Fifth Army had been sent west around the Argonne toward the south, and for the covering force set against Verdun to break contact farther away from the fortress, possibly along the eastern edge of the Argonne.

On the evening of 7 September the Fourth Army captured an order of the day issued by the French commander in chief, General Joffre. It read:

Commander in Chief's Order of the Day

> At this moment in the development of the battle, upon which the future of the Homeland depends, everyone must understand the fact that there can be no looking back. All forces must be used to attack the enemy and overthrow him.
>
> A unit that cannot advance any longer must hold the ground it has gained at all cost, and die in place rather than withdraw. Under the current situation the slightest weakness cannot be tolerated.
>
> This order is to be distributed to everyone all the way down to the front line.
>
> Joffre

We could not anticipate then that this order was linked with the French counterattack out of Paris and into the flank and the rear of the overall right wing of our army. That counterattack did, in fact, force the voluntary withdrawal of the German Army. At the time the only conclusion we could draw from the captured order was that despite all difficulties, the entire German Western Front had to attack strongly in order to tie down as many enemy forces as possible. In so doing, we would give our overall right wing—which we assumed was far superior in strength to the enemy—the support necessary to achieve a decisive victory. We did not know then that our overall right wing had been weakened by the detachment and redeployment to the east of the XI Army Corps and the Guards Reserve Corps. Quite the contrary, we were convinced that the right wing had been reinforced by several army corps from Lorraine forming a second echelon.

Our ignorance about the action in the sectors of the other field armies was a function of the compulsive sense of secretiveness that reigned at OHL, and even at the Fifth Army headquarters.

Exceptions were not made, even for the subordinate commanding generals. We had to rely on the reports that OHL prepared for release at home for our information on the fighting at other fronts. Those reports naturally only contained general news on the fighting, but no details about the composition and the missions of the field armies. We at that point were convinced that the German Army's overall right wing was operating at its initial strength, and that after the successful defense against the French breakthrough in Lorraine strong German forces were flooding from there north to the right wing. One can imagine how disappointed we were when we learned the truth about OHL's faulty operational decisions.

8 September 1914

Based on intelligence and aerial reconnaissance reports, the Fifth Army headquarters on 7 September developed the assessment that the enemy had strengthened their front opposite the VI, XIII, and XVI Army Corps. Opposite the Fifth Army's right wing, the French XV Army Corps appeared to be linked in with the French V and VI Army Corps. Opposite our XVI Army Corps it appeared that French forces that up until now had been positioned south of Verdun on the eastern side of the Meuse were intervening. Based on that assessment, telephonic orders were issued to prepare to defend to the Fifth Army's front. The attack would only continue when the Fourth Army moved up to secure our flank.

The XIII Army Corps would certainly take the brunt of any enemy attack. As reinforcements, the Fifth Army attached to the corps the 12th Reserve Division and the 11th Reserve Division's Detachment Dewitz from the VI Reserve Corps. The 12th Mörser Regiment was also attached directly from the Fifth Army. Accordingly, the divisions of the XIII Army Corps were ordered to echelon in depth for the defense.

During the entire day incredibly intense enemy artillery fire, which seemed to be growing even stronger, came down on our positions and our rear areas up to the line Vaubecourt–Pretz-en-Argonne and to the north. All low ground in which our combat squadrons in the rear were positioned took shrapnel and shell fire. Nonetheless, our troops stood fast in their improved positions and repulsed courageously the smaller enemy attacks. That afternoon the 12th Mörser Regiment northwest of Beauzée-sur-Aire went into battery and began firing against the enemy artillery, which had been spotted by aerial reconnaissance. The corps headquarters staff, which on 7 September had remained in the operations center near Èvres, took considerable artillery fire during that day. The 12th Reserve Division reached the area southeast of Brizeaux that evening. Detachment Dewitz, as the Fifth Army reserve, reached the area north of Èvres.

The support from the left wing of the Fourth Army that the Fifth Army had been expecting did not materialize on 8 September. The XVIII Reserve Corps did attack, supported by elements of the IV Cavalry Corps, but made little forward progress in the face of strong enemy resistance. To the north, the VI Army Corps caught up with the 11th Division in the vicinity of Louppy-sur-Loison, and with the 12th Division on the hills east of Villotte-sur-Aire.

In the XIII Army Corps sector, the 27th Division was attacked unsuccessfully southeast of Vaubecourt in the late evening. Meanwhile, the enemy forces opposite the right wing of the 26th Division did fall back a little from their forwardmost positions. In the XVI Army Corps sector the anticipated enemy attack failed to materialize. Toward the evening the enemy disengaged somewhat from the German lines. To the north of the XVI Army Corps, the VI Reserve Corps' 11th Reserve Division and Landwehr Division Francke secured the position opposite Verdun between Julvécourt and Avocourt.

The execution of the earlier Fifth Army plan to take the barrier forts south of Verdun with elements of the XVI Army Corps and attached engineer units, supported by very heavy howitzers, was no longer a viable option. Meanwhile, the V Army Corps units that had been deployed from the east against the barrier forts, supported by mounted foot artillery from Metz and an attached Austrian 305mm Mörser battalion, were only in the early stages of their long-anticipated attack.

The aerial reconnaissance reports on 8 September indicated that more reinforcements were heading toward the French positions in front of the XIII and XVI Army Corps. We expected very heavy fighting there. The overall assessment of the enemy by both the XIII Army Corps and our adjacent corps was that our infantry was prepared to move forward and that its stamina was superior to that of the enemy's infantry. The enemy artillery, however, dominated the battlefield almost completely. It had numerical superiority, superior aerial support, and unbelievable ammunition expenditure rates.

9 September 1914

When the Fifth Army commander, Crown Prince Wilhelm, arrived at our command post near Èvres in the early hours of 9 September, our corps commander briefed him on the assessment of the fight and suggested the elimination of the enemy's artillery fire through an attack to be conducted on the night of 9–10 September. The army commander concurred with the recommendation, and the corps chiefs of staff were called together for an orders brief at Triaucourt-en-Argonne. Before my departure the warning order was issued to prepare for a night attack.

In the meantime, the 12th Reserve Division had received the order from the V Army Corps headquarters to insert itself in the forward lines between the VI and XIII Army Corps. The division took over a sector between the two corps and was then attached to the XIII Army Corps. The VI and XIII Army Corps were thus able to echelon their inner flanks in greater depth.

Unfortunately, the Fifth Army headquarters took a long time to issue the operations orders for the night attack, which reduced the preparation time for the involved units. It undoubtedly would have sufficed to establish by telephone the attack sectors, the objectives, and the time lines for the coordinated attack. Instead, the Fifth Army did not even start issuing the orders until 1300 hours at Triaucourt-en-Argonne. First, the corps chiefs of staff had to brief the situations of their respective corps and had to coordinate the corps boundaries for the attack. The orders brief was not completed until 1500 hours, and so much valuable time was lost to the necessary detailed instructions for the corps, and especially for the measures at the lower echelons. The corps reserve was the 20th Engineer Regiment, which recently had been attached to us by the Fifth Army. The engineers were assembled northwest of Beauzée-sur-Aire, and positioned near the 12th Mörser Regiment. The objective of the night attack as specified by the XIII Army Corps headquarters was the destruction of the enemy artillery.

The enemy artillery fire lasted the entire day with uninterrupted and great intensity, until the onset of darkness. The fire reached all the way to the area around Pretz-en-Argonne. At that point in time the clear and hot weather changed, becoming cloudy, and from midnight on rain set in. Late that evening the Fifth Army headquarters ordered the VI Army Corps not to participate in the attack, because the left wing corps of the Fourth Army had been attacked by strong enemy forces. VI Army Corps, therefore, would have to secure the right flank of the XIII Army Corps. The VI Army Corps started digging in at its current position.

Because the order was issued late, and enemy artillery fire was heavy along the entire front, the forwardmost leaders of XIII Army Corps only received the Fifth Army order late that afternoon. As a result, the necessary preparations for the attack suffered accordingly. The 12th Reserve Division, which only recently had occupied its position, had a difficult time finding its bearings in the unfamiliar terrain.

10 September 1914

At 0200 hours the forwardmost line of infantry with unloaded rifles and fixed bayonets entered the lead enemy outposts by a surprise attack. Soon, however, the assaulting troops took fire in the darkness from the front and from the flank. The 12th Reserve Division attack did not even come close to reaching its designated objective line. One infantry regiment veered off the attack axis when for a while it was subject to friendly fire. By daybreak the 12th Reserve Division had made only small gains on the ground. At dawn the enemy launched a counterattack, which the division repelled. The 12th Reserve Division then pulled up its artillery and reorganized its tangled-up units. As a result of the failure of the 12th Reserve Division's attack, the 27th Division advanced only slowly with its right wing. The division's middle and its left wing, which had good contact with the 26th Division, made solid progress. Only the 26th Division managed to reach its designated objective line, with its left wing at Courcelles-sur-Aire, and then displaced its artillery forward as ordered. Soon after crossing its line of departure, Detachment Dewitz, which was linked in to the left, took fire from its left by troops of the XVI Army Corps' 26th Division. The detachment gained very little ground as a result.

The attack continued that morning in the face of increased enemy artillery fire. The enemy also launched a number of local hasty counterattacks, which were all repelled. The VI Army Corps, which initially had remained in its positions, advanced forward and gained approximately one thousand meters toward Louppy-le-Château and northeast of there. By that afternoon the 12th Reserve Division and the XIII Army Corps were tied in to a single line running west to north from the vicinity of Rembercourt-aux-Pots–Hill 309 (half way between Rembercourt-aux-Pots–Chaumont-sur-Aire)–Courcelles-sur-Aire–south east of Séraucourt. On the left, the XVI Army Corps was linked in along the continuous line, with its forwardmost elements between Séraucourt and Rignaucourt, and close to the west of Heippes. The corps' front line then bent back in the direction of Ippécourt, from where the front of the 11th Reserve Division ran close to and east of the road from Ippécourt to Julvécourt.

The 26th Division gained the most ground by seizing Hill 309. The entire attack front dug in at the positions they had reached by that point, regrouped in depth, and reorganized their units. However, the designated objective of the destruction of the enemy's artillery had not been accomplished. Only the 26th Division captured two batteries. Other than that, the enemy artillery had withdrawn all along the line as their infantry had been pushed back. Once in the new rearward positions, the artillery fire resumed that afternoon.

Even though they had been reduced to approximately one-third of their combat strength and had only a few officers left, our infantry units had once again proved themselves to be far superior to the French infantry. Our artillery too had supported the attack very well, and on its own initiative it often displaced its firing positions farther forward.

That evening I gave the corps commander my assessment of the day's successes, as such. I projected that our attack would force the French commander to sever his link with the Verdun Fortress because of the threat to his rear area and the potential loss of the barrier forts at Génicourt-sur-Meuse and Troyon. The German artillery had already started firing on these forts at 1400 hours on 8 September. In the event, the commanding general of the French Third Army had made just that decision, issuing the appropriate orders on the evening of 10 September.[29] Personally, I was convinced that our attack should be continued on 11 September with all means, but for reasons initially inexplicable to me the Fifth Army headquarters ordered the transition to the defense. We learned much later that this had been the result of OHL's withdrawal order to the First and Second Armies on the overall right wing of the German Army. Consequently, OHL also ordered the Fifth Army to halt. We had to comply with the Fifth Army order, but we still sent messages to our subordinate units to prepare continuously for future attacks. Captured French officers unanimously stated that the French infantry was completely exhausted and shaken up.

11 September 1914

We continued to improve our new positions. The enemy artillery did continue, but the fire was much less intense. In the evening the corps headquarters, based on the instructions from the Fifth Army, ordered that the current positions would remain manned without change on 12 September. We also ordered the displacement much farther forward of two heavy field howitzer batteries and one 100mm gun battery. But then the Fifth Army, based on instructions from OHL, gave the order for the entire army to withdraw, which had a devastating effect on us.

The Fifth Army order issued at 2000 hours on 11 September directed an immediate withdrawal. The VI Army Corps route was via Belval-en-Argonne and Villers-en-Argonne. The XIII Army Corps, with the 12th Reserve Division and Detachment Dewitz, was assigned the route via Triaucourt-en-Argonne toward Brizeaux. The XVI Army Corps was to remain in position until 12 September, and then at 1200 hours march toward Froidos to Clermont-en-Argonne. The VI Reserve Corps was to assemble later east of Clermont-en-Argonne and cover the area around Jubécourt–Aubérive. The general line of the rear guard was Chemin–Brizeaux–Waly–north of Fleury.

The echelons of the reinforced XIII Army Corps were assigned the march route Triaucourt-en-Argonne–Brizeaux–Les Islettes–Clermont-en-Argonne–Neuvilly-en-Argonne–Varennes-en-Argonne–Fléville, and then in a northerly direction. Departure time initially was set for 0600 hours on 12 September. At 0640 hours that morning the Fifth Army issued an amended order for Detachment Dewitz to march immediately via Fleury-devant-Douaumont[30] toward Rarécourt, in order to be available to support the VI Reserve Corps.

12 September 1914

At 0140 hours on 12 September, the XIII Army Corps issued the order to assemble for the withdrawal, now set to start at 0830 hours. At 0950 hours, based on reconnaissance reports from our aviation detachment, we reported to the Fifth Army headquarters that the enemy had marched off in front of the XIII and XVI Army Corps. Moving approximately five to six kilometers to the south, they had assumed and were now improving their new positions. Later that report was confirmed. On the morning of 10 September the commander of the French Third Army had ordered the withdrawal of his right wing to the general area of Courouvre–Longchamps-sur-Aire–Villotte-sur-Aire. He had withdrawn from his position on his own accord, and in the process severed his link with Fortress Verdun. At that point the fortress had only one division in its main reserve.

If on 11 September the Fifth Army had continued its attack with the VI, XIII, and XVI Army Corps, it would have only been against the French rear guard and undoubtedly would have thrown it back into its main positions. The XVI Army Corps, which was facing almost totally expended French territorial troops, could have cut into the right wing of the French main position at Courouvre. The result would have been a significant tactical victory at the Meuse. That, in turn, could have been expanded quickly into an operational success, if only OHL had decided to move forward the units of Sixth Army. The I, II, and III Bavarian Army Corps were already advancing toward Fortress Metz and could have had at least elements across the Meuse, preparing to attack on the left bank of the river on both sides of Saint-Mihiel. At that point the French High Command would have been forced to divert several more army corps to help the French Third Army, which already had sustained heavy infantry losses. The Fifth Army, tied in strongly on its right to the main line of the German Army during the withdrawal, would have been able to dissipate all of the enemy's strength.

It certainly was completely unnecessary for OHL to withdraw the middle of the German Army, consisting of the Third, Fourth, and Fifth Armies, to the line Reims–north of Verdun. Keeping those three armies on the general line from the Vesle (Third Army) to the Marne-Rhine Canal (Forth Army), and to Révigny–Saint-Mihiel–Metz (Fifth Army) was undoubtedly possible. Such a course of action would have tied down strong enemy forces in front of the three German field armies. It also would have facilitated the option of capturing Verdun in the immediate future, and all the blood that was spilled in excess during the attack on Verdun in 1916 could have been spared the German Army in the West. By holding that line, those three field armies would then have been united with the overall right wing of the German Army. After consolidating its forces, the German Army in the West could then have resumed an enveloping attack against the enemy's western wing.

OHL had already lost its nerve when it ordered the withdrawal from the Battle of the Marne, which handed to the left wing of the enemy's army an unearned operational success. And in my opinion, OHL really lost its nerve when it ordered the Third, Fourth, and Fifth Armies in the center of the overall German line to fall back. The ground that we had already won at the expense of much German blood should never have been given up voluntarily. Initially, OHL only intended to disengage the three central armies a short distance from the enemy. But the commander of the Second Army,[31] who already had exerted a decisive influence on the decision to withdraw from the Marne, convinced OHL that a French breakthrough against the Third Army was imminent. It was not until that assessment that OHL ordered the general withdrawal. It is my firm opinion that any French attack would have failed at great cost against our 11 September positions, which were echeloned back into the German Army's overall right wing. Certainly our brave infantry was quite exhausted after all the marching and the fighting, and they had sustained bloody losses reducing their combat power. Despite the exhaustion, the infantry's inner strength and vigor remained unbroken, and far superior to that of the enemy.

Along the entire fighting front of the German Army the will to win was the ruling emotion. But at the highest leadership level that firm and confident will was not predominant, because from their headquarters far from the front lines in Luxembourg they could not see the true picture of the German Army's heroism and will to resist. Because of that absence of direct frontline knowledge, they failed to understand the German Army's fundamental strengths. It was not the courageous German Army that had failed in the critical days of September 1914; rather, it was OHL that failed. Its faulty operational decisions directed the German Army in the West badly, and during the ensuing critical situation on the overall right wing OHL did not have that willpower that the troops never lost—not during the situation at that time, and not even up through the end of the war. I am not at all reluctant to state this quite candidly, even though I am aware I might offend some brave comrade who did not have the privilege of participating personally at the fighting front, but who was stuck at a map table and a telephone in the rear. If OHL had had more frontline spirit it would not have issued the general retreat order. With a strong will to win, OHL could have achieved a major and possibly a decisive victory in September 1914, despite the operational leadership mistakes that had been committed up to that point. But just as in the Battle of the Marne, where OHL had lost all its trust in the will of the German Army to attack, it now had even lost its trust in the German Army's will to defend. The fighting front did not understand the retreat ordered by OHL, and that undoubtedly had a negative influence on the will of the German troops to fight, and conversely strengthened the morale and the spirit of the enemy.

The Fifth Army headquarters did not decide wisely in its selection of the army's new defensive front. Initially, the inner wings of Fourth and Fifth Armies were to withdraw only to the hill at Sainte-Menehould. But the Fifth Army did not think the line from Sainte-Menehould to Verdun was favorable for a sustained defense, which resulted in the further withdrawal to the area north of the Argonne and north of Verdun. Admittedly, the area around the Argonne was very good defensive ground, as the French continued to demonstrate to us all the way to the end of the war. But both OHL and the Fifth Army saw the German Army's salvation only in the shortening of the front lines.

OHL and the Fifth Army planned to resume the operational attack from the new positions once the units were well rested and reconstituted. What both headquarters overlooked was the fact that the initiative had been handed to the enemy, who for the foreseeable future dictated the law of action (*Gesetz des Handelns*)[32] to the German Army in the West. Analyzing the situation correctly, the French High Command assembled all available forces to envelop the German Army's overall right wing. Thus, OHL had no other choice but to extend its own right wing continuously until it eventually reached all the way to the sea.[33] By the end of October 1914 the front lines between the German Army and the enemy ran from the sea in the north to the Swiss border in the south. The result was parallel trench war, from which an operational victory could only be achieved through the conduct of an operational breakthrough.

Retreat on 12 September 1914

At 0830 hours the withdrawal movements of the frontline combat forces started after all higher echelons had started the march toward the north during the night and had gained a sufficient head start. The retreat of the main body of the troops was initially covered by rear guards with strong supporting artillery. During the retreat, officer patrols maintained contact with the enemy, which continued firing on our abandoned positions until the afternoon. It was only that evening that the enemy started probing with rather weak infantry elements. The enemy's hesitance obviously was a reaction to the success of our previous night attack.

We were able to transport back all of our sick and wounded, with the exception of some fifteen German soldiers who were very badly wounded and had to remain in Èvres. Before we departed, the corps commander and I visited them and we tried to comfort them and prepare them for the fact that they would fall into the enemy's hands.

The roads in the Argonne Forest were soaked and in some places hardly passable because of the rain that had been falling since 10 September. Delays of several hours developed, but still the march was conducted in perfect order and completely unhindered by the enemy. During the march, however, our infantry became quite exhausted because it had not gotten much rest in the recent days of fighting.

By the evening of 12 September the 12th Reserve Division, marching via Triaucourt-en-Argonne, reached the area of Passavant-en-Argonne; the 27th Division, marching via Triaucourt-en-Argonne, reached the area of Brizeaux; and the 26th Division reached the area of Waly via Èvres. To the west of the XIII Army Corps, the VI Army Corps' trail elements reached the line Belval-en-Argonne–Senard. East of the XIII Army Corps, the XVI Army Corps' rear elements reached Fleury.

The Fifth Army order issued at 2100 hours on 12 September continued the retreat. On 13 September the 12th Reserve Division was to reach the area north of Varennes-en-Argonne via Les Islettes–Lachalade–Varennes-en-Argonne. The remainder of XIII Army Corps was to reach the area of Montblainville–Lachalade. The road near Varennes-en-Argonne was assigned to the 12th Reserve Division exclusively. The XVI Army Corps was routed through Varennes-en-Argonne. All further movements were organized by the XIII Army Corps order issued at 2215 hours.

13 September 1914

The march movements of 13 September were once again extremely exhausting for the troops, because of the bad road conditions in the Argonne Forest. You could tell that the troops were emotionally drained by the fact that after they had been feeling victorious following a constant and bloody fight for the ground gained, they now had to give it up to the enemy voluntarily based on orders from higher headquarters. The Württembergers are courageous and unspoiled people. All along the route of march you heard some strong language, like "damned mess." But still, the conduct of the troops remained fabulous.

In the late afternoon of 13 September the XIII Army Corps' command group received the Fifth Army order issued at 1330 hours. The general line of defense was designated west of the Meuse River, running from the Aire River east of Chatel-Chéhéry (which was to remain occupied)–Baulny–Charpentry–the hill southwest of Cuisy–the hill north of Forges-sur-Meuse.

When the VI Army Corps was placed on-call to OHL, the IV Cavalry Corps linked in west of XIII Army Corps and bivouacked in the area west of the line Saint-Juvin–Imécourt–Buzancy. To the east of the IV Cavalry Corps, the XIII Army, XVI Army, and VI Reserve Corps were bivouacked.

The Fourth Army's left wing XVIII Reserve Corps was to remain with its own left wing in the vicinity of Binarville, on the western edge of the Argonne. The XVI Army Corps was linked in to the east of the XIII Army Corps. That corps, however, initially had to leave strong forces deployed far forward of its front to prevent the enemy from disrupting the German movements through and around Varennes-en-Argonne. For the final stage of the retreat march the XIII Army Corps was assigned the road Le Four de Paris[34]–west past Varennes-en-Argonne–Montblainville. The 20th Engineer Regiment, scheduled to arrive in Bantheville the next day, was attached to the XIII Army Corps to reinforce its defensive line. On the eastern bank of the Meuse the defensive front of the Fifth Army ran along the general line Consenvoye–Azannes-et-Soumazannes–Étain–Orne River.

Upon receipt and analysis of the Fifth Army order, we recognized that our positive tie-in as the right wing of Fifth Army at Chatel-Chéhéry to the Fourth Army's left wing XVIII Reserve Corps at Binarville was missing. The army order only stipulated that the connecting road to the Fourth Army from Apremont to Binarville was to be secured by guard posts. The result, however, was that over time a gap between Binarville and Chatel-Chéhéry had to develop. Even though the Argonne Forest north of that line consisted of almost impenetrable underbrush, the French still knew that ground well. As I pointed out to the Fifth Army headquarters, I though it was urgently necessary to man strongly and improve the defenses along the Binarville–Apremont line. I estimated that would require half the respective strengths of the XVIII Reserve Corps and XIII Army Corps. The Fifth Army order, however, was not changed. As events later showed, if the Binarville–Apremont had been reinforced it would have been a great advantage to the German defense. Most likely there would have not been the heavy and costly fighting in the Argonne.

Based on the army order, the XIII Army Corps conducted a brief readjustment of the assigned defensive positions of its divisions. The 26th Division took up the position on the west, the 27th Division on the east. The corps staff rode forward to conduct a general reconnaissance of the defensive sector, which continued through the next day.

14 September 1914

Based on the corps order issued at 0855 hours on 14 September, the divisions moved into their assigned positions after having conducted their own reconnaissance. The sector assigned to the XIII Army Corps was in general well suited for the defense, even though the edge of the Argonne Forest was relatively close, directly opposite the 26th Division. The rolling and largely forested terrain to the rear provided good areas for covered artillery positions and assembly areas for the reserves. Artillery observation posts, however, always had to be positioned close to the forwardmost infantry lines.

Based on our peacetime training doctrine, the infantry in the first defensive line established fire zones that were as wide as possible. It was only in the further course of the war that we recognized that infantry positioned primarily on the forward slopes of hills were exposed and especially vulnerable to enemy artillery fire. It took a while to learn this lesson, but we eventually came to understand that defensive lines had to be selected and established on the principle of having the artillery observation posts on the high ground with good fields of observation and move the infantry main positions approximately one thousand to fifteen hundred meters forward of the artillery observation posts, in such a manner that the artillery could put well-observed barrage fire (*Sperrfeuer*) right in front of the infantry positions. From this experience we developed the concept of reverse-slope positions (*Hinterhangstellungen*),[35] which masked the infantry from enemy ground observation and artillery. A field of fire of only a few hundred meters was completely sufficient for infantry in the defense, especially if the heavy machine guns were well positioned to the rear of the infantry lines.

From the afternoon of 14 September on, the divisions organized and immediately started reinforcing their defensive positions. Elements of the attached 20th Engineer Regiment were allocated among the divisions.

15 September 1914

On 15 September the Fifth Army headquarters, positioned at Stenay, attached the 2nd Battalion, 6th Mörser Regiment, to the XIII Army Corps. The following day that unit occupied its firing positions south of Gesnes-en-Argonne. The mounted artillery battalion and the machine gun battalion of the 6th Cavalry Division also were attached to us. Those units were deployed within the 26th Division's defensive sector. The cross-attachment of those units indicated that the IV Cavalry Corps would most likely remain for a long time with the Fifth Army, where it was not able to use its mounted capabilities properly. In my opinion, the IV Cavalry Corps should have been redeployed as quickly as possible to the overall right wing of the German Army. Unfortunately, that decision was made only much later.

Aerial reconnaissance indicated that the enemy on 15 September had followed us on a wide front. Enemy march columns had been identified advancing on the Le Claon–Le Four de Paris road, the Neuvilly-en-Argonne–Varennes-en-Argonne road, and the Aubérive–Avocourt road. On 16 September the enemy opened artillery fire on the positions of the 27th Division without initially committing his infantry.

On 16 September we learned that on 14 September the Prussian minister of war, Lieutenant General Erich von Falkenhayn,[36] had been assigned as the chief of the General Staff of the German Army, replacing the physically and mentally exhausted Colonel General Helmuth von Moltke. In a private conversation with my corps commander I opined that it would have been better to fill this most responsible position with Colonel General Paul von Hindenburg, with Major General Erich Ludendorff as the chief of operations. Even in peacetime those two generals had justifiably high reputations throughout the whole German Army, and the trust in them increased even more by their purposeful and successful command of the German Army in the East.[37] Considering the critical situation in which the German Army in the West found itself in September 1914, the level of trust in the responsible army leaders had to play a decisive role. Hindenburg and Ludendorff had unlimited levels of this trust. General von Falkenhayn had yet to earn it.

Along with the news of General von Falkenhayn's appointment, we also learned—if only in broad detail—the reasons for the withdrawal of almost the entire front of the German Army, and the events as they had played out on the overall right wing. I then submitted in confidence to my corps commander my assessment of the decisions that now should be made. In my opinion, the option of achieving a decisive operational victory was now only possible on the overall right wing. It was there that a new operation with superior German forces would have to be prepared for the envelopment of the French left wing. Such a force only could be assembled at the necessary level of overwhelming strength at the cost of weakening all other fronts, which then had to assume a purely defensive role conducted from continually improved positions. The most important factor in the execution of such an operation was the German Army's poor ammunition situation. Initially we were informed in confidence of the ammunition shortages, although this later was pointed out more and more strongly. What ammunition we had available would have to be committed mostly at the operationally decisive point. Experience showed clearly that an abundance of ammunition was necessary for an attack, while in the defense it could be used more frugally.[38] All the fighting units that could somehow be spared from the defensive front line and the majority of the ammunition, in my opinion, should have been committed to the point where a decisive operational victory was possible. In September 1914 that point could have only been the German Army's overall right wing. That, too, was where all the army-level cavalry units belonged. It was only on the open right wing that the German Army had operational freedom, and it was there that the cavalry units would have served best by screening and securing the arrival and deployment of all other attack formations. Only after a tremendous superior force had been assembled on the right could an operationally decisive attack have been launched, even if while in the temporary defensive mode the right wing had to shift evasively to buy time.

Unfortunately, General von Falkenhyn did not execute such a course of action, even though as I learned later he initially considered it. Instead, he ordered that the First through Fifth Armies were to attack again in order to tie down the enemy forces to their front, and thus prevent them from shifting toward their own left wing. But those frontal attacks did not produce tangible results anywhere, and did not restrict the ability of the enemy commanders to thin out the front lines of almost all of their armies and then redeploy those forces to their left flank. The attacks that General von Falkenhayn ordered the First through Fifth Armies to make were not capable of affecting a penetration, primarily because the ammunition necessarily for such attacks was not available anywhere in the necessary quantities. As a consequence, the troops paid a heavy price in much unnecessarily spilled blood. The combat power of the attacking units was exhausted progressively, and even more significantly the timely extraction and redeployment of the reserves to support the overall right wing was prevented. Another resulting major disadvantage was that in order to attack, most of the German units on the left had to leave their defensive positions that had been well planned and adapted to the terrain, and in the end had to occupy far less favorable positions. And that made the later conduct of a long-term defense even more difficult.

The operation as I thought it should have been conducted was only executable if all of the fronts not involved in the operational attack, from the Second Army all the way to the Swiss border, transitioned immediately to the defensive in reinforced but broad and deeply echeloned positions.[39] Only such a firm course of action would have made it possible for OHL to assemble the necessary strong reserves. By thinning out the defensive sectors of the individual corps and divisions, the released forces could then have been extracted and redeployed to the German overall right wing by means of road marches and railroad transport. Once in position, they could be consolidated for a unified attack. So far the German Army had done exceptionally well in the attack, and it would have held any defensive position in which it could have established itself in a planned and deliberate manner. It undoubtedly could do so even against strong enemy superiority. Another factor in my proposed course of action was the high probability that the enemy initially would have followed the withdrawing German forces on the left in full strength. We later learned that he always did so, almost without exception. If such had been the case, we would have gained a considerable head start for assembling the strongly superior force on our right.

In the process of conducting the attacks from the right army wing to Metz, as ordered by OHL, we lost valuable time needed to consolidate the forces for a new strong attack from the overall right wing. The result was a more or less piecemeal deployment of the German Army's reserves, combined with almost constant fighting against equal and often superior enemy forces. Making the situation worse, the German army-level cavalry units that were consolidated on the right wing were only committed slowly to the frontal fighting on the left. Only rarely did they have the freedom of maneuver to attempt wide-sweeping envelopments against the enemy's flanks and rear. OHL's faulty decision to attack along the entire German front west of Metz while simultaneously assembling strong forces for an operational attack from the overall right wing ultimately robbed the German Army of the opportunity to achieve victory through an enveloping attack.

On 15 September, OHL ordered the Fifth Army to attack on both sides of Verdun, west of the Meuse. Specifically, the Fifth Army was to advance with its right wing through the Argonne Forest and with its left wing against the Meuse barrier forts at Troyon and Camp des Romains. The Fifth Army attack was supposed to cut off Verdun from the southwest. The Fourth Army was ordered to attack along its entire front, for which it was allocated the VI Army Corps, which had been withdrawn from Fifth Army. The Seventh Army headquarters had already been withdrawn from Alsace-Lorraine and redeployed between the First and Second Armies in the north. Within a few more weeks the Sixth Army also would be withdrawn from the south and redeployed on the overall right wing, to the right of the First Army. Army Detachment Gaede, commanded by General of Infantry Hans Gaede, and Army Detachment A, commanded by General of Infantry Ludwig von Falkenhausen, replaced the Sixth and Seventh Armies in the south as the command and control headquarters.

For the Fifth Army's scheduled 19 September attack against the barrier forts along the Meuse and to screen its southern flank against Toul, we were allocated the 33rd Reserve Division, which was the main reserve force at Metz. A little later the III Bavarian Corps and the Bavarian Cavalry Division, which had been in Lorraine, were also attached to us.[40] Those units were consolidated with the V Army Corps to form Army Detachment C, commanded by General of Infantry Hermann von Strantz, and subordinated to the Fifth Army.

The attack against the barrier forts at Troyon and Camp des Romains required a significant broadening of the Fifth Army's front. That could only produce operational results if the Fifth Army was able to advance far to the southwest of the Meuse, with the Fourth Army advancing sufficiently on its right. But both armies lacked the necessary force strength—and especially the ammunition—necessary for success. In my earlier comments about the kind of advance against the Meuse that I thought should have been conducted at the end of August and beginning of September, I also supported an attack by the Fifth Army south of Verdun. At that time such an attack could have had an operational effect. By the middle of September that was no longer possible. Because of the ammunition shortage and the greatly reduced combat strength of our corps, we could achieve at best only a tactical victory, and even then one that would have only minimal operational significance. Earlier the Fifth Army's VI Reserve Corps, and the XVI, XIII, and VI Army Corps west of the Meuse, had seized at the cost of a lot of blood the terrain south of the Argonne, forcing the French to sever their connection with Fortress Verdun. But then we had to abandon that ground because of an erroneous decision by the fainthearted OHL. It was difficult for the troops and their leaders to understand that they would have to repeat the earlier attack, but now under much more adverse conditions. In my opinion, the attack conducted in the middle of September on both sides of Verdun should never have been attempted. The units committed to that attack and the ammunition expended would have been better used on the overall right wing. By foregoing the Fourth and Fifth Army attacks, the III Bavarian Corps, VI Army Corps, one other corps from the Fifth Army, the IV Cavalry Corps, and the Bavarian Cavalry Division could have displaced immediately to the overall right wing.

In all of OHL's actions during the second half of September, Falkenhayn, as the new chief of the General Staff of the army, did not exercise his authority efficiently enough, and he often made his decisions based on the very differing opinions of the various field army headquarters.[41] The withdrawal of any troops from the combat front was almost always preceded by negotiations with the various army headquarters. But because of the unfavorable situations resulting from their tactical attacks, those headquarters often objected to any weakening of their forces, thus prolonging any action. That naturally delayed further the consolidation of a decisive combat force on the German Army's overall right, and that loss of time gave the enemy an advantage. I have no doubt that if General von Hindenburg had been the chief of the General Staff of the Field Army, he simply would have ordered the necessary extractions based on his recognized authority, and would have borne the responsibility for such actions.

16 and 17 September 1914

On 16 and 17 September the enemy in front of the XIII Army Corps remained relatively quiet. Enemy infantry was moving closer toward the 26th Division, apparently to secure artillery firing positions at the edge of the Argonne Forest. That would make the gap on the inner wings of the Fourth and Fifth Armies very dangerous for maintaining contact between the XVIII Reserve Corps and XIII Army Corps. The Fifth Army headquarters agreed with our recommendation to repel the enemy force. Initially a battalion of five companies supported by machine guns moved forward from the 26th Division's right wing. That force entered the Argonne Forest without a fight and advanced toward the Le Four de Paris–Varennes-en-Argonne road. From there it screened the right wing of the 26th Division's later attack. The 52nd Infantry Brigade advanced with elements of its artillery to the vicinity of Chatel-Chéhéry and across to the western bank of the Aire. It was replaced in its former positions by Landwehr units. The 52nd Infantry Brigade then attacked toward the south from between the eastern edge of the Argonne Forest and the Aire, immediately pushed the enemy back toward Montblainville, and seized eight guns, fourteen ammunition wagons, and assorted military equipment. Behind the new front line, eight field batteries and one heavy battery occupied firing positions from which they could enfilade the enemy in front of the 27th Division and the XVI Army Corps. The entire attack was very effectively supported by the 27th Division's artillery. The 9th Landwehr Brigade, which had been attached to the XIII Army Corps on 17 September, was assigned to the 27th Division.

18 September 1914

During the night of 17 December enemy counterattacks against the 26th Division were repulsed. On 18 September the 52nd Infantry Brigade was detached from the 26th Division. As a result, the 26th Division's front became narrower, but also acquired greater depth. To the east the 26th Division tied in with the 27th Division.

The XIII Army Corps had established its command post on the southern edge of the town of Baulny, which was situated close to the east bank of the Aire and high up on the slope of the river valley. From there we could better observe the progress of the 26th Division's attack and the French positions. Initially we were very close to the enemy. They apparently observed us in position and several times they directed strong machine gun fire on to the plateau that dropped steeply toward the Aire River. There was room for only a few of us at a time up there. After I had been up there for quite a while, observing with binoculars, I was about to withdraw when to my surprise I found the Fifth Army commander, Crown Prince Wilhelm, standing right next to me.[42] He asked me for a terrain orientation. I pointed out to him both front lines and described the outline of the attack plan, which was already in full swing. When we again started taking machine gun fire, I asked the crown prince to take cover, but he refused to do so. He remained forward with the corps staff until our attack concluded successfully. He was highly pleased not only with the results, but also with the opportunity to observe from such close range an attack conducted by his troops.

On 18 September a bad case of dysentery hit the units of almost the entire XIII Army Corps. There didn't seem to be any clear cause for the infection, but it severely affected the fighting strength of the troops. On the recommendation of the corps surgeon, we sent a telegram to the Württemberg Ministry of War requesting an expedited supply of the traditional Württemberg home remedy for such a disorder—dried blueberries. By the following day several motor vehicles arrived from the Homeland with the blueberries, which we then boiled down at the field kitchens. It worked surprisingly fast. I even got instant relief from this tried and true remedy that seems to be adapted especially for the Württemberg stomach. In just a few days all of the sick troops were once again fully combat effective.

19 September 1914

In the afternoon of 19 September all the corps chiefs of staff were ordered to the Fifth Army headquarters at Stenay for an orders briefing. There we were informed of the OHL order that directed the general attack by the Second, Third, Fourth, and Fifth Armies, for the purpose of trying down the enemy forces to our respective fronts. That morning the Fifth Army headquarters had already informed OHL by telephone that, owing to the prevalent shortage of ammunition, minimal combat strengths, and the poor health of the troops, it would be impossible to achieve any sweeping success through such an attack. This was especially the case for an attack west of the Meuse, which would have to be mounted frontally, and with the no-go terrain of the Argonne Forest on the right flank and the strong fortress of Verdun on the left.

Despite the situation, the liaison officer from OHL to the Fifth Army repeated the order to attack. In his presence the army chief of staff requested the corps chiefs to brief the situations and the conditions of their respective corps. I explained that our combat power, which at that time was severely reduced because of the dysentery outbreak, amounted to regiments composed of two battalions each, with company strength of less than one hundred men. Because of the illness, the corps' total infantry combat strength was less than eleven thousand men. I also reported that the attack almost certainly would run into difficulty in the almost impenetrable Argonne Forest, and that the corps' right attacking wing would come under threat from enemy forces reported to be located at Le Four de Paris. In contrast to the opinion of OHL that the enemy in front of Fifth Army had been considerably weakened, the other corps chiefs of staff and I emphasized that we all assessed the enemy strength to our respective fronts as being equally strong as we were. By the end of the briefing the question of whether or not the Fifth Army should attack remained unresolved.

In the face of strong enemy opposition, the attack by the Fourth Army was unsuccessful, and the Third and Second Armies had similar experiences. Thus, OHL retracted the order for a general attack and only assigned individual offensive strikes to tie down the enemy as required. But we concluded from that directive that OHL was still incapable of making the major decision to shift to the defense along all the field army fronts west of Metz, and then thin out those lines and use the released forces to reinforce the German Army's overall right wing for an operationally decisive attack. The number of units deployed either by train of by foot march to the German right was not nearly enough. The Sixth Army, which recently had been redeployed on the extreme German right wing, was forced to commit its units newly arriving in the sector to the frontal fighting piecemeal. The resulting lack of the Sixth Army's attack depth finally forced it to shift from the operational offensive to the tactical defense. OHL was not ready to decide to pull the First, Seventh, and Second Armies back for the purpose of regaining operational freedom, and then launch the Sixth Army to hit the enemy full in the flank. OHL believed that such an evasive maneuver could be interpreted by the enemy as a German failure. Following this line of thought, OHL maintained the general attack order for the First, Seventh, and elements of the Second Army even though those attacks so far had produced no tangible results and the troops were becoming progressively exhausted. OHL's order was executed, but success resulted only at isolated points, and those had no bearing on the overall operational situation.

In the Fifth Army sector, Army Detachment Strantz attacked east of the Meuse on 19 September to seize the Meuse forts at Troyon and Camp des Romains. In order to narrow the front by consolidating the III Bavarian and V Army Corps, the 33rd Reserve Division, the main reserve force at Metz, was inserted between the V Reserve Corps and V Army Corps. OHL also allocated the XIV Army Corps to secure the southern flank against Toul. At that point, then, there were two additional army corps and one cavalry corps the III Bavarian Corps, XIV Army Corps, and Bavarian Cavalry Corps—committed to a secondary action in Alsace-Lorraine instead of being deployed north to the overall right wing that was supposed to be making the operational main effort. The intent of the attack south of Verdun was to divert French forces that were redeploying to the overall French left wing, but that did not happen. The French, instead, engaged our attack with the defensive forces they already had in place in the sector.

20 September 1914

On 19 and 20 September Army Detachment Strantz initially made a rapid advance against the Meuse, prompting OHL to order the Fifth Army to prevent the enemy from withdrawing any forces from the fronts of the XIII Army, XVI Army, and VI Reserve Corps. Furthermore, General von Falkenhayn during an orders briefing at Stenay on 21 September ordered the Fifth Army to advance its right wing in an effort to envelop the flank and the rear of the enemy forces opposing the Fourth Army. The following day the Fifth Army ordered its right wing corps to advance through the Argonne Forest, southwest toward Vienne-la-Ville.

21–24 September 1914

On 21 September the Fifth Army issued the order for the attack between the Argonne and Verdun, which was to begin the next day at 0500 hours. The main effort of the XIII Army Corps was an advance with its left wing toward Cheppy–Varennes-en-Argonne. The corps' right wing would advance though the forest west of Boureuilles. On the left of the XIII Army Corps, the XVI Army Corps was to attack with its left wing in the direction of Avocourt, with Landwehr Division Francke following in close support.[43] The right wing of the VI Reserve Corps was to follow the XVI Army Corps.

The attack met with very intense resistance and advanced slowly in the face of strong and effective enemy artillery fire. Constantly fighting on the evening of 22 September, the 26th Division reached the Le Four de Paris–Varennes-en-Argonne road, and the 27th Division reached the area north of Varennes-en-Argonne. The right wing of the XVI Army Corps reached Véry, and later that night it advanced to Cheppy. Landwehr Division Francke deployed between the XVI Army Corps and VI Reserve Corps.

The 27th Division took Varennes-en-Argonne on 23 September, while only insignificant advances were made along the rest of the attacking front. The 26th Division encountered especially difficult fighting in the Argonne Forest. The Fifth Army headquarters then attached the Jäger battalions of the 3rd and 6th Cavalry Divisions to the XIII Army Corps for the forest fighting.

On 24 September the attacking left wing of the XIII Army Corps reached Boureuilles. The XVI Army Corps took Vauquois and the forest areas east of the town. Landwehr Division Francke and the right wing of the VI Reserve Corps occupied the forest west of Malancourt up to the Malancourt–Avocourt road.

The relatively small gains had come after hard fighting. The XIII Army Corps lost twelve hundred men in the three days. The enemy defended courageously and also suffered heavy losses. We captured three hundred prisoners. For 25 September, the Fifth Army headquarters ordered a pause in the attack to reorganize our units that had become mixed up mostly during the forest fighting.

The Fourth Army gained only little ground during 22–24 September as well. Enemy pressure from the Argonne Forest brought increasing flanking pressure on the corps' left wing. An attack by the VI Army Corps' 11th Division emerging from the rear of the 25th Division attempted to cut off the enemy from the north, but the attack failed. Nevertheless, OHL urged the Fourth Army to continue attacking along its entire front. The Fourth Army, in turn, requested support from the XIII Army Corps, attacking in the direction of Vienne-le-Château. The enemy, however, had strongly reinforced his positions in the forest west of Le Four de Paris and could only be eliminated by a deliberate attack. The XIII Army Corps, therefore, could not guarantee the required level of support. In order to tie down the enemy, the 5th Jäger Battalion was sent west along the Montblainville–Servon[44] road, with the 6th Jäger Battalion advancing toward the Varennes-en-Argonne–Le Four de Paris road. Both battalions, however, did not make much progress in the forest.

East of the Meuse, the V Army Corps and III Bavarian Corps made progress in the direction of the Troyon and Camp des Romains forts, bringing up their heavy artillery. But on that attack enemy resistance increased day by day. On 24 September the III Bavarian Corps took Saint-Mihiel.[45] From the direction of Toul the French attacked the XIV Army Corps, which was tasked with securing the Fifth Army's southern flank between Flury and Pont-à-Mousson. Serious fighting took place there also.

The results of the Fifth Army's attacks made it clear that the objective of cutting off Fortress Verdun from the southwest was no longer possible. In front of both the XIII Army Corps and XVI Army Corps the enemy evaded to the line Dombasle-en-Argonne–Aubérive, where he dug in and reinforced. A continuation of the attack would have been vulnerable to a flanking attack from Fortress Verdun, and the Fifth Army lacked the strength and mostly the ammunition. In the Argonne Forest the enemy was close up against the 26th Division and the left wing of the Fourth Army. They were dug into cleverly prepared and reinforced positions, which were invulnerable to artillery preparation fire because of the thick forest. Thus, the entire attack operation ordered by OHL ground to a halt.

The series of unsuccessful attacks to that point had lengthened the Fifth Army's front considerably, especially east of the Meuse, and the resulting necessary transition to the defense tied up considerably more forces than had been required to man the initial attack positions. The Verdun fortress remained unencumbered in enemy hands and continued to provide French forces with a relief gate to the southeast, east, north, and northwest. Almost all of the units of the Fifth Army had suffered heavy losses, and great amounts of attack ammunition had been expended for nothing. The excess levels of strength that the Fifth Army had before the start of the attacks would have better been redeployed to the German Army's overall right wing. But OHL gave the Fifth Army the mission of attempting to tie down the enemy by retaking the ground that previously had been abandoned voluntarily.

The other armies between the Argonne and the right wing of the German Army had experiences similar to that of the Fifth Army. Tangible successes were achieved nowhere. The enemy had reinforced his positions, thinned out his defensive front, and redeployed all his freed-up forces on his own left wing. But OHL still insisted on the frontal attacks and on 25 September ordered the continuation of the same to tie-down the enemy and facilitate the attack of the Sixth Army.

25–26 September 1914

On 25 September the Fifth Army ordered the XVI Army Corps to extend its front to the edge of the Argonne Forest. The next day one division of the XIII Army Corps was ordered to march from Cornay via Grandpré along the rear of the XVIII Reserve Corps. The other division was to be prepared to march toward the west on the Varennes-en-Argonne–Le Four de Paris–Vienne-le-Château road as soon as the left wing of Fourth Army had seized that road's western exit from the Argonne.

Still on 25 September, the newly assigned 27th Landwehr Regiment started the relief in place of the 26th Division's security forces. The 26th Division then started marching along the assigned route, and on the afternoon of 26 September it assumed its positions at the rear of the XVIII Army Corps. During 26 September the XVI Army Corps relieved the 27th Division. Because the road via Le Four de Paris was not open yet, the division moved via Apremont toward Binarville, where it could enter the fight on the left flank of the Fourth Army's 11th Division. The 27th Division reached Binarville without a fight on 26 September and relieved the combat elements of the VI Army Corps' 11th Division east of the Binarville–Vienne-le-Château road. In the meantime, the 5th and 6th Jäger Battalions were pushed back to the Roman road by superior enemy forces.

On 26 September I rushed ahead of the corps staff to Vouziers in order to be briefed on the situation and the intent of the Fourth Army. The Fourth Army chief of staff, Lieutenant General Walther von Lüttwitz[46] oriented me in detail and told me that the XIII Army Corps was to be part of the attack in the sector of the XVIII Reserve Corps. That day the Fourth Army had attacked along its entire front, gaining some initial success. By late afternoon and evening, however, enemy deliberate counterattacks had pushed it back to its starting positions almost everywhere.

The XIII Army Corps established its headquarters in Autry, where the XVIII Reserve Corps headquarters also was located. As I was briefing my corps commander in the open, an enemy aircraft dropped two bombs on the corps headquarters train, which had just arrived at the position. One of the bombs exploded close to us and also hit near the equipment, killing several horses and wounding two soldiers.

27–31 September 1914

Despite the failure of the Fourth Army's attack, OHL ordered the continuation of the general attack west of the Argonne. The XVIII Reserve Corps was attached to the Fifth Army and was to attack together with the XIII Army Corps. A supporting attack by the XVI Army Corps was supposed to advance through the Argonne Forest against the right flank of the enemy opposite the Fourth Army. Elements of the V Reserve Corps, which up to that point had been east of the Meuse, were pulled over on to the western bank to occupy the former positions of the VI Reserve Corps between Cuisy and the Meuse. The VI Reserve Corps, with Landwehr Division Francke, then took over the whole sector between the eastern edge of the Argonne and Cuisy. The entire XVI Corps was consolidated along and east of the Cornay–Varennes-en-Argonne road for the attack through the Argonne Forest, with the 34th Division advancing from Montblainville toward Servon, and the 33rd Division attacking from Varennes-en-Argonne toward Le Four de Paris. In the execution of that maneuver the XVI Army Corps engaged in heavy and costly fighting in the Argonne Forest that lasted throughout the war.[47]

East of the Meuse, the attack by Army Detachment Strantz quickly stalled from exhaustion of the troops and the lack of ammunition. The attack by the left wing of the V Army Corps failed to take the barrier fort at Troyon. The III Bavarian Corps succeeded in gaining a small bridgehead on the left bank of the Meuse west of Saint-Mihiel and seized the Camp des Romains fort. Over the course of the next several days the 33rd Reserve Division was relieved by elements of the V Reserve Corps' 10th Reserve Division. The 33rd Reserve Division then relieved the V Army Corps' frontline sector south of Étain. The V Army Corps thus gained greater depth for the continuation of the attack.

From 30 September through 2 October, the 5th Bavarian Division on the left of the III Bavarian Corps was relieved by the 10th Ersatz Division[48] and the XIV Army Corps was relieved by the Guards Division and 8th Ersatz Division. These three Ersatz divisions remained attached to Army Detachment Falkenhausen. All of these various relief movements established narrower sectors for the V Army Corps and III Bavarian Corps, which in turn facilitated their ability to continue their attacks. On 4 October the Bavarian Ersatz Division assembled in the vicinity of Thiaucourt as additional reserve. It also remained attached to Army Detachment Falkenhausen. As the battle progressed, however, the Bavarian Ersatz Division was not detached to Army Detachment Strantz for their attack because the fighting on the right wing of the Fifth Army did not produce the intended results.

The Fifth Army established two battle groups for the execution of the attack west of the Argonne ordered by OHL. West of the Aisne River the XVIII Reserve Corps had the 21st Reserve Division on the right and the 26th Division on the left. From the Aisne to the southeast of Binarville the XIII Army Corps had the 25th Reserve Division on the right, the 11th Division in the center, and the 27th Division on the left. The 27th Division relieved elements of the 11th Division that were positioned east of the Binarville–Vienne-le-Château road.

After conducting a reconnaissance of the attack sector and briefing the division commanders, the XIII Army Corps headquarters issued the attack order at 0930 hours on 27 September. Heavy fog, however, impeded the reconnaissance and occupation of the artillery firing positions, but they were finally in battery by the early morning hours of 28 September. A further corps order issued at 1800 hours on 27 September instructed the 27th Division to advance, following a thorough artillery preparation, with its right wing to the Binarville–Vienne-le-Château road, and with its left wing from Moulin-de-l'Homme Mort toward La Placardelle, clearing the enemy from the forest in the process.[49] Until the 27th Division successfully executed its mission, the two other divisions would remain in place. The 11th Division would then follow the 27th Division's attack only after its right wing caught up with the left wing of the 11th Division. After the reduction of the front, the excess elements of the 11th Division that were still forward would reassemble behind the division's left wing. The 25th Reserve Division was to attack in unison with the right wing of the 11th Division. The artillery preparation, which had started already on 27 September, was to continue on 28 September. That morning the 27th Division was ready for the assault at 0730 hours. The corps order also specified that the XVI Army Corps would assemble for the attack across the Roman road.

Soon after the start of 27th Division's attack it became obvious that the enemy in the thick of the forest south of Binarville had prepared for a stubborn defense. Thus, the 27th Division was forced to fight right from the start for every inch of forest ground. The enemy had constructed a large number of echeloned trenches in a checkerboard pattern that provided flanking support for one another. Their wire was interwoven into the thick underbrush. Effective rifle fire and—even more so—effective machine gun fire were largely impossible because the visibility was limited to only a few paces. The infantry fight had to be conducted primarily with hand grenades. Close observation of artillery fire was impossible, and the observers had to limit themselves to firing on the enemy's rearward positions. The fight against the enemy's forward line depended on mortar fire. French snipers positioned in tall trees also caused trouble. The 27th

Division's coordinated attack broke down very rapidly, requiring reconnaissance and single attacks against individual enemy strongpoints. The 27th Division advanced only very slowly. After three days of fighting, from 28 through 30 September, the 27th Division had penetrated only about one kilometer into the forest.

The XVI Army Corps' divisions encountered the same difficult conditions. Advancing from Montblainville toward Servon, the 34th Division by 30 September only reached the reinforced strongpoint in the vicinity of Bagatelle Pavillon. The 33rd Division, advancing from Varennes-en-Argonne via Le Four de Paris toward Vienne-le-Château, only made about one kilometer toward Le Four de Paris. Large elements of the division were forced to turn in the forest toward the south and transition to the defense to beat back tenacious enemy flank attacks.

1–6 October 1914

For the attack against Bagatelle Pavillon, the Fifth Army had assembled an ad hoc task group under the army's engineer commander, Lieutenant General Max Kämpffer. His group consisted of units from the 34th and 27th Divisions and special engineer and foot artillery[50] units. The 4 October assault on Bagatelle Pavillon failed, however, because of enemy obstacles. The 33rd Division had trouble fending off strong enemy attacks that came from the south on 2 October.

Within the XIII Army Corps' sector, the 11th Division, which followed the 27th Division and the 25th Reserve Division, made only very small progress. The 11th Division's left flank was forced to turn toward the southwest against enemy flanking fire from the forest. OHL finally decided that it would be impossible to clear the Argonne Forest. It halted the entire attack in and west of the Argonne and then shifted the units not needed for the defense to the overall German right wing, which had been struggling for some time.

The 26th Division and the 25th Reserve Division, along with the corps headquarters, were extracted from the XIII Army Corps and designated Corps Fabeck. The Fifth Army commander, Crown Prince Wilhelm, personally transmitted the reorganization order to General von Fabeck in Autry on the afternoon of 6 October. The crown prince commended the corps commander and the actions of the XIII Army Corps since the start of the advance, and he repeated those comments in a long telegram the following day.

The XIII Army Corps had fought courageously and successfully as part of the Fifth Army and could be proud of its accomplishments. The Fifth Army had conducted all its operations with a firm hand within the framework of the directives and missions assigned to it by OHL. I had made a number of operational recommendations to the Fifth Army headquarters during the advance to the

Meuse and during the attack on both sides of Verdun. And although all of those recommendations were not necessarily accepted, I understood fully that the Fifth Army at all times was bound by the directives it received from OHL. The subsequent compression of the Fifth Army on the western bank of the Meuse for the attack to the south was not the result of any decision by the Fifth Army headquarters, but rather it was a function of the attack direction assigned to the Fourth Army by OHL. Unfortunately, the space west of Verdun was too tight.

As the corps chief of staff, I conducted on a daily basis numerous conversations with the Fifth Army chief of staff, Lieutenant General Konstantin Schmidt von Knobelsdorf. Several times I also participated in situation and orders briefings at the Fifth Army headquarters. Between 1905 and 1907 I myself as a General Staff officer had served under the Fifth Army chief of staff in Hanover. Thus, a bond of mutual trust and cooperation already existed, which only grew stronger during the war. I continue to hold Lieutenant General Schmidt von Knobelsdorf in great esteem to this day. In him, the crown prince had a chief of staff who was loyal, diligent, and a proven pillar upon whom he could rely absolutely.[51] The crown prince often was at the fighting front, including at the command posts of the XIII Army Corps and the divisions. He frequently came within the range of enemy fire. Despite his relative youth, the crown prince was a well-educated soldier who commanded his army with purpose and confidence.[52] The crown prince later greeted me often in my various follow-on chief of staff assignments. I always had the impression that he trusted me completely.

With great regret the corps headquarters separated from its divisions and departed for the north. Technically, the XVIII Army Corps, with the 21st and 25th Reserve Divisions and the 11th Division, should have taken over the entire sector from its right wing to the XVI Army Corps boundary. The relief actions east of the Aisne would have taken perhaps a day longer, but then the 26th Division followed by the 27th Division could have been redeployed north. During the long period of peacetime, and even more so since the beginning of the war, the subordinate divisions of a corps operated together and were uniformly trained by the corps commander. Almost all the leaders knew each other personally and had developed strong bonds of trust. The integrity of the corps formations should have been maintained under all circumstances. By mixing up the corps headquarters and the subordinate divisions, they had to go through a completely new process of orientation. Unfortunately, almost all of the corps were split up during the course of the war.

The 25th Reserve Division, which was assigned to the XIII Army Corps in place of the 27th Division, was a division full of fighting spirit and well-led by its commander, General Wolf von Helldorf. The General Staff officer Ia, Captain von Unruh, was an especially courageous officer, well educated, and capable of surmounting any difficulty.[53] Right from the start of our association we developed complete trust and a close friendship. In the further course of operations, the corps headquarters always had good experiences with the 25th Reserve Division.

Before I turn to the discussion of my activities with the Sixth Army, I want to discuss my views on how we lost the Battle of the Marne. OHL was positioned far in the rear, with its headquarters initially in Koblenz and then in Luxembourg. As a result, the tight reins of the German Army slipped out of OHL's hands long before the Marne battle, and all operational control rested with the individual field army commanders. The opportunity to destroy the French-British army near Mons through the conduct of a frontal attack by the Second Army, to which the First and Third Army were at the time subordinated, was lost because of the peculiar independence of mind of the Second Army's commander.[54] Similar conditions allowed the enemy to slip away at Saint-Quentin. Instead of learning from those experiences and rapidly establishing a small forward command post behind the main effort on the overall right wing, OHL remained in Luxembourg and issued only very general directives to the field armies. And those directives were based on the false assumption that the victory had already been won. This is the only explanation why OHL withdrew the XI Army Corps and the Guards Reserve Corps from the German overall right wing, and the V Army Corps from the Fifth Army, and then redeployed those corps to the east.

It was only after the war that it became fully clear to me that OHL at the time intended for the Sixth and Seventh Armies to break through the French southern wing and advance in the direction of Toul–Épinal. As the German extreme right wing passed east of Paris and then in a southerly direction deep into the heart of France, the two wings of the German Army would be able to envelop and destroy the French-British army. Only this can explain the forward echeloning of the First Army to the Second Army, as well as the compression of the Fourth and Fifth Armies toward the Meuse.

The failure of the breakthrough attack toward Toul–Épinal gave the French Army leadership the opportunity to assemble strong forces in and around Paris, and then to advance those forces against the flank and rear of the First Army. It was, in fact, an operational masterpiece on the part of the First Army to neutralize the threat to the German overall right wing by first evading to the north and then swinging toward the west to get into position to attack any French force advancing from Paris. Even as this grand operational maneuver opened up a gap between the First and Second Armies, that gap was filled provisionally by the I and II Cavalry Corps. The French Army leadership committed the British

Expeditionary Force (BEF) of six weak divisions against the gap. So far in the war the English had evaded any decisive fight to avoid losing their links to the Channel ports. For that same reason, the BEF's thrust into the gap between the First and Second Armies was neither rapid nor energetic.

In this situation it would have been the duty of the Second Army's commanding general, either acting in conformance with, or even contrary to, specific orders from OHL, to extend the front line of his army far toward the west and then transition to a deliberate defense in the immediately reinforced positions in order to secure the southern flank and the rear of the First Army. Instead, the Second Army shifted the 14th Division of its VII Army Corps, which was positioned on the right flank, to the Second Army's left flank. That action increased the gap between the two field armies, as the Second Army then attacked on 8 September with its left wing. It was a grave operational mistake.

On 9 September the First Army was close to achieving a clear victory over the French force advancing from Paris. That left the First Army positioned squarely on the flank of the BEF. Without a doubt, however, the situation on the German right had become serious. In such situations, the decision always must be made by the responsible commander on the ground. I, therefore, am of the unwavering opinion that the decision should not have been made by Lieutenant Colonel Richard Hentsch, who lacked frontline experience and who was pessimistically inclined. He later was blamed for the withdrawal order. That decision only should have been made by the chief of staff of the Field Army, General von Moltke.[55]

Moltke by this time was physically spent, but he still had sufficient energy on 11 September to cover long the distances by motor car to participate in briefings at the headquarters of the Third, Fourth, and Fifth Armies. If Moltke had rushed to the right wing of the German Army in a timely manner and had given the order to the Second Army commander to hold under all circumstances and to extend the defensive front of his army far to the west, the Battle of the Marne would have been a German victory.

I can only describe Hentsch's directive to withdraw behind the Marne as a grave operational mistake. I reached that conclusion only later, after long conversations with the commanding general of First Army, General Alexander von Kluck, his chief of staff, General Hermann von Kuhl, and his assistant chief of staff, General Walter von Bergmann. All three of them assured me that they never would have abandoned the Marne battle, but they had to follow the directive issued by Hentsch in the name of the OHL. The blame for this incomprehensible order certainly falls on OHL. But the commanding general of the Second Army, General Karl von Bülow, is also not without guilt, because he failed to make the decision on his own initiative to cover the gap between the First and Second Armies with his own units.

It is not the courageous German Army that was to blame for the withdrawal from the Marne, but rather OHL and General von Moltke, who from the beginning of the war made one mistake after another. The Second OHL, under General Erich von Falkenhayn, also did not make the drastic operational decisions necessary to achieve victory in the west in 1914 by temporarily pulling back the German overall right wing while simultaneously moving forward as many as possible of the available German combat units to execute a sweeping operational envelopment of the enemy's left wing.[56]

The weakening of all the defensive front lines in the west to the maximum level possible, while at the same time mounting a stubborn defense to support the buildup of a strong and deeply echeloned attack force on the German right, would not have involved a great degree of risk. Never during the entire war did an enemy force, no matter how superior, manage to break through a German defensive line. Despite the enemy onslaught [in 1918], the German Western Front remained locked until the conclusion of the war.[57]

During the grave situation following 9 September 1914, the only important issue was the ability to assemble a superior force for the German right wing to attack with. Whether or not the right wing should have been pulled back farther was immaterial, because in a mobile war one does not fight for terrain, but for the total destruction of the enemy.

The XIII Army Corps with the Sixth Army

On the evening of 6 October 1914 we received the Fifth Army transportation order for our movement to Valenciennes. We immediately sent for one officer from both the 26th Division and the 25th Reserve Division to report to the Sixth Army headquarters at Mézières[58] as orders couriers. We issued the corps order at 2200 hours and coordinated with the XVIII Reserve Corps headquarters, also located in Autry, for the reliefs of our units in place. The infantry units moved by rail, the mounted troops by road march. We started the loading process in Autry and Challerange at 1000 hours on 7 October. Advance party officers coordinated with the rear area inspectorates of the Fourth, Third, Second, Seventh, First, and Sixth Armies for quartering and rations for the mounted march units and the supply columns. We had four march days to make the approximately 150-kilometer move to Valenciennes. The movements of the foot units initially went as planned, but then we ran into delays because there were insufficient rail cars for their vehicles. We were not able to load the infantry of the 26th Division until 8 October. The movements were routed via Mézières, but then mudslides there blocked the tracks. We had to unload everything and then reload beyond the blockage. We lost eight hours in the process. By the evening of 8

October some half of the troops had arrived in Hirson, but the rail line there had been destroyed and had not yet been rebuilt. After another process of offloading and reloading, we finally continued the movement to Valenciennes and Saint-Amand.

On 8 October the XIII Army Corps headquarters moved by motor cars from Autry to Hirson via Mézières. In Mézières, General von Fabeck met with the chief of staff of the Field Army, Lieutenant General von Falkenhayn. I used the short pause in Mézières to orient myself to the situation on the Western Front's overall right wing.

The OHL Operations Division gave me a short briefing on the Sixth Army's failed attack to envelop the enemy's overall left wing. I realized that almost from the start the attempted envelopment had evolved into a frontal attack, and because it had not been echeloned in depth sufficiently, almost the entire front of the Sixth Army was forced to transition to the defensive. I could not help but think with a sense of bitterness that the attacks OHL had ordered the Fifth Army to mount from its defensive positions had resulted in predictably minor results, and in the process had cost a great deal of blood with little decisive effect on the operations on the German Army's overall right wing in the north. In any case, my assessment of our situation since the withdrawal of the German front confirmed my conclusion that the frontal attacks we had launched from our defensive positions had not prevented the enemy from shifting major forces against us to the north. OHL's attempt to pin down the enemy with frontal attacks had been an operational blunder. Not only did we not fix the enemy in place, we also tied down a significant number of our own forces that would not have been needed for the conduct of so simple a defense in an operationally nondecisive sector. Thus, the Sixth Army had not had the forces necessary for a decisive operational attack, and was now also stalled in a defensive posture.

While at OHL I also learned that a reorganized Fourth Army would be staged on the German far right flank on the coast for an enveloping attack. I hoped at the time that Corps Fabeck would have the honor of a decisive role in such an attack. I also assumed that the newly formed XXII through XXVII Reserve Corps consisting of fresh replacements would initially relieve veteran corps in quiet battle sectors, and that the planned operational offensive would be conducted with the latter. Had all this been the case, the attack in Flanders most likely would have been more successful. As every frontline soldier knew, the young replacements required time to adjust themselves to the horrors of war before they could be fully combat effective.

The Corps Fabeck headquarters staff spent the night of 8–9 October in Hirson. The following morning the commanding general and I drove to Cambrai to establish contact with the Sixth Army, commanded by Crown Prince Rupprecht of Bavaria, with Major General Konrad Krafft von Dellmensingen as his chief of staff. There we learned that, along with our corps, the Saxon XIX Army Corps was being redeployed from the Third Army to the right wing of the Sixth Army.

On the evening of 9 October the staff of Corps Fabeck occupied our headquarters in Valenciennes. The majority of the infantry units of the 26th Division had arrived there and in Saint-Amand that day. The divisional staff of the 25th Reserve Division was also in Valenciennes already. According to the incoming messages, the march movements of the mounted formations and the columns were going according to plan. On the evening of 10 October our infantry units completed their movement and occupied their assigned bivouac area. At noon that day the commanding general of the XIX Army Corps arrived in Valenciennes to establish personal contact with General von Fabeck. By the evening of the following day our mounted units and supply columns closed and settled into their quarters.

On order of the Sixth Army headquarters, the infantry units of the 26th Division were moved forward by rail and road marches from Saint-Amand to the area southeast of Lille. The 25th Reserve Division followed. Farther to the west, the XIX Army Corps moved up from the south to closer to Lille. The intent was to attack at 1400 hours against the Lille citadel from the south, the west, and southeast. Simultaneously, a detachment under the command of Major General Franz Wahnschaffe would attack from the north with three infantry battalions, two artillery battalions, and one cavalry squadron from the 41st Combined Landwehr Brigade. The forwardmost elements of the 26th Division were alerted to support on order the XIX Army Corps on its right flank. In the event, the XIX Army Corps managed to take Lille on 12 October.

Corps Fabeck reconsolidated southeast of Lille on 13 October. The Sixth Army then ordered us to march to the north in two columns, past Lille's eastern side. The 26th Division's objective was the line Menen–Wervik, and the 25th Reserve Division's was the area north of Lille. That same day the right wing of the XIX Army Corps reached Warneton.

At 1430 hours the Sixth Army ordered Corps Fabeck to defend the line Menen–Wervik–Warneton, on the right of the XIX Army Corps. After a rapid reconnaissance of the ground, the divisions received a verbal warning order and then a written corps order designating their respective defensive sectors, to which they started moving immediately. Our reconnaissance elements reported no enemy in the area north of the Lys River. We established advance posts two to three kilometers out. The Sixth Army informed us that aerial reconnaissance reported stronger enemy forces had moved in the direction of Lille from Antwerp, which had capitulated on 9 October. In the event, however, those enemy forces apparently changed their march direction toward Ypres to counter the advance of the XIII and XIX Army Corps.

On our left, the XIX Army Corps assumed a defensive front line oriented toward the west, with its right flank at Warneton and its left flank west of Lille. The VII Corps' 14th Division was on their left, to the east of La Bassée. The XIX Army Corps was short one infantry brigade at that point, but they nonetheless sent out advance units to Armentières. Initially, the forward areas of the Flanders front were screened by the IV, II, and I Cavalry Corps. During the night of 15–16 October all of the forward cavalry was withdrawn to rest areas in the vicinity of Lille. We were a little nervous when the cavalry withdrew, because it meant that the intervening ground would be relinquished to the enemy. As a consequence, the XIX Army Corps became tied down in its defensive positions as the enemy pushed forward, and the corps thus was unable to participate in the attack toward Ypres.

By the middle of October the 26th Division and the 25th Reserve Division received several replacement levies, which brought Corps Fabeck's combat strength up to sixteen thousand men. The other Sixth Army corps also received replacements.

The reason Corps Fabeck was given the mission of defending the Lys sector was that both the Sixth Army and OHL no longer believed it possible to conduct a successful decisive attack on both sides of Arras. The ground between Arras and the Lys River had many coal mines and large, built-up villages. The enemy made very effective use of those positions to establish a long-term defense. Despite having excellent esprit de corps, all of the Sixth Army's corps only advanced slowly in that sector, because any attacks required extensive artillery preparation. Our ammunition supply was becoming increasingly low. Thus, all of the advancing corps sustained heavy losses.

From 13 October on, aerial reconnaissance reports increasingly indicated that major enemy forces from the south were assembling on both sides of the Lys between La Bassée and Bailleul. The enemy also managed to link up with the Belgian Army after it withdrew from Antwerp. We also received reports of stronger enemy forces marching from Ostend south toward Dijksmuide and Torhout. As a consequence of this serious threat from the north and northwest, OHL abandoned its plan to deploy the XIII and XIX Army Corps on the overall German right wing for the purpose of mounting an attack toward the west in the general direction of Lillers. Instead, OHL formed a defensive flank, with the XIII Army Corps facing north and the XIX Army Corps facing west. Another factor in this change of plans was the redeployment of the Fourth Army from the German center to the area around Brussels, from which it was to advance toward the west.

OHL's estimate of the situation, which later failed to correspond with the actual events, was that the enemy would attack from the west and north against the newly formed defensive line on the Sixth Army's right flank, which ran from Menen via Warneton to La Bassée. Under that scenario the Fourth Army could then attack by advancing toward the west on both sides of Gent, penetrating the enemy's eastern flank and rear. The original plan was for the III Reserve Corps, which had besieged Antwerp, to deploy on the Sixth Army's right flank. Instead, the III Reserve Corps was ordered to deploy toward Bruges as the forward echelon of the Fourth Army. The corps reached the Bruges area on 14 October, and that same day the Fourth Army was ordered to assume staging positions along the line from Urselto to Anzegem. Then on 18 October the Fourth Army would attack with its left wing via Menen in the direction of Merville. Along with the III Reserve Corps, the Fourth Army was assigned the 4th Ersatz Division and, somewhat later, the IV Cavalry Corps.

OHL ordered the Sixth Army to defend along the line Menen–Armentières–La Bassée, but in the face of an overwhelming enemy attack it was authorized to withdraw to the line Tourcoing–northern forts of Lille–La Bassée. OHL also ordered the Sixth Army to prepare to conduct a follow-on breakthrough in the vicinity of Arras, advancing to the west-northwest in order to hit the rear of any enemy forces withdrawing from the Fourth Army. The OHL plan also required the Sixth Army to transfer forces from its right wing to the Fourth Army. The Sixth Army headquarters correctly estimated that there was a very low probability of breaking through the enemy's well-developed positions, especially around Arras. It almost certainly would have been better if OHL had concurred with the Fourth Army's request for operational control of the XIII and XIX Army Corps for its attack toward the northwest.

We had assumed that both the XIII and XIX Army Corps would support the Fourth Army's attack in Flanders, but we later learned that a different decision had been reached during a planning conference with OHL and the Sixth Army. At the time we were convinced that all available forces and ammunition should be committed to a decisive attack north of the Lys. We expected, therefore, that the two corps would be echeloned in depth and advance as the attack's right wing toward Ypres. That, in turn, would facilitate the Fourth Army's attack across the Yser River. As an operational objective, we surmised that we would throw the enemy back toward the Channel coast west of the mouth of the Yser, and then destroy him there.

Based our map analysis, we anticipated that the deeply echeloned main effort of the Fourth Army's strong left wing would be between Dijksmuide and the Ypres–Menen road. The enemy's front from the sea to Langemark would only be held lightly, because they could flood the entire area by damming the Yser and the canal. The chief of the General Staff at OHL should have known this. The longer the enemy resisted in that sector, the greater would be our probability of cutting off his retreat by making a deeply echeloned attack on both sides of Ypres. We also hoped that after analyzing our experiences to date, OHL finally would decide to transition the remainder of the Western Front to the defensive. Then they would redeploy all available forces behind the overall German right wing for a decisive thrust in Flanders. Doing so also would have freed up the urgently needed supplies and ammunition for the Flanders attack. To this day I remain convinced that had OHL acted rapidly and decisively to assume overall control of the Fourth and Sixth Armies' operational attack, directing the action from a command post established close to the front, we would have achieved decisive results in Flanders.

Unfortunately, OHL clung to its preconceived notion that the enemy in Flanders would swing to the southeast against the Lys, and that the attack of the Fourth Army would then hit his flank and his rear. But even then it was obvious that the British would do everything possible to hold Flanders, otherwise they would lose their lines of communication with England via Dunkirk and Calais. The basis for any German decision in the given situation, therefore, had to be to concentrate all available forces and ammunition supplies against the British and the Belgians in Flanders. Such a course of action was feasible, and with an acceptable level of risk. OHL's subsequent decisions proved this. After the Fourth Army's attack ground to a halt, OHL redeployed the XV Army Corps, the II Bavarian Corps, the Guards Corps, the 6th Bavarian Reserve Division, and heavy artillery units from other sectors to Flanders. OHL also moved the XXIV Reserve Corps from Metz into position as a reserve in the north. That corps had recently been deployed from Germany with the apparent intent of committing it to continue the attack across the Meuse, south of Verdun.

OHL had far too optimistic an assessment of the combat effectiveness of the Fourth Army's newly formed XXII, XXIII, XXVI, and XXVII Reserve Corps. These corps, consisting of young volunteers, had high morale and esprit de corps, but the troops and their leaders lacked the necessary battle experience. Their aggressiveness in the attack, therefore, resulted in horrendous casualties. Nonetheless, their reckless heroism will always be held in high esteem by every brave German soldier.[59] In the later course of the war the younger troops almost always fought well and effectively.

In reviewing the results of the attack in Flanders, it is impossible to recognize an OHL that exercised clear leadership and made decisions based on the prevailing situation. OHL could not bring itself to make the decision to abort the attacks in Flanders. Withdrawing forces from the First and Seventh

Armies, OHL planned to attempt a breakthrough near Roye, on the boundary between the Second and First Armies. But the planned attacks at Roye and near Arras were never launched. The latter was cancelled based on the Sixth Army's objections. The Sixth Army instead recommended that the XIII and XIX Army Corps conduct a holding attack to the west, south of and past Warneton, to tie down and further draw off the British there, and thus facilitate the attack of the Fourth Army. OHL did not approve that recommendation until 17 October.

Returning to the actions of the XIII Army Corps, we reinforced our designated positions between Menen and Warneton from 15 October on, with the 26th Division on the right and the 25th Reserve Division on the left. The XIX Army Corps was linked in to the west. According to reconnaissance reports, the enemy's northern wing seemed to extend to Ypres. In the evening of 15 October a liaison officer from the Fourth Army headquarters briefed us on the Fourth Army's situation and intent.

The following day, on order of the Sixth Army, our second-echelon troops started establishing a second defensive line approximately two kilometers south of the Lys. Weak enemy forces were identified to the 26th Division's front, and weak cavalry and bicycle patrols in front of the 25th Reserve Division. In the XIX Army Corps' sector the enemy was probing carefully against Warneton and Armentières.

As we continued to reinforce our positions on 17 October, the enemy probes with infantry, cavalry, and bicycle patrols worked their way closer to our forward positions by that evening. The following morning the 26th Division captured a British operations order directing their 7th Division to advance on both sides of the Ypres–Menen road. Our intelligence also tentatively identified the British 2nd Division to the west. Our two divisions had orders to hold their positions. The corps reserve was in ready position behind the 26th Division. When the British made a weak thrust against our advance guards, they were repulsed after a short fight. The British then started to dig in at their current positions everywhere, all the while harassed by our artillery fires.

We hoped to receive the order soon to attack in the direction of Ypres, but on 18 October at 1500 hours the Sixth Army headquarters issued the surprising order for the IV Cavalry Corps to relieve in place our two divisions during the night of 18–19 October. Corps Fabeck then would assume a ready position west of Lille. We quickly made all the preparations to execute the reliefs. The 3rd and 6th Cavalry Divisions occupied the 26th Division's sector, and the Bavarian Cavalry Division relieved the 25th Reserve Division. By the morning of 19 October we had accomplished all the relief actions without incident, and we also linked up with the 54th Reserve Division of the XXVII Reserve Corps of the Fourth Army in Courtrai.

Corps Fabeck went into quarters west and southwest of Lille on 19 October. On the way there we visited the command post of the XIX Army Corps. Around 1500 hours we received an order from the Sixth Army for an attack toward the west on 20 October. That attack was to be conducted with the XIX Army Corps on both sides of the Lys, advancing its left wing via Prémesques–Fleurbaix. Corps Fabeck was to advance its left wing via Beaucamps[60]–Aubers. The VII Army Corps was linked in to the south, and to its south the XIV Army Corps was also linked into the attack. The IV Cavalry Corps with the subordinated I Cavalry Corps and the 9th Reserve Division had the mission of pinning the enemy down to the southeast and south. Otherwise, those enemy units could threaten the northern flank and rear of the XIX Army Corps. The II Cavalry Corps remained south of Lille in Sixth Army reserve. The I Bavarian Reserve Corps to the south of the XIV Army Corps was ordered to exploit on 21 October by spearheading the breakthrough north of Arras.

We issued warning orders by telephone to both of our divisions, directing them to reconnoiter their designated attack sectors and coordinate for the reliefs of the elements of the XIX Army Corps currently in those positions. The British, meanwhile, did not continue to attack on 19 October. They dug in approximately eight hundred to one thousand meters in front of the German lines. At the onset of darkness, the 25th Reserve Division on the left and the 26th Division on the right started relieving the Saxon units in their attack sectors. During the relief actions the British put out some strong probing patrols, but we repulsed them all.

During the early darkness hours of 20 October both of Corps Fabeck's divisions started advancing in attack formation closer to the enemy positioned along the line Prémesques–Escobecques–Château de Flandre–Bas Flandre–La Voirie–Le Riez du Biez. After our artillery registered and fired a strong preparation, the infantry jumped off at 0900 hours via the line Prémesques–Erquinghem-Lys. The corps reserve was positioned on the alert at Le Marais, where Corps Fabeck also had its command post. The XIX Army Corps and the 4th Division started to attack at the same time. Communications with those units was secured by telephone line and liaison officers.

By 1230 hours the 25th Reserve Division had advanced to Prémesques and Mont de Prémesques, where a British hasty counterattack forced the division's right wing on to the defensive temporarily. The strongest point of the enemy position was the village of Ennetières-en-Weppes. We finally managed to seize the village at 1900 hours with a combined attack by the inner wings of the 25th Reserve Division and the 26th Division. Making a rapid advance, the 26th Division took Escobecques and then pushed its right wing forward in the direction of Ennetières-en-Weppes and La Vallée. Its left wing continued to attack toward Château de Flandre.

By the evening of 20 October the corps had captured approximately 450 British troops and was in possession of the line west of Mont de Prémesques–La Vallée–northwest Escobecques–Château de Flandre–Le Fresnoy–Bas Flandre. To our right the XIX Army Corps made only very minimal progress. Its left wing was able to hold Prémesques against strong British attacks. To the left of us the 14th Division had taken Bas Flandre and Rosembois.

The attack continued at 0700 hours on 21 October. By 0830 hours the 25th Reserve Division reported that it had taken Le Touquet and was continuing to advance on both sides of Paradis. At 0930 hours the XII Army Corps command post displaced forward from Le Marais to La Couture, accompanied by the corps reserve. By 1000 hours the 26th Division had taken Le Bas and Radinghem-en-Weppes, and was continuing to advance toward Bas Maisnil. About that time we received reports that the enemy was actively retreating on both sides of the Lille–Armentières road.

Toward 1100 hours the commander of the Sixth Army, Crown Prince Rupprecht of Bavaria, arrived at Corps Fabeck's command post, from which he reported the rapid advance of the Sixth Army to the Fourth Army's headquarters, and urged them to increase the pace of their own advance.

Following positive reports from the front, the Sixth Army at 1245 hours issued the order for a rapid follow-on advance. We moved the corps command post and the corps reserve toward Englos. By the evening of 21 October, Corps Fabeck held the line Fleur d'Écosse–west of La Vallée–Le Bas–Radinghem-en-Weppes–the eastern part of Le Maisnil–Bas Flandre. The advance of the corps' right wing, however, was limited because we lost contact with the left wing of the XIX Army Corps and came under enemy flanking fire as a result. Our left wing remained tied in tightly with the 14th Division at Bas Flandre. We spent the night with the corps command post in Grande Ville Château, with the corps reserve in Englos and Sequedin.

During the night of 22 October the situation remained calm along the fronts of the XIX Army Corps and Corps Fabeck. Elements of the VII Army Corps on our left came under attack twice, but with no significant results for the enemy. At that point we estimated that although the enemy had sustained heavy losses, their forces remained intact. We continued attacking on 22 October. We jumped the corps command post and the corps reserve forward to the vicinity of Englos at 0700 hours.

That day the 25th Reserve Division made little progress because they suffered high casualties from enemy flanking fire from the northeast. The XIX

Army Corps decided to continue the attack only after the arrival of its fourth infantry brigade, which had been detraining in Lille between 21 through 23 October. Nonetheless, the XIX Army Corps made little headway, even though the 25th Reserve Division on their flank supported them with artillery fire. Thus, the 25th Reserve Division failed to take their objectives, the villages La Houssoye, Le Quesne, and Bois Blancs. On 22 October the 26th Division seized the villages of Bas Maisnil, Bacquart, and La Voirie and with the right wing of the VII Army Corps reached the line Le Riez–Herlies.

We continued attacking on 23 October, but newly emplaced enemy obstacles prevented the 25th Reserve Division from taking the villages of Le Quesne and Bois Blancs. By 0800 hours, however, the 26th Division captured the village of Fromelles. That afternoon they reached the line Bas Maisnil–Le Touquet–western edge of Fromelles. They then moved weak forces to Le Bas to establish a linkup. The 25th Division, meanwhile, continued to take heavy artillery fire from their front and right flank, as the XIX Army Corps still had not advanced, even though its fourth infantry brigade had closed. The VII Army Corps' right wing managed to reach Aubers.

On 23 October Corps Fabeck's command post and the corps reserve reached the Erquinghem-Lys rail station. Soon after our arrival the commanding general and I went far forward to the command post of the 25th Reserve Division. We only managed to reach there by infiltrating through almost constant heavy enemy artillery fire. That convinced us that the artillery fire hitting the division from the front and flank made it impossible for them to advance until the XIX Army Corps started moving forward. We then moved directly to the 26th Division's command post and determined that the enemy's front was oriented more to the southeast than to the east. When we sent our situation report to the Sixth Army at 1030 hours, we therefore requested the adjustment of the corps' assigned sector in accordance with the situation. At 1215 hours the 26th Division reported encountering enemy trench works along the line Fleurbaix–Fauquissart. Aerial reconnaissance confirmed that report by identifying the enemy's construction of bridges and trench works on the Lys River.

At 1415 hours the Sixth Army issued a telephonic order to continue the attack in a northwesterly direction. We then ordered the 26th Division to advance toward Aubers and Laventie, and then to the La Boutillerie–Six Blanche road as the ultimate objective. We ordered the 25th Reserve Division to advance its left wing the direction of La Boutillerie. Unfortunately, we made no headway that day.

At about 0930 hours on 24 October we at the command post heard heavy infantry and artillery fire. Both of our divisions, however, reported no activity in their sectors. At the time we assumed that the XIX Army Corps was under attack along their entire front north of the Lille–Armentières rail line. It later turned out to be a false alarm, a not unusual occurrence in tense combat situations.

The continuation of our attack was set for 0710 hours. The corps headquarters, along with the corps reserve, regrouped at the Erquinghem-Lys rail station. The 25th Reserve Division prepared to attack La Houssoye with its right wing in coordination with the left wing of the 24th (Saxon) Division. The 26th Division's objectives were the villages of Rouges Bancs and Deleval Farm, in the vicinity of Fromelles. That would be the limit of the advance because we did not have sufficient ammunition to push farther. By the evening the 26th Division had worked its way close to the heavily fortified villages.

During the past few days we had been waiting tensely for news on the progress of the Fourth Army in Flanders. The lack of information bothered us greatly. We later learned that the Fourth Army's attack had been halted on 23 October.

On the morning of 25 October, the 25th Reserve Division seized parts of La Houssoye and reported the continuation of its attack. The 26th Division seized Deleval Farm and reported that strong enemy forces were located in positions reinforced by wire obstacles directly opposite the center of the division's front line in the vicinity of La Cardonnerie Ferme. The 26th Division then was ordered to shift the main effort of their attack to the left wing. The corps reserve advanced to Le Fresnoy after several officers from the corps headquarters reconnoitered the terrain for their deployment. They reported that the ground between Fromelles and La Cardonnerie Ferme was most suitable for the advance. By 1145 hours the 25th Reserve Division seized the entire village of La Houssoye, but Le Quesne still remained in enemy hands. By the evening the 26th Infantry Division had made only very little progress. For the night the corps reserve moved back to Ligny.[61]

The 25th Reserve Division took Le Quesne on the 26th. It then prepared for a follow-on attack on Bois Blancs and Le Bridoux, which were seized soon after 1300 hours. We then ordered the division to shift the main effort of its attack to the left wing. During the period from 20 to 26 October the hard-fighting 25th Reserve Division lost some twenty-five hundred men. That same day the 26th Division prepared to attack the enemy positions at La Boutillerie and La Cardonnerie Ferme, and worked their way close to those objectives. During the night of 27 October a General Staff officer from the XXIV Reserve Corps delivered a Sixth Army order stating that that corps' 48th Reserve Division would immediately relieve our 26th Division. At that point the 26th Division was positioned almost everywhere within close storming distance of the enemy. Such a relief in place by very young and inexperienced troops would have been accomplished with very heavy losses. Thus, at 0200 hours on 27 October we ordered the 26th Division to disengage from the enemy and pull back to a distance that would make the relief possible without heavy casualties. The 48th Reserve Division then moved forward to Beaucamps and smoothly relieved the 26th Division during the night of 28 October.

The 25th Reserve Division remained in its current positions and on 28 October came under the command of the XXIV Reserve Corps, which relieved Corps Fabeck. The Sixth Army's attack to the west with the XIX, XIII, VII, and XIV Army Corps and the I Bavarian Reserve Corps produced no operationally significant results at the cost of a great deal of blood and ammunition. The entire attacking front had to pass through a battle zone that had been recognized as difficult for a long time. It was heavily interspersed with reinforced villages that gave all the advantage to the defenders. Thus, we achieved no significant gains on the overall German right wing. OHL's hope that the enemy in Flanders would swing major forces southeast against the Lys between Menen and Warneton, and thus expose their flank and rear to attack by the Fourth Army, failed to play out that way. It is hard to comprehend OHL's thinking that Corps Fabeck, positioned on a wide front along the Lys, could be relieved in place by OHL-level cavalry forces whose combat strength would certainly not be sufficient to hold off a major enemy attack.

Along its wide sector from the sea to Courtrai, the Fourth Army had deployed all five of its corps in line. The attack, therefore, had lacked any depth from which as the attack progressed a main effort could be formed against the tactically correct point. In the event, the Fourth Army's attack met equally strong resistance along the entire front. Right from the start the enemy progressively reinforced their defensive positions, eventually deploying an entire British and a Belgian field army, plus French units. The bulk of the enemy forces fell against the Fourth Army's two left wing corps, which were pushed back a considerable distance. Rather than that unsuccessful attack, a far better scheme of maneuver would have been for the Fourth Army to attack across the Lys between Menen and Warneton, just as the Fourth Army had recommended originally. OHL, however, did not think they could free up sufficient forces from other sectors to mount such an attack.

Following the Fourth Army's failure, the XV Army Corps and II Bavarian Corps, the 6th Bavarian Division, and later the Guards Corps, II Army Corps, and the 9th Reserve Division were redeployed to support the offensive operations in Flanders. But we had lost precious time that allowed the enemy to organize a defensive front along the Lys. Thus, any new German attack across the Lys would meet strong enemy resistance. But such an attack was still necessary because there now was a large gap between the left wing of the Fourth Army and the right wing of the Sixth Army, which was only filled by OHL cavalry units. If the enemy could muster enough forces to push through that gap, he could create a very serious situation on the German overall right wing.

Army Task Group Fabeck

On 28 October 1914, OHL put General von Fabeck in command of an ad hoc army task group, which, under the operational control of the Sixth Army, was to break through the enemy's defenses between the Fourth and Sixth Armies and attack to the northwest in the general direction Ypres–Poperinge. The army task group consisted of the headquarters of the XIII Army Corps, the 26th Division, the XV Army Corps, the II Bavarian Corps, and the 6th Bavarian Reserve Division.

That same day the 26th Division started advancing. By approaching from the south, the forces reached the following locations by that evening: the XV Army Corps, the area east of Lille; the II Bavarian Corps and the 26th Division, the area northeast of Lille. On 27 October the 6th Bavarian Reserve Division was still initially assigned directly to the Fourth Army, and was moving toward Dadizele via Menen. The following day one of the division's infantry regiments and the two heavy batteries deployed on the XXVII Reserve Corps' left wing.

On 28 October, meanwhile, I went with General von Fabeck to make the initial contact with the commands that had just been attached to his army task group. We especially needed to know the situations of the Fourth Army and the OHL cavalry forces positioned north of the Lys. While we were gone the headquarters of the army task group was established in Linselles, and the telephonic connections were made to the subordinate command posts.

The heavy artillery allocated to the army task group, which unfortunately had very little ammunition, consisted of the following:

- The 3rd and 4th Batteries of the 1st Battalion, Guards Foot Artillery Regiment, and the 3rd and 4th Batteries of the 1st Battalion, 4th Foot Artillery Regiment (heavy field howitzer), to the II Bavarian Corps.
- The 1st Battalion, 14th Foot Artillery Regiment (very heavy howitzer), and the 1st and 2nd Batteries of the 1st Battalion, 19th Foot Artillery Regiment (heavy field howitzer), and a 30cm very heavy howitzer battery to the 26th Division.
- The 2nd Battalion, 3rd Bavarian Reserve Foot Artillery Regiment (four very heavy howitzer batteries), remained initially in reserve.

The Sixth Army also gave General von Fabeck the I Cavalry Corps, consisting of the Guards and 4th Cavalry Divisions and the 11th Landwehr Brigade. The 4th, 9th, 10th, and 1st Bavarian Jäger[62] Battalions were deployed on the right wing of the OHL cavalry units. On order of OHL, the II Army Corps' 3rd Division moved by rail to Lille and came under Army Task Group Fabeck. The division started off-loading on 29 October. Up to that time the OHL cavalry units were positioned north of the Lys, with their right flank supported by the 11th Landwehr Brigade and the four Jäger battalions. Those units were attached to the XV Army Corps.

The army task group order issued at 1930 hours on 28 October directed the XV Army Corps and its heavy artillery to attack with its right wing along the Menen–Ypres road, and with its left wing along the Comines-Ypres Canal. The main effort of the task group's attack would be the II Bavarian Corps, with its left wing at Garde de Dieu.[63] The 26th Division was to attack with its left wing west of Warneton, along the Douve River.

On order, the remainder of the Sixth Army on Army Task Group Fabeck's left was to attack with the I Cavalry Corps supported by three battalions of the XIX Army Corps against Sint-Yvon and the forest north of Ploegsteert. Army Task Group Fabeck's reserve consisted of the 6th Bavarian Reserve Division, the 11th Landwehr Brigade, and the 2nd Battalion, 3rd Bavarian Reserve Foot Artillery Regiment.

On 29 October the XV Army Corps, II Bavarian Corps, and 26th Division moved into their attack assembly areas. The 6th Bavarian Reserve Division moved with its two heavy batteries to Menen, minus one infantry regiment, which remained at the XXVII Reserve Corps and was essential for a local attack planned at Gheluvelt.

During the night of 29–30 October the cavalry formations positioned in the attack sectors of the XV Army Corps, II Bavarian Corps, and the 26th Division were relieved in place. The I Cavalry Corps already was positioned in its attack sector and was reinforced by three battalions of the XIX Army Corps.

Almost all of the assault units had moved into completely unknown terrain by making long marches to their jump-off positions in the dark. Based on our prior experience, we still did not have enough ammunition to register our artillery and stage the infantry. General von Fabeck, therefore, requested that the Sixth Army postpone the attack until 31 October. The troops needed the additional time to prepare. But OHL, with little understanding of the frontline realities, insisted that we attack on 30 October. The Fourth and Sixth Armies were scheduled to attack simultaneously with Army Task Group Fabeck.

We were convinced that our attack would run into strong resistance. The enemy had used the time delay between our previously planned but never executed attack toward Ypres and now to move up additional reinforcements. He also strengthened his defensive positions to his east by opening the flood gates on the lower Yser River. That freed up units he could commit against Army Task Group Fabeck and the left wing of the Fourth Army. With the exception of the 6th Bavarian Reserve Division, almost all of Army Task Group Fabeck's units were at reduced combat strength because of the earlier fighting. More significantly, we expected that as our ammunition supplies decreased after the first day of the attack, we would encounter correspondingly heavy resistance by the strongly reinforced and stubbornly defended towns and the forested areas.

Aerial observation on 29 October reported strong enemy forces near Ypres, heavy activity on the rail lines between Dunkirk to Hazebrouck, and increased road march traffic toward Poperinge. On the morning of 30 October the XV Army Corps took Zandvoorde and then the strongly reinforced Castle Zandvoorde. The corps' right wing made less forward progress because the XXVII Reserve Corps failed to take Gheluvelt. The commanding general of the XV Army Corps, General Berthold Karl von Deimling, requested operational control of the 2nd Battalion, 3rd Very Heavy Howitzer Regiment, which had pushed forward to Comines. General von Fabeck, however, had designated the main effort of the attack as the narrow sector of the II Bavarian Corps, where the breakthrough was supposed to be made. He therefore attached only one very heavy howitzer battery to the XV Army Corps, and three batteries to the II Bavarian Corps. The XV Army Corps also was restricted from opening fire on Gheluvelt because the XXVII Reserve Corps' infantry units were too close to the town. Thus, the XV Army Corps with the support of the units on its right flank advanced several battalions toward Gheluvelt. But by the evening they still had not taken the stubbornly defended town.

The II Bavarian Corps with its 4th Bavarian Division seized Hollebeke on 30 October. The 3rd Bavarian Division on the left reached the area northwest and west of Wambeek. The 26th Division managed to advance its right wing to approximately twelve hundred meters southeast of Wijtschate. It then mounted a deliberate attack against strongly defended and reinforced Mesen by advancing its infantry slowly toward the town under heavy artillery cover. Tied in on the left, the I Cavalry Corps took the town of Sint-Yvon on the evening of 30 October despite suffering heavy losses from strong flank fire from the forest of Ploegsteert. However, an enemy deliberate counterattack retook the town.

That same day the 6th Bavarian Reserve Division (minus the one infantry regiment still with the XXVII Reserve Corps) from the army's reserve moved to Wervik. We took some three hundred prisoners from the British 4th and 7th Infantry Divisions and the 1st through 3rd Cavalry Divisions. We also found dead Indian troops north of Mesen.

Our general assessment was that Army Task Group Fabeck's attack on 30 October mainly hit enemy forward positions. Only Gheluvelt, Wijtschate, and Mesen seemed to have been strongly defended. Aerial observation identified strong enemy forces assembling in Ypres and Poperinge and also reported heavy train traffic between Dunkirk and Hazebrouck.

The fighting on 30 October fell short of our expectations. A key reason was that after our troops had made long approach marches on the night of 29–30 October, they first had to relieve the OHL cavalry forces, and then go straight into the attack without proper artillery preparation.

For the resumption of the operation on 31 October, the XV Army Corps was ordered to hold more securely against the left flank of the main effort. The previous day the main effort had not been concentrated enough because of the diversion toward Gheluvelt that was caused by the advance from the area around Zandvoorde toward the bend in the canal north of Hollebeke. The left wing of the II Bavarian Corps' main effort was reinforced with an infantry regiment and one light field howitzer battalion from the 6th Bavarian Reserve Division.

The hotspots of the fighting on 31 October were Gheluvelt and Mesen. Gheluvelt was seized after bitter fighting by the XV Army Corps and elements of the XXVII Reserve Corps—primarily by the one infantry regiment of the 6th Bavarian Division that had remained with the corps. The attacking forces captured some nine hundred prisoners, including a regimental commander and seventeen officers, three field guns, and one machine gun. The XV Army Corps' left wing and the II Bavarian Corps' right wing only gained a little ground on 31 October, as they encountered stiff resistance in the forested areas north of Zandvoorde–Hollebeke. The left wing of the II Bavarian Corps took Oosttaverne and then on order attacked Wijtschate and the strip of ground five hundred meters south of the town. Along the canal on the boundary between the XV Army Corps and the II Bavarian Corps, we identified the French XX Corps' 69th Infantry Regiment. Meanwhile, the 3rd Bavarian Division committed the infantry regiment that was attached to it from the 6th Bavarian Reserve Division against strongly reinforced Wijtschate. In order to weight this attack, we committed almost all the remainder of the 6th Bavarian Division, which then sent another of its infantry regiments against Wijtschate. At that point the army task group had in reserve at Bas-Warneton only the 11th Landwehr Brigade and one infantry regiment and one battery from the 6th Reserve Division.

After very bitter fighting the 26th Division took the eastern half of Mesen. The attacking forces suffered significantly from machine gun fire from the south because the I Cavalry Corps failed to retake Sint-Yvon. We committed what we had left of the army task group's artillery reserve to the I Cavalry Corps, but Sint-Yvon remained in enemy hands.

Aerial reconnaissance yielded few results. It seemed, however, that the enemy identified in the vicinity of Ypres was advancing toward the southeast and south. After a telephone conference between General von Fabeck, OHL, and the Sixth Army, the latter attached the II Army Corps' 3rd Division to us. We committed it to the attack between Wijtschate and Mesen, under the operational control of the 26th Division. In so doing, we were able to narrow the II Bavarian Corps' sector.

On the evening of 31 October we received a situation report from the Fourth Army. Despite several attempts to take Dijksmuide, it still remained in enemy hands. But by 29 October major elements of the XXII Reserve Corps advancing north of Dijksmuide crossed the Yser and linked up to the north with the III Reserve Corps, which was approaching the Nieuwpoort–Dijksmuide rail line. The enemy still held Nieuwpoort. The 4th Ersatz Division, operating under the III Reserve Corps, took heavy losses from British naval gun fire while attempting to attack toward Nieuwpoort. After the enemy opened the canal locks at Nieuwpoort and the flooding inundated the III Reserve Corps' area of operations, it was forced to withdraw behind the canal during the night of 30–31 October. The XXIII Reserve Corps' left wing attacked and took Bikschote on 30 October, but then lost it to a French deliberate counterattack. The XXVI Reserve Corps remained on the defensive. Only the left wing of the XXVII Reserve Corps participated in the attack at Gheluvelt. All of these situation reports made it clear to us that the Fourth Army's advance in the general direction of Ypres was now unlikely to succeed. That would leave the enemy free to throw his available forces against Army Task Group Fabeck.

We therefore were not surprised when our continuing attack on 1 November encountered increased enemy resistance across the entire front of the army task group. The XV Army Corps gained only a little ground. In the II Bavarian Corps' sector an attack by the 3rd Bavarian Division was repulsed. The 4th Bavarian Division advanced only very little. The 6th Bavarian Reserve Division stormed the town Wijtschate twice, but was thrown back both times by enemy hasty counterattacks. The 26th Division occupied all of Mesen. The I Cavalry Corps made no progress.

After General von Fabeck consulted with the Sixth Army headquarters and OHL, the 156-meter height of Mont Kemmel became the attack objective of the army task group's left wing. At 1345 hours we issued the order for the II Bavarian Corps, including the 6th Bavarian Reserve Division, to attack Kruisstraat with its right wing. Under the operational control of the 26th Division, the 3rd Division on the left flank of the attack was ordered to push its right wing north past Mesen, toward the northern slope and the main ridge of Mont Kemmel. The 26th Division, commanded by General Wilhelm Herzog von Urach, was ordered to advance against the southern part of Mont Kemmel, between Mesen and the Douve River. The 3rd Division's attack would be supported by strong artillery fire from the II Bavarian Corps and the 26th Division. All of the army task group's divisions were now committed, with the exception of the 11th Landwehr Brigade in reserve.

The Fourth Army did not attack on 1 November because the enemy in their sector had reinforced significantly. The XXII Reserve Corps also withdrew back across to the eastern side of the Yser Canal as the flooding expanded. The inundated ground now made an attack north of strongly reinforced Dijksmuide impossible. The only unit that the Fourth Army still had in the fight was the III Reserve Corps' 4th Ersatz Division, while the rest of the corps east of the Yser displaced on 1 November south toward Staden.

On 2 November the XV Army Corps' right wing advanced against constant enemy contact. Close to Veldhoek they took seven hundred prisoners and two guns. Other than that, only the 6th Bavarian Reserve Division made any progress, capturing Wijtschate and five hundred prisoners. The 26th Division advanced several hundred meters to the west, but then had to pull back its left wing because the enemy still held Sint-Yvon and Ploegsteert Woods in the I Cavalry Corps' sector. We then committed our last available reserve, the 11th Landwehr Brigade, to the 26th Division for deployment on its left wing and it continued to attack in full force to the west.

Army Task Group Fabeck received operational control of the 2nd and 4th Cavalry Divisions, and attached the latter to the XV Army Corps so that it could close the gap with the left wing of the XXVII Reserve Corps, which was lagging behind. Simultaneously, the XV Army Corps' sector was extended to the canal. The 2nd Cavalry Division was attached to the II Bavarian Corps for commitment south of the canal, where the corps narrowed its sector but increased its depth on both sides of the Warneton–Voormezele road. Along the army task group's front, the enemy reinforced his artillery, which was well supplied with ammunition and had excellent fields of observation from the high ground around Mont Kemmel. Our ammunition stocks, meanwhile, continued to shrink.

On 3 November we only managed to make minor advances in isolated sectors in the face of the increasingly strong enemy artillery fire. The XV Army Corps seized Veldhoek. The II Bavarian Corps made only minor gains and repulsed strong enemy attacks in the 6th Bavarian Division's sector. An ad hoc attack group consisting of the 3rd Division, 26th Division, and 11th Landwehr Brigade and commanded by General von Urach advanced very slowly against heavy enemy artillery and infantry fire. By 3 November everything had been reduced to constant back-and-forth fighting for minor pieces of ground. Our stout infantry had to bear the main burden of the fighting, and suffered heavy losses because we remained chronically short of artillery ammunition.

The Fourth Army made only minimal progress on 3 November, even though it had consolidated all available forces in the XXIII Reserve Corps' attack sector. Only the XXVII Reserve Corps was able maintain contact with the right flank of our XV Army Corps.

Resulting from the actions on 3 November, all of the command echelons up to OHL recognized that any operational success in Flanders was no longer possible. The necessary reserves—and especially the ammunition—were just not there for the continuation of the operational-level attack.

OHL missed the opportunity to achieve a major operational victory in Flanders. To have done so would have required masses of ammunition and the timely redeployment of large reserves from other sectors of the Western Front. All of the corps that could have been freed up should have been redeployed on the Fourth Army's right flank to mount a major attack in depth on the enemy's still weak forces between Dijksmuide and Armentières. But as it had ever since the Battle of the Marne, OHL fell short by only hesitantly redeploying excess forces from the secondary sectors. The result was an unfavorable correlation of forces in Flanders, which the enemy was able to exploit by shifting his own forces. After we failed in Flanders, the entire German Army on the Western Front was more or less relegated to protracted trench warfare.

By 3 November the purely frontal fighting that the Fourth Army had been forced into had cost us approximately 39,000 dead and wounded and 13,000 missing. The Sixth Army's losses were approximately 27,000 dead and wounded, of which between 30 October and 3 November 17,250 alone were from Army Task Group Fabeck.

Our last reserves of ammunition had been used up. The combat strength of the German Army in the West was considerably weakened. For the time being the German Army was no longer capable of major operations on the Western Front. We were forced, then, to go over to a deliberate defensive in the West so we could free up the forces necessary to shore up our weakening Austrian allies in the east. The intent at the time was to mount a major operational offensive against the Russians to eliminate the threat in the east.

That decision was self-evident, but OHL still could not force itself to come to the conclusion, and it continued to cling to the idea of making a major attack in the west. But any such attack could only have yielded tactical and not operational results, because our troops were too worn out and our ammunition was too low.

OHL's hesitating operational leadership and its failure to remain focused on the objective cost it a great deal of trust with the troops and their leaders. The commanders that the troops of the German Army still trusted implicitly were then in command on the Eastern Front.[64] Their operational victories in the east[65] had earned them the highest levels of respect from the entire German Army. Unfortunately, they were not given the overall command of the German Army until much later, by which time more of the combat power of the German Army in the West had been wasted unnecessarily.

Even though OHL could no longer achieve an operational success, they nonetheless decided to continue attacking in Flanders, with the tactical objective of seizing Ypres. That would move the German positions forward that currently were bent far back and establish a straighter north-south front line. Once that was accomplished, OHL would redeploy forces to the Eastern Front.

It certainly was desirable for us to reduce the salient that bulged in toward the east at the inner boundary of the Fourth and Sixth Armies. That would both straighten and shorten our overall line from Bikschote to Ypres to Wijtschate. But with unjustified optimism, OHL assumed we could accomplish that in fourteen days. Experience to that point should have told them that such a purely frontal attack would encounter very strong resistance. The enemy's position could only be broken if we had enough fresh troops and, most of all, sufficient ammunition. These two preconditions for success existed only to a limited extent. OHL nonetheless decided to attack for purely tactical reasons. But in so deciding, it knew all too well what the cost would be to our units that already were down to 50 percent combat strength.

For the maintenance of unity of command, it certainly would have been better if OHL had given the Fourth Army operational control of the entire attack front, from the sea to the Douve River. The Fourth Army then could have designated a single commander for the Ypres salient attack sector. That commander in turn could have then planned to focus the attack into an overwhelming main effort, massing the necessary forces and ammunition. In the event, the responsibility for the attack sector remained split between the Fourth and Sixth Armies, with the two headquarters determining independently their attack objectives and the extent to which they would coordinate their operations with one another.

On 5 November OHL reinforced the Sixth Army in Lille with the II Army Corps' command staff, the 4th Division, and a heavy howitzer battalion detached from the First Army. On 9 November the Fourth Army in Courtrai was reinforced with the 9th Reserve Division, detached from the Fifth Army. The Sixth Army also redeployed to Flanders the 25th Reserve Division from the sector south of Armentières, and the headquarters of the Guards Corps with the 2nd Guards Division from the sector south of Arras. With this additional infusion of forces, the coordinated attack was scheduled for 10 November. Until then, however, the Fourth and Sixth Armies had to continue attacking with the forces available.

The Fourth Army reorganized itself. The Naval Division reinforced by a Landwehr Brigade was deployed on the coast, with its front oriented toward Nieuwpoort. To the south the 4th Ersatz Division was tied in with the Guards Cavalry Division, which had deployed behind the inundated ground, and the

43rd Reserve Division south of Dijksmuide. That sector came under the command of the XXII Reserve Corps. The XXIII Reserve Corps was deployed toward the west and southwest, against the enemy at Drie-Grachten and Bikschote. The Fourth Army's main effort was in the III Reserve Corps' sector, which consisted of the 44th and 5th Divisions, the 6th Reserve Division, and the 9th Reserve Division that was still en route. To the south, the XXVI Reserve Corps had a Landwehr brigade and an Ersatz brigade. The XXVII Reserve Corps was on the Fourth Army's left wing. Army Task Group Fabeck remained under the operational control of the Sixth Army. Our attack objective remained the line from the west of Ypres to Mont Kemmel. The Sixth Army assigned a high priority to the capture of Mont Kemmel.

It was clear here that the attack as ordered by OHL lacked unity of effort. The Fourth Army's main effort was with the III Reserve Corps, east of the Poelkapelle–Ypres road, and along it in a southwesterly direction. Army Task Group Fabeck under the Sixth Army was ordered to attack in a more westerly direction, for the purpose of taking Mont Kemmel and the surrounding high ground.

In my opinion, OHL should have established a unified command for the attack, or at the least they should have coordinated and synchronized the Fourth and Sixth Armies. The Fourth Army's main effort should have been on both sides of the Poelkapelle–Ypres road; the Sixth Army's on both sides of the Comines–Ypres rail line. Up until the start of the attack the front of the entire attack sector should have been on the defense, and the troops should have been improving their recently taken positions. The time preceding the attack should have been used to advance all the arriving reinforcements up behind the main effort. All the other reserves and the heavy and field artillery freed up from the quiet sectors should have been consolidated to support the main effort.

Prior to the start of the attack ammunition should have been economized and then redistributed to the forces making the main effort. The actual jump-off date should have been determined based on the completion of the preparations. In the meantime, the artillery should have registered on the key targets in the main effort sector, in advance of firing a heavy preparation in support of the attack.

Small infantry patrols should have been used to locate key enemy positions. The follow-on forces behind the main effort should have had their flanks echeloned in depth. With such a scheme of maneuver, the main efforts of both armies could have driven at least one deep wedge into the enemy's front, therefore forcing the enemy units between the two main efforts to withdraw to the west. If the attack produced significant results on the first day, there was a good likelihood we could clean the enemy out of the entire Ypres salient.

OHL's order that the Fourth Army and the Sixth Army's Army Task Group

Fabeck were to continue attacking from 4 November on with their own resources was a grave restriction on the operational initiative of both army headquarters. It forced us to continue attacking in the same direction without sufficient infantry strength or ammunition. The result was that our combat power progressively weakened. Had we been allowed to conduct an operational pause, we could have built back up somewhat.

The Sixth Army reorganized its attack sector against the Ypres–Mont Kemmel line, forming two attack groups. Attack Group Linsingen under General Alexander von Linsingen, commanding general of the II Army Corps, deployed from the Fourth Army boundary to the Comines-Ypres Canal. The Guards Corps, under General Karl von Plettenberg, formed Linsingen's right wing, with the 2nd Guards Division and the 4th Division. The XV Army Corps was on Linsingen's left flank. On Linsingen's left wing Attack Group Fabeck deployed the II Bavarian Corps, with the 3rd and 4th Bavarian Division on the right; Corps Gerok, commanded by General Karl von Gerok, was in the center, with the 6th Bavarian Reserve Division and the 25th Reserve Division; and Corps Urach was on the left wing with the 3rd and 26th Divisions and the 11th Landwehr Brigade. Because we had no reserves available, we were not able to designate an explicit main effort. Our strongest force was Corps Plettenberg, whose two divisions were still being transported forward and had little time to familiarize themselves with the battle space.

The Fourth Army had made only minor and sporadic gains during the attacks up through 10 November. The Sixth Army's XV Army Corps had been able to advance its positions at Klein-Zillebeke on 6 and 8 November. Corps Gerok gained some ground on 6 November north of Wijtschate, after Corps Urach the previous day had driven a wedge into the enemy lines between Wijtschate and the Douve River. None of these advances, however, were of any tactical significance for the coming major offensive. They had cost us too much in casualties and ammunition. These minor operations did, however, determine that British troops were positioned only in front of the XXVII Reserve Corps, Corps Plettenberg, and the XV Army Corps. French troops opposed the remainder of our front from the coast to the south of Wijtschate. Aerial reconnaissance also reported that enemy troop trains were running constantly to Ypres, Poperinge, and Bailleul. Large enemy units were observed moving toward the front near Ypres. In most places the enemy was improving his rearward positions.

The attack that started on 10 November from Dijksmuide to the Douve River did not produce any decisive results. The Fourth Army's 4th Ersatz Division and 43rd Reserve Division did manage to take and hold Dijksmuide. On the left, the XXIII Reserve Corps and the 44th Reserve Division also gained considerable ground northwest of Bikschote. The 5th Reserve Division gained some ground as well. The 9th Reserve Division attacked after being inserted on the III Reserve Corps' left flank. Facing effective fire and enemy positions protected by wire obstacles, the division lost twenty-five hundred men. It had to be pulled out of the line and went into corps reserve. The XXVI Reserve Corps only gained some ground on its extreme left wing. The XXVII Reserve Corps remained in position, as Corps Plettenberg on its left flank reported that it could not attack until 11 November.

Corps Plettenberg had not been able to integrate into the Sixth Army's attack front until very late, making it impossible to attack on the 10th. Thus, only the XV Army Corps of Attack Group Linsingen attacked that day, but made no headway. In Attack Group Fabeck's sector the II Bavarian Corps took Sint-Eloi. Corps Gerok and Urach made only little progress.

On 11 November the Naval Division seized Lombardsijde. The Fourth Army ordered the XXII and XXIII Army Corps to attack in a southerly direction, and the right wing of the III Reserve Corps to take Boezinge. Those attacks, however, made little headway as well. The XXVI Reserve Corps did not advance at all, and the XXVII Reserve Corps only very little.

In the Sixth Army's sector, Group Linsingen's Corps Plettenberg made good progress initially, but then was pushed back by an enemy hasty counterattack, taking heavy losses in the process. Attack Group Fabeck's XV Army Corps only made minor headway as well.

In the Fourth Army's sector the Naval Division on 12 November pushed the enemy back toward Nieuwpoort, and then on order assumed the defensive. With very low levels of combat strength, the XXII Army Corps and XXIII Reserve Corps made no progress at all. Similarly, the III Reserve Corps, which OHL had ordered to advance rapidly, made only insignificant gains against strong enemy resistance. The inner wings of the XXVI Army Corps and the XXVII Reserve Corps gained little ground.

In the Sixth Army's sector, Group Linsingen's Corps Plettenberg encountered very stiff resistance and aborted the attack. The XV Army Corps improved its positions slightly on its left wing. In Group Fabeck's sector the II Bavarian Corps made a strong thrust forward and took some one thousand French prisoners. In Group Gerok's sector the 25th Reserve Division advanced considerably between Sint-Eloi and Wijtschate. Corps Urach did not have any successes. Group Gerok's 6th Bavarian Reserve Division was completely expended after its aggressively pushed attacks and had to be relieved in place by the 11th Landwehr Brigade. The Bavarians then went into reserve near Comines. As a result, however, the 26th Division had to extend its sector toward the south, which dissipated much of its attack power.

By the evening of 12 November the Fourth and Sixth Armies concluded that the attack on Ypres was stalled and could only be continued after reinforcement by fresh forces and much ammunition. OHL then ordered the transfer of a Seventh Army division to the Sixth Army, and one division from the Third Army and an infantry brigade from Attack Group Strantz[66] to the Fourth Army. Only the infantry units from these two and a half divisions were to be deployed. OHL believed that those reinforcements finally would produce victory in Flanders. But that was a grave miscalculation. As OHL was well aware, the combat strength of the Fourth Army's new and inexperienced divisions was only about two thousand men, and the various commanding generals were requesting urgent relief of several completely expended divisions.

The Fourth Army told OHL that it was incapable of continuing the attack. The Sixth Army's Attack Groups Linsingen and Fabeck had mostly experienced units, but the divisional combat strengths were no longer adequate against the growing strength of the enemy resistance. Only the somewhat fresher 3rd Division was able to attack the area west of Wijtschate on 13 November. Otherwise, we were forced to suspend the offensive along the whole front. The XV Army Corps' attack by Division Hofmann, which had been attached from the Seventh Army, failed to achieve any tangible results and lost twenty-five hundred men in the process. On 18 November aerial reconnaissance reported that the enemy was moving forward additional replacements, organizing his defenses in depth, and improving his existing positions.

Thus, in the evening of 18 November OHL was forced to abandon the plan that it had clung to stubbornly for far too long. With a victory in Flanders no longer possible, we had to go over to the defensive. The Sixth Army was ordered to withdraw the XIII and II Army Corps from its sector for redeployment elsewhere. Included with the XIII Army Corps headquarters were the 26th Division and the 25th Reserve Division. The disengagement started on the night of 19 November, and the following day we started marching to our transportation points.

The continuation of the attack in Flanders since 3 November failed to achieve any decisive results. Rather, it only caused further losses in our already weakened units. Between 10 and 18 November alone, the Fourth Army lost some 13,000 men. During the same period the Sixth Army's Groups Linsingen and Fabeck lost 10,500. When Corps Fabeck's 26th Division and 25th Reserve Divisions left Flanders they had a combined combat strength of close to ten thousand men, but that number included replacements that were still moving up.

The high losses we suffered in Flanders were proof of the energy and the courage of the troops, who always gave their best to accomplish the mission. OHL's continued insistence on launching rapid attacks betrayed their total lack of frontline experience. There was never sufficient time to conduct proper reconnaissance of the attack sectors, nor to register the artillery and plan the fires. As the enemy strongly improved their positions, our ammunition supply, especially for heavy artillery, declined with predictable consequences.

We left Flanders feeling that we had put everything into accomplishing an impossible mission. But we also could not shake the idea that OHL's continued tactical and operational interference was the result of perceptions that had not been grounded in reality.

The relief from the front line of the 26th Division and 25th Reserve Divisions came off with no problems. The II Bavarian Corps, the 6th Bavarian Reserve Division, and the 11th Landwehr Brigade took over the whole sector that had been held by Attack Group Fabeck. On 25 November General von Fabeck relinquished command of the sector to the commanding general of the II Bavarian Corps. Up to that point we had a great deal of work planning in detail for the relief, transport, quartering, and loading of the units. The movement of the 26th Division started on 25 November, and the following day the XIII Army Corps headquarters integrated into their transports. At the time we did not know our ultimate destination, but we were looking forward to our new mission. I accompanied General von Fabeck during the out-briefing with Crown Prince Rupprecht, the commander of the Sixth Army. The crown prince expressed his gratitude and high regard for our period of service with the Sixth Army. The Sixth Army's chief of staff also expressed regret at losing such a combat-experienced corps.

To my wife, to whom I wrote almost daily during the course of the war, I wrote on 25 November in a cautious tone, "We are wrapping up our mission here, and preparing to assume a new one in another place. Where, we don't know yet." I advised her to seek out our new address with the deputy general command in Stuttgart.

On 26 November General von Fabeck and I finally were told that we were headed to the east. The exact location remained unknown to us, however. We nonetheless were excited, because we hoped to return to an environment of mobile warfare after our period of trench fighting.

General von Fabeck wanted the 25th Reserve Division to relieve our old 27th Division in the Argonne, in order to reform both the XIII Army Corps and the XVIII Reserve Corps back into their standard wartime structures. Unfortunately, the Fifth Army refused to release the 27th Division. We did, at least, get some artillery reinforcement for the 25th Reserve Division in the form of the command staff of the 27th Field Artillery Brigade with the 13th Artillery Regiment and two heavy batteries.

To our great regret, the entire XIII Army Corps was transported from the Sixth Army before we could replenish our ammunition trains. Making matters worse, we failed to be resupplied when we reached our new destination. The combat strengths of our divisions were very low. We therefore detached two officers from the corps staff and sent them by car to Stuttgart to hand-carry our requests for resupply and replacements.

Our troop train passed through Liège, Aachen, Cologne, Hannover, Magdeburg, and Berlin, then took a northeasterly direction. After we reached Bydgoszcz we finally learned that our final destination was located to the south of Toruń. For the longest time we could not help but think that we would continue traveling via Silesia in order to be integrated then into the Austrian front. We were greatly relieved to learn that we would come under the command of the Commander in Chief, East, General von Hindenburg, and his highly respected chief of staff, General Erich Ludendorff.

From Toruń the train continued moving along the banks of the Vistula River via Aleksandrów to Nieszawa. During the course of the trip we all received inoculations against cholera and typhoid. Some members of the staff got sick because of the repeated inoculations, but they were back on their feet quickly. Only one of our transportation officers suffered so much that he had to be sent home.

Along the way I wrote to my wife, "It is with happiness that I travel through the Homeland again, prior to engaging a new enemy. Instead of burning villages I see flourishing towns. That is the difference between us and our enemies. In Toruń the officers met us whom we had sent to Stuttgart by car. They had managed to reach Toruń ahead of us.

The XIII Army Corps with the Ninth Army

Corps Fabeck[67] was assigned to the Ninth Army, commanded by General of Cavalry August von Mackensen. I had already worked for him as his first General Staff officer from 1910 to 1912 at the XVII Army Corps headquarters in Danzig.[68] The chief of staff was Major General Paul Ferdinand Alexander Grünert. We had been instructors together at the war academy in Berlin from 1908 until 1910.

On its arrival in Nieszawa, Corps Fabeck received the mission to advance quickly via Włocławek to support the I Reserve Corps positioned in the vicinity west and northwest of Łowicz. The I Reserve Corps was deployed facing southward and eastward and heavily engaged against superior Russian forces. Immediately upon off-loading, the lead regiment of the 26th Division with some artillery advanced from Nieszawa on the left bank of the Vistula River, pushing back weak enemy forces as far as Włocławek. Corps Fabeck established its command post there.

Soon thereafter another General Staff officer and I took a staff car to the Ninth Army headquarters in Łęczyca. I intended to familiarize myself with

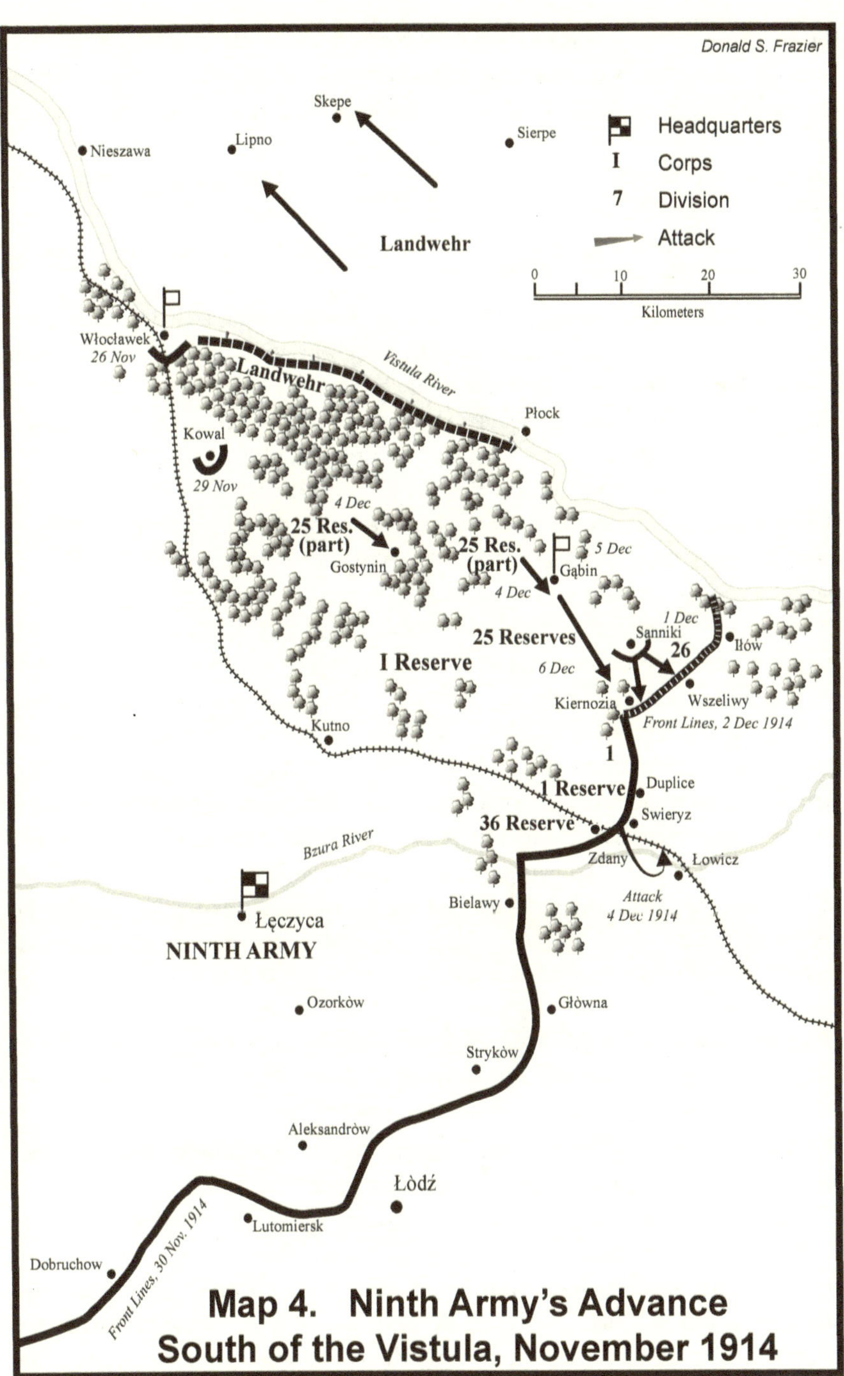

Map 4. Ninth Army's Advance South of the Vistula, November 1914

the situation there. The route was horrible because all the hardtop roads had been destroyed and we constantly had to drive around the blast craters. Often we could only use secondary routes, whose ground across the heath was littered with difficult-to-negotiate mud holes. After several hours of driving we got stuck in a muddy ditch. To our relief an empty ambulance convoy came up from behind. The drivers, who were from Berlin, pulled us out of the mud with much humor and gave us information about the passable roads. It took us more than five hours to go the approximately 120 kilometers to reach the Ninth Army headquarters. We were welcomed by General August von Mackensen and his chief of staff, and I received a thorough briefing on how the situation had developed since the start of the Battle of Łódź. The I Reserve Corps on the Ninth Army's left flank was engaged in heavy fighting north of the Bzura River. From there the army front ran toward the southwest, past Łódź on its north and west side, and then bent toward the south. The Russians had assembled very strong forces and clearly were attempting to envelop the Ninth Army's northern flank. To block this threat against the I Reserve Corps it was necessary for Corps Fabeck to advance quickly. I then discussed with the appropriate staff sections at the Ninth Army headquarters all the logistical support issues and learned that they also were very low on ammunition. We were only able to replenish our supply columns and maintain the supply flow for the attack at the minimum levels.

On the return trip I also visited the I Reserve Corps headquarters. Only the corps chief of staff was there, but he briefed me on the corps' organization and structure. I now had reliable information on which to base the actions of Corps Fabeck. The I Reserve Corps had three divisions, with the 36th Reserve Division positioned on the southern wing, and the 1st Reserve Division in the center. Both divisions faced toward the south against the Bzura River. The 1st Division on the corps' left faced toward the east, with its left flank in the vicinity Kiernozia. All three divisions were opposed by a strong enemy, especially the 1st Reserve Division and the 1st Division. The Russian units to their front had been identified as I and II Siberian Corps, the 1st Russian Rifle Brigade, another division only recently arrived from Siberia, and superior Russian cavalry. The objective of the I Reserve Corps was Łowicz, and during the last several days of intense fighting the corps had captured fifty guns and a large number of prisoners. In the process, however, the corps' combat strength had been reduced greatly.

The 26th Division did not complete off-loading until 1 December, and during that time it remained deeply echeloned. It was ordered to make contact with the enemy quickly, and then to maintain a defensive posture against the superior enemy forces. Corps Fabeck could only launch a coordinated attack after the arrival of the 25th Reserve Division, which could not come on line with the 26th Division any earlier than 6 December.

On 29 November the 26th Division's lead elements reached Kowal. The Landwehr brigade directly subordinated to the Ninth Army headquarters was in position there. Its mission was to provide security for Corps Fabeck's arrival and deployment along the Vistula River, with the corps' southern flank in the vicinity of Płock. Another Landwehr brigade directly attached to Ninth Army headquarters had been forced by a superior enemy to retreat on the right bank of the Vistula in the direction of Toruń. Otherwise, we had only weak forces on the northern bank of the Vistula facing the Russian cavalry. Our 4th Cavalry Division was scheduled to off-load at Toruń starting on 30 November, but they had to remain there initially to fit the horses with winter horseshoes.

As soon as the Nieszawa–Włocławek rail line was repaired, we were able to advance our unloading point. We did not receive any ammunition resupply until 2 December. From 5 December on, the rail line to Kutno was scheduled to be in operation, and from then on Kutno would be our main supply railhead. But we had to use our own resources to move the supplies forward from there. Right from the start and throughout the operation we constantly were short of ammunition, which made it extremely difficult to fire effective artillery preparations to support the infantry.

Soon it became apparent that our ammunition and ration column wagons were much too heavy for the extremely bad and muddy routes. It was only possible to get through everywhere with the light Russian farmer's carts harnessed to the local horses that were accustomed to the climate and the bad routes. We put pressure on the Włocławek town administration to provide us with several such columns. Although we guaranteed payment, we got no response. I then summoned a good number of the Jewish businessmen from Włocławek and energetically negotiated with them with the help of a translator fluent in Russian and Polish. That translator was a cunning NCO from the mounted 4th Jäger Regiment.

I demanded ten columns of fifty farmer's carts each, all harnessed with two good horses. I offered the frightened Jews 500 rubles (approximately 1,000 marks) for each column. After some extended back and forth discussion, the Jews promised to do their utmost, and a few days later we had the columns. I assume that the carts and the horses came from the local farming population, many of whom had fled into the forests. I later learned that some of the carts and horses came from the northern bank of the Vistula, where the Jews had bought horses for money and Schnapps from the Russian cavalry positioned there. We did not pay for the ten columns with cash, but rather (as with all requisitions in enemy territory) we paid with securities issued against the Russian government.

Motorized traffic became impossible the farther we moved south, and we had to leave our cars behind. The four members of the Voluntary Motor Corps

(*Freiwilliges Kraftfahrkorps*) were all experienced tradesmen driving their own cars. I sent them under the command of an energetic administrative official (*Verwaltungsbeamter*) with the light farmer's carts to Kutno to collect all the supplies dedicated to Corps Fabeck. That measure paid off well.

The NCO translator later proved to be a valuable asset, especially in questioning prisoners, translating captured orders, and negotiating with the members of the civilian population who had not fled.

We immediately established telegraph communications with the I Reserve Corps headquarters. A staff officer we sent to the corps as a liaison reported that the V and VI Russian Corps had been identified in the vicinity of Łowicz, and farther north the III Russian Corps and elements of the VI Siberian Corps. Reports received by the Ninth Army headquarters indicated we could expect that the Russians would continue to strengthen their northern wing. From the very start, then, we anticipated heavy fighting against a strong enemy.

On 1 December a combined brigade[69] from the 26th Division reached Sanniki, and from there pushed a detachment forward to Kiernozia. These forward elements of the 26th Division were placed under the operational control of the I Reserve Corps, which was the best judge of its support requirements in its very precarious situation. On 2 December the 26th Division's forward-deployed 52nd (combined) Brigade of the 26th Division marched from Sanniki toward Wszeliwy, where it ran into a far superior enemy force north of the town. The brigade commander correctly limited himself to tying down the enemy, preventing him from attacking the I Reserve Corps. The Ninth Army deployed a follow-on Landwehr brigade coming from Toruń to further secure the line of the Vistula from Płock to Włocławek. Russian cavalry forced the weak Landwehr troops north of the Vistula to retreat toward Toruń. Corps Fabeck ordered the 26th Division to secure the left flank of the Ninth Army north of the Bzura. Coordinating with the Ninth Army headquarters, the I Reserve Corps decided to attack Łowicz because it wanted to beat back the enemy there before mounting an offensive against the Russians' left flank.

The 26th Division closed up piecemeal in the direction of Wszeliwy and on 3 December fended off enemy attacks that were directed against their front and left flank. During the course of the fighting the division had to occupy the entire sector from Wszeliwy to Iłów. From Iłów it bent its left wing back, facing the Vistula. On 4 December the I Reserve Corps' attack on Łowicz failed, tying down in the process large portions of the corps. The Ninth Army then ordered Corps Fabeck to support the I Reserve Corps with the strongest force possible.

On 4 December, meanwhile, the 26th Division was attacked multiple times on its entire sector by superior enemy forces. By launching deliberate counterattacks, the division repelled all the enemy's attempts, and in several places actually gained ground. Aerial reconnaissance indicated additional enemy forces advancing against the 26th Division. The enemy obviously had recognized the danger to his northern wing and was reinforcing it. For the most part, Austrian units were deployed south of the Ninth Army and Army Detachment Woyrsch.[70] The movement of strong enemy forces to the north was detected, and on 5 December the 26th Division was given the option of launching a spoiling attack to weaken the enemy before he could reinforce. A shortage of ammunition, however, made such an attack impossible. On 5 December the headquarters of Corps Fabeck displaced to Gąbin.

The 25th Reserve Division had started unloading on 3 December in Włocławek and Nieczawa. It was closely followed by the III Reserve Corps, coming from Flanders. On 4 December a brigade of the 25th Reserve Division reached Gąbin, and the other brigade marched in the direction of Gostynin. Artillery and cavalry were distributed among the individual march elements. On 5 December the 25th Reserve Division closed in on Gąbin and continued the march on 6 December. On that day two ammunition barges from Toruń arrived for Corps Fabeck, deployed on the Vistula at Płock. In response to urgent calls for help from the I Reserve Corps, which had suffered heavy losses during its unsuccessful 4 December attack on Łowicz, the 25th Division was deployed to the right of the 26th Division. The 25th Division's assigned direction of march was the sector between Kiernozia and Wszeliwy via Sanniki. The advantage of that route was that there was a forested area along the Vistula north of Iłów and to the east. That would be the III Reserve Corps' assigned area of operations.

On 1 December the Ninth Army had initiated its attack south of the Bzura. Its follow-on objective was the seizure of Łódź. The main effort of the attack was made by the II Corps, which had been redeployed to the east from Flanders. Its mission was to make a breakthrough south past Łódź. The units of the Ninth Army (XI, XVII, XX Army Corps, XXV Reserve Corps, and Cavalry Corps Richthofen) deployed west and north of Łódź to join the attack. By 4 December the Ninth Army's attack reached the line Mzurki–west of Łódź. To the south it was linked in with the left wing of Army Detachment Woyrsch, which had committed mainly Austrian units to the attack and was lagging far behind. It was especially important that we preempt the threat to the Ninth Army's left flank. For the time being we had to scale down our attack and limit ourselves to tying down the enemy opposite us. I also suggested to my commanding general the option that the Ninth Army might not attack on its northern wing until the III Reserve Corps had moved up. The more forceful the attack from the north, the greater probability we had of smashing the enemy and crossing the Bzura in the rapid pursuit action. The actual events, however, played out differently.

Quite soon the Ninth Army headquarters had indicators that the enemy near Łódź was in retreat. The II Army Corps' Attack Group Linsingen was now pushing forward and the entire army front up to the Bzura joined in the attack. With the enemy in retreat, it became necessary for the Ninth Army to establish a definite main effort (*Schwerpunkt*)[71] to complete the pincer movement on the northern wing. We therefore pulled the XVII Army Corps out of the sector that was narrowing at Łódź and redeployed it to the army's left wing with orders to relieve the division on the left wing of the I Reserve Corps and tie in with Corps Fabeck.

During the fighting of 5 December the 26th Division took eight hundred prisoners, seized several machine guns, and identified to its front the enemy's 50th Division and 74th and 79th Reserve Divisions. On 6 December the 26th Division was ordered to consolidate on the defensive. The attack by Corps Fabeck was then scheduled for 7 December, after arrival of the 25th Reserve Division. But the 7 December attack encountered such strong resistance that Corps Fabeck ordered a pause in the attack. In the first place there was an ammunition shortage. It also was necessary to give the troops more rest time because they were still worn out from the fighting in Flanders, the long rail travel, and then the subsequent long and exhausting approach marches. The fighting strength of the entire corps was down to nine thousand men, and 50 percent of that number were only recently arrived replacements who were not yet broken in and acclimatized to the horrors of war. Nonetheless, it was very difficult for the troops to get any rest in the towns, where the quarters consisted mostly of wood and mud cabins that were incredibly dirty and smelly.

On 7 December the enemy tried to envelop the 26th Division's left wing farther north. During that action we identified enemy cavalry units that had crossed from the northern side of the Vistula. We hoped that the III Reserve Corps would soon intervene along the Vistula, but they reported that their advance party could reach Gąbin no earlier than 8 December, and the main body of the corps would close on 9 December.

South of the Bzura the enemy withdrew farther in the face of the Ninth Army's attack. Aerial reconnaissance detected the arrival of enemy reinforcements at Sochaczew. The Ninth Army headquarters identified additional enemy units in front of the I Reserve Corps and Corps Fabeck that included the II Caucasus, I Siberian, and VI Russian Corps. Heavy fighting lay ahead of us.

Even though the Ninth Army headquarters constantly urged us to advance quickly, the Corps Fabeck headquarters ordered both divisions to close in on the enemy positions only gradually, because neither the XVII Army Corps nor the III Reserve Corps were close yet, and we still did not have enough ammunition to conduct a decisive attack.

I had to go to the Ninth Army headquarters on the morning of 8 December for a briefing with all of the corps chiefs of staff. The Ninth Army staff informed us of the intent to defeat the enemy west of the Bzura, and to then pursue him across the river and push him southward while screening to the Vistula. The XVII and XIII Army Corps and the III Reserve Corps were to attack on a twenty-five-kilometer-wide front, with the I Reserve Corps joining in the attack later. The 4th Cavalry Division, already on the march south from Toruń, was to deploy in a ready posture behind the attack front. The Landwehr troops were to continue to screen along the Vistula. The attack date for Corps Fabeck was set for 9 December. The other corps would attack on 10 December. The corps had specific orders to move forward independently, rather than waiting for their adjacent units to be ready to start their attacks.

It would have been better if the Ninth Army headquarters had established a unified command for the entire forced crossing of the Bzura, which was now the main effort and where the decision would be made. The most senior corps commander, General Hans Hartwig von Beseler of the III Reserve Corps, was an experienced commander who could have designated the general attack date. We were attempting to achieve a decisive success, and such centralized control would have resulted in a unified attack, rather than piecemeal attacks. Even though the enemy opposite the center and the southern wing of the Ninth Army would have continued his withdrawal toward the east, the Russian formations north of the Bzura initially would have held their positions and would not have withdrawn across the river until the Russian front linked in to the south had reached the approximate line from Łowicz running south. A farther withdrawal of the Russian front across the Vistula, which the Ninth Army headquarters thought a possibility, could have been secured by the Russians' northern wing at the naturally strong Bzura position, where they had numerous available forces. The primary task, then, was to destroy Russian formations north of the Bzura with a unified German attack, compress them into the Bzura bridgeheads, and then force our own crossing over the river. Even if that plan had not succeeded fully, the Russians would have suffered severe losses by any German victory west of the Bzura, which then would have facilitated our planned follow-on attack across the river. The Ninth Army headquarters, however, insisted on sticking to its original plan, and within that framework Corps Fabeck had to plan to conduct its attack on 9 December.

On 9 December we had some success in the attack, especially near Wszeliwy. In many places the attack hit wire obstacles, and our experienced unit leaders instantly reduced the tempo of the advance. That day the III Reserve Corps' 5th Division reached Słubice and the 6th Reserve Division reached Gąbin. Both divisions had suffered significant march attrition after advancing more than thirty kilometers across poor roads. The corps' heavy artillery was not able to get into position until 12 December. Aerial reconnaissance indicated that additional enemy reinforcements had arrived at Sochaczew and that six hasty bridges had been constructed below Sochaczew. Unfortunately, the Ninth Army's continuous attacks made the ammunition shortage worse.

The Ninth Army headquarters ordered the III Reserve Corps to reinforce Corps Fabeck rapidly with one division. During the night of 11 December, however, the III Reserve Corps limited itself to extending to our left wing, which eliminated the constant threat to our left flank. Other than that, General Hans Hartwig von Beseler reported that he would not be able to attack until 13 December because his heavy artillery had not closed yet. Nonetheless, the Ninth Army insisted that Corps Fabeck rapidly continue its attack. On 10 December we only continued the preparations for the attack, because the ammunition we needed to assault the reinforced enemy positions had not yet arrived. On 10 December Corps Fabeck displaced its headquarters to Sanniki. By that day our troops had brought in more than two thousand prisoners, most of whom were covered with dirt, lice, and vermin.

On 11 December we finally started the attack with our 25th Reserve Division, along with the XVII Army Corps and the I Reserve Corps' 1st Division. Although we only made small progress, we did capture more than twenty-eight hundred prisoners. The 26th Division was deployed on a very wide front and participated in the attack only with its extreme right wing. The III Reserve Corps did not attack, reporting to the Ninth Army headquarters that it could not attack until 14 December because of the delay in its deployment. The III Reserve Corps wanted to advance along the Vistula and then thrust to and possibly across the Bzura. Some of its elements also would advance north of the Vistula.

The Ninth Army constantly kept urging us to increase the tempo of the attack, and so did the XVII Army Corps. As a result, I recommended an extreme measure to my commanding general, to which he concurred. During the night to 12 December the elements of the 26th Division located between Wszeliwy and Iłów were relieved by dismounted riflemen of the 4th Cavalry Division who had been resting behind our front. Eagerly accommodating our request, they were assembled west of Wszeliwy as a reserve. During that same night the 25th Reserve Division massed its troops on the left wing. By consolidating almost our entire artillery and ammunition in the vicinity of Wszeliwy, we were able to form a main effort with our artillery and infantry to break through the enemy position. The XVII Army Corps agreed to attack with us simultaneously, but the III Reserve Corps insisted that it could not start to attack until 14 December.

After thorough artillery preparation fired on the morning of 12 December, Corps Fabeck broke three kilometers deep into the enemy position at and south of Wszeliwy. We captured more than four thousand prisoners, many machine guns, and some field guns. North of Wszeliwy to Iłów the Russians held their positions without moving. After we swung against their southern flank and their rear with relatively weak forces, they either surrendered or retreated quickly. North of Iłów, opposite the III Reserve Corps, the Russians retreated approximately three kilometers. They were pursued by the 5th Reserve Division while the 6th Reserve Division remained in reserve. But although the situation had changed completely, the III Reserve Corps still insisted that they could not mount a decisive attack until 14 December. On 12 December the XVII Army Corps achieved only small gains against strong enemy resistance.

During the night of 12–13 December the enemy in front of Corps Fabeck and the XVII Army Corps retreated. We maintained close contact and by 13 December we had moved forward some nine kilometers. Only the center of the corps met strong enemy resistance, defending stubbornly from positions that they apparently had prepared earlier. The III Reserve Corps spent 13 December preparing to conduct its deliberate attack against the enemy holding on to the forest north of Budy.[72] The Ninth Army headquarters did not believe that the enemy would try to hold on to the Bzura Position. On 14 December, therefore, they ordered general march routes for the I Reserve Corps to Łowicz; for the XVII Army Corps tied in east of Łowicz to the mouth of the Rawka to the Bzura; for the III Reserve Corps to and north of Sochaczew; and for Corps Fabeck to follow in zone, up to but not including Sochaczew. The XVII Reserve Corps and Corps Fabeck were to cross the Bzura and open the crossing at Sochaczew for the III Reserve Corps, which had orders to advance rapidly. The warning orders were issued telephonically and later confirmed by written orders.

The Russians were still located north of the Bzura in the vicinity and northwest of Łowicz, but south of the Bzura west of Łowicz. Their fighting front was oriented to the west. Based on that situation, it was predictable that the Russian right wing would have to put up decisive resistance in the vicinity of and below Łowicz, or in a last extreme at the Bzura. We prepared our orders based on that assumption. Initially it was important to throw the enemy forces that were still in position back approximately ten kilometers west of the Bzura. We would accomplish that with a unified attack by the XVII and XIII Army Corps and the III Reserve Corps. On 14 December we made the preparations for such an attack, confident that the III Reserve Corps would defeat its enemy that day and then move up on line with us. That in fact happened when the III Reserve Corps took the forest north of Budy against weak enemy resistance and then continued to advance farther to the east.

On 14 December the enemy attacked Corps Fabeck, the XVII Army Corps, and the I Reserve Corps at multiple points. He was repelled everywhere, suffering heavy losses. We took many prisoners, including soldiers from divisions that up to now had been reported to be in East Prussia. That fact, combined with aerial reconnaissance indicating the approach movements of Russian units heading toward the Bzura, lead to the assessment that the enemy was determined to put up an extended resistance. On the other hand, we did not believe that the enemy who had been beaten along his entire front would still conduct a deliberate defense forward of the Bzura, with the river in his back. Corps Fabeck therefore advised both divisions to thrust forward immediately against the weakened enemy front.

On the morning of 15 December Corps Fabeck, along with the XVII Army Corps and the III Reserve Corps, resumed the attack immediately. According to the Ninth Army order, the III Reserve Corps was to advance with its southern wing toward Sochaczew, and they deployed their 6th Reserve Division to the south of the 5th Reserve Division. Our 25th Reserve Division was ordered to maintain close contact with the enemy, and set with its center advancing toward Dachowa. The 26th Division, which had its left wing stretched to Łąki Kujawskie, was pulled out of the front line gradually and then advanced in the direction of Kozłów Szlachecki, on the Bzura and to the rear of the 25th Reserve Division. That day the enemy still put up a strong resistance on the western bank of the Bzura.

On 16 December the enemy remained in force on the left bank of the Bzura River. The 25th Reserve Division advancing with its main effort along the Rybno–Lubiewo road could not break the Russian resistance. Only that evening did the right wing of the III Reserve Corps, advancing on Sochaczew, reach our line. We started our preparation for the river crossing on that day. The bridging engineers had already been brought forward close to the front lines.

Simultaneously with the enemy forces across from us, the Russians opposite the center and the right wing of Ninth Army started their retreat toward the east. The Ninth Army headquarters expected that the Russian front would be pulled back behind the Vistula, and thus gave all the corps on the left wing objectives that were far behind the Bzura. The ultimate objective was to push the Russian northern wing away from the Vistula. The Ninth Army's center was to maintain close contact with the enemy. The right wing, linked to Army Detachment Woyrsch, was to swing against the enemy's southern wing.

On 17 December the enemy continued his retreat in the center and on the right wing of the Ninth Army. The I Reserve Corps was then ordered to attack with its right wing toward Bolimów.

The 26th Division crossed the Bzura at Kozłów Szlachecki by a coup de main and established a bridgehead on the right bank of the river. The enemy across from the 25th Reserve Division and the III Reserve Corps continued to hold his positions west of the Bzura. The XVII Army Corps and I Reserve Corps were still fighting on the left bank of the Bzura.

On the morning of 18 December the Russians in front of the 25th Reserve Division and the III Reserve Corps retreated across the Bzura on several hastily constructed bridges. The reliable and steady 25th Reserve Division stayed right on top of the retreating enemy and forced a crossing of the sixty-meter-long wooden bridge at Dachowa. The withdrawing enemy had wrapped the bridge with petroleum-soaked canvas. But the 25th Reserve Division immediately established a broad bridgehead on the right bank of the Bzura. With the support of its rapidly advanced artillery, the division held the bridgehead against strong enemy attacks.

Corps Fabeck had succeeded in pushing advance elements of both of its divisions across the Bzura and on to the eastern bank. The more slowly advancing III Reserve Corps followed the enemy only close to the Bzura. Our corps command post came under repeated and very heavy artillery fire on 18 December. Normally when members of the staff visited the forward units, which they did almost every day, they rode at a walking pace. We did not lose any of the staff during this current action. The Russian artillery was generally very inaccurate, and for the most part the Russian infantry fired too high. Our rearward elements, however, suffered some losses. On 18 December we displaced the corps' main headquarters to Rybno.

In front of the Ninth Army's center the enemy had withdrawn to the Rawka. The German forces pursuing the enemy came close to the Rawka. Nonetheless, the prevailing assumption at the Ninth Army headquarters was that the enemy's main body would retreat across the Vistula. The Ninth Army's left wing was ordered to stay close on the enemy. But as we soon realized, the enemy was not retreating across the Vistula. Correctly recognizing the dangerous situation, they were facing at the Bzura, the Russians brought forward significant reinforcements. Heavy fighting ensued against those forces, and also at the Rawka. It was clear that the enemy was determined to hold the Bzura–Rawka line, which were strong natural obstacles, including the adjacent marshy areas.

During the night of 19 December the enemy launched a very strong attack with superior forces against the elements of the 26th Division that had crossed at Kozłów Szlachecki. Several times during the attack our troops heard from the Russian lines the call, "*Deutsche! Nicht schiessen!*" ("Germans here! Don't shoot!"). Unfortunately, the troops fell for this malicious ruse. When the enemy rushing in several waves was recognized only at a very close distance, a very bloody fight evolved during which rifle butts and bayonets were the primary weapons. During the long struggle the 26th Division lost more than one thousand men, including prisoners, and six machine guns. But the division held the bridgehead by launching a courageous hasty counterattack, which netted more than six hundred prisoners. When daylight broke, our artillery could finally be effective, and the guns forced the Russians to retreat with heavy losses. During that night the enemy mounted multiple attacks against the 25th Reserve Division's bridgehead at Dachowa. All were beaten back bloodily.

On 19 December the III Reserve Corps took a west-facing outcropping in the river bend north of Sochaczew. In the process it faced very stiff enemy resistance everywhere else along its front. Based on the actions of 19 December, the Ninth Army headquarters concluded that the reports of strong enemy resistance at the Rawka did not indicate a Russian withdrawal behind the Vistula for the time being. On the right of Corps Fabeck the XVII Army Corps had crossed the Bzura, and in coordination with the I Reserve Corps it started to swing toward the line from Bolimów to the mouth of the Rawka. By advancing across the Rawka, the left wing of the XVII Army Corps affected a linkup with the 26th Division, eliminating any threat to the division's right flank. Corps Fabeck and other corps reported to the Ninth Army that the enemy had conducted a deliberate withdrawal behind the Bzura.

During the night of 19–20 December and until the afternoon of the 20th, the Russians launched a continuous string of attacks against our two bridgeheads. Our stout troops repelled all the attacks bloodily, but the fighting left them considerably worn down. With all means available the positions at the two bridgeheads were reinforced with obstacles. The necessary wire came from former Russian positions that our rear echelon troops dismantled and sent forward.

On 21 December the Ninth Army's attacks made only small gains against the enemy positions along the Rawka. The left wing of Army Detachment Woyrsch was pushed far enough back by a Russian attack that a gap opened up, which the Ninth Army had to plug. On that day and the days and nights that followed, the Russians attacked almost uninterruptedly against the bridgeheads, but we managed to hold them. The strongest assaults always came at dusk, then around midnight, and again close to dawn. All the Russian attacks failed because of the courage of our infantry and the artillery fire that we delivered into the Russian lines beyond the immediate bridgeheads, Although the Russian assaults were deeply echeloned, they suffered very high losses because their forces were tightly massed. The III Reserve Corps, however, was forced to abandon its position on the river bend north of Sochaczew.

According to the daily prisoner interrogations, approximately twelve divisions of the Russian First Army were deployed in front of the III Reserve Corps and Corps Fabeck. Roughly six of those divisions had sustained very heavy losses in the fighting west of the Bzura. The other divisions on and east of the Bzura had been held in reserve. Any gaps that occurred in the Russian lines were quickly plugged, and many of the prisoners we captured were young replacements.

On 24 December the Ninth Army intercepted a Russian radio transmission and distributed the resulting intelligence to the subordinate corps. It indicated a large general attack during the night of 25 December. The corps, therefore, remained at a very high alert status on Christmas Eve. In our immediate sector, however, the enemy only launched weak thrusts, which we repelled without much effort. Late that evening the thoughts of everyone in the German army turned to our families at home. People in the Homeland had mailed large quantities of Christmas gifts to the frontline soldiers. But owing to the long and bad routes from Kutno to our front lines, most of the larger packages did not arrive until January. The smaller gifts and letters did arrive on time.

Combat losses and illness had reduced the combat strength of all of the Ninth Army's corps. The horses, too, suffered greatly in the bad weather. We were no longer capable of mounting a general attack with major objectives. The Ninth Army headquarters therefore decided to conduct only one more limited attack from the army's southern wing on 28 December. That attack, however, did not achieve any tangible success, nor did other limited attacks change the overall situation. The Ninth Army's entire front line increasingly solidified into trench warfare conditions. The Russian attacks also became less frequent. We took advantage of the relatively quiet time to conduct systematic reliefs of out units in the bridgeheads and give the troops some rest and relaxation. The slowly arriving but only partially trained replacements underwent initial combat training at the special academies established by both divisions. Only then were the new troops sent to the front line. The rear rest areas were also improved to the extent of the available material. The troops, therefore, were protected from the cold weather and the constantly alternating rain and snow. Warm underwear, fur gloves, and other useful equipment were sent forward, primarily from the Württemberg War Ministry.[73] In the decline of fighting activity we could also save ammunition for later attacks.

During these quiet days my thoughts often returned to OHL's very questionable operational and tactical decisions that had not produced decisive results. During the fighting in Flanders since the Battle of the Marne, much of the German Army's strength and ammunition had been wasted. As I had emphasized earlier, the fight in Flanders was continued far too long. Had OHL decided earlier to give up this wrestling for tactical advantage, and at the same time shifted the German Army in the West (*Westheer*) to the defensive, all the units not needed in the west could have been transferred to the command in the east. Such a surge in forces would have made it possible for the Commander in Chief, East (*Oberost*), to attack on both sides of the Vistula.

If such an attack had been made, there would have been much greater operational freedom in the east and a good probability of pushing the Russians back farther east from the Vistula line. That indirectly would have brought much needed relief to the Austrian front. Unfortunately, OHL had been incapable of making such sweeping decisions in a timely manner, which might have had a decisive influence on the course of the war. The very questionable decisions that OHL made in the fall of 1914 consequently led to the transition to trench warfare in the west. They had much the same effect in the east, because we no longer had sufficient combat strength there to conduct large operational-scale attacks.

As I only learned later, General von Falkenhayn during this decisive period of time believed in the possibility of reaching a special peace accord with Russia and was taking steps in that direction. Such efforts, however, could not have been effective until we had achieved a devastating victory against the Russian Army. Such a major operational victory against the Russian Army possibly could have kept Romania and Italy permanently out of the war. It also would have strengthened Turkey, which had entered on our side, and more importantly it would have increased the strength and confidence of the Austrian Army. Then Germany and Austria, possibly in coordination with Bulgaria, could have brought the Serbs under control.

As 1914 turned into 1915, the intensity of the fighting on the Ninth Army's front decreased progressively. Both we and the enemy were in prepared positions. The main effort of the defense in the Corps Fabeck sector was at the bridgehead positions, which also were the focus of repeated Russian attacks. To the rear of the front lines we continued to improve the troop quarters and improve the road network. The work required the help of the local population, which was slowly returning to their dwellings from the forests where they had fled. Almost daily we were able to gain useful information from Russian soldiers who defected to us. Often those cowards brought their machine guns with them in the belief that they would be treated better.

On 5 January 1915 we conducted a deliberate attack that enlarged considerably our bridgehead near Kozłów Szlachecki, capturing more than one thousand prisoners and five machine guns in the process. All the Russian counterattacks, meanwhile, stalled almost immediately in front of our emplaced obstacles.

On 8 January, I was ordered to a briefing at Ninth Army headquarters, which recently had displaced to Łódź. After all the corps chiefs of staff briefed their respective situations, nothing changed and we remained in the trench warfare posture.

Life at Corps Fabeck headquarters increasingly turned into a routine. At 0700 hours we had breakfast together. Then after telephone conversations with the divisions and an 0800 hours meeting with the commanding general, I dictated the morning reports to the Ninth Army. I always accompanied the corps commander when he rode out to visit the troops. At the communications centers en route, I collected information from the front line. We had to ride very fast to cover the large and deeply echeloned area of our defensive sector. At 1300 hours we had a lunch of soup and a warm meal.

Then work continued until the late evening. We had very little space in the squalid estate manor we occupied in Rybno. The commanding general and I each had a very small room. Otherwise, the entire staff was spread throughout two large rooms used as living and work space. We did not have beds, only straw and sleeping bags. At our arrival in Rybno we found all the window glass had been shattered by the concussion from artillery fire. We took glass from picture frames to reglaze the windows in the commanding general's room. We covered the other windows with paper and wooden shutters. At the end of January we were finally able to requisition window panes and putty in Łódź. The shell craters in the estate's large park were reconfigured as latrines. There was plenty of barn space for the horses. The lower-level staff members were well established in the estate's housekeeping rooms. The family that owned the estate were left to the upstairs rooms of the manor. There was no coal, but the wood fires gave off enough heat. Health-wise I was in great condition, even though I was constantly under great stress. I was able to sleep for only short periods because I had much work that lasted late into the evening hours, and I frequently had to make many phone calls, especially when the Russians were attacking. We generally had tea and coffee available.

The opposing front lines were between one hundred and four hundred meters apart. All trenches were filled with groundwater, and almost everywhere we had to build wooden plank paths to keep the rapid cross traffic open. The groundwater made the construction of shelters possible only at certain locations. For the most part the troops had to make do in reinforced dugouts, into which they built small brick stoves to protect themselves against the constant cold. Drainage pipes served as chimneys. We produced our own material for building the positions after we put an old, run-down saw mill back in operation. The local population removed large amounts of wire from the Russian positions that we had seized earlier. The sixty-kilometer-long road to Kutno, where we had to pick up all our supplies, ran mostly across muddy ground, which made it impossible to load the farmers' carts to full capacity.

The units generally occupied the bridgehead positions for forty-eight hours and were on a fixed rotation schedule. The equipment in the Russian positions was similar to ours, but we took better care of our gear. When we conducted our limited attacks and sent patrols across the Bzura between the bridgeheads, we capture many Russians still in their foxholes. Our artillery fire was very effective; that of the Russian was not. We always used precision fire against the enemy positions; the Russians limited themselves to random interdiction fire that inflicted few losses on us. I got along well professionally and personally with General von Fabeck. While he had some rough edges, he was also an excellent soldier. Our thinking on required decisions and orders generally came together automatically. That made the entire working atmosphere much easier. The commanding general almost never changed anything in the orders that I drafted.

My most wonderful distractions were always the letters from home, mostly from my wife, who like me wrote every day. On very calm days I sent officers of the staff out hunting. The bag they brought in served to improve our meal plan.

On 24 January at about 0700 hours an OHL telegram sent from Charleville arrived at Corps Fabeck headquarters informing me that I was reassigned as department chief on the staff of General Erich von Falkenhayn, the chief of the General Staff of the army in the field. My successor as chief of staff of XIII Army Corps was the capable and intelligent Major Reinhardt, who had been my General Staff officer (Ia). I handed everything off to him after I gave my final report to the commanding general. It was quite hard for me to say farewell to my commander and my colleagues. The entire staff still consisted of the same persons as the day we first deployed. All of them were excellent and courageous officers, and all the supporting personnel also were exemplary. Since the beginning of the war the XIII Army Corps had almost constantly been on the offensive. Its courage and the understanding and focus of its leadership resulted in many successes and a solid reputation. The troops trusted their leaders and also knew that their leaders took care of them as much as possible. Mutual relations had been built upon this great understanding. To this day I still look back with gratitude to my days as the corps chief of staff, where I was able to devote my energy to the welfare of the troops. A desk job as section chief, even though it was at OHL, did not at all correspond with my spirit. I was a frontline soldier through and through. The thought of being away from the front lines, possibly for a long time, did not suit me at all. Nonetheless, I was hoping to bring my frontline experiences gained on so many battlefields to this executive position and apply it productively at the center from which all operations were commanded.

About an hour after receipt of the telegram I got on a limber with four horses and was taken with my bags at high speed to the spot where I had ordered a corps staff car to pick me up. I had sent a telegram to my wife telling her to travel immediately to Berlin, which I would come through on my way to the west.

At around 1500 hours I arrived in Poznań and reported in to the staff of Oberost. Unfortunately, General Erich Ludendorff was not there, but rather at briefings in Wrocław. His deputy, Lieutenant Colonel Max Hoffmann, told me that OHL was planning to establish two operations sections, one for the east and one for the west. Supposedly I was to take over the Operations Section, East. Reporting to Field Marshal Paul von Hindenburg, whom I had met during peacetime in Karlsruhe, I touched on the possibility of my being assigned to the Operations Section, East, and I asked him, in that case, to give me copies of certain documents relating to Eastern Front operations. He told me in essence, "Make sure that we maintain freedom of action. We will manage quite well."

That evening I was General von Hindenburg's dinner guest. His serene calmness and confidence made quite an impression on me. Later that evening I took a scheduled train to Berlin, where on 25 January I met with my wife. That evening I continued on to Charleville-Mézières. My wife accompanied me as far as Kassel. There my old regimental comrade from the 2nd Foot Guards Regiment, Lieutenant General Hugo Freiherr Freytag von Loringhoven joined me on the train. Up to that point he had been the German liaison officer to the Austrian High Command, and now he had been assigned as the deputy chief of staff in Charleville-Mézières. We had a lot to talk about and the rather slow trip passed very quickly. I arrived at noon on 26 January in Charleville-Mézières.

2

Division Chief of the General Staff of the Supreme Command of the Field Army (OHL)

In the afternoon of 6 January, I reported to the chief of the General Staff of the Field Army, Lieutenant General Erich von Falkenhayn, at Mézières.[1] I already knew him during peacetime. During the years 1900 through 1903, when von Falkenhayn as a major was an advisor to the Chinese Army, we lived in the same building as his family, who had remained in Karlsruhe. We had frequent contact with Frau von Falkenhayn, whom I was able to assist often with advice and help. During my time as an instructor at the War Academy in Berlin I demonstrated a war game with my tactics class to a Chinese Military Mission, to which Major von Falkenhayn was assigned. Through this and other subsequent experiences I got to know Falkenhayn quite well. In the fall of 1908, during the five-day-long Kaiser Maneuver in Lorraine, I was the communications officer in the maneuver cell of the XVI Army Corps headquarters. The chief of staff then was Lieutenant Colonel von Falkenhayn. In later years, when Colonel von Falkenhayn was commander of the 4th Foot Guards Regiment, when he was the chief of staff of the IV Army Corps, and when he was the Prussian minister of war, I dealt with him on a frequent basis. Certainly, Falkenhayn was a superb soldier, a very diligent and capable worker, and he had an expansive mind. The decisions he had to make after the Battle of the Marne were made during a difficult time for the leadership of the German Army. He undoubtedly intended the best, but by fragmenting the army's combat power he failed to achieve the objective of decisively defeating the enemy in the west.

Previously in this book I offered my opinion on the operational decisions that Falkenhayn made up through the end of 1914. During the subsequent months I came to the conclusion that Falkenhayn failed to gain much respect and trust because of the inconsistency of his operational leadership and his frequent flip-flopping, despite his very self-confident demeanor. Even though he did listen to reasonable suggestions and recommendations, he mostly chose to go his own way. Extremely animated in his temperament, very deft and self-assured in his manner, he all too often quickly glossed over the consequences of any mishaps resulting from his leadership. As I soon realized, the unconditional trust that the troops and their leaders at the fighting front should have had in their supreme headquarters and its leader was reserved at best.

General von Falkenhayn personally requested my assignment to his staff. When I reported in he greeted me very cordially. He recognized that giving up the independence of a corps chief of staff must have been a great personal sacrifice for me, but that now the mission had to be the priority. To my disappointment, the separation of the Operations Division into eastern and western sections had probably only been considered as a temporary measure. There was no mention of such when I reported in, nor at any time later. Rather, I was put in charge of three sections of the Operations Division–Ia (operations), Ib (organization and tactics), and Ic (order of battle). I came under the Operations Division chief, Colonel Gerhard Tappen, as his deputy.

I also had known Colonel Tappen during peacetime. During the years 1907 and 1908 I was an instructor with him in Berlin at the War Academy. Upon his reassignment to the XVII Army Corps, I took over his mid-level courses in tactics and military history. When in the fall of 1910 then-Major Tappen became the Ia of the Great General Staff's 2nd Division (called the Operations Directorate during wartime), whose chief was Colonel Ludendorff, I became Tappen's successor in Danzig[2] as the Ia of the XVII Army Corps. When Ludendorff later took command of the 39th Fusilier Regiment, Tappen became the chief of staff of the 2nd Division.

As far as I can remember, the Railroad Department was supposed to be consolidated into the War Operations Directorate under Ludendorff. During the period when he was the commander of an infantry brigade in Strasbourg, Ludendorff was under consideration for assignment to the position of deputy chief of staff. I do not know why that did not happen immediately upon the start of the World War. Colonel General von Moltke would have had an excellent advisor in the person of General Ludendorff, who was superbly schooled in operations. Instead, Colonel Tappen at the outbreak of the war remained in charge of the Operations Division. All of my experiences in the war so far led me to the conclusion that very grave mistakes in the operational command of the German Army had been made by Moltke and Tappen, for which in the final analysis General von Moltke bore the blame. The greatest blunders on which to focus here were the release of the Sixth and Seventh Armies for the attack in Lorraine, combined with the commitment of reinforcing divisions to that effort which were supposed to have been dedicated to the seizure and occupation of the Belgian and French fortresses. Furthermore, the continuation of the German offensive in Lorraine against the front of the reinforced fortresses at Toul–

Épinal was misguided, which in turn made impossible the timely redeployment of strong German forces from the left to the right wing of the German Army in the West.

An especially grave mistake was the withdrawal of the XI Army Corps and the Guards Reserve Corps from the overall right wing of the German Army for redeployment to the Eastern Front, which resulted in a lack of forces necessary to organize our overall right wing in depth. Moltke, naturally, bears the overall responsibility for these decisions. Whether Tappen, as Moltke's primary advisor, had a decisive influence in such decisions I am not able to judge. Both of them, however, must have believed that the initial victories we had achieved during our advance had already secured the German Army's victory in the west. In the final analysis, such a mind-set led to a gravely false conclusion. As the result of all the foregoing, I could not bring myself to trust Colonel Tappen completely.

Upon reporting to Tappen, I could sense that he did not welcome the fact that I had been inserted into his direct chain of communication with the Ia, Ib, and Ic sections. He never dropped that attitude during the period of our collaboration, instead of recognizing that I often could relieve his more than heavy workload. He obviously was not pleased that I also attended the daily general briefings scheduled in the morning for Falkenhayn. Also attending the daily briefings were the deputy chief of staff, Lieutenant General Hugo Freiherr Freytag von Loringhoven, with his assistant chief of staff, Colonel Zoellner; the Prussian war minister, Lieutenant General Adolf Wild von Hohendorn; the chief of railroad affairs, Colonel Wilhelm Groener; the chief of communications, Lieutenant Colonel von Rauch; the chief of personnel, Colonel von Fabeck; and often the chiefs of ammunition, telegraphs, and reconnaissance. These daily briefings were intended primarily for mutual orientation, and formed the foundation for the work that had to be done cooperatively. I, of course, was always very considerate of Colonel Tappen's peculiarities of personality. Owing to his general disposition, however, it was difficult for me to develop a trusting relationship with him, even though I tried everything possible for the sake of the mission.

I got along very well with all of the members of the sections. All of these General Staff officers were capable and smart men with a good grasp of the big picture and a solid work ethic. After some initial friction they soon accepted that I sometimes would modify their recommendations prior to presentation to Colonel von Tappen.

On 27 January 1915 we held a field service and a pass in review by the staff guards and a *Landsturm* battalion in honor of the Kaiser's birthday. Afterward, I reported to the commander in chief, and General von Falkenhayn presented me to the Kaiser as the new division chief. Turning to von Falkenhayn, the Kaiser said, "What, you picked the freshest lieutenant from Berlin as a member of your staff? Well, congratulations!" He was at his humorous best. I had had frequent contact with the Kaiser during my time at the front with the 2nd Guards Foot Regiment. That also gave me the opportunity for contact with all the sections of the Supreme Headquarters. I received an especially warm welcome from the chief of the Prussian military cabinet,[3] General of Infantry Moriz Freiherr von Lyncker, with whom I had served from 1905 to 1907 as a divisional General Staff officer in Hanover. I had maintained constant contact with him since then.

For quarters I was assigned a nice, bright room close to the prefecture building in which OHL had its offices. My two orderlies also were installed in the same house. They were glad to get into a bed again for the first time since the start of the war. My two good horses arrived in Mézières from the east on 28 January. As an early riser, I took a refreshing morning ride before the start of my duty hours whenever it was possible with my tight schedule.

At noon and in the evenings we ate at the OHL mess in the prefecture, at small tables on our own schedule. The meals were always very simple. We usually took our morning breakfast in our quarters; the afternoon coffee usually was served in the large conference room of the Operations Division, with all members present. This was always announced by the staff duty officer with the little ditty, "The coffee gets cold and the pie will be old, so now is a break and a snack we take!" The pastries usually came from packages that the officers' wives had mailed to them. My wife quickly picked up on this custom. The talk at OHL was very comradely and stimulating, because most of the gentlemen were efficient officers quite willing to accept responsibility. In the evenings, whenever the heavy workload allowed, everyone met at small tables in the grand salon of the officers' mess. General von Falkenhayn was there every evening, unless he was on the road. The inner circle of the more senior officers who belonged to his round table were called the "Whispering Club," as quite often during these evening conversations matters of business were discussed in low voices.

The Operations Division worked on the commands issued in all the theaters of war, and for the Army in the West in detail. The Commander in Chief, East (Oberost), generally received only general directives that gave him great latitude in their execution. OHL maintained constant telegraphic or written contact with the Austro-Hungarian Army Supreme Command (*K.u.K. Oberkommando*). General von Falkenhayn himself dealt almost exclusively with this written correspondence. The German liaison officer at the Austrian Supreme Headquarters, General August von Cramon, sent reports concerning the situation and intentions of the Austrians on an almost daily basis. We frequently received from the Austrian chief of the General Staff, General Franz Conrad von Hötzendorf, requests for German units and combat assets to shore up the very volatile Austrian front. I have no personal impressions of General Conrad von Hötzendorf, as I never met him. I am certain that he was an operationally well-schooled leader, but he vastly overestimated the combat strength and the will to resist of the Austro-Hungarian Army, which was greatly inferior to the capabilities of the German Army. General von Falkenhayn correctly turned down the increasingly urgent calls for support from the Austrians. Such requests were granted in only the most serious of emergencies. We used the term "corset stays" for the generally smaller German units that were inserted into the Austrian front. It was a most apt term. Whenever we inserted such units the Austrian front unfailingly and quickly stabilized against the Russian attacks.

General von Falkenhayn also issued directives influencing the operations in Turkey, which had joined the Central Powers in October 1914. His intervention made it possible for a Turkish thrust toward Georgia to counter the serious threat against Armenia. The stalling tactic bought enough time until the winter preempted any larger Russian operation there. At the initiative of General von Falkenhayn, the main effort of the Turkish operations was then shifted against Egypt. That effort, however, never achieved its objective of taking the Suez Canal. Nonetheless, the operation forced the British to send stronger defensive forces to the Middle East, which drew them away from our western front.

During the course of that winter the Ministry of War stood up four and a half new army corps, with especially well-trained replacements and good leaders. This infusion of forces improved our overall situation to such a level that General von Falkenhayn decided to transition again to a large-scale offensive. From the start of 1915, the German Western Front was firmed up by our constantly improved positions. The enemy, too, remained relatively calm. Our railroad network in the west also was improved constantly, making it possible to reinforce rapidly those frontline sectors under attack, despite the relative weakness of the army reserves. This also improved the flows of ammunition and the necessary materiel for the improvement of the positions.

But Britain and France also stood up new units and strongly improved their fighting positions. According to the reports coming in at the beginning of 1915, the new units totaled an estimated seven French and twelve British divisions. The German Third Army at the beginning of January identified French attack preparations on its left wing. According to intelligence reports from agents, the British wanted to wait until the completion of the fielding of the Kitchener's Army divisions before attacking.[4]

At the turn of the year General von Falkenhayn initially planned to launch a large-scale attack in the west. More detailed calculations, however, showed that approximately twelve additional army corps would be necessary, and those units could not be stood-up immediately. The forces then available were sufficient for an effective defense of the west. But the situation in the east had deteriorated daily, primarily on the Austrian front, and especially on the Austrian southern wing. The danger there was that all of Hungary would fall into Russian hands. That meant not only that the German supply line to Turkey would be interrupted, but also the possibility that Romania and Italy would enter the World War on the side of the Entente. Based on these factors, General von Falkenhayn at the beginning of January decided to launch a large-scale attack against the Russian Army, converging from both wings of the Eastern Front. In preparation, a new Southern Army under General Alexander von Linsingen was formed in Hungary from three German and several Austrian infantry divisions and a strong cavalry force, including two German divisions. General Ludendorff was temporarily attached to General von Linsingen as an advisor for the attack preparations. On the northern wing of the Eastern Front a new Tenth Army under General Hermann von Eichhorn was formed in East Prussia, consisting of the newly formed XXXVIII, XXXIX, XL Army Corps, and the XXI Army Corps that had been replaced by the XLI Army Corps in the west. The staging for these attacks had already started by the time I assumed my new duties in Mézières.

Right from the start of my work at OHL, I aspired to master completely all aspects of my new duties. Colonel Tappen and I had separate offices. The other General Staff officers worked together in a large hall. That arrangement had some disadvantages for uninterrupted work, but it also had some advantages. Many of the incoming tasks required group efforts to develop the orders drafts for submission for decision. That could be accomplished faster in the common office. I had to evaluate all drafts and then present them to Colonel Tappen. He signed routine matters himself. Only the very important issues ultimately went to General von Falkenhayn for signature.

Falkenhayn correctly believed that it was necessary for him to be physically as close as possible to the upcoming large-scale operations. On 28 January he and Colonel Tappen traveled to Berlin for briefings, and then they continued on to the east. As his deputy, Colonel Tappen directed me to forward to him all incoming matters along with developed orders drafts, and to maintain constant telephonic contact with Berlin. Important urgent matters were to be forwarded in code by telegraph. All other matters were sent by courier. This kind of arrangement naturally delayed the rapid handling of even the smallest issue, but Tappen insisted on maintaining control of everything.

With one exception, I was the only officer in the Operations Division who at that point had any frontline experience. The other was the especially capable Captain von Harbou, who as a liaison officer from OHL had participated in the attack on Liège, where through his special prudence and personal courage he earned the *Pour le Mérite*. Thus, I often encountered, especially among the more junior officers, arrogant assessments concerning the command and the capabilities of the troops, which clashed strongly with my own frontline experience. From the beginning I corrected such attitudes openly and forcefully, and with good effect.

The absence of General von Falkenhayn and Colonel Tappen lasted longer than expected. During that period, I worked from the early morning to the late evening to meet all requirements. Commanding generals with their chiefs of staff often came to Mézières to speak with me. I could only forward in writing or telegraphically their mostly modest requests, as I had not been given the authority to make such decisions personally.

Foreign officers also came to Mézières, including six American officers on 9 February, who, with the permission of OHL, were visiting the Western Theater of War. I dined with those gentlemen, who spoke only English, and I had to conduct the conversation through an interpreter. After telephonic confirmation from General von Falkenhayn, I sent them to a spot at the front line where the French for quite a while had been firing artillery rounds against us that had been manufactured in America.[5]

Once in a while large numbers of members of the German press and war correspondents also appeared, with the approval of OHL. I had to exercise special restraint in answering their many questions, and I limited myself to describing events that were in the past. I never addressed any future operations plans that I had knowledge of. Unfortunately, such visits always cost precious time, which resulted in less sleep for me. I still had my work to do.

On 13 February 1915 we received reports of the great success of the attack launched in East Prussia on 8 February by the Tenth Army under General von Eichhorn, supported by the Eighth Army under General Otto von Below. The Kaiser, General von Falkenhayn, and Colonel von Tappen had observed the fighting directly. I had known the broad outline of the attack plan. I nonetheless was surprised at the extent of the victory, which included the capture of approximately 10,000 prisoners, 162 guns, and 200 machine guns. The efforts made by our troops in the ice and snow had to have been incredible, but I knew from my own experience what good troops under good leadership were capable of accomplishing. During that period, I had an overwhelming feeling of wanting to be back at the front line again, where you could have, albeit on a smaller scale, the satisfaction of direct experience and independent action.

The attacks executed by the Southern Army under General von Linsingen and the Austrian Army's right wing yielded only minor successes. We had not been able to accomplish the intended relief of the Austrian fortress at Przemyśl, which was encircled by the Russians. The Austrian attack front very quickly solidified once more into a defensive posture. Thus, General Conrad von Hötzendorf's high hopes that the large-scale attacks by the two wings of the entire Eastern Front would force the Russian Army to collapse and withdraw failed to materialize. General von Falkenhayn never believed such a large-scale success was possible. He was more practical and calmer in the development of large-scale attacks than General Conrad von Hötzendorf, who constructed large-scale attacks in theory on paper but always overestimated the real capabilities of his troops.

The German attack on the northern wing had cleared the enemy from all of East Prussia. The situation there was consolidated firmly, and all Russian deliberate counterattacks were repelled. But the follow-on German attacks in the northeast failed to yield any further significant success. On the Eastern Front's southern wing the Russians attacked so powerfully that the Austrian lines in the Carpathians were forced to pull back into a purely defensive posture.

During those actions in the east, the French and British conducted relief attacks in the west, primarily in the Champagne region against the Third Army; north of Arras against the Sixth Army; and between Verdun and Metz at Combres Heights, near Saint-Mihiel, and at the Bois-le-Prêtre against Army Detachment Strantz.[6] In the Vosges Mountains fighting also flared up again in the sector of Hartmannswillerkopf,[7] held by Army Detachment Gaede. All of these enemy attacks were fought through with fierce determination on both sides, but they produced only minor successes because our stout troops everywhere fought heroically.

Quite often during this period the commander of the Fifth Army, Crown Prince William of Prussia, came to see me from his headquarters in Stenay to receive updates on the actions at the fighting fronts in the east and the west. As with all visitors to OHL, I maintained the utmost restraint with him during the descriptions of the events.

On 3 March 1915 General von Falkenhayn and Colonel Tappen returned to Mézières, after visiting several headquarters in the east and attending briefings in Berlin. Immediately upon their arrival I briefed them on the current situation and my assessment of the fighting in the west. Soon thereafter General von Falkenhayn sent me on a personal reconnaissance mission to evaluate the situation at the Third Army, which had been engaged in defensive action against strong French attacks since 9 February. In the process the Third Army had maintained its positions, except for some minor losses of ground. I informed the Third Army headquarters telephonically that I would be arriving, and I requested a large-scale situation map and an escort with a good knowledge of the fighting positions. I arrived at Vouziers in the very early morning hours and drove directly to the battle zone with the escort. I visited all the corps and division headquarters, conducted several recon trips from there to the forwardmost lines, and verified the situation on the spot. Toward the evening I briefed the Third Army headquarters on my positive assessment of the fighting front and I promised to communicate the wishes expressed to me at the front line directly to General von Falkenhayn. Immediately upon my return to Mézières I briefed Falkenhayn on the situation map. I voiced my strong conviction that the Third Army would hold its positions. The very modest requests of the Third Army headquarters, which I forwarded to General von Falkenhayn, were answered quickly. I had come under enemy fire several times that day, but it was a most welcome break from my office routine.

On 6 March I was invited to breakfast with the Kaiser, who spoke with special pride and gratitude about the actions of the German troops in the east, who with heroic recklessness had cleared the Russians from East Prussian soil. I also briefed the Kaiser on my inspection tour of the Third Army and its courageous and successful perseverance against a strongly superior French force. We had a simple but well prepared meal. The Kaiser himself ate only fruit. I was able to excuse myself immediately after the meal, because the Kaiser understood the high volume of work to be accomplished by the Operations Division. On 7 March Colonel Tappen was detached for approximately three weeks to the Seventh Army headquarters to reconnoiter the ground there for a large-scale attack in that sector. During his absence I functioned as the primary operations advisor to General von Falkenhayn. I very quickly acquired full insight into his thoughts and plans for the future. In the process, I frequently had to spend the nighttime hours working through the current issues. I did not get more than two or three hours of sleep during those days. I soon gained the feeling that General von Falkenhayn trusted me, and that conviction made my work much easier.

General von Falkenhayn was open to any informed opinion. He accepted opposing views, and he even welcomed them. Thus, I influenced significantly Falkenhayn's telegraphic and written communications with Oberost, which he always wrote personally. Quite often this written correspondence contained passages that antagonized General von Hindenburg and his chief of staff, Ludendorff. When I pointed this out to Falkenhayn, he started giving me his drafts for review. I often made changes, not in content but in tone. To my deep satisfaction, the result was a better relationship between Falkenhayn and Hindenburg and Ludendorff.

My assignment as deputy chief of the Operations Division was very satisfying, because I handled the larger operational and organizational work, while the routine daily business was accomplished by the General Staff officers who were my subordinates. I reported only the most necessary of the latter work to Falkenhayn; everything else I signed myself.

Daily at 1200 hours General von Falkenhayn, accompanied by the chief of the Operations Division, briefed the Kaiser in his villa in Charleville. These meetings were always attended by His Majesty's personal adjutant general, Colonel General Hans Georg Hermann von Plessen, and the chief of the military cabinet, General Freiherr von Lyncker. Occasionally the minister of war, General Adolf Wild von Hohenborn, also attended. During the 30 March Kaiser briefing my former commanding general at the XIII Army Corps, General von Fabeck, reported in. He had been appointed commanding general of the Eleventh Army. The Kaiser had him brought into the conference room immediately and said to him, "So, Fabeck, now don't be so rude of a commander and quarrel with all your subordinates, as you always do." Fabeck's quick-witted and amusing answer was, "Your Majesty, that is not the case at all. I never quarreled with Lossberg, and thus I won't quarrel with anybody else." After the briefing I had breakfast with the Kaiser and Fabeck in the OHL officers' mess. Fabeck and I reminisced about a few of our common experiences.

The four and a half new army corps formed by the War Ministry in the winter of 1914–1915 consisted entirely of divisions with only three strong infantry regiments. Toward the end of February, Colonel Ernst von Wrisberg, chief of the Army Department (*Armeeabteilung*) at the War Ministry, suggested to General von Falkenhayn during a briefing in Berlin the establishment of new divisions initially on the Western Front by reorganizing all the infantry divisions from four to three infantry regiments. General von Falkenhayn took up this proposal immediately, and with the approval of the Kaiser he started on 25 February the preparation for the reorganization on the Western Front.[8] All the preparation work to accomplish this was done by the Operations Division. The establishment of the new divisions was delegated to the staffs of those divisions. According to plan, one infantry regiment was detached from most of the divisions in the quiet sectors of the front, and their remaining three infantry regiments received as reinforcements twenty-four hundred well-trained replacements and two machine gun platoons with three machine guns each. Those frontline divisions and all the newly formed divisions had then three strong infantry regiments, one field artillery brigade, one foot artillery battalion with two field howitzer batteries, two engineer companies, and ammunition columns and trains. The newly formed divisions were given the numbers 50th, 52nd, 54th, 56th, 58th, and 10th Bavarian. This increase of reserves behind the Western Front had the major advantage that the number of transfers of units from the Eastern to the Western Fronts could be reduced.

The reorganization of the entire German Army proceeded in a similar manner. The pool of trained and available replacements, as well as the stocks of materiel and ammunition, were only sufficient initially to form another eight new divisions behind the Western Front. Those divisions were numbered 111th, 113th, 115th, 117th, 119th, 121st, 123rd, and 11th Bavarian. The Army in the East also was ordered to initiate the reorganization of its divisions with three infantry regiments, and in the interim to form three new divisions with the numbers 101st, 103rd, and 105th.

Very soon after Colonel Tappen's detachment, General von Falkenhayn conferred with me on operational questions and stated his intent to execute a large-scale operational attack in the spring of 1915. The question whether it was to be launched in the west or in the east remained open initially. During my time at OHL I had written an operational staff study that addressed that very question, based on my own experiences in the east. I gave General von Falkenhayn a copy of that study, as reproduced below:

Operational Study

> A decisive attack on the Western Front will only be feasible after strong German forces can be released from the Eastern Front. Such a movement of numerous corps from the east to the west can only be considered after a crushing blow against the Russians. The conduct of the operations in the east focusing on this critical objective thus becomes the precondition for the beginning of a decisive attack in the west.
>
> The number of army corps that can be moved to the west depends on the extent of the success in the east. If we can achieve the ideal objective of throwing back the destroyed Russian forces into the area between the border of eastern Galicia and the Pripet Marshes, the German Landwehr, Landsturm, and replacement troops that will remain in the east will be sufficient to maintain the status quo, together with the Austrian forces. Behind that front it will be necessary to maintain a mobile army reserve that will be capable of enlisting local replacements. Such units, for example, would be the I Army Corps, I Reserve Corps, and the 3rd and 35th Reserve Divisions. All other corps in the east could be considered for redeployment.
>
> If the overall operational situation in the east requires actions against Serbia or Romania, or defense against an attack by Italy, then it will be necessary to leave a force of combat-capable OHL reserves in the east. In such a situation, it would be advisable to transfer to the west primarily those army corps which have during the fighting in the east thoroughly mastered the principles of the attack

against a strongly reinforced field position. The recently formed XXXVIII, XXXIX, and XL Army Corps are better left in the east. Those corps, even after the completion of major operations in the east, will still have had only little experience in conducting deliberate attacks against reinforced positions. Thus, ten army corps could be considered for redeployment from the east to the west, as well as those corps that had been transferred from the west to the east in the spring for the operational attack. An especially favorable scenario might include some Austrian army corps that could be redeployed to the west to relieve German formations in quiet sectors of the front. Those Austrian corps would occupy prepared and hardened positions, freeing up the relieved German corps for the large-scale attack in the west.

The planning width for the deeply echeloned operational attack in the west depends on the number of corps that can be moved to the west after a breakthrough victory in the east. To establish a firm foundation for the attack, we should plan on the reinforcement of the Army in the West with eight army corps from the east by approximately March 1915. To that we will add one corps that is constantly resting behind the lines, and the six new divisions that are currently being stood up. Those forces combined will give us three more corps. The result will be twelve corps to reinforce those corps already deployed in the sector selected for the operational attack in the west.

The Location of the Large-Scale Attack

The first objective of the attack must be to rupture the enemy front with a tactical breakthrough at one point, conducted with strong forces. That will separate the enemy forces and set up the operational breakthrough in the initial penetration sector. Such an operation is impossible for the most part between the Meuse and the Swiss border. Any breakthrough there would be restricted by the French fortress system and the space restrictions.

Along the front between the Meuse and the sea, two locations where we could achieve a significant success seem obvious. The first is from the Champagne to Verdun. The second is immediately north of the Somme. We do not have the forces or the necessary ammunition to attempt a simultaneous attack in both sectors. Victory can only be guaranteed if we mass all of our combat assets against one sector. On that basis, I suggest an attack north of the Somme.

Breakthrough at the Somme

The objective of this operation must be to reach the sea north of the Somme, thus splitting the enemy armies into two groups, with the British in the north and the French in the south. The French and the British currently have the four primary lines of communication for transporting troops through the area on both sides of the Somme.

- The rail line from Montdidier to Albert.
- The rail line via Amiens to Doullens.
- The rail lines via Abbeville to Saint-Pol-sur-Mer and Boulogne-sur-Mer.
- The sea route.

If we take the rail lines across the Somme, and if we reduce the traffic at sea through the actions of our submarines, and we then advance north of the Somme from our breakthrough, the British Army will then have to fight with its back toward Dunkirk, Calais, and Boulogne-sur-Mer; and the French Army with its back toward the Somme crossing points at and below Amiens. The forced opening of the route to the sea by the spearhead of our breakthrough wedge will strain the political ties of our opponents, both of whom will be fighting with their backs toward their own homelands and their strategic bases.

We will accomplish much if we succeed in physically separating the allied armies. That will give us a certain degree of operational freedom that we can use in the defense facing south from the Somme, and our advance to the north with strong forces. If we manage to push the British off the Continent, it would be quite improbable that they would return to France by new landings at or south of the mouth of the Seine. Britain then will be completely separated from France, and France on its own is no match for Germany.

By executing a breakthrough north of the Somme, we quite possibly might decide the outcome of the war. Any offensive by the Army in the West must focus on achieving such results from the very start.[9]

Width of the Attack Sector

A key question when planning the breakthrough is the final trace of the south-facing defensive line after the breakthrough. I believe the line Roye–Avre River–Somme is the most suitable. If we establish the breakthrough's flank security for follow-on operations against the British as the line Roye–Bray-sur-Somme–Amiens, that line will have to be secured as it becomes longer. The resulting angle jutting out into our defensive front in the direction of Bray-sur-Somme will become the point of strong and consistent French attacks against the left flank and the rear of our penetration zone. Our attack, therefore, would have to be conducted initially on both sides of the Somme. South of the Somme the attack would have only the limited objective of the Avre River line between Amiens and Roye. From there it would transition to the defense facing south along that line. The simultaneous attack north of the Somme would have the Channel coast as its objective, and after reaching Amiens it would be reinforced with some of the attack units from south of the Somme, which should be releasable by that point.

The distance that the northern wing of the combined attack can advance will depend on the number of available attack corps. A rapid advance of the breakthrough forces could be extended to the area north of Arras. A major factor in determining the width of the attack sector will be the mass of artillery and the availability of ammunition for the sustainment of a presumably long offensive operation.

Staging for the Attack

The attack must be very deeply echeloned if it is to have any prospect of success. I recommend initially organizing the staging into two attack echelons. In the area north of the Somme the commanding generals of the Second and Sixth Armies will command the first echelon of the tactical breakthrough. Between Bapaume and Roye a new Eleventh Army headquarters should be formed which will control the fighting sectors on both sides of the Somme, and in that sector command the attack to seize the areas of the Avre and the Somme south of Amiens.

The army corps of the leading echelon must be capable of fighting independently and in depth. Depending on the terrain and the mission, this necessity requires narrow fighting sectors, of 4.5 to 5.5 kilometers per corps. The commanders must be able to draw strong reserves from the elements assigned to them in order to move reinforcements into the fighting lines quickly in that sector which shows the most promise for achieving tactical breakthrough. As soon as the tactical breakthrough has been accomplished, the forward attack echelon with its remaining reserves will destroy the enemy lines on the left and right of the breakthrough sector. Through that ever-widening gap, the units of the follow-on attack echelon, which must follow the first echelon closely, will then achieve the operational breakthrough. OHL will command the entire attack from the beginning, and will order the commitment of the second echelon. The flanks of the operational breakthrough will be secured by the units of the leading attack echelon.

Preparation of the Attack

During the deployment phase we must avoid any mixing of the corps already in the line with the newly inserted attacking corps. Our experiences so far indicate that the troops fight better under their familiar leaders than when they are thrown all together with other units. I recommend, therefore, that we link a corps currently occupying the front lines side by side with a newly inserted corps of the first attack echelon, but only when they are deployed at the attack base line, and only then just prior to the start of the attack.

This assumes that the corps currently in the line will brief the newly inserted corps on the terrain, the attack possibilities, and the enemy's infantry and artillery positions. Therefore, the corps already in the line must conduct all the reconnaissance missions required for the attack prior to the insertion of the new attacking corps. Such information must be documented in writing in the attack orders, supported by sketch maps as required. All of these preparations in detail should be supervised by the Sixth and Second Armies' headquarters.

Diversionary Attacks

Total quiet must be maintained along the entire attack front, other than the normal patrol activity. Along the other sectors of the front, units using their organic resources should stage well-prepared small-scale attacks with limited tactical objectives. Their purpose will be to tie down the enemy and, if possible, draw enemy reserves into that area.

I initially submitted this attack recommendation in an oral briefing to General von Falkenhayn. Then I submitted it in writing, with the above wording and a sketch map. I knew that General von Falkenhayn also had tasked the Sixth, Second, First, Seventh, Third, and Fifth Armies' headquarters with developing attack scenarios, and that Colonel Tappen had been sent to the Seventh Army for that purpose. The chief of staff of the newly formed Eleventh Army headquarters based in Maubeuge, Colonel Hans von Seeckt,[10] was also given the task of reconnoitering the attack options between La Bassée and the Somme. The content of these recommendations, however, remained unknown to me. I did know that the Fourth Army was planning to launch a large-scale gas attack, but they had to wait for favorable winds blowing in the direction of the enemy positions.[11]

During the period I worked with General von Falkenhayn I came to appreciate his special talent for grasping quickly the key issues of all the questions posed to him, and his ability to make rapid decisions accordingly. He had a rare command of language, which was a characteristic feature of his daily briefings to the Kaiser and in his multiple conferences with the senior commanders. He never lost his confidence and his trust in the troops and their leaders, even in critical situations. He insisted, even to the point of sharpness, that the frontline sectors threatened by the enemy be held with the minimum necessary forces. Such a procedure was necessary for us to be able to hold multiple sectors while retaining sufficient forces for us to conduct attacks. That, however, resulted in frequent and strong differences of opinion with the commanders on the Western Front and with Oberost on the correct balance of forces for the defensive. The Austrian High Command almost constantly begged for German support, but General von Falkenhayn was especially reluctant to commit such support, except in the direst of circumstances. In person and on the telephone, General von Falkenhayn could be very temperamental, and he frequently caused hard feelings without intending to. That was the main reason he had only a few friends and supporters. His whole demeanor was the reason he never quite earned the absolute trust of the Kaiser and the commanders of the field armies.[12]

Communications between Falkenhayn and Chancellor Theobald von Bethmann-Hollweg, whose slow decision making created many problems, were especially strained. That resulted in a lively direct telegram exchange between Falkenhayn and General Conrad von Hötzendorf over political issues and the conduct of Austrian diplomacy. Falkenhayn continually demanded that Austria yield its southern border regions to Italy. Falkenhayn hoped that the result would be to preempt both Italy and Romania from joining the Entente. In my opinion, it was only Falkenhayn's firm position on this issue that postponed Italy's and Romania's declaration of war against the Central Powers.

General von Falkenhayn was especially careful in operational matters. The war that had to be fought on two fronts, however, required bold and sweeping decisions with the far-reaching objective of destroying our opponents sequentially by launching powerful offensives. But General von Falkenhayn could never quite muster the necessary will to the necessary decision, either in the east or in the west.

As early as March 1915 Falkenhayn started withdrawing five army corps from the Western Front: the Guards Corps; the XLI Army Corps; the II Bavarian Army Corps with the 11th Bavarian Division; the III Army Corps with the 113th Division; and the X Army Corps with the 111th Division. Additionally, a new corps was formed with the 119th and the 121st Divisions and a division withdrawn from the X Reserve Corps. All of these formations, including the cavalry divisions still positioned in the west, were given an extended period of intense training in attack procedures far behind the front lines. Thus, the capability of the Western Front to resist enemy attacks was severely weakened. An additional forty harnessed heavy field howitzer batteries were also withdrawn from the west and replaced with the same number of the older type unharnessed field howitzer batteries.[13]

Toward the end of March, the situation along the Austrian Carpathian front increasingly became serious. After Fortress Przemyśl capitulated on 22 March, the Russians quickly shifted their excess forces from that sector to the Carpathian front and launched strong attacks that the Austrians were incapable of resisting. Conrad von Hötzendorf sent us appeals for support on an almost daily basis. General August von Cramon, the German liaison officer at Austrian General Headquarters, reported that the situation was so serious that General von Falkenhayn took three German divisions then in the east—the 25th Reserve Division from the Ninth Army; the 35th Reserve Division from Army Detachment Woyrsch; and the 4th Division from the Southern Army—and formed an ad hoc unit designated the Beskids Corps[14] under the command of General Wolf Rudolf Freiherr von Marschall von Altengottern. The timely attack launched by that corps prevented Austria's Beskids and Carpathian fronts from collapsing.

When Russian successes in the Carpathians and into Hungary made it likely that Italy would enter the war, Austria at Falkenhayn's urging offered to cede to Italy Southern Tyrol, including Trento. Italy rejected the offer as inadequate and made additional demands in Austria's coastal region. Simultaneously, Italy started to move troops to its border with Austria, finally demanding all of Tyrol up to the Brenner Pass. Falkenhayn advised Conrad von Hötzendorf to appease the Italian demands as a way of gaining the freedom of action necessary for launching large-scale operational attacks on both the Eastern and Western Fronts. Conrad von Hötzendorf rejected Falkenhayn's pressures, insisting that with German support ten Austrian divisions could be assembled for an Austrian attack against Serbia. For obvious reasons, General von Falkenhayn did not support the Austrian request. By that point he had lost all confidence in the efficacy of any Austrian attacks. Furthermore, any commitment of German divisions to Austria's defensive front in the east would have made impossible any option for transitioning to a large-scale operational attack that would have sufficient force. It seemed to me that during that critical period General von Falkenhayn was considering taking down Serbia primarily with German troops, and only then launching a large-scale attack in the west.

As a result of the increasingly serious situation in the east, General Conrad von Hötzendorf increased his urgent demands for the war to be decided in the east. General von Falkenhayn therefore grew more and more doubtful about tying down strong German forces in the west by committing them to a large-scale attack, which undoubtedly would take a longer time. The danger to the Austrian monarchy would thus grow larger. A Russian breakthrough in Hungary most likely would be followed by Italy and Romania joining the enemy alliance. The overall situation also caused more difficulties in our alliance with Turkey. The Turks, on 18 March, had managed to repel an attack by British and French naval forces against the Dardanelles, but the serious danger there had not been eliminated completely. Turkish Army commander Enver Pasha had formed an army of five Turkish divisions under German general Otto Liman von Sanders[15] for the defense of the Dardanelles. That force, however, was only combat capable if it could be equipped with German materiel, especially ammunition for the heavy guns.

Thus the plan developed to open the passage to Turkey by seizing Serbia, thereby bringing Bulgaria in on the side of Germany and Austria. Bulgaria refused, however, even though Turkey offered to commit two army corps to the attack on Serbia. Field Marshal Colmar von der Goltz was deeply involved in all these negotiations, but as the representative of Enver Pasha he never gained direct access to the king of Bulgaria. Field Marshal von der Goltz consequently went to Romania for talks with General Conrad von Hötzendorf, and from there he traveled to Mézières.

In the meantime, Falkenhayn of his own volition made the decision to launch a large-scale operational attack in the east. Based on the experiences from the February attack in the east, he came to the conclusion that an attack from both wings of the Eastern Front would not catch the Russian Army in a destructive pincer. He therefore decided on a breakthrough north of the Carpathians along the Tarnów–Gorlice line, advancing in a generally easterly direction. The objective would be to eliminate the ever-increasing danger to the Carpathian front. Falkenhayn intended to exercise direct command over the entire attack in the east. The actual breakthrough was to be accomplished by a newly inserted German field army composed entirely of German units, supported by the Austrian Fourth Army on the northern flank. The newly inserted German Eleventh Army would be commanded by General of Cavalry August von Mackensen, who had been in command of the Ninth Army. Colonel Hans von Seeckt would continue as Mackensen's chief of staff. The already existing Eleventh Army headquarters was moved from Maubeuge to Kassel initially. The former commanding general of the Eleventh Army, General von Fabeck, was reassigned as the commanding general of the First Army, replacing Colonel General Alexander von Kluck, who was severely wounded on 28 March 1915.

General von Falkenhayn personally developed the staging and attack plan. He tasked me to develop a concept map showing the recommended march routes and attack sectors of the five involved army corps. I also was tasked to develop recommended courses of action for the destruction of the Russian front in the Carpathians following the breakthrough. I briefed the concept map to General von Falkenhayn the following day. I emphasized that right from the beginning of the breakthrough attacks the adjacent sectors north and south would have to use their own assets to tie down the enemy forces to their fronts, thereby preventing them from attacking the flanks of our breakthrough.

Falkenhayn concurred with the attack in the northern sector, but he thought it would make more sense to pull back the Carpathian front on the southern flank of the breakthrough sector shortly before the start of the attack. That would draw in the Russians, who certainly would pursue into the rough and trackless terrain of the Carpathians. Such an evasive action and subsequent Russian pursuit in the Carpathians, combined with a quick and very deep breakthrough in the primary attack sector, would produce several advantageous results. But if we did not succeed in a decisive breakthrough, there was a danger that the Russians would penetrate deeply into Hungary, and that the Austrian resistance would crumble. The experiences in the east had taught us that it was very difficult to halt the Austrians once they started falling back. I recommended instead to Falkenhayn that the Carpathian sector with all of its reserve forces should move forward from their current positions. If the main breakthrough succeeded, these forces could then attack immediately and prevent the Russian reserves from shifting against the southern flank of our breakthrough.

In March, Falkenhayn started the preparations for the breakthrough attack at Tarnów–Gorlice. The staff of the Railways Department reconnoitered in detail the options for the transportation and deployment, and calculated the required staging times. German General Staff officers conducted terrain reconnaissance for the approach march into the attack positions. Toward the middle of April all of the reconnaissance was to be completed.

In the evening of 31 March, Colonel Tappen returned from the Seventh Army, where he had reconnoitered the ground for a large-scale attack operation in that sector. He immediately reassumed the functions of the chief of operations, and I reverted to my previous position as his assistant. The period when I was in charge during Colonel Tappen's absence had been professionally rewarding for me, because I carried a high level of responsibility, which was very gratifying. My old tasks, nevertheless, remained interesting. I heard everything, saw everything, spoke with many senior-level leaders, and influenced the preparation phase for the highest-level decisions.

On 1 April, General von der Goltz Pasha[16] arrived in Mézières and immediately had long meetings with General von Falkenhayn. In the evening he dined at the officers' mess with a small circle, which included me. The large pot of caviar he had brought with him was quite a treat for us. He departed on 2 April. That same day General Conrad von Hötzendorf raised the question of a special peace between Germany-Austria and Russia, and he wanted to discuss the issue with Falkenhayn. The latter left for Berlin on 3 April and returned on 5 April. During that same period the Beskids Corps attacked and stabilized the situation in the Carpathians.

On Easter Sunday, 4 April, I wrote the following letter to my wife, which summed up my firm convictions at the time:

> Easter Sunday! The bells are ringing, but so is the rolling of the cannon thunder. Strange contrasts! The peaceful heart and the warrior's heart are in conflict; sometimes the one and sometimes the other has the upper hand. The routine of the office reminds me constantly of the naked reality, and without complaint the soldier soldiers on. Rain and fog are prevalent in the Meuse valley. There is no Easter sun. Just like this Easter weather, the prospects for peace are equally bleak. The future is veiled in darkness. The few neutral states are ready to strike against us. Italy is mobilizing its troops. Romania may start anytime now. Since yesterday China is at war with Japan. The whole world is ablaze. Almost every state is fighting for its survival; but Germany is also fighting for its prevalent role in the world. Our means are plenty and our weapons are deadly. We shall never give up what we have seized. It is a form of firm security, a heavy prize in any peace negotiations. That is the main advantage of our current situation. Our submarines are continuing to do their duty. Their average kill rate per two-week mission is ten steamers. The British naval establishment is in shock. Food prices and wages in Britain are increasing daily. Their industry is already showing big, open wounds. Our main enemy has been hit in his main artery. Slowly but consistently his trade on the high seas will bleed to death, and on land his militia army will do likewise in our lines. This bloodletting takes time, but it has a sure effect.[17] Victory is ours, but it cannot be accomplished overnight. The beautiful words "Peace on Earth" are still a long way off.

On 9 April, right after the general briefing, Falkenhayn sent me off to reconnoiter the situation of Army Detachment Strantz. It was fighting between Verdun and Metz, where it was dealing with heavy French attacks. I was supposed to be back by midnight and then report immediately. I took off in a fast staff car. After a short report to General Hermann von Strantz, who had been my former commander in the 2nd Guards Regiment, I visited all the corps commanders whose front lines were affected by the attack. From there I conducted individual probes and terrain walks into the forward lines. Everywhere I was met with confidence and the full trust that the positions would be held. As in my earlier reconnaissance visit to the Third Army, the troop leaders were especially delighted by the appearance of an OHL officer, who exposed himself recklessly to the fire and who promised to champion their modest requests. Shortly after midnight I was back in Mézières and immediately gave General von Falkenhayn an oral report of my thoroughly positive impressions of the leaders and troops. He immediately authorized the support requests that I had brought back from the front lines.

It was not until 13 April that General von Falkenhayn informed General Conrad von Hötzendorf about his breakthrough plan north of the Carpathians. He sent him a long telegram, also suggesting that during the staging phase of the attack formations the Carpathian front should gradually disengage from the enemy just before the attack, thereby drawing the enemy into the Carpathians. The telegram also reemphasized the necessity of Austria's accommodating Italy's demands to the maximum extent possible, to keep that country calm until at least the completion of the planned attack operations in the east. General von Falkenhayn suggested a conference for the evening of 14 April in Berlin. During that conference the breakthrough attack at Tarnów–Gorlice was decided on, and Conrad von Hötzendorf agreed, albeit reluctantly, to overall German command of the attack. The attack date of 2 May was agreed on. General von Falkenhayn assumed overall command of the operation in the east; General von Mackensen was assigned the command of the breakthrough attack. Besides his own Eleventh Army, he also had operational control of the Austrian Fourth Army, linked in on his northern flank. The initial attack objective was a breakthrough of the Russian front, which would make the Russian positions up to the Łupków Pass in the Carpathian Mountains untenable.

On the morning of 16 April, General von Falkenhayn and Colonel Tappen returned to Mézières from Berlin, where they had briefed the Kaiser following the conference. Before leaving Berlin they also had a long discussion with Colonel Hans von Seeckt[18] about the staging and execution of the attack. Meanwhile, the enemy had grown a little more active along the Western Front. Part of a position on the Loretto Ridge was lost in the Sixth Army sector. Six bombs fell on Charleville, causing only minor damage. An enemy airship dropped bombs over Strasbourg, injuring a number of civilians but causing minimal damage. Enemy aerial activity also increased in several army sectors.

On 17 April, General von Falkenhayn left Mézières for talks with the army and unit commanders at Metz, Strasbourg, and Colmar. I accompanied him, while Colonel Tappen remained in Mézières. We made the round trip in a special troop train, with a salon car to serve as the conference room. The information presented at the conferences indicated quite clearly that there was no immediate threat on the Western Front between Verdun and the Swiss border. The commanders in all sectors were confident of their ability to repulse any enemy attacks with their own assets.

On the evening of 18 April we returned to Mézières, where General von Mackensen had arrived earlier in the day. The following day he and Falkenhayn had a long meeting, after which I was able to say hello briefly to General von Mackensen. I asked him to take me with him back to the east, but all the General Staff positions at Eleventh Army headquarters were currently filled. I asked him to suggest to General von Falkenhayn my assignment as a General Staff officer for special duties—for example, as a liaison officer with the adjacent armies. Mackensen did this, but Falkenhayn initially was noncommittal. He promised to send a telegraphic answer to Metz, where General von Mackensen intended to meet with the Kaiser. Within hours after Mackensen's departure, Falkenhayn sent the telegram saying I was indispensable to OHL. Thus, my quiet hopes to get back to a frontline assignment failed, to my regret.

On the morning of 20 April, General von Falkenhayn and Colonel Tappen departed again to check on the situations at the Fourth, Sixth, and Second Armies. They returned on 22 April, confirmed in Falkenhayn's assessment that no large-scale enemy attacks were imminent and that the Western Front required only a small number of OHL reserves during the upcoming large-scale German attack in the east. General von Falkenhayn had requested that all of the western army commanders conduct in the near future a series of smaller and larger attack operations with their own available forces, to tie down the opposing enemy and to feign the coming of larger attacks in the west. In the evening of 23 April, I was invited to a very pleasant dinner with the Kaiser.

On 24 April, Army Detachment Strantz attacked successfully with its right wing against the Combres Heights, taking twenty-four French officers and sixteen hundred soldiers prisoner. They then held the ground against strong, deliberate counterattacks. On 25 April, Army Detachment Gaede captured nine hundred prisoners during an attack at Hartmannswillerkopf in the Vosges Mountains in Alsace. On 27 April the Third Army conducted a successful local attack, cleaning out a French pocket in their sector that had been there since the winter battle. On 27 April the northern wing of the German Army on the Eastern Front launched a large diversionary attack. The 78th Reserve Division, 3rd Division, and Bavarian Cavalry Division achieved a rapid success.

In Flanders, the Fourth Army had for some time been preparing to conduct a gas attack along a wide sector. A large number of gas cylinders had been installed along the front line of the XXIII Corps and XXV Reserve Corps, which were oriented south between the Channel and Poelkapelle. The release of the gas, however, was only possible when the wind was blowing directly toward the enemy positions. After a long wait, that finally happened on the afternoon of 22 April. Once the gas was released, the troops moved out and followed the gas cloud forward, taking three to four kilometers of ground. They then held those gains against British deliberate counterattacks starting on 24 April. That same day the wind was again favorable, and gas was released from the cylinders along the frontline trace of the XXVI Reserve Corps, which had not participated in the 22 April attack. The right wing of the adjacent XXVII Reserve Corps to the south also supported that attack. More gains were made along the entire sector by rapidly moving forward reserves that were drawn from the XXII Reserve Corps to the north, and also from the Naval Corps.[19] Enemy resistance then rapidly increased with the approach of the British reserves, supported by arriving French divisions. Another gas attack released on 2 May yielded only small ground gains. On 3 and 4 May, however, the enemy retook his positions that were threatened by pincer arms from two sides, pushing well forward on both sides of the Ypres–Zonnebeke road. The German counterattack immediately thrust forward in coordination with the XXVII Reserve Corps and the right wing of the XV Army Corps to the south. The Fourth Army attack order established the objective as the line of the Ypres Canal, but increasing enemy resistance prevented us from advancing that far. The new enemy positions ran in an arc five to seven kilometers east of Ypres. On 5 May the XV Army Corps succeeded in occupying and holding the earlier much-contested Hill 60, which was important for artillery observation. On 4 May, General von Falkenhayn and Colonel Tappen went to reconnoiter the situation at the Fourth Army, whose front lines had contracted considerably. During its attacks the Fourth Army suffered approximately thirty-five thousand killed and wounded. The British and the French lost more than twice that number.

On 2 May, following a thorough artillery preparation, the German Eleventh and Austrian Fourth Armies on the Eastern Front launched the breakthrough attack at Tarnów–Gorlice. They made good progress right from the start. The reports during the subsequent days were so favorable that General von Falkenhayn, with the consent of the Kaiser, decided to execute the already planned move of OHL from Mézières to Pless.[20] Along with seven other General Staff officers, I was instructed to remain in Mézières as OHL's principle liaison officer on the Western Front.

I knew that initially only two major communications stations were available to handle direct connections between Mézières and Pless. The station at Pless still had quite a few limitations that could not be upgraded before the displacement of OHL on 7 May. In the afternoon of 6 May, I asked Colonel Tappen for precise clarification of what *Vollmacht*[21] authority I would have in case of unforeseen events in the west. His short answer was that everything would be controlled and directed from Pless. I pointed out the very poor communications between Mézières and Pless, plus the fact that OHL would be out of communications during the period it was displacing to the east, but Tappen said that his decision stood. I then tried to get some clarity on the extent of my authority by asking General von Falkenhayn directly. He cut me off with the brief words, "I trust you completely and you will do the right thing." In the event, the bad communications connections to Pless very quickly forced me to act independently in the west.

During the period that OHL was in Pless, the Western Front had a strength of ninety-seven German divisions. According to OHL's Intelligence Division, we were facing 110 to 112 enemy divisions. Of our ninety-seven divisions, seven and a half divisions were in OHL reserve. They included the 58th Division behind the Sixth Army at Lille and the 115th Division at Douai; a combined infantry brigade behind the Second Army at Péronne; a combined infantry brigade behind the Seventh Army at Laon; the 117th Division behind the Third Army at Rethel; the VIII Army Corps (minus one infantry brigade, which was deployed with the III Bavarian Army Corps) behind Army Detachment Strantz; and the X Reserve Corps behind Army Detachment Falkenhausen at Strasbourg.

Shortly before OHL's displacement to Pless, General von Falkenhayn issued directives to the Fourth, Sixth, Second, First, and Third Armies instructing them to improve their forwardmost fighting positions continually, and also to establish a second rearward position approximately two kilometers from the front line. The armies, however, did not have the necessary labor troops to construct such positions, and they had to resort temporarily to reconnoitering and marking out those positions on the ground. Nonetheless, the standing order to hold the forwardmost line at all costs remained in effect. General von Falkenhayn and Colonel Tappen, accompanied by a large operational staff, left Mézières by train on the morning of 7 May.

On the morning of 9 May a gigantic British-French attack against the Sixth Army sector broke loose between Loos and Arras. The indicators of such an attack started appearing on 1 May, when the enemy increased his preparatory fires. By the morning of 9 May the fire tempo increased into a full-scale barrage in the center of the Sixth Army's sector, held by the VII and XIV Army Corps and the I Bavarian Reserve Corps. The enemy fire flattened the forward German trenches and caused very heavy losses. Toward 1100 hours a vastly superior enemy infantry attack advanced under an artillery umbrella. A staunch resistance, combined with hasty counterattacks launched by the local reserves, allowed the Sixth Army to hold its lines generally, although we did lose some ground. The strongest attacks were against the left wing of the XIV Army Corps, fighting on both sides of the Loretto Ridge. We managed to even out our lines by conducting a deliberate counterattack with the reserve forces that we brought up rapidly. Nonetheless, the 5th Bavarian Reserve Division in the south was pushed back approximately three kilometers along a seven-kilometer-wide front, suffering very heavy losses.

As soon as the initial reports started coming in, I knew immediately from my own frontline experience that the Sixth Army's situation was serious. They no longer had their own consolidated reserves. That afternoon the Sixth Army headquarters correctly requested the immediate forward commitment of the 58th and 115th Divisions. It was impossible to get a rapid decision from General von Falkenhayn. I knew that on 8 May he had been with the Kaiser at the Eleventh Army headquarters, and he would not be back in Pless with Colonel Tappen until 9 May. The remainder of the OHL operational staff was on a train between Berlin and Pless. Falkenhayn would not be back in a position to approve Sixth Army's request until the evening of 9 May at the earliest.

Thus, I decided without hesitation to approve on my own responsibility the Sixth Army's request, and I ordered the attachment of the 58th and 115th Divisions to the Sixth Army. I sent a radio message and a telegram to Pless reporting my actions. Throughout the afternoon and evening I tried constantly to establish a telephonic connection with Pless via the telephone center of the Deputy General Staff in Berlin. I was not able to get through until the night of 10 May. The connection, however, was so bad that although General von Falkenhayn could understand my description of the situation and my directive, his words came back completely unrecognizable. I had to ask the female telephone operator in Berlin to relay the conversation. I told her to ask Falkenhayn if he concurred with my directives. After a short break the answer came back, "General von Falkenhayn is in agreement with everything." That night the telegraphic approval of my directive arrived, including the approval of my recommendation to move the 117th Division, which was then was located behind the Third Army, from Rethel to Douai as the OHL reserve behind the Sixth Army. My directive, which was already prepared, also reinforced the Sixth Army with a larger number of heavy batteries from the OHL reserve.

I want to recall here a noteworthy experience that made my duties in Mézières rather difficult. General von Falkenhayn had given his full support to my independent actions on 9 May. Colonel Tappen, however, saw my independent action as undermining his authority, and he ordered me to desist from issuing further independent directives on the Western Front. When on 8 June General von Falkenhayn came to Mézières for a short period, I told him about Colonel Tappen's directive to me, and I asked him for clarification of my authority. General von Falkenhayn was very surprised by Colonel Tappen's order. Falkenhayn in turn gave me the order to continue as before. I later heard from Pless that Colonel Tappen was very upset that Falkenhayn had overruled him. Nonetheless, sometime later he sent me the following personal telegram from Pless: "Directives and inquiries to army headquarters in the west will only be issued from here, not from there. In the future I insist that you only forward orders that have been generated here." Since my independent action on 9 May, I had not issued any more directives to the armies' headquarters. Colonel Tappen's order to desist, therefore, had no real practical effect. But the order to refrain also from requesting information directly from the armies' headquarters meant a complete restriction of my duties that was completely incomprehensible. In order to keep OHL in Pless updated beyond the scope of the routine morning, noon, and evening reports, I constantly had the chiefs of staff of the armies that were in contact with the enemy give me situation updates. I had to develop a work-around of Tappen's order by having one of my staff officers ask the army chiefs on their own accord to call me directly in the case of sudden, unforeseen events. During General von Falkenhayn's next visit to the Western Front I told him in no uncertain terms the difficulties that Colonel Tappen's order was making for me. General von Falkenhayn fully understood my dilemma, and he again authorized me to communicate directly with the armies' headquarters.

Colonel Tappen and I had completely opposite personalities. For me, objective action was the primary operating principle, and on that basis I always had good relations with my superiors and my subordinates. Colonel Tappen was focused above all else on protecting his position as the chief of the Operations Division. That was his right, of course. But with his highly developed sense of self-confidence it was rather difficult for his subordinates to get along with him.[22] I cite here yet another example. All of my colleagues in the Operations Division who stayed behind in the Mézières rear detachment had never been in the front lines. In order to develop these gentlemen professionally, I frequently during calm periods sent one of these young General Staff officers from Mézières to the Argonne Forest, to observe the limited attack operations of the XVI Army Corps. They always came back ecstatic about their experiences. Naturally, in their temporary absence their workload had to be carried by other staff officers, or by me personally. When Colonel Tappen learned what I was doing, he completely forbade any further trips to the front. His mind-set was totally incomprehensible to me. General von Falkenhayn apparently knew that there was no real bond of trust between Colonel Tappen and me. When on 26 September 1915 he told me about my reassignment as chief of staff of the Third Army, which was then heavily engaged in the autumn battles in Champagne, he said to me, "You must be happy to get away from Tappen." I could only agree heartily. Having to work on a daily basis with Tappen much longer would have been a serious strain on my nerves.

At this point I want to return to the heavy and costly fighting of the Sixth Army. I will describe in more detail that action which was consuming virtually all of my time at Mézières. Even though I was only in an advisory capacity, I ensured through frequent telephone conversations and reports that the Sixth Army always had sufficient reserves available. The four divisions of the XIV Army Corps and the I Bavarian Reserve Corps were defending, as we soon learned, against twelve French divisions that were supported by a greatly superior artillery force. The 5th Bavarian Division initially was supported by the 115th Division, but in very short order two-thirds of the 58th Division had to be moved into this sector. The planned deliberate counterattack was made more difficult, time-wise, because large losses of ground had forced elements of our artillery to displace behind Vimy Ridge, from where they had to register again. On 10 May the situation in the 28th Division and the 5th Bavarian Reserve Division sectors remained quite critical. That evening the 58th and 115th Divisions launched a deliberate counterattack. It made good progress at first, but it was not able to push through the far superior enemy. Farther north, then, the left wing of the 28th Division, reinforced by a regiment from the 58th Division, remained threatened in the sector of Carency and the Loretto Ridge north of that town. So did the right wing of the 1st Bavarian Reserve Division, which was linked in to the south.

The situation was critical, but good nerves prevailed at the Sixth Army headquarters. OHL committed the 117th Division to the Sixth Army and ordered the movement of the VIII Army Corps headquarters and 16th Division to Douai as the OHL reserve

On 12 May the situation at the 5th Bavarian Reserve Division became so serious that two-thirds of the 117th Division were attached to it. OHL therefore attached the corps headquarters of the VIII Army Corps and the 16th Division to the Sixth Army and redeployed an infantry brigade of the VIII Army Corps' 15th Division to Douai as an OHL reserve unit.

Despite all of these reinforcements allocated to the I Bavarian Reserve Corps, the situation in the 5th Bavarian Reserve Division's sector and the adjacent sectors remained very tense. On 12 May, strong enemy attacks were repulsed and parts of the positions on the Loretto Ridge were retaken.

In order to ensure a unified command along the main battlefront, Army Task Group[23] Fasbender was formed with General Karl von Fasbender's own I

Bavarian Reserve Corps and the XIV Army Corps. Fasbender was ordered to hold and improve the current positions. On 12 May the enemy took the town of Carency, enveloping it from three sides. As a result, the left wing of the XIV Army Corps lost its positions along the Loretto Ridge–Ablain-Saint-Nazaire–Souchez line.

By 13 May the Sixth Army had lost approximately twenty thousand men. All of the units that had been involved in the fighting so far were very worn out. Based on the Sixth Army's report, OHL moved additional reinforcements forward, including the Fourth Army's 85th Reserve Brigade, attached to the XIV Army Corps; and the Second Army's 52nd Reserve Brigade, attached to the I Bavarian Reserve Corps. The X Reserve Corps' 2nd Guards Reserve Division was deployed to Douai as part of the OHL reserve. The commanding general of the III Army Corps, General Ewald von Lochow, and his chief of staff, General Walter von Bergmann, were also detached to the Sixth Army to assume command of one of the battle sectors.

The reliefs of the exhausted units started during the night of 13–14 May. The completely spent 5th Bavarian Reserve Division was replaced by the 16th, 58th, and 115th Divisions and half of the 15th Division, all under the VIII Army Corps. During the night of 15–16 May, General von Lochow assumed command of the main battle area, which he organized into three subsectors. The XIV Army Corps, with the 28th, 29th, and 117th Divisions and the 85th Reserve Brigade, was assigned to the sector north of Carency. The VIII Army Corps, with the 16th, 115th, and 58th Divisions and half of the 15th Division, assumed the sector from Carency to the Lens–Arras road. The I Bavarian Reserve Corps, with 1st Bavarian Reserve Division and 52nd Reserve Infantry Brigade, took over the adjacent sector to the south. The center sector also received the other half of the 15th Division, with the mission of retaking the heavily reinforced village of Neuville,[24] a large part of which was still held by the enemy. That attack started on 22 May, but it was only partially successful.

Since 12 May, the Sixth Army headquarters had received several telegrams from General von Falkenhayn demanding in no uncertain terms that the positions be held. He stressed the fact that large numbers of reinforcements had been committed to the Sixth Army. Nonetheless, the commanding general of the Sixth Army, Crown Prince Rupprecht of Bavaria, had complained directly to the Kaiser. General von Falkenhayn expressed his regret about the misunderstanding, considering the wishes of the Kaiser.

While the French initially refrained from conducting large-scale attacks, the British on 16 May moved against the VII Army Corps' positions and pushed the German lines back north of the La Bassée Canal on a three-kilometer width. With the help of reinforcements committed by the XIX Army Corps and the

6th Bavarian Reserve Division, and the deployment of the Fourth Army's 38th Landwehr Brigade, we lost no further ground until about 21 May.

I had sent my most senior General Staff officer, Major von Barttenwerfer, to the Sixth Army as a liaison officer. Through his very reliable reporting I was able to keep OHL in Pless continually informed about the Sixth Army's situation and the condition of its troops. In response, OHL allocated the 2nd Guards Reserve Division to the Sixth Army to reinforce the VII Army Corps. OHL also withdrew the 111th Division from Army Detachment Strantz and redeployed it to Douai as OHL reserve. The 15th Division's 80th Infantry Brigade also was withdrawn from Army Detachment Strantz and redeployed to the VIII Army Corps, fighting south of Souchez. Soon thereafter, the 123rd Division was withdrawn from the Seventh Army and shifted to Lille as the OHL reserve behind the Sixth Army. Artillery reinforcements also were attached to the Sixth Army, partially from the OHL reserve and partially from the other armies. The former chief of staff of the Sixth Army, Lieutenant General Konrad Krafft von Delmensingen, was assigned as the commander of the newly formed *Alpenkorps*.[25] Colonel Gustaf Graf von Lambsdorff, the former chief of staff of the X Army Corps, was assigned to the Sixth Army as his successor.

On 23 May the French resumed large-scale attacks, primarily against Army Task Group Lochow.[26] The French were thrown back with deliberate counterattacks only after a period of back-and-forth fighting. Our losses in dead and wounded were heavy, but the French losses were even heavier. OHL redeployed the 111th Division from Douai and attached it to the Sixth Army. Then OHL withdrew the IV Army Corps' 8th Division, which had been weakened during the fighting as a part of Army Detachment Strantz. The 58th Division replaced the 115th Division, which had suffered heavy losses at Neuville. At the beginning of June, the 5th Bavarian Reserve Division relieved the IV Army Corps' 7th Division. The entire IV Army Corps then reverted to the OHL ready reserve at Douai.

In the meantime, the French continued to commit their infantry relentlessly against Army Task Group Lochow, and we lost the village of Ablain.[27] We had to abandon Ablain voluntarily, because we did not have the forces necessary for a deliberate counterattack. The French continued to press their attacks and took parts of the town of Souchez. The British also resumed attacking farther north, but did not make any gains.

Based on the assumption that the Sixth Army would have to be reinforced with all the forces it needed, General von Falkenhayn ordered all of the other armies on the Western Front not to conduct any large-scale attacks, but to limit themselves to the defensive. The predictable but manageable consequence of that order was that the enemy started conducting diversionary attacks in many sectors, especially those of the Second and First Armies. The First Army suffered some considerable losses, requiring OHL to position the newly formed 183rd Infantry Brigade in the First Army's rear. On the other hand, the Fifth Army's XVI Army Corps achieved considerable success in the Argonne Forest with an attack that had been prepared for some time. The French sustained heavy losses. The Army Detachments Strantz, Falkenhausen, and Gaede had to fend off strong French attacks, but they were able to hold their positions or regain lost ground with their own assets.

In June the main battle area remained the sector of the Sixth Army and Army Task Group Lochow. With an almost uninterrupted sequence of both smaller and larger attacks, the French focused on the much-contested village of Neuville. The 15th Division was finally ordered to abandon the village to avoid further losses. The French also attacked again with fresh and strong forces in the Loretto Ridge sector. Heavy German losses there prompted the Sixth Army to commit elements of the IV Army Corps to relieve the exhausted units of the XIV Army Corps.

In the evening of 7 June, General von Falkenhayn returned from the east to the Western Front to assess personally the fighting. After a short stay with the Fourth Army, he held longer talks with the troop leaders of the Sixth Army. He concluded that the Sixth Army could hold its positions but, in light of the great superiority of the enemy, would need significant reinforcement with strong units. General von Falkenhayn then visited the headquarters of the Second, First, and Seventh Armies. During the afternoon of 8 June he returned to Mézières, where the chief of staff of the Third Army briefed him on the situation. After about a two-hour stay in Mézières, I accompanied General von Falkenhayn to the Fifth Army and Army Detachments Strantz, Falkenhausen, and Gaede for briefings on their situations. I was able to discuss many current questions with General von Falkenhayn on his special train. He gave me his assessment of what he considered my reliable work, and he directed me to continue in the same vein.

A relative calm started to settle in along the Sixth Army's sector toward the middle of June. While we were still in Mézières, General von Falkenhayn, after consulting with me, ordered the relief of the worn-out 115th Division by the First Army's 5th Division; of the 117th Division by the 123rd Division positioned near Lille; and of the XIV Army Corps by the IV Army Corps. The XIV Army Corps in turn was ordered to relieve the VI Army Corps on the right wing of the Third Army, which was then redeployed to the rear of the Sixth Army as OHL reserve. The short calm period in the Sixth Army sector made this relief very feasible. On 14 June the IV Army Corps took over the sector of the XIV Army Corps. The 117th Division, which had been fighting at the Loretto Ridge, then moved into the quieter right wing of the corps' sector. Simultaneously, the 7th Division was repositioned in the center and 8th Division on the left wing. Farther south, in the VIII Army Corps' sector, the 16th Division was positioned on the right, and the 5th Division on the left. In the I Bavarian Reserve Corps' sector the 58th Division was positioned on the right, and the 1st Bavarian Reserve Division on the left. Two approximately two- to five-kilometer-wide rearward positions were prepared behind our forwardmost positions, which were required to be held.

Starting on 14 June very heavy enemy artillery fire destroyed our newly constructed positions. At noon on 16 June a very strong and deeply echeloned French attack hit the center of Army Task Group Lochow. As we later determined, the French had intended to make a large-scale breakthrough. At first the French had some success, and at individual locations they penetrated deeply into the German positions. During that night the German troops fighting fiercely were able to regain almost everything through deliberate counterattacks. The French breakthrough attempt had failed. During the course of the fighting General von Falkenhayn detached the VI Army Corps from the Third Army and attached it to the Sixth Army. He also issued a directive to all the other armies on the Western Front that they would now have to make do with their own available forces because of the heavy fighting in the Sixth Army's sector.

On 17 June the French again launched an attack against Army Task Group Lochow, but they made only minor gains. In the meantime, the severely worn-out 16th Division was relieved by the VI Army Corps' 11th Division. General von Falkenhayn then attached units of the OHL reserve positioned in the rear of the Sixth Army directly to that army to reinforce its own reserve. Those units included the 123rd and 15th Divisions. Additionally, the Fifth Army's 187th Infantry Brigade, with two regiments, and Army Detachment Strantz's 5th Ersatz Brigade were shifted directly behind the Sixth Army as OHL reserve. The Fourth Army had to withdraw the XXVII Reserve Corps' 53rd Reserve Division to free up the Sixth Army's 3rd Bavarian Division, which was to relieve the 58th Division fighting on the right wing of the I Bavarian Reserve Corps. The Sixth Army also was reinforced with more heavy artillery.

Army Task Group Lochow had borne the brunt of the large-scale attacks. After the execution of all the relief actions, the line-up in the Army Task Group Lochow sector was, from right to left: the IV Army Corps with the 123rd, 117th, 7th, and 8th Divisions, and with the 5th Ersatz Brigade as corps reserve; the VIII Army Corps with the 11th and 5th Divisions. The plan was to insert the 12th Division north of 11th Division and thus shorten the sector of the IV Army Corps and the I Bavarian Reserve Corps, which consisted of the 3rd, 1st, and 5th Bavarian Reserve Divisions. The Sixth Army reserve was the III Army Corps'

6th Division, positioned at Douai. The VIII Army Corps, consisting of the 15th and 16th Division, was alerted pending OHL orders to redeploy behind the First Army.

From 18 June on, the enemy attacks weakened and only flared up occasionally along the inner boundary of the IV and VIII Army Corps. The 12th Division was deployed there at the time. On 28 June the commanding general of the VI Army Corps, General Kurt von Pritzelwitz, assumed operational control of the 12th Division and the former sector of the VIII Army Corps. That same day, Army Task Group Lochow was dissolved. In July the French only made occasional and futile forward probes, mostly against the VI Army Corps. Toward the end of July aerial reconnaissance detected active enemy transport movements across the Somme and toward the south. The assessment at this point was that the French had broken off their large-scale attack against the Sixth Army.

General von Falkenhayn decided that the heavy commitment of forces on the Western Front required a reinforcement by combat-ready units from the east. Thus, the 8th Bavarian Reserve Division and the 56th Division redeployed from the Eastern Front to the Western Front. The largely depleted 54th and 58th Divisions were then redeployed from the west to the east. In July OHL started a reorganization of the Western Front, with the objective of rebuilding complete and combat-effective units as reserves.

The former commanding general of the VII Army Corps, General Eberhard von Claer, was appointed General of the Engineer and Pioneer Corps, with orders to ensure uniform construction and improvement of the positions based on recent experience. One by one he visited all of the western armies. His energetic activities were beneficial, but in the process he was tagged with the nickname "trench devil."[28] General Ludwig von Lauter was appointed the General of the Artillery[29] at OHL, with the authority to supervise and coordinate the artillery operations of all the field armies. The skillful use of artillery was equally essential in the defense and the offense.

In my position as the OHL liaison officer at Mézières, I had no influence on the developments in the east and the other theaters of war. I did, however, monitor the tactical events in the east on a daily basis through the daily reports from Pless that were sent to Mézières, where we maintained a current situation map on the eastern operations. I followed the eastern operations closely and made assessments on the future actions in the east. At the time my thoughts on the Eastern Front were as follows:

The attacks by the German Eleventh Army and the Austrian Fourth Army initially had been planned only as tactical breakthroughs, but they quickly became operational successes. The adjacent sectors in the east then shifted to the attack in sequence. The most significant of those follow-on attacks was in the south, which greatly relieved the pressure on the Carpathian front, and also pushed the southern part of the Russian front in Galicia gradually back far to the east. The continuity of the Russian line was never broken, however. Przemyśl capitulated on 3 June and we reached Lwów on 22 June. We made significant tactical gains, which indirectly had the operational effect of the Russians giving up their planned attack on Turkey and the Bosporus. They were forced to use their troops in the east that had been earmarked for the Turkey attack. The German successes in Galicia also intimidated Romania into maintaining its neutrality. General von Falkenhayn correctly decided to expand the large-scale tactical success against the Russians into follow-on larger operations. He therefore turned the German Eleventh and Austrian Fourth Armies to the north for an attack at the beginning of July. He also reinforced this attacking force with the Beskids Corps, an infantry division that had been positioned on the Serbian border, and a cavalry division redeployed from Belgium. He also established the new Army of the Bug on the right wing of the attack. The operational task was to attack the flank of the Russian-held sector around Warsaw. It was a practical course of action. In my opinion, however, such an attack could only result in the absolutely necessary encirclement and destruction of the center and the northern part of the Russian Army if simultaneously the northern wing of the German Army made a wide encircling attack in a southerly direction toward the Rokitno Marshes. That would cut off the Russians' route of withdrawal to the east. Only the combination of the two operations could result in the destruction of the Russians. In order to give such a pincer attack from the north and the south the necessary resources for success, OHL had to assume the necessary risk by ordering all the sectors in Oberost that were not committed to the northern arm of the pincer to release as many of their major units as possible to support that operation. There was little possibility that the Russians would attack from their Warsaw salient to the west and north, because of threat from the south by Army Group Mackensen.[30]

The scenario I described above was the only course of action capable of achieving a successful breakthrough. As the German northern wing advanced, the Russians would have been forced to weaken the other sectors of their front. A rapid German thrust from the south, then, would most likely have forced the Russians to evacuate rapidly their salient at Warsaw. By withdrawing to the east they would have to abandon all their fortifications between the Bug and the Narew. With the German Eastern Front then considerably shortened, we would be able to reinforce our northern wing. Once that northern wing had gained maneuver space in the south, large parts of the Russian Army would not be able to evade destruction. Only then would the German Army in the West have sufficient forces to conduct large-scale and decisive offensive operations in the west.

General von Falkenhayn could not bring himself to make the decision for such an audacious operation. As I learned later, General von Hindenburg had recommended much the same thing. General von Falkenhayn was never focused on the destruction of the Russian Army as an objective, rather only on significantly weakening the Russians by pushing our eastern front forward far enough to establish a straight line between the Romanian border at Chernivtsi and the Baltic Sea.

On 2 July, Oberost headquarters in Posnań conducted a decision briefing on the operational course of action. Unfortunately, the Kaiser approved General von Falkenhayn's recommendation for all further actions in the east. According to that plan, the German northern wing would not form the northern arm of our encirclement pincer, but rather that arm would be launched from the area east of the Vistula against the Narew line. Army Task Group Gallwitz[31] would start the attack on 12 July on both sides of Przasnysz, advancing toward the southeast.

General von Falkenhayn believed that such an attack toward the north and south would defeat the Russians in their salient around Warsaw. That hope failed to materialize, however, as the Russians recognized the dangerous threat they faced. They evaded to the east in sufficient time to avoid destruction. The consequence was a frontal and very time-consuming pursuit, during which the Russians suffered heavy losses but remained combat effective. An attack finally launched from the German northern wing came much too late and did not break through, because after their withdrawal the Russians were able to muster superior forces.

Despite the great loss of time resulting from Falkenhayn's eastern operations, we still managed to transfer just in time reserves from the east to the severely threatened Western Front. We also had sufficient forces for the more urgently required attack on Serbia.

The long-planned and -prepared attack on Serbia required initially a crossing of the wide Danube in the face of the enemy. Such was necessary because of the Austrian failure during the Russian attacks in Galicia and the redeployment of strong Austrian forces to Italy. By that point Italy had declared war, but so far against Austria only. Italy then attacked at the Isonzo and into Tyrol. The operation against Serbia, therefore, had to be executed primarily by German and Bulgarian troops. General von Mackensen commanded, and he almost completely destroyed the Serbian Army. I shall now return to the discussion of the operations on the Western Front.

On 29 July 1915, I accompanied General von Falkenhayn to a conference in Metz with all of the Western Front army chiefs of staff. Falkenhayn started by conveying the Kaiser's gratitude to all of the army headquarters. He then briefly summarized the fighting in the east, without going into the details of the German operational decisions. The Russians were fighting tougher now than previously. They strongly occupied every hill in their sectors. The blood toll was low, however, because whenever the Germans attacked the Russian infantry almost always gave up as soon as their artillery pulled back. The German losses were manageable. Our progress, however was slow because of terrain difficulties, supplies, and the Russian way of fighting. A specific timeframe for ending the eastern operations was not yet clear. In the meantime, the German armies in the west would have to hold their positions with their available forces.

The army chiefs of staff then briefed in detail on the situations in their sectors and their assessment of the enemy to their fronts. Most of the armies had no cohesive reserves. Only elements of the battalions of the individual infantry regiments that were in a rest status were available for immediate commitment by the various army headquarters. Despite those reports, General von Falkenhayn insisted that the army chiefs withdraw additional forces to form cohesive reserves, and make detailed preparations to reinforce immediately any sectors that came under attack. Even though the chiefs of staff of the Third and Sixth Armies reported on the enemy's attack preparations in their sectors, General von Falkenhayn considered a large-scale enemy attack improbable. The British had participated only in the first phase of the French Arras Offensive. Current indicators suggested that the British were especially suffering from a lack of ammunition. The British political objective currently was focused on the Dardanelles. On the Continent they were satisfied with standing on the defensive and, along with the French, holding on to whatever ground they had gained in their offensives to date. A British attack on their own volition was only conceivable in the event of a total collapse of the Russian northern armies, and even then only as long as our current forces on the Eastern Front were still tied down in Russia. In terms of numbers, the British were hardly capable of conducting a large-scale offensive at this time. On the Belgian front the six British divisions (including one Kitchener division) were tied firmly to their positions. Of their twenty-six other divisions, six were from Kitchener's New Army and were still in training.

General von Falkenhayn also did not believe that the French would launch a large-scale offensive. They might make an attempt in Alsace and in Lorraine to gain bargaining chips for the conclusion of the war. Falkenhayn believed that the movements in this sector reported by the Third Army's chief of staff were only relief operations of the units in the French lines. Falkenhayn then directed all the army chiefs of staff to maintain constant situational awareness of the enemy's actions, and to conduct small-scale advances to develop the situation, even at the cost of blood and ammunition. Along with all the chiefs of staff, I was rather surprised by General von Falkenhayn's views at the time. Less than two months later he had to admit that he had been overly optimistic. General von Falkenhayn also reemphasized the details of the conduct of the defensive battle, which did not really give the army chiefs of staff anything new.

Soon after the 29 July briefing, Army Group German Crown Prince was formed with the Fifth Army and the Army Detachments Strantz, Falkenhausen, and Gaede. From the beginning of August almost the entire Western Front settled into a period of calm. That prompted OHL to shift the III Army Corps' headquarters and its 6th and 115th Divisions from the Western Front. The 85th Reserve Brigade, which was positioned in the Third Army's sector, also was redeployed to the XXII Reserve Corps in the east. I was most uncomfortable with that decision, because I thought increasingly that our enemy in the west was marshaling new forces for a large-scale attack. If that happened, OHL had only three complete and two weak divisions in reserve on the Western Front. The 54th Reserve Division was behind the Fourth Army; the 123rd Division was behind the Sixth Army; the 113th Division was behind Army Detachment Strantz; the 183rd Infantry Brigade was behind Army Detachment Falkenhausen; and the 185th Infantry Brigade was behind Army Detachment Gaede.

During the first half of August British troops took over the positions north of the Somme that had been manned by the French. The French, however, continued to hold the positions on both sides of Arras. At the end of August our Intelligence Division estimated the enemy reserve to total fifty French and British divisions. As we continued our operations in the east, it was predictable that these enemy reserves would be committed to attacks on the Western Front to relieve the pressure on the Russians.

From the beginning of September reports from the Sixth and Third Armies increasingly indicated imminent and large-scale enemy attacks in their sectors. In all the other army sectors the enemy only conducted limited attacks and made feints by shifting his infantry positions and increasing his artillery fire. In August a French attack in Army Detachment Gaede's sector resulted in extended fighting into the middle of September. Despite the back-and-forth results, it did not evolve into large-scale operations.

As I later learned, General von Falkenhayn, during a meeting in Metz at the end of July, had tasked the chief of staff of Army Group German Crown Prince, General Konstantin Schmidt von Knobelsdorf, with reconnoitering a German attack to clear the Entente out of Alsace. Supposedly, this directive had something to do with General von Falkenhayn's hopes for reaching a peace agreement, initially with the Russians, and then with the Western Powers. If he could achieve that, it would be important for us to have complete control of Alsace.[32] This purely political reason for an attack in Alsace, however, was mooted when the hopes for peace failed to materialize.

At the end of August 1915, Falkenhayn attached the 123rd Division to the Sixth Army to strengthen its reserve. He also decided, finally, to reinforce the entire Western Front. He ordered the Guards Corps and the X Army Corps to redeploy from the east, but both units faced long march routes to reach their points of embarkation. Their movement to the west only started on 11 September. Both corps initially moved into rest quarters in the area of the General Government of Belgium.[33] The XXII Reserve Corps was to follow later from the east. The redeployment of twenty-six heavy batteries from the east also started at the beginning of September, but in turn the Western Front had to release the same number of more modern heavy batteries to support the planned attack against Serbia. The batteries from the east did not arrive in the west until 20 September.

On 17 September the First Army headquarters was withdrawn from the Western Front and redeployed to the east.[34] The First Army's IX Reserve Corps was transferred to the Second Army, and the IX and VIII Army Corps to the Seventh Army. On 22 September OHL had the following reserves on the Western Front: the 53rd Reserve Division, which had been relieved by the 54th Division, was behind the Fourth Army; the newly formed 192nd Infantry Brigade was behind the Seventh Army; the 5th Division was behind the Third Army; the 113th Division was behind Army Detachment Strantz; the 56th Division was behind Army Detachment Falkenhausen; and the 19th Reserve Division and 181st Infantry Brigade were behind Army Detachment Gaede.[35] By that date the Guards Corps had arrived Belgium, as well as the headquarters of the X Army Corps and its 20th Division. The corps' 19th Division was still in transit to the west. For an artillery reserve OHL had only thirteen modern heavy batteries and eleven batteries that did not have their own organic horses for transport.

During September, the Sixth Army and especially the Third Army reported increasingly strong indicators of large-scale attacks developing against their sectors. From 12 September both armies reported the increasing registration of enemy artillery and the buildup of forces behind the enemy's front lines. The Sixth Army expected an attack north of Arras against the front lines of its VII, IV, and VI Army Corps; the Third Army on its left, against the XII and VIII Reserve Corps. The Fifth Army also thought that an attack was possible against the XVIII Reserve Corps on its right wing. These assessments later proved to be correct. The Sixth and Third Armies also forecast that the large-scale enemy attacks would be attempted breakthroughs.

Colonel General Karl von Einem, the commander of the Third Army, met with me several times in Mézières during September. With an increasing sense of urgency, he noted the indicators pointing to the approach of a wide and deeply echeloned major French attack, supported with far superior artillery. I could only advise him to turn directly to OHL [which was still in Pless], as I lacked the right kind of authority. Even though he did so with great urgency, the Third Army was still required to withdraw its 85th Reserve Infantry Brigade—which it had only recently received—for redeployment elsewhere. In order to fill out its front lines, then, the Third Army had to insert three battalions withdrawn from its XIV Army Corps on the right wing, and two battalions formed from the army's cavalry. The Sixth Army also reported increasingly the buildup of an enemy large-scale attack.

On 22 September a powerful French artillery barrage started in the Third Army's sector against the XII Reserve Corps' 24th Reserve Division, the VIII Reserve Corps, and to the left the adjacent 21st Reserve Division of the Fifth Army's XVIII Reserve Corps. The barrage destroyed all of the fighting trenches and most of the dugouts, and overwhelmed the German artillery. It also destroyed many communications land lines, making it necessary to use signal light detachments to transmit orders and unit reports. That same day the Third Army reported reliable intelligence indicating that their four weak divisions—the 24th Reserve Division, Division Liebert, the 50th Division, and Division Ditfurth—were facing six French corps in the forward lines, with still more corps and cavalry divisions in reserve. When the accuracy of the intelligence was confirmed, the Third Army was reinforced with the 183rd Infantry Brigade, which had been positioned behind the Seventh Army. But General von Falkenhayn could not decide on this day, or on any of the following days, to move behind the Third Army at least one of the army corps in the process of unloading in Belgium. On 24 September the Third Army received operational control of only the 5th Division, which was then positioned in its rear at Attigny as part of the OHL reserve. The 5th Division's three infantry regiments moved forward by foot march, taking up positions in reserve at Pauvres, Bessincourt, and Vouziers. The 5th Division's artillery did not arrive until the afternoon of 26 September.

The Sixth Army reported that its I Bavarian Reserve Corps, VI Army Corps, and the left wing of the IV Army Corps were facing six French corps; and the rest of the IV Army Corps and the VII Army Corps were facing nine British divisions. Although the enemy had a huge force ratio superiority against the Sixth Army, it was less than the superiority they had massed against the Third Army. Based on the type of preparatory artillery barrage, the Sixth Army forecast a French attack on both sides of Arras, with the main effort against Vimy Ridge, and a British attack between Loos and the La Bassée Canal. This assessment proved rather accurate. In the Sixth Army sector the enemy's preparatory fires started on 15 September and increased in intensity to 22 September. Then, from 24 September on, an intense barrage hit the Sixth Army's forward positions from the La Bassée Canal to almost to the Sixth Army's left wing. The strongest fire was against the VI Army Corps. On 24 September General von Falkenhayn attached the 8th Division, which had been pulled back to Douai as OHL reserve, to the Sixth Army as an emergency force. On that day, then, OHL no longer had any reserves behind the Third and Sixth Armies. Nonetheless, Falkenhayn left the Guards Corps and X Army Corps in Belgium, despite the seriousness of the situation.

On the evening of 21 September General von Falkenhayn left Pless with the Kaiser's entourage. Colonel Tappen remained there as the deputy of OHL until further notice. On 23 September the Kaiser and Falkenhayn conducted troop inspections in Colmar and Strasbourg, and in Metz on the 24th. Those trips and stops at the said locations made it very difficult for me to communicate with OHL. Despite all the reports available to him, General von Falkenhayn did not believe that the enemy would launch a large-scale attack in either the Sixth Army or Third Army sectors. Even when he arrived in Montmédy with the Kaiser on the morning of the 25th, he still maintained that opinion, even though the reports of the enemy artillery barrages continued to pour in. By noon on the 25th, when they arrived at the Fifth Army headquarters in Stenay, he continued to assure the Kaiser.

The Kaiser remained in Stenay with the crown prince while General von Falkenhayn and the Fifth Army chief of staff went forward for a briefing with the unit commanders. Just before he left, the Fifth Army chief of staff received a message from the Third Army reporting a French breakthrough in the direction of Souain–Sommepy.[36] The penetration was made in the sector of Division Liebert, which formed the right wing of the VIII Reserve Corps. The Third Army was requesting support from the Fifth Army. But the Fifth Army was under attack on its own right wing and therefore needed its own reserves there. The Fifth Army chief of staff immediately passed the Third Army message to General von Falkenhayn. Almost at the same time a telegram arrived from Sixth Army reporting that the enemy had penetrated into the VII and IV Army Corps' positions and that all available reserves were allocated to those corps. Falkenhayn immediately called the Third Army commander, General von Einem, who told Falkenhayn in no uncertain terms that he needed a rapid infusion of several divisions. General von Falkenhayn then finally rushed to Mézières by car, where, in my opinion, he should have been in the first place.

Unaware of the situations at the Third and Sixth Armies, the Kaiser that afternoon drove to the Third Army near the Maison-Rouge. The headquarters was located in a castle close by Vouziers. General von Einem immediately briefed the Kaiser on the situation. But since General von Falkenhayn repeatedly had described the situation to the Kaiser in the most optimistic terms, the Kaiser gave General von Einem a very odd answer that bore no relation to the overall situation: "Just have them plant their bayonets and kick those people out again." General von Einem later spoke with me often about this very disturbing episode with the Kaiser, which he attributed to Falkenhayn's inadequate briefings.

When General von Falkenhayn arrived in Mézières, I showed him the maps on which the terrain losses reported by the Sixth and Third Armies were plotted. In the Sixth Army sector the British had pushed in the 117th Division's front lines two to four kilometers on a breadth of about eight kilometers. The British used large quantities of gas and smoke, and an unfavorable wind (for us) reduced our visibility and fields of observation. In the center of the IV Army Corps sector the 7th Division managed to keep the situation under control. The 123rd Division's left flank was pushed back at Souchez. In the center of the VI Army Corps sector the enemy made a penetration of about one kilometer on a breadth of about four kilometers.

In the Third Army sector the XII Reserve Corps' 24th Reserve Division lost its front lines on the right wing on a breadth of about one kilometer, and on the left wing on a breadth of about 3.5 kilometers. The penetration was not very deep. The situation at the VIII Reserve Corps, however, was very serious. Division Liebert and the 50th Division lost their front lines on a breadth of more than twelve kilometers, and were pushed back north of Souain[37] and north of Perthes up to 3.5 kilometers and into their secondary positions. Those secondary positions, which were based on a reverse slope, had been improved only at sporadic locations, and otherwise were only marked out on the ground. The outer left wing of the 50th Division and the right half of Division Ditfurth held their positions. The left half of Division Ditfurth was thrown back about one kilometer.

Both armies had committed their available reserves. The Third Army even brought up troops from the recruit depots to man the secondary positions. General von Falkenhayn told me that even before he left the Fifth Army for Mézières he had ordered the 192nd Infantry Brigade to redeploy from the rear of the Seventh Army to the rear of the Sixth Army; and the 56th Division from the rear of Army Detachment Falkenhausen to the Third Army sector. He also issued warning orders to prepare to move to the Guards Corps and X Army Corps in Belgium. Based on my situation brief, he then immediately ordered the Guards Corps to move to the Sixth Army sector, and the X Army Corps headquarters and its 20th Division to move to the Third Army sector. By the evening of 25 September all the units ordered forward were under the control of both army headquarters. After a telephone call with General von Einem, who correctly described the situation of his army as very serious, and who once again demanded in the strongest terms sufficient reinforcements, the 192nd Infantry

Brigade was attached to the Third Army rather than the Sixth Army. Truck columns were assigned to facilitate its rapid movement. Additionally, the Seventh Army, whose sector was calm at that point, detached two of its infantry battalions and two light machine gun battalions to the Third Army.

During the afternoon of 25 September, I pointed out to General von Falkenhayn that the fight on the inner wings of the Third and Sixth Armies required a unified command, and I recommended that the Third Army should be attached to Army Group German Crown Prince. I emphasized that this army group had not been attacked, and therefore it could support the fight with large infantry units and with large portions of its artillery. General von Falkenhayn accepted my recommendation and subordinated the Third Army to Army Group German Crown Prince.

I spent the night of 25–26 September in my office. I had plenty of work to do, and I maintained constant contact with the Third and Sixth Armies. At noon on 26 September, I accompanied General von Falkenhayn to a briefing with the Kaiser. During the short car trip to the Kaiser's villa, Falkenhayn told me that earlier in the morning he had a long conversation with the chief of staff of the Third Army, Bavarian[38] lieutenant general Maximilian von Höhn, who described the serious situation in his sector. He recommended a general withdrawal of the front lines, which had been penetrated deeply in many places. The withdrawal would allow us to straighten our lines and could be executed in two phases, during the nights 26–27 and 27–28 September. I vehemently nonconcurred with that recommendation, which would have handed victory to the enemy. During the car trip, however, I did not have enough time to justify my position. I stressed emphatically that in the current situation the present positions had to be held at all costs.[39]

General von Falkenhayn routinely briefed the Kaiser himself. But after he gave a short overview of the operations in the east, he asked the Kaiser's permission for me to give a more detailed report on the situation on the Western Front, since I was far more familiar with the details. The Kaiser agreed. Using the maps I had brought along, I described in detail the kind of attacks against Sixth and Third Armies. Both could be classified as attempted breakthroughs.

The Kaiser questioned whether the two armies would be able to hold. I answered by emphasizing that the Sixth Army with their own reserves had held the enemy quite well at the beginning of the attacks. With the support of the Guards Corps, whose lead elements had already arrived in sector on the morning of 26 September, the Sixth Army undoubtedly would succeed in not only preventing the enemy breakthrough, but it also would regain much of the lost ground through a deliberate counterattack. I described the Third Army's situation as very serious, considering the enemy's large numerical superiority, their very strong infantry and artillery, and their deeply echeloned attack formations. I emphasized that mastery of the current difficult situation required an iron will on the part of Third Army headquarters. Voluntary withdrawals must not be made under any circumstances. The Third Army would have to hold and fight for every inch of ground, because that was the only way to prevent an enemy breakthrough. The troops of the Third Army had fought heroically, would continue to do so, and would certainly continue to hold with the support of the arriving reserves, all under a unified and energetic command.

My briefing had a visible and strong impact on the Kaiser. General von Falkenhayn then asked me to leave the briefing room. Shortly thereafter, Falkenhayn left the Kaiser. Immediately after our departure by staff car, General von Falkenhayn turned to me and said, "Now my dear Lossberg, we will have to go our separate ways. His Majesty has appointed you chief of staff of the Third Army." It was completely surprising news for me, but I was thrilled. For months it had been my silent wish to get back to the front and serve in a position of high responsibility. The desk work at OHL did not satisfy at all my thirst for action.

As I later learned, General von Falkenhayn had lost his trust in my predecessor at the Third Army when he made the suggestion to disengage from the enemy voluntarily. Out of a sense of loyalty to General von Höhn, however, Falkenhayn merely told him that he did not expect him to bear the indignity of working under the younger chief of staff of Army Group German Crown Prince, General Schmidt von Knobelsdorf. The Kaiser, therefore, had appointed Höhn commander of the 2nd Guards Division, which for a Bavarian general was a high honor.[40]

Immediately after I returned to the headquarters building I made some quick preparations for my rapid departure. I did take breakfast with General von Falkenhayn, and we discussed one more time the situation at the Third Army and the necessity of inserting strong and combat-capable reserves, most immediately the X Army Corps' 19th Division. Immediately after breakfast I rode by staff car to Vouziers.

At the time I had only been a full colonel for two months, while almost all the chiefs of staff at the army level were lieutenant generals or major generals. I could, therefore, interpret my appointment as a special recognition. I was driven by a firm intent to justify the trust placed in me by applying all of my energy to the care of the troops. My rich combat experience to that point would serve me well in my new, highly responsible position. My inner thoughts at the time were best summarized in a short letter I mailed to my wife from Mézières. I told her about my appointment as an army chief of staff and added, "Here the dusty files rule, in Champagne there is fresh air and soldiers. There, I will be in my element and can breathe more easily, because I will be standing on my own two feet again. I will have responsibility and the ability to accomplish something on my own. I am not that easily defeated, especially not by these damned Frenchmen. I will show them my teeth. Now the only thing that matters is to beat as many of them to death as possible."

3

Chief of the General Staff of the Third Army (Champagne, 1915)

During the car trip from Mézières to the Third Army headquarters at Vouziers, I made an action plan for my new assignment. My decision was based on an iron resolve to hold the new positions created by the enemy's break-in (*Einbruch*) and to fight for every inch of ground. A voluntary withdrawal (*Ausweichen*) was completely contrary to my approach and my own combat experience. In order to be able to act, I of course needed the approval of the Third Army commander, General of Cavalry Karl von Einem. Before I left Mézières I signaled that I would arrive in Vouziers at 1500 hours, and requested a meeting with the commander shortly thereafter. Before reporting to him, however, I wanted to talk to my predecessor, Lieutenant General Maximilian von Höhn, about the developing situation resulting from the renewed French attack on 26 September. Once I did report to the commander, I immediately intended to go forward to the front to conduct my own reconnaissance and talk to the troop leaders, thereby gaining a clear picture upon which to base the continued conduct of the defense.

I arrived in Vouziers a little before 1500 hours. The former prefecture building housed the offices of the army's staff. A staff officer who received me told me that General von Höhn had already relinquished his post and currently was in his quarters preparing to depart shortly.

As I walked into the chief of staff's office the telephone rang. Lieutenant General Paul Friedrich Fleck, the commanding general of the VIII Reserve Corps, was on the phone. He wanted to know if his corps should start the planned evasive action during the night of 27 September. The orders had been prepared and would have to be sent out soon. With the intent of establishing immediately an atmosphere of complete transparency I answered, "The withdrawal is cancelled. The VIII Reserve Corps will die in place exactly where it is now positioned."

General Fleck apparently recognized that he was not hearing General von Höhn's voice, and he asked who was giving the order. I answered, "The new chief of staff of the Third Army, Colonel von Lossberg." When General Fleck asked if the army commander knew about the order, I answered, "I assume full responsibility and will visit your corps headquarters very soon."[1]

Major von dem Hagen, the first General Staff officer (Ia) then reported to me. I had known him since the days when I had been a lieutenant serving in Berlin. He briefed me on the Third Army's current situation using a specially prepared map. On 25 September five German divisions had been attacked by eighteen French divisions, supported by artillery three times the size of ours. They fired gas rounds extensively, which the southerly winds blew into our positions. Our five divisions included the Third Army's 24th Reserve Division, Division Liebert,[2] the 50th Division, and Division Dithfurth.[3] The Fifth Army's 21st Reserve Division was also in the French attack sector. Despite the relentless courage of our troops, we sustained large losses of ground. Each of the trench divisions suffered some five thousand casualties. Initially the reserves only arrived piecemeal and were deeply intermixed with the other formations. Despite these great complications in the management of the battle, the newly formed combat lines had held more or less against strong French piecemeal attacks on 26 September.

During drawn-out, back-and-forth fighting the 24th Reserve Division launched courageous hasty counterattacks to retake its original 26 September positions. In the VIII Reserve Corps' sector a new Corps Wichura[4] was established for the operational control of Division Liebert and the right regimental sector of the 50th Division. The eastern boundary of this area of operations was a designated as a line running from Perthes[5] to the north. That reduced the width of the 50th Division's sector. Corps Wichura consisted of the right half of the 15th Reserve Division reinforced with several battalions and the 5th Division (minus the 8th Grenadier Regiment), in whose sector were positioned several reinforcement battalions and the largest part of the 50th Division's heavily depleted 39th Infantry Regiment. On 26 September Corps Wichura launched hasty counterattacks that successfully beat back the repeated piecemeal French attacks. That effort was especially commendable because the infantry and almost of all the artillery of the 5th Division had to move into their fighting positions under very difficult combat conditions.

The VIII Reserve Corps now only consisted of the 50th Division and the Division Liebert. The 50th Division's reduced frontage was reinforced by two newly arriving battalions. Putting up a stalwart defense, the division repulsed very strong and repeated French attacks, which were launched in the direction of La Butte de Tahure, one kilometer north of Tahure.[6] Division Ditfurth (16th Reserve Division) was supported by the 5th Division's 8th Grenadier Regiment and an additional battalion. Later, the only partially arrived 56th Division was committed there. In the 16th Division's left sector strong French attacks were directed primarily against Hill 199. After initial terrain losses, we retook large portions of our old fighting positions with hasty counterattacks, supported by the initial reinforcements that arrived just in time. The XVIII Reserve Corps' 21st Reserve Division, which was tied in on the left, was able to hold its position with the support of reinforcements from the Fifth Army.

Taking the situation map that had been prepared for me, I went into the commanding general's adjoining office. General von Einem had just arrived from his quarters. He appeared to be quite affected by the costly fighting and the difficult situation of his army. After a brief personal talk, I told the commander about my telephone conversation with General Fleck. General von Einem answered, "I hope, my dear Lossberg, that this order will reflect honor upon the Third Army." My prompt response was, "That is why I issued it, your Excellency, and I ask you now to give me retroactive approval for this only viable course of action." Deeply moved, General von Einem then shook hands with me. As I learned only much later from General von Einem, General von Höhn, without General von Einem's knowledge, had made the recommendation to General von Falkenhayn to withdraw the VIII Reserve Corps' fighting front three to four kilometers, to behind the Dormoise River.

I then asked the commanding general to allow me to go immediately to the front lines. I also requested Vollmacht, which, based on my assessment of what I saw, would authorize me to issue any necessary orders without first obtaining his approval. General von Einem agreed. I can say that in this first official conversation between General von Einem and me a bond of trust developed that could not have been better. During the period of our collaboration at the Third Army, General von Einem was always a most trusting superior.

On my trip to the front I first went to the VIII Reserve Corps' headquarters in Savigny-sur-Aisne, only a few kilometers away from Vouziers. Arriving at 1600 hours, I encountered a quite serious but confident atmosphere. The staff, the subordinate commanders, and Lieutenant General Feck especially concurred enthusiastically with the order I had issued to hold the current positions. During my talks at the VIII Reserve Corps, the chief of staff of the Fifth Army and Army Group German Crown Prince, Lieutenant General Konstantin Schmidt von Knobelsdorf arrived at the corps headquarters.[7] He too was in absolute agreement with the Third Army's decision to hold the positions at all costs. He told us that the XVIII Reserve Corps would be able to hold its positions with its own assets. General Schmidt von Knobelsdorf then accompanied me back to the Third Army headquarters to confer with General von Einem. That meeting at Vouziers did not last very long and concluded in complete agreement.

From Vouziers I took a staff car and continued on to Blaise,[8] and then south toward Sommepy to the fighting front of Corps Wichura's 15th Reserve Division. The 25 September French attack there had pushed us back farther than in any other of our sectors. I left the car in Sommepy and then advanced south by foot, making short dashes under enemy artillery fire along the torn-up road. Between Sommepy and the forward line I spoke with several leaders of the reinforcement units moving forward. They had occupied a thin line of reverse-slope positions that were only partially prepared, and minimally echeloned. All of the leaders were unanimously of the opinion that another strong French attack was imminent for 27 September. I too thought that it was possible, assuming the enemy had managed to move his artillery positions forward successfully on 26 September. I immediately recognized that a coordinated French attack could only be repelled if we could manage with the time available to organize strong defensive fires with our own artillery. I was glad to see that General Wichura had already recognized this necessity, and accordingly he already had executed the forward displacement of the 5th Division's artillery, including several reinforcing batteries from his corps' sector north of the Py River.

From the hills north of Sommepy I had a good field of observation over Corps Wichura's entire battle area. I was able to ascertain that many artillery observation detachments were advancing on the ground south of the Py. With confidence, then, I anticipated the renewed fighting along this especially important sector.

The towns of Sommepy and Sainte-Marie-à-Py and a large cantonment area in a forest north of Sommepy had been heavily shot up. The terrain farther north had few settlements. I concluded that we had to build a new encampment in the forested area north of Sommepy.

The position now occupied by the left wing of the XII Reserve Corps and Corps Wichura was the only remaining German position that was inadequately fortified. Exactly against that sector the French had launched their main effort. Everything possible, therefore, had to be done to establish new positions there. South of the Py the construction would have to be done by the combat troops. North of the river the improvement of a continuous position could only be done by special construction units.

I then rushed on by staff car to the headquarters of the XII Army Corps. General Günther von Kirchbach was in command, and the mood there was one of confidence following the good results of the fighting on 26 September. The 24th Reserve Division on the corps' left had lost its positions east of Aubérive—on the division's own left wing—during the fighting on 25 September. A deep penetration into the sector of the 15th Reserve Division, on the left flank of the 24th Reserve Division, forced the latter to pull back during the night of 25–26 September in order to maintain contact with the 15th Reserve Division. On 26 September the corps held its positions almost completely. To my delight, the corps commanding general told me that with the help of the already arrived reinforcements he would be able to continue to hold his positions.

I then drove on to the command posts of the 23rd Reserve Division, commanded by Lieutenant General Bernhard von Watzdorf, and the 24th Reserve Division, commanded by General of Infantry Oskar von Ehrenthal. At both divisions I was met with the same confident attitude that the positions could be held with the available forces. On 26 September the 24th Reserve Division had conducted a deliberate counterattack east of Aubérive to reconquer the positions it had lost on 25 September. In the process, the division took one thousand prisoners. The following day the division retook all its remaining lost ground with a series of hasty counterattacks.

Unfortunately, the fading daylight prevented me from acquiring little more than a general overview of the 24th Reserve Division's forward ground. I drove back to Vouziers, where I briefly updated the commander on my observations. I then immediately started to develop all the necessary directives for the continuation of the fight. During that process I met all the officers of the Third Army headquarters staff.

The deputy chief of staff, Saxon Major General Otto Löffler; the general of the engineers, Major General Schulz; and the general of the artillery, Colonel Schulenburg, were senior to me. All three answered in the affirmative whether they could work for a more junior chief of staff.[9] I worked with these three very capable officers very well during the battle and well afterward.

Major von dem Hagen, the Ia of the Third Army, was an excellent General Staff officer. He substituted for me almost daily during my extensive trips to the front. He always accomplished the work of his intensive and responsible position quite superbly. The other General Staff officers, the adjutants, and the administrative staff officers were all reliable and responsible. After only a short time there developed a bond of total trust and good camaraderie between the entire headquarters staff and me.

In difficult times during the battle, objective-oriented and well-coordinated staff work is essential. I coordinated with a strong hand the synchronization of all the directives that almost always involved multiple sections of the staff. All action officers had access to me at all times, because that was the only way to ensure rapid and focused effort. My personal workload was heavy and full of responsibility, but I did it happily and willingly. Thanks to my solid health and strong nerves, I overcame all challenges easily, despite many short nights and sometimes no sleep at all. I always maintained the conviction that the commander has the responsibility for all actions. Thus, all basic orders were never issued until I first briefed them to General von Einem, who in most cases concurred with my recommendations. Important Third Army orders always were signed by the commander.

Because of the initial and infrequent trickle of reserve forces, the result was a wide-spread mixing of units that made the management of the battle difficult for the division commanders. I recommended, therefore, the reorganization of the formations and the insertion of newly arriving reinforcements into the front lines as cohesively as possible. I knew from earlier experience that the troops always fought better under their own leaders than under unknown ones.

The broadest sector by far was the heavily contested one held by Division Ditfurth. Right from the start, then, my objective was to deploy the whole of the arriving 56th Division there. For the present, we did not have adequate strength to reorganize the units in the other sectors. We only had the immediate capability of supporting the front lines with our few available reserves, but that would enable us to echelon those sectors more deeply and fend off with hasty counterattacks any deeper advances by the numerically superior enemy. All the relevant directives were issued during the night of 26–27 September.

Soon after my return to Vouziers I had a telephone conversation with General von Falkenhayn, describing my observations from my visits to the front line. I stressed to him that further strong French attacks certainly could be expected. Accordingly, I asked him to send as many consolidated combat formations as possible to the Third Army, additional heavy batteries with sufficient ammunition, aviation units, replacement guns, and equipment for the field and heavy artillery. I also requested the deployment of laborers, building materials, and trench railway equipment for the construction of a new continuous rearward position north of the Py River.

On 26 September I tasked the general of the engineers to reconnoiter a continuous position north of the Py, between Suippes and the northern boundary of the Fifth Army. I asked him to make a rough initial estimate of the workforce and material requirements. I also told the general of the artillery to prepare an estimate for requesting additional artillery forces and the replacement of destroyed artillery equipment. I gave the assistant chief of staff the mission of reconnoitering the rear area for the locations of new cantonments and forward depots, and calculating the required materials for a trench railway leading there. I also tasked him with the construction of billeting in the towns that were behind the fighting front.

In the late evening of 26 September OHL informed us that the Third Army would receive the 19th Division from the X Army Corps as well as six bomber squadrons. The commanding general of the X Army Corps, Lieutenant General Walther Freiherr von Lüttwitz, arrived in the meantime and assumed control of Corps Wichura's former sector, which included the 15th Reserve Division and the 5th Division.

During the large-scale fighting on 25 September rain had set in, which continued with only short interruptions. This weather change was advantageous for us as the defenders. The terrain on which the battle was fought had a deep chalk bed under a narrow layer of humus. All the positions, the connecting trenches, and the shell craters were outlined sharply by the underlying chalk. They could be spotted easily by ground and aerial observation. The rain dissolved the chalk into a dirty and sticky mush, which made all movement very difficult. The ground between our positions consisted of a uniformly muddy field of craters that the French would have to cross during any new advance. All movement would be slowed, of course. Our troops welcomed the rain, even though they too had to endure the wet conditions. The heavy precipitation increased on 26 September and came down even harder during the night of 26–27 September.

According to a French order captured on 26 September, the French intended to launch a renewed breakthrough attack on 27 September. Therefore, during the night of 26–27 September the XII Reserve Corps, Corps Lüttwitz, and Corps Fabeck were reinforced with an additional infantry regiment and artillery from the 20th Division. The Third Army headquarters ordered Corps Fleck to establish three divisional sectors, which would be occupied by the 50th Division on the right, Division Dithfurth (16th Reserve Division) in the center, and Division Sonntag (56th Division) on the left. All of the available and the still arriving construction troops from the Third Army were assembled behind the especially vulnerable sector held by the 24th Reserve Division, Corps Lüttwitz, and the 50th Division. Their mission was to construct a rearward position north of the Py River.

From the early morning of 27 September on, an incredible enemy barrage rained down on our positions and the ground to the rear. The French attacks did not begin until 1700 hours, and then not along a continuous front. Rather, they were only piecemeal and limited attacks against the 24th Reserve Division and Corps Lüttwitz and Fleck. A long and bitter struggle ensued, during which a series of German hasty counterattacks held the positions for the most part. The French gained ground only on the right wing of Division Liebert (15th Reserve Division) and in the sector of the 50th Division near Tahure. Despite several deliberate counterattacks, we could not retake that ground. We then reinforced those sectors with newly arrived reserves. Ground losses by the 15th Reserve Division forced the 24th Reserve Division on its left to move back and to lengthen its positions. It received a reinforcement of one battalion respectively from the XIV Army Corps' 28th Division and the X Army Corps' 20th Division. Division Ditfurth was reinforced by battalions from the 56th Division. On the right wing of the Fifth Army, the XVIII Reserve Corps' 21st Reserve Division also received reinforcements from its army, and held its positions.

Our hasty counterattacks netted a considerable number of French prisoners, including some cavalry officers. Upon interrogation they indicated that they had been sent into the infantry lines to reconnoiter the terrain for a breakthrough by major French cavalry formations that were in readiness. We concluded from that intelligence that the French leadership had overrated significantly their current successes. Our aircraft and balloon observers reported that strong French cavalry units had advanced as far as the vicinity of Souain.[10] At that point they were forced back by our observed and strong artillery fire. Prisoners also indicated that in several locations the French infantry had refused to leave their initial attack positions.

The success that the enemy achieved against Division Liebert and the 50th Division on 27 September encouraged the French leadership to continue the attack on 28 September. The principal attacks were planned against the boundary between the 24th Reserve Division and Division Liebert, at Tahure against the 50th Division, and at the boundary of the Third Army's 56th Division and the Fifth Army's 21st Reserve Division. According to a French order captured on 27 September, the objective of the overall attack was the elimination of the entire German second defensive line.

On 28 September the French infantry assault began in the afternoon, following a tremendous artillery barrage. The main thrust against the inner boundary of the 24th Reserve Division and Division Liebert penetrated rather deeply. Immediate German hasty counterattacks did not succeed. The break-in sector could only be closed by the commitment of the rather expended units of the XII Reserve Corps, which only recently had been pulled out of the line. As soon as I received the reports of the terrain losses I hurried immediately to that sector and organized the preparations for a well-planned deliberate counterattack, which would be commanded by General Liebert on 29 September.

I had not had any sort of sleep since the morning of 25 September. Around midnight on 28 September I finally was able to get some sleep. Although the window in my quarters was wide open, I slept so soundly that I did not hear a French air attack on Vouziers. Even the huge detonation of a bomb that landed about one hundred meters from my open window did not wake me. I learned of the aerial attack only after I woke up around 0500 hours. Some sixty bombs had been dropped on Vouziers. There had been some civilian casualties and we lost some of the horses in a stable; otherwise there was only damage to buildings.

In the morning of 29 September the commanding general and I drove to the front, as we did on all battle days. Our initial destination was the sector of the 50th Division. On 28 September that division had suffered some minor ground losses in the vicinity of Tahure. For the time being they refrained from launching a deliberate counterattack because they lacked sufficient fresh forces. We then continued on to Division Liebert. Along with the commander of the X Army Corps, we verified all the preparations for a deliberate counterattack to be conducted in the evening of 29 September. The consolidated artillery fire plan for the attack was almost completed, and the guns were already registering. The infantry assault would be launched later toward the evening, after a thorough artillery preparation.

The attack was a complete success, owing to the exemplary courage of the troops, and we recaptured all of our old positions. We took some one thousand prisoners, primarily from the French 157th Division. By the evening of 29 September we had retaken completely our second defensive position (*R-Stellung*). This attack proved the efficacy of the German reverse-slope defense technique. We were able to coordinate our artillery preparatory fires with ground observers, while the French were forced to use aerial and balloon observers to adjust their fires. On 30 September our artillery broke up multiple French deliberate counterattacks. The ground we took and our former positions were littered with French dead, an indicator that we had been fighting against a courageous enemy.

Things calmed down a little during the subsequent few days. The French limited themselves to heavy artillery fire and local attacks conducted mostly in the dark. These thrusts forced our purposely thinly manned forward lines to fall back initially, but then our hasty counterattacks launched immediately against the enemy's front and flanks always broke up their attacks and we regained our positions.

The enemy's aerial activity remained constant, with observation, fighter, and bomber aircraft. Vouziers was bombed again by about twenty planes during the day of 2 October. That same day we shot down a French airship in our rear area in the vicinity of Rethel. A German airship dropped approximately three thousand kilograms of bombs on the railroad junction at Châlons-sur-Vesle.

In the meantime, the X Army Corps' 19th Division arrived in sector. It initially assembled to the rear of the boundary of the XII Reserve Corps and Corps Lüttwitz, as an army-level reserve in the vicinity of Machault. Very shortly elements of this division were committed in the sector of Corps Lüttwitz. Army Group German Crown Prince assigned the 113th Division to the Third Army, which previously had been assigned to Army Detachment Strantz. That division too initially assembled in the area west of Vouziers as an army-level reserve, behind the boundary of Corps Lüttwitz and Corps Fleck. Army Group German Crown Prince also indicated the possibility of soon assigning to us an infantry brigade from the 53rd Saxon Division. This brigade was gradually assembled behind the 50th Division, in the vicinity of Manre.

In the front lines the commander of the 15th Reserve Division, Lieutenant General Liebert, was replaced by Major General Arthur Freiherr von Lüttwitz, the commander of the 20th Division. To the extent that sufficient local reserves were available, worn-out units were relieved. Whenever possible, such units also were reconstituted. The troops worked with all of their strength on improving their positions and emplacing wire obstacles forward of the front lines. In the air, the French managed to maintain a superiority of three to four times. Thus, the reinforcement of our positions was mostly only possible at night. Our bomber squadrons regularly conducted night attacks against the positions behind the enemy's front lines. The French conducted many relief actions of their own forces, as reported by our aerial observers. To establish greater clarity on that intelligence, our troops conducted small-force patrol operations every night. Based on the interrogations of the prisoners brought back, we deducted the following deeply echeloned enemy order of battle:

- 6 French Divisions in front of the 24th Reserve Division
- 5 French Divisions in front of the 20th Division
- 5 French Divisions in front of the 5th Division
- 4 French Divisions in front of the 50th Division
- 3 French Divisions in front of the 16th Division
- 3 French Divisions in front of the 56th Division
- 3 French Divisions in front of the Fifth Army's 21st Reserve Division

This picture of the overall situation made it clear that we had to anticipate further strong attacks. This assessment was also confirmed by aerial observers, who reported that the French artillery was working its way forward through the cratered terrain. Our artillery had been reinforced by additional batteries attached from OHL. With sufficient ammunition we therefore were able to disrupt forcefully the assembly of the French for their increasingly obvious new attacks.

During this stressful period, however, I did not just think about defensive operations, but also about conducting our own attacks. As soon as I briefed the commander, I worked out an attack plan for the purpose of straightening out the salient that had been pushed in on us from the north and northeast, and was north of the line Souain–Perthes. The intent was to retake our positions of 25 September. For the objective of such an attack I designated the Hill 185 ridgeline, which ran from west of Ferme de Navarin–Hill 190 (near Baraque)–Hill 185 (near Trou Bricot)–Hill 188 (two kilometers north of Perthes). We needed several additional fresh divisions. Those divisions would be positioned in a ready status behind our front lines. Then, once we repelled the anticipated large-scale French attack, our coordinated and deliberate counterattack would overrun the enemy positions. The plan never materialized because OHL could not provide the necessary reinforcements. OHL detached only two gas regiments to us, but it was impossible to deploy them in the front lines because of the strong French artillery fire. We shifted those regiments to the sector of the XIV Army Corps, on the Third Army's right wing. Our intent was to conduct a diversionary gas attack south of Reims. But for that attack, too, there were no sufficient reinforcements available for the XIV Army Corps. All available units were needed in the main battle sector. I also planned an attack from our left wing, with the objective of recapturing the key Hill 199 and the lower heights on both sides. But once again, OHL could not allocate the necessary additional forces.

On 4 October an incredible French barrage opened up against our main battle sector. The fire continued without interruption until 6 October. In the morning of that day our forward positions and rear areas were contaminated with a gas attack, similar to the gas attack we received on 25 September. At 0630 hours the large attack began in thick fog, which made visibility very difficult. The sectors hit included the 24th Reserve Division, Corps Lüttwitz, Corps Fleck, and the Fifth Army's 21st Reserve Division. Earlier that morning, in anticipation of the attack, we had moved all our available reserves forward, close to the front lines. The recently withdrawn 15th Reserve Division also was alerted.

Our artillery fire concentrated primarily against the French line of departure trenches (*Sturmausgangsgräben*). At the first indicator that the enemy was starting to move forward, we initiated our interdiction fire. The French attackers suffered tremendous losses, with only fragments of units entering our trenches. Many of the French assault troops fled back to their own trenches, only to be driven forward again by their own leaders. Uninterrupted fire continued from both sides. Wherever the French managed to enter into our lines, we threw them out immediately with a hasty counterattack. Nonetheless, the French attacked again and again. The struggle lasted into the late evening, when the French major breakthrough attempt finally collapsed.

During this especially difficult day of fighting, our German troops performed like heroes. The 24th Reserve Division successfully repulsed six French attacks, between which the French artillery fired one barrage after another. In the sector of Corps Lüttwitz and its 20th Division, French Moroccan troops broke through our infantry positions and advanced all the way to the German artillery observation posts. There they stabbed out the eyes of many artillery observers and then massacred them. During the ensuing hasty counterattack, the German infantry reserves gave no quarter to the Moroccans in the hand-to-hand fighting. After we recovered our positions, more than two thousand dead black French troops covered the battlefield. In the sector of Corps Lüttwitz's 5th Division the long back-and-forth fighting lasted late into the night. When it was over, the French still held a three hundred-meter-wide section of trench line.

In Corps Fleck's sector the French directed the main effort of their attack against the 50th Division. Attacking with strong, deeply echeloned forces against the completely destroyed village of Tahure and the La Butte de Tahure high ground to the north, the enemy initially seized both locations. We pushed the French back out of both places with hasty counterattacks, but they retook both the village and the high ground with a follow-on attack. That night a regiment of the 53rd Reserve Division launched a deliberate counterattack against the key high ground of La Butte de Tahure. That attack, however, was poorly prepared and failed. The loss of La Butte de Tahure, and especially the village of Tahure, created a serious threat to the 50th Division's left flank. Although the division had been able to hold its positions south of Tahure, the enemy forces in the village itself were well positioned against the division's northern flank. During that night, however, the 53rd Reserve Division managed to seal off the penetration. Division Ditfurth (16th Reserve Division) and Division Sonntag (56th Division) managed to hold their positions in hand-to-hand combat or with hasty counterattacks. The Fifth Army's 21st Reserve Division on the Third Army's left flank also held.

I had been up and active without interruption since the morning of 5 October. On difficult battle days like these I could not get away from Vouziers. Reports and requests came in by telephone from the front lines almost constantly. I had to answer all those immediately. All reports from our aviators had to be analyzed quickly in order to direct our artillery fire on known enemy concentrations and movements. On 6 October we shifted a few units of the army-level reserves to the most threatened sectors. All other sectors had to make do with their own available forces. A certain toughness in such decisions was essential. How much we would have liked to help everywhere, but economizing the available forces was absolutely necessary. Reserves had to remain under the control of the Third Army headquarters for the relief of worn-down units and for the conduct of counterattacks to retake lost positions. During the back and forth of the fighting, rapidly executed hasty counterattacks by the local reserves supported by well-registered artillery succeeded for the most part. Whenever a hasty counterattack failed and the attacking enemy force entrenched, only a well-planned deliberate counterattack after thorough preparation by concentrated artillery fire yielded results. The Third Army headquarters quite successfully based its decisions on these principles, which were derived from experience.

Without a doubt the attack on 6 October was a definite French failure. They failed to break through at any point. French losses were several time higher than ours, and our troops captured more than one thousand prisoners. The Third Army had achieved yet one more great defensive victory. With absolute trust in our battle-proven troops, we looked confidently toward new battles.

In the evening of 6 October the Third Army headquarters shifted the 36th

Infantry Regiment from army-level reserve to the XII Reserve Corps, which also was reinforced with the artillery of the arriving 113th Division of Army Detachment Strantz. The X Army Corps was reinforced with the 78th Reserve Infantry Regiment and elements of the 74th Infantry Regiment. Corps Fleck received the headquarters and staff of the 37th Infantry Brigade, the 73rd Reserve Infantry Regiment, and the 53rd Reserve Division's 241st and 243rd Reserve Infantry Regiments. An almost combat-ready infantry regiment of the 15th Reserve Division was moved to the vicinity of Vouziers as the army-level reserve.

During the night of 6–7 October enemy fire hit our positions almost without interruption, but our troops in accordance with existing directives were echeloned in depth and had been reconstituted as much as possible. The troops had established new trenches opposite the few break-in locations, and they were settled in and ready to defend.

Based on our reports regarding the expenditure of forces, OHL assigned additional reinforcements. The 4th Division and the 5th Bavarian Division's 185th Infantry Brigade were just arriving from the east. At our request the Seventh Army exchanged their worn-down battalions that had been temporarily assigned to the Third Army with fresh ones. Soon thereafter OHL assigned two additional infantry regiments from Army Detachment Strantz. One each went to the X Army Corps and the VIII Reserve Corps.

On 7 and 8 October the French continued their strong attacks, almost without interruption. Primarily they attempted to expand their 6 October break-in against the 50th Division in the vicinity of the village of Tahure. They succeeded at only a few locations. All other French attacks against the 24th Reserve Division, the X Army Corps, and the center and the left wing of the VIII Reserve Corps broke down in the face of our well-registered artillery.

Among the arriving reserves, elements of the 185th Infantry Regiment and the 5th Bavarian Division were positioned behind the VIII Reserve Corps. OHL also sent the 7th Reserve Division in exchange for the seriously depleted 15th Reserve Division, which had fought heroically during the heavy fighting. On 7 October OHL also deployed an infantry brigade behind the X Army Corps. That brigade was formed by Army Detachment Strantz from the 7th Grenadier Regiment, the 164th Infantry Regiment, and the 364th Infantry Regiment.

With these reinforcements the Third Army finally had the capability to reorganize our thoroughly mixed-up combat formations. The X Army Corps received the 185th Infantry Brigade and the 7th Grenadier Regiment; the VIII Reserve Corps received the 53rd Reserve Division's 241st and 364th Reserve Infantry Regiments and the newly arriving 7th Reserve Division to relieve the completely exhausted 50th Division. After the completion of these relief operations the army-level reserves consisted of two infantry regiments of the X Army

Corps, supported by three batteries positioned far to the rear of the right wing of the X Army Corps; the 77th Infantry Regiment behind the XII Reserve Corps; the 5th Bavarian Division behind the VIII Reserve Corps' 16th Reserve Division; the 8th Life Guards Regiment at Vouziers; and the 50th Division after its relief by 7th Reserve Division northeast of Vouziers.

In the meantime, we made all preparations to retake Tahure. This deliberate counterattack could not actually be executed until 9 October, owing to the constant French advances and also the rain-soaked ground. The counterattack was executed by elements of the 73rd, 241st, and 243rd Reserve Infantry Regiments and units of the 50th Division. At almost the same time we started our attack, however, the French attacked us and our advance stalled some one hundred meters in front of Tahure. When the fighting ended on 9 October we held a position to the east the French and to the west of the almost completely destroyed village. Tahure itself remained almost constantly under fire from both sides.

On 10 October, General von Falkenhayn and the chief of staff of Army Group German Crown Prince came to Vouziers for a conference. At the briefing General von Falkenhayn issued the directive for the sector in the current battle to concentrate henceforth on the pure defensive. General von Falkenhayn did not object to us conducting the limited objective attacks that we already had planned and prepared. During the entire briefing we could hear a French artillery barrage, the strength of which came as quite a surprise to Falkenhayn. The artillery preparation was followed by a strong French attack, which we bloodily repelled that day, and again on 11 October. On 13 October the French executed a sequential series of seven strong attacks at Tahure. Those attacks, however, all broke down with heavy losses in the face of our defensive fires. From that day on, the French suspended their attacks and reinforced their fighting positions at Tahure.

On 13 October the Kaiser visited the Third Army headquarters. I gave a longer briefing on the course of all of the previous fighting, and I had the impression that the Kaiser only now understood the difficult situation of the Third Army. When the Kaiser asked if we would be able to hold our positions, I responded confidently that the reports from large sectors of our main fighting front had become increasingly positive for the last several days, and that the enemy had started to improve both his forward and rearward positions. The overall picture reinforced the conclusion that the enemy intended to abort his large-scale attacks in Champagne. As we learned much later from statements made by prisoners, the French High Command ordered the termination of the attacks in Champagne on the evening of 6 October.

Based on our corresponding report, OHL attached to the Third Army the 5th Bavarian Division and the 4th Infantry Division, which previously had been OHL reserves. OHL also ordered the relief of the X Army Corps by the IX Army Corps. The X Army Corps and the 50th Division, which already had been relieved by the 7th Reserve Division, were reassigned as OHL reserve behind the inner boundary of the XIV Army Corps and the XII Reserve Corps. Those relieved units initially went into rest quarters. South of Tahure the right wing of the 5th Bavarian Division relieved the 16th Reserve Division, which had been deployed in the center of the VIII Reserve Corps. The 16th Division then became the army-level reserve and went into rest quarters northeast of Vouziers. The division had fought especially courageously during the large-scale attacks. On 12 October the lead elements of the 50th Reserve Division moved into their positions southwest of Rethel.

The Third Army headquarters estimated that between 22 September and 14 October 1915 we had lost approximately 1,700 officers and 80,000 troops. Later intelligence reports indicated that the French had lost 3,750 officers and 140,000 men. Those numbers indicate the dimensions of the French major offensive in Champagne, but also prove the difficulty of conducting a breakthrough penetration of a well-organized defensive front.

During the relief operations the Third Army headquarters decided to conduct deliberate counterattacks to eliminate the salients that had been pushed into our main fighting front, thereby improving our unfavorable positions at various points along our front lines. The XII Reserve Corps, IX Army Corps, and VIII Reserve Corps were ordered to draw up tentative attack plans and calculate the required forces. I and the officers of the army staff reconnoitered all potential attack sectors and then evaluated the attack plan drafts submitted by the corps.

Following a short but intense artillery preparation, the 24th Reserve Division launched the first of these attacks on 15 October, destroying a French strongpoint east of Aubérive. That attack achieved quick success, capturing more than six hundred prisoners, including eleven officers. Several French counterattacks failed. The prisoners who had been brought back to the XII Reserve Corps marched by the Kaiser, who was at the corps headquarters that day. They were the first French POWs the Kaiser had ever seen. During his three-hour visit I explained to the Kaiser in great detail the preparation and execution of the attack. I also had a long talk with the chief of the Kaiser's military cabinet, General of Infantry Moriz Freiherr von Lyncker, with whom I had served between 1905 and 1907, when I was a General Staff officer in the 19th Division, based in Hanover.

After the Kaiser left, our happiness about the success of 24th Reserve Division's attack was deeply overshadowed by a report from the 7th Reserve Division. The spontaneous detonation of hand grenades in a railroad tunnel that had served as shelter for the division reserves resulted in a great fire that killed roughly 850 brave German soldiers.[11]

I went to the front lines to conduct personal reconnaissance trips and meet with the unit leaders during any morning or afternoon that had a slight lull in the fighting. I assigned to each officer on the Third Army staff sectors of the divisional front lines, and I required them to walk their assigned ground twice a week. Aside from reconnoitering the fighting sectors, they had to visit all the unit leaders and ask them about their requirements. After the requests were reported to me by telephone, I coordinated with the other officers of the divisional staff to ensure that the frontline requests were fulfilled immediately. Most of the requests were for rations, ammunition, the rapid transport forward of materials for trench construction, etc.

About this time the commanding general planned to shift the Third Army headquarters to Rethel. I advised against it, because we then would be too far from the front lines. General von Einem concurred, and Vouziers remained the headquarters location. We then started a thorough improvement of the facilities at Vouziers.

On 18 October the relieved 16th Reserve Division started moving to the Seventh Army sector. The 4th Division that was slowly arriving from the east also started moving into quarters near Vouziers. In the meantime, all the preparations had been made for the gas attack that was to be executed by the XIV Corps' 35th and 36th Engineer Regiments. The release of the gas depended solely on a straight northerly wind, which occurs only rarely in the Champagne region. The gas cylinders were emplaced in the forward infantry positions of the XIV Corps' 28th and 29th Divisions and the right regimental sector of the 23rd Reserve Division. The gas line ran from north of Saint-Léonard to south of Pontfaverger.[12] For the execution of the follow-on infantry attack, OHL had allocated to us until 16 October the X Army Corps and the 50th Division, supported by four heavy batteries. The 50th Reserve Division was assigned as an army-level reserve behind the XIV Army Corps. The objective of the attack was the elimination of the enemy's infantry and battery positions. The effective combat strength of the X Army Corps and the 50th Division were quite minimal at the time. Those units were very short of officers, owing to recent losses. The replacements in the slowly arriving flow were not yet trained well enough to be effective.

The winds were still unfavorable for a gas attack when on 17 October OHL started to withdraw the X Army Corps and the four reinforcement batteries. The original attack objective was then reduced. The 50th Reserve Division had been allocated to the Third Army only for the gas attack. It was ordered into position between the 29th Division and the 23rd Reserve Division. Fort de la Pompelle was then designated as the only remaining attack objective. Other than that, because the attack was short on infantry and artillery strength, only raiding detachments were to advance to the Vesle River and across the Roman road, recover valuable material, and then return to their original positions after two and a half hours.

When the prevailing northern winds finally set in on the evening of 18 October, the commanding general of the XIV Army Corps ordered the release of the gas at 0800 hours on 19 October, in the sector north from Saint-Léonard to the south of Pontfaverger. The resulting gas cloud moving toward the south covered only the lower lying ground, while the higher elevations and especially Fort de la Pompelle remained well above the gas cloud. The gas, therefore, had little effect on those positions. In the event, our advancing raiding parties encountered strong enemy infantry fire and only managed to enter the enemy trenches in a few places.[13] Only the right wing units of the 29th Division, following a carefully planned artillery and trench mortar preparation, achieved any significant success, capturing some three hundred French troops. Fort de la Pompelle remained in French hands, with its garrison suffering no effects from the gas. The enemy artillery apparently suffered more from the gas, because it remained almost completely inactive from 0900 hours on. On 19 October we repositioned the unexpended gas cylinders directly opposite Fort de la Pompelle. We released the gas on 20 October, but the attack produced no effect.

On 20 October the Third Army started receiving the lead elements of the 22nd Reserve Division, which OHL had withdrawn from the Seventh Army. The division took over the position that previously had been occupied by the X Army Corps. Simultaneously, OHL ordered the transfer of the 113rd Division to Army Detachment Strantz, the 53rd Reserve Division (initially without the 241st and 243rd Reserve Infantry Regiments) to the Fourth Army, and the 37th Reserve Infantry Brigade to Army Detachment Gaede. The 183rd, 185th, and 192nd Infantry Brigades were deployed as OHL reserve, deep in the Third Army's rear.

On 21 October 1915, I was awarded the Knight's Cross of the Royal Order of Hohenzollern with Swords, in recognition for my services as chief of Staff of the Third Army. That afternoon I received the decoration from Colonel von Fabeck, who came from OHL to make the presentation. Later that afternoon I took him along to a series of briefings at the front lines.

I was on the road almost all day on 22 October. I spent most of my time at the VIII Reserve Corps, which, like the Third Army headquarters, had been concerned about its positions south of Tahure that were threatened by envelopment from the north and the south. The troops appropriately called that sector "Bad Weather Corner." The deeply echeloned 5th Bavarian Division was deployed there. Thus, it came as no surprise when on the morning of 24 October heavy enemy artillery fire started, followed at 1130 hours by a strong French infantry attack from all sides. Initially, several Bavarian companies in "Bad Weather Corner" were destroyed. The immediately executed hasty counterattack did not get very far. Soon thereafter, the 7th Reserve Division, positioned north of Tahure, also came under a strong but unsuccessful attack. That afternoon and evening the 5th Bavarian Division transitioned into a deliberate counterattack, which almost everywhere turned into bloody hand-to-hand combat with hand grenades and bayonets. The fighting continued well into the night before we finally retook the positions that we had lost that morning. The enemy attack had been conducted by the French XX Army Corps.[14] The French tried again on the night of 29 October. The heavy preparatory trench mortar fire had significantly attritted several Bavarian companies. Launching immediate hasty counterattacks, we were able to retake only some sections of the lost ground.

After standing on the overall defensive for several weeks, the VIII Reserve Corps launched a well-planned and -prepared attack with the objective of retaking the key elevation Hill 192 (La Butte de Tahure), the village of Tahure, and the hills immediately to the south. The Third Army headquarters attached the 4th Division to the VIII Reserve Corps for the attack.

On the morning of 30 October the attack preparation started with trench mortar fire and approximately sixty artillery batteries. The enemy answered only with weak counterfire, mostly from field howitzers. At 1600 hours the deeply echeloned assault was started on our right by the 7th Reserve Division, reinforced by the 14th, 50th, and 149th Infantry Regiments, and on our left by the 5th Bavarian Division, reinforced by the 47th, 49th, and 150th Infantry Regiments. On its first attempt the 7th Reserve Division crossed La Butte de Tahure and captured twenty-one officers and 1,215 French soldiers. During the 5th Bavarian Division's attack, only the 49th Infantry Regiment reached the enemy trenches, but then had to withdraw under heavy flanking fire. During the fighting on 30 and 31 October, I was at the VIII Reserve Corps' command post in the mornings and again in the afternoons. On the night of 30–31 October the 5th Bavarian Division attempted another enveloping attack on the village of Tahure, but the attack failed. The VIII Reserve Corps then started preparations for a new attack on Tahure on 31 October.

On the morning of the 31st, French fire increased and developed into a barrage against La Butte de Tahure. At 1700 hours the French launched a ground attack against La Butte de Tahure and pushed back the center of the 7th Reserve Division. Intelligence later indicated that the attack was carried out by major elements of the French XI and XVI Corps. At 1815 hours the 7th Reserve Division commander reported that the French had broken through and were pushing north with strong forces. The VIII Reserve Corps' 147th Infantry Regiment was shifted immediately to reinforce the 7th Reserve Division. The Third Army committed from its army-level reserve the 158th Infantry Regiment and elements of the 8th Light Grenadier Regiment and the 52nd Infantry Regiment. Only the elements of the 8th Light Grenadier Regiment engaged, as it soon became clear that La Butte de Tahure, contrary to earlier reports, was still firmly held by the 7th Reserve Division. They would continue to hold that key high ground.

In order to avoid further losses, the Third Army headquarters ordered the termination of the attack. The enemy to that point had suffered heavy losses, including more than thirteen hundred prisoners. Strong rain started to set in and the roads quickly became impassable. That, combined with exhaustion on both sides, forced a relative calm to set in along the battle sector.

Despite the heavy fighting on both sides of Tahure, our aggressive esprit still held. On 3 November the 56th Division deployed on the left army wing. Supported by elements of the 21st Reserve Division positioned on the right wing of the Fifth Army, they assaulted Hill 191 north of Massiges. "Cannon Mountain," as the troops called it, was held by the French 2nd Cavalry Division. The attack had been rehearsed thoroughly in the rear. After a proper fire preparation, the attack succeeded quickly, supported by accompanying flamethrowers. We then retained control of the hill despite several enemy deliberate counterattacks.

The loss of Hill 191 deprived the enemy of his fields of observation to the north, which had given him overwatch of our troop movements around Rouveroy. We then turned "Cannon Mountain" into a reinforced position, including the construction of a large number of dugouts on the steep north-facing slope. Those positions had room for two or three battalions. We also gradually improved and expanded the heavily torn-up road network around and north of Rouveroy.

Since October the Third Army headquarters had been receiving intelligence based on prisoner interrogations and agents' reports of increasing troop movements behind the enemy front lines. All this indicated further large-scale attacks, most likely against our present main battle sectors. Thus, we committed all available means to improving our main fighting positions and their connecting lines. The well-rested XIV Army Corps' 29th and 28th Divisions were positioned to reinforce the sectors of the 7th Reserve Division and the 5th Bavarian Division. The corps commander, Lieutenant General Karl von Hänisch, assumed operational control of the Third Army's left sector, which included the 56th Division. After they had a short rest period, the 7th Reserve Division took over the sector from the 5th Division, which along with the 5th Bavarian Division was withdrawn. The XIV Army Corps' sector on the Third Army's right wing was taken over by the commanding general of the VIII Reserve Corps, Lieutenant General Fleck. He had the 4th and 50th Divisions. Within the XII Reserve Corps, the exhausted 24th Reserve Division was relieved by the still fresh 23rd Reserve Division. The artillery units that during the fighting had become heavily intermixed were reorganized, which allowed the corps headquarters to form special artillery groups with clearly defined combat missions. Aerial observation detachments also were attached to those corps-level artillery groups. We continued to commit all available resources to the improvement of our positions. The efforts paid off with a reduction in our losses. Despite heavy enemy artillery fire, the Third Army lost only 845 killed and wounded between 11 and 20 November.[15]

Further analysis of the enemy gradually established a picture that the French had transitioned to the defense. From some parts of their positions they still had deep fields of observation into our positions, and thus good observation posts for their artillery. The XII Reserve Corps and the IX and XIV Army Corps, therefore, received orders to start drafting orders for limited attacks to eliminate those French positions.

On 17 November the king of Saxony visited the headquarters of the Third Army, which had been stood up by Saxony and whose staff still consisted of many Saxon officers, including the crown prince of Saxony, who was serving as an administrative staff officer. I frequently had taken the crown prince with me as an escort officer during my trips to the front. The king's second oldest son was serving in the front lines as an officer in the XII Reserve Corps. The king of Saxony made a good impression on us with his upbeat and unique way of speaking. When he visited the headquarters communications section, which consisted almost exclusively of Saxons, he asked many of the soldiers about their duties. A good looking NCO answered his question by saying, "I am Your Majesty's court chamber singer." The king quickly replied, "Well then, glad to hear you have a real job!" The king only stayed at the army headquarters for a short while, and then he spent a few days with the Saxon XII Reserve Corps.

The sun finally came out on 18 November, following a long rainy period that handicapped the construction of our positions and made all routes impassable. On 27 November the division aviation staff officer and I accompanied the commanding general out to inspect a shot-down French plane that was of their newest construction. Later we met the prince of Hohenzollern, a former regimental commander in the 2nd Guards Regiment, who was the commander's guest for the evening.

On 29 November General von Falkenhayn, who some time ago had gone to the OHL forward headquarters in Pless, returned to Mézières. He ordered all chiefs of staff of the western armies to attend a briefing in Mézières on 30

November. General von Falkenhayn first reviewed briefly the course of the operations against Serbia, which had almost completely destroyed the Serbian Army. Only small remnants had been able to escape to the mountains, without their artillery. The enemy did not impede our operations. The Entente landing at Salonika was designed primarily to win over Greece, but it was a political failure. To this point the Entente did not know what to do in the Balkans, and it did not even have the necessary mountain artillery for operations in mountainous terrain. For the present, therefore, any large-scale Entente operation from Salonika would be impossible. Falkenhayn did, however, describe Salonkia as a "Balkan Gibraltar." For the most part, Bulgarian and Austrian units were maintaining the overwatch in the Balkans for us. Only small numbers of German troops were positioned in the Balkans, to secure General von Mackensen's army headquarters and act as a liaison with Turkey.

On the Eastern Front the overall situation was favorable for us, even though the Russians had not been completely subdued. Any peace feelers extended by the Central Powers would be a devastating error, and surely would be seen as a sign of weakness. We had to continue the war forcefully until our enemies concluded that they could not force their will on us. The way in which we should continue our operations, however, was very difficult to decide. Falkenhayn doubted that we would be able to destroy the enemy militarily. Nonetheless, the leadership of our enemies were fighting for their survival.

The cutting edge of our own operations would remain our army. The most important focus for all our leaders would have to be the maintenance of the troops' warrior spirit, because everything depended on the proficiency of our army. This would require a high level of discipline, but without harassment. The highest levels had to be maintained in and just behind the front lines. Five percent of the troops would be allowed to go on Christmas leave. He emphasized the timely preparation for the transport of the troops to and from the Homeland (*Heimat*). All units would have to be brought up to full combat strength, and the number of officers in the staffs would have to be reduced in favor of frontline duty. The quality of officers would be critical for the units. The resupply of replacements and equipment was secure. Raw materials, except rubber, were available in sufficient quantities. There was only a lack of horses. Thus draft horses would have to be replaced by trucks. We also had started importing horses from Asia Minor. All ammunition requisitions submitted by the army headquarters would be filled. A newly designed 150mm gun with a range of twenty kilometers would be issued first to the Third Army, and then to Army Detachment Gaede.

The primary task of the Third Army was to bring Suippes, Souain, and Mourmelon under fire. New 75mm shells with delay fuzes were being issued to the armies for destructive fires against covered positions. Heavy field howitzer ammunition with time fuzes also was issued. The latter was effective against personnel, but not for destructive fire against materiel.[16]

After General von Falkenhayn finished, all the chiefs of staff briefed the situations in their army sectors. Orders also were issued for the cross-leveling of some units between armies. The Third Army had to detach only individual batteries, which would be replaced with batteries of captured Russian guns capable of both flat-trajectory and high-angle fire. None of the Russian gun batteries would come with assigned horses.[17]

Toward the end of the meeting General von Falkenhayn noted that any opportunity to hurt the enemy must be taken advantage of. Simultaneously, we must exploit every opportunity to raise the morale of our own troops to ensure their readiness to fight the next battle. General von Falkenhayn that day did not discuss any operations being planned by OHL.

On 2 December strong rain and winds set in again, lasting through 18 December. The barely dried-out roads once again became bottomless, hindering the construction of positions. We already had started laying down duckboard in the forwardmost trenches, and now we started to do likewise in the communications trenches.

On 3 December the 47th Landwehr Brigade, holding our extreme right flank, was detached from the Third Army and reassigned to the Seventh Army. That same day OHL ordered the reattachment of the 5th Division to the III Army Corps, and the 5th Bavarian Division to Army Detachment Strantz. The 22nd Reserve Division and the 185th Infantry Brigade also were put on call to the Third Army, which would develop the orders for the rapid forward deployment of the two units. OHL, however, would give the order to start the movement.

At 2200 hours on 6 December the XII Reserve Corps launched a well-prepared attack south of Saint-Souplet-sur-Py, with its 23rd Reserve Division taking a key observation point from the enemy in the process. Several subsequent enemy deliberate counterattacks failed. On 7 December the IX Army Corps attacked and took Hill 185, which was key observation terrain for the enemy. The German troops then held the ground successfully against a series of five strong counterattacks on 7 and 8 December. I was at the front on both days, and we captured a large number of prisoners. The fighting on both days brought to a close the 1915 autumn battle in Champagne. That sector remained quiet from then on.

On 8 December, the Third Army was released from the temporary operational control of Army Group German Crown Prince and returned to direct subordination under OHL. The following day General von Einem fell ill. I reported to him in his sickbed daily, keeping him continuously updated on the situation. He finally returned to full duty on 28 December.

On 12 December the Third Army headquarters reported to OHL the intelligence assessment that large- scale enemy attacks were no longer likely. Thus, OHL on 18 December ordered the detachment of the 50th Reserve Division. That left us without an army-level reserve force behind our right wing. The Saxon 183rd Infantry Brigade that was already positioned there as OHL reserve was reassigned to the Third Army.

After a few sunny days the horrible weather consisting of rain, snow, and fog rolled back in on 21 December, lasting until 3 January. In the afternoon of 26 December, I was at Mézières for a briefing that primarily revolved around logistical issues, and I saw again quite a few of my close comrades from my time at OHL. We were delighted on 27 December when five German soldiers who had been captured by the French in the November fighting returned to our lines. They had escaped from the French, and with great dexterity they infiltrated back through the French lines. The army commander awarded the Iron Cross, 2nd Class, to all five.

From 28 December 1915 until 9 January 1916 the commanding general went on medical leave to recover more fully from his recent illness. During that time the most senior subordinate commander, General von Kirchbach of the XII Reserve Corps, was the acting commander. Even though he gave me Vollmacht to run the daily operations, I still reported to him quite frequently at his headquarters in Saint-Neuville. Unfortunately, that meant a lot of lost work time for me. During the long period of fighting that started on 26 September 1915, my primary sphere of activity was directly on the battlefield. But the initially rare and then later more frequent days of quiet at the front gave us time for reorganization of the of the Third Army's rearward areas.

Owing to the Third Army's extensive loss of ground during the first part of the autumn battle in Champagne, the Bazancourt–Bétheniville–Sommepy–Challerange rail line was useless as a through route because the section from south of Bétheniville to south of Challerange was within the range of enemy artillery fire. Only a few days after taking over as chief of staff of the Third Army, I had requested the accelerated construction of a rail line from Bazancourt, past the northern side of Semide, to Vouziers. Fortunately, this rail construction was executed quickly by the chief of field rail operations, and thus the resupply of ammunition, rations, and other combat supplies was greatly facilitated. We connected into that line several branch lines running south, on which the largest part of the resupply moved vertically toward the front lines. That significantly reduced our horse requirements.

At the beginning of October we started completely reorganizing our rear areas to support the front lines. Initially, I personally put together a program to acquire as many rations and supplies for the front lines as possible. After finalizing all the plans, the execution rested in the hands of the staff sections. Nonetheless, I devoted every free hour to check personally on the progress of the construction of the positions, the improvement of the roads, the fortification of the built-up areas, the construction of new and camouflaged encampments, the establishment of field hospitals and rest centers, artillery and engineer maintenance shops, delousing points, chicken and rabbit farms, etc. Even during the fighting, we made significant progress in all of these areas. We were racing against time to establish good winter quarters for the troops before the cold weather set in. The staff worked harder than they ever had, but they all did their duty happily. Despite the high levels of stress and the very limited time available, we managed to do a lot of good. Both the commanding general and I appreciated all their hard work, of course, but it was most appreciated by the troops for whose welfare all this activity was directed. From 1 February on, we even printed a local newspaper, called *Der Champagne-Kamerad.* At my request the Kaiser sent us his picture for the paper, which we printed with the caption, "To my brave comrades of the Third Army." We printed that issue in large numbers, enough for every Champagne combatant to receive a copy.

Once the fighting let up, we could resume granting home leave. I refrained from taking Christmas leave because the commander was ill and then went on sick leave over New Year's. On the afternoon of 24 December all the officers of the staff and I paid a visit to the commanding general in his sick quarters to convey our best Christmas wishes. General von Einem thanked us all deeply for all of our successful efforts, and he gave all the officers of the staff a silver cup with his coat of arms and an enameled commander's flag. Then gathering around the tree we sang Christmas carols in harmony and remembered our loved ones at home. That evening we all gathered together for a festive dinner, which the commander unfortunately could not attend because he was still too weak.

At the beginning of October, I had initiated a program of cultivating the mostly fallow fields in the Third Army's rear areas. We sowed a considerable amount of winter seed. Landwehr soldiers in the rear echelon units who were experienced in agricultural matters were distributed throughout the villages, and we tasked them to organize the cultivating efforts. Retired *Rittmeister*[18] von Zitzewitz, whom I had known from when I was a lieutenant, and who was a close friend of the commanding general, was recalled to active duty and assigned to the Third Army as an agricultural staff officer to manage the agricultural and associated efforts. This officer, highly qualified in all agronomic matters, achieved significant results for us. He established in the rear areas a large number of dairies, whose milk, butter, and cheese output was devoted almost exclusively to the troops in our front lines.

Zitzewitz also requisitioned from the Homeland frame saws for the steam-powered sawmills that cut the wood from the tree trunks we took out of the French forests. We used that lumber for the construction of dugouts, duckboard walkways, and new construction of billets. The processed lumber was transported to the front via the existing rail lines and the branch lines. Over time we had some six thousand Russian prisoners of war provided by OHL to work construction of the road network in our rear area.

Our large number of German agricultural personnel were issued a small German-French dictionary to help them communicate with the local people. Using this dictionary, which also listed phonetic pronunciations, our stalwart Landwehr soldiers very quickly became comfortable with the French population. All the larger installations in the rear areas were tied into the local telephone network, which facilitated rapid requisitions and deliveries. All these huge rear-area efforts to provide for the frontline troops paid off in their satisfied faces.

So far, the staff at the Third Army headquarters in Vouziers had always messed in the building of the commanding general's quarters. At the start of January we established a simple but comfortable officers' mess in the old building of the former prefecture, directly across from the headquarters' building. There were several apartments on the floor above the mess, one of which I occupied. It consisted of a sitting room, bedroom, bathroom, and small anteroom, which served as the quarters for my orderly. The horses were stabled close by, but I only rarely had the opportunity to go riding. The work hours in Vouziers and my many trips to the front and to the rear areas consumed almost all of my time. In the evenings we frequently had guests from outside the command. For the troops and the lower level staffs we established several NCO and enlisted canteens. We also converted a large riding hall into a theater and conference center. On several occasions the members of the staff put on a production of *Wallenstein's Encampment.*[19] Singers and comedians from the staff performed as well.

As early as the middle of December, I had been contemplating the continuation of the war at the operational level on the Western Front. Our successes in the east and in the Balkans clearly would allow us to regroup strong forces in the west. There was no doubt in my mind that those forces must be used for an offensive on the Western Front. I knew that General von Falkenhayn frequently ordered the various army headquarters to develop plans for offensives in their area of operations. From my experience in the autumn of 1914, I knew the ground on both sides of the Argonne Forest, as well as the forest itself. On my own initiative, therefore, I drew up a rough draft plan for a Third Army attack, thrusting far into the enemy. Then, in coordination with the Fifth Army's right wing, we would encircle the French forces in the Argonne from the east, west, and south and destroy them. Secondary attacks would cut off Fortress Verdun from the south and demolish it with fire from our heaviest artillery. I specifically discounted the probability that the enemy would break through our positions in the south, because they had not been able to penetrate us so far. According to my rough estimates, OHL by the spring of 1916 would have a reserve of at least twenty-five fully combat-ready divisions. When we launched our attack, both the French and the British would have to consolidate their reserve divisions to defend. Then the reserves of the German western armies not committed directly to the attack could be used to mount an operational-level attack. Initially I developed following operational plan for the Third Army:

1. Attack toward Prunay with the army's right wing on a fourteen-kilometer-wide front with six divisions and very strong artillery; with the left wing from the center of 24th Reserve Division toward the south to the Vesle River, which would serve as a flank and rear security barrier. The follow-on operation would be an advance with the army's left half toward the Marne.
2. South of Suippes an additional six divisions would attack to the east and southeast into the flank and rear of the enemy forces positioned north of Suippes. The enemy's left wing would be fixed in position by a holding attack launched by another division.
3. Another six divisions from the army's left wing would attack via Souain.
4. Then Attack Groups 2 and 3 would advance farther toward the east and southeast, with main effort on the right wing. The result would be a penetration between Souain and Massiges by the Third Army and the right wing of the Fifth Army. Depending on the situation at that point, a follow-on attack would then continue to exploit in the direction of Châlons-en-Champagne–Vitry-le-François.

I calculated the necessary forces for the attack at 6 + 6 + 1 + 6 = 19 divisions, of which the Third Army could contribute five divisions: the 4th, 50th, 18th, 24th Reserve, and 23rd Reserve. Thus, we would have to be reinforced by fourteen divisions with strong artillery.

I reviewed this attack plan with the commanding general, who voiced no concerns or objections. There was at this time no reason to submit the plans to the OHL. As I learned only much later, General von Falkenhayn had submitted a position paper to the Kaiser identifying England as the main enemy. In order to defeat Britain, Falkenhayn recommended an offensive on land and sea, starting with initiation of unrestricted submarine warfare. Grand Admiral Alfred von Tirpitz and Admiral Henning von Holzendorff reported that the submarine operations could begin in March 1916, and they predicted that Britain would be ready to negotiate a peace toward the end of the year. Chancellor of the Reich Theobald von Bethmann-Hollweg disagreed with any initiation of unrestricted submarine warfare, pointing out that it would then lead to war with America.

The Kaiser decided against unrestricted submarine warfare, which probably is the main reason that General von Falkenhayn abandoned a large-scale offensive against the British. In the meantime, some twenty-five divisions had gradually reached combat-ready status as OHL reserves, but Falkenhayn did not believe that number sufficient to win a decisive victory over the British—one which would succeed in pushing the British off the Continent. About the same time Falkenhayn also rejected a recommendation from the Austrian chief of the General Staff for an attack to destroy the Italian Army. Falkenhayn thought that such an operation would require the diversion of too many German divisions away from the Western Front.

Failing the other options, General von Falkenhayn decided to launch an attack against the French. He did not, however, think that we had sufficient forces available to achieve a breakthrough. He therefore considered a more localized attack, either against Verdun or in the direction of Belfort. He tasked Army Group German Crown Prince to develop attack plans and force estimates for both alternatives.

By the beginning of December of 1915 General von Falkenhayn decided on the Verdun attack. He believed that the French would try to hold Verdun at all costs, and consequently would commit large numbers of reinforcements against such an attack. Despite the operationally sound recommendation by Army Group German Crown Prince to attack on both sides of the Meuse, General von Falkenhayn decided to conduct the attack only on the eastern bank of the river. That was a critical mistake. Although the attack along the eastern bank initially would make good progress, it would have to stall as soon as it encountered French artillery flanking fire from the western bank. That, in fact, is exactly what happened.

From the beginning of January 1916 on, the enemy remained quiet across the Third Army's front. In order to maintain a continually updated French order of battle, our subordinate corps conducted many small patrol operations that brought in several prisoners. The interrogations of the prisoners helped us maintain a rather accurate assessment of the enemy's strength. The conclusion was that the French front was manned only minimally. Our aerial observers confirmed this information and also reported large transport movements headed south, away from our sector. To our delight, almost all of the prisoners stated that the French positions were full of water. We also had water in our more elevated positions, but everywhere in our trenches we laid down duckboard, constructed from locally cut lumber. Our troops also used pumps to remove the water.

On 9 January 1916 the XIV Army Corps conducted a well-executed attack that had been rehearsed meticulously in the rear area. Attacking northwest of Massiges, the corps succeeded on the first attempt, capturing seven officers and 480 French troops. We found about twice that number of dead in the French positions. We suffered only minor casualties. Our assault troops then immediately improved the former French trenches facing south. In the evening of 9 January, I met General von Einem at the train station upon his return from sick leave. He was quite pleased with the result of the XIV Army Corps' attack. On 11 January the French launched a counterattack, but they were bloodily repelled. Heavy firing continued to rage at Massiges until 15 January, and then the sector became quiet again.

After a long rainy period, the sun finally came out on 14 January. On 17 January, I accompanied the commanding general to a series of briefings at the Seventh Army headquarters. On the trip there and back we visited two of our corps headquarters and their divisions. The following day the heavy rains returned. On 27 January, the Kaiser's birthday, we held a parade in the market square at Vouziers. That evening we had a more formal than usual dinner in the officers' mess, during which General von Einem delivered an especially nice speech. In the meantime, I had picked up indicators that the Fifth Army's preparations were in full swing for its attack against the northern face of Verdun's defenses. Consequently, we briefed the Third Army estimate of the situation to OHL on 29 January. We reported that it would only be possible to fix in place the French divisions in the Champagne sector if we could conduct a larger holding attack. We could not conduct such an attack, however, without additional troops and ammunition. On 1 February we received a follow-on request for information from General von Falkenhayn. He wanted to know if, where, and with what additional forces the Third Army could launch a larger thrust in the event that the French thinned out their line opposite the Third Army. Such an attack would have to advance at least as far as Vitry-le-François.

On 4 February the Third Army briefed the detailed attack plan to OHL. The key point was that after pushing the French back into the Argonne Forest, the type of follow-on operation in the direction of Vitry-le-François would depend on the development of the overall situation. In all likelihood, additional reinforcements would be necessary to extend the operation farther to the south. We also forecast that this operation to the south most likely could become the decisive battle on the Western Front, against which the French would have to consolidate all of their available forces. As the enemy weakened their forces opposite our other sectors, we then would be able to consolidate any and all forces available for the decisive battle. At the end of the briefing General von Einem noted that, since transitioning to a trench warfare posture, his Third Army had been fighting heavy defensive battles almost constantly and sustaining heavy losses in the process. The troops, therefore, would be more than happy to go over to the offensive.

General von Falkenhayn, however, already had decided on a frontal attack against Fortress Verdun. I thought as much when on 5 February as I was driving to Stenay for a briefing. I could see that increasing numbers of attack troops for the Verdun operation had already arrived in the Fifth Army's sector. Still, I did not learn any of the details of the attack that day. Understandably, the Fifth Army headquarters was rather reluctant to share information. Under the circumstances, then, we were not surprised that General von Falkenhayn had not authorized our requests for reinforcements. As he noted, "Our problem is to inflict heavy damage on the enemy at the decisive point, with a relatively modest effort." That clearly was a reference to the planned attack on Verdun. Falkenhayn, however, wanted a new recommendation from the Third Army for a breakthrough to the south, between Prunay and Saint-Hilaire-le-Grand. Such an attack would be launched from the sectors of the 50th Division, 24th Reserve Division, and 23rd Reserve Division, with a follow-on advance to the east against the enemy shoulder. General von Falkenhayn wanted to allocate for this attack only five to six divisions in the first echelon, and two or three in the second, with a howitzer battery supporting each 150-meter segment of the attack front. Three to four of the eight divisions would have to come from the forces that the Third Army already had on hand. We immediately submitted a new attack plan based on the parameters laid down by General von Falkenhayn. We never got an answer from OHL.

On the morning of 11 February General von Falkenhayn and the Kaiser arrived in Charleville from Pless. That same morning all the army chiefs of staff (with the exception of the chief of staff of the Fifth Army) were ordered to attend a conference in Mézières with General von Falkenhayn.

After all the chiefs of staff briefed the situations of their respective armies, General von Falkenhayn spoke. Based on notes I took at the time, his comments were as follows:

> The decision in this war can only be achieved on the Western Front. For large-scale operational planning the question is less what needs to be done, but how and when. The German Army is now moving into a phase of operations in the west that should bring about the decision. Thus, the General Headquarters will be moved from Pless back to Charleville. It is necessary to transition to the conduct of forceful

> strikes on the Western Front, because mere episodes are the only things we have achieved in the east, nor is there any reason to continue operations in the Balkans. A decisive strike against Italy is possible, but it would have no influence on German interests and could not result in the ending of the war. Now, during this winter, we must conduct offensive operations in the west. The French are not yet worn out, but the harsh winter weather will degrade their capability. During the winter of 1914–1915 it had not been feasible for us to conduct a large-scale attack, but we now have the necessary reserve forces.

Falkenhayn did not like any of the recommendations that had been submitted by the western armies, because the twenty to thirty divisions needed for a major strike in the west were not available. The armies not involved in such an attack could not be weakened, because their front lines then would be too thin and could be easily broken through by the enemy. Setbacks on the Western Front were unacceptable. The assembly of strong forces takes a long time. Based on experience, such an attack only advances slowly, which gives the enemy time to conduct counter operations. We, therefore, had to abandon the basic principle of pulling everything together prior to launching a large-scale attack.

The command of such large attack operations would be very difficult. The attempts by the enemy to break through at Arras and in Champagne failed largely because the enemy's leadership failed to control their massed formations. Thus, there was no clear proof to this point that a mass breakthrough would necessarily be more effective than smaller-scale operations. In any case, the assembly of massed formations for an attack invites a massive reaction by the defender.

Falkenhayn's comments were not meant to be a criticism of the military merits of the recommendations submitted by the armies, but rather to serve as the starting point for continued deliberations. In order to break the deadlock on the Western Front, it would be necessary to inflict a deep wound on the enemy at a decisive point. Verdun was the only major point where we had the necessary reach. For quite some time we had been considering an attack on Belfort, but that would be too difficult. Nonetheless, preparations for that major attack in Alsace would serve as a good deceptive measure. OHL, therefore, had selected Verdun as the attack objective. And although it would be good if we actually managed to capture Verdun, even a serious threat to the fortress would be a major setback for the French. The problem facing the enemy, then, would hinge on the impact on the rest of his front that our attack on Verdun would cause.

If the French had the nerve for it, they could put their trust in the ability of the fortress to resist. Such an enemy course of action would be least advantageous to us. We then would be faced with the alternative of continuing the attack on Verdun, or shifting to an operation in another army's sector. The French most probable course of action, however, would be to pull strong forces in toward Verdun. That is essentially what we did in the face of major attacks. If they did that, then we would have the opportunity to inflict a major wound on the French Army.

A third option for the French would be to reinforce Verdun only to the minimum extent necessary to hold on, and then mass for an attack against us in another sector, such as Artois or Champagne. Alsace and Lorraine were also options for French attacks.

General von Falkenhayn's then asked us if there were any indicators that the enemy was preparing for such actions, to which all of the armies' chiefs of staff replied in the negative. Even so, Falkenhayn offered the opinion that a major enemy attack anywhere other than the Verdun sector would really be to our advantage, because we always had succeeded in defending against such attacks. Our thrust toward Verdun, then, would have an even greater chance of succeeding.

The fourth enemy course of actions would be for the French to consolidate their main forces at Verdun while the British launched a major attack elsewhere. At the time, however, the British were in a weak position, because they were in the process of consolidating their old professional army with their newly formed Kitchener divisions. A large-scale British attack, therefore, was somewhat unlikely.

As General von Falkenhayn then summarized his discussion, our operation against Verdun had a high probability of success. All the field armies, therefore, should conform their operational planning with that of OHL. Unity of effort was essential for the success of the Verdun operation, and the primary reason why Falkenhayn had called the meeting.

The army chiefs of staff all knew that the attack would be conducted only on the eastern bank of the Meuse. Most of us knew how strong the Verdun defenses were, and there probably was not one of us who did not foresee that as the attack advanced only down the eastern bank of the Meuse it sooner or later would come under French artillery flanking fire from the western bank. I knew that ground on the western bank of the Meuse very well from when I was the chief of staff of the XIII Army Corps. I simply could not conclude that that attack as planned by OHL would result in the seizure of the fortress. My commanding general agreed with me. I will not discuss here the details of the attack on Verdun. I was not involved in the operation, and I only learned the facts at a much later date.

Now that OHL had made the decision, the Third Army had to pin down the enemy forces on our front to the maximum extent possible. We could only do so by launching small and limited objective attacks. On 12 and 13 February we successfully conducted two such attacks, which already had been planned. The attack on 12 February yielded 202 French prisoners; the attack on 13 February yielded seven officers and 304 enlisted soldiers. In response, the French restricted themselves to laying heavy fires on the positions we captured. But we strongly reinforced those positions, which proved very valuable for artillery observation. Starting on 12 February we could hear continual fire from the direction of Verdun.

The initial results of the Verdun attack fell short of expectations. Across from us the French artillery fire increased constantly, probably based on the fear that the Third Army would attack. On 16 February the French attempted several unsuccessful deliberate counterattacks into the ground we had taken on 12 and 13 February. On 23 February we lost a small salient in our line, but prepared immediately to retake it with a deliberate counterattack. During that time I went to the front mornings and afternoons on an almost daily basis. My purpose was to check on the preparations for the series of limited attacks that we were still planning. I also reconnoitered the ground for the potential offensive with the five additional divisions General von Falkenhayn indicated we might get. That attack, however, never materialized.

On 27 February the IX Army Corps achieved some very respectable results with a well-planned attack on both sides of the Ferme de Navarin, capturing in the process twenty-six French officers, 1,125 troops, fifteen machine guns, and a large number of trench mortars. The corps was led by its especially capable commander, General Ferdinand von Quast, supported by his chief of staff, Colonel von Klüver, and his General Staff officer Ia, Major von Platen. In reaction, the French launched several deliberate counterattacks, all of which were bloodily repelled. The ground we gained in that attack provided us with a wide and deep field of observation into the enemy positions. On 4 March the Kaiser personally reviewed the IX Army Corps' assault troops. The weather that day was excellent. General von Einem and I later met the Kaiser in the field, where I used a map to brief His Majesty in detail on how that attack had been executed. The Kaiser eloquently expressed his appreciation and gratitude to the troops and their leaders.

On 7 March we launched a broad and deliberate counterattack to retake the section of trench line that we had lost on 23 February. The attack succeeded immediately, resulting in two officers and 150 French troops captured. Three days later the weather changed. Heavy rain set in at first, and then turned to snow as the temperature dropped. Then everything started to thaw, turning all the roads and paths into small creeks.

On 11 March three naval officers visited the Third Army headquarters in

Vouziers and gave us an interesting briefing on submarine warfare and other fleet operations. On 13 March, I took them with me on a reconnaissance trip into our forwardmost positions. They were quite impressed with such a rare experience, and they repeatedly expressed their gratitude. That night in the officers' mess we celebrated the event with quite a few drinks. The friendship I established with these three naval officers continued well after the end of the war.

On 15 March the French launched a deliberate but abortive counterattack against the ground we had taken from them on 7 March. The following day, General von Falkenhayn called me personally to express his satisfaction with the high tempo of the Third Army's local operations. When I asked him when we could expect the five divisions to mount a larger attack, he answered so evasively that it was clear me that we most likely would never see them.

The sun finally returned on 20 March. The ground dried out quickly and soon the roads and paths were covered with an unpleasant layer of chalky dust. During those days I went forward almost daily to reconnoiter the front, or to the rear areas to check on the logistical support. On 30 March I made a long terrain walk through sections of the trenches. I then returned to my office by car, where I was hit with a sudden and very painful attack of lumbago in my back. Any movement at all was extremely painful, and therefore the commanding general had to come to my office to do all the signing. I had a large and very hot mustard pack applied to my back, which was surprisingly effective. After only about two hours I was able to move again. That evening I surprised General von Einem and my comrades when I showed up in the officers' mess. I fully intended to fight off the remaining effects of the lumbago with some internal remedy. General von Einem, who always thought that he too had back problems, asked the army surgeon to give him a mustard pack, although there was really nothing wrong with him. As a consequence of the hot pack, General von Einem ended up with a raw back that took quite a while to heal. My thick hide had been more resilient against the mustard.

During this period the Third Army had a lot of visitors, especially members of the high nobility. The grand dukes of Baden, Mecklenburg-Schwerin, and Mecklenburg-Strelitz visited their troops serving in the Third Army. The duke of Meiningen, the crown prince of Bulgaria, and the Turkish military attaché also showed up. One especially noteworthy visitor was Prince Oskar of Prussia, who earlier had been in Stenay to visit his brother, the German crown prince. Prince Oskar described to us in much detail the course of the heavy fighting around Verdun. Other visitors included Wilhelm Solf, the state secretary of the German Colonial Office, and Karl Prince of Ratibor and Corvey, the executive president of the province of Westphalia. On many occasions I had dinner in

Vouziers with various colleagues I had known from before the war, and who now were serving in the Third Army. We took advantage of that period of relative calm to make continuous improvements to our positions and reinforce our rearward lines.

After one year and eight months of war I went on leave for the first time between 8 and 10 April, to visit my family in Stuttgart. The occasion was the confirmation of my oldest daughter. During my return trip on 10 April, I learned via a telephone call I made from Charleville that everything had remained calm at Third Army. The weather was good, so I used the remainder of that day to visit many of the agricultural production sites in our rear area. I finally arrived back in Vouziers that evening. From 14 to 23 April we had rain again almost uninterruptedly, which played havoc with the hay harvest in the rear areas. General von Falkenhayn ordered me to attend a briefing in Mézières in the afternoon of 30 April. He instructed the Third Army to submit an attack plan based on receiving two divisions and corresponding artillery as reinforcements. Falkenhayn designated the attack as a diversionary operation to tie down French forces. The choice of the attack sector he left to the Third Army.

Just a few days later we submitted the attack plan to be conducted on an approximately seven-kilometer-wide front on both sides of the boundary between our XII Reserve Corps and IX Army Corps. The right wing would advance in the direction of Saint-Hilaire-le-Grand, and the left wing in the direction of Souain. Based on our available forces, the limited objective of the attack would be three kilometers beyond our positions. The intent was to inflict heavy losses on the enemy and to destroy his artillery. That, in turn, would force the French to rebuild their defensive positions opposite us by withdrawing divisions from Verdun.

If the French did not conduct strong deliberate counterattacks, our attack would then be widened toward the east, in order to establish a defensive line conforming to the terrain. That line should run as straight as possible between Aubérive and the "Bad Weather Corner" south of Tahure. In submitting our plan to OHL, we emphasized that by reconquering a large part of the ground we had lost during the autumn battle of 1915, we would place heavy pressure on the French, who then would respond with strong deliberate counterattacks. The end result almost certainly would be a reduction of the French forces fighting the Germans at Verdun. General von Falkenhayn never responded to the Third Army's attack plan draft, either orally or in writing.

According to reports coming in at the beginning of May from our rear area agricultural production sites, 160,000 *Morgen* [100,000 acres] had been cultivated for the provisioning of the Third Army's combat troops. Our saw mills were cutting lumber for construction at a daily value of 50,000 marks. The rear area production of meat, milk, butter, cheese, and eggs completely covered the requirements of the Third Army. Every soldier going on leave took a large food package home with him.

On 8 May the Kaiser returned to review the Third Army troops. Between 8 and 16 May General von Einem was on leave with his family in Münster in Westphalia, from where he had first assumed command of the VII Army Corps in 1914.

On 10 May, I received the welcome news that our only son at age sixteen and a half had graduated from high school with good grades. He already was accepted as an officer candidate in the 2nd Foot Guards Regiment, with a report date of 1 July 1916. That was the same regiment that my father, my brother, and I had all served in.

During the commanding general's absence several other of the senior staff officers also were on leave, which tied me down to the office a great deal. I used whatever slack time I had for trips to the front lines and to plan in all detail the assembly and the execution of the attack that we had recommended to General von Falkenhayn.

After General von Einem returned from leave, he and I between 18 and 25 May made daily visits to the front lines and to the rear area agricultural production sites. On 24 May we celebrated the birthday of the king of Saxony in the officers' mess and in the enlisted canteens. The commanding general made an especially good speech that day.

General von Falkenhayn ordered all the Western Front army chiefs of staff to report to Mézières on 26 May. Initially, he reviewed the operations in the other theaters of war. The Russian offensive in February and March had been repulsed quite effectively. The Russians apparently were preparing to launch a new offensive, but time and location were not yet clear. They might not even execute their plans because of the deteriorating domestic situation in Russia. If they did attack, however, they most likely would aim against the southern sector of our eastern front.

Although the Russians were attacking aggressively in Turkey, the operations there would have no decisive influence on the outcome of the war. A Russian attack on Persia, however, could prove dangerous. There were clear indications of an operational-level synchronization in the Middle East between the Russians and the British, who were now approximately twenty kilometers north of the Suez Canal. General von Falkenhayn stressed his confidence in the Turkish leader, Enver Pasha, even though the latter's operational capability was limited to the present.

In the Balkans, General von Mackensen was holding his advance line with his German Life Guards units and his Bulgarian troops. The situation was serious, however, in the Italian theater of war. The independent Austrian advance had weakened the Italian Army, and in so doing contributed to our overall strategic position; but in the process the Austrian Army's combat power had been reduced significantly.

On the Western Front, the French were being worn down increasingly. Their reserves had been strongly attritted, and their replacement pool was only between three hundred thousand and four hundred thousand men. The Verdun operation had been a success in that respect. Our heavy artillery, however, had only been as effective as we anticipated during the initial stages of the operation. As the attack progressed, the concentrated heavy artillery had been less effective against the major forts and especially against the smaller, concrete-reinforced *ouvrages.*

The main objective of the attack at Verdun was still the degradation of the French army, and not necessarily the seizure of the fortress. Nonetheless, were we to actually capture Verdun, it naturally would be an even more serious blow to French morale. Any plans of confronting the British directly on the high seas were not viable. We could only achieve a decision on land. However, General von Falkenhayn did not talk at all about operational plans against the British. He stressed in only the most general terms the necessity of defeating the British, whose present outlook was very gloomy because of Verdun.

Falkenhayn concluded by issuing directives for the training of the troops, and he stressed the overall importance of lifting morale and instilling the spirit of attack. A key factor, in his opinion, would be the officers getting closer to the troops and sharing in their living conditions. He also talked about the need to coordinate the fires of all the artillery, with the field artillery units increasingly engaging targets at longer ranges. Ammunition was available in sufficient quantities, but that did not mean it should be expended recklessly. The standard daily rates of fire should not be exceeded, otherwise the necessary ammunition would not be available for the large battles.

With the exception of the chief of staff of the Fifth Army, the rest of the army chiefs of staff remained behind for a while and talked over General von Falkenhayn's remarks. We all thought they were disappointing. We knew that according to OHL's intelligence reports the French alone still had thirty divisions in reserve, and that the British were growing stronger all the time. We had all hoped, therefore, that our attack on Verdun would be suspended in favor of a new operation against the British. The Fourth, Sixth, and Second Armies, opposite the British, had all submitted draft attack plans to General von Falkenhayn, but he did not, in our opinion, know himself what had to be done. His hesitating attitude was starting to reduce our confidence in him.

Immediately after my return to Vouziers I briefed General von Einem on the meeting with General von Falkenhayn. Einem then ordered all the Third Army subordinate commanding generals and their chiefs of staff to attend a briefing at the Third Army headquarters on 30 May. During that meeting we discussed all the basics for the training of all troops and the coordination of artillery flanking fires between the corps.

On 2 June we finally received detailed reports of the victorious outcome of the naval battle at Skagerak on 31 May 1916.[20] That evening General von Einem celebrated the glorious victory by delivering a fiery speech at the officers' mess. During the night of 2–3 June we conducted a planned minor attack operation, capturing two hundred French troops. At the beginning of June, Captain von Santen, a member of the Third Army General Staff, published a very good memorandum on the 1915 autumn battle in Champaign. A total of four hundred thousand copies were printed and distributed to all the troops.

On 11 June we conducted a small attack in the vicinity of Tahure, capturing one hundred prisoners and four machine guns. A small advance patrol brought in another twenty prisoners and several more machine guns. All of these operations had the simple purpose of reconnoitering the enemy's order of battle and verifying the information from prisoner interrogations. During the night of 18–19 June, enemy aircraft dropped several bombs on Vouziers, causing only slight damage.

Along with the rest of the army, we looked with ever increasing concern at the ongoing attacks at Verdun. The chief of staff of the Fifth Army,[21] who had a great deal of influence with General von Falkenhayn, was the driving force behind continuing the operation. This meant that not only were all the OHL reserves available in February engaged at Verdun, but also the rapidly depleted divisions had to be replaced by fresh divisions that were withdrawn from the other field armies on the Western Front. Incredible amounts of German blood were spilled at Verdun without our ever achieving the objective of the attack. When the Austrian attack in Galicia failed toward the middle of June, we also were forced to redeploy additional German divisions from the west to the east.

That, however, still did not cause General von Falkenhayn to make the obvious decision to end the fighting at Verdun. On 25 June at a briefing I attended in Mézières, Falkenhayn told me that he intended to continue pressing the Verdun attack as long as the French were sustaining higher losses than we were. That, in my opinion, was based on a completely incorrect estimate of the situation. Our enemies in the west had far greater reserves than we did, and the British Army was growing ever stronger with the arrival of the many new Kitchener divisions. While we were engaged completely at Verdun, those new divisions were able to train and adjust to the conditions in the front lines without any interference from us. General von Falkenhayn put his last hope for a decisive success at Verdun on artillery fires using the new Green Cross gas shells.[22] Since Green Cross was fired primarily by light field artillery, a large number of light field batteries were withdrawn from the other armies and reassigned to the Fifth Army. In the Third Army we had to detach almost half of our light field batteries.

On 27 June we received reports of the French bombing raids on Karlsruhe that killed many German children. I arranged with my wife to turn the thickly walled, vaulted basement under our house in Stuttgart into an air-raid shelter. My family spent many nights in that shelter during the numerous bombing raids on Stuttgart.

On 24 June 1916 heavy artillery fire started falling on the positions of our Second Army, on both sides of the Somme. The intensity of the enemy fire increased constantly, becoming a preparatory barrage during the final days of June. On the morning of 1 July 1916 the French[23] launched a wide and deeply echeloned multicorps attack, which initially pushed our thin lines back a good distance with heavy losses.

On 2 July the chief of staff of the Second Army recommended a voluntarily withdrawal from the torn-up ground in the deep salient south of Péronne. The purpose of such a withdrawal would be to straighten the overall line. General von Falkenhayn, who was at Second Army headquarters that afternoon, did not concur.

Later that night, around 2330 hours, I received a phone call in Vouziers from Lieutenant Colonel von Tieschowitz, the chief of the General Staff's Personnel Section. He told me that I was being reassigned as the chief of staff of the Second Army, and I should come to Mézières as quickly as possible to talk to General von Falkenhayn. Tieschowitz asked me if I could recommend a capable successor for the Third Army. I recommended Colonel Martin Freiherr von Oldershausen, the chief of staff of the VIII Army Corps. He knew the situation in the Third Army sector. He was very energetic and a well-rounded General Staff officer. He succeeded me on 3 July 1916 and proved to be a very good choice.

The call reached me in my quarters above the officers' mess, just as I was going to bed. I sent for the commanding general's son, who was still at the mess, and asked him to wake his father. I got dressed quickly and reported to the commander, after taking my quick leave of my comrades who were still at the officers' mess. I asked them to send my gear as quickly as possible to Saint-Quentin. General von Einem was quite upset that he was going to lose me, but he warmly thanked me for my work. He also expressed his firm belief that my energy would contribute to a German victory in the Somme defensive battle. Ever since our time serving together in the Third Army, General von Einem remained a benefactor and a friend. I faithfully stayed in contact with him until his death.

Making a fast trip by car, I reached Mézières at about 0100 hours on 3 July.

General von Falkenhayn had already gone to bed, but he received me at his bedside and expressed the hope that I would gain control of the fighting at the Somme. I told General von Falkenhayn very frankly that the Second Army would need a significant reinforcement of divisions, artillery, aviation, and supporting elements. Sufficient reinforcements for the Second Army, however, could only become available if the attack on Verdun was aborted immediately in a planned and deliberate manner. Upon disengagement, our forces would have to establish immediately a straight and defensible line. Only then could we move adequate reinforcements to the Somme sector. The French-British attack was wide and deeply echeloned, and their most probable objective was a breakthrough with massive force.

General von Falkenhayn was very reluctant to abort the Verdun offensive. After I continued to push the issue, he finally gave me a hand-shake promise to discontinue the attack on Verdun. Unfortunately, Falkenhayn did not keep his promise. He continued to press the Verdun offensive right up until he was relieved as the chief of the General Staff of the German Army on 28 August 1916.

I left Mézières for Saint-Quentin about 0145 hours, traveling in General von Falkenhayn's very fast staff car. I was accompanied by Falkenhayn's personal adjutant, who set up a bed for me with blankets and pillows in the open car. Thus, I was able to get some sleep during the trip. Just after 0500 hours I arrived at the Second Army headquarters in Saint-Quentin, refreshed and ready for action. I immediately assumed my duties as chief of staff.

General of Infantry Fritz von Lossberg, shortly before his retirement. (Mittler und Sohn, Berlin)

General Helmuth Johann Ludwig von Moltke the Younger, Chief of the General Staff, 1914. (Library of Congress, LC-B2-3173-7)

General Erich Georg Anton von Falkenhayn, Chief of the General Staff, 1914–1916. (BArch/146-2004-0023)

Field Marshall Paul von Hindenburg and General Erich Ludendorff, Chief of the General Staff and First Quartermaster General, 1916–1918. (BArch/146-1970-073-47)

Crown Prince Wilhelm of Prussia, Commander, Army Group German Crown Prince. (BArch/146-1988-089-06)

Crown Prince Rupprecht of Bavaria, Commander, Army Group Crown Prince Rupprecht. (Library of Congress, LC-B2-5302-6)

General Hermann Josef von Kuhl (right), Chief of Staff of Army Group Crown Prince Rupprecht in 1917 and 1918. Kuhl is pictured here with First Army Commander General Alexander von Kluck (center), under whom he served as chief of staff during the Battle of the Marne in 1914. (The Prussian Machine)

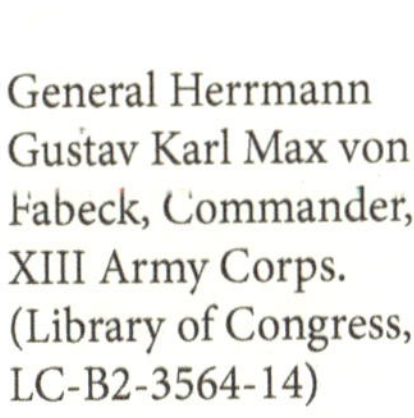
General Herrmann Gustav Karl Max von Fabeck, Commander, XIII Army Corps. (Library of Congress, LC-B2-3564-14)

General Karl von Einem, Commander, Third Army. (Library of Congress, LC-B2-3292-14)

General Friedrich Bertram Sixt von Armin, Commander, Fourth Army. (Wikimedia Commons)

General Max Ferdinand Karl von Boehn, Commander, Army Group Boehn. (Wikimedia Commons)

Field Marshal Erich von Manstein, World War II. (BArch/183-H01757)

Captain von Manstein as a General Staff officer during World War I. (Used by permission of the von Manstein family.)

4

Chief of the General Staff of the Second Army (The Somme, 1916)

By the time I arrived at the Second Army headquarters in Saint-Quentin on 3 July 1916 shortly after 0500 hours, my predecessor, Major General Paul Grünert, had already departed. The senior General Staff officer, Major Faupel, briefed me on the previous conduct of the battle, which he described approximately as follows:

The Battle of the Somme did not catch the Second Army by surprise. In February German flyers had already reported numerous troop bivouacs in front of the northern sector of the army on both sides of the line from Albert to Bapaume. A short time later there was an increase in the number of divisions on the English front north of the Somme. According to the observations of German patrols, most of these units were relieved again after a few weeks in the line. Toward the end of April, the number of English divisions north of the Somme had grown to twelve, which originally were opposed by only four German divisions—the 2nd Guards Reserve Division, 26th Reserve Division, 28th Reserve Division, and the 12th Division. The standing plan at that time to counter the expected enemy offensive with a counteroffensive was found to be unworkable because of the draw on our forces at Verdun. In April only one division, the 52nd Division, was allocated as a reinforcement to the Second Army. That unit was positioned between the 2nd Guards Reserve Division and the 26th Reserve Division, where the English were particularly strong. The divisional fronts on the right wing of the Second Army were thus 6 kilometers in width, while along the remaining army sector the divisional frontages remained between 7.5 and 9 kilometers.

In May two of the Second Army's infantry divisions were pulled out of the front and replaced by one division, which following a short rest period still had not made up its losses from Verdun. A significant number of German modern heavy batteries also were replaced with captured batteries. Until May the assumption was that the French would not participate in the expected attack. At the beginning of June, the indicators of the impending attack increased. Two French divisions appeared north of the Somme, where up to that time the Eng-

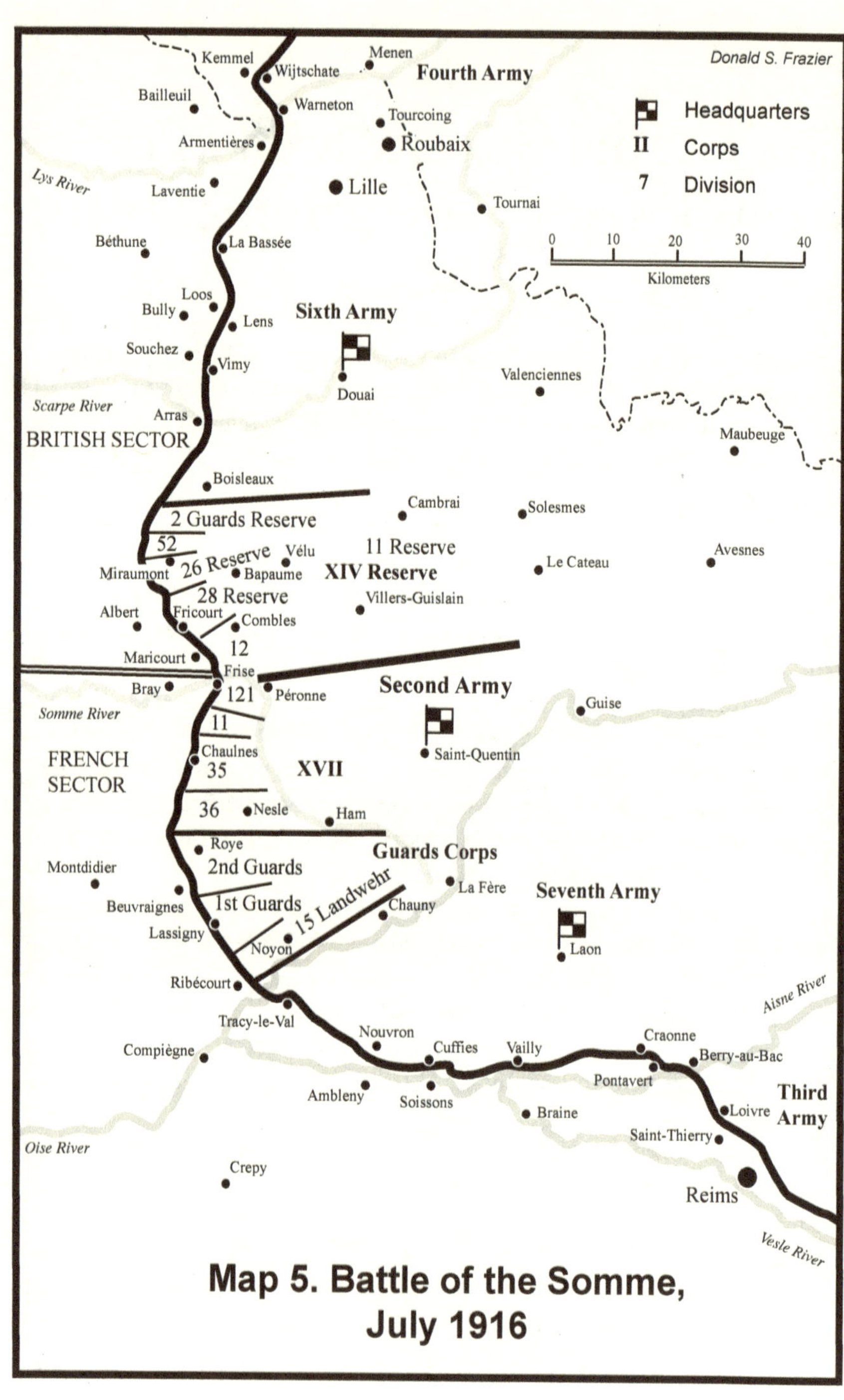

Map 5. Battle of the Somme, July 1916

lish had been in position. The initial assessment was that this was a defensive measure to give more depth to the English attack to be staged farther north. That assessment proved incorrect as soon as patrolling activity identified the French XX Army Corps north of the Somme. That unit was known to be an excellent attack corps. We also identified increased attack preparations south of the Somme. Thus, in the course of June the expected expanse of the enemy attack from the right wing of the 52nd Division to the left wing of 11th Division became apparent. In June the Second Army received an infantry division, the field artillery assets of another division, and toward the end of June seventeen light field howitzer batteries. On 22 June the enemy fire started to become increasingly strong. On 24 June an almost uninterrupted barrage started, with the enemy firing their heaviest caliber guns and their long-range, heavy, flat-trajectory guns.

The situation map that was prepared for me upon my arrival indicated that on the morning of 1 July the Second Army was deployed as follows: From the army's right wing to the Somme, the XIV Reserve Corps had the 2nd Guards Reserve Division, the 52nd Division, the 26th Reserve Division, the 28th Reserve Division (reinforced by one-third of the 10th Bavarian Division), and the 12th Division (reinforced by another third of the 10th Bavarian Division). The remaining third of 10th Bavarian Division was positioned behind the left wing of the 28th Reserve Division. As the army reserve, the 185th Division was positioned behind the XIV Reserve Corps. The OHL reserve[1] was the VI Reserve Corps, consisting of the 11th Reserve Division and 12th Reserve Division. South of the Somme, the XVII Army Corps had the 121st Division, 11th Division, 35th Division, and 36th Division. South of the XVII Army Corps and down to the left wing of Second Army, the Guards Corps had the 15th Landwehr Brigade. Behind the XVII Army Corps, Division Frentz[2] was the army reserve, and the 22nd Reserve Division was the OHL reserve.

On 1 July, about 0830 hours in the morning, the English and French attack started on a forty-kilometer front, from the right flank of the Second Army's northern wing south to the left flank of the 35th Division.[3] The attackers laid down overlapping artillery fires on both sides of the attack sector. In their forwardmost line the enemy had a three-to-one force superiority ratio. The enemy artillery fire quickly flattened our forward positions, large sections of our rearward positions, and inflicted heavy losses on our artillery. In the air the attacker also had a huge superiority over our sixteen fighters and fifty-two short- and long-range reconnaissance aircraft. The boundary between the English and the French was in the middle of the 12th Division sector, near Maricourt.

The XIV Reserve Corps, commanded by Lieutenant General Hermann von Stein, was attacked by thirteen enemy divisions. His three northern divisions, the 2nd Guards Reserve, the 52nd Division, and the 26th Reserve Division, managed to hold their positions during the back-and-forth fighting. The 28th Reserve Division on the left flank of XIV Reserve Corps managed to hold on with its right wing, but its left wing and the 12th Reserve Division in the south were pushed back one to one and a half kilometers with heavy losses after putting up a courageous resistance. The French attack started two hours later in the sector of the XVII Army Corps, commanded by General of Infantry Günther von Pannewitz. On the corps' right wing the 121st Division was attacked by three French divisions, losing its forwardmost positions completely and being pushed back two to two and a half kilometers. The 11th Division to the south was pushed back on its right flank. Our rearward elements, however, were able to stop the enemy breach. The left half of the 11th Division held its position. On the southern end of the Second Army sector elements of XVII Army Corps and the Guards Corps were not attacked, but they were heavily gassed.

During the course of 1 July the Second Army headquarters allocated the 185th Division to the XIV Reserve Corps and Division Frentz to XVII Army Corps. OHL attached the VI Reserve Corps to the Second Army, and that corps was positioned with the 12th Reserve Division on the right. On the left, the 11th Reserve Division was integrated into the 12th Reserve Division's sector. OHL also attached the 22nd Reserve Division to the Second Army, which was moved expeditiously and attached to the XVII Army Corps. On the afternoon of 1 July, OHL reported the accelerated movement of the 3rd Guards Division via Cambrai and the 44th Reserve Division via Ham. Additionally, OHL moved sixteen heavy batteries and three fighter squadrons forward.

According to the 1 July frontline reports, fourteen English and seven French divisions had attacked seven German divisions. Behind this first attack echelon—as we later ascertained—there were another eight English and nine French infantry divisions, as well as three English and two French cavalry divisions. However, the enemy's intended breakthrough did not succeed despite their commitment of overwhelming power. All they managed to do was to push in a twenty-kilometer front.

On 2 July the very exhausted German front was forced to remain on the defensive. South of the Somme, in the XVII Army Corps sector, the back-and-forth fighting for the second line of German positions required reinforcing the 121st Division and 11th Division with one infantry regiment each from the 22nd Reserve Division. North of the Somme the enemy continued pushing their earlier advances with superior forces. The frontline units of the XIV Reserve Corps by and large held their positions. During the course of 2 July, General Fritz von Below formed on the left flank of General von Stein's XIV Reserve Corps a defensive battle group under the command of the VI Reserve Corps'

General Konrad von Gossler. That group consisted of the 11th Reserve Division, 12th Reserve Division, and 12th Infantry Division. Elements of the 10th Bavarian Division that up to this point were still engaged were moved behind the 28th Reserve Division. The 3rd Guards Division, meanwhile, reached Cambrai with its forward elements. The 44th Reserve Division started unloading operations at Ham and was assigned to the XVII Army Corps.

The 121st Division lost a large part of its artillery and many of its troops were taken prisoner. The commanding general of the XVII Army Corps reported that the division's positions were untenable. The Second Army headquarters decided to withdraw the division to the line Biaches–Barleux, with its left flank tied in to the 11th Division along the line Barleux–Belloy–Estrées. The Second Army headquarters planned to launch a counterattack from that position. This voluntary withdrawal, however, exposed the left flank of the VI Reserve Corps, and that unit subsequently had to occupy the northern bank of the Somme from Ham to Cléry. General Erich von Falkenhayn,[4] who arrived in Saint-Quentin early in the evening of 2 July, did not concur with the planned course of action of the Second Army headquarters, which had wanted to facilitate with this action the staging of a counterattack south of the Somme. Falkenhayn laid the blame for what he considered a bad plan on General Grünert, and he replaced him with me as the chief of staff of the Second Army.

After the situation briefing by Major Faupel, I reported on 3 July at approximately 0600 hours to the commander of the Second Army, General of Infantry Fritz von Below, who I knew from a previous assignment and respected. General von Below greeted me very warmly. He assessed the situation as very serious, but also with confidence. I immediately requested and received permission to make a reconnaissance drive along the entire front line in order to develop a more in-depth situational understanding from the local commanders and orient myself on the battle terrain, with which I was not familiar. Unfortunately, General von Below was suffering from painful stomach cramps and could not accompany me. Based on my personal reconnaissance and the briefings I would receive, he gave me Vollmacht to issue the necessary orders for the deployment of the very scantily arriving reinforcements.

Upon my return to the headquarters building the complete staff of the Second Army was already assembled and I greeted them with warm words. There were only two other qualified General Staff officers on the staff, Major Faupel, the Ia,[5] and Captain von Bredow, the Ib.[6] There was no assistant chief of staff. Even before my departure to the front I requested from OHL two additional General Staff officers and an assistant chief of staff. For the latter position I specifically requested the competent Colonel von Redern, whom I knew from my time at OHL. Redern was assigned per my request. Using the situation map, I then directed the scarce reserves which were arriving by foot march or by transport to the most threatened sectors of the front line.

Around 0730 hours I departed by car. The driver and assistant driver knew all the routes through the army's area of operations to the front lines. South of Péronne, the first divisional commander I met with was General Konstantin von Altrock, commander of the 44th Reserve Division. He already had proved himself during the Allied Second Champagne Offensive in the autumn of 1915. Altrock greeted me with the words, "Well, my dear Lossberg, we continue to meet in places where the dirt (he used a stronger word that starts with sh . . .) runs in streams." He was quite right, because my reconnaissance tour of the front confirmed that the situation of the Second Army was incredibly serious. But during my long drive along the front line, during which I met with all the corps, divisional, and many of the subordinate leaders, I did not meet a single officer who had given up hope. On the whole front line the troops and their leaders were strongly committed to holding at any cost. I also got the impression that my appointment as chief of staff of the Second Army was welcomed by the leadership. They apparently trusted my energy, with which I had mastered the difficult situation in Champagne the previous autumn.

During my reconnaissance trip I developed a clear assessment of the combat conditions and the terrain. The ground in many places was overgrown with mostly rolling wheat fields and plots of forests, which made it highly compartmentalized terrain. During my approximately one-hour stay under heavy enemy fire on the ground overlooking Hill 110 north of Péronne, I recognized its importance as an observation point for our artillery. The rolling terrain, especially north of the Somme, offered many possibilities for frontal and flanking observation and artillery fire. The ground also was good for infantry defensive operations, especially because of numerous solidly built-up settlements, which were well suited for points of resistance. On this first reconnaissance trip I also recognized the enemy's unbelievable aerial superiority. His aircraft were constantly flitting about over German-held terrain, strafing our infantry with machine gun fire from low altitudes and dropping bombs in the rear areas on any recognized movement. Our flyers were powerless against this incredible superiority.

Everywhere I went on my reconnaissance of the front I issued the order on behalf of the commanding general to fight for every foot of ground and under no circumstances withdraw—even against the strongest fire and superior infantry attacks. Such an order had worked well during the battle in Champagne the previous autumn, and it also served us well in the Somme battle.

My initial consultations with the subordinate commanders revealed great flaws in the Second Army's wire communications system. The main trunk line ran parallel to the front line and much too close to it. By 3 July it already had been cut in many places. I therefore decided to order the construction of a new communications system whose trunk line would be far to the rear of the front line, with perpendicular branches running off to the frontline command posts.

Everywhere I detected that the enemy on 3 July had for the most part made only limited attacks. The English made a strong attack in the XIV Reserve Corps sector against the inner boundary of the 26th Division and 28th Reserve Division. Those units were reinforced by elements of the 10th Bavarian Division and 185th Division, repelling the attack in hand-to-hand combat and inflicting heavy losses on the enemy.

During a telephone conversation with army headquarters, Major Faupel reported to me that in the XVII Army Corps sector the depleted 121st Division had been relieved in place by the 22nd Reserve Division along the line Biaches–Barleux, and by Division Frentz along the line Barleux–Belloy–Estrées. The 11th Reserve Division had moved its right wing back to the line Estrées–Soyécourt. The enemy had advanced only slowly against the line Biaches–Barleux and attacked with little effect against the line Estrées–Soyécourt. OHL reported that the 183rd Division would arrive at Bapaume and be assigned to the Second Army, and that the IX Army Corps would be the OHL reserve behind the XVII Army Corps. Step by step, the Second Army was to be reinforced with aircraft and artillery. We urgently needed both. As I learned from my personal reconnaissance, the heavy losses in guns we had sustained meant that the batteries had to cover interdiction zones eight hundred meters in width. OHL also assigned the 3rd Guards Division to the Second Army. It arrived in sector on 5 July and was positioned behind the left wing of the 28th Reserve Division.

I did not return to Saint-Quentin until late evening on 3 July, and I found to my delight the commander had fully recovered from his stomach cramps. I reported back to him at the headquarters building, described in the presence of the Ia my impressions from the reconnaissance trip to the front line, and reported the directives that I had issued along the way. General von Below fully agreed with my assessment that the fight had to be conducted by clinging absolutely to the forwardmost lines, and in case of losses by launching hasty counterattacks—or if that did not work, by deliberate counterattacks.[7] He signed a draft of a Second Army order that I had prepared confirming these measures, and it was sent out immediately to all command posts. The order stated: "I prohibit the voluntary abandonment of positions. Every leader is responsible that the firm will to fight is ingrained in every member of the [Second] Army. The enemy will only make his way forward over [our] dead bodies."

General von Below and I deliberated over a counterattack plan, which was only feasible after we brought forward sufficient numbers of combat-ready divisions, strong artillery, and sufficient ammunition. During the entire Battle of the Somme we never managed to achieve those conditions. The reinforcements provided by OHL were always only barely sufficient to replace just in time the battle-weary divisions fighting forward. Thus, the same pattern was emerging that I had already experienced during the autumn battle in Champagne. The divisions bled to death and most often lost their best soldiers. The German Army suffered irreplaceable losses of NCOs and courageous fighters that could not be replaced during the course of the war.

On 4 July the enemy restricted himself to individual attacks that failed everywhere. On 5 July in the XIV Reserve Corps sector small portions of positions south of Thiepval were lost by the 26th Reserve Division, and south of Contalmaison by the 28th Reserve Division. In the XVII Army Corps sector the enemy occupied the southern bank of the Somme across from our troops, who had already interdicted the northern bank along the line from Ham to Cléry, blowing all the bridges. The French attacked our positions from Biaches to Soyécourt. The 22nd Reserve Division bloodily repulsed an enemy attack between Biaches and Barleux. Division Frentz lost Belloy and Estrées while the 44th Reserve Division was rushing toward it. A hasty counterattack of the 44th Reserve Division's infantry did, however, succeed in pushing the enemy back again. Only the village of Belloy remained in French hands.

OHL assigned the IX Army Corps and the 183rd Division to the Second Army, reported the arrival of 123rd (Saxon) Division via Cambrai, and attached to us fifteen field batteries and two batteries each of heavy howitzers and heavy flat-trajectory guns. During a long telephone conversation with General von Falkenhayn I detailed the heavy losses of the Second Army, but I also told him that in my opinion the enemy's heavy concentration of forces on the Somme made it very unlikely that he would be able to attack at other locations. I therefore suggested that OHL allocate fresh reserves to the Battle of the Somme from unengaged forces along the Western Front. The general evaded my question on whether the attack on Verdun had been aborted.[8]

On my recommendation General von Below established from the northern part of the XVII Army Corps a new defensive battle group under the command of General Ferdinand von Quast, the commanding general of the IX Army Corps. Group Quast took up the line Biaches–Vermandovillers. The 22nd Reserve Division, Division Frentz with the 44th Reserve Division (which was relieving Division Frentz), and the 11th Division were deployed in this sector. General von Quast was given assurances that his 17th Division and 18th Division would be used in his sector. The commander of the XVII Army Corps was left with only his own 35th Division and 36th Division. In order to support the northern sector of our defensive front, where the English had made their breach, the XIV Reserve Corps was allocated the 183rd Division, in addition to the 3rd Guards Division and the elements of the 10th Bavarian Division that had already deployed in that sector. Those reinforcements allowed us to withdraw the 28th Reserve Division and the 185th Division and to reduce the front of the 26th Reserve Division to where its left flank only reached to south of Thiepval.

I used the relatively quiet period of 4 and 5 July to organize for large-scale battle the Second Army staff, the communications network, and the logistics system. I did away with consolidated staff assessments as too time consuming. Instead, all staff section chiefs were given direct access to me at all times. All reports from the fighting front had to reach me quickly so that the appropriate orders could be issued immediately. We established a special telephone circuit within the staff for just that purpose. The circuit allowed me to talk to all the staffers who were involved in a given order. The Second Army artillery commander was directed to organize flanking fires against the attacking enemy, especially by using Hill 110 north of Péronne.

The commander of the engineer troops was ordered to provide large quantities of materials, especially barbed wire and trenching timber, for the construction of rearward positions. All inhabited dwellings and villages behind the front line were to be prepared for defense and covered with wire obstacles. This work was to be done by the people living in the towns, under the direction of the engineer staff. The division engineer also was directed to construct army-level observation posts on high points and towers that had visibility of the forward lines. These observation posts were to be tied in to the army headquarters with a special communications network that also included the corps and divisional command posts on the front lines.

The aviation commander was directed to organize his flight assets for deep and close-range reconnaissance, photographic reconnaissance, fighter aircraft attack missions, and bomber aircraft bombing missions. The *Ordonnanz* officers[9] had to be prepared to rush immediately to the affected command posts in the event of a large-scale attack, to develop a clear picture of the situation by using the observation posts and direct visits to the forward lines, and then to report back to the army headquarters by telephone.

From 3 July on, my workload became immense. After making a night drive from Bouziers via Maizières to Saint-Quentin I got my first three hours of bed rest during the night of 6 July. During the whole Battle of the Somme my nightly rest periods were rarely much longer. But I had the gift of being able to use every free moment for a short nap. Even during car trips I could catch up on sleep. My health at the time was exceptionally good and I was able to endure such exertions, which sometimes lasted for months.

From 5 July on, I was at the front almost daily with General von Below and the senior adjutant (IIa), Major von Trotha.[10] We remained at the army headquarters only during days of the most intense fighting, because we were able to receive all of the telephone reports there. We routinely departed the headquarters at 0730 hours. By that point in the day I had already worked for a few hours and had prepared the morning reports to OHL. General von Below during his long career had served at all levels of the General Staff and had acquired a great appreciation for the workings of the General Staff.[11] When urgent telephone calls prevented me from being at the staff car at 0730 sharp, he would wait, or he would come into my office when urgent decisions were required. Our cooperation during and after the Somme battle was smooth in every respect and I still remember this magnificent soldier and marvelous human being with deep gratitude.

Initially we always traveled to the locations of the previous day's fighting. There we met with the responsible leaders at their command posts and battle positions. Those consultations formed the basis for the army orders of the day. After consulting with the commanding general, I immediately dictated such orders on the spot. Those orders that involved troop reinforcements were then immediately transmitted by telephone in summary form to the affected units. The leaders on the front line developed a great trust in the army headquarters through this kind of quick action.

On 1 July the English had driven a deep salient into the front lines of the 28th Reserve Division and the 12th Reserve Division. We were sure they would continue to press their main effort in that sector, which they soon did. Similarly, we expected the main effort of the French attacks to come on both sides of the Somme.

On 6 July the enemy offensive continued, but initially only with limited objective attacks. The English attacked the inner wings of the 26th Reserve Division and the 28th Reserve Division, but all those efforts failed in the face of the strong resistance put up by our closely packed together and intermixed units, including the 26th Reserve Division, 28th Reserve Division, 10th Bavarian Division, 185th Division, and 3rd Guards Division. The 12th Reserve Division and 11th Reserve Division also were attacked by the English south of Longueval at the Trônes Forrest and near Hardecourt, and also by the French on the northern bank of the Somme in the direction of Ham. The enemy attacks had little effect on our positions. On 6 July we established a new battle group from the 11th Reserve Division and 12th Reserve Division, under the command of General von Gossler. That sector of the front line was split out from the rather wide area of operations of Group Stein. The French attacked Group Quast with strong forces only at Estrées, held by the 44th Reserve Division. Despite support from the 11th Reserve Division, we lost that town after a long period of close-quarters combat.

Our significant losses on 6 July were caused by the long-lasting, close-quarters combat and the horrific enemy artillery fire along the whole front line. In response, we reinforced Group Quast with the 17th and 18th Divisions. OHL allocated the 123rd (Saxon) Division to the Second Army as reinforcement. OHL also reported that a division under Lieutenant General Eduard von Liebert would be detached from the Seventh Army and would move to the Second Army as the OHL reserve.[12] OHL also allocated to us an additional five heavy field howitzer batteries and two batteries of heavy, flat-trajectory guns. The combat-weary 121st Division was made ready for withdrawal.

During the night of 6–7 July, elements of the 10th Bavarian Division commanded by General Hermann von Burkhardt relieved the left wing of the 26th Reserve Division. That allowed the 26th Reserve Division, which had been fighting brilliantly under the leadership of General Franz Freiherr von Soden, to echelon its positions more deeply, thereby improving its capability to resist longer. The 28th Reserve Division also was relieved in place during the night of 7 July by the 183rd Division and 3rd Guards Division, and went into cantonment positions far behind the line. Simultaneously, the worn-down 185th Division was pulled out of the line and went into reserve behind the left wing of the XIV Reserve Corps.

Preceded by strong artillery fire, the English attacked on 7 July in the direction of Ovillers, Contalmaison, and Longueval. After a long and bloody fight, they pushed the German front into a line running east and west of Contalmaison. We still held the town of Ovillers, but it was encircled from three directions. The town's stalwart defenders repulsed an English attack supported by flamethrowers on 8 July. The French also attacked south of the Somme on 7 July, fighting along the line Biaches–Barleux. The 22nd Reserve Division, however, held its position. During the night of 8 July, Division Frentz was relieved by the 17th Division

On 8 July the French attacked almost the entire sector of Group Gossler. The enemy captured the town of Hardecourt, but all of our other positions held. Heavy fighting again took place on 9 July. In the Group Stein sector heavy English attacks failed to take Ovillers against the heroic resistance of the 10th Bavarian Division. In the Group Gossler sector the 12th Reserve Division on the right wing managed after a long fight to hold on to the forest west of Guillemont. In the Group Quast sector the French did not attack until that afternoon. Their main effort was directed against the 22nd Reserve Division. After long back-and-forth fighting we lost the village of Biaches and the 22nd Reserve Division's center was pushed back. Elements of the 17th Division counterattacked to hold the hills south of Biaches. We lost Barleux temporarily, but then we retook it, capturing more than 150 French soldiers in the process. The French attacks against the frontline positions of the 17th Division and 11th Division also failed. On the evening of 9 July the Second Army headquarters attached the freshly arrived 123rd (Saxon) Division to Group Gossler.

The 7th Division of the IV Army Corps, meanwhile, had been designated as the Second Army reserve. Marching on foot, that unit reached Cambrai on 10 July. Forward elements of the 5th Division as OHL reserves arrived east of Caulaincourt, and the 8th Bavarian Reserve Division reached Ham. OHL also ordered ten additional heavy batteries, construction units, and a fighter squadron to move into the Second Army sector. The fighters immediately destroyed an enemy balloon.[13]

The enemy attacks continued uninterrupted night and day until 12 July. They concentrated on all of the battle zones of 6 through 9 July. Our troops fought heroically, but despite their courageous resistance some positions were lost because of the enemy superiority in numbers and materiel. In Group Stein's sector we lost the village of Contalmaison and parts of the forest east of the village; in Group Gossler's sector we lost the ground west of Guillemont and north of Hardecourt. After a long struggle, Group Quast managed to hold the villages of Belloy, Estrées, and Soyécourt. Group Quast's 22nd Reserve Division was relieved by Division Liebert; the 44th Reserve Division was relieved by the 18th Division. OHL meanwhile ordered the command group and later the entire headquarters of the IV Army Corps to move forward to Havrincourt to assume control of the Second Army reserves. The IV Army Corps with the 24th (Saxon) Reserve Division and the 123rd (Saxon) Division was positioned directly behind Group Gossler. Eventually the IV Army Corps took over the left half of Group Stein's sector. As requested by the Second Army, OHL also reported the attachment of several machine gun companies and machine gun marksman battalions,[14] twenty-six heavy and two super-heavy howitzer batteries, five flat-trajectory heavy gun batteries, one field artillery battalion, and three artillery observation aviation detachments.

On 13 July the worn out 22nd Reserve Division and Division Frentz were readied for withdrawal from the lines per OHL orders. As a replacement, the Second Army was allocated the IV Corps' 8th Division. The completely worn-out 183rd Division was to be replaced by the 7th Division and then reassigned to the Sixth Army. OHL also reported the pending attachment of Division Dumrath,[15] which had been assembled from troops of the Seventh Army, as well as five heavy batteries and twenty-six construction companies. During the course of 13 July the enemy artillery fire greatly increased on our positions on both sides of the Somme, in preparation for an enemy attack.

On the morning of 14 July, General of Infantry Friedrich Bertram Sixt von Armin, the commander of the IV Army Corps, assumed command of Group Armin, which included the sectors of the 10th Bavarian Division, 183rd Division, and 3rd Guards Divisions. Just as that was taking place and as the 7th Division was still moving forward, seven English divisions started an attack between Ovillers and Hardecourt. Their main effort was near Pozières and Longueval, which hit the whole of Group Armin and the right wing of Group Gossler. Under constant and heavy artillery fire, the initial enemy assault made a deep penetration into the German positions. After protracted close combat that lasted into the night, Group Armin and the right wing of Group Gossler, reinforced by the most forward elements of the 123rd (Saxon) Division, were pushed back to the line running from the southern edge of Pozières to the northern edge of Bazentin, to the northern edge of Longueval, to the western edge of Guillemont, and to the east of Hardecourt. Between Bazentin and Longueval there was an open gap into which the English cavalry pushed. At Group Quast, meanwhile, the French attacked the line Barleux–Soyécourt with far superior forces, including African colonial troops.[16] After prolonged fighting, the 17th Division, 18th Division, and 11th Division managed to hold their positions.

Shortly after midnight on 14–15 July, I received in short succession telephone calls from two frontline command posts north of the Somme. Both reported that the English had broken through at Flers, between Bazentin and Longueval. I already knew about the gap between Bazentin and Longueval, and I did not doubt the accuracy of these new reports. After I held a brief telephone consultation with the commanding general, the Second Army committed the 5th Division and 8th Bavarian Reserve Division from the south against the breakthrough point. The divisions moved by night march, with large elements of their infantry transported in trucks. The 8th Division, which at the time had some of its units committed to a relief action in the Sixth Army sector, moved down from the north in the direction of Flers. The 5th Division moved up from the south. Both units had orders to attack the English penetration simultaneously from the north and south.

Meanwhile, I immediately sent off two officers in staff cars with orders to move from the south and the north toward the reported breakthrough point near Flers, assess the situation, and report back to me by telephone. Then I called General von Falkenhayn that night and reported the breakthrough. General von Falkenhayn was rather agitated at first, but he calmed down as I summarized the resulting Second Army orders. Our actions included attaching to Group Armin one regiment from the 12th Division, which had been resting near Louveral, the 8th Division, and the 5th Division, which had been advancing toward Rocquigny. Group Gossler was assigned the 24th (Saxon) Reserve Division, which reached Sailly-Saillisel on the morning of 15 July, and the 8th Bavarian Reserve Division, that deployed via Templeux. Groups Armin and Gossler were to counterattack with these reinforcements.

During the night and the early morning of 15 July I had several telephone conversations with Groups Armin and Gossler, but I was not able to develop any more clarity on the breakthrough situation. Finally, at about 1000 hours we received clear, similarly worded reports from the two officers I had sent to the breakthrough point. Both reported that the English had not advanced beyond Flers, and that approximately five hundred English prisoners had been taken and were being transported to the rear. That was a huge load off my mind, as well as the commanding general's. I reported the situation immediately to General von Falkenhayn.

The initial reports had been somewhat exaggerated. I had received such exaggerated reports in earlier battles as well. You had to accept them initially at face value and act on that basis. Any experienced practitioner of large-scale battles will agree with me that such combat can fray the nerves of the troops as well as the leaders. Before the enemy infantry attack, the massive artillery fires reaching deep into our defensive positions had shot up and cut almost all of the connections to the rear. The troops were then very much on their own and had no knowledge of how the adjacent units were doing. From the rear forward and then from the forward line to the flanks, the only connecting links between the leaders and the fighting troops were the runners. That was a job that required the most courageous and most intelligent soldiers. On every trip these runner-heroes were exposed the heaviest artillery and infantry fire, but all orders forward and reports rearward were based on their getting through. These courageous runners accomplished great things in all the large-scale battles, and they deserve the highest praise and unlimited recognition. But there were also the despondent soldiers in these large-scale battles, who much too easily misjudged the true seriousness of the situation. Soldiers such as these were the initiators of the reports of the breakthrough at Flers. The Second Army headquarters later investigated rigorously the false reports of the breakthrough, but the investigation yielded no concrete results.

A rapid series of reports we received from the local command posts on the morning of 15 July indicated that during the evening of 14 July the line from Pozières, to the northern edge of Longueval, to the western edge of Guillemont, and to the eastern edge of Hardecourt had been held, partly through local counterattacks. On the basis of these reports the 5th Division and the 8th Bavarian Reserve Division reverted to their roles as the army reserve, with the 5th Division positioned behind Group Armin and the 8th Bavarian Reserve Division behind Group Gossler. But the reports also indicated that both the English and the French had continued their strong attacks. Group Armin was again heavily engaged between Bazentin and Guillemont. That action was decided in our favor only after a hasty counterattack by elements of the 8th Bavarian Reserve Division. In the process, we retook a significant part of the terrain between Bazentin and Guillemont that we had lost on 14 July. In Group Gossler's sector the only attacks were mostly localized and after some initial successes were beaten back with the help of elements of the 24th Reserve Division. The 123rd (Saxon) Division, which was deployed in the middle of the group's sector, and the 11th Reserve Division, which was fighting to the south of it, also held their positions in the face of heavy combat. A deliberate counterattack planned there was cancelled because sufficient forces were not available. In Group Quast's sector the French limited themselves to local attacks. Division Liebert conducted a hasty counterattack and recaptured the village of Biaches, taking almost four hundred French prisoners in the process. That afternoon the French attacked the whole line from Biaches to Soyécourt, but they only bloodied themselves.

In the evening of 15 July, Group Armin started the relief of the 3rd Guards Division by the 8th Division, and Group Gossler started the relief of the heavily worn-out 12th Reserve Division by the 24th (Saxon) Reserve Division. Meanwhile, Division Dumrath, which had arrived south of Nesle, became the Second Army reserve. The Fourth Army's 233rd Infantry Brigade, 117th Division, and eight Jäger[17] bicycle companies of the Fifth and Sixth Armies were brought forward as the OHL reserve. OHL also ordered the Third Army's 22nd Reserve Division to relieve the 23rd (Saxon) Division, and Division Frentz was to be transferred to the Seventh Army in order to free up a formation for the Second Army that was made up of nine Saxon battalions under General Franke. OHL also attached two aviation officers to Second Army to coordinate the air defense battle.

Only localized fighting took place on 16 and 17 July, which made the relief operations easier. But during this period Ovillers, one of the villages that had been encircled for quite a while, was lost in the 10th Bavarian Division's sector. In the Group Quast sector the French also managed to take Maisonette Ferne, situated southeast of Biaches. The Second Army headquarters attached Division Dumrath to Group Quast. OHL further attached to the Second Army the 28th Division, coming from Saint-Quentin, and the rest of the 117th Division, coming from Cambrai.

On 17 July General von Below and I had several telephone conferences with General von Falkenhayn, who was considering dividing the Second Army's very wide front into a northern sector under a newly re-formed First Army commanded by General von Below, with me as chief of staff, and a southern sector under the Second Army commanded by General Max von Gallwitz, with

Colonel Bernhard Bronsart von Schellendorff as chief of staff. Both armies were to be formed into an army group under the command of General von Gallwitz. This arrangement was necessary because the First Army would have to establish a new rear area and support structure. The plan had several disadvantages, because all the reinforcements for the large-scale battles would have to be attached first to Army Group Gallwitz, which would then allocate reinforcements to the First Army. The proposed boundary between the two armies was the Somme south of Cléry. I recommended to General von Falkenhayn that it would be more advisable to move the right boundary of the Second Army farther to the north, which would give the Second Army the option using its own artillery to counter any French attack south of the Somme. General von Falkenhayn insisted on the boundary as he had planned it.

Nonetheless, General von Below and I agreed that splitting the Second Army into two armies was justified. The very broad front and the intensity of the enemy attacks had imposed a huge responsibility and a heavy workload on the Second Army headquarters. Compounding our problems, the position of the army headquarters in Saint-Quentin made it difficult to exercise proper control over the northern part of our area of operations. We consumed a great deal of time making our necessary daily trips to the command posts of the northern defensive groups. General von Below and I thus welcomed the OHL decision to divide the Second Army into two armies. The change of command was set for 19 July. We immediately conducted a reconnaissance and selected Bourlon (west of Cambrai) as the new headquarters of the First Army. It had good road connections to the frontline sectors. The preparations for the move to Bourlon and the construction of a new telephone network started on 17 July and were completed by the evening of the following day.

General von Gallwitz and General von Below were both very independent personalities. They were not especially close friends. Colonel Bronsart von Schellendorff and I had been the General Staff officers of the two divisions of the X Army Corps in Hanover from 1905 to 1907.[18] We had become close. General von Gallwitz had recommended to General von Falkenhayn that the French penetration south of the Somme should be attacked and eliminated prior to the transfer of command. General von Below had considered such a course of action earlier. The execution of that plan, however, required a considerable number of additional forces, which would not be available to the First Army because OHL had few reserves left. General von Falkenhayn, therefore, correctly rejected General von Gallwitz's plan and ordered that both armies would initially limit themselves to defensive operations. As the Battle of the Somme progressed, the main effort of the enemy attacks was directed almost exclusively against the new First Army, while the Second Army sector gradually became quiet.

On 18 July, General von Below's last day in command of the old Second Army, he produced a nice success. That evening Group Armin counterattacked with their newly attached 8th Division along with the support of elements on the right wing of the Group Gossler and the 24th (Saxon) Division. They seized the town of Longueval and the ground to the east and west, and then held this line against strong English counterattacks. In the process we captured about one thousand English prisoners. This successful operation improved our situation very much.

5

Chief of the General Staff of the First Army (The Somme, 1916)

On the morning of 19 July the new First Army headquarters occupied Bourlon. Remaining with the Second Army were Major Faupel, the Ia, and Captain von Bredow, the Ib. Colonel von Redern, who had just been assigned as the assistant chief of staff, moved to the First Army, along with Major von Trotha, the IIa, and some of the more junior officers. Otherwise, we had to organize the First Army staff from the ground up. Major Max Stapff became the Ia, and Captain Erich von Manstein[1] was assigned as the Ib. The positions of general of the artillery, general of the engineers, commander of aviation, and almost the entire lower staff were newly filled. It was a difficult rebuilding task for me. I had to get familiar with the members of my new staff and train them in the conduct of the large-scale battle. To my great satisfaction, it was a very rapid process. All of my colleagues were energetic and knowledgeable officers, with whom I soon developed a sense of close comradeship. General Otto von Below moved into quarters at Castle Bourlon with his senior and personal staff, which included the chief of staff, the General Staff officers, the adjutants, and the special duty staff officers. The remainder of the quite large staff was quartered close by in the town of Bourlon. The various sections were able to find spacious offices and quarters. That same day General von Below and I visited all the subordinate command posts in our new operational sector. We could tell that a new and major battle was imminent.

Following a massive barrage on 20 July, the enemy attacked along almost the entire former sector of the old Second Army, from Pozières to Soyécourt. In the First Army sector the right half of Group Armin, consisting of the 10th Bavarian Division and the 7th Division, managed to repel the attacks after a long struggle. Against the left half of Group Armin, the British main effort hit the line Bazentin–Longueval. The 8th Division and the only partly inserted 5th Division had a tough time of it. Although the enemy initially broke into our lines, the two divisions made a heroic stand, pushing the enemy back with a combination of hasty and deliberate counterattacks. The French also attacked in the Group Gossler sector with strongly superior forces, but the 24th (Saxon) Reserve Division

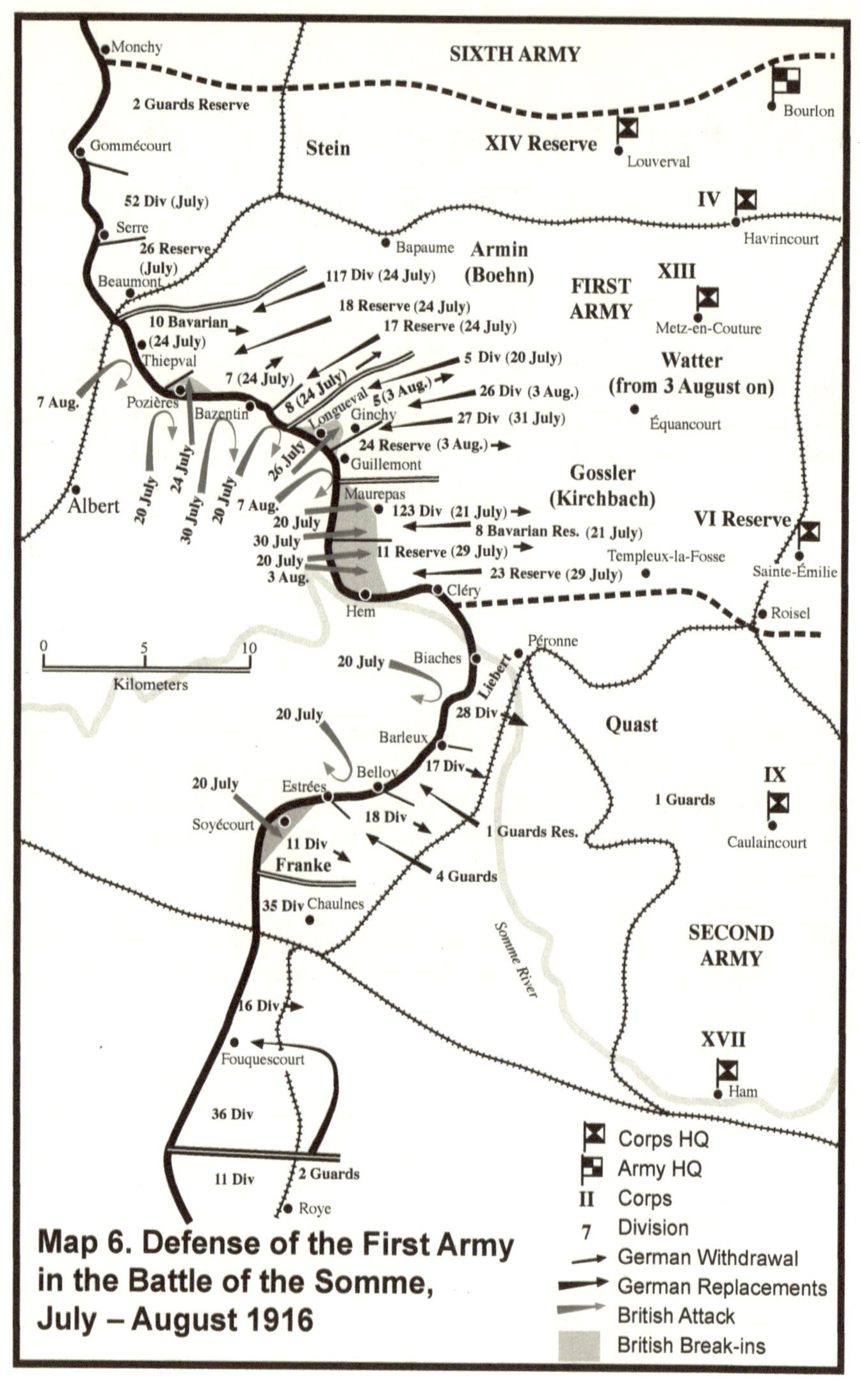

Map 6. Defense of the First Army in the Battle of the Somme, July – August 1916

fought courageously and held their lines. Farther south the 133rd (Saxon) Division and the 11th Reserve Division lost their positions after heavy fighting, and were pushed back to a line running from west of Maurepas to east of Ham.[2] The First Army headquarters assigned the 8th Bavarian Reserve Division to support Group Gossler.

According to the reports from the Second Army, it had been attacked along its entire sector. Following a long struggle, Group Quast managed to hold its positions almost everywhere. Only the inner wings of the 11th and 35th Divisions had been pushed in somewhat. Both the First and the Second Army took many prisoners. According to prisoner interrogations, eight British and nine French divisions had attacked Army Group Gallwitz on 20 July. All eight of the British and half of the French divisions had fought against the First Army. We knew then that the enemy's main effort was north of the Somme.

During the following days the enemy limited himself to individual operations supported by constantly strong artillery fire, mainly in the area of Pozières and Maurepas. The 7th Division at Pozières fought for individual sections of their position. It was important for us to hold Pozières, because any enemy advance there would threaten the left flank of Group Stein. After days and days of bitter fighting, the British finally took the town of Pozières, as well as the high ground to the north, which gave them long-range observation. The depleted 10th Bavarian Division, which had held its position for three weeks, was relieved by the 117th Division. The 123rd (Saxon) Division, which had been roughly handled on 20 July, was relieved by the 8th Bavarian Reserve Division, which then performed brilliantly.

OHL shifted the IX Reserve Corps, the Guards Reserve Corps, the XIII Army Corps, and the infantry of the 16th Division to Army Group Gallwitz, as well as nine field batteries and twelve heavy batteries. Of those units, the First Army received the IX Reserve Corps to relieve the IV Army Corps, and also some artillery reinforcements. The XIII Army Corps became the OHL reserve. Initially it assembled far to the rear of the First Army, and then marched to the vicinity east of Équancourt. In the Second Army sector, General von Gallwitz relieved Division Liebert with the 28th Division, and the IX Army Corps with the Guards Reserve Corps. He also reinforced the 11th Division with an infantry brigade and inserted the 16th Division between 35th and 36th Divisions. Then, when the 44th Reserve Division deployed to replace the 1st Guards Division, he established his own reserve west of Caulaincourt. When OHL deployed the relief forces, they also informed the subordinate commands that from that point on major units could only be withdrawn from other army sectors if they were replaced by previously depleted units that had since been reconstituted. Based on that, the First Army released the 183rd, 185th, 3rd Guards, 10th Bavarian, and 123rd (Saxon) Divisions for reassignment. Unfortunately, we also learned that we had not broken off our attack at Verdun.

The IX Reserve Corps started to relieve the IV Army Corps on 24 July. General of Infantry Max von Boehn assumed command of Group Armin. On 25 July the 18th Reserve Division conducted a very carefully prepared deliberate counterattack against Pozières, but it failed in the face of strong British force superiority. After an attack against Estrées in the Second Army sector also failed, General von Gallwitz issued an order to the First Army stating that in the future only tactically decisive points should be retaken. That order quite understandably upset General von Below, and he told me that General von Gallwitz had not correctly assessed the importance of holding Pozières.

Even after 25 July the fighting never stopped, but the enemy limited himself more to local small operations. Aggressive reconnaissance in the Group Stein sector indicated a probability that the British would extend their attacks to the north. The British artillery opposite of the left wing of Group Stein clearly had been strengthened and was now registering. Thus, we assigned more heavy artillery to Group Stein.

On 26 July the enemy's artillery fire increased to great strength, mostly against Group Boehn and the right wing of Group Gossler. Following preparation fires, the enemy launched several strong local attacks. The 5th Division fighting on the left wing of Group Boehn and the right wing of the 24th Reserve Division lost the town of Longueval and the ground west of Ginchy.

From the reconnaissance reports of our patrols and the ever-increasing artillery fire, we concluded that a new large-scale enemy attack was imminent. We therefore replaced Group Gossler's 11th Reserve Division, which had been in its positions since 3 July, with the 23rd (Saxon) Reserve Division. At the same time the commanding general of the XII Reserve Corps, General Günther Graf von Kirchbach, assumed command of Group Gossler.

On 27 July the First Army headquarters requested and received disposition authority over the XIII Army Corps' 27th Division. That unit then was designated as the relief for the 24th Reserve Division, which had fought extremely bravely and suffered heavy losses. The relief was completed by 31 July. On 29 July the headquarters of the XIII Army Corps and its 26th Division also were reassigned to the First Army.

On 30 July the British and French major attacks that we had anticipated started between Pozières and the Somme, with the main effort from Guillemont to the Somme. In the Second Army sector the French limited themselves to strong artillery fire, which was directed mainly from the southern bank of the Somme against our positions at Ham and Cléry-sur-Somme. The British only attacked against Group Boehn, which held its positions during the back-and-forth fighting of the 117th, 18th Reserve, 17th Reserve, and 5th Divisions. As the attack started, General von Kichbach was just in the process of assuming command of Group Gossler. With strong artillery support, the British and the French managed to break in on their first attempt. The 24th Reserve Division (with elements of the 27th Division), the 8th Bavarian Reserve Division, and the 23rd Reserve Division then launched hasty counterattacks, which ejected the enemy forces. During that fighting we captured thirteen machine guns and eight hundred British and French soldiers. Thanks to our stalwart troops, we prevented the enemy both from breaking through and from enlarging his break-in. The enemy resumed the attack on 31 July but accomplished nothing.

Prior to 30 July we already had suffered large losses from the enemy's artillery fire, but our casualties on 30 and 31 July were even greater. We then requested Army Group Gallwitz to make certain that OHL would provide us with additional relief forces. OHL shifted the XIX (Saxon) Army Corps, which up to this point had been assigned to the Sixth Army. Reports indicated that only worn-out British divisions were now opposite the Sixth Army, and that their artillery was also reduced. We concluded, therefore, that the British would continue their attack against the First Army with full force. But we also assumed it would take them some time to shift their forces. Indeed, the British did not launch their major attack until the beginning of August.

Despite strong preparatory fires, the French did not attack south of the Somme on 30 July. From that we concluded that the French main effort also would shift to the sector north of the Somme, with the objective of executing a breakthrough in coordination with the British. We reported this assessment to Army Group Gallwitz. The natural course of action now was to move all available reinforcements to the First Army sector, but that only happened in part.

On 1 August, the second anniversary of the beginning of the war, the Kaiser sent a long telegram to the leaders and troops of the First Army, citing us for our heroic fight. During the first days of August the enemy restricted himself to individual and limited advances, which we repelled almost everywhere. Our only loss was Monacu Farm,[3] located farther north, close to the Somme and east of Ham. Our troops holding that position previously had come under heavy fire from the French guns on the south bank of the Somme. The relatively quiet period, otherwise, made it easier for us to relieve the 5th Division and the 24th Reserve Division—positioned on the inner wings of Groups Boehn and Kirchbach—with the entire XIII Army Corps. Their 26th Division was on the right, and their 27th Division on the left. We improved our command and control structure by establishing Group Watter on 3 August, with General Theodor Freiherr von Watter in command. On 4 August the XIX (Saxon) Army Corps was assigned to the First Army.

Our entire front line was subjected to constant enemy artillery fire. Our forward battle zone consisted almost entirely of shell craters. All of the dugouts were destroyed, and the wire obstacles were swallowed up in the craters. The enemy also brought concentrated fire down on our rearward positions as soon as their trace was identified by aerial reconnaissance. Those conditions made the conduct of the battle and the resupply of our troops increasingly difficult. But the defense based on the craters did have the advantage of depriving the enemy's artillery of a clearly identifiable target. They therefore had to saturate the entire depth of the battle space, which consumed incredible amounts of ammunition. The enemy fired on all of the villages and the wooded areas in our rear, which one after the other were wiped off the face of the earth. In contrast to the incredible amounts of ammunition used by the attacker, our defensive ammunition stocks were very limited right from the beginning of the battle. Nor would an increase of ammunition be allocated to us.

Since the beginning of July we had been preparing to improve our rearward positions and the connecting trenches to the front lines. Initially, the necessary construction companies and the materials were not available. We were able to start the work only toward the end of July. Once we started, we worked steadily and energetically, and gradually we connected our multiple rearward positions with a series of interlocking trenches. The selection of those positions was based primarily on optimal artillery observation. Then, we sited the infantry defensive zone one to two kilometers in front of the artillery observation line. Wherever possible, the forwardmost infantry line was on a reverse slope. Such reverse-slope positions only had a field of fire of two hundred to four hundred meters deep. On the forward slope of the ridgeline we established a line of individual screening points that were not connected laterally. The infantry positions themselves consisted of several lines. Almost all the dugouts were established in the rearwardmost trench. In those areas where the water table was known to be high, we brought dowsers in from the Homeland to detect any problems we might have with groundwater. As we gradually and continuously increased the depth of our defensive sector, we increased our ability to resist the enemy's attacks. We also improved the defenses in the towns behind our front lines, which housed most of our staffs. The work was done by the officers' orderlies, and we called those defensive works "orderly positions" (*Burschen-Stellungen*). The First Army headquarters in Bourlon was strongly fortified with a continuous position of strong wire obstacles and several concrete dugouts, all of which encircled the village and the castle. The deep and strongly vaulted basements so common in France were reinforced as dugouts and served as bomb shelters for enemy aerial attacks. Later, when we established the Siegfried Position, Bourlon became an artillery defensive strongpoint, which played a key role in stopping the major British tank attack in November 1917.[4]

The First Army headquarters was deeply involved in the planning of deliberate counterattacks. We concluded that it was necessary to retake the town of Longueval and the surrounding key terrain. Unfortunately, that operation and others remained unfeasible because we had neither the infantry strength nor the necessary ammunition to prepare and execute such attacks.

Both the First Army and Army Group Gallwitz believed that the enemy would resume a major attack, with the First Army sector as the main effort. OHL, on the other hand, believed that the enemy would shift any future attacks to another sector. Army Group Gallwitz, therefore, was ordered to release combat assets. OHL's assessment of the situation, however, soon proved to be incorrect.

The quiet period at the front during the first days of August gave the German troops a much welcomed opportunity to reorganize the units and to make all the necessary preparations for the coming attacks—but it also gave the enemy time to bring forward additional attack forces, including a considerable reinforcement of enemy aviation. Even though we were reinforced with several aviation units, the enemy still had at least a threefold air superiority.

The new major enemy attack that we at First Army Headquarters had forecast began on 7 August against the sector from Thiepval to the Somme. As always in such powerful attacks, we initially lost parts of our forward zone. Hasty counterattacks on 7 August and deliberate counterattacks on 8 August reestablished the lines in the Group Boehn and Group Watter sectors, and almost all of the lines in the Group Kirchbach sector. Group Kirchbach only failed to recover ground on its left wing, close to the Somme, west of Cléry-sur-Somme. The primary reason was that the 23rd (Saxon) Reserve Division came under heavy flanking fire from the south bank of the river. On both days the Second Army was subjected to heavy artillery fire, but no attacks. The First Army suffered heavy losses and we were reinforced with the XIX Army Corps and the I Bavarian Reserve Corps' 16th Division.

The enemy's activity in the Second Army's sector continued to decrease after 8 August. In the First Army sector, meanwhile, we were subjected to constant enemy attacks, always supported by preparatory fires expending incredible amounts of ammunition. The enemy's obvious primary objective during all these attacks was to push in from all sides against the salient southeast of Thiepval. The fighting was especially intense at Mouquet Farm,[5] which had deep cellar rooms. That position held out for a long time thanks to the tough perseverance of our local commander there, Major Walter Freiherr von Schleinitz,[6] with whom I had served in the 2nd Guards Regiment. After he was severely wounded at Mouquet Farm, Schleinitz was awarded the Knight's Cross with Swords of the Hohenzollern House Order. At the end of October 1917, when I was then the chief of staff of the Fourth Army, I had the pleasure of telephoning him at his command post to tell him that he had been awarded a well-deserved Pour le Mérite.

The hotspots in the never-ending fight after 8 August included our positions northwest of Longueval and west of Guillemont. Starting on 10 August, Group Boehn was relieved by Group Laffert, which consisted of the 16th Division and the XIX Army Corps' 24th and 40th Divisions. The 23rd (Saxon) Reserve Division also was relieved by the 1st Bavarian Reserve Division. The commanding general of the I Bavarian Reserve Corps, General Karl von Fasbender, assumed command of Group Kirchbach.

On 11 August the Kaiser came to the First Army to inspect the troops, but we were not able to muster the customary parade. We did, however, have the 24th (Saxon) Reserve Division, which had fought so gallantly and was moving back to its rest area, march past him in full combat gear as an impromptu pass in review. Despite the troops' state of exhaustion from the major battle they had just fought, they marched in good order and made a deep impression on the Kaiser. After the pass in review the Kaiser presented the Oak Leaves to the Pour le Mérite to General von Below for the courageous leadership of his army. We then had a simple breakfast served in a tent for the Kaiser and his entourage. Generals von Falkenhayn, von Gallwitz, von Below, and some of the combat commanders were present. I, however, requested permission to return to the headquarters, where my presence was urgently needed to oversee the continuing fight. When General von Below returned from the breakfast he told me about a very sharp and embarrassing exchange of words between the Kaiser and General von Falkenhayn, which almost certainly would undermine Falkenhayn's position as the chief of the General Staff of the army.

On 12 August the British launched an especially strong and cohesive attack against Groups Laffert and Watter, which nonetheless were able to hold their positions during the back-and-forth fighting. That same day the French directed a strong attack against Group Fasbender. Although the 8th Bavarian Reserve Division fought as bravely as they always did, we lost the southern part of Maurepas. The 1st Bavarian Reserve Division, linked in farther to the south, was pushed back considerably by superior French forces. After a few days of fighting the Bavarians suffered such high losses that they had to be relieved by the 1st Guards Reserve Division, which had been attached to us by Army Group Gallwitz. The I Bavarian Corps' 5th Bavarian Reserve Division relieved the 8th Bavarian Reserve Division.

A rather serious dispute arose between General von Gallwitz and General von Below. The army group commander thought that Below had relieved the 1st Bavarian Reserve Division too quickly with the 1st Guards Division. General von Gallwitz sent a rather sharp but unjustified directive to General von Below. Initially, General von Below intended to lodge a protest, but he reconsidered and accepted my offer to see General von Falkenhayn to try to resolve the dispute. After making an appointment, I drove to General von Falkenhayn's location. He was quite understanding about the conflict. He first talked with General von Below on the telephone, and then asked him to meet him at a certain location east of Saint-Quentin to discuss the matter personally. Thanks to General von Falkenhayn's intervention, the matter was resolved to General von Below's satisfaction.

In the meantime, Army Group Gallwitz made the preparations to relieve the Guards Reserve Corps in the Second Army sector with the recently reconstituted IX Army Corps. The IX Army Corps was moving into positions it was familiar with already, but the exchange of the two corps still consumed a considerable amount of time. The movement of the Guards Reserve Corps to the First Army sector was particularly difficult because the enemy's main effort was concentrated there.

On 14 August General von Falkenhayn ordered all the army group and army chiefs of staff on the Western Front come to Mézières for a conference at 1600 hours. I made the following notes from General von Falkenhayn's comments:

> During the most recent briefing we had assessed that any immediate breakthrough on the Western Front was unlikely. The enemy attacked on the Somme with larger forces and more ammunition than we committed at Verdun, once again proving the difficulty of achieving a breakthrough. Approximately fifty enemy divisions were committed on the Somme, and they also had a three-to-one superiority over us in artillery and aviation. They apparently had an unlimited supply of ammunition. Nonetheless, a British and French breakthrough remained unlikely.[7] On the Eastern Front a Russian breakthrough was partially successful. Conditions there were different, however. An operational breakthrough still had not been achieved there.
>
> Development of Operations in the East: In May the Austrians started major operations against Italy.[8] At that point two-thirds of the Russian forces were north of the Pripet Marshes. To the south, the Russian forces were inferior in numbers to the Austrians. The Austrian AOK,[9] therefore, was capable of operating in Italy. The Austrian positions in the east were good. Any Russian movements to the south were estimated to take four weeks, which gave the Austrians that window

of opportunity in Italy. Falkenhayn nonetheless has advised the Austrians against their Italian operation.[10] His concerns were military and military-political. Operations in Italy are difficult, and British support of Italy made it almost impossible for the Austrians to achieve decisive results.

Italy also faced the threat of a socialist overthrow of their government, prompting the Russian forces south of the Pripet Marshes to attack the Austrians without waiting for reinforcements. The Russian attack succeeded in opening a forty-kilometer gap west of Lutsk.[11] The Austrians then cried to us for support. The Russian offensive finally was stopped by German forces redeployed from the west. In the meantime, the Russians managed to move large forces rapidly from the north to the south. The movements of German forces were slowed by the poor conditions of the Austrian railroads. Our counteroffensive thus lost momentum, but the Russian offensive finally was brought to a halt. In the meantime, more Russian forces attacked the Austrians farther south, on the Dniester River, which in turn forced us to send more German forces to that sector. The Russian drive finally was stopped, but Russian superiority was now so great there and in the Carpathians that we had to commit even more German troops to the East.

The recent events in Galicia can only be explained by Austrian internal instability. The Russians always manage to break into weak positions. Thus, no operational-level progress is possible for us in the East. Initially we had to prop up the Eastern Front to restore Austrian morale. The Austrians must now hold; otherwise Romania will certainly enter the war in support of Russia. This has been a threat for quite a while now. It is becoming increasingly difficult to provide the Austrians with more support, but the Eastern Front must be propped up. We must do everything possible to achieve that, and if we do then there is still hope for victory in the East. Consequently, however, that will have a very serious impact here in the West. For the meantime, we must remain on the defensive, conducting only a few small and local attacks. The West must remain the iron wall that will ensure greater success in the East.

Having gained new courage, the Italians attacked on the Isonzo and achieved some success. The Austrians were forced to deploy fresh forces to that front, and we had to fill the holes in the Austrian lines. Thus, the German armies in the West are now forced to operate with minimum forces. All our armies in the West must understand this situation and support OHL accordingly. Along many sectors of the front the French are even weaker than we are. (French battalions typically have only three companies of 120 men each.) So far the armies have complied with any requests from OHL to release units to form reserves. This will continue, but do not wait for such requests. Offer any detachable units for release.

Details:

1. Can our forwardmost positions be held under today's enemy artillery fire? We must continue to do so. Keep the forward lines thinly manned. Respond to the enemy with deliberate counterattacks. That requires the correct decisions at lowest command levels. Commanders must be trained to operate accordingly.
2. Our artillery depends on aerial observation, and we are not doing well there. We frequently hear complaints. Perhaps our aviation is being deployed incorrectly; perhaps OHL has organized our aviation assets incorrectly. A single command should be responsible for our aerial artillery observers and their protection by fighter aircraft. The level of protection must be adequate. Only our remaining aviation assets, then, should be used for interdiction missions, and those units should be based close to the front.
3. New formations: There is a proposal to replace the combat units in some positions with garrison personnel.[12] That will free up combat troops to form new units. This will thin out our soup even more, but the enemy's soup is thin too. We must increase our combat assets.
4. We must economize our personnel and ammunition. This is critical. At many points along the enemy's front their artillery is weak, consisting mostly of old guns and trench mortars. We must do something similar. We must avoid giving our troops the impression that we actually have an ammunition problem. We always must emphasize focused and tight fire discipline. In quiet sectors interdiction fires should be limited to periods of two to five minutes.
5. Our heavy artillery must be coordinated and integrated into a seamless fire plan.[13] Our young battery commanders should be trained accordingly, and our more senior commanders are responsible for developing training regulations and trainers. Keep a tight control on our fires and evaluate our performance.
6. We can only keep our recruit depots full to a limited extent. We therefore must avoid losses as much as possible to be able to fill the replacement requirements in the sectors with the most critical fighting. In quiet sectors

> we only will be able to maintain small recruit depots until more replacements are trained in the Homeland.

General von Falkenhayn's comments made an uncomfortable impression on us, the army chiefs of staff. They were in sharp contrast to the optimism, which at the time we felt was unjustified, that had prevailed when he developed his attack plan for Verdun in February 1916. Following his summary of the overall situation, General von Falkenhayn then had all the army chiefs of staff report on the situations of their respective armies. I had prepared notes for my report, which ran as follows:

> The fighting on the Somme remains very heavy—heavier than during the autumn battle in Champagne. The attacks in our sector are pretty much constant. The enemy fires massive preparations that consume a great deal of ammunition. The enemy has an absolute numerical superiority in the air. They constantly direct planned fires on our infantry and artillery positions, which obstruct any movement to and from our positions during the day. Constant random searching fires hit our rear areas at night, while planned fires continue to hit our infantry positions. That makes it extremely difficult to improve our positions at night. Thus, our forwardmost line is made up almost entirely of shell craters. The constant fire wears our infantry down very quickly. Routine reliefs are extremely difficult because the rearward battalions have to be brought forward during the never-ending attacks. We only have a real reserve available immediately following the relief of a division or a corps. So far, the relieving units have not been able to get into position on time. It is absolutely necessary that we are provided with relief units much earlier. Attacks will certainly still continue for a long time. Of the fifty-seven British divisions now in France, thirty-three have attacked. Twenty-four British divisions overall are still available. Currently they have eighteen divisions capable of attacking us. In the meantime, their divisions that already have been in the fight have been reconstituted and are once again combat ready. The most dangerous point at this time is Pozières. If the enemy makes any progress there, our already constricted artillery positions on both sides of the Albert–Bapaume rail line will be threatened. We must improve our situation there by attacking, but we currently lack the troops and ammunition to do so. Prior to attacking at Pozières, we should improve our situation between Longueval and Guillemont, in order to draw the enemy artillery toward Longueval. We currently are developing both attack plans and ammunition estimates.

I also noted that Germany's overall casualty reports on the Western Front from 24 June to 8 August showed losses of 1,977 officers and 84,766 enlisted, of which 854 officers and 41,077 enlisted were lost by the First Army between 19 June and 8 August.

On 15 July OHL moved from Mézières back to Pless. Even before his departure, General von Falkenhayn, as I heard later, told Army Group Gallwitz that it would have to make do with the units it currently had on hand.

Up until 15 August the enemy limited himself to local attacks and very strong artillery fires against our entire fighting front. On 16 August the fire increased, and under its cover they launched strong attacks in several locations; but their attacks lacked cohesiveness. During the following days the attacks continued almost uninterruptedly between Pozières and the Somme. The enemy also fired artillery against the ground on both sides of the Albert–Bapaume rail line, from Serre Lès Puisieux to Pozières. In the latter location the British pushed their battle lines close to our positions, and we anticipated that they would widen their attack front. On 17 and 18 August the enemy's fire increased even more, and on the afternoon of the 18th they launched a cohesive attack with several fresh divisions. The British pushed forward against Groups Laffert, Watter, and Fasbender, between the Albert–Bapaume rail line and the Somme. Our combat strength in those group sectors had been reduced considerably by the enemy's daily artillery fire. The fighting there raged back and forth for three days. But despite their thin combat strength, our stalwart combat troops weathered the situation rather well. We only lost some ground at Pozières, Guillemont, and Maurepas. Otherwise the lines held or were reoccupied by hasty and deliberate counterattacks.

During these rather critical days for the First Army the French made only individual and limited advances in the Second Army's sector at Belloy-sur-Somme and Soyécourt. The Guards Reserve Corps, which had been promised to the First Army as a replacement for the IX Army Corps, suffered heavy losses in that attack.

There now were no relief forces available for the First Army. The 27th (Württemberg) Division was under heavy pressure. Elements of the 1st Bavarian Reserve Division, which only recently had been pulled out of the front line, had to be moved forward to reinforce the 27th Division. Since OHL had no replacement units to provide the First Army, it ordered Army Group Gallwitz to shift reinforcing units to us. The army group gradually moved to our sector the Guards Reserve Corps, the 2nd Guards Division (which was withdrawn from the XVII Army Corps), and the 111th Division. The First Army in turn released the IX Reserve Corps and the 23rd (Saxon) Reserve Division. OHL then attached the II Bavarian Army Corps and the 56th Division to Army Group Gallwitz.

The enemy actions against the First Army slackened until 23 August, although they kept up strong and constant artillery fire, augmented with multiple local attacks. Our frontline troops got no rest. By 24 August the relief forces we had been promised had not yet arrived. The British that day launched another major attack against our front from Thiepval to the Somme. Our tired troops that had been in the trenches for so long bore the brunt, but they managed to recapture most of the lost positions with hasty counterattacks. Our stalwart garrison at Mouquet Farm beat back multiple British attacks launched with numerically superior forces. The rest of Group Laffert also held almost all of their positions in the face of heavy, close-quarters combat. Only the left wing of the 40th (Saxon) Division and the 26th (Württemberg) Division on Group Watter's right wing lost some ground. Otherwise, Group Watter firmly held on to its position. In Group Fasbender's sector the 5th Bavarian Reserve Division lost the hamlet of Maurepas, but otherwise the whole line held. The enemy committed strong bomber wings to this major attack. Our infantry and artillery suffered heavy losses from the bombing and from aerial machine gun fire. The First Army did not have enough aviation assets to defend effectively against the enemy's aerial attacks. We only managed to shoot down a very few of the enemy's bombing and strafing aircraft with rifle and machine gun fire.

The enemy barrage continued almost uninterruptedly through the night of 24 August and into the 25th. All of our communications trenches to and on the front lines were cut. We could not plan and organize deliberate counterattacks in the face of the heavy enemy fire. The enemy artillery finally slackened somewhat on the night of the 25th. Our frontline troops had suffered heavy losses and the survivors were so exhausted that they no longer had the strength to mount the deliberate counterattacks to recapture our lost positions. When General Below and I went forward to the front, he ordered the First Army to stand temporarily on the pure defensive.[14] Strong rains on 26 and 27 August softened up the ground and helped us to beat back the British attacks at Thiepval, Maurepas, and Cléry-sur-Somme. In Group Stein's sector we had indicators that the enemy was preparing to launch a gas attack against our positions at Hébuterne and Beaumont. In response, the army group withdrew ten trench mortar battalions from quieter sectors and attached them to the First Army to reinforce our defensive and interdiction fires. We also redistributed our machine guns for better defensive fires against low-flying enemy aircraft.

On 25 August OHL in Pless issued an order establishing a new army group consisting of the Sixth, First, and Second Armies. Under the command of Crown Prince Rupprecht of Bavaria, with Lieutenant General von Kuhl as chief of staff, the new army group came into effect on 28 August, with headquarters in Cambrai. Its primary mission was to coordinate and execute troop movements within its area of operations independently, while keeping OHL informed. Replacing Crown Prince Rupprecht of Bavaria, Colonel General Ludwig Freiherr von Falkenhausen took command of the Sixth Army, with General Friedrich Graf von der Schulenburg as chief of staff. Three months later, however, Schulenburg was reassigned as the chief of staff of Army Group German Crown Prince, commanded by Crown Prince Wilhelm of Prussia. Schulenburg's successor at the Sixth Army was Bavarian general Karl von Nagel zu Aichberg.

The in the meantime, the Guards Reserve Corps arrived and was gradually deployed by Group Laffert in the former sector of the 16th Division and half of the 24th Division's sector. The XIX Army Corps' sector was narrowed, and the corps was then relieved in place by the arriving II Bavarian Army Corps. The commander of the Guards Reserve Corps, General Wolf Rudolf Freiherr von Marschall von Altengottern, took command of Group Laffert. Relief operations for Group Watter also started when the XIII Army Corps was replaced by the 56th and 111th Divisions. The sector was taken over by the commanding general of the XII Reserve Corps, General von Kirchbach. Farther south, the 5th Bavarian Reserve Division was relieved by the 2nd Guards Division, coming from the Second Army.

From the evening of 27 August on, the First Army consisted of Group Stein (2nd Guards Reserve Division, 52nd Division, 26th Reserve Division), Group Marschall (Guards Reserve Corps and II Bavarian Army Corps), Group Kirchbach (56th Division and 111th Division), and Group Fasbender (2nd and 1st Guards Divisions). Reserve forces that had arrived or were arriving were the 185th Division, the XXIII Reserve Corps, and the XXVII Reserve Corps.

Together with General von Below, I spent long hours traveling to the fighting front in order to prepare everything for the defense against the new attacks we certainly expected. Up until 30 August we endured rain and strong thunderstorms, during which two British observation balloons were destroyed by lightning.

On 29 August we received the news that Romania declared war on the Central Powers. Almost at the same time we received a telegram from Pless reporting that General von Falkenhayn had been replaced as the chief of OHL by Field Marshal von Hindenburg, with General Ludendorff as first quartermaster general.[15] We welcomed the news and we hoped that from now on we would receive more focused support for the heavily engaged First Army. We were convinced, correctly, that more heavy fighting lay ahead. We were not disappointed by the new command structure.

As I have addressed already, General von Falkenhayn made many mistakes as the chief of the General Staff of the Field Army. His attack at Verdun was still in progress and had not yet achieved its objective. The countless German troops deployed there were fighting against a courageous and tough enemy who defended from steel and concrete positions, inflicting great losses on the German Army. With complete confidence in my abilities, General von Falkenhayn had transferred me to the OHL staff in January 1915. On 26 September 1915 he assigned me to the Third Army as chief of staff; on 3 July 1916 as the chief of staff of the Second and then the First Army. On 31 August I sent General von Falkenhayn a long letter thanking him for his trust. Soon after his relief at OHL, General von Falkenhayn was reassigned to command an army deployed against Romania. In Romania and then later in Turkey he proved to be a highly successful troop commander. I did not see him again until 1919. I met with him at his apartment in Berlin, where he was writing his book *Die Oberste Heeresleitung von 1914–16.*[16]

Heavy enemy fire continued almost uninterrupted until 31 August. Almost every day the enemy made local attacks, which captured small sections of ground. On the afternoon of 31 August Group Kirchbach launched a carefully prepared deliberate counterattack in the direction of Longueval. Group Kirchbach was reinforced by the II Bavarian Army Corps, which had been detached from the left wing of Group Marschall. Despite the heaviest enemy pressure, the attack was successful and the troops then managed to hold their newly won ground against multiple hasty counterattacks.

That same day we learned to our great relief that the new OHL leadership[17] ordered the termination of the attack on Verdun. General von Falkenhayn had insisted on pressing that attack right up until the day he was relieved. We now had high hopes that Army Group Crown Prince Rupprecht would receive sufficient forces to conduct the fight on the Somme.

The enemy's artillery fire continued almost without interruption. On 3 September, following a drumfire barrage of several hours, the British and French attacked. The assault, however, was not cohesive and was directed against different locations. The left wing of Group Stein came under heavy pressure, but they repelled all the attacks. In Group Marschall's sector the British made some small progress at Mouquet Farm, but we nonetheless retained control of the position. In Group Kirchbach's sector the British captured the almost completely flattened village of Guillemont. In Group Fasbender's sector the 2nd Guards Divisions lost Leforest, as well as their connections to our lines north and south of the town. The 1st Guards Division, meanwhile, completed its relief by the 53rd (Saxon) Reserve Division.

On 4 September the British and French launched another huge attack following some of the heaviest preparatory fires we had encountered so far. This was a cohesive attack on both sides of the Somme, with the main effort against Groups Kirchbach and Fasbender. The massive and violent attack covered a frontage of forty kilometers. In their reports, both the First and Second Armies described it as a renewed breakthrough attempt. As the enemy pressure increased, the 24th (Saxon) Division, which was in reserve and still needed to rest and refit, had to be committed to support Groups Kirchbach and Fasbender. As an additional precautionary measure, elements of the I Bavarian Reserve Corps and the 1st Guards Division, both of which had been reconstituted, were moved forward as reserves and given the mission of improving the already established rearward position behind Group Fasbender. The enemy continued attacking on 5 September, but they failed to break through. The German defensive line remained intact.

In the First Army sector the main attack hit Group Kirchbach's 56th Division, which held its position. However, the 111th Division did not. Group Fasbender's 2nd Guards Division and the 53rd (Saxon) Reserve Division also lost their positions. By 5 September their front lines were pushed back to a line west of Combles–east of Leforest–west of Cléry-sur-Somme. The back-and-forth struggle cost us considerable losses in dead, wounded, and prisoners. We were greatly relieved when the new OHL immediately started moving adequate reserves to the embattled Somme front. Army Group Crown Prince Rupprecht also reacted quickly, assembling new reserves for the relief of the worn down formations. There was now a new and fresh sense of energy that had been missing under the always hesitating General von Falkenhayn.

On 6 September the commanding general of the XXVII Reserve Corps, General Oskar von Ehrenthal, assumed command of Group Fasbender, which was renamed Group Ehrenthal. Within that group the 13th Division was newly deployed north of the Somme. Gradually the following units were relieved: In Group Marschall's sector, the infantry of the 4th Guards Division were relieved by the 89th Brigade of the 207th Division, and the 1st Guards Reserve Division was relieved by the 45th Reserve Division. In Group Kichbach's sector, the 56th Division was relieved by the 5th Bavarian Division, and the 111th Division was relieved by the 185th Division. In Group Ehrenthal's sector, the 2nd Guards Division was relieved by the 54th Reserve Division. During these relief operations the enemy kept our fighting positions under almost constant heavy fires. We learned that the XVIII Army Corps would arrive via Cambrai on 9 September and become the army group reserve.

On 8 September General von Hindenburg and General Ludendorff arrived in Cambrai for a conference at the headquarters of Army Group Crown Prince Rupprecht. The commanders of both army groups, the commander of the Fourth Army (Duke Albrecht of Württemberg), and all the army chiefs of staff on the Western Front also were in attendance. General von Hindenburg told us that an attack to overpower Romania was planned and he expressed his firm confidence that in the meantime the Western Front would repel all enemy attacks and hold. His calmness, serenity, and confidence made a big impression on all of us. Then General Ludendorff took the lead in the conference and told me to brief the situation of the First Army. Earlier that day I had discussed with General von Below the requests we would present, because we assumed that was the main reason for the conference.

Initially I summarized the course of the fighting to date and emphasized my firm conviction that the First Army would continue to put up the utmost resistance and prevent an enemy breakthrough. Because of the attacker's great superiority in all combat assets, however, it would be hard to avoid losing some additional ground, even if we defended every inch. Owing to the overpowering fires of the enemy's artillery, with its 10-to-1 ammunition superiority, all our trenches, approach routes, wire obstacles, and most dugouts in our forward combat zone and most of our first line of rear positions had disappeared into the crater field. We were determined to continue to improve constantly our rearward positions. A large-scale active defense based on a major deliberate counterattack was not possible, because we lacked the necessary infantry, artillery, ammunition, and aviation. Such an attack also would be difficult to conduct across the wide and deep crater field.

I then briefed the respective combat tactics of the attacker and the defender. After the attacker made the first deep break-in on 1 July, he initially followed up with local consolidating attacks. Then he followed with major attacks on a wide front that he prepared with consolidated fires, preceded by barrages lasting for days. In order to minimize our losses from such fires, we held our foremost line very thinly, which by that point was nothing but a series of craters. From those positions we fought an active defense in depth. That kind of fight minimized our losses significantly. Once the enemy's artillery started displacing forward, we then launched hasty counterattacks at the initiative of the lower echelon leaders. We thus often managed to throw the enemy back to his line of departure.

Our infantry had been generally superior to the enemy's when it came to the sort of close-quarters fighting that is conducted with bayonets, hand grenades, and entrenching tools with sharpened blades. In the cases where a hasty counterattack did not succeed, we immediately started to prepare a deliberate counterattack. Those generally succeeded when we could concentrate our artillery fires against the enemy's break-in point.

I emphasized that all our divisions were being required to fight to the end of their strength, resulting in losses of 50 to 70 percent. In the process, our most courageous soldiers suffered the greatest losses, and our divisions were bled white. Any divisions so attritted could only rebuild their combat strength very slowly with the young replacements coming in. The maintenance of our infantry combat strength was especially critical. I recommended, therefore, a timelier relief of the divisions in the line. That in turn would reduce the amount of ground we were losing when we tried to relieve divisions in the line after they had lost their basic combat effectiveness.

Overall, our field artillery was sufficient, but the gun crews were overstrained and exhausted. We were taking substantial equipment losses from the constant and heavy enemy fire. I therefore recommended that we preposition sufficient replacement materials immediately to the rear of the army's sector. Our heavy artillery, on the other hand, was not sufficient, especially in terms of ammunition supply. The improvement of our entire combat effectiveness, especially that of our artillery, depended heavily on increasing our aviation assets. The attacker had air superiority, and therefore made more effective use of his artillery and ammunition.

Even though the First Army headquarters always provided in advance to the relieving divisions a situation map and the operations orders necessary for the conduct of the battle, such divisions nonetheless needed a period of time to orient to the terrain and to allow their artillery to occupy and register from their new firing positions. I recommended, therefore, that each relieving division prior to moving forward receive an orientation briefing on their new sector. Such briefings would be conducted jointly by knowledgeable General Staff officers and knowledgeable artillery officers. Such officers would impart a great deal of critical information for the relief, and also for the continued conduct of the battle.

Both General Ludendorff and General von Hindenburg concurred completely with my recommendations, and expressed thanks to General von Below and me. The other army chiefs of staff then briefed their respective situations.

General Ludendorff then told us that a defensive position had been constructed in the northern part of Schleswig-Holstein to secure against potential enemy landings in Denmark. Also, the right flank of the Western Front's northernmost Fourth Army would be secured by an improved position along the Dutch border. To the rear of our forward positions on the Western Front we were constructing two continuous sets of operational defensive positions: one position to the east of the Arras–Laon line was behind the Sixth, First, and Second Armies; and the other along the Verdun–Metz line to the rear of Army Group German Crown Prince.

Most significantly, General Ludendorff told us that the attack on Verdun would be aborted. He also said the most immediate and urgent task was to establish new reserves. Of the eight newly raised divisions, five would be assigned to the Western Front and three to the east. More divisions, meanwhile, were in the process of being raised. One division each would be withdrawn and not replaced from the sectors of the Fourth Army and Army Detachment Strantz.

It was urgently necessary for us to launch the attack on Romania rapidly, and we could expect quick success. General Ludendorff also emphasized the importance of thoroughly training all the troops. In order to achieve an equal level of training across the Western Front, every field army would be required to stand up a storm troop battalion, which then would run the training courses for that army.[18]

During September, Army Group Crown Prince Rupprecht's seven field artillery, four foot artillery, and almost all of the super-heavy howitzer ammunition trains would be supplied on a daily basis; the remaining artillery ammunition would be distributed to the other frontline firing units. The heavy artillery of the First Army would be reinforced. The protection of all artillery equipment was of critical importance. Barrage fires were absolutely necessary, but should not be overdone. Trench mortar fire should primarily be defensive in order to avoid wasting costly ammunition. We already had started increasing our aviation assets, but it would take time to accomplish the buildup. A social gathering followed the conference, but General von Below and I left shortly and returned to Bourlon because the enemy's fire had increased.

On 9 September the British started new attacks between Thiepval and Combles. We lost the completely destroyed village of Combles, but other than that we managed to hold our positions. General von Below and I spent almost all of 9, 10, and 11 September at the front, where we briefed all the corps and division commanders on the key information we had learned from the conference at Cambrai. Returning to army headquarters, I found plenty of desk work awaiting me. I did not get much sleep, but I got through it rather well.

On the morning of 12 September the enemy's constant artillery fire increased to a gigantic crescendo between the Albert–Bapaume rail line and the Somme. It was particularly strong in Group Ehrenthal's sector, where the French followed up with a strong and deeply echeloned attack. They captured the village of Bouchavesnes[19] and the ground to the north and south. By the evening of 12 September Group Ehrenthal was pushed back to a line running east of Combles, to the eastern edge of Bouchavesnes, and to the east of Cléry-sur-Somme. Group Ehrenthal held that line when the French attacked the following day, but suffered heavy losses, especially in prisoners. As a result, we had to deploy the 24th Reserve Division on the group's right flank.

Army Group Crown Prince Rupprecht allocated the XVIII Army Corps for the relief of the XXVII Reserve Corps and the 24th Reserve Division, and moved the corps forward expeditiously. During the fighting on 12 and 13 September the 53rd (Saxon) Division failed completely. Both General von Below and I confirmed that personally. After the division came out of the line, I sent several officers from the army staff to the rest area to gauge the division's morale. They reported unanimously that the unit's cohesion was questionable. After mingling with the troops around their campfires, the staff officers returned and reported statements such as, "Well, they're not gonna send us to dangerous spots like that a second time."

On the other hand, the XXVII Reserve Corps' 54th (Württemberg) Reserve Division had fought well. The only reason it was relieved was the fact that it was reporting very low combat strengths. But when the division came off the line, we saw that the strength of their movement columns was much higher than reported. General von Below was upset primarily by the failure of the 53rd (Saxon) Reserve Division, which led to a rather serious discussion with the commanding general of the XXVII Reserve Corps.

OHL and Army Group Crown Prince Rupprecht moved quickly to provide more reserves to the First Army. The army group assigned to us as relief forces the IV Army Corps; the headquarters of the III Bavarian Army Corps, with the 6th Bavarian Division and the 50th Reserve Division; and the XVI Army Corps. OHL in turn allocated to the army group the 214th Division, the 37th Reserve Infantry Brigade of the newly formed 213th Division, and the 211th and 212th Divisions, which were still being stood up. Concurring with our plan to retake Bouchavesnes, OHL allocated to us the 212th and 214th Divisions and plenty of ammunition. The experienced General Alfred Ziethen was assigned to the First Army as the artillery advisor.

OHL established a rear area inspectorate for the First Army in Valenciennes, which made our logistics operations more self-sufficient. General Max Graf von Montgelas was appointed the area inspector, and his chief of staff was Colonel Hans Schenck zu Schweinberg. The latter was an old, faithful friend of mine who was a veteran General Staff officer. I specifically requested him for that position because I knew and valued his competence and sense of responsibility. Major von Zitzewitz, who had served well under me at the Third Army, was assigned as the logistics officer. In very short order, the First Army had a well-organized system for rations, trench construction material, and other logistics functions.

Our intelligence reports indicated that many of the enemy units that had been committed to the 12 September attack were replaced by fresh British and French divisions. Accordingly, we anticipated that the enemy would continue their massive attacks, especially since they heavily outnumbered us in artillery, ammunition, and aircraft.

On the morning of 15 September, following massive preparatory fires, the enemy launched another major attack against the First Army between the

Albert–Bapaume rail line and the Somme. Group Stein held its position at Thiepval. In Group Marschall's sector the 4th Guards Division and the 45th Reserve Division were pushed back to the line Mouquet Farm–Courcelette, which the British took. Linked in to the eastern flank of their attack, the British made a deep break-in by launching a surprise attack with a large number of tanks. The stoutly defending II Bavarian Army Corps was pushed back past Flers, and Group Kirchbach was pushed back to Lesboeufs and Morval. Group Schenck,[20] which from right to left consisted of the 54th Reserve Division (supported by large elements of the 24th Reserve Division), the remaining elements of the 53rd Division (supported by considerable elements of the 25th Division), and the 13th Division, managed to hold its positions against the back-and-forth close-quarters combat. According to the reports that came in that night, the First Army's line now ran Mouquet Farm–north of the town of Courcelette (in enemy hands)–Martinpuich–Flers–southwest of Lesboeufs–west of Morval–east of Combles–east of Bouchavesnes–east of Cléry-sur-Somme. The Second Army also lost some ground along its front oriented to the northwest.

On 16 and 17 September the enemy tried to exploit his successes through limited objective attacks. Although the enemy's fire continued day and night, all the attempts to turn the break-ins in the First Army sector into a breakthrough failed in the face of the stout German resistance. The enemy's various break-ins, however, had lengthened our front lines considerably. Our heavy losses also forced us to postpone our planned deliberate counterattack at Bouchavesnes. All our available reserves had to be committed to relieve our exhausted front-line units.

General von Below had considered temporarily pulling back our right and left flanks into a rearward position that was partially still under construction, but based on my advice he decided to continue to hold out in the present lines. During the previous year's battle in Champagne, I had advocated conducting an unrestricted fight to hold every inch of ground. I was convinced that was the correct course of action here too. A voluntary withdrawal from the enemy could produce some temporarily relief, but it also could give the enemy a significant morale advantage.

On 17 September we reorganized our defensive sectors. General Friedrich Sixt von Armin, the commanding general of the IV Army Corps, took over Group Marschall. General Otto von Hügel, the commanding general of the XXVI Reserve Corps, assumed command of Group Kirchbach. In Group Armin's sector the 50th Reserve Division gradually relieved the 3rd Bavarian Division, and the 6th Bavarian Division relieved the 4th Bavarian Division. That same day our fighter pilots shot down twelve enemy aircraft during a big air battle.

OHL, meanwhile, issued the order to start reconnoitering and constructing the operational rearward positions that General Ludendorff had spoken about at the 8 September conference in Cambrai.[21] Army Group Crown Prince Rupprecht was responsible for establishing the new line, which would run from Arras, to the west of Cambrai, and to the west of Saint-Quentin. OHL stressed that our current lines must be held meanwhile, and assigned the V Reserve Corps and the 7th Reserve Division to Army Group Crown Prince Rupprecht for that purpose. OHL also made preparations for the VI Army Corps, the IX Reserve Corps, and the 6th Bavarian Division to relieve the First Army's depleted II Bavarian Army Corps and XXVII Reserve Corps, followed by the 5th Bavarian Division. Our 45th Reserve Division and 185th Division also would be relieved by the Seventh Army's 15th and 113th Divisions. The Fourth Army offered to exchange their 4th Replacement Division and a Marine infantry brigade for the First Army's 58th Division—currently in a rest position—and our 89th Infantry Brigade, fighting as part of the 4th Guards Division. Executed gradually, those relief actions restored the First Army's operational strength. Army Group Crown Prince Rupprecht, meanwhile, established to our rear a position along the line Bapaume–Manancourt–Bussu, manned by the 9th Reserve Division, 7th Reserve Division, and 211th Division, which were withdrawn from the front lines.

During the first half of September our aviation force was increased significantly. Our combat wings attacked courageously and aggressively, destroying some fifty enemy aircraft. Fighter Wing Boelcke was especially effective in confining the aerial dogfights to the space above the enemy's lines.

The air support was particularly effective during our 20 September deliberate counterattack at Bouchavesnes. The counterattack was conducted by Group Ehrenthal with elements of the 214th Division, the 213th Division, and the 54th Reserve Division. All available artillery fired in support, including sixty high-angle and sixteen flat-trajectory batteries. Our counterbattery fires made extensive use of Green Cross gas. For the first time our infantry assault was supported by infantry-support aircraft,[22] which attacked the enemy with bombs and machine gun fire and radioed back reports on the progress of the attack. Although our counterattack achieved some initial success, the French recovered their losses with strong hasty and deliberate counterattacks. By evening our attacking units were back at their lines of departure. The fighting continued until 22 September, at which point Group Ehrenthal broke off the attack. We then started relieving the 45th Reserve Division, the 5th Bavarian Division, the 4th Guards Division, and the 185th Division with the newly arriving fresh divisions.

On 21 September 1916 the Kaiser awarded me the *Orden Pour le Mérite.*

After making a speech to the First Army's senior staff, General von Below hung the decoration around my neck. He noted my outstanding contributions in managing the gigantic Battle of the Somme. That evening I received congratulatory telegrams from Field Marshal von Hindenburg, the crown princes of Prussia and Bavaria, the duke of Württemberg, almost all the army commanders, General Ludendorff, many generals, good friends, and courageous fellow soldiers. I was the first of my clan to be awarded the Prussian Pour le Mérite. Until 1866 my ancestors all had been officers in the army of the Electorate of Hesse. The former Electorate of Hesse did have a high wartime decoration, which was awarded only very rarely. Two of my direct ancestors and one of their brothers received this decoration.[23] Two of them had been commanders of the Hessian 2nd Infantry Regiment, designated "Old-Lossberg" and "Young-Lossberg."[24] I was proud of the fact that I was following the tradition of this old military family. My father served in the 2nd Foot Guards Regiment from 1878 to 1886, and I had entered that regiment as an officer candidate. My father later commanded the 3rd Guards Regiment, finishing his career as a brigade commander in Holstein. Unfortunately, he died in 1904; but my mother was still alive and was very excited that her son had become a Knight (*Ritter*) of the Pour le Mérite. She lived to the ripe old age of ninety, and died peacefully in 1926. My wife, who came from the old military family of Herwarth von Bittenfeld, and my four children all wrote me proud congratulatory notes. In my heart I believed, and I still believe, that I served the German Army merely doing my duty, just like any other stout soldier.

On 22 September the front line of Group Stein was held by the 12th Division, the 2nd Guards Reserve Division, the 52nd Division, and the 26th Reserve Division. Group Armin's line was held by the 8th Division, the 7th Division, the 6th Bavarian Division, and the 50th Reserve Division, with the 7th Reserve Division to their rear. Group Hügel's line was held by the 52nd Reserve Division, the 51st Reserve Division,[25] and the 213th Division. To their rear the V Reserve Corps was still moving up. Group Schenck's line was held by the 214th Division, the 21st Division, the 25th Division, and the 212th Division, with the 211th Division and the depleted 54th Reserve Division to the rear.

On 23 September heavy enemy artillery fire started falling between Thiepval and the Somme. Two days later the enemy launched a major attack, again supported by many tanks. Enemy aircraft engaged in both close ground support and air superiority dogfights with our aircraft. Group Stein and the largest part of Group Armin held their positions. The left wing of Group Armin, all of Group Hügel, and approximately the northern half of Group Schenck were pushed back after putting up a spirited fight. On the southern wing of Group Schenck the 25th and 212th Divisions managed to hold their positions.

On 25 September the British took the villages of Lesboeufs and Morval. The hamlet of Fregicourt (which no longer exists) and Rancourt fell into French hands. On 26 September the enemy resumed his major attacks. Thiepval, Mouquet Farm, and the ground south of Le Sars fell to the British. The French then pushed forward between Combles and Bouchavesnes to the southwestern edge of the Saint-Pierre-Vaast Forest (Bois de Saint-Pierre-Vaast), situated east of Rancourt and in the direction of Moislains. The enemy continued attacking the following day. The British tried to break through in the direction of Bapaume, the French in the direction of Moislains. We managed to beat back those attacks.

The gigantic British and French breakthrough attempt that had started on 25 September failed. Our front was not broken anywhere, but along an approximately twenty-five-kilometer-wide sector we were pushed back some two kilometers. Heavily outnumbered, our troops fought heroically from the water-filled shell craters that covered the battleground. Conducting an active defense, they repeatedly launched hasty counterattacks. By the end of that fighting the 50th Reserve Division, the 213th Division, and the 214th Division were no longer combat effective, and were relieved quickly by the 7th Reserve Division, the 15th Division, and the 10th Reserve Division. In the meantime, OHL launched the campaign against Romania in the east.

OHL had reassigned six divisions to Army Group Crown Prince Rupprecht from Army Group German Crown Prince, which in turn was assigned worn-out divisions. OHL also assigned the 6th and 11th Divisions to Army Group Crown Prince Rupprecht and moved forward the 5th Replacement Division, the 29th Division, and the 111th Division as the First Army reserve.

We reported to Army Group Crown Prince Rupprecht our assessment that the enemy would continue to attempt a breakthrough in the same direction. Based on our reconnaissance results, we also concluded that there was the possibility that the British would expand their attack against Group Stein's entire sector to support the western wing of their breakthrough push. The army group endorsed our assessment to OHL. Since all the indicators pointed to a relatively low level of threat to the Second Army, OHL then detached several of their artillery batteries and reassigned them to support the First Army.

In addition to our routine morning, noon, and evening situation reports to the army group, General Ludendorff usually called me several times daily. I reported in great detail my overall assessment of the situation based on the daily trips General von Below and I made to the front. Those daily conversations established a firm bond of trust between General Ludendorff and me, which strengthened continually until the end of the war.

On 29 September General von Boehn, commanding general of the IX Reserve Corps, assumed command of Group Hügel. The IX Reserve Corps'

52nd Reserve Division was relieved by the 18th Reserve Division, and the 51st Reserve Division by the 17th Reserve Division. During the last days of September and the beginning of October the enemy launched only limited attacks in the Thiepval sector against the 26th Reserve Division, and against the 8th Division along the boundary between Groups Stein and Armin. Group Armin lost some ground to a stronger British attack against the boundary between the 6th Bavarian Division and the 50th Reserve Division. During that time period the French extended their left flank to Morval.

On 2 October General Otto von Garnier, commanding general of the V Reserve Corps, assumed command of Group Schenck. In Group Armin's sector the 8th Division and the 7th Division were relieved by a Marine infantry brigade and the 4th Replacement Division. In Group Boehn's sector the 15th Division replaced the 213th Division. In Group Garnier's sector the 21st Division was relieved by the 113th Division, and the 25th Division by the 9th Reserve Division. On our southern flank the Second Army took over Group Garnier's southernmost divisional sector.

At the beginning of October OHL transferred the 103rd Division, the 28th Reserve Division, the 8th Replacement Division, and the I Bavarian Army Corps to Army Group Crown Prince Rupprecht. The 19th Reserve Division and the 38th Division were designated the First Army's reserve. Along the quieter sectors of the Western Front OHL reduced the field artillery brigades from four to three battalions each. The excess battalions were then formed into a Field Artillery General Reserve (*Heeres-Feldartillerie-Reserve*) that OHL could use to support relief actions in the main battle areas. The First Army received a number of trench guns[26] and naval gun batteries, both of which proved highly effective.

Group Stein's 26th Reserve Division was relieved by the arriving 28th Reserve Division. After a short rest and reconstitution period, the 26th Reserve Division moved to the quiet sector at Monchy-le-Preux and relieved the 12th Division, which then was reassigned as the First Army's reserve behind Group Stein. A growing number of indicators pointed to an enemy buildup against Group Stein's southern sector. Group Armin also started the preparations to deploy the 6th Division between the 6th Bavarian Division and the 7th Reserve Division, both of which were depleted. Additional aviation and ground units were attached to our right wing from the Second Army. We anticipated that the main effort of the enemy's renewed attacks would be against Groups Stein and Armin. In response, the newly arriving 5th Replacement Division, XIX Army Corps, 16th Division, and 211th Division were deployed in our rear positions as reserves. Heavy batteries from the Artillery General Reserve were deployed on our right wing, and we received another eight aviation detachments and a fighter squadron. Our number of aviation units now stood at forty-six.

Heavy enemy artillery fire opened up against our entire front on 3 October. From experience we knew that a major attack was coming. The Second Army, meanwhile, had taken over the left divisional sector of Group Garnier, positioning the fresh 29th Division with strong artillery there. On 6 October the Second Army beat back a French attack south of the Somme, during which the attackers used flamethrowers.

By 6 October the enemy artillery fire against the First Army had increased significantly. After a gigantic preparatory barrage on 7 October, a strong and deeply echeloned major attack broke lose between the Albert–Bapaume rail line and Bouchavesnes. The enemy committed large numbers of tanks and aircraft. After a protracted period of back-and-forth fighting, we managed to hold our defensive lines for the most part. We only lost the village of Le Sars in Group Armin's sector, and Group Boehn's front line was pushed back to Le Transloy and Sailly-Saillisel.

On 8 October the enemy infantry attacks continued, supported by heavy artillery fire. The British restricted themselves to limited advances at Le Sars. The French, however, launched a strong, cohesive attack on both sides of Rancourt. We managed to repel that attack after protracted fighting, during which both sides suffered heavy losses.

Shortly before the battles on 7 and 8 October, OHL ordered the 215th Division, 222nd Division, Bavarian Replacement Division, and XV Army Corps to deploy to Army Group Crown Prince Rupprecht as relief units. At First Army headquarters, meanwhile, all the indicators pointed to the continuation of the major enemy attacks. The army group concurred with our assessment to OHL, also pointing out that the attacks in the Second Army's sector seemed to be decreasing.

Gradually, our units on the front line were relieved. In Group Armin's sector the Marine infantry brigade was replaced with the 5th Replacement Division, whose battle sector then was reassigned to Group Stein; the 4th Replacement Division and the 6th Bavarian Division were replaced with the 24th Division and the XIX Army Corps' 40th Division; and the 7th Reserve Division was relieved by the 19th Reserve Division. In Group Boehn's sector the 18th Reserve Division was relieved by the 2nd Bavarian Division, the 17th Reserve Division by the 16th Division, and the 15th Division by the 1st Bavarian Division. In Group Garnier's sector the 10th Reserve Division was relieved by the 211th Division, the 113th Division by the 103rd Division, and a short time later the 9th Reserve Division was relieved by the 8th Replacement Division.

All those relief operations were disrupted constantly by enemy limited attacks, but we managed to beat them back everywhere. Group Stein came under very heavy artillery fire with poison gas near and south of Gommecourt. On 12 October our relief operations were disrupted by a strong enemy attack from the west of Le Sars to Bouchavesnes. The French captured the northwestern part of Sailly-Saillisel, but we managed to hold along the rest of the front.

The enemy's limited attacks continued on 13 October. Group Stein's 28th Reserve Division lost part of its position. A French limited attack against the 16th Division on 15 October took the northern part of Sailly-Saillisel. On the evening of 16 October the enemy's limited attacks subsided, but as we anticipated, a major attack followed.

Our ground and aerial reconnaissance detected British efforts to strengthen their forces significantly directly opposite the southern sector of Group Stein. The French also extended their left wing north, toward Le Transloy. Everything indicated a coordinated major attack toward Bapaume, with the British thrusting from the west and south, and the French toward the east. Based on that assessment, we reinforced Group Stein with several batteries from the OHL general reserve. OHL also promised to assign the 208th and 221st Divisions to Army Group Crown Prince Rupprecht.

On 17 October the new major enemy attack we had been anticipating started against the First Army. They hit us on a wide front between Le Sars and Rancourt, but initially they made only small gains. The British captured some ground east of Le Sars. After a long fight, the French seized the completely destroyed village of Sailly-Saillisel.[27] On 18 October, following a long preparatory barrage, the British resumed their full-scale attack along the line from Le Sars to Rancourt. They penetrated into the positions of the 40th and 6th Divisions, and the 19th Reserve Division between Le Sars and Le Transloy. Their tanks initially pushed our front line south of Bapaume back some three kilometers. By launching hasty counterattacks everywhere along the entire front we managed with a few minor exceptions to recover our original positions. We also captured several tanks.[28] Our brave troops put up a determined fight and once more they came through.

In response to our situation report on the fighting to that point, the Kaiser visited the First Army on 19 October. When he arrived at the First Army headquarters in Bourlon, the Kaiser praised my work as chief of staff and conveyed the respects of Field Marshal Hindenburg and General Ludendorff. He told me that they both had absolute confidence in me. The Kaiser, accompanied by General von Below, then made a long inspection trip to almost all the subordinate command posts. Meanwhile, I remained in Bourlon working on the preparation of operations orders. The Kaiser spoke with many of the troops during his trip. He had the following to say to a large gathering at Group Stein:

> I have traveled here from the Eastern Front to express my heartfelt thanks to the troops that have been fighting this protracted battle on

> the Somme against an overpowering enemy for three months now. Both the Fatherland and your comrades on the Eastern Front also send their gratitude. In these tough battles the German people are fighting against half the world in all directions. The sons of Germany are doing well everywhere against the enemy's superiority, but nothing compares with the fighting on the Somme. It is without precedent in the history of human conflict. Thus, I thank you as your supreme commander (*Oberster Kriegsherr*)[29] and in the name of the German nation for your courage, your willingness to sacrifice, your trust in God, and for your devotion to your last breath. This Battle of the Somme will in later centuries be seen as a symbol of a whole people in arms. The manner in which you have fought can only be called superhuman.

After the long inspection tour, Crown Prince Rupprecht invited the Kaiser to a simple dinner in Cambrai. General von Below and I also were invited. I sat next to General Freiherr von Lyncker, with whom I reminisced about old times. He told me that his second son, who had been assigned to the First Army as a fighter pilot and then was transferred to Romania, had shot down two enemy aircraft. During the second dog fight, as he dove closer to the ground to observe his opponent crash, he collided with the burning enemy plane. He too crashed and he died instantly. That was General von Lyncker's second loss of a son during the war.

There were only minor engagements on 19 and 20 October, but Group Armin's 40th Division managed to retake a small piece of ground at Le Sars that the British had captured on 17 October. While the fighting was still in progress on 18 October, OHL initiated the necessary relief actions. The Guards Reserve Corps and the 58th (Saxon) Division were moved to the First Army. The 212th and 221st Divisions and the XV Army Corps were attached to Army Group Crown Prince Rupprecht. The army group also was allocated for future relief actions the 4th Division, the 14th Division, the 21st Reserve Division, the 111th Division, the 22nd Reserve Division, and the 32nd (Saxon) Division. The 56th Division and the XIII (Württemberg) Army Corps became part of the OHL general reserve.

The army group initially assigned the 38th Division and the 23rd (Saxon) Reserve Division to the First Army. The 38th Division relieved Group Stein's 28th Reserve Division. The 23rd Reserve Division relieved Group Armin's 6th Division. The 19th Reserve Division also was relieved by the Bavarian Replacement Division. The 12th Division remained behind Group Stein as the First Army's reserve, which was reinforced further with five heavy batteries from the OHL general reserve.

But even before the completion of the reliefs, Groups Armin and Boehn and the left wing of Group Stein were hit with a major attack on 21 October. The direction of the British main attack was toward Bapaume, while the French directed their main effort toward Sailly-Saillisel. In Group Stein's sector the British attack hit the heavily depleted and not yet relieved 28th Reserve Division and the 5th Replacement Division with great force. Both units were pushed back about one kilometer, east of the Albert–Bapaume rail line. On our left, Group Armin's 24th Division, 40th Division, and the not yet relieved 6th Division held their positions. That same day Group Boehn tried to retake the northern part of Sailly-Saillisel. However, that attack failed in the face of overpowering French artillery fire.

On 22 October the enemy widened their attack sector southward toward Rancourt. Following a gigantic drumfire barrage that started at noon, the French attacked via Rancourt southwest of Le Transloy. Simultaneously, the British made their attack toward Le Sars. Despite the enemy's artillery fires targeting our forward lines and our immediate rear area, we managed to hold for the most part. The British and the French resumed their attacks the following day, but they failed to make any significant headway. The gigantic fight of 21 through 23 October was a major German defensive victory. We suffered great losses in the process, but the enemy lost even more.

A period of calm settled in over the battlefront following 23 October. That made our relief operations easier, despite the sporadic enemy interference. The British still conducted limited attacks against Group Armin on 25, 27, and 31 October. The French too made minor attacks north of Rancourt on 24 and 27 through 29 October. The enemy attacks failed in all sectors.

According to plan, Group Stein's 5th Replacement Division was relieved by the 58th Division, and the 12th Division was inserted into the line between the 52nd and the 38th Divisions. Group Boehn's 16th Division was replaced by the 30th Division, and the 1st Bavarian Division by the 39th Division. On 26 October General Berthold von Deimling, commanding general of the XV Army Corps, took command of Group Boehn.

On 28 October the courageous Captain Oswald Boelcke was killed in action resulting from a tragic midair collision over German lines.[30] He had shot down twenty-two enemy aircraft during the Battle of the Somme. Thanks to the tactical principles he developed, the air battles that at first were almost always fought over our lines were later fought primarily over the enemy's lines. The entire First Army and the rest of the German Army deeply mourned the loss of this true hero. I had met Captain Boelcke several times. I paid my final respects to him as he was lying in state in the cathedral at Cambrai.

On 29 October General von Stein was appointed the Prussian minister of war. His combat group, which he had commanded with such great prudence and energy, was taken over by the commanding general of the X Reserve Corps, General Georg Fuchs.

With the 222nd Division added to our reserve pool, we continued to conduct the necessary reliefs of our divisions in the front lines. On 2 November the commanding general of the Guards Reserve Corps, General of Cavalry Wolf Rudolf Freiherr von Marschall von Altengottern, assumed command of Group Armin. The XIX Army Corps was then relieved by the Guards Reserve Corps, with the 1st Guards Reserve Division on the right and the 4th Guards Division on the left. In Group Deimling's sector, the 2nd Bavarian Division was relieved. That group's line now consisted of, from right to left, the 222nd Division, the 30th Division, and the XV Army Corps' 39th Division. In Group Garnier's sector the right and center divisions were relieved, and the front line now consisted of the 16th Reserve Division, the 111th Division, and the 8th Replacement Division. The enemy remained quiet during the relief operations, most likely because of the heavy losses they had suffered. The rainy weather also contributed to the lull, with the clay soil of the Somme battlefield turning into mud and the shell craters filling with water. As we reinforced our front lines, we waited with confidence for the enemy to resume his offensive operations. We anticipated attacks from the west and south, with the main effort in the general direction of Le Transloy–Bapaume.

To the great advantage for the management of our artillery defensive fires, every division gradually was assigned a special aerial artillery observer squadron and a fighter squadron for its protection. Groups Fuchs, Marschall, and Deimling each had a special fighter squadron assigned. That improved our artillery capability greatly. Immediately following the 8 September briefing at Cambrai, artillery commanders and General Staff officers also were attached on the ground in the forward echelons. They greatly improved the reliability of our relief operations. On 1 November Group Deimling committed its 30th Division to a limited attack against the village of Sailly-Saillisel. Despite several days of preparatory fires and the commitment of flamethrowers, rain and fog hampered the operations of the aerial artillery observers, and the division failed to achieve its objective. Initially they were able to hold some of the quarters of Sailly-Saillisel, but they lost them on 2 November.

On 3 November the British and the French initiated probing attacks between Le Sars and Rancourt, during which the French made some insignificant gains between Le Transloy and Sailly-Saillisel. As we had experienced several times before, those probing attacks were followed by a large-scale attack, well prepared with heavy artillery drumfire that expended gigantic amounts of ammunition. The fire also extended to the southern half of Group Fuchs's sector, in which we also anticipated an infantry attack. On 5 November at 0900 hours a cohesive, very strong, and deeply echeloned infantry assault broke lose against the front between Le Sars and Bouchavesnes. Everywhere along that line the enemy's artillery followed their infantry forward. Our stalwart troops put up a tough and heroic fight and once again emerged victorious from the close-quarters fighting. Aside from a small loss of ground south of Sailly-Saillisel, our front lines held completely. And despite their strong artillery fire, the British never did attack Group Fuchs.

Committing relief units forward, OHL moved the X Army Corps and the 43rd Reserve Division to Army Group Crown Prince Rupprecht and informed us they also were moving up the 10th Replacement Division, the 14th Bavarian Division, the 111th Division, and the headquarters of the V Army Corps. The XIX Army Corps, which already had been withdrawn, and the 38th Division were to be relieved in an expedited manner by the XIII Army Corps and a Marine infantry brigade.

When the ground froze over on 9 November, the enemy resumed their probing attacks, but they made only minor gains in the vicinity of Le Sars, near Sailly-Saillisel, and in the forest to the south. The British then were moving closer toward Group Fuchs. Our reconnaissance identified the emplacement of enemy gas cylinders across from Serre Lès Puisieux. On 11 November the enemy resumed heavy artillery fire against almost the entire front of the First Army, just at the time the 185th Division was in the process of relieving the 39th Division in Group Deimling's sector. The lead elements of the 208th Division also were arriving in the vicinity of Cambrai.

The British mounted a large-scale attack on 13 November, which this time overlapped far beyond the Albert–Bapaume rail line. Unfortunately, there was a very heavy fog that day and our otherwise well-placed and reliable barrage fires started too late. In Group Fuchs's sector that alone allowed the British to surprise the 12th and 38th Divisions at Beaumont-Hamel and Divion and push them back as far as two kilometers. Despite a gas attack, the rearward units—the 52nd Division to the north and the 58th Division to the east—managed to hold their positions. In Group Marschall's sector the Guards Reserve Corps also held on.

The French did not start their attack from the Rancourt–Sailly-Saillisel line until 14 November. Our barrage fires broke up that attack. Our local attack toward Sailly-Saillisel in Group Deimling's sector succeeded initially, but then was beaten back by the enemy's deliberate counterattacks. Our troops attacking in Group Garnier's sector were able to regain the parts of the forest north of Rancourt that we had lost earlier. They successfully held on to the new ground and captured more than three hundred French soldiers in the process.

In Group Fuchs's sector the 12th Division was relieved by the 208th Division and the 38th Division by the 223rd Division. In Group Marschall's sector the Bavarian Replacement Division was relieved by the 24th Reserve Division. All the relief actions were conducted under constant enemy fire.

Preceded by many days of artillery preparatory fire, the British on 18 November launched a major attack against Groups Fuchs and Marschall, between Serre Lès Puisieux and Le Sars. Simultaneously, the French hit the inner wings of Groups Deimling and Garnier. Group Fuchs repelled all the attacks north of the Albert–Bapaume rail line, but the front lines of the 223rd Division and the 58th Division south of the rail line were pushed back. The British also gained ground from the 1st Guards Reserve Division and the 4th Guards Division in Group Marschall's sector. Group Deimling's 30th and 185th Divisions and Group Garnier's 16th Reserve and 111th Divisions managed to beat back four strong French attacks. From 13 November on, the fighting was mostly close quarters. The German troops captured almost one thousand prisoners and more than thirty machine guns, demonstrating the reckless courage of our brave troops, who themselves suffered heavy losses in dead and wounded.

The Battle of the Somme ended on 18 November 1916. Despite the ground we lost, it was a clear defensive victory for the dauntless German Army. The enemy's multiple breakthrough attempts had failed in the face of the German Army's power of resistance, and the energy of its leadership. On 18 November it was not immediately clear to us that the battle had ended, and we therefore conducted several relief actions in anticipation of new attacks.

At the end of November, the First Army's front lines were held by Group Fuchs, with the 26th Reserve Division, 2nd Guards Reserve Division, 14th Bavarian Division, 208th Division, 50th Reserve Division, and 56th Division; Group Marschall, consisting of the 1st Guards Reserve Division, 4th Guards Division (both reinforced by a Marine infantry brigade), 23rd Reserve Division (later relieved by the 214th Division), and 24th Reserve Division; Group Watter (XIII Army Corps), with the 26th Division, 27th Division, and 185th Division; and Group Garnier, with the 22nd Reserve Division, 111th Division, and 32nd Division.

It was relatively calm during the relief operations. The French continued to attempt some small thrusts between Rancourt and Sailly-Saillisel, but they were all repelled. The British also tried also some unsuccessful probing attacks on both sides of the Albert–Bapaume rail line. Group Fuchs's 208th Division consolidated its position with a well-prepared attack on 25 November, capturing 150 British soldiers.

Then the rains came and the ground softened, making any movement on the shell-cratered battlefield most difficult. Our ground and aerial reconnaissance, meanwhile, produced strong indicators that the entire enemy front was starting to thin out. First Army headquarters, therefore, immediately ordered the improvement of the forward zone and the reestablishment of the rearward positions, which had suffered heavy damage from the enemy artillery fire. Only gradually, however, were we able to conclude that the great Battle of the Somme had come to an end.

According to our after action analysis, the Battle of the Somme had cost the First and Second Armies a combined loss of approximately half a million brave soldiers, while the British lost around 410,000 and the French approximately 300,000. Our tactical principle of holding every inch of ground had indeed stood the test during the battle. During the close-quarters fighting that was conducted man-to-man with bayonets and hand grenades, the German soldier proved far superior to the British and the French soldier. Our numerical inferiority during the battle was compensated for by the courage and superior abilities of the German infantryman, superbly supported by our artillery.

For years the German Army had been trained by its leaders in a planned and focused manner, while most of the British Army had started the battle with only a few month's training behind it.[31] The British Army, nonetheless, performed quite courageously during the Battle of the Somme and in subsequent battles, despite its shortcomings. The French Army was better trained, but it had suffered great losses in 1914 and 1915, and then at Verdun. Those losses increased significantly on the Somme. As a result, the major French offensive in the spring of 1917 failed largely because the French Army was then lacking the necessary inner strength.[32]

Our artillery had a difficult task countering the enemy's numerical superiority in guns and especially ammunition. The infantry direct support mission was facilitated by collocating the infantry and artillery command posts. That greatly improved the infantry-artillery coordination.

As long as General von Falkenhayn was the chief of the General Staff of the German Army, battle management was a difficult process at all echelons down to the platoon leader level. During the Battle of the Somme, OHL habitually committed the OHL-level reserves at the last possible moment in the heavy fighting. That bled our divisions to such an extent that they only slowly recovered after they were pulled out of the line. During Falkenhayn's time the First Army only very rarely had a viable army-level reserve. OHL even considered—if only temporarily—withdrawing forces from the Somme battlefront.

It was not until Hindenburg and Ludendorff assumed the leadership of OHL that this situation changed drastically. Reserves were now always available for the conduct of the necessary relief actions. The artillery too was reinforced properly from the army-level reserves. The width of each battery's sheaf for barrage fire was reduced from four hundred to two hundred meters. That increased the weight of shell that could be delivered in support of the infantry during the defense or during the conduct of hasty counterattacks.

During the final phases of the Battle of the Somme every divisional sector was assigned an aviation detachment of aerial artillery observers and one fighter squadron. That significantly improved the effectiveness of our artillery fires, which improved even more when close air support aircraft became available.[33] During the battle our aviators destroyed 350 enemy aircraft while losing only 114. Under the new OHL leadership our air arm grew numerically and its state of training and fighting spirit increased. The credit for these results goes to Lieutenant Colonel Hermann Thomsen, who was then the chief of staff of the air force.

The artillery gained the most from this reorganization. Up until then our artillery for the most part had to deliver their destructive, harassing, and barrage fires blindly, because both our guns and the enemy's were deployed in covered and camouflaged firing positions. Only gradually were we able to reorganize our air assets for both the artillery observation and the air superiority missions. The enemy had more aircraft and greater resources to strengthen their air forces. The enemy's aerial advantage became very clear to us on the Western Front during the 1915 battles at Arras and in Champagne. During the Battle of the Somme the enemy command massed a significantly superior force on the ground as well as in the air. The enemy's air superiority during the first phases of the battle posed a serious threat to us both on the ground and in the air.

All that started to change with the new leadership at OHL, but the improvements came only gradually. Nonetheless, we managed to achieve air parity and then air superiority in a relatively fast time thanks to the fighting spirit of our combat flyers. Under leadership of the air ace Captain Oswald Boelcke, our aviators pushed the aerial combat from the space over our lines to that over the enemy. At that point, our aerial observers could operate over the enemy to direct the fire of our guns. Captain Boelcke was a hero in the truest sense of the word and an innovator in aerial combat.[34] Many combat pilots followed his example. Of special note were the brothers Lothar and Manfred von Richthofen[35] and Captain Hermann Göring, who assumed command of Manfred von Richthofen's squadron after the latter was shot down and killed. Göring today is the commander in chief of the German Luftwaffe.[36]

The troop commanders had an especially difficult time on the Somme. The divisional commanders moved in and out of the line with their respective divisions, but the commanding generals of the groups consisting of several rotating divisions remained in command of their sectors for much longer periods. Those commanders developed a detailed knowledge of the peculiarities of the terrain in their sectors and were able to manage the battle accordingly. During the battle the headquarters of the First Army underwent only minor changes in its internal structure.

On an almost daily basis I accompanied General von Below on his visits to the front. We therefore maintained a firsthand and real-time picture of the situation. During those trips to the front the first General Staff officer (Ia) at the headquarters covered for me. I received great support from first Major Stapff, and then Major von Platen. The assistant chief of staff, Colonel von Redern, and the generals of the artillery and the engineers were great experts. The remaining staff consisted throughout of competent and responsible officers. An excellent sense of camaraderie and mutual trust prevailed throughout the entire staff. After the long morning trips with the commanding general, I often went back to the front in the afternoon. Once in a while I moved up into the forwardmost fighting positions during early morning hours in order to observe the situation for myself. I also required all the General Staff officers to walk the ground in the divisional sectors twice a week. They often brought back reliable information for the management of the battle and for the resupply of combat assets and rations. According to the calculations of my very reliable and competent signal officer, First Lieutenant von Unruh, who is now a forester at the Göhrde State Forest, my daily average sleep time was three hours and seventeen minutes during the Battle of the Somme. I bore up rather well during that period, although I did lose twenty pounds.

The British commitment of tanks came as a total surprise to us. It did not take us very long, however, to overcome the so-called "tank-terror" (*Tankschrecken*). At first our infantry fought the tanks with clusters of hand grenades, which courageous soldiers threw under the tanks' treads. Shooting at the vision slits rarely worked in the heat of battle. Any tanks that broke through were most often eliminated by our artillery. Once we started to field antitank guns, the threat reduced quickly.

The signal troops had to accomplish their very difficult work under the enemy's massive artillery preparatory fire, which often cut all the connections within the battle sector. At that point our courageous runners (*Meldegänger*) took over. In such situations we also relied on specially trained reconnaissance troops, who as they probed forward laid phone lines to send back their reports.

Despite all the difficulties, the "battle of material" on the Somme was won by the heroism of the German Army. Based on my own experiences in Champagne and on the Somme, I understood the great operational difficulties involved in effecting a breakthrough. In the final analysis, the German Army could only win an operational victory if we could make a tactical breakthrough of the enemy lines. That would be followed by an exploitation leading to the destruction of the enemy's front. This was the primary situation on the Western Front, and also the other theaters of war. I will come back to this question later when I discuss the war in 1918.

In November OHL ordered the First Army headquarters to submit an after action analysis report, which then would be distributed to all the field armies. After briefing the commanding general, I immediately started working on the analysis with the officers of the staff. We finally completed it toward the end of January 1917. I organized the report into two parts, a tactical section and an administrative and logistical section. The staff specialists worked on their respective sections, and I spent several hours each day in close discussion with the action officers. During the period of the report's preparation I averaged as little sleep as I had at the height of the battle.

As early as the middle of September, Army Group Crown Prince Rupprecht had received the order to start construction work on rearward defenses that would become the Siegfried Position. The design and layout of the new position was to be based on the lessons of the Somme. Army Group Crown Prince Rupprecht was tasked with the overall management of the construction of the entire Siegfried Position. At that point in time, however, the First Army had only very general instructions to tie the flanks of its new line into the Sixth Army to the north and the Second Army to the south. When it actually came to laying out the forward lines of the new rearward position, the First Army headquarters was at odds on more than one occasion with Army Group Crown Prince Rupprecht. Finally, we conducted a combined inspection on the ground itself. The survey party included Crown Prince Rupprecht, his chief of staff, General von Kuhl, General von Below, myself, and a number of staff technical specialists. After a long and rather drawn-out discussion, we finally decided to use the forward trace originally recommended by the First Army because it offered wider fields of observation for our artillery. We knew from experience the importance of having good observation over the ground forward of our positions. That was a critical prerequisite for our guns to support the infantry with well-observed fires. Based on the specific characteristics of the ground, the artillery observation line ran from five hundred to fifteen hundred meters to the rear of the infantry's forwardmost line. The infantry's reverse-slope positions were established three hundred to four hundred meters down from the crest of the high ground.

Once we fell back to occupy the Siegfried Position, every divisional sector was to receive in addition to the division's own organic artillery another three heavy field howitzer batteries, a super-heavy howitzer battery, three flat-trajectory batteries (10–13 centimeters), and various captured guns. The infantry battle zone consisted of three to four defensive lines with strong wire obstacles and numerous deep dugouts. The approach routes were secured with wire obstacles to one side. The dugouts were integrated mostly into the second and third zones of trenches.[37] The location of the dugouts was checked by dowsers brought in from the Homeland to assure that no water veins were present under the surface. The dugouts, infantry and artillery command posts, artillery observation posts, and ammunition storage bunkers were reinforced with concrete.

After the construction of the Siegfried Position was completed, OHL ordered the general withdrawal of the First and Second Armies, the left wing of the Sixth Army, and the right of the Seventh Army. Any pursuit by the enemy would be slowed down by a thorough destruction of everything in the intervening ground—most of which already had been destroyed by enemy fire—to include villages, route networks, rail lines, bridges, etc. The withdrawal operation was code-named ALBERICH. The preparations for the withdrawal started on 9 February 1917 and were completed by 15 March. The first day of the retrograde movement into the Siegfried Position was 16 March 1917. The headquarters of the Sixth, First, Second, and Seventh Armies had managed the construction of the Siegfried Position in their respective areas of operation. Special construction staffs were established for that purpose. The two army groups distributed the labor force and the materials for the construction of the positions to the armies and determined the number of divisions to man the new line. Depending on the nature of the ground, the width of the divisional sectors was between four and seven kilometers. Initially, all available labor units were used to construct the Siegfried Position. A second rearward position to be constructed behind the Siegfried Position was reconnoitered and marked out on the ground, but work on it started only after the occupation of the Siegfried Position was complete.

When we recognized that the enemy was thinning his battle lines and was conducting large retrograde movements into his rear areas, we also started thinning our lines in order to allow our exhausted troops to move into rest quarters farther to the rear. The commanding general and I at this point redirected our almost daily trips from the front to the rear. It gave us both great satisfaction to see how quickly our units recovered. Meanwhile, we continued to emplace new obstacles forward of our planned new front lines. In some places, however, the condition of the ground made a thorough improvement impossible. The commanding general and I spent most afternoons personally supervising the construction of our section of the Siegfried Position.

On 3 December 1916, OHL issued a communique on our successful operation in Romania and the seizure of Bucharest. The entire First Army staff celebrated, emptying a considerable number of bottles that only recently had arrived as a donation from a vineyard on the Moselle. On 12 December we received an army-wide message from the Kaiser reporting that Germany had made a peace

Map 7. Withdrawal to the Siegfried Position, February–March 1917

overture to its enemies. There certainly was a great deal of rationale for doing so. Romania was almost completely defeated. France and Britain were reeling from their failures on the Somme. The Russian Brusilov Offensive had bled itself to death. Italy had no chance for an operational victory. Thus, the speech that the Kaiser delivered in Berlin gave us new hopes. It was clear to us that Germany would dictate mild conditions for peace. But we also foresaw that the Entente would make such high demands that the willingness of Germany, Austria, and Turkey to meet them would be highly questionable.

On 14 December General von Below and I went to Army Group Crown Prince Rupprecht's headquarters for a briefing, where for the most part we only discussed current issues. Soon thereafter I participated in a briefing at OHL in Stenay during which General Ludendorff wanted to hear my assessment of the Fifth Army's recent dismal failure at Verdun against the French counterattacks. I arrived a day before the briefing, oriented myself on the situation maps, and made a trip to the Fifth Army's forward lines. During my inspection I could not identify any mistakes that had been made in the conduct of the defense. The French attack had come as a surprise and with such force that no blame could be assigned to the German leadership. Our divisions hit by the attack were positioned correctly in depth. The barrage sheafs were only 150 meters per battery. The distribution and positioning of the machine guns and the establishment of the communications network were faultless. As I later learned, General Ludendorff initially put the blame on the chief of staff of Army Group German Crown Prince, Colonel Friedrich Graf von der Schulenburg, and he planned to make me Schulenburg's successor. But he abandoned that idea after I gave my report at Stenay. Personally, I was particularly happy about the outcome, because Colonel von der Schulenburg was an expert through and through and a magnificent, courageous, and proven soldier. He also was a good personal friend of many years' standing, and remains so to this day.

On 20 December my brave horse groom, Corporal Brietzke, who had been with me since 1910 as a long-term enlistee (*Kapitulant*), was hit by a motorcycle in Bourlon and broke his leg. After a long recovery in a field hospital in Cambrai and then back in Germany, I finally brought him back in July 1917 into the headquarters guard force of the Fourth Army. Later, after the war, he served under me as a sergeant at the headquarters of Border Defense Command South in Breslau,[38] and then at the Reichswehr's Group Command II at Kassel. After he had served for twelve years I found employment for him at the *Reichsbank*, where he still works today. Brietzke was a good soldier, and he remains a close comrade.

Through the end of 1916 the enemy restricted himself to limited operations, most of which we repelled. We only retook lost ground by deliberate counterattack if the enemy's gains disrupted the continuity of our battle line. The Christmas celebration that year was quite cheerful. All the officers of the senior staff received a very pretty cigarette case from the commanding general, with Below's name in silver. General von Below also gave me a copy of his picture with a very complementary inscription. The senior staff gave General von Below a poodle. His old poodle, to which he had been especially attached, had been run over by a car at the beginning of December. General von Below put considerable pressure on me to take leave right after Christmas. Thus, I spent the days between 26 and 31 December in Stuttgart with my family, including my son, who was an officer candidate (*Fähnrich*) in the 2nd Guards Regiment.

At the beginning of January the Entente responded to the German peace initiative. Russia demanded Constantinople, Poznan, and Silesia; France wanted Alsace-Lorraine; and Britain wanted our colonies. Such demands were unacceptable. On 5 January General von Below and I were invited to a pleasant and stimulating dinner with the commanding general of the Sixth Army, Colonel General Ludwig Freiherr von Falkenhausen. I had no idea at the time that about three months later I would be the chief of staff of the Sixth Army.

On 17 January a briefing took place at Cambrai with General Ludendorff and all the army group and army chiefs of staff. General Ludendorff emphasized that the West would be the decisive theater of the war.[39] Unfortunately, sufficient troops would not be available for the limited offensive by the Sixth, First, and Second Armies that General von Kuhl had proposed. A limited and narrow offensive by the Seventh Army might be a possibility. General von Kuhl briefed us in detail on the extension of the British front toward the south. I reported that our intelligence assessment pointed to the British preparing an attack against the salient jutting out toward the southwest in Group Fuchs's sector, and that we had made all preparations to defend against such an attack.

General Ludendorff told us that our successful operations in Romania would be drawn down in a planned and deliberate manner. Five infantry and three cavalry divisions would then be redeployed to the West. Thirteen new German infantry divisions also were in the process of being stood up. The First and Second Armies would have to release some aviation units, but there was no need to weaken our artillery at that point. General Ludendorff then asked me to brief my ideas on how to counter an enemy attack with our artillery. I made the following comments:

> The defense against an enemy major attack must be prepared in detail in all defensive sectors, and the artillery must be trained thoroughly for this mission. The basis for an effective artillery fire plan is an exact knowledge of the enemy's artillery and infantry positions and their level

of reinforcement. This can be accomplished by aerial photography, aerial direct observation, balloons, observation posts on the forwardmost battle lines, patrolling, and the interrogation of prisoners brought back by the patrols. Using maps and patrol reports, every artillery leader must develop a clear picture of the key elements of the enemy's attack sector—hollows, gaps, built-up areas, ground cover, tree lines, ravines, etc. Furthermore, they must maintain current situation maps showing all the details of the enemy's infantry positions, as inevitably the infantry prepares to assault from the trenches.

As soon as an imminent enemy attacks is recognized, the sustained rate of fire barrage fire already in progress should intensify to maximum rate of fire. The primary targets will be the enemy's artillery and infantry positions. The destructive fires should all be precision[40] and observed. The rate of fire should be increased as soon as it has been confirmed that the attacker is ready in his forward trenches. As the attacker is deploying prior to the assault, destructive fires should be delivered with full force against targets that have already been registered. The fire plan also should include unobserved fires, especially at night, during which the enemy most often prepares for the assault. As soon as the enemy's attack preparations are recognized, the barrage fire should start. In most cases, the request for fire will come from our infantry forward lines using signal flares. The barrage fire must be registered precisely, and its accuracy must be verified periodically.

All battery commanders and their higher headquarters must maintain constantly detailed and current maps for all kinds of fire missions. In case of an enemy break-in and local deliberate counterattacks, the artillery fires always must be observed. For defense against enemy penetrations, a number of batteries right from the start should be displaced to firing positions with good observation closer to our forward infantry defensive lines. In the case of an enemy break-in, those batteries will have to operate independently, as in most cases there will not be sufficient time to transmit orders from the rear. Those forward batteries are in the best positions to support our local hasty counterattacks quickly and efficiently with observed fires. When supporting planned and deliberate counterattacks, the artillery fire should be concentrated from all sides. Such coordinated action must be rehearsed periodically.

The correct firing data for the different fire missions must be verified periodically. It is important that the divisional artillery commanders be collocated with the divisional staff at their operations centers (*Gefechtsstände*). Similarly, the artillery subordinate commanders must establish their command posts close to the infantry regimental command posts. Officers at all batteries must supervise closely the firing, discipline, ammunition storage, ammunition resupply, and the recovery of shell casings and projectile baskets. The artillery observation posts must be decentralized in a systematic manner. Battery personnel should rehearse the rapid movement from their dugouts to their guns.

General Ludendorff informed us that there was little material left available for the field railroads. The ammunition program also was lagging. A large number of logistics units would be formed by reassigning frontline soldiers suffering from physical limitations and health issues but who were still capable of work.[41] Every divisional sector would in time receive two locally based logistics companies of two hundred men each. Ninety new batteries would be stood up monthly. Mount and draft horses were being requisitioned, mostly from Belgium.

By the end of January all infantry regiments would have eighteen heavy machine guns, which would be increased to thirty-six over a period of time. The effectiveness of the MG 08/15 light machine gun had been improved significantly.[42] General Ludendorff particularly emphasized that the relief of machine gun units must be prepared in detail and closely supervised, which at Verdun apparently had not been the case. Replacement crews would be needed for standing up of the new units, but until 1 April 1917 there would be a shortage of machine gun crews in the front lines. The replacement crews would have to be drawn from returning wounded soldiers, which might result in reduced combat strength for the infantry.

Our fuel supply situation would improve with production from Romania as soon as transportation issues were resolved. The training of the troops was especially important and must be given priority of effort. The training of infantry was primarily an army-level task. The training of artillery officers would be conducted at training centers established by OHL.

At the end of the conference General Ludendorff gave us the welcome news that on 1 February 1917 Germany would resume unrestricted submarine warfare.[43] Germany had to have contingency measures to deal with the neutral countries. Ludendorff said that six brigades had been earmarked for defense against Denmark. If Holland should declare war on us, five German divisions were designated to seize Zeeland. America already was supplying the Entente with large amounts of money, rations, war material, and tonnage. Most likely it would soon commit soldiers. Following the briefing we had a simple but pleasant dinner that evening in Cambrai.

On 21 January 1917, I completed editing the lessons of the Somme report. It was printed immediately by OHL and distributed to all command centers.

Based on my recommendation, OHL established a training area near Valenciennes at which all troop leaders up to regimental commanders would be trained in the basics of the defense. The commander of the 27th (Württemberg) Division, Lieutenant General Otto von Moser, became the commandant, and his division supplied the school troops. When General Ludendorff asked me to recommend an operations officer for the 27th Division, I suggested the competent and intelligent Captain Walther Wever, who did an excellent job. Wever and I became friends. He was killed in an airplane accident in 1936 while he was chief of staff of the new Luftwaffe General Staff. He was a man who would have had a great future.[44]

On 23 January 1917, I accepted an invitation from Colonel General Karl von Einem to dinner at Vouziers. I was received quite cordially and spent a few very pleasant hours in the circle of my old comrades from the Third Army. Upon my return to Bourlon on the afternoon of 24 January I found that General von Below had fallen quite ill with a stomach flu. He was in bed and had to remain very still. I gave him the daily report at his sickbed and always described in great detail my assessment from my daily trips to the front and into the Siegfried Position. He recovered very slowly. Following medical advice, General von Below decided to take three weeks of convalescent leave at a spa in Germany, but he was not able to leave until 11 February.

On 3 February 1917 General Ludendorff called another briefing with all army group and army chiefs of staff. General von Kuhl recommended withdrawal into the Siegfried Position as soon as possible. I concurred with General von Kuhl, because reliefs were no longer being conducted in our area of operations and the likelihood of a British attack against the northern sector of the First Army was increasing. General Ludendorff did not make any decisions during this briefing. Everyone agreed, however, on a code word that could be transmitted by telephone to signal the decision to start the withdrawal into the Siegfried Position.

On 8 February 1917 America broke off diplomatic relations with Germany. That meant war with America, and I therefore hoped that our unrestricted submarine warfare would be effective. On 10 February General von Below turned over acting command of the First Army to his deputy, General Karl von Fasbender, the commanding general of the I Bavarian Reserve Corps. The following day Below left for his convalescent leave in the spa town of Wiesbaden.

The weather had been rather frosty for quite a while, and it therefore came as no surprise that the British launched larger attacks against our northern group. Our positions were held overall, and as soon as the weather thawed, things got quiet again. I had a rather painful experience during a daily trip to the front lines with General von Fasbender. As we left the staff car at a divisional command post, General von Fasbender slammed the door on my right thumb. It was extremely painful, and the divisional surgeon had to bandage my bleeding thumb. After we left the division, General von Fasbender, who never did apologize, told me a story about an incident between a Bavarian farmer and a Bavarian railroad conductor. The farmer had leaned out of the open railcar door and had his thumb in the door frame. The conductor slammed the door from outside and smashed the farmer's thumb. In response to the farmer's screams the conductor answered in Bavarian dialect, "Why do you idiots always have your dirty fingers in everything!" I gave General von Fasbender an appropriate answer, and I was very glad that only a few days later General von Below returned to his command, fully recovered.

At the end of February OHL relocated to Kreuznach.[45] In order to streamline the command and control structure, we established a third army group on the Western Front. Army Group Bavarian Crown Prince Rupprecht (chief of staff General von Kuhl) had the Fourth, Sixth, First, and Second Armies; Army Group German Crown Prince Wilhelm (chief of staff General von der Schulenburg) had the Seventh, Third, and Fifth Armies; and Army Group Duke Albrecht of Württemberg (chief of staff General Konrad Krafft von Dellmensingen) had Army Detachments C, A, and B.[46] Duke Albrecht was replaced as the commanding general of the Fourth Army by General Friedrich Sixt von Armin, who relinquished command of the IV Army Corps.

After an extended lull in the fighting, stronger British attacks against our northern group resumed at the beginning of March. We ignored minor losses of ground because our movement back to the Siegfried Position was imminent. We already had established the advance party at our new army headquarters in Solesmes.

On 4 March heavy dog fighting developed over our northern group, during which nine British planes were shot down. During this time the British attacked again on the ground and made some small advances. As planned, we refrained from launching any deliberate counterattacks. In the middle of March 1917 the czar of Russia was deposed through revolution. Unfortunately, our hope that Russia would leave the Entente did not materialize. Up through 15 March General von Below and I were at the front every morning and afternoon. We verified the completion of all the First Army's preparations for the withdrawal from our front lines to the Siegfried Position and the destruction of the intervening ground.

The withdrawal movement commenced on 15 March. The units that had the longest routes back to the Siegfried Position started moving first. Rear guards covered the withdrawal. The retrograde movement was a slow process. Shortly before each sector was abandoned, the prepared destruction actions were executed. When the enemy did advance, his movement was slow and difficult because all the rail lines, roads, bridges, villages, etc. were destroyed. Long before we started our withdrawal we had evacuated all the local inhabitants. Along with their belongings and even some art treasures, they were moved far to the rear of the Siegfried Position.

Our entire movement operation ran very smoothly. The First Army headquarters stayed at Bourlon until 30 March and then jumped to Solesmes.[47]

The enemy followed our withdrawal only slowly and carefully. That gave our troops sufficient time to settle into the well-prepared Siegfried Position and to recover from their exhaustion. Our artillery used the quiet period to register from their new firing positions. Everything was prepared to give the enemy a hot welcome, but he improved his own positions at a respectful distance from our lines and kept quiet.

Before the end of March the British started delivering heavy artillery fire from the vicinity of Arras against the Sixth Army, which was on the right of the First Army. Intelligence also indicated that the French were preparing an attack from the south, in the direction of Rethel. OHL gradually developed the assessment that the enemy was preparing major attacks in those two areas, with the intent of breaking through north and south of the Siegfried Position. If they succeeded, both wings of the Siegfried Position would be threatened with envelopment. OHL decided, therefore, that the First Army headquarters would be pulled out of the line and redeployed to a fighting sector between the Seventh and Third Armies on both sides of Rethel. The First Army's right wing XIV Reserve Corps would be reassigned to the Sixth Army and the remaining units on the left wing would be reassigned to the Second Army.

General von Below concurred with my recommendation to establish the new First Army headquarters at Rethel, and OHL also agreed. I knew Rethel quite well from my time as the chief of staff of the Third Army. Many well-developed roads intersected there. We immediately began setting up the new headquarters and establishing the telephone network.

On 5 April 1917 America declared war on Germany. On 9 April 1917 a gigantic British attack in the vicinity of Arras broke lose against the Sixth Army. The assault began after a long period of preparatory fire against the German infantry and artillery, followed by a short but very strong drumfire barrage. The British also fired a great many gas rounds. I was completely convinced that the British attack would not succeed, because I knew that to the rear of the Sixth Army there was a large number of divisions in reserve from Army Group Crown Prince Rupprecht and OHL. I estimated that the Sixth Army had enough attack divisions to conduct an active defense against the British attack. Despite my assessment of the situation, Army Group Crown Prince Rupprecht committed the reserves much too late, and even then released them to the Sixth Army for relief operations only. Thus, the relatively thinly manned front of the Sixth Army, which already had suffered very heavy losses from the British artillery fire, faced a very difficult situation. During the enemy's initial thrust on 9 April 1917, the Sixth Army lost Vimy Ridge and the hills at Roeux, and was pushed back considerably on a wide front. On the mornings of 10 and 11 April the British limited themselves to only minor attacks.

6

Chief of the General Staff of the Sixth Army (Arras, 1917)

On 11 April 1917, I had a long conversation with General von Below about the basics of the defense for the newly redeployed First Army, positioned between the Seventh and Third Armies. At about 1000 hours I got in the staff car to leave for our new army headquarters in Rethel. The motor had already been cranked up when a staff officer came running out of the building and told me that General Ludendorff wanted to talk to me urgently. I got on the phone immediately and Ludendorff told me, "His Majesty has appointed you chief of staff of the Sixth Army. Report to your new assignment immediately. The Sixth Army is in a serious situation and has lost a great deal of ground since the British launched a large-scale attack on 9 April. I trust that you will master this situation."

From my time as the First Army chief of staff, I knew full well the then neighboring Sixth Army's difficult situation. In order to deal with the problem, I requested that General Ludendorff give me Vollmacht for the conduct of the battle. Once I had made a close personal scrutiny of the situation, that authority would give me the freedom of action to make all the necessary decisions and issue the appropriate directives. General Ludendorff concurred immediately. I then asked him to inform my new commander, Colonel General Ludwig Freiherr von Falkenhausen, as well as the commander of Army Group Crown Prince Rupprecht and his chief of staff, General von Kuhl. It was essential for them to know about the decision-making authority OHL had given me. I also told General Ludendorff that I would immediately reconnoiter the Sixth Army's entire defensive front line. I therefore asked him to notify the commander of the Sixth Army that I would not be able to report in at the headquarters in Tournai until the evening of 11 April.[1]

General Ludendorff also told me that the operations officer at Sixth Army headquarters, Major Rudolf von Xylander, would be replaced by a new Ia. Since it was my normal procedure to visit the front lines every day during tense situations, I needed an especially competent and effective Ia. I asked General Ludendorff to reassign to the Sixth Army my old Ia, Major Axel von Platen. General Ludendorff agreed to that, too, and asked me to recommend my own successor as chief of staff of the First Army. Without hesitation I recommended Major von Klüber, who I knew from his assignment as the chief of staff of the IX Army Corps during the Champagne and Somme battles. I had a great deal of respect for this competent and energetic officer. Klüber at the time was the chief of staff of Army Detachment A. He was reassigned to the First Army, and he did a superb job.

I then told General von Below about my reassignment. I could tell that he was not happy to see me go, but he thanked me very warmly for my service with him. After a short farewell with the officers on the First Army staff, I left for the Sixth Army by car.

That same day I managed to visit all of the Sixth Army's corps commanders and many of the division commanders on the defensive front. I also made a number of trips to the front lines to study the ground and to develop personally a deeper understanding of the requirements to continue the fight. I realized very quickly that the enemy had unrestricted fields of observation into our defensive sector, having seized Vimy Ridge and the high ground on both sides of the Scarpe River. That meant that the British would push their artillery forward and establish their observation posts on the high ground. That would give them the capability of calling down well-observed fire on all movements in and behind our lines. On the other hand, I recognized that the firing positions of the British artillery, especially behind Vimy Ridge, would have to be far enough back from the ridgeline to achieve the trajectories necessary to clear the intervening high ground. I then estimated the maximum ranges to the east of Vimy Ridge that their artillery creeping barrage (*Feuerwalze*) would be able to reach.[2] The British had made very effective use of the creeping barrage technique during their initial attack on 9 April. After visiting all the command posts and confirming my estimates with the artillery commanders, I was then able to plot on the map the enemy artillery's most probable maximum range line.

At all command posts I was told that the large ground losses from 9 April on, which were as deep as six kilometers in some areas, happened primarily because the reinforcements promised by the army group had not been available in time. My personal reconnaissance and discussions with the commanders on the spot convinced me that a pure defensive conducted from our present positions facing Vimy Ridge would be very difficult and would only result in even German greater losses. I thought, therefore, that it would be far better to base the upcoming defensive fight more on hasty and deliberate counterattacks. That, however, was impossible presently because our forward infantry positions were too close to Vimy Ridge. The conduct of an active defense (*offensive Abwehr*) requires sufficient depth of battle space from which to mount counterattacks. In the current situation, those counterattacks while assembling would be vulnerable to constant and well-observed enemy artillery fire. I concluded, therefore, that our active defense required lightly manned forward lines, with the mass of the infantry deeply echeloned farther in the rear. Strong artillery support required that our firing positions be pulled back far enough to be able to place heavy destructive and interdiction fires forward of our most advanced infantry lines, and also be able to support our hasty and deliberate counterattacks with well-observed fires.

I understood, of course, that such strong echeloning in depth was risky. But, if this form of deployment proved successful, it would be very difficult for the British artillery to break up our infantry assault while at the same time supporting their own infantry. It was obvious to me, then, that we would have to abandon the technique of rigidly defending every piece of ground to the last man. That kind of fighting had little chance of success in this situation. Consequently, I decided to man with only weak forces the current infantry positions that consisted almost exclusively of shell craters with only a few dugouts left standing. The remaining forward forces would have the mission of thwarting small local attacks, but in the event of a large-scale attack they would evade and withdraw ahead of the enemy barrage.

I was convinced that the enemy would launch a deeply echeloned infantry force immediately behind their creeping barrage. After the creeping barrage lifted, our entire infantry force supported heavily by artillery would have to launch a deliberate counterattack from their rearward staging positions. The objective of the counterattack would be to throw the enemy back to our original forward positions. During the night following the attack, the mass of our infantry would then pull back to their initial positions prior to the attack. To do otherwise would expose our infantry to the enemy's overpowering and well-observed artillery fire. I issued verbal orders to the troop leaders in the forward areas and told them that written orders from the Sixth Army headquarters would follow on 12 April.

I arrived in Tournai that evening and reported to Colonel General Ludwig Freiherr von Falkenhausen. I outlined in broad strokes the basics of my decisions. He concurred with everything and gave me the freedom to act accordingly. Then I immediately familiarized myself with the Sixth Army's staff. My predecessor, General Karl von Nagel, and his Ia, Major Rudolf von Xylander, had left already. Of the remaining staff officers I want to mention especially the assistant chief of staff, General Braun, and Captain Enders. Both were outstanding officers. Major Axel von Platen arrived at the headquarters on 14 April and immediately took over as the Ia.

During the night of 11–12 April, I drafted the orders for the future conduct of the battle. Based on my experience, I estimated that the enemy artillery would take four to five days to move into new firing positions to support a large-scale attack, and then they would need one to two days to register their guns and bring up their trail elements. In the event, the staging of enemy artillery took longer. The second stage of the enemy's set-piece attack did not start until 23 April.

I summarized the reasons for the failure of the Sixth Army as follows from the command's war diary:

Since the beginning of March the Sixth Army constantly reported that a British large-scale attack was building up opposite its front. On 31 March it reported to Army Group Crown Prince Rupprecht that the attack was imminent. Long before this the subordinate corps commands had been advised several times to conduct intensive counterfire operations, and they were given exact target areas for their destruction and interdiction fires. Since ammunition was plentiful, the artillery fire was to be continued without regard to shell expenditure. We did not start to experience heavy losses in artillery equipment until 9 April. Reinforcing artillery did not start to arrive until 2 April even though urgent requests for reinforcing artillery had been submitted. On 9 April forty-five of the promised reinforcement batteries still had not arrived. Nor had the gas rounds that had been requested for use against Arras arrived by that day, despite the constant and urgent requests submitted by the Sixth Army headquarters.

On 5 April the Sixth Army headquarters sent an urgent request to Army Group Crown Prince Rupprecht to push forward reinforcement divisions by rail. The army group headquarters did not approve the request until the evening of 6 April. Even then, it was not until the following morning that the orders were issued, after the Sixth Army reported that the attack was imminent. Army Group Crown Prince Rupprecht ordered the following units to move forward to the Sixth Army's sector:

1. The 111th Division was assigned to the sector of Group Loos. This division arrived so slowly that by 9 April only four battalions and a few batteries were in the battle area.
2. Advance elements of the Guards Reserve Corps (1st Guards Reserve Division and 4th Guards Division) arrived on 8 and 9 April, moving up to the Lille–Douai road.
3. The 17th and 18th Divisions started arriving in the sector of Group Vimy on 7 April, their advance elements coming up from Douai. The 17th Division was assigned the mission of improving the rearward positions, with one-third of the division in the Sixth Army sector and two-thirds in the First Army sector. The 17th Division did not become available to the Sixth

Army as a combat force until it was relieved by the advance elements of the 47th Landwehr Division, arriving on 10 April.

4. The 26th Division arrived in the sector of Group Arras on 8 April, with its advance elements moving to the Douai–Cambrai road.

Thus, on 9 April only the 111th Division, the 1st Guards Reserve Division, the 4th Guards Division, the 18th Division, and the 26th Division were available. Of those five divisions, the 18th and 26th Divisions were still temporarily under the command of the First Army. According to the order issued by Army Group Crown Prince Rupprecht, the inserted divisions were not to be committed to combat directly, but only committed later as reliefs. The hasty and deliberate counterattacks would have to be conducted with the currently available units, with their own reserves.

The Sixth Army requested two divisions more than the number finally approved. On 9 April there were no cohesive attack divisions available, except for an ad hoc formation of two infantry regiments that had been formed from the two northern trench corps. The movement by trucks of those two regiments from the Sixth Army's northern wing was planned and smoothly executed, with the forces arriving in the battle sector on the morning of 9 April.

Reconnaissance reports from south of the La Bassée Canal indicated that 12 German divisions with 108 battalions were facing 19 British divisions with 228 battalions. The British artillery had an estimated tube superiority of 3-to-1. The Sixth Army situation on 9 April was very serious.

The British had started their preparatory fires for the attack toward the end of March.[3] Initially the primary targets were the German artillery positions. From the start of April, the fires were directed against our infantry positions, which were shot to pieces. On 8 April the British artillery fire increased to a drumfire (*Trommelfeuer*) barrage against the entire German battle sector. Almost all the German dugouts were destroyed and the trenches and wire obstacles were flattened. Simultaneously, all the German artillery positions from the right wing of Group Vimy to the left wing of Group Arras were gassed. The gas severely disrupted our own artillery fire, as well as our ammunition resupply.

On 9 April at 0500 hours British artillery drumfire opened up against the German artillery and infantry positions on both sides of Arras, from the vicinity of Givenchy-en-Gohelle–Neuvillle-Saint-Vaast, to the First Army's northern wing. At 0700 hours the British infantry attack, preceded by a creeping barrage, started against the entire Group Vimy sector and between the Scarpe River and Neuville-Saint-Vaast. Group Souchez managed to hold the right half of its positions. In the center and on the left wing of Group Vimy the British broke through west of Thélus, and in the vicinity of Saint-Laurent. The British committed tanks between the Scarpe and Thilloy,[4] forcing us to yield a considerable amount of ground. At the break-in points the British destroyed the German fighting lines, entered Vimy and Farbus, and advanced toward Bailleul-Sir-Berthoult. Farther to the south our fighting line was thrown back to the line Gavrelle–Roeux and to Monchy-le-Preux. A deliberate counterattack retook the village of Vimy. Only three battalions from the I Bavarian Reserve Corps and the forwardmost regiment of the 111th Division managed to intervene in the fight.

By the evening of 9 April the Sixth Army held the following line: Givenchy-en-Gohelle–southern edge of Vimy–rail line from Vimy to Farbus–southern edge of Bailleul-Sir-Berthoult–Gavrelle–Fampoux–west of Monchy-le-Preux–western edge of Wancourt–Siegfried Position. Sixth Army headquarters ordered that line held. All of the divisions previously designated as relief units by the army group were pushed forward.

The British artillery fire subsided during the night of 9–10 April, after which they only conducted fire strikes (*Feuerüberfälle*) against the German infantry and artillery positions. At noon on 10 April the British resumed their infantry attacks, primarily south of the Scarpe. Supported by cavalry units, they took Monchy-le-Preux. The fight lasted into the evening against the line Roeux–Monchy-le-Preux–Wancourt, but the position held. North of the Scarpe, British attacks failed at Bailleul and Fampoux.

During the night of 10–11 April three combat-weary divisions were replaced by fresh ones. Heavy British fires made the reliefs very difficult to execute. Army Group Crown Prince Rupprecht also moved three more relief divisions forward to the Sixth Army. The XIV Reserve Corps, which had up until now held the right wing of the First Army, was reassigned to the Sixth Army.

On 11 April the British resumed heavy attacks against Group Arras and the XIV Reserve Corps (which also was designated Group Quéant). In that sector the British broke in east of Bullecourt, but the First Army's training paid off. Initially the break-in was sealed off, and then the enemy was ejected with a well-prepared deliberate counterattack. The British suffered a great many of their troops killed and lost some eleven hundred prisoners, fifty-three machine guns, and seven tanks. Farther to the north, however, the British managed to take Monchy-le-Preux, but they failed to take Héninel, Wancourt, Roeux, and Vimy. British cavalry units attacked against Pelves in the Scarpe Valley, but they were driven back with heavy losses.

When the Sixth Army chief of staff, General von Nagel, and his Ia, Major von Xylander, were relieved on the morning of 11 April, Colonel General von Falkenhausen also submitted his own resignation. Responding by telegram, however, the Kaiser graciously declined to accept it.

I had not been directly involved in the Battle of Arras up to the point where

I arrived on 11 April. That evening the commanding general approved my recommendations to move our front line back from Vimy Ridge and on both sides of the Scarpe. During the night of 11–12 April, liaison officers hand-delivered the necessary orders to the individual battle groups. Disengagement from the enemy was to start during the night of 12–13 April, along the line east of Loos–western edge of Lens–Avion–Méricourt–Arleux[5]–Gavrelle–Roeux–Guémappe, and then farther east to Fontaine-Notre-Dame in the Siegfried Position up to the Sixth Army's left wing at Inchy.

I returned to the front lines on 12 April, and the following day the commanding general came with me. His enclosed staff car moved so slowly, however, that from then on I preferred to go by myself, because the loss of time on the trip meant the loss of productive work for me.

On 13 April the British conducted a series of weak and unsuccessful attacks against the picket troops we had left in our old forward positions. The fragmentary nature of the British artillery fire indicated that they were displacing their guns forward. From 14 April on, I spent a long period each day in the front lines, organizing our active defense. All the troop leaders cooperated completely. Our planning was based on responding to the British large-scale attacks with deliberate counterattacks. Meanwhile, I was able to get Army Group Crown Prince Rupprecht to agree to replace by 20 April almost all the seriously depleted divisions that had been in the fight since 9 April. The relieved divisions went into reserve, partly for the army group and partly for OHL. They remained in positions behind the individual combat groups, however, which in turn were responsible for their reconstitution and training.

The positions we abandoned during the night of 12–13 April remained only lightly manned by weak elements, primarily officer patrols with numerous machine guns. These elements had the mission of deceiving the enemy into believing that the old positions were strongly manned, but they also had orders to withdraw to our new main battle positions ahead of the enemy creeping barrage in the event of a major attack. We did not plan to make any significant improvements to our new main positions. The infantry occupied the existing shell craters and added camouflaged wire obstacles. Behind that line the deeply echeloned infantry was camouflaged in a similar way. Nor did our artillery improve their new firing positions. The guns were positioned in rolling terrain in such a manner that they could displace forward to firing positions from where the gunners could engage with direct fire the enemy infantry as it was moving forward behind its creeping barrage. Once the enemy creeping barrage lifted, our deeply echeloned divisional infantry would launch a deliberate counterattack under strong artillery covering fire. Fortunately, heavy rains between 16 and 19 April softened up the ground that was already churned up by British artillery fire. The rain also limited visibility, making it more difficult for the British guns to register.

I still had a great deal of paperwork to go through when I returned to headquarters following my daily trips to the front lines. The workload increased significantly when on 16 April an OHL memorandum arrived addressed to all army group and army headquarters on the Western Front. It was based on reports submitted by Army Group Crown Prince Rupprecht assessing the Sixth Army's fiasco on 9 April. The OHL memorandum addressed three main points: (1) the failure of several divisions caused by reduced combat effectiveness; (2) the advancement of reserves too late for the execution of deliberate counterattacks; and (3) inadequate use of artillery and ammunition. My commanding general quite rightly was incensed by the harsh criticism directed at the Sixth Army, instead of at Army Group Crown Prince Rupprecht.

During the nights of 17–18 and 18–19 April I drafted a response, based on my analysis of the war diaries. I argued conclusively that the debacle of 9 April happened because Army Group Crown Prince Rupprecht had held back the reinforcement divisions for too long, and even then restricted their use as relief divisions only, rather than as attack divisions. I also pointed out the belated reinforcement of the Sixth Army's artillery and the late supply of gas rounds. I concluded that it was not the Sixth Army, but rather Army Group Crown Prince Rupprecht that was responsible for what had happened on 9 April. I strongly supported my commanding general, who made only a few minor changes to the report, signed it, and sent it to OHL. On 22 April Colonel General von Falkenhausen was appointed governor general of Belgium, to replace the deceased Colonel General Moritz Freiherr von Bissing. He received the following telegram from the Kaiser:

> I have appointed you effective today to be the governor general of Belgium. I would have preferred to keep you at the head of the Sixth Army in view of your capabilities as a troop commander, widely recognized within the German army. The death of Colonel General von Bissing, however, makes it imperative to appoint his replacement as the governor general of Belgium, and I therefore have selected you. Your career record and your superb accomplishments in all of your assignments, and your knowledge and energy, all assure me that you will execute your duties in this especially important and significant position. My selection indicates my extreme trust in you, and I am certain that you will serve in the best interests of the Fatherland. I again express my special satisfaction with your superb duty performance during the war, and I assure you of my royal gratitude.

The Kaiser did order Colonel General von Falkenhausen to remain in command until relieved by his successor, who was General of Infantry Otto von Below.[6] At the time he commanded an army in Macedonia, and he would not be able to assume command of the Sixth Army until 28 April.

The British launched their anticipated major attack against the Sixth Army on the morning of 23 April. Their main effort was directed against the sector that we had evacuated as planned. When the British creeping barrage lifted close to our forwardmost main battle lines, and the British infantry continued to advance, our infantry then stormed forward in a deeply echeloned, deliberate counterattack, heavily supported by our artillery. The close-quarters combat along the entire front lasted well into the evening, and our stalwart infantry proved much superior to the British. No quarter was given in the fight. Those who continued to resist were pummeled to death. We took many prisoners in hot pursuit. The battle of 23 April was a major and clear victory for the Sixth Army. General Ludendorff called me late that evening, and I described the course of the battle to him in detail. Ludendorff thanked me much for my own contribution, and also expressed thanks on behalf of Field Marshal von Hindenburg.

During the night of 23–24 April our troops fell back and reoccupied the same positions that we had held on the morning of 23 April. That prevented the unnecessary losses that would have been unavoidable if the troops had remained close to the beaten enemy and within the range of the British artillery. On 24 April the Kaiser presented me with the Oak Leaves to the Order of Pour le Mérite.[7] That same day the commander of Army Group Crown Prince Rupprecht issued the following order:

> During the fight yesterday the soldiers of the Sixth Army conducted themselves superbly, paralleling the earlier achievements of their comrades at the Aisne and in Champagne. The success resulted from steady and energetic leadership, the courage of all of our troops, and the superb coordination of all arms. Our infantry has proved once again that it can attack and that it is superior to the British. I would like to express my highest appreciation and my most sincere gratitude to the command, to all the leaders, and to the troops of the Sixth Army. The enemy's first powerful push has been broken. Continue to fight like this, comrades, and the spoils of victory will soon be ours.

The chief of the General Staff[8] also received the following message saluting the troops, signed by the leaders of all the parties in the Reichstag: "The undersigned members of the Reichstag Appropriations Committee thank the incomparably courageous German heroes at Arras, at the Aisne, in Champagne, and wherever they are fighting and bleeding for the welfare of the People and the Fatherland. Their accomplishments are quite unique in the history of the world. They are committed by their oath to sacrifice relentlessly with all their power, to defend the German People until there is peace."

At the time this acknowledgment from the Homeland delighted us. Unfortunately, during the final months of the war approximately one-third of the signers of that message broke their own oath most shamefully.

Immediately following 23 April several of our depleted divisions were relieved by fresh divisions. At daybreak on 28 April the British drumfire opened up again. That same day General of Infantry Otto von Below arrived in Tournai. I picked him up at the train station and greeted him with the words, "British barrage in progress. Expecting a large-scale attack." Below answered, "Fabulous! That means I got here just in time." He beamed all over. At the headquarters he had a brief talk with General von Falkenhausen, and then he immediately assumed command. I gave him a summary briefing on the situation.

On 28 April the Sixth Army scored its second major defensive victory. The British attacked in the same manner as they had on 23 April. We again let them advance, and then launched our planned deliberate counterattack, which succeeded completely. The British again suffered heavily in dead and captured.

General von Below was a man after my own heart. He openly admitted that he was not sufficiently familiar with the techniques of the large-scale defensive battles. Since it would take him some time to learn the system, he initially gave me a great deal of operating freedom. Naturally, I submitted to him drafts of all the important orders, and he always signed them.

From 29 April on, I always accompanied General von Below on his daily visits to the front. At first he asked me to run the situation update briefings at the various command posts. After a few days General von Below, who had a keen intelligence, mastered the tactical nuances of the large-scale defensive battle. Based on my recommendation, then, he assumed personal control of the briefings. He did ask me to continue be on hand and to offer all necessary advice. Such was characteristic of his generous attitude and his down-to-earth and focused manner of thinking and acting. The friendship we developed during the Battle of Arras has lasted to this day.[9]

Another major British attack failed on 3 May 1917. It lacked the great impetus of their previous attacks on 9, 23, and 28 April. We conducted an active defense in the same manner as on 23 and 24 April, and once again we inflicted high losses on the British. After that a greater calm gradually set in over the front. We immediately took advantage of the break to make energetic improvements in the forward line of our former positions, which had been the line of departure for our own attacks. We strengthened the position in depth, while pulling back our forwardmost troops from their final positions at the end of our counterattack.

Throughout the rest of May, the British still conducted occasional attacks, which almost everywhere failed completely. We successfully eliminated any minor break-ins with well-prepared and deliberate counterattacks, usually capturing many British troops in the process. Gradually a complete calm settled in, and we made greater progress improving our positions. Rearward units strengthened our secondary lines and the farther-back Wotan Position, which was at operational depth.

On 19 May the Kaiser visited the Sixth Army. That morning he inspected the troops at Tournai. Then I gave the Kaiser my assessment on the course of the Battle of Arras. Following that we had breakfast on the royal duty train. I sat next to my old mentor, General Moriz Freiherr von Lyncker, who was now the chief of the Prussian military cabinet. That afternoon the Kaiser inspected other units, during which he delivered appropriate speeches to the troops. After he returned to the Sixth Army headquarters, the Kaiser sent the following telegram to the commander of Army Group Crown Prince Rupprecht, for further dissemination to the troops:

> On the battlefields of Arras and under your leadership your units composed of troops from all the German provinces have thwarted the aggressive British intentions during the heavy fighting of the last two months. A will of steel and firm conviction of victory is reflected in the eyes of those I have visited during this trip. That same spirit is at the core of the whole army. Through me the Fatherland thanks its courageous sons for their willingness to sacrifice for the German cause. Extend my gratitude to all leaders and troops, with the trust that with God's help the coming battles also will be won.

A few days later at Tournai, Crown Prince Rupprecht awarded me with the Knight's Cross of the Military Order of Max-Josef, the highest Bavarian wartime decoration. In his comments he emphasized my contributions to the war.

To my delight I received only good news from my old First Army after 16 April. On that day they very courageously defended their positions east of Reims against superior French attacks. By applying the tested combat principles, they lost only a little bit of ground. The Seventh Army lost slightly more ground east of Soissons, but they held the important high ground of the Chemin des Dames Ridge. We only learned much later that, after suffering heavy losses, entire divisions of the French Army mutinied. Even though these mutinies were put down with brutal force, it took a long time before discipline was reestablished in the

French Army. Had OHL known about the French situation at the time, we most probably would have launched a major offensive against the French. Following the mutinies on 17 April, the commander in chief of the French Army, General Robert Nivelle, was relieved. His successor was General Philippe Pétain, and Ferdinand Foch became the chief of staff of the French Army.[10]

The intensified German submarine campaign yielded good results. In April more than a million gross registered tons were sunk, half of which were British ships. In May the total was 869,000 gross registered tons.[11] To our great delight, our field artillery batteries starting in May were rearmed with the 1916 gun models, which gave us significantly greater range.[12]

On 26 May Field Marshal von Hindenburg came to visit the Sixth Army. General von Below and I met him at the train station. After we arrived back at headquarters I gave him a briefing on the situation and current operations. The Field Marshal had nothing but praise and thanks for our accomplishments.

Aerial reconnaissance detected strong British troop movements to our north, primarily in the sector of the Fourth Army's left wing. We concluded that there was a high probability of an attack against the Fourth Army. On 27 May the Sixth Army headquarters submitted an estimate of the situation to the army group. We described the overall situation in the Sixth Army sector, and then touched on the probable British actions in the near future. We forecast the following possible enemy courses of action:

1. The enemy will break off his continuing attacks against the Sixth Army and regroup for a main effort against the Fourth Army. There are clear indicators of a pending attack in their sector, including the reinforcement of British artillery and the improvement of troop cantonments and ammunition dumps opposite the Wijtschate Salient.
2. The enemy will launch a new large-scale attack against the Sixth Army. Both ground and aerial reconnaissance confirms strong manning of the British forward zone, strong artillery, and continuing improvement of troop cantonments, airfields, and ammunition depots, primarily in the northern part of the Sixth Army sector.
3. Enemy will attack both the Sixth and Fourth Armies, with his main effort initially against the Wijtschate Salient.

Based on this estimate of the situation, Army Group Crown Prince Rupprecht ordered the Sixth Army to release selected divisions, heavy and field artillery, aviation, and intelligence units. We also were ordered to be prepared to release two Landwehr divisions and engineer and construction companies that were involved in improving the Wotan Position. Almost all of the released units were positioned behind the Fourth Army.

As the days passed it became increasingly clear that the British were preparing a major attack against the Fourth Army. The British front opposite the Sixth Army thinned out, and the withdrawn units were shifted north. The Fourth Army recognized that a strong British attack was imminent against the Wijtschate Salient on their left wing. The Fourth Army's chief of staff was now Lieutenant Colonel Max Stapff (my former Ia at the First Army), who had replaced General Emil Ilse. The troops deployed in that sector knew full well that much of their forward zone was undermined by British tunnels. Countermining efforts had been unsuccessful. Most likely the British would blow the mines before they launched their attack. In a telephone conversation with General Ludendorff I recommended that the threatened German positions should be abandoned and that all defensive measures should focus on launching a deliberate counterattack. General Ludendorff concurred, but the Fourth Army rejected the recommendation.

On 7 June 1917 the coordinated detonations demolished very large segments of the German forward positions. The British infantry attack that followed immediately was heavily supported by artillery, pushing the German lines back some four kilometers.[13] (This catastrophe affected me profoundly. When I was the chief of staff of Corps Fabeck during the autumn of 1914, we had taken the Wijtschate Salient at the cost of much blood.) That same day the British also attacked the Sixth Army between Lens and La Bassée, but they achieved nothing. Most likely those were diversionary attacks for the purpose of tying down troop movements from the Sixth Army to the Fourth Army.

Immediately after the start of the battle General Ludendorff told me on the telephone that he intended to swap out the chiefs of staff of the Fourth and Sixth Armies, which would send me to the Fourth. All the current indicators pointed to a major British attack against the Fourth Army on both sides of Ypres. I recommend that the army commanders be exchanged as well, to maintain the continuity of the commander-chief relationships. After conferring with Field Marshal von Hindenburg, Ludendorff rejected the idea.

On 12 June 1917, I took over as the chief of staff of the Fourth Army, and Lieutenant Colonel Stapff replaced me at the Sixth Army. I was now faced with a new and difficult situation. I parted company only very reluctantly with General von Below, with whom I had an excellent personal and professional relationship.

7

Chief of the General Staff of the Fourth Army (Flanders, 1917)

On the morning of 13 June, I drove in a staff car from Tournai to the Fourth Army headquarters at Courtrai, Belgium. I reported immediately to the commanding general, General of Infantry Friedrich Sixt von Armin, who received me very warmly. As the commanding general of the IV Army Corps, General Sixt von Armin twice had commanded a battle group centered on his IV Army Corps, and in the process he proved himself brilliantly as a capable senior leader. Right from the beginning I got along marvelously with him. He and I were both convinced that the British together with the French were preparing a massive large-scale attack against the Fourth Army.

After a long meeting with the commanding general I met with the staff of the Fourth Army headquarters. They were all capable and responsible men, but the army staff did not have enough officers to meet the demands of facing a large-scale attack. In a phone call with General Ludendorff I requested and received a reinforcement to the operational staff, which I then distributed as follows:

Department I (Operations): Major von Voss (Ia) with six General Staff officers, plus a reports collection officer, a front office officer, a map officer, and several liaison officers.

Department II: Deputy Chief of Staff, Colonel von Redern with two General Staff officers.

- Artillery[1] Advisor: General Meckel
- Engineer Advisor: General Schulz
- Aviation Advisor: Lieutenant Colonel Milberg

Additional augmentation went to the communications staff, the motor vehicle staff, the logistics staff, the chemical staff, the surveying staff, the agricultural staff (Major von Zitzewitz), and the naval liaison staff (Captain Fritz Taegert of the German Navy).

On the afternoon of 13 June, I drove to the front lines and visited the corps commanding generals. I also visited with many divisional commanders, and by random inspection trips forward I developed a general feel for the potential battlefield. From my service in the fall of 1914 I knew part of the ground, but only south of the Menen–Ypres road. North of that road the terrain was mostly flat, only occasionally interrupted by hills and rolling terrain.

The ground in Flanders is made up of a very soft and rich humus layer of one to three meters thickness. Under the topsoil is an impermeable layer of clay of about one meter thickness. When artillery fire hits that ground, the impact pushes the groundwater upward, which then fills the shell crater to the brim. Almost all defensive positions had to be built on top of the humus layer and were therefore easily identifiable by the enemy. In extended dry weather the topsoil becomes very hard, which is very advantageous for the attacker. During periods of rain, which are frequent in Flanders, the humus layer turns into a marshy muck. Then the defender has the advantage.

During the Champagne, the Somme, and the Arras battles I assumed my duties as the army chief of staff in those sectors only after the enemy break-ins had already occurred.[2] For the Battle of Flanders[3] I had sufficient time from 13 June to 31 July to organize in detail the defense for large-scale attack.

During the night of 13–14 June, I calculated the number of trench divisions (*Stellungsdivisionen*) and attack divisions (*Eingreifdivisionen*) needed for the defense of the enemy's anticipated large-scale attack, as well as the additional artillery, aviation, and other combat assets (*Kampfmittel*) that would be needed. My requests were approved quickly by OHL. One by one, significant numbers of additional divisions arrived in the Fourth Army's rear area, to be available as corps and OHL reserves that could relieve as necessary battle-weary divisions. OHL likewise approved without hesitation all my other requests.

The basis for conducting large-scale battles is a good communications network. I immediately started to improve the existing network, the main trunk line of which ran parallel to and was far removed from the front line. From this main trunk line numerous branch lines split off perpendicularly to the front line, to the higher command posts, and to the three consolidated army artillery groups in the center and the two flanks of the potential battlefield. They reported directly to the Fourth Army headquarters. All the airfields also were tied into the network, which comprised thousands of kilometers of wire. The system proved to be very effective during the Battle of Flanders. From the army command post I could communicate with all the corps and divisional headquarters, the artillery groups, and the airfields. I could talk to them all simultaneously by plugging together all of the connections. The individual department chiefs of the army staff were always tied in during such conversations. They monitored, and then acted according to my orders, which I had already discussed with the commanding general.

During less intense trench fighting the divisions generally had the freedom to commit two or three infantry regiments in their forward zone. This depended on the width of the divisional sector and the state of the improvement of the forward combat zone. If only two regiments were forward, then the third had a longer period for recuperation and training. During a large-scale battle, however, all the combat divisions had to be organized in the same manner to ensure a safe and uniform relief of the worn-out divisions by fresh ones. On 27 June, therefore, an order went out that made this a requirement for the Fourth Army's entire defensive front. I quote that order in its entirety, because it was the foundation of our successful conduct of the Battle of Flanders. That order remains relevant to this day as guiding principles for the organization of defensive battles.

27 June 1917

1. The strength of the defense lies in screening our combat assets from enemy observation. Combat emplacements (trenches, dugouts, machine guns, battery positions) which appear on the enemy's aerial photography become targets for the enemy's fire. Their protection during the battle becomes impossible after the enemy initiates destructive fires in preparation for his attack.

As the fighting strength of our troops becomes exhausted, the defense must be reorganized. That reorganization must be prepared ahead of time, during lulls in the action and based on the factors of the terrain and the objectives.

The transition to the newly organized defense must be executed as soon as our losses mount. Based on experience, the troops have a tendency to remain stuck in their positions and dugouts, which become death traps or result in high numbers of captured troops. The troops are only fully combat effective outside of their dugouts. There is, therefore, a potential need to blow up the dugouts and exercise close control of the order to evacuate. Evasive movements of the infantry out of the positions and dugouts and into the open terrain—preferably forward—must be planned and prepared well in advance, and should be executed on order as soon as the enemy starts his preparatory fires. This includes ready units and reserves.

During periods of low-intensity trench warfare, it is necessary to man the forward lines at a certain level of strength. Echelonment in depth may be impossible in broad sectors, which can easily lead to the wrong organization of the defense. Thus, in the organization of the defensive battle the divisions should assume narrow fighting sectors of 2.5 to 3 kilometers. Based on this plan, all preparations should be made, including for command centers and communication networks.

2. The infantry should be echeloned by combat battalion, ready battalion, and reserve battalion. This triple echeloning is well proven, similar to the triple flank formation into three regimental zones. Every regiment will be assigned zones of depth for its three defensive echelons.

Combat Battalion: From the most forward shell crater line in a depth of five hundred to one thousand meters, depending on the terrain and the width of the sector.

Ready Battalion: Forward in the zone, in and behind the artillery defensive position.

These two types of battalions comprise a battle formation. Units returning from a quiet sector do not transition easily to such a battle formation, which must be rehearsed before execution of the mission. Not doing so will result in many unnecessary losses.

Reserve Battalion. This unit is held back initially for reconstitution and training, and for commitment later in relief of the forward battalions. The term "resting battalion" must be discarded immediately whenever a large-scale attack is imminent. Reserve battalions are then moved forward into previously reconnoitered positions at an elevated level of readiness. This is based on the situation of the enemy's artillery fire, which must be monitored constantly. (Daily maps of low-fire sectors should be maintained continually!)

Within the combat and readiness battalions, companies should be echeloned, preferably adjacent to each other. The companies themselves should be echeloned in depth.

The forward shell crater line should be manned by approximately half a platoon, with a full platoon behind it, another half platoon in the third echelon, and a platoon in the fourth echelon. This, however, is not a rigid formula! Everything depends on the requirements of the terrain. A similar formation should be used for the ready battalion, where the platoons should be kept together if possible.

The reserve battalions in an elevated combat readiness posture should be configured based on the terrain and combat mission. Throughout the depth of the entire sector security detachments should be deployed from the start with sufficient strength and responsible leaders.

3. Machine Guns

Some light machine guns should be deployed to the front of the most forward shell crater line to provide for interdiction fire (Sperrfeuer). Each regimental sector should deploy not more than five to six machine guns there. The remainder should be held at the company level to support hasty counterattacks. The MG 08 should be echeloned in depth in such a manner that no terrain within its own position remains uncovered. They always should be deployed in pairs, and if possible supported by troops with rifles. The command posts of the combat battalion, the ready battalion, and the regiment should be secured with at least one machine gun each. A machine gun reserve should be maintained at division or brigade.

Machine Gun Marksman (*Maschinengewehr-Scharfschützen—M.G.Ss.*) battalions[4] should only deploy two companies, keeping one in rest status for relief. The forward limit of their deployment should be no farther than in the artillery defensive position, otherwise farther to the rear. These units also can be used to provide antiaircraft support for the artillery. They are subordinated to the divisions, and are assigned only for precisely described and nonvarying missions.

Machine guns should not be deployed in rigid formation, rather they should be highly maneuverable throughout their assigned sectors, adapting to the enemy's fires. Sufficient amounts of belted machine gun ammunition and standard steel core armor-piercing bullets must be provided in sufficient time. After rainy weather the ammunition belts should be dried adequately.[5]

4. Trench Mortars

Light trench mortars should be echeloned in depth in the forward zone. Their mission is interdiction fire and delivering gas shells. The usage of medium and heavy trench mortars depends on the ammunition supply. These weapons are relative immobile and very difficult to move forward. Medium trench mortars, therefore, will be deployed in the artillery defensive positions. Fires will be initiated only after the enemy breaks in. Forward movements will be made on a case-by-case basis. Medium trench mortars should then be positioned in shell craters and supplied with prepositioned ammunition. After firing they should be repositioned. Heavy trench mortars are only rarely deployable. They are used in forward positions for very special purposes, such as the elimination of enemy machine gun nests.

5. Communications

The correct and terrain-appropriate organization of communications resources is decisive for the conduct of the battle. At a minimum there should be one direct line from the commander of the combat troops to the division staff or the divisional observation post. Branch lines preferably start at the infantry brigade commander and extend to the forward lines.

The main communications network should be supplemented by ground telegraph stations, homing pigeons (at forward posts use gas protection housing), messenger dogs, runners, mounted messengers, light signal stations, divisional observation posts, and reconnaissance squads. The entire organization should be established in such a manner that assumes that during the battle the telephone network will not function forward of the brigade command post.[6]

6. Artillery

Based on experience, the following points are necessary for the proper distribution of field and heavy artillery batteries:

For interdiction fires, field artillery batteries should be deployed with a width of 200 to 250 meters; heavy artillery at four batteries across one kilometer, consisting of two heavy field howitzer batteries, one very heavy howitzer[7] battery, and one flat-trajectory battery.[8]

Based on the forces available, artillery will be distributed by the army headquarters to the subordinate corps, and then down to the divisions. One foot artillery regiment should be allocated to support every division. The foot artillery regiment's staff will not be co-located with the divisional artillery commander, but farther forward, possibly with the infantry brigade commander. The staff should monitor the heavy batteries very closely for gunnery technique, observation, fire control, treatment and replacement of materiel, and storage of ammunition. The registration of the batteries must be supervised personally. The foot artillery staff will only infrequently meet with the divisional staff for briefings.

Artillery must be echeloned in depth. Its forward boundary should be approximately two kilometers from the forward shell crater line, with the rearward boundary approximately five to six kilometers back. The heavy artillery should be organized into deep battle and close battle groups.

The bulk of the flat-trajectory guns and all howitzers allocated for counterbattery fire should be assigned to the deep battle group. The close battle group will primarily fire destruction missions. The deep battle group, therefore, must be deployed decisively forward in order to shoot far into the enemy's depth. The close battle group should be echeloned in greater depth in such manner as to deliver deep destructive fire zones in front of the forward shell crater line.

Ground observation should be established everywhere. When that is not possible, auxiliary systems should be used for both heavy and field artillery, to include aviation, balloons, and survey plans. These systems must be used in a decisive manner, and directly subordinated to the artillery commander. Verbal contact is necessary between aviators, balloon observers, and the battery commanders. Therefore, the aviation detachment[9] with its security squadron[10] must be located as close to the division command center as possible.

All the operations of the divisional artillery commander must be conducted in close coordination with divisional General Staff officer Ia. Their duty stations always should be established in the same building, preferably next door to each other. Constant oral communication simplifies battle management and evaluation of incoming reports, as well as facilitating rapid action.

The deputy commander at the infantry regimental command post and the artillery regiment commander at the infantry brigade command post should maintain their dugouts closely together. During large-scale attacks coordination via liaison officers only is insufficient. Command posts should be inconspicuous and positioned away from population centers, road junctions, etc. The observation posts of the subordinate commands (*Untergruppen*) must be established with good observation and especially with reliable communications.

The entire control of artillery fires before a large-scale engagement and during the battle is of the highest importance. Thus, written artillery orders must be issued after coordination with the artillery commanders. The orders must include: targets, deployed batteries, and ammunition calculations. In urgent combat situations written artillery orders are usually necessary in the morning, at noon, and in the evening.

High mobility of artillery is essential to maintain combat strength during large-scale engagements. The expert use of terrain and the rapid shifting of positions by compromised batteries is also important. Smoke screens should be planned to obscure enemy destructive fires.

7. Artillery Action

(a) Before the battle intense countermeasures against enemy artillery are of special importance. Do not spare ammunition.

Besides the heavy artillery, light field howitzers also should be used against newly detected enemy batteries, and the heaviest flat-trajectory guns should fire against distant, deep batteries.

Use precision fire initially. As soon as enemy battery groupments are detected, transition to less precise shooting methods. Shift such fires from the registration points on to each of the enemy battery positions. After firing on an enemy battery always shift back to the registration point, and from there shift planned fires on to new enemy battery positions. This method is necessary in order to be able to fire adequate ammunition against the enemy.

(b) The proper distribution of destructive fires is especially important. It should not be rigid, but adjustable in conformance with the enemy's attacking maneuvers and into the enemy's depth. Indicate the enemy's potential lines of departure on the map. This becomes the basis for the target sketch for the distribution of destructive fires. Experience shows that the British often get ready for an attack in front of their trenches.

(c) Before the distribution of interdiction fires, form detachments of batteries and platoons as a mobile artillery reserve. The fires of those units are then layered for regular interdiction fires. Plan subgroup interdiction fires for individual regimental sectors. Whenever possible combine field guns and light field howitzers.

Interdiction fires should advance sharply toward the enemy's forward shell crater line. Make all efforts to resist unnecessary interdiction fires, and constantly instruct infantry leaders and the troops about this. They must understand the means and purpose of destructive fires in comparison to unnecessarily requested interdiction fire.

Destructive fires are directed not only against enemy artillery, but also heavily against all of the enemy's other combat positions—in other words, trench mortar positions, machine gun nests, observation posts, command centers, ready trenches, and bridges, but not against the enemy's wire obstacles. Primarily use field guns against enemy wire.

(d) Use harassing fires primarily at night and deep into the enemy's rear. Heavy flat-trajectory fire is normally insufficient for this purpose; therefore, the field gun batteries should be moved far forward every night, close to the friendly front line, to conduct harassing fire. Those batteries then should be pulled back before daybreak.

(e) Carefully prepare chemical gas fires against large enemy battery groupments and against sections of enemy infantry positions. Fire sudden destructive strikes during favorable weather conditions, especially shortly before enemy infantry attack, but also when the enemy is delivering his own destructive fires. Establish forward chemical gas positions, from which firing is conducted only at night.

(f) Of special importance is the organization of our fires against an opponent who has broken into our area of operations. Such fires must be planned specifically to support adjacent divisional sectors. If possible, every terrain sector must be covered with fires, preferably with direct fires from the battery positions. The interlocking of the batteries' fires is frequently necessary. Regular, primary, and auxiliary observation posts cover the front of our positions, but generally will be lost if the enemy breaks in. Therefore, establish completely separate observation positions to cover our own battle terrain between forward of the leading shell crater line and the battery positions. These observation posts should be positioned as close as possible to the battery positions. Trees and elevated, well-masked ground make good observation posts. From such positions the forward observer monitors with binoculars the enemy's combat movements and those of friendly infantry, then directs his battery's fires against the enemy with voice commands. Never use planned fires in such situations, otherwise firing on our own troops is inevitable during the give and take of battle.

Wherever sectors of terrain cannot be observed directly by friendly batteries, keep mounts ready for the rapid forward displacement of the batteries, or commit mobile artillery reserves that have been prepared in advance for such a mission. Prepare ready positions for the occupation by such guns when "Increased Readiness Status" has been declared. Also prepare the supporting observation positions.

Maintain the second echelon (field and heavy artillery) in readiness to the rear of the committed artillery units. The primary mission of that second echelon is to engage enemy forces that break in. Batteries must remain undetected; therefore, they should be pulled forward for destructive fires only in the direst of emergencies. Their initial positions must be maintained in the case of very heavy equipment losses forward. Guns are never pulled forward for the rapid replacement of lost equipment. At the army level consolidate the heaviest flat-trajectory guns into a special artillery group. Assign a group commander with a separate communications network and staff car. The fire missions for the heaviest flat-trajectory guns come from army headquarters, and in extremely urgent situations from the corps.[11] The consolidation of such fires is extremely important shortly before large-scale combat action. Priority targets are large battery groupments, large built-up areas, enemy railroad guns positioned far in the rear, ammunition dumps, and troop concentrations. Ground observation must be established for these guns in order to facilitate firing into built-up areas close to the front line, even during bad flying weather.

(g) The heaviest high-trajectory howitzers (42cm, 30.5cm, 28cm) are assigned to the corps artillery groups for special missions. Frequently, such batteries are located quickly by the enemy. Therefore, alternate positions must be prepared and the guns displaced rapidly.

8. Aviation Actions

Aircraft are assigned to conduct offensive actions against enemy aircraft, enemy balloons, ammunition dumps, debarkation railheads, and battery groupments. These missions must be executed despite enemy air superiority. Therefore, aviation strength must be conserved before large-scale combat to avoid unnecessary attrition. Fighter squadrons are distributed among the corps.[12] One fighter squadron will be available to each army headquarters for the reinforcement of aviation assets at the decisive point.

9. Army-Level Reserves

Reserves are positioned to the rear of any threatened sectors of the army front. They are attached to the corps for the purposes of quartering, training, and preparation for combat. Quartering before the battle will be positioned beyond the range of enemy fires. At the divisional level one-third of the division will be positioned forward and two-thirds to the rear. Upon the order "Assume heightened combat readiness posture!" elements will move forward promptly. Such an order will be given by the corps headquarters and reported to army headquarters. Tactical commitment will be executed only with specific approval of the army headquarters. The forward movement from rear quartering areas by railroad, narrow-gauge railroad, and wheeled vehicles must be well planned and trained for. In such situations additional time cannot be gained, but strength can be maintained.

At the Fourth Army one infantry regiment and one artillery battalion were designated as the forward-positioned echelon. An additional artillery battalion served as the mobile artillery reserve and was available to the corps. Additionally, every division of the combat reserve assigned four hundred troops (four companies) to move forward to construct quarters for the forward-positioned elements.

In preparation for the mission the Fourth Army headquarters provides detailed directives for the eventual deployment. It is essential to plan for movement in more than one direction. Based on these directives detailed reconnaissance of the future area of operations is conducted, down to company and battery leaders. It is essential to know the battery positions of the trench divisions, their distribution, their command posts, their communication, and their sectors of fire, and their the low-fire sectors. The divisions of the combat reserve or elements thereof need to know the potential area of operations well and establish their own communications network. The attack divisions must duplicate the maps maintained by the trench divisions. To accomplish this, officers of the attack divisions must be sent forward to the command posts of the trench divisions.[13]

The primary purpose of the combat reserve divisions is to give the army's subordinate corps the flexibility to commit their trench divisions completely while having a new backing of reserves that are being moved forward. Such a system greatly increases the speed and strength of any hasty counterattacks. Behind particularly threatened sectors echelon the combat reserve divisions into two waves. The divisions of the second wave become attack divisions for the second day of the large-scale battle. Therefore, their rapid movement to the battlefield must be planned and prepared for execution on the first day of the large-scale battle.

10. Conduct of the Battle

The timely recognition of the enemy's staging for the attack is of the highest importance. For the most part the necessary troop mass for the fight can only be transported forward and emplaced at night. Therefore, the enemy uses the early morning hours for the beginning of his large-scale attack. If he waits until later in the day, his infantry will be destroyed.

For large-scale battle actions, therefore, pay very close attention to the nightly movements of the enemy. This is done especially by listening posts in the forwardmost shell crater positions. They must report any suspicious noise. The increase of such reports usually indicates enemy staging activity.

During early dawn routinely send out low-altitude aviation patrols over the enemy's staging areas. If enemy staging is identified by the aviators, during their return flight they should give the destructive fire signal while over our infantry and battery positions.

In tense situations during which enemy attacks can be expected at any time, the conduct of a destructive fire strike should be executed routinely every morning, even in the case of no reports of enemy staging. Such actions will heighten the attention of all our combatants.

One must expect that after delivering massive destructive fires the enemy will break into our positions. Nonetheless, all available troops must defend to the last man, even in the forwardmost shell crater positions, and even during an encirclement. The enemy forces that have broken in will then be caught in the cross fires of interlocking machine guns.

From experience, enemy break-ins at different locations will occur at varying depths. That makes it very difficult for the enemy to maintain his own situational awareness. Support by his own artillery for follow-on attacks will not immediately be possible. His forward elements must first establish communications with his rear. Enemy infantry that has broken in, therefore, will almost always fight for a certain time without effective support from its own artillery. The defender must exploit this situation with the earlier described organization of our artillery fire against a partially penetrated enemy. Then the enemy infantry will be forced to fight in unfamiliar terrain without artillery support. We, however, will be fighting in familiar terrain with artillery support. This is the main advantage of the active defense and the immediate hasty counterattack.

The sooner the hasty counterattack is executed, the greater the advantage. Once the enemy has consolidated his position with his machine guns and has established communications with his artillery, we will have lost the primary advantage of the hasty counterattack. Consequently, it is of decisive importance for the offensively conducted defense to train our artillery and every infantry NCO to execute hasty counterattacks immediately, without waiting for orders.[14]

Once the enemy has been ejected, it is essential to reorganize our units and reestablish echelonment in depth. In the offensive battle a concentration of forces by nature develops in the forward lines as the reserves move forward. If we maintain this high concentration of forward forces after the enemy has been pushed back, it offers mass targets for the enemy's artillery, which will result in great friendly losses. The rapid execution of echelonment in depth at the conclusion of a fight must be trained for just as the hasty counterattack. Deep echelonment is only possible for the most part after darkness.

The enemy often commits several waves during the attack. He often echelons two divisions behind each other. After the enemy has broken in, therefore, interdiction fires will be necessary in front of old shell crater positions in order to make the advance of the enemy's reserves more difficult. The interdiction fire must be coordinated and conducted by those batteries which are not committed in their own battle sectors.

The enemy infantry attack often is accompanied by tanks. The rapid engagement of tanks at long range is important. All available means must be used. One gun per battery can be designated for antitank fire, while the remaining three continue their planned fires. Special guns necessary for fighting tanks can include infantry gun batteries, individual mobile field artillery platoons, light trench mortars, and machine guns with armor-piercing ammunition. The tank threat has almost completely been eliminated these days, but close attention is still necessary.[15]

11. Behind the Front

The strictest order must be maintained throughout the entire rear area. Movements should be organized so that all vehicles moving forward and those moving rearward do so on separate routes in order to avoid unnecessary detours. Such route discipline must be enforced during calm periods so that the convoys get used to the routes. Plan convoy routes by avoiding built-up areas, which experience shows are always under fire. Forward and rearward routes should be changed as soon as the usual harassment fires start at night on the established routes. Special teams should be assigned to maintain the trafficability of the routes around battery positions.

The well-organized forward movement of artillery supplies is very important. A mount pulling a damaged gun back to a forward-positioned maintenance shop must immediately bring back forward a newly repaired gun. Minor maintenance procedures by ordnance experts, armorers, and battery fitters should be conducted directly in the battery positions.

Intense supervision must be devoted to the return transport of empty shell casings and dunnage, as ammunition resupply depends on the quick turnaround of the expended material. This is especially important following large-scale attacks.

According to the ground and air reconnaissance reports, the Fourth Army was facing British forces from its southern wing to the edge of Boezinge, and the French from Boezinge to the sea. Intelligence analysis indicated that the enemy attack was prepared in the area between Hollebeke and Bikschote, with the direction of attack toward the northeast. There also was a serious possibility that the French would attack along the coast. The French there had established a bridgehead east of the canal, near Nieuwpoort. If they attacked out from the bridgehead along the coast and then turned south on the eastern side of Nieuwpoort, the German front could be penetrated and destroyed from the north at the Yser Canal line between the sea and Bikschote.

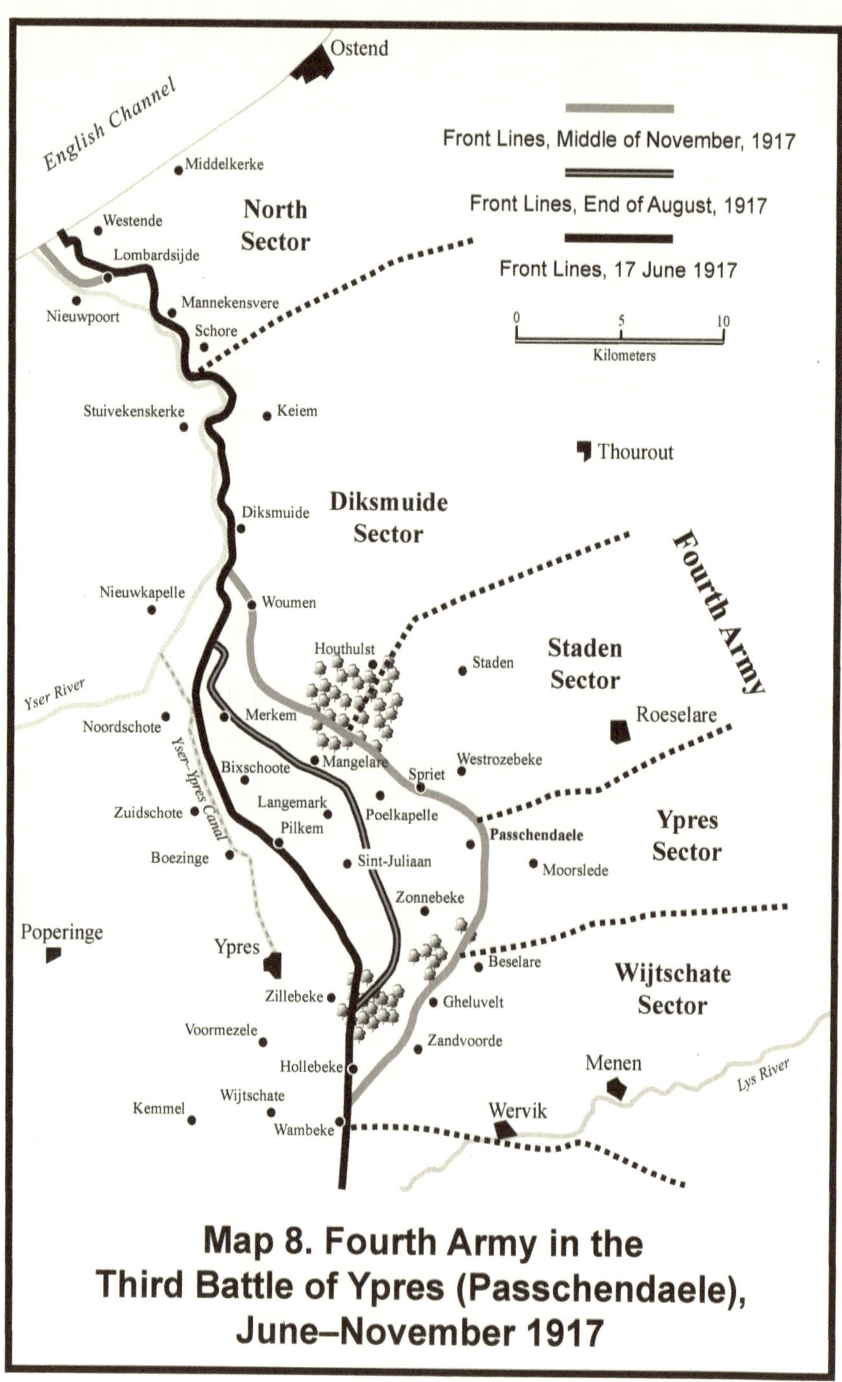

Map 8. Fourth Army in the Third Battle of Ypres (Passchendaele), June–November 1917

This created the additional danger that the navy subsequently would lose its submarine bases in the harbors of Ostend and Zeebrugge. Soon after taking over as the chief of staff, therefore, I drove to Bruges to report to Admiral Ludwig von Schröder and discuss the situation with him. The Naval Corps, even though it was not directly subordinate to the Fourth Army, was nevertheless required to follow the directives of the Fourth Army headquarters.[16] Admiral von Schröder was a very down-to-earth and responsible man who understood the importance of his special position. When I reported to him I pointed out the threatening danger near Nieuwpoort, which he fully agreed with. I suggested that the enemy should be pushed back with Fourth Army forces in order to prevent any enemy attack along the coast. Admiral von Schröder immediately concurred with my recommendation.

Shortly thereafter, General Sixt von Armin, accompanied by General Meckel, Admiral von Schröder, and me, conducted a reconnaissance of the area in the vicinity of Lombardsijde. We made the decision to eliminate the French bridgehead there. That same evening, I discussed this decision with General von Kuhl and General Ludendorff, who both immediately agreed with our plan. For the execution of this attack OHL made available one army corps under the command of General of Infantry Ferdinand von Quast, the commander of the Guards Corps. His chief of staff was my old, proven Ia at the First and Sixth Armies, Major von Platen. On 11 July the Guards Corps eliminated the bridgehead in the first try and destroyed all bridges that the French had constructed near or north of Nieuwpoort. Thus, we permanently eliminated the great danger faced by the right wing of the Fourth Army and the Naval Corps.

During this time the divisions, artillery units, and other combat assets requested by the Fourth Army headquarters arrived one by one. The Fourth Army headquarters divided the anticipated attack front into three sectors, assigned to Combat Groups Dijksmuide, Ypres, and Wijtschate.[17] To the north, Group North was tied in and remained only minimally manned, mostly by naval troops. The formations of the defensive front were organized as follows:

- Group Dijksmuide (commanding general of XIV Army Corps, General Martin Franz Chales de Beaulieu)
  Front: 19th Landwehr Division, 20th Landwehr Division, 40th Division, 111th Division.
  Rear: 79th Reserve Division, 2nd Guards Reserve Division
- Group Ypres (commanding general of III Bavarian Army Corps, General Hermann Freiherr von Stein)
  Front: 3rd Guards Division, 235th Division, 38th Division
  Rear: 50th Reserve Division, 221st Division

- Group Wijtschate (commanding general of IX Reserve Corps, General Karl Dieffenbach)
  Front: 6th Bavarian Reserve Division, 22nd Reserve Division, 10th Bavarian Division
  Rear: 119th Division, 12th Division, and 207th Division

In the later course of the battle, when the battlefront widened, Combat Group Staden was inserted between Groups Dijksmuide and Ypres.

To our delight OHL assigned a large number of aviation assets to the Fourth Army. Every combat division received an artillery aviation squadron and a bomber squadron. Additionally, OHL assigned several fighter squadrons and the 1st Fighter Wing under Captain Manfred von Richthofen.[18] That unit was located in the vicinity of Menen and was directly subordinated to the Fourth Army headquarters. In order to ensure a reliable basis for aerial reconnaissance and rapid reporting on the enemy, the entire anticipated combat sector was divided into sequentially numbered grid squares. The primary grid squares were further divided into grid sub-squares identified by letters. The reconnaissance and fighter aviators reported from the air or immediately after their landing the enemy movements with exact reference to the grid squares and sub-squares. This arrangement was decisively effective for engaging the enemy with our artillery and our infantry.

The Fourth Army headquarters formed three special artillery groups from the heavy flat-trajectory artillery units that were attached to us. These groups were directly subordinated to the Fourth Army headquarters. They were positioned directly behind the three combat groups, Dijksmuide, Ypres, and Wijtschate. Their mission was to concentrate fires frontally and on the flanks against identified enemy movements. This system paid off quite well in the course of the long fight.

It took me several days to organize the defensive front, and I was forward every day, sometimes with the divisional commanders and sometimes by myself. I checked on the implementation of the Fourth Army directives by the frontline combat divisions, as well as by the counterattack divisions.

The counterattack divisions were to plan and prepare their counterattacks in the forward direction, as well as to the right and left oblique. The basis for their commitment was an exact knowledge of the terrain. They conducted terrain orientation walks down to the company and battery commanders. Thus, both the frontline combat divisions as well as the counterattack divisions developed a synergy based on the complete knowledge of the unique characteristics of their anticipated battle sectors. During the course of several briefings at the front, the chief of staff of Army Group Crown Prince Rupprecht, General Hermann von

Kuhl, and also General Ludendorff, personally verified the effectiveness of the Fourth Army's defensive preparations.

From the beginning of July on, we could detect most clearly the enemy's staging for his attack. On the line from Bikschote to Hollebeke he massed an artillery force far superior in numbers to our own. In many places the enemy artillery stood hub to hub.[19] Incredible amounts of ammunition were stocked at the enemy's artillery positions. Toward the middle of July we recognized that the attack would be imminent from 19 July on. At that time, however, our defensive preparations were not yet completed. I therefore requested and received from OHL a special allocation of two heavy and four light ammunition trains. With this additional ammunition we commenced on 17 and 18 July firing a strong destructive counterpreparation against the identified enemy artillery positions. I was able to observe our fires from an army observation post with good, wide-range visibility. I clearly observed that we blew up many of the enemy's ammunition stockpiles. As a result of our decision to expend ammunition from our reserve stocks, we delayed the start of the enemy's large-scale attack until 31 July. OHL later replenished our reserve stocks.

The enemy started his large-scale attack on 31 July, preceded by an artillery preparation that lasted several days.[20] The ground of Flanders shook under the massive fires, which tore up the terrain extensively in width and depth. That morning the fire grew into a crescendo along a twenty-five-kilometer-wide front. When the enemy infantry finally attacked, they were preceded by a creeping barrage of such a dimension as I had never seen before. Owing to the force of these fires, the enemy infantry initially broke into our forward positions, which were only thinly manned. The Fourth Army headquarters received reports of heavy losses in positions one after another. The heaviest losses were reported in the sector of Group Ypres, against which the enemy's main effort was directed, supported by large numbers of tanks. Group Dijksmuide also reported large losses of ground resulting from French attacks. Group Wijtschate lost its forwardmost line, but the second German line still held.

Soon after 1200 hours the Fourth Army headquarters developed a rather clear picture of the situation, which I then briefed to the commanding general. I recommended deploying the already staged attack divisions for a deliberate counterattack. The commanding general concurred. Within minutes, communications were established with the combat groups, the defending divisions, the counterattack divisions, the three artillery groups, the fighter squadrons, and the individual sections of the Fourth Army headquarters. With a firm voice I issued on behalf of the commanding general the order for the attack divisions to counterattack, supported by the defending trench divisions.

The counterattack was to be supported by our entire artillery and all available aviation assets. I sent staff officers to the especially threatened positions, with orders to report continuously on the situation. Both the British and the French met the counterattack with strong resistance. Much of their artillery, however, was in the process of repositioning forward. Bloody, back-and-forth, close-quarters combat ensued, during which our reckless infantry brilliantly supported by our brave artillery gained the upper hand. The heavy fighting raged on without interruption across the wide battlefield, but our troops fought with a stubborn rage. Everywhere our lines advanced and regained back large sectors of the ground we had lost initially during the bloody, close-quarter fighting. The heavy fighting continued as darkness set in.

It was only toward midnight that the Fourth Army headquarters developed a complete picture of the situation: The enemy's attempted breakthrough had failed completely. Much of the ground we had lost initially was regained. The final break-in areas measured between one to two kilometers. The Fourth Army headquarters issued the order to hold the current lines and reorganize the entire defensive front in depth during the night. Some of the defending divisions that had high losses were relieved by some of the divisions that had counterattacked. New counterattack divisions that had been the army group reserve were then attached to the Fourth Army. The worn-out defending divisions were sent to reconstitute their units and were filled with arriving replacements.

Soon after midnight General von Kuhl and General Ludendorff called me one after the other. I gave detailed reports to both, and both were satisfied with the favorable results of the initial phase of the large-scale defensive battle. I reported the details of the extensive fighting and emphasized the heroism of our brave troops, who deserved all the credit for repulsing the break-in. I also reported that the Fourth Army headquarters was well prepared to repulse the follow-on attacks that could be expected soon.

During the next few days we conducted small attacks, during which we were able to straighten out bulges at several locations in our front lines. The enemy apparently reorganized in depth and replaced many of his worn-out units with fresh troops.

On 3 August 1917, I was promoted out of sequence to major general, a particular honor since I had only been a colonel for less than one and three-quarters of a year.[21]

I will not describe the massive defensive battle of Flanders in every detail, as I did for the Second Battle of Champagne of 1915 and the Somme Battle of 1916. I will emphasize only the key events. Map 8 shows the terrain losses that occurred during the longer course of the battle.

For both us and the enemy, the Battle of Flanders was the most monumental battle of the World War in terms of length of time and the size of the forces committed. It consumed an incredible portion of the strength of the German Army, but our losses were still much less than the losses of the enemy. They broke off the battle in the middle of November 1917, completely exhausted. From that point until the start of December they conducted only small-scale operations. Our great defensive victory in the Battle of Flanders resulted from the heroism of the German Army and the energy of the German leadership. Not a single one of our divisions failed during the Battle of Flanders. Every piece of ground was fought for stubbornly. The gigantic fight played out in an almost uninterrupted field of craters, turning the battleground into a muddy morass, as water seeped up from the craters and more rain fell from the skies. In many places on the battlefield one could move forward only on wooden plank walks. The enemy, of course, identified those walkways through aerial reconnaissance photography, and then brought them under sweeping fire.

The British and the French had put great hopes into their attack in Flanders. Numerous British tanks participated in the attacks. Those weapons, however, were usually neutralized by our artillery as soon as we observed them. The enemy also staged several cavalry divisions, but they were not committed during the course of the battle.[22]

A follow-on large-scale attack by the enemy on 10 August achieved only very minimal success. On 16 August, however, we initially lost a great deal of ground in the vicinity of Poelkapelle,[23] much of which we regained through deliberate counterattacks. Nonetheless, the enemy's attack continued almost without a pause. Large-scale fighting also took place on 22, 25, and 27 August. From that point on the Battle of Flanders slowed down gradually. The enemy thinned out his lines and we did the same. A considerable number of divisions remained in the rear of our front lines for reconstitution and training. During this time General Ludendorff visited the Fourth Army headquarters on several occasions. He was always full of understanding for our serious situation.

Toward the middle of September the enemy started manning his frontline positions again. OHL once more made available the necessary defensive forces, and we again organized our front into combat defensive divisions and counterattack divisions. It was the same system we had used successfully since 31 July. On 20 September the enemy again started large-scale attacks, which in rapid sequence lurched forward repeatedly on 21, 26, and 27 September. The main effort of these attacks was clearly in the direction of Passchendaele–Gheluvelt, against Group Ypres and the right wing of Group Wijtschate. Over time the British shifted to conducting attacks on smaller frontal sectors. During their preparations they always concentrated huge amounts of artillery. The most serious battle occurred on 4 October. Starting on 1 October the enemy rained intense artillery fire on us nonstop night and day. When they finally attacked on 4 October we held our lines for the most part. The enemy's new breakthrough attempt failed.

On the recommendation of OHL we started fighting primarily in our outpost zone from 5 October on. We maintained only patrols and many light machine guns in our forwardmost areas. Depending on the terrain, the main line of resistance was echeloned in depth several hundred meters to the rear. With this type of deployment we gained more time for the commitment of our reserves to the deliberate counterattack, which was launched after the enemy's creeping barrage had reached its maximum range. The procedures we had formulated previously for the defensive battle continued to be effective.

There was large-scale fighting again on 9 and 12 October. We lost ground, but the front always held. Massive attacks resumed on 22 October, and again on 26 and 30 October and 6 November. The attacks extended north to the forest south of Houthulst. Their main effort was directed toward Poelkapelle and farther south along the line Gheluvelt–Zandvoorde. Considerable bulges in our lines developed, but our front line held despite all of the enemy's attempts to break it. OHL constantly supplied relief units, so that we always had two waves of rearward divisions available, forming the army and the OHL reserves.

On 3 November the Fourth Army headquarters displaced to Tielt because Courtrai was within range of the enemy's long-range artillery and was frequently subjected to aerial attack. One day after we displaced to Tielt the building where I had been billeted in Courtrai was destroyed by artillery.

The attacks in Flanders only slowed down toward the middle of November. Then we immediately began to reinforce our fighting positions. As we came to realize that the enemy opposite us was also digging in, we thinned out our own front lines. From the beginning of December, the fighting in Flanders came to an almost complete halt. At that point we also began to improve our rearward positions. On 5 December we received the following message from Army Group Crown Prince Rupprecht:

> The great battle for Flanders seems all but over. The moment, therefore, has come for me to express my gratitude and appreciation to all the leaders and troops that took part in the Battle of Flanders.
>
> Eighty-six divisions, including 22 that were committed twice, and the mass of our artillery and other weapons systems contributed to this most monumental of all battles to date. The sons of all the German tribes have competed here in heroic courage and stubborn tenacity, preventing all the breakthrough attempts of the French and British. It was their intention to win the war by capturing Flanders and our submarine base. Despite their incredible mass deployment of men

and materiel, the enemy accomplished nothing. A small, completely destroyed field of shell craters is all he gained. He paid for this gain with extremely high losses, while our losses were far less than in any defensive battle so far.

Thus the Battle of Flanders is a serious defeat for the enemy and for us a great victory. All who participated in it can be proud to have earned the title of "Flanders Fighter." Each individual combatant has earned the gratitude of the Fatherland. Only because our front in Flanders withheld against every attack was it possible for the High Command to attack the Russians in the east and the Italians in the south.

Special thanks to the army leadership in Flanders, the commanding general of the Fourth Army, and his seasoned chief of staff, whose strong wills and objective-oriented tactical and organizational efforts had a decisive impact on the success of the battle.

I also must thank the other armies of the army group. They limited themselves and were fully willing to make extreme sacrifices in contributing large numbers of forces, and in the process overcame immense difficulties in order to support the combatants in Flanders.

May our enemies prepare for new onslaughts! We know how to deal with them.

Signed/ Commanding General:
Rupprecht, Crown Prince of Bavaria
Field Marshal

During the night prior to 7 December a strong enemy aerial attack against the Fourth Army headquarters in Tielt resulted in the partial destruction of the commanding general's villa. The general's adjutant was wounded so seriously in the arm that it required amputation. I immediately made my quarters available to General Sixt von Armin and moved into a small house close to my office.

In the middle of September 1917, during the height of the massive battle, I received a message from the 2nd Guards Regiment, which was part of the 1st Guards Division, near Riga. My son, who at the time was an officer candidate (Fähnrich), had been severely wounded in the stomach during a patrol.[24] He initially was treated at a field dressing station for six weeks and then in two field hospitals in East Prussia. Only after he was transferred to Berlin did the military doctors determine that all his vital organs were undamaged. The bullet had been deflected by a rib and then burrowed in just below his shoulder. Our almost two meters-tall son, who soon after his wounding received the Iron Cross, 2nd Class, was then commissioned as a lieutenant. But for the longest time he could only ingest liquid food and he was reduced to a skeleton. In order to nurse him back to full health, and with the permission of the commanding general, I had him transferred to Tielt, where he also underwent further training courses at a communications school and an assault school.[25] On 18 February, I accompanied him back to the 2nd Guards Regiment, which at the time was resting in the vicinity of Charleville. From there I briefly visited my two former commanding generals, General von Einem of the Third Army and General von Below of the First Army. The latter, unfortunately, I found very sick, but he received me at his bedside.

During the entire Battle of Flanders OHL had made available to the Fourth Army all the necessary replacements and reserves. This is all the more deserving of recognition because OHL also faced high levels of requirements in the other theaters of war. In addition to the imperative in the east to attrit the Russians continually, on the northern flank in the east OHL also planned and ordered an attack across the Daugava River, southwest of Riga. That attack, launched on 1 September 1917, was completely successful and resulted in a significant shortening of our lines in that sector.[26] The Italians, meanwhile, had attacked successfully in August and September along the Isonzo River, which required the Austrian Isonzo front to be reinforced with German troops. The situation of the Austrians became more and more serious, however. OHL finally decided to commit more German troops and go on the attack.[27] In Macedonia the Entente started attacking at the beginning of November and achieved minor successes. In Romania minor fighting also started up again. All in all, the events in the east allowed us ultimately to thin out our front against the Russians and thus gain some reserves for a deliberate attack against the Italians at the Isonzo River. For the execution of that attack a new Fourteenth Army was formed under the command of General Otto von Below, whose successor at the Sixth Army was General Ferdinand von Quast. Six German divisions, well equipped with strong artillery and all the other necessary combat resources, were transported to the Isonzo River sector on both sides of Tolmin. During the preparation for the attack against the Italians, several supporting offensive actions were carried out in the east. In the middle of October, a well-prepared attack by the army and the navy captured the Estonian islands of Osel, Moon, and Dagoe, which commanded the entrance of the Gulf of Riga.[28]

The British and the French in the west also launched attacks outside of the Battle of Flanders sector. On 9 August the British attempted unsuccessfully to advance against the Sixth Army on both sides of the Scarpe River. On 15 August near Lens, however, we lost ground to a British attack. At the end of August the French unsuccessfully attacked the Second Army near Saint-Quentin. From 20 to 26 August the French attacked the Fifth Army north of Verdun on both sides of the Meuse, and pushed the German front back rather significantly. On 22

October the Seventh Army lost the deep Laffaux salient and its connecting lines southwest of Laon. We elected not to make a deliberate counterattack, and thus withdrew our front line back behind the Oise-Aisne Canal and into the area north of the Chemin des Dames Ridge. The repulse of all these attacks cost a great deal of blood and required the relief of the expended divisions. Only the unlimited confidence of OHL and Ludendorff's trust in the German Army's ability to resist enabled us to weather all these crises, despite an incredible loss of forces.

Ludendorff exerted his iron will, especially when on 20 November 1917 the British attacked from the southwest with massed tanks in the direction of Cambrai. The initial British wave overcame a German Landwehr division and broke deeply into the Siegfried Position, taking many prisoners in the process. During the battle for the fortifications of Bourlon, the headquarters of our old First Army acquitted itself well. The British tanks became bogged down in that fortified zone, and OHL then launched an immediate deliberate counterattack on 30 November, regaining large sectors of the lost ground, and even gaining some new ground south of the initial penetration point. A hasty counterattack launched by the British on 5 December failed.

Earlier, on 24 October, the attack against the Italians at Tolmin started when the German 12th Division broke deeply into the Italian front lines. Then this initial success was exploited greatly, as the Fourteenth Army advanced to the Piave River. Approximately one hundred thousand Italians were captured. A simultaneous but poorly conducted attack on both sides of the Adige River in the direction of Verona conducted by Austrian field marshal Franz Conrad von Hötzendorf was largely unsuccessful. But our situation against the Italians greatly solidified. As a consequence of our victory, the Entente was forced to support the Italians with multiple French and British divisions pulled from the Western Front. In Palestine, meanwhile, Turkish troops under General Erich von Falkenhayn were pushed back between 23 November and 25 December 1917, far to the north beyond Jerusalem, by greatly superior British forces attacking from the south. The German Asia Corps was then committed to reinforce the Turkish front line.

During the same period the Bolshevik Revolution broke out in Russia. As large sectors of the Eastern Front were taken over by Austrian troops redeployed from Italy, OHL finally was able to transfer many German divisions to the west starting in November 1917. Once those units redeployed, they all were thoroughly trained for the style of combat in the west. The armistice with Russia was signed on 15 December 1917.

The hope that France and Britain would finally be ready for peace now proved in vain. The leaders of those nations only thought of continuing the war, and they now had the support of America. Those three countries also urged Italy to hold out. The peace initiative advanced by the German Reichstag and the new chancellor, Georg Michaelis, failed completely, and he was succeeded as chancellor by Georg Graf von Hertling. Unfortunately, he was not the strong leader that Germany needed.

For the longest time my commander, General Sixt von Armin, had been urging me to return to Stuttgart to see my family over Christmas. Since the front was completely calm I decided to go. Shortly thereafter General Ludendorff called me and told me that the Kaiser wanted to inspect the troops of the Fourth Army in Flanders on 23 December. I immediately told him that under the circumstances I would cancel my leave, which had already been approved. I stuck to this decision despite all of Ludendorff's urgings to the contrary. About half an hour later Ludendorff called me back and told me that he had just seen the Kaiser and that the Kaiser himself ordered me to take my leave. I went home, of course, where I was reunited with our wounded son. On the evening of 23 December in Stuttgart I received a long telegram from the Kaiser. He noted my meritorious contributions in the fortunate outcome of the fighting in Flanders and promoted me to his *General à la suite.*[29] I first sent a reply telegram to the Kaiser, who had returned to Berlin from Flanders. I then followed up with a letter expressing my gratitude for this high honor. Colonel General Moriz Freiherr von Lyncker[30] also congratulated me in writing and suggested that later I should report directly to the Kaiser. Toward the end of January, when the Kaiser moved from Berlin to Homburg-vor-der-Höhe, I drove there to report to him personally. The Kaiser kept me there for several days. Homburg-vor-der-Höhe was my birthplace, and at the end of March 1918 the town bestowed honorary citizenship on me.

As early as the end of 1917 OHL made the decision to not limit operations in the west to the defensive, which consumed too much strength. We had to assume the operational offensive in the west. The entire German Army greeted the OHL decision with enthusiastic support. It was obvious that Germany could only win the war through successful attack, and the Western Front was the only place where an operationally decisive attack would be possible. The execution of such an attack required that all available forces in the east and south should be consolidated in the west. The necessary and time-consuming transport movements started at the end of 1917.

OHL strongly pressed for a conclusive peace accord between Russia and the Central Powers. But the final peace negotiations with the Russians were delayed repeatedly. Despite the armistice, the only viable option was to go on the attack against Russia. In the middle of February a force of mostly German Landwehr units advanced to the approximate line from the northeastern tip of the Sea of

Azov to the west of Saint Petersburg. A special administration was established for the fertile Ukraine, with the task of securing the rich wheat supplies for transportation back to the Central Powers. The offensive action against Russia had its effect, and at the start of March 1918 the peace accord was signed.[31] At the beginning of May the peace with Romania also was finalized. Any troops that could be released from the east were transferred to the west during the spring 1918. After all the troop movements were completed, OHL estimated that the German Western Front had numerical superiority of twenty to thirty divisions.

The numbers and effectiveness of replacements for the German Army had been decreasing for some time. In terms of raw numbers, we had reached the bottom by that spring. But when America entered the war the Entente started to receive a constantly growing number of fresh reinforcements. The Entente also had a considerable superiority in terms of guns, ammunition, and aircraft, which continuously increased with the addition of American units. German submarines were constantly successful, but there was still a great uncertainty about their ability to delay significantly the movement of the American army. The naval forces of both sides were probably equal in combat power.[32] The German Army's decisive advantage was its unified command structure. Initially the senior leadership of the Entente military forces was divided. Only after we started our great 1918 Offensive did the Entente unify its military command under French general Ferdinand Foch.

General Ludendorff was primarily responsible for the planning, preparation, and execution of our operational attack. Together with Field Marshal Paul von Hindenburg, Ludendorff was accountable to the supreme commander of the German Army, as well as to the German people. In the final analysis, however, it is my personal opinion that General Ludendorff largely exercised his own will.[33]

The most important decisions for the operational offensive in the west were the time, the type, and the location of the attack. Soon after the end of the Battle of Flanders I put together a detailed assessment of the situation, based on my extensive frontline experience. As soon as I knew about the decision for the upcoming operational attack, I consolidated my thoughts into a position paper, which I handed to General Ludendorff. My position paper stressed the following points:

> 1. Timing of the Offensive.
>
> The quiet period on the Western Front since the end of the Battle of Flanders and the end of the fighting at Cambrai is not only advantageous to the German Army, which has been reinforced from all the other fronts, but also serves the enemy. At the beginning of our offen-

sive the German Army will certainly engage an enemy army that has been reinforced in its combat strength. In addition, the enemy will continue to be reinforced throughout 1918 by the American influx. For the present, the Americans are taking their time with the training and movement of their new formations. As soon as our offensive shows any initial tangible success, the Americans will increase the formation of new units and will accelerate their deployment. Whether the successes of our submarines will be sufficient to influence decisively the American transports is uncertain, based on earlier experiences. If our attack does not produce a decisive operational breakthrough, we will be at the end of our operational capability and must transition to the operational defensive. It will be necessary then to face an enemy superior in numbers and in combat power.

The war can be decided in our favor only through the offensive. Such a decision is not only inevitable according to the reasoning by our highest leadership, but most especially because of the will and the efforts of our troops and their leaders to abandon this grueling trench warfare. The possibility of the failure of the operational offensive must be taken into consideration, which will leave the German Army no option but to go back on the defensive. The later during the year that we might be forced back on the defensive, the greater the prospect of resuming such operations in the fall. That will allow us to continue the fight successfully under weather and terrain conditions that will be more difficult for the enemy to attack in. I, therefore, have concluded that our offensive should be launched approximately in the middle of May. At that time the attack terrain forward of almost all of our front lines that consists of a deep field of shell craters will be dryer, and therefore more negotiable for larger troop movements. This is especially true in the Flanders region, with its low water table, and especially for the Lys River flood plains.[34]

Delaying the start of the offensive until May will also make it possible for us to move to the Western Front almost all of our divisions still remaining in the east. Based on their relative combat value they can either participate in the attack or relieve divisions currently in defensive positions that are more experienced in the style of combat on the Western Front. Eastern Front divisions that consist of older-aged Landsturm and Landwehr troops could form the cadre for the improvement of our rearward positions. Some of those divisions also could be dissolved and their effective elements made available as replacements for western units after undergoing thorough training.

It is unlikely that the enemy will attack before May. All the indicators are that they will wait for the German attack.

2. The Conduct of the Offensive

During the years 1915–1917 the enemy's large-scale attacks in the west did not result in operational success, despite their considerable superiority in troops and materiel. In all our defensive battles, at least in 1915 and 1916, the German troops which were not always fully combat ready prevented the attacker's tactical breakthrough. Our success resulted primarily from the heroic tenacity of our troops, and also through our clever exploitation of the maneuver difficulties that the attacker faced in the crater fields that he himself had created.

If you compare these experiences in the past defensive battles with the situation for our offensive in 1918, the German senior leadership must recognize clearly that the offensive must be directed against an enemy who has well-rested trench divisions and many fully combat-ready divisions and other weaponry in reserve. The numbers of their combat divisions will increase constantly with the arriving American reinforcements. For the time being they are deploying in well-prepared and not heavily threatened sectors, which in turn frees up French and British units. The enemy will face far fewer troop and materiel replacement shortages than we will. We also must take into consideration the fact that the enemy has considerably greater transportation assets, including his efficient railroad network and his numerous motor vehicles. Thus, we must assume that our opponents can reinforce their attacked or threatened front lines in a much shorter time than was possible for us during our defensive battles.

If a German operational attack runs into a fully combat-ready enemy who can quickly move his well-rested reserves, the difficulties for a tactical or an operational breakthrough will increase immensely. Whether the German troops can manage to achieve the necessary scale of complete victory in the face of such force ratios remains very uncertain.

I therefore am of the opinion that multiple small-scale attacks with planned, limited objectives will force the enemy to commit a large portion of his reserves, thus weakening his combat power. Only then can we conduct a large-scale operational attack.

My recommendation to launch a series of limited-objective attacks in preparation for the main effort is based on my extensive experiences in our own defensive battles. In my opinion an attack preceded by an incredibly intense artillery preparation and the element of surprise will always produce strong initial results. The losses of the defenders during the first days of such attacks are approximately one thousand men per kilometer killed or taken prisoner, along with the loss of large quantities of materiel. During the days following the initial assault, the remnants of the trench divisions that are hit often lose their combat effectiveness because of the highly destructive effects of the enemy's artillery. The initial days of the attack almost always create deep salients, which on the average reach all the way to the defender's artillery belt.

The Battle of Flanders was an exception to this rule. The enemy's attack did not come as a surprise, and our defensive preparations were well in hand. Most importantly, the necessary attack divisions were positioned behind our front. They were completely familiar with their missions and had access to a special communications network specifically designed for the purpose. In the Champagne, Somme, and Arras battles the enemy attacks came as a surprise. The German reserves were not available in sufficient quantity, or they were positioned too far to the rear.

During the battles for the Champagne and Somme it took more than two weeks before a combat effective front could be rebuilt in the face of continuous enemy attacks. During that period we had to withdraw divisions from other fronts. Those sectors had to be taken over by adjacent units, which took five days. It then took the displacing divisions five days for loading, transportation, and unloading; two more days to march to the front lines from the de-training points; and finally three days to enter and occupy the new positions. Thus, the entire process took some fifteen days. But in a situation where we already had units positioned close by in reserve status, we could get them into the defensive front lines within eight to ten days.

Using these figures as a basis for calculation, I estimate that in the course of a large and wide-ranging offensive the tactical breakthrough by the leading attack wave must be accomplished at the latest within eight days. At that point, fresh leader reserves[35] at the tactical breakthrough point must to be ready to assume control of the execution of the operational breakthrough, and the fight through the enemy forces that will be converging from all sides.[36]

With the large number of enemy reserves now available, it seems too risky to me to base all on a single massive offensive. I think it necessary first to weaken the enemy reserves through smaller scale attacks in order to at least approximate an enemy situation that prevailed during our own defensive battles from 1915 to 1917. These smaller scale attacks should be prepared and executed as follows:

All of the army groups and armies on the Western Front should be solicited for recommendations and plans for limited attacks. The width of these attacks should be approximately fifteen kilometers. The objective of an attack will be the destruction of the enemy artillery; thus the depth of the attack will be seven to ten kilometers. If local conditions allow, the depth of the attack can be extended temporarily to harass the enemy further. Before the attack the line for the new forward defensive position must be designated on the map and according to the contour lines. So doing will establish a positive linkage in the attack to the adjacent front lines based on the terrain. The new forward position will be established by specially assigned construction units (staffs, engineers, construction troops, labor battalions, etc.) that follow the attacking forces. The attacking forces will withdraw to those new positions as soon as the continuation of the attack seems fruitless, or the preparation of the enemy counterattack is evident. As a precaution against strong enemy counterattacks, plans should be made for withdrawal to the initial attack position if necessary. OHL will select the most optimal recommendations received from the armies and then order the execution of the attack in short order. These attacks should start in the middle of May.

On average, the German Army deploys three divisions on a fifteen-kilometer-wide front. Every sector that is preparing to conduct a limited attack should be augmented with one attack division for each three kilometers of attack front, or five additional divisions for fifteen kilometers. OHL also will establish a reserve force of three divisions, held in close proximity, to exploit any especially favorable situation. Even in such cases, however, plans must be in place for withdrawal in the face of a strong enemy reaction.

The artillery preparation for the attack will include not only the batteries of the attack divisions, but also the artillery of the trench divisions, but which will only fire out to their maximum ranges from their original positions. The army-level artillery units committed by OHL will also fire in the preparation. The intensity of the fires must completely destroy the enemy positions and troops. Therefore, calculate one battery for approximately every twenty meters of the attack sector; and one battery for every fifty meters for adjacent units that are tied in to the attack sector. Once a deep break-in has been accomplished, the army-level artillery units will be pulled back. The trench divisions do not participate in the attack, except for their artillery, which will temporarily remain forward. The trench divisions will be pulled back after they are relieved in the line by the attack divisions, where they will rest, reconstitute, and retrain. Once the newly gained forward positions have been reinforced, the trench divisions will then pass through the attack divisions that are withdrawing from a strong enemy and occupy the new positions. The attack divisions thus become available again to form the OHL reserve, after receiving replacements, reconstituting, and retraining.

Each of the approximately four limited German attacks should accomplish the following:

a. Each attack will achieve the almost complete destruction of an estimated three enemy trench divisions.
b. The enemy will be forced to deploy at least five divisions in order to defend against each attack.
c. The enemy also will be forced to move up five more divisions to reestablish the depth of his defense and support the necessary relief actions in his lines.
d. The enemy's other assets (artillery, ammunition, engineers, armored vehicles, aviation, etc.) held in reserve also will be weakened.
e. Our own attacking forces will be conserved through the timely withdrawal into the new and reinforced attack positions, or back into the initial attack positions.
f. In the process we will gain the time necessary for the reconstitution and training of the old trench divisions.
g. The initially committed attack divisions can then be returned to the OHL reserve.

As a result of these four limited attacks, which should be conducted as geographically far apart as possible, I estimate that approximately forty enemy divisions they currently have in reserve will be forced to deploy, and twelve enemy trench divisions will be destroyed.

For these four attacks we will need to draw from the OHL reserve five divisions each, for a total of twenty divisions. Those units, however, will be returned later to the OHL reserve. Our attacks must be sequenced rapidly, one after another. The length of the pauses will be dictated only by the army-level artillery, which will have to be shifted to new positions to support each new attack. The additional artillery must be able to occupy firing positions that have been completely prepared, surveyed in, stocked with ammunition, and with pre-developed firing plans for the new attack. Given the exceptional level of training of our leaders, such preparations should not be difficult at all.

3. Location of the Main Operational Attack

Only after our four limited attacks have thoroughly disrupted the enemy and weakened his reserves can our large-scale operational attack be launched on a broad front. The objective of that attack will be a penetration of the enemy's front lines in the attack sectors and the consequent tactical and operational breakthroughs. This large-scale attack should be planned and prepared at different locations along the Western Front, which will give us the option to exploit the conditions that result from our development of the situation. The feasibility of a tangible operational success will be the final factor in determining the location of the attack. The width of the attack sector depends on the number of available divisions. Right from the start a strong reserve must be formed to conduct the operational breakthrough after the tactical breakthrough is achieved. It is important to make the decision on the location of the operational attack in such a timely manner that it can be launched as soon as possible after the completion of the four limited attacks.

My recommendations were not accepted. As I found out later, they were assessed as not being far-reaching enough. Looking back even now I am still convinced that my recommended course of action would have been more likely to have led to a victory than the decision ultimately made by OHL. In the end, however, it was my self-evident duty to support OHL's decision with all of my powers.

General Ludendorff apparently had decided from the start to open the offensive campaign with a major attack. Based on that and the mission I was given, I then recommended an attack in the vicinity of Lens, with the objective of disrupting the British line, destroying their northern sector, and then taking the strongly reinforced enemy defensive positions in the vicinity of Arras from the west—that is, from the rear. After that the offensive would continue in the direction of Amiens. I warned specifically against a frontal attack in the direction of Arras, which according to aerial photography had a front orientated toward the east, and with its flanks facing to the north and south. It was a virtual fortress. Despite this warning, the Seventeenth Army was scheduled to follow-up the Great Battle of France[37] with a frontal attack toward Arras on both sides of the Scarpe River. This attack ultimately failed with heavy losses.[38]

I also warned against attacking across the old Somme battlefield. Hardly anyone knew this terrain as well as I did. It consisted largely of shell crater fields that were almost impossible to get across. I had, after all, been the chief of staff of the field army that fought the Battle of the Somme from July 1916 to April

1917. The time required to achieve a tactical breakthrough in this kind of terrain would be excessive, owing to the difficulties of troop transportation and ammunition resupply. The enemy reserves, therefore, would have more time to rush from both the north and the south in an effort to close the penetration gap.

General Ludendorff kept his decision for the attack on very close hold for the longest time. At the end of February 1918 I was ordered to report to the headquarters of the Eighteenth Army for a briefing scheduled by Ludendorff. There I learned that OHL intended to attack across the Somme battlefield as early as the end of March. It was my impression that Ludendorff selected the attack sector between Cambrai and La Fère mostly because he believed that the enemy front was weak there. At that point, however, I was no longer involved in the preparation for the Great Battle of France.[39]

When I later saw well after the fact OHL's directives for the Great Battle of France, I formed the following assessment:

1. The commitment of two army groups (Crown Prince Rupprecht and German Crown Prince) created serious problems in the orders process during the battle, despite OHL maintaining overall control. In my opinion, one commander should have been the head of the attack force. Based on a clear mission given to him he would issue his directives to the subordinate attacking field armies, both for the preparation and the execution phases. It would have been best if OHL had designated a specifically selected general officer with a sufficient staff as the overall attack commander. That commander should have received all the necessary means for the attack, to include the necessary reserves for the strategic breakthrough.[40]
2. Right from the beginning all three armies involved in the attack should have been given attack objectives reaching deep into the enemy's territory. Instead, the Eighteenth Army only had an objective of the Somme south of Péronne and the Crozat Canal. In the event that they made good progress, they also were to seize the crossing points across those waterways.
3. Where and in what direction the operational breakthrough was to be conducted depended on where and if the tactical breakthrough succeeded initially. At that location—only apparent in the course of the attack—the operational breakthrough was to be directed.

   In my opinion, it was a poor decision to designate the objective of the operational breakthrough as the direction toward Boulogne right from the start of the offensive. That plan—in comparison to the tactical attack mission—resulted in the Seventeenth Army being over-strength, which led in turn to an unnecessary compression of that army in a restricted space. The troops staged there in too large numbers should have been under the control of the commander of the reserve force.

4. There was no designated leaders' reserve for the execution of the operational breakthrough. Its absence was a decisive handicap when the strong Seventeenth Army got bogged down and failed to achieve its tactical breakthrough.

The battle plan, therefore, had to be changed in the middle of the fight, and the main effort of the attack shifted in the direction of Amiens. That, however, could only have been accomplished at the absolutely required speed by committing an untapped leaders' reserve, which should have been fed directly on to the actual breakthrough point that the constantly advancing Eighteenth Army achieved, despite its initially limited attack objective.[41] As a stopgap measure instead, the uncommitted or partially committed divisions of the Second and Seventeenth Armies had to be shifted toward the breakthrough sector. Precious time was lost, which gave the enemy an advantage. An opportunity was lost because from the beginning, just like at the Marne in 1914, the required depth for operational maneuver was lacking. If it had been possible to gain control of the line of the Somme and the area south of Amiens, it then would have been possible to destroy all of the enemy's formations north of the Somme.[42] The failure to achieve a complete victory was not the fault of the troops, but of the senior-level leadership.

On 30 March 1918 OHL designated as a new attack sector the area between Armentières and La Bassée. A planned attack had already been prepared there by the Sixth Army.[43] I knew this attack sector and its tactical conditions quite well from my experience there in 1914 and 1917. I knew that sector had been strongly reinforced by the enemy. The many built-up areas created strong points of resistance for the defense and were excellent positions for machine guns. The road network in the attack sector ran largely contrary to the attack direction. The larger roads ran mostly to our positions, and the towns and built-up areas along those roads enfiladed our attack direction. The attack sector south of the line Armentières–Bailleul–Hazebrouck was very flat, and because of its extensive built-up areas offered only limited observation options for our artillery. Only the areas north of the main line of the attack were hilly and in some parts mountainous.[44] Mont Kemmel northeast of Bailleul dominated the terrain on all sides. Running through the very flat terrain along the rivers Lys and Lawe were main channels of the drainage system during peacetime, but by 1918 the drainage system had been destroyed. The shallow subsurface of the ground in the flats was an impenetrable clay layer. Thus, that ground was often very marshy until far into the spring, which severely restricted the forward movement of

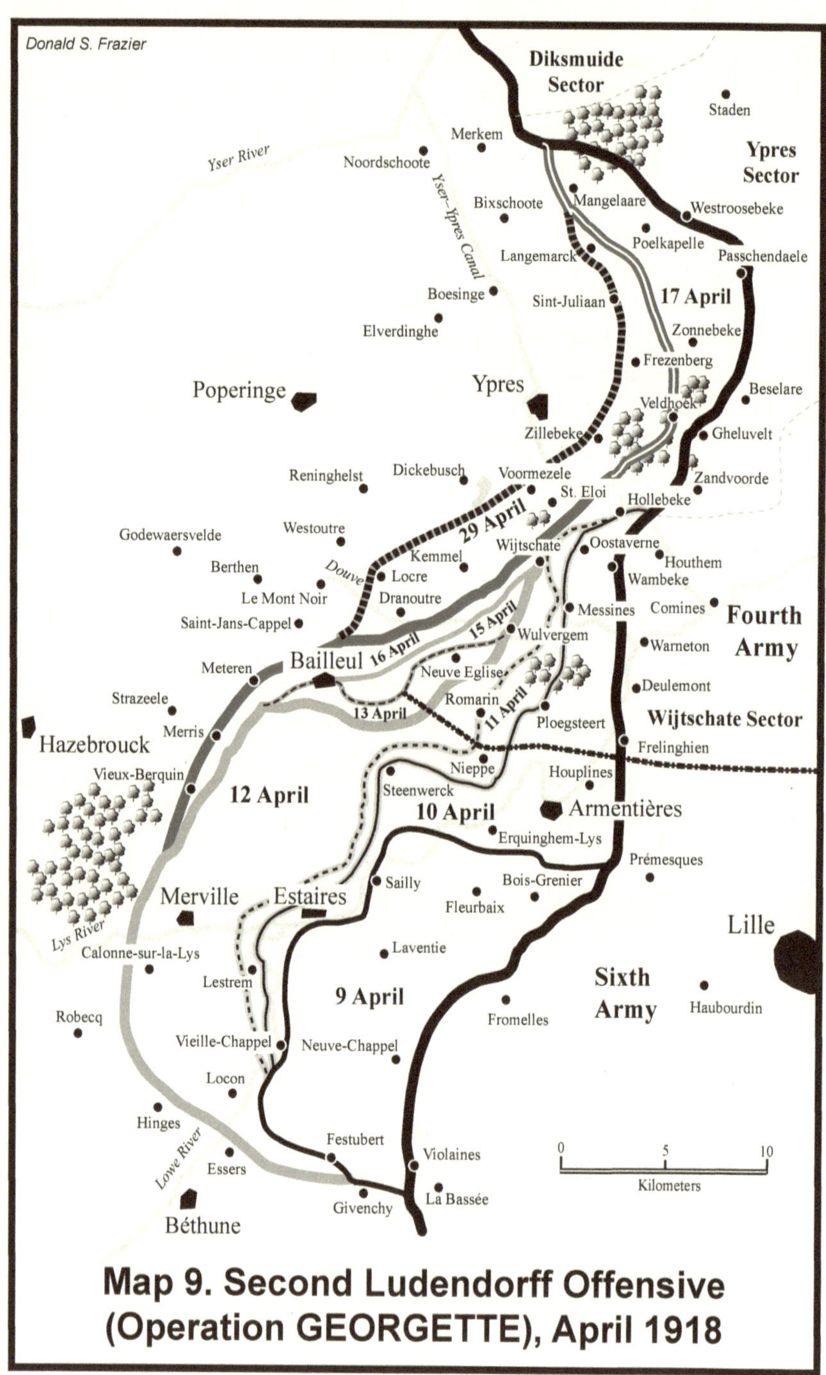

Map 9. Second Ludendorff Offensive (Operation GEORGETTE), April 1918

the attack artillery following the infantry, as well as the ammunition resupply. Generally, the ground did not dry out until the end of May. It was, therefore, very risky to attempt a breakthrough attack in such terrain at the beginning of April. In the event, the terrain difficulties slowed down the attack significantly, although there had been unusually dry weather at the beginning of April 1918. Even so, the artillery could not follow the infantry rapidly enough through marshy crater fields.

The Sixth Army was scheduled to attack out of its frontline positions from La Bassée to its northern wing, which then reached to Houplines. The Fourth Army headquarters recommended widening the attack front to include the southern wing of the Fourth Army, and also indicated our capability to pull all available forces from our front and consolidate them on our southern wing.[45] But we also requested fresh divisions, artillery with adequate ammunition, and other combat assets. OHL concurred with our recommendation. Thus, we were delighted to be participating in the Sixth Army's attack, in whose sector, however, the main effort remained. The Fourth Army's mission was only to support the advance of the Sixth Army by attacking in parallel and screening the Sixth Army's right flank during the advance. I am describing this attack in more detail, as during the course of the action the main effort shifted progressively to the Fourth Army's sector.

The Fourth Army assumed the highest possible level of risk by consolidating its attack forces on its southern wing. We were rather confident, though, that the enemy across from the front sections that were not involved in the attack would also withdraw all their available forces to repulse the attack. Thus, we concluded that the enemy would pose no serious threat to our thin defensive lines.

The overall control of the attack was in the hands of the Army Group Crown Prince Rupprecht, which remained headquartered at Mons. OHL reinforced the army group primarily with trench divisions and only very few combat divisions. In my opinion an operational staff from the army group (including the commanding general, chief of staff, and supporting General Staff officers) should have been much farther forward in order to coordinate between the Fourth Army and the Sixth Army via daily personal briefings with the commanding generals. The Sixth Army's headquarters remained in Tournai. The Fourth Army, in the meantime, shifted its headquarters from Tielt to Roubaix. We also established a forward command post for the attack. On 3 April 1918 Army Group Crown Prince Rupprecht received the following directives from OHL:

> The Sixth Army attack initially will reach the general line Godewaersvelde–Hazebrouck–Béthune.

> The Fourth Army follows the continued attack of the Sixth Army by advancing in the general direction Messines–Wulvergem.

Initially only one field artillery regiment had been attached to the Fourth Army as reinforcement. The existing army boundaries remained in effect. A boundary between the advances of the Fourth and Sixth Armies was not designated initially, even though I urgently requested such. The Sixth Army was to bypass Armentières with its right wing. Shortly before the attack the town was to be cut off and contaminated with Yellow Cross artillery fire.[46] The effect of Yellow Cross gas lasted about twenty-four hours. The first attack objectives for the Sixth Army's right wing were the seizure of the enemy positions in the Lys River bend from Houplines to Sailly-sur-la-Lys, and the opening of the crossing site across the Lys. The Sixth Army's attack was scheduled to start on 9 April.

On 10 April the Fourth Army's strong left wing was scheduled to follow the attack of the Sixth Army from the line Hollebeke–Frelinghien.[47] The attack front of the Fourth Army consisted of the XVIII Reserve Corps on the right and the X Reserve Corps on the left. The latter had only one of its trench divisions in the forward lines.[48] Another trench division and a newly assigned division were held initially in reserve. The X Reserve Corps' trench division had to make all the preparations for crossing the Lys between Deûlémont and Frelinghien. The evening before the attack it was tasked to establish bridgeheads on the western bank of the Lys. Also on the night before the attack the leftmost of the two attack divisions was to cross the Lys with large elements and occupy the western bank of the river. The Douve River, running from Wulvergem to Warneton, was designated the boundary between the two corps.

The designated attack objective for the XVIII Reserve Corps was Messines,[49] and for the X Reserve Corps the enemy batteries at and west of the Messines–Ploegsteert–Armentières road. During oral briefings at the Fourth Army headquarters we concluded that it would be sufficient to reach the line Sint-Eloi–Wijtschate–Kemmel and the Ypres–Poperinge road. That would give us fire observation on Ypres. In support of the Fourth Army's attack, we were scheduled to receive eleven batteries of heavy artillery from the Sixth Army after they made their initial break-in. Since the Sixth Army was to begin its attack on 9 April and the Fourth Army not until 10 April, we made all the necessary preparations to commit this additional firepower to the start of our attack that day.[50] As a precaution, the Fourth Army headquarters ordered that both of our attack corps should be ready to attack on 9 April, in the event that any great initial successes by the Sixth Army might also collapse the enemy in front of the Fourth Army. Right from the start of the preparations plentiful rations, ammunition, and other combat assets were assembled behind the Fourth Army's front.

On 9 April at 0415 hours the Sixth Army started its artillery preparation in very heavy fog. At 0815 hours the assault force broke into the enemy's forwardmost lines. By 1000 hours the attack force had already crossed the enemy's third line of defense. The Fourth Army, meanwhile, supported the Sixth Army with all its own organic artillery and silenced the enemy artillery in front of the Sixth Army's right wing. By the evening of 9 April the Sixth Army had reached the line indicated on Map 9. During the infantry's rapid advance, however, only small artillery elements could follow in support because of the cratered and muddy ground.

Owing to the Sixth Army's good initial progress, Army Group Crown Prince Rupprecht authorized the Fourth Army to attack on 10 April. If our advance went well, we were promised two reinforcing divisions by that afternoon. On 10 April the Fourth and Sixth Armies attacked simultaneously. The right wing of the Sixth Army continued attacking in the direction of Nieppe, bypassing Armentières, which was still in enemy hands. In the process, the Sixth Army maintained contact with the left flank of the Fourth Army.

All of the Fourth Army's attack directives had already been passed down to the lowest leadership echelons. Special orders regulated the start of the artillery preparation, designating targets and coordinating the timing and support for the infantry assault. The assault of both attacking corps was scheduled for 0515 hours. The conduct of the entire attack was based on a time table starting from that point in time.

The line reached by the Fourth and Sixth Armies on 10 April is shown on Map 9. Armentières, still occupied by the enemy, was enveloped from all sides. The attack beyond the 10 April line depended on the forward displacement of the artillery. But those movements in both army sectors were impeded greatly by the extensive crater fields and the poor, wet advance routes. Army Group Crown Prince Rupprecht assigned an additional division to the Fourth Army for the reinforcement of the X Reserve Corps and ordered the Sixth Army to shift additional artillery assets to the Fourth Army.

At the Fourth Army headquarters we assumed that the enemy north of the Yser Canal would attempt to evade any further German successes. Therefore, we ordered the commander of Group Ypres (the commanding general of the Guards Corps) to consolidate all available forces for an attack across the Yser Canal to the north of Boezinge. We previously had planned and prepared such an attack, which was designed to cut off the enemy's general withdrawal route west toward Poperinge.

During 10 April OHL ordered the left wing of the X Reserve Corps to shift its direction of attack toward Bailleul. OHL also attached to the X Reserve Corps an army-level field artillery regiment that was then moving up. General Ludendorff issued guidance directly to me to gain control of the Armentières–Bailleul road by the end of that day. That road, however, was in the Sixth Army's area of operations. I then communicated directly with the chief of staff of the Sixth Army, who shifted his army's right wing toward Bailleul. Thus, the Sixth Army would try to cut off Armentières and force it to surrender without attacking the town directly. I emphasized to him that it was the Sixth Army's job to mop up quickly the two towns of Houplines and Armentières that were still held by the enemy. Otherwise, the advance of the Fourth Army's left wing would come under enemy flanking fire. I also requested that Army Group Crown Prince Rupprecht establish a new and clearly delineated boundary between the Fourth and Sixth Armies. Initially, however, nothing happened.

During the next few days General Ludendorff continued to interject himself, bypassing Army Group Crown Prince Rupprecht and issuing orders directly to the Sixth Army. I had the impression that such interference was almost always based on the spot reports of intelligence officers sent out by OHL. Naturally, it was impossible for them to have a picture of the complete situation. Although Ludendorff undoubtedly only wanted the best degree of control for the attack, his interference and issuing direct orders in fact made the situation more difficult for Army Group Crown Prince Rupprecht and especially for the Fourth and Sixth Armies. When OHL designated Bailleul as an objective for the Fourth Army and Army Group Crown Prince Rupprecht designated it an objective for the right wing of the Sixth Army, the inevitable friction resulted. On 10 April both armies received boundaries and clear attack objectives from Army Group Crown Prince Rupprecht, and thus acted in accordance with those clear directives.

It would have been better to trust the leadership of both armies and to leave them the full responsibility for the conduct of the attack. Both army headquarters were in constant communications with the front lines and had much better situational awareness of the fight than did OHL. Both army headquarters never lost track of the overall situation and thus were much better capable than OHL of reacting with detailed orders to any developing irregularities, which mostly resulted from the difficult terrain and the varying intensity of the enemy's resistance. General Ludendorff always directed his interference at the chiefs of staff of the armies. For the most part, however, Ludendorff apparently trusted me inherently. During my conversations with him he almost always concurred with my well thought-out but contrary assessment, which I based on the facts.

It was different with the younger army chiefs of staff, who despite their competence did not yet possess Ludendorff's complete trust. The often gruff tone that Ludendorff used with those chiefs made them angry and was completely uncalled for. The chief of staff of Sixth Army, Bavarian Lieutenant Colonel von

Lenz, complained bitterly to me at the time about Ludendorff, who in almost every telephone conversation addressed him in such a sharp manner that he considered asking to be relieved. As Lenz was a very capable chief of staff and a respected soldier who I regarded highly, I gave him the advice to use the same tone toward Ludendorff as I used successfully in similar earlier situations. Lenz must have followed my advice very energetically, but in his blunt Bavarian way. Immediately following a subsequent telephone conversation with Lenz, Ludendorff called me and told me that he thought Lenz had lost his nerve because he had yelled at him during the conversation in such a manner that he should be removed. I was able to calm Ludendorff down quickly by telling him that I had given Lenz the advice to follow my example and to reciprocate in kind. Ludendorff in his good soldierly manner must have accepted that he had gone too far with Lenz, and with that the incident was completely forgotten.

The best support that the Fourth Army could give to the Sixth Army was, in my opinion, to attack straight on into our attack sector with the entire X Reserve Corps and the southern half of the XVIII Reserve Corps, gaining as much ground as possible with our strong left wing. That would force the Armentières garrison to capitulate eventually. With that in mind I coordinated with our two attacking corps, after consulting with my commanding general, who had the same thoughts.

The Fourth Army order of 11 April instructed all attacking forces to maintain close contact with the enemy, especially at night, so that he would not have sufficient time to pull forward any of his reserve forces. The XVIII Reserve Corps was ordered to exert strong pressure with its left wing in the direction of Wulvergem. The X Reserve Corps was ordered to follow closely along the whole front, maintaining the main effort on the left wing and establishing a link with the right wing of the Sixth Army, which was advancing via Nieppe toward Bailleul. The orders required rapid action until at least the capture of the enemy batteries directly to our front. We had to prevent any escape by the enemy from Armentières. In case the enemy in the north attempted to evade, Group Ypres already had orders to pursue forward in full force. Behind the two flanks of Group Ypres we had positioned our heavy flat-trajectory batteries. Those firing units had orders and detailed fire plans to engage the enemy withdrawing via Ypres toward Poperinge.

On 11 April the XVIII Reserve Corps advanced a little farther with its right wing, reaching to within some eight hundred meters of Wijtschate, where it then ran into stubborn resistance. South of Wijtschate the enemy attempted four deliberate counterattacks with strong forces, all of which failed. The X Reserve Corps was attacked by the enemy repeatedly but unsuccessfully on the evening of 10 April in the vicinity of Ploegsteert. From there and farther to the north the enemy resistance remained rather stubborn on 11 April. During the course of that day the X Reserve Corps did succeed in crossing the forest north of Ploegsteert, seizing Nieppe, and thus cutting off the retreat route of the Armentières garrison. That same day the X Reserve Corps also was ordered to shift its main effort past the west of Neuve-Eglise,[51] toward Mont Kemmel, shown on the maps as Hill 156. That provided the X Reserve Corps with flank security, as the right wing of the Sixth Army had stormed Armentières, taking three thousand prisoners and capturing forty-six guns, and still had managed to advance past Steenwerck. Army Group Crown Prince Rupprecht designated the Armentières–Bailleul road as the Sixth Army's right boundary.[52] Based on the situation that day, the X Reserve Corps was ordered to exploit its successes by cutting off the enemy north of Nieppe.

Group Ypres reported that there was yet no observable weakening of the enemy force opposing them, and they therefore requested some additional divisions for the conduct of their attack via Bikschote toward Poperinge. Such an attack could have great operational effect if it reached the western bank of the canal quickly. That, however, required Group Ypres to be reinforced strongly with additional divisions and artillery. The Fourth Army headquarters passed the Group Ypres request up to the headquarters of Army Group Crown Prince Rupprecht. We concurred with the conditional requirement for a sufficient number of divisions to remain constantly available to relieve worn-out units in the main attack sectors of both the Fourth and Sixth Armies. With the concurrence of OHL, Army Group Crown Prince Rupprecht provided Group Ypres with two additional divisions for the attack. The Fourth Army headquarters immediately made all the necessary preparations to ensure the success of Group Ypres's attack.

The Fourth Army attack order for 12 April emphasized that the line Wijtschate–Wulvergem–Nieuwkerke must be reached. From that line we would then launch the unified attack against the very dominating Mont Kemmel. During the course of the day the XVIII Reserve Corps successfully pushed its front line close to Wijtschate. The X Reserve Corps pushed elements of the opposing enemy force back toward the northwest. This facilitated the advance of the Sixth Army's right wing. The middle and the left wing of the Sixth Army also made progress.

Based on the situation on 13 April, the Fourth Army ordered the XVIII Reserve Corps to eliminate the enemy flanking the X Reserve Corps by concentrating fires on to the hills in the vicinity of Wulvergem and to seize Wijtschate and Wulvergem. The X Reserve Corps was ordered to seize the ridgeline from Nieuwkerke west in the direction of Bailleul. The Sixth Army also attacked with its right wing, with orders to seize the hills east of Bailleul.

To make the Group Ypres attack as strong as possible, we withdrew from Group Nord without replacement one Landwehr Regiment with two batteries, which took over the northern sector of Group Dijksmuide. The 6th Bavarian Reserve Division that was positioned there up to that point became the reserve of Group Ypres, which had to extend its southern wing to include Zandvoorde. Thus, all of the Fourth Army sectors not involved in the attack were weakened to the maximum in order to be as strong as possible in the attack sector.

On 13 April at 0945 hours OHL ordered Army Group Crown Prince Rupprecht to integrate the newly assigned Guards Reserve Corps and IX Army Corps into the attack sector of the Sixth Army, which had grown rather wide by that point.[53] Army Group Crown Prince Rupprecht complied with OHL's directive at approximately 1400 hours. That was accomplished in such a manner that the two divisions fighting on the right flank of the Sixth Army came under Fourth Army operational control. The Fourth Army was then directed to give the control of that attack to the X Reserve Corps. Only after the attack succeeded was the Guards Reserve Corps to assume command of those two new divisions.

In the meantime, the fighting continued along the Fourth Army's former left wing. Unfortunately, the situation there deteriorated. The left wing of the X Reserve Corps started its attack at 0700 hours, after it learned that the adjacent unit on its left also would attack at that time. The right wing of the X Reserve Corps attack got to within three hundred meters of Nieuwkerke, while the corps' center stormed the hills west of the town. The corps' left wing, however, came under strong flanking fire, because the right wing of the Sixth Army had been conducting relief operations and did not attack at all. As a consequence, the left wing of the Fourth Army was forced to retreat to its initial attack positions in the face of a strong enemy attack. The Fourth Army's decision that the X Reserve Corps would be committed to the Sixth Army's attack planned for the afternoon of 13 April was the logical course of action. The result was a successful combined attack by the inner wings of both armies.

By the evening of 13 April the situation stood as follows: the XVIII Reserve Corps had been able to bring forward their artillery through the crater fields only under great difficulties; the X Reserve Corps had penetrated the enemy position east of Nieuwkerke, destroying it partially and seizing Nieuwkerke and the ridgeline up to one kilometer west of Nieuwkerke. On the Fourth Army' left flank the follow-on troops of the Sixth Army were still lagging behind. However, the newly deployed Alpenkorps reportedly had entered Bailleul. The follow-on echelon of the Sixth Army also appeared to have had made progress.

At 2240 hours Army Group Crown Prince Rupprecht ordered the continuation of the attack. The Fourth Army was ordered to continue putting the main effort on its left wing in order to gain a secure footing on the ridgeline northeast of Bailleul. We also were to continue to make plans and preparations for an attack on the line Wijtschate–Kemmel. The Sixth Army was to shift its main effort on to its right wing, seize the hills north of Méteren and the vicinity of Strazeele as rapidly as possible, and then gain ground in the direction of Godewaersvelde–Hazebrouck. The Fourth Army headquarters issued the orders for 14 April accordingly. The main effort remained as before on the army's left army wing, whose advance would be supported by all other forces on the attacking front. Based on the actions of 13 April, the Fourth Army headquarters issued detailed directives for liaison with the staffs of the adjacent units.

Forward of the left half of our attacking front, the enemy had reinforced his infantry positions, positioned in depth. As new enemy artillery also was identified, we assessed that the enemy was determined to hold those positions at all costs. The troops of the X Reserve Corps had attacked well into the night of 13 April. Their attacks on 14 April, therefore, were initially only prepared through reconnaissance and the forward repositioning of the artillery. On 14 April the Sixth Army as well had only made preparations to continue the attack. At 1320 hours Army Group Crown Prince Rupprecht ordered the Fourth Army to advance as rapidly as possible against the ridgeline northeast of Bailleul and cut off Bailleul from the north and east. The Sixth Army was ordered to cut off Bailleul from south and west, bypassing Bailleul on the west and continuing in the direction of Berthen. The boundary between the Fourth and Sixth Armies was designated tentatively as the line of the creek running from Bailleul to Berthen. The headquarters of the Guards Reserve Corps took control of the divisions detached from the right wing of the Sixth Army. Army Group Crown Prince Rupprecht also ordered the Fourth Army to attack in the Group Ypres sector, and to report the anticipated time of this attack. Army Group Crown Prince Rupprecht attached another infantry division to the Fourth Army, plus two heavy howitzer battalions, two trench mortar battalions, and a flamethrower company.

The very heavy enemy resistance caused the 14 April deliberate attack to abort. The Fourth Army headquarters then ordered that the attack was not to resume until 15 April. The Sixth Army headquarters also decided not to conduct its planned attack on the Méteren–Strazeele ridgeline until 15 April, and issued orders accordingly. It designated 1100 hours on 15 April as the start time. All the subordinate corps of the Sixth Army considered that too early because the necessary artillery ammunition could not be brought forward by that time. The Sixth Army therefore delayed the start of their attack until the early morning of 17 April.

During a telephone conversation with General von Kuhl at Army Group Crown Prince Rupprecht, he told me that in his opinion the Sixth Army offensive had bogged down because their troops were exhausted and needed recovery time. I was very opposed to the Sixth Army decision, and I recommended a strong continuation of the attack. I knew well that the attacks were very difficult, but if we paused attacking for several days on a broad front it would give the enemy time to consolidate his very sketchy defenses and to move his reserves up. Naturally we had to move our own artillery with sufficient ammunition forward to continue the attack against a stubborn enemy. We then had to consolidate our firepower against the designated breakthrough point, to penetrate the enemy and destroy him. I considered it the wrong course of action for the situation to halt our attack across a broad front for more than two days.

On 15 April the XVIII Reserve Corps seized the town of Wulvergem and the enemy positions northeast of the town, and then advanced across the line Wulvergem–Wijtschate. To the left, the right wing of the X Reserve Corps followed this attack and advanced as far as the XVIII Reserve Corps. On the afternoon of 15 April the remaining elements of the X Reserve Corps resumed that attack and pushed the enemy back. That afternoon I myself rushed forward in order to reconnoiter the attack options for the seizure of Mont Kemmel.

In the meantime, Army Group Crown Prince Rupprecht received a telegram in the early morning hours of 14 April, personally composed by General Ludendorff and signed by Field Marshal von Hindenburg:

> Yesterday the Fourth Army with superb leadership and exemplary attack spirit seized the hills of Nieuwkerke. I expect the Sixth Army with its well-commanded corps to gain ground north of the Lys, with the XIX Army Corps initially making the main effort.
> /Signed/
> von Hindenburg.

In the event, the Sixth Army did not achieve those objectives on 14 and 15 April. Thus, when I returned to my own command post I was even more surprised to learn from General von Kuhl that General Ludendorff had concurred with the recommendation that the Sixth Army not continue to attack until 17 April.

On 15 April the commanding general of the Fourth Army held a series of briefings with the commanders of Group Ypres and the attack divisions assigned to this group. As a consequence, all of the leaders had full confidence in the attack in the direction of Bikschote. The overall attacking strength, however, was reduced. The 6th Bavarian Reserve Division, for example, had company-size units with a combat strength of only fifty men.

During a telephone conversation with General Ludendorff, he told me that the attack at Bikschote timed simultaneously with the attack near Bailleul would hardly achieve the breakthrough, but it could still result in a significant tactical success. I told him that I thought the reduction of the Ypres salient would in itself be a desirable result.

During a telephone conversation on the evening of 15 April, I again asked the chief of staff of Army Group Crown Prince Rupprecht to resolve the boundary between the Fourth and Sixth Armies. Question about the location of the boundary resulted from the establishment of the newly integrated Guards Reserve Corps. After the boundary question was resolved, the Fourth Army headquarters on 15 April issued a set of warning orders to our subordinate units. It was not until that night, after the reports from the front lines had trickled in piece by piece, that we could issue a comprehensive army order. The subordinate corps received the following orders for 16 April:

> The XVIII Reserve Corps will seize the enemy positions in the vicinity of Wijtschate.
>
> The X Reserve Corps will advance its artillery rapidly in its center and on its left wing to exploit the favorable situation and advance into the Douve Valley.
>
> The Guards Reserve Corps will assume control of its own troops tonight, after coordination with the X Reserve Corps. The Guards Reserve Corps will then advance its guns rapidly to mass a strong as possible artillery force that can cover the high ground of Mont Noir.[54] Depending on the development of the situation, the corps will gain ground in the direction of Mont Noir. Bailleul will be encircled from the north, east, and south. The corps' rear boundary will run from the creek west of Bailleul to the western edge of Steenwerck.

The Fourth Army headquarters marked all the sector boundaries on the maps attached to the orders to eliminate any doubts.

The specific tasks assigned to all three of the attacking corps were as follows:

> The XVIII Reserve Corps will hold in place on the objective and conduct reconnaissance in preparation for the continuation of the attack. The key element of information is the line where the enemy establishes his main defensive position after repositioning his artillery and echeloning his infantry in depth. The corps also will mass strong artillery fire against the canal crossing sites north and south of Ypres.
>
> a. The X Reserve Corps will be prepared to attack with its left wing along the Douve toward the high ground between Kemmel village and

> Mont Noir. The corps also will tie down the enemy with strong pressure against Loker and Mont Kemmel.
>
> b. The Guards Reserve Corps will attack against the line Mont Noir–Berthen. The left boundary will temporarily remain the creek line between Bailleul and Berthen. Bailleul will be encircled.
>
> The Sixth Army intends to attack on 17 or 18 April with its right wing across the general line Méteren–Strazeele and seize the high ground north of that line. The left wing of the Fourth Army will attack simultaneously from the line reached the previous day. All preparations must be made on this basis.

On the morning of 16 April General von Kuhl and I attended briefings at the Guards Reserve Corps, the X Reserve Corps, and the XVIII Reserve Corps. I first described the missions of the three attacking corps, and then gave my assessment of how the enemy likely would react to the German advance. Battle experience let us assume that the enemy would defend every inch of ground stubbornly, and thus a further advance of the German lines most certainly would cost us a lot of blood. I also forecast that the enemy in front of the Fourth Army would not voluntarily give up Mont Kemmel. If the attack of Group Ypres in the vicinity of Bikschote turned into a significant success, the enemy inevitably would tie his defensive line to Mont Kemmel. As we knew from aerial reconnaissance, he had two improved rearward positions along the line Kemmel–east of Zillebeke–Frezenberg–Sint-Juliaan–Langemark–west of Ypres–Elverdinge–Loos Canal. General von Kuhl recommended the immediate seizure of the line from Mont Kemmel to the high ground north of Mont Noir. I did not concur fully because our combat strengths had diminished significantly. (Regimental strengths now stood between six hundred and one thousand men).[55] It was obvious, however, that the immediate follow-on thrust would be conducted against a failing enemy. Thus, I requested an additional replacement division for the Guards Reserve Corps, which General von Kuhl took under consideration.

The morning of the attack, the XVIII Reserve Corps seized the village of Wijtschate and the hills in the direction of Wulvergem. The four hundred prisoners captured during this fight belonged to four different British divisions. In front of the X Reserve Corps the enemy withdrew across the Douve. The Guards Reserve Corps occupied Bailleul, which the enemy had abandoned voluntarily. A new division arrived in our sector and we positioned it behind the Fourth Army's left wing. The Sixth Army also made progress with its left wing. Group Ypres continued the preparation for its attack, which was scheduled tentatively for 20 April.

In the evening of 16 April we detected that the enemy was faltering between

Hollebeke and Poelkapelle. Our troops immediately pushed forward and maintained close contact with the enemy. In the vicinity of Bikschote the enemy stood fast, and the attack advanced initially as planned. Group Ypres reported that, based on the situation, it would attack on 17 April at 0900 hours, following a thirty-minute artillery barrage. That evening the intelligence service detected for the first time French listening posts in front of the Fourth Army. That meant the French were arriving to support the British.

Army Group Crown Prince Rupprecht informed us that behind the inner boundary of the Fourth and Sixth Armies three fresh divisions had been deployed as army group reserve, and another two divisions as OHL reserve. That evening the Sixth Army also reported after the enemy had withdrawn from Bailleul that its right wing corps had broken through the enemy and advanced past Méteren. On 17 April the corps tied in on the left would also attack. That day the Fourth Army headquarters issued the following orders:

> Group Ypres will cross the canal north of Boezinge as soon as possible. The XVIII Reserve Corps will consolidate the fires of its long-range guns toward the area of Ypres, but will continue the attack only if the situation is favorable. The X Reserve Corps will advance swiftly with its right toward Mont Kemmel, and continue the attack with its left. The Guards Reserve Corps will pull its reserves up closely and attack along the entire front line. The X Reserve Corps and Guards Reserve Corps attacks will start at 1000 hours on 17 April.

Group Ypres's reinforcement divisions had not arrived yet, so it could only attack with its trench divisions—the 6th Bavarian Reserve Division and the 1st Landwehr Division, reinforced with a naval infantry regiment. The attack was only a limited success. During the attack and the follow-on consolidation, the frontline trace of Group Ypres reached approximately the line north of Langemark–west of Zonnebeke–vicinity of Veldhoek–Castle Hollebeke. The enemy reestablished their positions in front of that line.

After consolidating its artillery in the vicinity of Ypres, the XVIII Reserve Corps was only able to advance its infantry lines in limited spots. The X Reserve Corps advanced its positions slightly along the southwestern slope of Mont Kemmel, and farther west at Douve River. The Guards Reserve Corps only made minor progress with its very depleted divisions. The enemy resistance in front of the X Reserve and the Guards Reserve Corps was very strong and supported by machine guns. The Fourth Army headquarters, therefore, decided to bring the attack to a temporary halt in a controlled manner. Stronger artillery support would be needed to resume the attack.

After telephone conversations with the chiefs of staff of the corps, I briefed the commanding general. Then I transmitted the Fourth Army's assessment of the situation to General von Kuhl at Army Group Crown Prince Rupprecht. I explained that the attack against the Mont Kemmel–Mont Noir line had not penetrated. Five battle weary divisions would have to be relieved by fresh divisions in order to resume the attack and reach the operational objective. Until that happened, any resumption of an operational-level attack would fail. Until the spent divisions were relieved, we would be able to conduct only local attacks to keep the enemy off balance.

The situation at Group Ypres was different. The new divisions had not been deployed because the enemy had managed to take evasive action by withdrawing. Despite stubborn enemy resistance and the predictable difficulty of pushing our artillery forward through the crater fields, we could resume the attack with the available forces, and with a reasonable probability of success. The Fourth Army headquarters intended to maintain an offensive posture along the entire attack front.

General von Kuhl told me that the Sixth Army also was demanding the relief of its depleted divisions. After reviewing the entire situation and consulting with OHL, the army group would issue further orders. There was no consideration of abandoning the unified operational attack, only its postponement. Late that evening I had a similar telephone conversation with General Ludendorff. He concurred with our intent to continue the attack of Group Ypres. If that effort did not achieve success, the available relief divisions for the group would be committed at another location.

The Sixth Army faced the following situation by 17 April: In the evening of 16 April the enemy had attacked Méteren several times in vain. Farther south the enemy appeared to have strengthened himself substantially, mainly with artillery. All of the Sixth Army's attacks in that sector had met with strong enemy resistance, primarily from machine guns. The attacks gained very little ground. French forces had been identified without any doubt to the front of the Sixth Army's attack.

In the evening of 17 April the Fourth Army headquarters ordered Group Ypres to continue the attack. The XVIII Reserve Corps attack was halted temporarily. The X Reserve and Guards Reserve Corps were ordered to conduct local attacks against key points in their sectors. The Sixth Army headquarters also ordered the continuation of their attack, but only after the completion of the preparations.

During the night of 17–18 April Army Group Crown Prince Rupprecht reported that they were considering shifting the main operational attack to another sector of the Western Front. The Fourth Army, therefore, was warned that a reduction of Group Ypres's forces along its front lines might be required. This was our first indication that the entire attack of the Fourth and Sixth Armies might be terminated. Based on the current situation, the condition of our attacking forces, and the necessity for establishing a well-situated and defensible front line in the event the attack halted, I concentrated all my attention on the requirements for the potentially new situation. I discussed the issue with the corps chiefs of staff and then developed an assessment and presented in it writing to my commanding general, who concurred. The assessment read as follows:

> The attack of the Fourth and Sixth Armies ordered by OHL did not result in the expected operational-level victory. The main reason that we did not achieve initially the large-scale seizure of ground is that the supporting artillery had immense difficulties moving forward across the muddy crater fields. As the advance was delayed significantly, it gave the enemy the time to reestablish his defenses to his rear and to move up additional units. The enemy leadership anticipated the vulnerability in Flanders and thus reinforced the British front with French formations. If we continue or attack in an effort to reach an operational objective heavy fighting will develop, and we will not be able to achieve that objective without committing fresh forces and incredible ammunition expenditures. The operational-level failure did not result from any lack of fighting spirit of the German troops, but rather because that attack was scheduled too early and without adequate consideration of the terrain conditions.
>
> For the present the attack has stalled in the sector of the Fourth Army and on the right wing of Sixth Army. We therefore face significant problems in preparing to resume the defensive. The long stretch of hills in the Kemmel area and the mountainous area to the west and southwest gives the enemy the best observation positions for his artillery to the east, southeast, and south, and thus into the ground in which our forward positions are now located. Our only two options are to attack to take all of the dominating high ground, or reposition our defensive positions. The latter option means that we must voluntarily relinquish ground we have gained at the price of a great loss of our blood. I conclude, therefore, that it is absolutely necessary for us to improve our present forwardmost line by conducting additional limited attacks to the front.
>
> For the Fourth Army it is absolutely necessary to seize Mont Kemmel and the high ground to the west. If we capture Mont Kemmel, it most likely will force the enemy to pull his lines back to avoid being

> flanked. A complete seizure of Mont Kemmel and the adjacent high ground can only be achieved by a deliberate attack. During the initial phase of the attack our forces must occupy the high ground to preempt the enemy's ability to bring flanking fire on us. The initial attack objective should be the line Lindenhoek (approximately one kilometer south of Kemmel village)–the terrain east of Dranoutre. From that line we can then launch our attack on Mont Kemmel itself. The Sixth Army will have to seize the hills north of Méteren to prevent enemy flanking action from those hills.

I submitted this assessment of the situation to General von Kuhl and to General Ludendorff when they solicited my recommendation on the continuation of the battle. On 18 April Group Ypres's attack toward Bikschote was pushed back almost everywhere by enemy deliberate counterattacks. A division was alerted and moved forward to support Group Ypres. The planned attack, however, was postponed until 20 April because the enemy detected the readiness posture of the X Reserve Corps. The enemy reinforced his positions to the front of the Fourth Army's entire attack sector. We also clearly identified French artillery fire, integrated into the enemy's positions.

The Sixth Army failed to make any progress on 18 April. At noon on that day Army Group Crown Prince Rupprecht ordered the left wing of the Fourth Army and the right wing of the Sixth Army to halt the attack, which would be resumed only after sufficient preparations. The main effort of the renewed attack was to be made by the Fourth Army, with Group Ypres attacking in the direction of Bikschote toward Poperinge and the XVIII Reserve and X Reserve Corps attacking from Wijtschate up against Mont Kemmel. The intent of this concentric attack was to force the enemy to withdraw from the Ypres salient and reestablish the momentum on the inner wings of Fourth and Sixth Armies. One of the divisions newly assigned to the Fourth Army had a rifle strength of only three thousand. It was attached to the XVIII Reserve Corps. We expected two additional divisions to follow by approximately 22 April.

The corps received their orders for 19 April. Group Ypres would continue its advance toward Poperinge. The objective of the XVIII Reserve Corps was the Voormezele–Kemmel village ridge. The main effort would be on its left wing, and the newly attached division would be deployed there, but only for the start of the attack. The X Reserve Corps was to attack with its main effort toward Mont Kemmel, seizing the high ground in the vicinity of Dranoutre. As soon as the XVIII Reserve and X Reserve Corps completed their preparations, they were to report the day on which they would be ready to attack.

In the evening of 18 April we had to make a change to the Group Ypres operations order. Reconnaissance patrols had discovered a strong enemy position of concrete-reinforced machine gun nests running across the attack front in the vicinity of Bikschote. It would take several days of heavily concentrated artillery preparation fire before the attack would have any hope of succeeding. When I reported the situation to Army Group Crown Prince Rupprecht and to OHL, General Ludendorff initially proposed staging the attack farther north. But according to reports the same situation existed there. Besides, postponing the attack would have taken several days in order to execute the necessary repositioning of the artillery. I did not have confidence in a rapid breakthrough in the direction of Bikschote, and I therefore recommended OHL cancel the attack and reattach the still fresh relief divisions to the Fourth Army in order to strengthen the attack south of Ypres. After OHL concurred, Group Ypres initially received one division to relieve the very worn-out 6th Bavarian Reserve Division, which OHL positioned to the group's rear. The other divisions released from Group Ypres became the army reserve, positioned behind the XVIII Reserve and X Reserve Corps. Both corps reported that 25 April would be their earliest possible attack date.

On 19 April the commanding general visited the divisions of the XVIII Reserve Corps. When he returned he told the staff that the fighting strengths of the regiments had shrunk down to between three hundred and six hundred men. In the meantime, I had worked over the attack plan for Mont Kemmel, which the commanding general approved. I then briefed the plan to General von Kuhl and General Ludendorff by telephone. The designated attack objective was the line Voormezele–northwestern hills of the village and Mont Kemmel–northern edge of Dranoutre. Shortly before the beginning of the attack the XVIII Reserve Corps was to seize the ground southeast of Kemmel village, and the X Reserve Corps the hills west of Dranoutre. That would give us maneuver space to seize the line Kemmel village–Mont Kemmel–Dranoutre. Up until the day of the attack the enemy's infantry and artillery positions were to be subjected to heavy artillery destructive fire by day and harassing fire at night. On the day of the attack the infantry assault would be preceded by two hours of gas fire against the enemy batteries, followed by forty-five minutes of destructive fire. Generals Ludendorff and von Kuhl concurred. I also requested and they approved the attachment of two more battalions of reinforcing heavy artillery, plus a 42cm battery to fire against the heavily reinforced village of Kemmel.

On 20 April OHL ordered the Sixth Army to transition to the defensive. Relief in the forwardmost lines was authorized only in urgent cases. The defensive sectors were to be widened and organized in depth. Artillery was to be pulled back to be on-call to OHL and as army group reserve. Army Group Crown Prince Rupprecht attached many of those firing units to the Fourth

Army to reinforce the attack on Mont Kemmel.

On that same day the Fourth Army headquarters issued the order: "The attack of Group Ypres will be halted. The front line must be held with the group's remaining divisions. The essential task is to tie down constantly the enemy forces along that front. All resources must be devoted to deceiving the enemy into believing the attack will continue."

The Seizure of Mont Kemmel

On 20 April the preparations began for the seizure of Mont Kemmel and its adjacent terrain. The XVIII Reserve and X Reserve Corps were tasked with the conduct of the attack in the following order from left to right:

- XVIII Reserve Corps 1st echelon: 7th Reserve Division, 13th Reserve Division, 19th Reserve Division, 56th Division. 2nd echelon: 3rd Guards Division, 233rd Division.
- X Reserve Division 1st echelon: Alpenkorps, 4th Bavarian Division, 22nd Reserve Division. 2nd echelon: 214th Division, 31st Division.
- Army reserve: 49th Reserve Division, 10th Ersatz Division.

Together with the Fourth Army's general of the artillery I worked out the staging and the fire plan of the attack artillery. We were able to mass a significant level of firepower with much of the artillery that was reassigned to us from the Sixth Army and attached to us by Army Group Crown Prince Rupprecht and OHL. The sector for the XVIII Reserve Corps ran from the right of the canal between Hollebeke and Ypres, left to the line Wulvergem–Kemmel village the road to Reningelst. The X Reserve Corps' sector followed the line to approximately fifteen hundred meters west of the Dranoutre–Loker road.

The main effort of the attack was Kemmel village for the XVIII Reserve Corps' 56th Division; and Mont Kemmel itself for the X Reserve Corps' Alpenkorps.[56] The attack objective was the line from the bend in the canal east of Voormezele–Voormezele village–the lake east of Dikkebus–the creek northwest of Kemmel village–the hill slopes north and northwest of Dranoutre. If the attack succeeded on a large scale initially, the exploitation would be in the general direction of Ypres–Poperinge.

The entire artillery deployment and the reliefs of the worn-out divisions by fresh ones took place only at night. I was at the front every day, reviewing with the corps and the divisions their assigned tasks. During this process I recognized that before the XVIII Reserve Corps' main attack, the ridgeline running southeast of Kemmel village had to be taken; and in the X Reserve Corps' sector, the hills southwest of Dranoutre. The latter attack was conducted successfully on 23 April. The former attack was scheduled for fifteen minutes before the main attack on 25 April.

The artillery preparation for the 25 April attack was scheduled to start at 0330 hours, with two hours of gas projectiles against the enemy infantry and artillery. From 0600 hours on the guns would fire for effect against all enemy positions with high-explosive projectiles (*Brisanzmunition*). At 0645 hours the creeping barrage would start opposite Kemmel village. The remainder of the creeping barrage would start at 0700 hours, with the infantry echeloned in depth following closely. Accompanying guns,[57] towed trench mortars, and flamethrowers were assigned to all infantry units. Aerial artillery observers would direct the counterbattery fire against any enemy batteries still firing. The 42cm battery was assigned the complete destruction of the heavily fortified Kemmel village.

On 25 April the Fourth Army attacked and seized all of Mont Kemmel and its rearward support lines. The continuation of the attack required the forward displacement of the supporting artillery, which had great difficulty negotiating the intervening ground. The British and French divisions launched strong deliberate counterattacks, which we repulsed. During the follow-on fighting until 29 April we gained additional ground. North of the canal the enemy pulled his positions back closer to Ypres, with the troops of Group Ypres following in close pursuit. After 30 April the fighting started to die down, and an almost complete calm settled in. Map 9 shows our new forward line. Both we and the enemy reinforced our new lines.

On 23 April the Kaiser observed the assault on Mont Kemmel from a highly elevated fortification at Lille. A few days later he visited the Fourth Army headquarters at Roubaix. I gave the Kaiser a detailed briefing on large-scale maps, explaining the preparation and the execution of the attack on Mont Kemmel.

Shortly before the start of the Kemmel attack we received the sad news that the famous fighter pilot Manfred von Richthofen, who had eighty aerial victories, crashed over enemy lines because of engine failure during a dogfight with an enemy aviator.[58] Together with the whole German Army, I mourned deeply the tragic fate of this fighter ace.

Along the Flemish coast on 22 and 23 April the British conducted a series of demolition attacks against our submarine ports at Zeebrugge and Ostend using obsolete cruisers packed with explosives. At Zeebrugge the pier attached to the harbor was severely damaged; otherwise the attacks failed. Three British ships and their crews were destroyed. But as the possibility remained of further attempted landings along the Flemish coast, General Ludendorff tasked me to coordinate with Admiral von Schröder for the construction of a fallback position, parallel to and set back from the coastline, with concrete-reinforced machine gun nests. When I passed the OHL mission on to Admiral von Schröder, he refused with the comment, "I prefer an iron heart over a concrete dugout." I answered, "An iron heart in a concrete dugout is also nothing to sneeze at." The admiral then gave in and ordered the position to be built.[59]

Our seizure of Mont Kemmel and its adjacent lines was the basis for OHL's decision to launch another large operational attack around the beginning of August, with the Fourth and Sixth Armies advancing in the direction of Calais and Boulogne.[60] Army Group Crown Prince Rupprecht was tasked with the development of an operational plan, in coordination with the Fourth and Sixth Army headquarters. This attack, however, was to be preceded initially by several diversionary attacks against the French in the Chemin des Dames and Champagne sectors.[61] Their purpose was to draw all the French formations and even some British divisions away from Flanders. All of the divisions that had been extracted from the front lines of the Fourth and Sixth Armies were to remain behind those fronts, where they would receive replacements and undergo training. Then, in combination with additional fresh divisions, they would execute the planned large-scale attack. Major elements of the army-level artillery that had been supporting the Fourth and Sixth Armies were withdrawn and redeployed for other missions.[62]

During the meetings with General von Kuhl to plan the staging of the new attack, I was of the opinion that an attack over the old Flanders battlefield would meet with incredible difficulties. I therefore recommended bypassing that deeply churned-up ground and instead staging the attack from the approximate line Armentières–Lens. From there the Fourth Army would attack with concentrated forces on both sides of Mont Kemmel, in the general direction of Dunkirk. The Sixth Army would advance in the general direction of Saint-Omer, toward Calais. An attack echelon following the left wing of the Sixth Army would then gradually shift in the general direction of the line Boulogne-la-Grasse–Saint-Pol-sur-Ternoise–Arras. If that attack succeeded, the British would lose their main ports and their rearward lines of communication.

The main features of this operational plan generally were approved by Army Group Crown Prince Rupprecht and also OHL. Army Group Crown Prince Rupprecht was tasked with the preparation of the attack. The starting time depended on the success of the major diversionary attacks against the French. Initially our entire army-level artillery had to be used to support those attacks. OHL developed a plan to shift the bulk of the army-level artillery from the Champagne sector back to the Fourth and Sixth Armies. The movements, tentatively planned for mid-July, would start immediately after the attack against Reims.[63] Meanwhile, all battery positions for the Fourth and Sixth Army attacks were to be reconnoitered and established well beforehand, and the fire plans for the entire artillery and the trench mortar forces were to be developed. This process started at the beginning of May and was completed by the beginning of July.

I focused all my attention and efforts on the preparation of this attack. I spent almost every day at the designated attack front, managing the execution of the preparation down to every detail. All the battery and trench mortar positions were emplaced very tightly behind the forwardmost lines. The follow-on forward displacement of the supporting artillery and trench mortar units was planned in detail and marked on the maps. All approach routes from the rear were improved. We were confident in our planned operational attack.

On 27 May the diversionary attack started against the Chemin des Dames ridgeline. That same day the center of the attacking forces reached the Vesle River, in the vicinity of Fismes. Constantly moving forward, our forces reached Fère-en-Tardenois on 29 May, and shortly thereafter the Marne near Château-Thierry.[64] On 9 June the Eighteenth Army attacked between Montdidier and Noyon in order to reinforce the angle that had developed at the base of the new salient.[65] The attack gained ground initially, but then it stalled in the face of strong enemy deliberate counterattacks. The Eighteenth Army did manage to hold the new line it had reached. By the middle of June this sector became calm, interrupted only by small enemy attacks, which were repulsed. The front lines of the Eighteenth and Seventeenth Armies had widened considerably during the course of the offensive operations in the south. OHL thus formed a new Ninth Army on the inner wings of those armies, which then took over the sector between the Rivers Oise and Ourcq.

In Italy, meanwhile, an Austrian attack between Lake Garda and the Adriatic Sea stalled after some initial small successes, and the attacking forces had to fall back to their original positions. Austria-Hungary, then, after long urging by OHL, agreed to send four of its divisions to the German Western Front. During that same period, however, twenty American divisions arrived in France. More followed, so that the Entente increasingly gained in force superiority. The American formations were fresh and highly resourced, had high operating budgets, and each division had a strength of twelve battalions.[66] Initially the American divisions took over only calm, well-prepared positions along the Western Front, where they could adjust to combat conditions. The British and French divisions relieved from those sectors received rest and training. Thus, the balance of usable forces shifted more and more from the German side to the Entente. Degrading our combat effectiveness even more, the German Army from the middle of June on increasingly suffered from the spreading and virulent flu epidemic.[67]

During this period OHL faced difficult decisions. Considerable portions of the German Army in the West had been reduced significantly. Replacements, for the most part, came from recuperated sick and wounded soldiers returned to duty. Although we had gained considerable ground up through June 1918 during the Great Battle of France, in Flanders, and during the attacks of the Seventh Army in Champagne, our defensive front lines had increased by seventy-five kilometers in the process. All of those new lines had to be improved by the trench divisions, whose sectors of the front increased to 4.5 kilometers each. This in turn required us to increase the number of trench divisions by about sixteen. Thus, the army, army group, and OHL reserve divisions decreased by the same number. Naturally, the Entente forces had roughly the same number of divisions deployed against us along the new salient line; but the Entente was constantly reinforced with American divisions, which were all at full strength.

Considering this situation, OHL assumed a great degree of risk when it decided to prepare and execute an approximately eighty-kilometer-wide and deeply echeloned attack in Champagne, between Château-Thierry and the Argonne.[68] After that attack OHL would then shift rapidly to the attack to be conducted by the Fourth and Sixth Armies.[69] But OHL firmly believed that the attack on both sides of Reims would result in a great success, and possibly even accomplish a breakthrough followed by the subsequent destruction of the enemy front.[70]

Unfortunately, the enemy learned about our scheme of maneuver and the exact day of the attack on both sides of Reims, betrayed by German deserters and the statements of German prisoners captured in small-scale enemy operations.[71] We learned of this after the attack. In recognition of the threatening danger, the commander in chief of the Allied armies, General Foch, issued the order that on the battlefields on both sides of Reims the forwardmost lines would be held only by thin forces. Everything else was to be pulled back to a second well built-up position.[72] Thus, the German attack failed right from the start on 15 July 1918, and was discontinued as soon as the German commanders understood the situation.

The failure of the attack at Reims, which OHL had intended as a feint to draw enemy forces from the sector north of the Somme and especially from Flanders, was a major disappointment for us in the north. OHL suspended the movement of combat assets from Champagne to Flanders that had started on 16 July. That same day we at the Fourth Army headquarters received the initial reports of the enemy's successful evasion of the attack on both sides of Reims. During the night of 16 to 17 July our combat patrols verified that the enemy positions to our front were still heavily manned.

OHL issued a warning order for subsequent actions. Early on the morning of 18 July General Ludendorff arrived in Flanders for briefings with Army Group Crown Prince Rupprecht and the Fourth and Sixth Armies. During the briefing the chiefs of staff reported on the current status of the attack preparations.[73] Ludendorff was confident, and to our delight he still intended to order the execution of the attack in Flanders. All preparations were to continue. The start day of the attack would be based on the completion of the force movements from the Champagne sector to Flanders. The current situation required some adjustments to those plans.

Toward the end of the briefing, at approximately 1130 hours, Ludendorff received an urgent report from the Operations Section at OHL in Avesnes. The enemy was attacking from the Villers-Cotterêts forest against the right flank of the Marne salient, in the sector held by the Ninth and Seventh Armies. As Ludendorff passed this information on to us, he expressed his trust in the ability of our engaged forces to hold, and he considered the situation as not dangerous. Shortly, however, more serious intelligence came in from Avesnes reporting large losses of ground and the certainty of large-scale enemy successes. I encouraged Ludendorff to return to Avesnes immediately. In the afternoon I asked OHL about the situation at the Ninth and Seventh Armies, but I was given information only very reluctantly. Toward midnight I received a message from Ludendorff to come to Avesnes as soon as possible. After reporting my orders to my commanding general and consulting with my staff on the Fourth Army's actions for the next few days, I took a staff car to Avesnes that night, arriving about 0800 hours on 19 July.

When I reported to Ludendorff I found him rather nervous and agitated. To my regret, he unjustifiably made accusations against the chief of the Operations Section, Colonel Georg Wetzell, and his staff. Ludendorff believed that they had "failed" to evaluate the combat power of the Seventh Army correctly. It was a rather embarrassing scene. Wetzell remained silent, as a good soldier, but it was obvious that he took the reproach very hard. His eyes started to water, but he controlled his emotions rather well.[74]

Ludendorff described briefly to me the situation in the Seventh Army sector, and also on the left wing of the Ninth Army. He asked me for recommendations on how to proceed, but he was then called away for some time to answer telephone calls. I used that welcome pause to go the Operations Section, where I oriented myself in detail on the situation. I also took a look at the map updated by the Intelligence Section showing the reported positions of the enemy divisions, both in the line and in reserve. The field army and corps headquarters received updated printed copies of this map on an almost daily basis. On the most current version of the map, which I had taken with me from Fourth Army headquarters, a large number of enemy divisions were indicated as not identifiable, possibly dissolved, and in any case not combat ready. To my surprise, approximately twenty of those divisions were now shown as fully combat ready on the OHL map, which had been updated by hand. The positions of the enemy divisions were based on human intelligence reports. The enemy situation now plotted on the OHL map clearly indicated an attack in the direction of Soissons, most likely echeloned in depth. The enemy had enough divisions available to make a strong exploitation of their initial success.

What I saw on the map reinforced the conclusion I had reached earlier. In the Aisne–Vesle sector it was high time to pull back the Ninth Army, linked on its left with the Seventh Army. We also had to withdraw from the forward line that we had reached in the Great Battle of France.[75] We were planning no further attacks from there, and we had to establish a straight line that was favorable for the defensive. Based on my own experience, I concluded that the units positioned there now could no longer be fully combat effective. They had been holding on too long in unimproved positions and command posts, and their forward supply systems were complicated with many problems. Along those frontline sectors where preparations were being made for subsequent attacks, morale remained positive in expectation of a successful advance. But along those front lines where the troops recognized that they were condemned to remain in poor positions without hope of relief by attacks by their own or adjacent friendly units, the situation was deteriorating.

They were subjected increasingly to the inner pressures of enemy propaganda and political manipulation from the Homeland, diminishing their will to resist. This alarming condition affected most of those sectors of the front lines from which most of the 1918 offensives were launched—the Seventeenth, Second, Eighteenth, Ninth, and Seventh Armies.[76] A large number of the trench divisions in those armies had remained in the front line without relief since the attacks had stalled. Based on my own experience over the years, I assessed that their combat effectiveness had to be severely diminished. It was not unusual for some of the divisions to remain in unimproved positions for up to three months, lice ridden and physically and psychologically ground down. Furthermore, those sectors had only small reserves, which themselves were in need of rest and were short on ammunition. It was quite clear to me that they would fold in the face of a massive enemy attack.

Analyzing the enemy break-in between Soissons and Château-Thierry, I came to a much different conclusion than OHL. During the short time I had to scrutinize the OHL situation maps it became quite clear to me that the enemy's break-in on 18 July was not a limited attack, but rather it indicated the intent of the enemy's leadership to seize the initiative through a major attack. The linkage between the enemy's withdrawal from our attack on 15 July and their own counterattack on 18 July was as clear as daylight. That formed the basis of my recommendations to Ludendorff.

Ludendorff called me back in after about half an hour. He had just received reports from the Ninth and Seventh Armies that the enemy's morning attacks on 19 July had continued and widened. Large gaps apparently existed in the front lines of both of our armies. It was clear that as the enemy made further progress in the direction of Soissons, the Seventh Army's lines of communication would be threatened.

When I entered the room Ludendorff struck me as very depressed. Unlike his normal self, he interrupted my briefing several times, digressing into details that, considering the seriousness of situation, were irrelevant. I gave him a comprehensive briefing, focusing on my assessment of the overextension of our front lines, which were still in an attack posture. I then made a recommendation, summarized as follows:

1. Put the Seventh Army and the left wing of the Ninth Army under a unified command and direct them to conduct an orderly withdrawal back to the Aisne–Vesle Position. The reserves positioned behind that front should remain in place and be reinforced as needed. They should be committed mainly to prevent a rapid advance of the enemy toward Soissons and to restore stability to our own front. The execution of the retrograde movement and its time line should be up to the Seventh Army. The recovery of the supply depots (ammunition, other combat assets, rations) should not be allowed to retard the rapid withdrawal. Where supplies cannot be recovered, they should be destroyed in place.
2. The attack front resulting from the Great Battle of France should be given a warning order to withdraw within approximately three weeks to the old Siegfried Line. As many divisions as necessary should be held in reserve and maintained as close to combat ready as possible. They should be moved into the Siegfried Line to rebuild and later occupy the position. Each of those divisions should improve their future sector on a broad front. The divisions currently in the front lines should then be withdrawn incrementally, preceded by the recovery of their equipment. Once behind the Siegfried Position they should be reconstituted and then become the new OHL reserve.
3. All of the remaining available and fully combat-ready divisions should be shifted to Flanders, where they will be committed to the already planned and prepared attack there.[77] Nonetheless, it is most probable that the planned attack sector on both sides of Mont Kemmel with the limited number of attack divisions[78] available will result in only a limited tactical success, and certainly not a major opera-

> tional success that could decidedly influence the end of the war. If we decline to attempt such a purely tactical success, then the Fourth and Sixth Armies should also be pulled back into their previous reinforced positions. The entire Western Front will then assume the defensive. The time gained will be used primarily for reconstitution and rest and training of the troops. Simultaneously, the improvement of deeply echeloned operational defensive sectors should extend all the way to the Meuse–Antwerp Position, as well as in Lorraine and in Alsace behind ground that can be flooded, and along the line Metz–Strasbourg–Rhine River. The formations used for the rearward improvement of these defensive sectors should come preferably from units released from the winding down of combat operations in the east. Those units will form a buffer between the combat zone and the Homeland. They also will round up the large numbers of malingerers and return them to order and discipline.

My assessment of the situation and my recommendations clearly made an impression on Ludendorff. He thought for quite a while and then told me that he thought my recommendations were sound, but he could not accept them for political reasons. When I asked him what those political reasons were, Ludendorff indicated the conclusions that would be drawn by the enemy, by our army, and by the Homeland. I responded that if we do not adopt and properly execute a militarily correct course of action in this situation, then we are going down the wrong path. Ludendorff clearly took umbrage at my response. I could sense his inner tensions as he told me that if that was my position, he would ask the field marshal[79] to accept his resignation.

I advised him against doing such, because I firmly believed it was the wrong thing to do. Ludendorff had earned a well-deserved reputation in the army and among its leadership. His resignation at that time would have sent the wrong message to the army, and would have reinforced the enemy's resolve. The moral consequences were inestimable in their effect. I was close to Ludendorff, both as a human being and as a soldier. I thought it would be a disaster if he withdrew himself in this time of crisis. In the end he put his trust in me, as he had done so often before. I had told him what I thought with all candor. If he could bring himself to do the same and apply his energetic and acknowledged leadership skills, the overall situation could improve quickly. We had to abandon the objective of an operational victory against the enemy; but if we conducted a systematic defensive war with tactical attacks that were within the capabilities of our forces, we could prevent the enemy from achieving victory. Those were my thoughts as I talked Ludendorff out of requesting his relief.

Objectively, I later came to regret that I had not encouraged Ludendorff to resign at the time. His behavior on 19 July 1918 should have proved to me that he was incapable of making the urgently required decision to withdraw from the untenable front line and pull back to improved positions from which we could continue to resist. Instead, fate led the German Army down its catastrophic path. In retrospect, it would have been better if a new first quartermaster general who was not tainted by the failures of our offensives had taken the reigns of the new defensive operations.[80]

Despite my advice, Ludendorff did actually offer his resignation to the field marshal, but when he came back he told me that Hindenburg had refused his offer. I do not know if in his conversation with the field marshal Ludendorff mentioned my recommendations on the conduct of future operations. Without letting me know what his final decision was, Ludendorff then ordered me to go immediately to the Ninth and Seventh Armies to survey the situation there and report back to him by that evening. He also told me that the attack in Flanders had been cancelled and that orders to that effect would be issued. Ludendorff also authorized me to take over immediately from the chief of staff of the Seventh Army if in my opinion he had lost his nerve.

That concluded my approximately two-hour stay in Avesnes. I left Ludendorff under the impression that my recommendations had been accepted and would be executed accordingly. It was painful for me not to be able to return immediately to the Fourth Army. I believed that the transition from preparation for the attack to the defense required the presence of the chief of staff that everyone knew and who held in his hands all the necessary reins. To my great relief I later learned that my very capable Ia did an outstanding job advising the commanding general.

Immediately after the conclusion of the briefing at OHL on 19 July 1918, I took a staff car to the Seventh Army. Making a plan while on the road, I decided that I had enough time to visit first the break-in sector of the front line and to speak with the leaders there. What I learned reinforced my impression about the very strong impact of the enemy attack, as well as the condition of our worn-out troops. I was used to such things from my experience as an army chief of staff during our major defensive battles. I gave the leaders on the spot my best advice based on my experiences in similar situations. After I had visited the corps headquarters and the majority of the divisional staffs that had been involved in the main battle, I made a short probe in the direction of the combat front. I then drove to the Seventh Army headquarters. To my relief, I found solid people there whose nerves were good. The commanding general, General Hans von Boehn, the chief of staff, Colonel Walther Reinhardt,[81] and the Ia, Major Werner von Blomberg,[82] responded to my questioning about the appropriate course of action now that holding on to the Marne salient could only be possible with numerous fresh divisions. Such an attempt would cost a lot of blood, and even then there was no guarantee that we would succeed in holding the position.

All three gentlemen thought it was more practical to withdraw the battlefront in a planned and sequenced move to the Aisne–Vesle Position. I then called Ludendorff and gave him my own assessment of the situation at the Seventh Army headquarters. I urged him to issue the necessary orders to plan and execute the withdrawal. To my surprise Ludendorff seemed unwilling to make such a decision quickly. He described to me his measures that would move divisions and other combat assets from Champagne and from Flanders. I got the impression that he wanted to let the situation play out. I considered such a half-measure to be a mistake, and I stressed the necessity of a withdrawal based on the situation. Ludendorff, however, did not give in. He ordered me to remain with the Seventh Army and to brief him daily on the situation.

When I passed the information on to the commanding general and chief of staff of the Seventh Army, I sensed their disappointment, and I felt it even more. As good soldiers, however, both accepted the directive as issued. The Seventh Army headquarters subsequently issued execution orders that were well thought out, clear, and energetic.

After a short nap I drove back to the front on 20 July, and during the dawn hours I reconnoitered the main break-in sector. The fertile ground to the front of our pushed-back positions consisted of many high-standing wheat fields, which made observation very difficult. Many enemy tanks had used the limited visibility to their advantage as they broke into our positions, creating a petrifying psychological effect in our ranks. During my visits to the front line on the morning of 20 July, I was able to observe for myself the effect created by such tanks. One of the tanks drove past me about fifty meters away, through a high wheat field that I was just crossing on my way to the forwardmost front line. Only by throwing myself down in the wheat field was I able to avoid getting hit by the constantly firing tank.

The Ninth and Seventh Armies had started their battle from their forwardmost sectors and main positions. That type of defensive combat had proven effective in the later months of the Battle of Flanders, where the battlefield was flat and ravaged. It was, however, completely inadequate for the battlefields on which the Ninth and Seventh Armies fought. In the heavily overgrown terrain the forwardmost troops were doomed to either death or capture, and few escaped one fate or the other. In addition, the significantly reduced combat strength of the line companies was not sufficient to organize the sector into a forward zone and a main line. Wherever I went I cancelled the application of this form of deployment, although the units felt obligated to follow the general orders from OHL. I quickly coordinated with OHL to suspend their directive on this form of defense. It naturally took a long time until that change reached the troops.

My stay with the Seventh Army and the left wing of the Ninth Army linked in on its right lasted from 19 July to the morning of 26 July. My actions consisted of daily visits to the front lines and meetings with the staffs, with whom I shared my own combat experience. Two or three times daily I reported my observations to Ludendorff, continually urging the withdrawal from the front line, which in many places had been pushed in deeply. All the leaders on the spot agreed that such was the correct course of action. To my surprise, however, new divisions were sent forward every day to relieve the combat-ineffective frontline troops. As the salient progressively narrowed from the enemy's action, those relief operations became more and more difficult because the enemy's long-range fire reached deeply into our rear areas. Those artillery strikes directed by aerial observers and the heavy pounding in our rear from the enemy's bomber squadrons caused the discipline of our troops to start to unravel. Numerous malingerers tried to make their way to the rear. Soon, even our ammunition depots came under enemy fire. Twice I observed convoys approaching those depots for resupply scatter in all directions as soon as the enemy's artillery opened up. As a consequence, frontline troops at some points suffered severe ammunition shortages.

I kept Ludendorff current on the ever-increasing and clearly visible deterioration of the condition of some of the troops. Still, the much hoped for OHL order for a deliberate withdrawal to the Aisne–Vesle Position never materialized. By the evening of 27 July the level of fighting on the front lines had intensified to such a degree that I could no longer rule out a catastrophe. Our forwardmost troops had fought valiantly for the most part, but their heroism carried a heavy price in blood. During the night of 25–26 July, I again reported my observations and assessment to the headquarters of the Seventh Army, and I asked the commanding general for authorization to return to OHL in Avesnes to try to get an order for a deliberate withdrawal. The commanding general agreed immediately, and I left that very night. I did not get very far very fast, because all the roads were jammed. The experiences during my journey that night reinforced my conclusions that the discipline of the troops was diminishing, and especially that the organization of the supply trains was too bloated. In the latter case energetic and proactive leaders were lacking for the most part.

I only managed to get close to Avesnes toward noon on 26 July. I knew that every day around 1200 hours the field marshal appeared in Ludendorff's office to receive the daily situation briefing. Nobody was admitted to Ludendorff's office during that period. When I finally reached the OHL headquarters building shortly after 1200 hours I found that the field marshal was already in with Ludendorff. Without knocking I entered Ludendorff's office and found him arguing loudly with the field marshal. I assumed it was over the situation at the Seventh Army. In any case, as soon as I entered the field marshal asked me to give my assessment of the situation at the Seventh Army. I described it in short terms and emphasized especially that based on my own observations I thought the condition of the troops was cause for serious concern. For the past few days the Seventh Army commanding general, the staff, and I had all been recommending a withdrawal from the increasingly untenable front lines. I told Hindenburg that I had come to Avesnes with the concurrence of the Seventh Army commanding general to secure such an order. The field marshal turned to Ludendorff, saying something to the effect of "Now Ludendorff, make sure that that order goes out immediately." He then left Ludendorff's office rather upset.

Ludendorff also struck me as being rather upset. He told me in no uncertain terms that he was not at all pleased that I had given my assessment so openly to the field marshal without first going through him. He still tried to stall in issuing the order. I objected, and he finally gave in. The order for the deliberate withdrawal was first issued by telephone and then in writing to the Seventh Army.

My mission at the Seventh Army was complete. I drove back to Flanders on the afternoon of 26 July to resume my duties as chief of staff of the Fourth Army. Prior to leaving I had learned from a briefing by the OHL Operations Section that—as far as I can remember—approximately thirty-five fresh divisions and many batteries of army-level artillery had been thrown into the fight in the Seventh Army sector. Meanwhile, OHL had done nothing with the resources available to them to reconstitute the Aisne–Vesle Position. The forward lines from the Great Battle of France were still in their old positions. Nothing had been ordered and nothing had been prepared for the deliberate withdrawal.

The field armies in that sector were forced to replace their expended frontline units with their own weak reserves. It was my impression that Ludendorff had not been able to force himself to make the hard decision. He left the entire German frontline trace unchanged. A large number of divisions and other combat assets had been thrown into the Seventh Army's hopeless fight instead of using the reserves that OHL still had available for either a new attack in Flanders or to transition to the deliberate operational defensive. All these formations had been bled to death unnecessarily. As I later learned, the shortage of replacements forced us to disband ten divisions.

The disaster at Villers-Cotterêts could repeat itself any day in other sectors, at which point our lack of combat-ready reserves would prove disastrous.[83] Ludendorff's decision was based on a deplorable compromise. That is not to suggest that I thought he was only fighting to preserve his reputation. Nonetheless, he had not recognized that by 18 July 1918 the overall initiative had shifted to the enemy. By then they had sufficient reserves available, which were constantly reinforced by the influx of American units. Ludendorff certainly had overestimated the fortitude of our army, and thus he believed that he could still impose the law of action upon the enemy. It was a grave mistake. The exact turning point of the war did not come on 8 August 1918, but rather on 18 July 1918.[84] OHL failed to recognize that the German Army's combat power had been depleted and gravely shaken in July 1918. We needed to conduct a deliberate reconstitution, which would have been possible if only our troops had been able to rest in tenable positions. This failure forced us into the situation in which we found ourselves at the end of the war.

In the evening of 26 July, I briefed my commanding general on the broad outline of my experiences with the Ninth and Seventh Armies. Soon thereafter I also briefed General von Kuhl. The front line of the Fourth Army was completely quiet. As our combat forces continually improved their positions, their overall condition improved. Only very few divisions remained in our rear area as army and army group reserves.

At the beginning of August General Sixt von Armin urged me to use the quiet period to take some home leave. I finally gave in to the suggestion after ascertaining that the enemy opposite us was continuously thinning out his lines. During the night of 7 August, with the concurrence of General von Kuhl and General Ludendorff, I left for several days of leave. When I arrived in Stuttgart on the morning of 8 August my wife handed me an urgent telegram from OHL. "Return immediately!" it said. I took the next train back. In Namur an officer from OHL got me off the train and told me that I was to report to General Ludendorff in Avesnes immediately.

8

Chief of the General Staff of Army Group Boehn

When I arrived at Avesnes-les-Aubert, General Ludendorff made a rather depressing impression on me. He immediately informed me that I had been appointed as the chief of staff of the newly organized Army Group Boehn, which consisted of the Second, Eighteenth, and Ninth Armies. He then briefed me on the map about the current situation. On the morning of 8 August in a heavy fog the Second Army had been pushed back as much as ten kilometers by British and French forces launching a strong surprise attack between Albert and the Avre River. The enemy had committed many tanks. The Eighteenth Army was forced to bend back its right wing in order to maintain contact with the Second Army. The troops of the Second Army suffered very heavy losses. Divisions from the reserve had to be pulled forward to fill the gaps in the fighting front. Additional divisions were now moving up to the battle zone. Army Group Boehn had the mission of coordinating the operations of its three subordinate armies. Command and control was to be initiated as soon as Colonel General Hans von Boehn arrived in the already established army group headquarters at Le Cateau. He most likely would arrive on 12 August.

General Ludendorff then asked me to get more detailed information about the developed situation from the OHL Operations Section. I realized quickly that the situation of the Second Army was very serious. Based on the reports coming in, it certainly could be expected that strong enemy attacks would also soon be launched against the Eighteenth Army. In front of the Ninth Army the situation was quiet for now. The Seventeenth Army, which tied in with Army Group Boehn in the north, also reported that it was expecting an enemy attack between Arras and Albert. No action had been taken to reinforce the Siegfried Line. During a follow-up briefing with General Ludendorff, I repeated the recommendation that I had made on 19 July to occupy the Siegfried Line immediately with newly arriving reserves and to have them improve the position, while directing only the most necessary replacements to the forwardmost front line for the present. I justified my recommendation again by explaining that the initiative of action by now had certainly shifted to the enemy's leader-

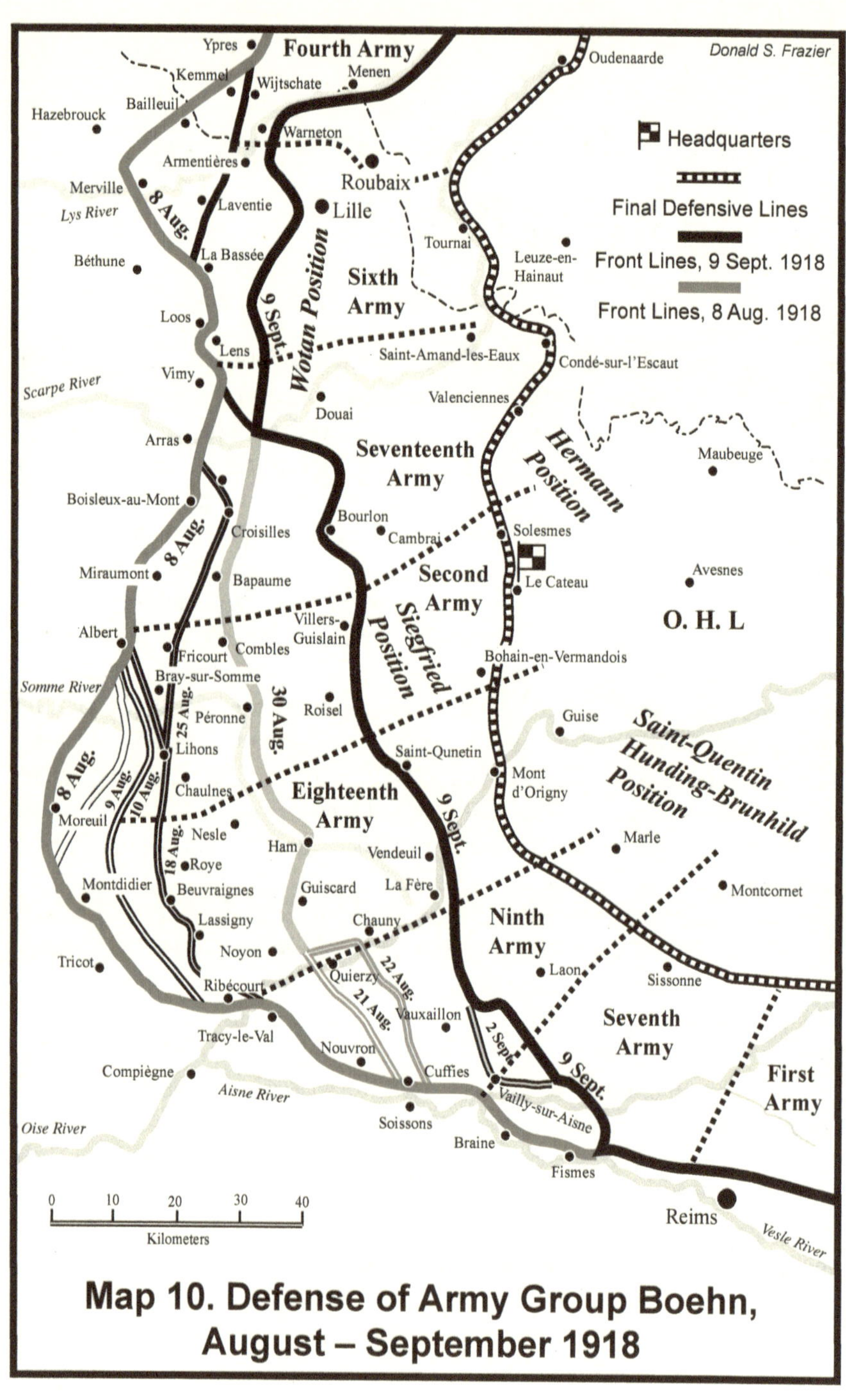

Map 10. Defense of Army Group Boehn, August – September 1918

ship, and their attack had hit a very weak spot in the German front. But General Ludendorff stuck with his decision to conduct the defensive fight in our forward battle lines. He only ordered the immediate reconnoitering of a new contour position along the Combles–Péronne–Noyon line as a fallback position. He would not change his mind, even when I made it clear to him that the reconnaissance and improvement of this position would take a long time. That position played no role later on because it was quickly overrun in the course of further enemy attacks. Meanwhile, still nothing was done to reinforce the Siegfried Line.

From Avesnes-les-Aubert I made a long telephone call to my previous commander, General Friedrich Sixt von Armin, informing him of my transfer. Major Humser, who had proven himself in all of his previous General Staff assignments, was appointed as my successor at the Fourth Army.

I then left for Le Cateau, where I met with several officers of the newly established staff. Among them was the very capable Major Joachim von Stülpnagel,[1] who was appointed Ia of the army group. General von Boehn sent us a message that he would assume command of the army group on 12 August, after first reporting to Field Marshal von Hindenburg at OHL.

I left the establishment of the army group staff in Le Cateau to the officers of the staff who were arriving one after the other. I myself used the time until the evening of 11 August to make contact with our three subordinate army headquarters.

The commanding general of the Second Army was General of Cavalry Johannes Georg von der Marwitz. His chief of staff, Colonel Erich von Tschischwitz, had been assigned the blame by General Ludendorff for the grave defeat of the Second Army. In my opinion, that was unjust. On 8 August the losses of the Second Army had been very heavy. They lost approximately 700 officers, 27,000 men, more than 400 guns, and large amounts of machine guns and mortars. It was probably the greatest defeat of a German field army during the World War. In the final analysis, however, this catastrophe fell back on General Ludendorff, who greatly overestimated the ability of the German fighting front to resist in the Great Battle of France, and who did not accept my recommendation on 19 July to pull back to the Siegfried Position.

The commanding general of the Eighteenth Army was General of Infantry Oskar Emil von Hutier, who had Lieutenant Colonel Bürkner as his chief of staff. On 8 August the Eighteenth Army had been attacked unsuccessfully on its extreme right wing, but it was forced to bend its line back to maintain contact because the Second Army had lost so much ground.

The commanding general of the Ninth Army was General of Infantry Hans Carl Adolph von Carlowitz. His chief of staff was Lieutenant Colonel Faupel, a very energetic General Staff officer who was appointed to the position on 22 August. So far the Ninth Army had not been attacked.

On 9 August the enemy pushed back the Second Army along its entire front for another three to five kilometers. Again many troops were captured by the enemy, and again a wave of German divisions had to be fed to the Second Army in order to reinforce its resistance. As the Second Army lost more ground, the Eighteenth Army was dangerously exposed on its flank. OHL therefore ordered the Eighteenth Army to disengage its right wing from the enemy during the night of 9 to 10 August, leaving only rear guards in the former positions. On 10 August the French attacked the Eighteenth Army with strong forces between Montdidier and the Oise River, but they could not shatter the very courageously and well-led Eighteenth Army.

On 11 August the British and the French reduced their operations to limited attacks against the newly established German line between Albert and the Oise. For the most part the new positions held. On 12 August Colonel General von Boehn assumed command of his army group following a long meeting with Field Marshal von Hindenburg. As soon as Boehn arrived in Le Cateau I gave him a thorough briefing on the situation and my assessment of the three subordinate armies. I urgently recommended that General von Boehn insist to OHL that the Siegfried Line be reconstituted by manning it immediately with the reserves that were now moving up. But again, even General von Boehn's efforts were unsuccessful. Totally misjudging the seriousness of the situation, General Ludendorff steadfastly insisted on defending every inch of ground. I also reported to General von Boehn the poor condition of the Second Army's combat troops, who had failed so seriously on 8 and 9 August.

By 12 August the reserve divisions that had been positioned behind Army Group Boehn on 8 August were completely deployed by OHL. Additional divisions withdrawn by OHL from all the other army groups were also approaching. In the subsequent fighting all of the divisions attached to the army group had to be used as immediate replacements in the heavy struggles along the front lines. During all of Army Group Beohn's entire existence we never had a dedicated reserve force.

From 13 August on, General von Boehn and I went to the front almost daily in order to assess the situation personally and assign accordingly the ever decreasing trickle of replacement divisions to the most urgently threatened points. The enemy, however, gave us no reprieve. He committed more and more of his own reserves, and by 18 August he had pushed back the Second and Eighteenth Armies with heavy losses to the line Albert–west of Bray-sur-Somme–Lihons–west of Roye–south of Noyon. On 20 August the enemy also attacked the Ninth Army with superior forces. Despite courageous countermeasures, the

Ninth Army by 21 August was pushed back to the line east of Noyon–west of Soissons—and by 22 August to the line south of Chauny–Soissons.

From 21 August on, the British expanded their attack front from the northern wing of the Second Army to the area east of Boisleux, and a few days later all the way to the vicinity of Lens. Those attacks affected almost the entire front of the Second Army, as well as the Seventeenth Army of Crown Prince Rupprecht's Army Group. By 25 August the British broke through the Seventeenth and Second Armies and reached the approximate line Croisilles–west of Bapaume–east of Fricourt–Lihons. Soon thereafter the combined British and French attacked on a broad front and pushed the Seventeenth, Second, and Eighteenth Armies back to the line south of Lens–east of Hénin[2]–east of Bapaume–east of Combles–Péronne–along the Somme to west of Ham–east of Noyon. At that point the German line tied in with the Ninth Army, which had not yet come under attack. In the Second and Eighteenth Armies' area of operations the front ran along the position that general Ludendorff had ordered reinforced on 9 August. From the east of Hénin the line ran toward the north to the east of Lens, to the Wotan Position.

During these tremendous onslaughts by the enemy several German combat divisions suffered very heavy losses and were reduced so much that they had to be dissolved by OHL after their relief. Their remnants were then used as replacements for other divisions.

On 2 September the British attacked with a large number of tanks and overran the Wotan Position in the Seventeenth Army sector. Based on this serious situation, which also affected Army Group Boehn, OHL ordered the withdrawal to the Siegfried Position of the largest part of the Seventeenth Army's front, the whole of the Second and Eighteenth Armies, and the right wing of Ninth Army. Unfortunately, the Siegfried Position still had not been rebuilt. Although the left wing of the Ninth Army had held out so far against all enemy attacks, OHL quickly decided to withdraw it behind the canal north of Vauxaillon that ran east of Vailly-sur-Aisne between the rivers Oise and Aisne. Consequently, the Seventh Army also had to pull back its right wing behind this canal. All of these retrograde movements were accomplished by 9 September. Since the British attacked on 8 August, the Seventeenth, Second, Eighteenth, and Ninth Armies had lost more than one hundred thousand men.

It was clear that the German Army's inner strength and will to fight was decreasing more and more. Soldiers on leave back home were increasingly harassed by agitators. When they returned from leave to the positions in the field they had left, their divisions often had already moved. The troops tried to follow their units, but most had little success. The registration, collection, and information points that were established everywhere often could not give reliable advice on where the units were located. Meanwhile, the propaganda leaflets that enemy aviators dropped over the front line and in the rear were taking their toll. Thus, a large number of malingerers developed. They poisoned even the most committed fighters with their bad example. Things became so bad that soldiers-turned-agitators yelled the foul word *Streikbrecher* (strike breaker) at their comrades who were still willing to fight.

In order to preserve our forces, we withdrew our forward lines on the inner wings of the Fourth and Sixth Armies, making a straighter and shorter line from Ypres to La Bassée. The ground that the Fourth and Sixth Armies had gained with such fighting spirit on 18 April thus fell back into British hands without a fight. It was a bitter disappointment for me.

OHL wanted to establish new operational defensive positions behind the shortened front line. To determine the exact locations of the positions, the chiefs of staff of Army Groups Crown Prince Rupprecht, Boehn, and German Crown Prince were ordered to report to Avesnes-les-Aubert on 6 September. General Ludendorff had already traced the first line of these positions, the Hermann Position, on the map. The line was to start at the coast north of Gent, and then run from there behind the Schelde and Skarpe to south of Tournai and farther toward Condé-sur-l'Escaut, Valenciennes, Solesmes, Le Cateau, and west of Guise. From there, as the Hunding-Brunhild Position, the line was to run west of Guise and to the south past Marle and east toward Rethel along the course of the Aisne, linking it to the existing line north of Verdun. Army Group Gallwitz was positioned on both sides of Verdun. From the east of Verdun to directly south of Metz the line formed a deep salient pointing southwest at Saint-Mihiel. The relatively straight Michael Position running across the base of the salient had already been prepared. Army Group Gallwitz was scheduled to evacuate the Saint-Mihiel salient starting on 8 September.[3] Meanwhile, OHL ordered the reconnoitering of a farther rearward operational position starting at the North Sea northwest of Antwerp and running along the course of the Meuse between Givet and Verdun. All the fortified positions in Alsace-Lorraine were to be rebuilt. By the end of the war, however, no real improvement of the Meuse–Antwerp Position had been made.

During the briefing with the three army group chiefs of staff on 6 September in Avesnes-les-Aubert, Field Marshal von Hindenburg initially spoke briefly about the seriousness of the situation. He then handed the conduct of the meeting to General Ludendorff, who struck me as being very nervous. It was a drastic change from his usually firm personality. He had quite a few critical things to say about the troops. He blamed the soldiers and their leaders for the recent events, without acknowledging that his own misguided leadership was in large part the reason for the failures. He announced an OHL directive reducing the battalions from four to three infantry companies because the required officer and enlisted replacements were no longer available. The supply trains also were to be reduced. General Ludendorff demanded severe punishment for malingerers. Then he described OHL's plans for the Hermann and Hunding-Brunhild Positions, as well as the Meuse–Antwerp Position. When he invited input from the three army group chiefs of staff, I reported that General von Boehn and I during our daily trips to the front lines had determined that the Siegfried Position was in a serious state of disrepair. It had only a few wire obstacles in place. Considering the current state of the troops, I said that we would not be able to conduct any lengthy resistance from there. The improvement of the Hermann Position had not started yet, and therefore no long-term resistance was likely after a withdrawal to that line. Based on these facts, the official recommendation of Army Group Boehn was that after we lost the Siegfried Position we should withdraw immediately from the sea to Verdun in one jump to the Meuse–Antwerp Position. That line was seventy kilometers shorter, but it required immediate improvement. Ahead of the main retrograde movement we should transport back as much equipment and supplies as possible. During the main retrograde movement we should destroy all railroads, bridges, and other lines of communication facilities. I justified my recommendation primarily on the fact that the German Army could only gain the necessary time to reestablish order and reconstitute its units by disengaging from the enemy at the greatest possible distance.

General Ludendorff rejected my recommendation and stuck with his plan to improve the Hermann and Hunding-Brunhild Positions, occupying them upon the loss of the Siegfried Position. This was an erroneous decision. The Siegfried Position was overrun as early as 8 October, and then the northern part of the German Army broke down under the constant enemy pressure as it withdrew toward the Meuse. By the time we reached the Meuse–Antwerp Position, the German Army had lost approximately four hundred thousand troops and six thousand guns since 8 August.

We completed our withdrawal to the Siegfried Position by 9 September. A few days later the enemy's advance elements appeared all along the line. Obviously their mission was to mask the deployment for the large-scale attack. Toward the end of September the enemy attacks began against almost all of our line. The Ninth Army was reassigned from Army Group Boehn to Army Group German Crown Prince, whose left wing and the right wing of Army Group Gallwitz were under strong enemy attack (mostly American) from both sides of the Argonne Forest.[4] Step by step the enemy extended his attacks against the entire German front, from the North Sea to Metz. The enemy broke through at many places, forcing OHL to displace from Avesnes-les-Aubert to Spa shortly after the

6 September chiefs' conference. On 9 October OHL ordered the withdrawal into the still little-improved Hermann and Hunding-Brunhild Positions.

Almost at the same time that order was issued, Army Group Boehn, which in the middle of September had moved its headquarters from Le Cateau to Avesnes-les-Aubert, was disbanded. The Second Army was assigned to Army Group Crown Prince Rupprecht and the Eighteenth Army to Army Group German Crown Prince. General von Boehn went on leave and at the end of October, at his request, assumed command of Seventh Army. I remained for the time being in Avesnes-les-Aubert at the disposal of OHL and dissolved the army group staff. I sent my horses and my luggage to Namur. Spending long hours in a staff car, I visited many command posts and units.

In the meantime, we learned that Entente troops had broken through the Bulgarian Army, which had withdrawn and all but dissolved. Soon thereafter, the Turkish Army also collapsed in Palestine and withdrew in panic. Realizing that victory was no longer within reach, Germany made an offer for an armistice.

On 26 October 1918 General Ludendorff resigned as first quartermaster general of the German Army. At that time I learned that he had offered his resignation previously, on 8 August. This was Ludendorff's own decision, which the Kaiser accepted, because Ludendorff could not support the intentions of the government under Chancellor Prince Max von Baden to seek peace at any price.[5] Ludendorff was succeeded by Lieutenant General Wilhelm Groener, who had been the chief of staff of Army Group Eichhorn in the Ukraine.

I deeply deplored the resignation of General Ludendorff. After Graf von Moltke [the Elder] and Graf von Schlieffen, General Ludendorff was certainly the greatest strategist that the German Army had produced.[6] His most important accomplishment had been the victory at Tannenberg in 1914. Unfortunately, his and Hindenburg's recommendation in the summer of 1915 to attack the Russians with our extreme left wing on the Eastern Front, push them into the Pinsk Marshes, and annihilate them there had been disapproved by Falkenhayn. In the further course of the war Ludendorff after his appointment as first quartermaster general was certainly the mainstay of all the war decisions. He accomplished the utmost. Under his strong hand the organization, training, and numerical strength of the German Army improved. He transformed the German Army into a sharp-edged war machine again, following the many failures under Moltke [the Younger's] and Falkenhayn's leadership. Ludendorff injected new fighting spirit into the German Army. During the years 1916 and 1917, and most of all in the spring of 1918, the Entente armies were dealt many serious blows in the west, in the south, and in the east. The German Army and its leadership developed an unrelenting trust in Ludendorff.

But then came the turnaround on 18 July 1918, when the British and French, increasingly reinforced by the Americans, went on the offensive. From that point on, Ludendorff's leadership of the German Army was based on inaccurate assumptions, as I have explained in my discussion of my own experiences. At the time Ludendorff was most certainly convinced of the correctness of his decisions, but he underestimated the weakness of large portions of the German people back in the Homeland, and he likewise overestimated the remaining strength of the German Army. With his highly developed sense of self-confidence, Ludendorff stuck uncompromisingly to his unfortunately incorrect inner conviction that the enemy attacks could be repulsed. In the final analysis, only this can explain Germany's total military collapse. Ludendorff failed because of the way he overstretched the forces. It was a tragic misfortune, both for him and the German Army. I had the highest respect for Ludendorff the soldier, even after his resignation. After the war, however, it became impossible to understand Ludendorff the man. I could not approve of his ideas about religion and Christianity, and his attitude toward Field Marshal von Hindenburg.[7]

On 30 October 1918, I drove to Spa and reported to the Kaiser, Hindenburg, and Groener. I was devastated by the conditions I found at OHL. Under Ludendorff iron discipline and procedure ruled. Now the strong leadership was lacking. All the wannabes were talking big. Everyone had his own opinion and offered it all too willingly. Consequently, I was glad that in place of General Emil Hell, who was assigned to replace Groener in the Ukraine, I was appointed on 31 October as the chief of staff of Army Group Duke Albrecht of Württemberg, and thus returned to the fighting front.

In the early morning hours of 1 November, as I was getting into my staff car for the drive to Strasbourg, I received a telegram from the chief surgeon of the military hospital in Antwerp. It read: "Your son—ill with double pneumonia. Life threatening!" After receiving his fourth wound, a severe shot through the lower thigh, my son was not yet ready to go back to the front line. In the fall of 1918, therefore, he had been performing duties as an administrative officer in a department of OHL. Despite the telegram, I still drove immediately to Strasbourg. From there I telephoned my wife in Stuttgart and asked her to travel to Antwerp. There she assumed the care of our son, whose condition slowly improved. But when the revolution in the Homeland broke out, it quickly affected the rear areas of the army as well. My wife had to leave Antwerp, and it took her five days to get back to Stuttgart on trains that were filled with crazed soldiers. Transporting our son back became a problem because the medical evacuation trains were stormed by riotous rear echelon soldiers. Any orderly transport of the wounded and sick was not possible. Our son and another sick officer were finally able to secure a seat in one of those medical evacuation trains, and they finally made it through Holland to a military hospital in Lübeck. On 23 December 1918 my son and I arrived almost at the same time in Stuttgart. As did I, he remained faithful to the army after the war. Today [1939] he is a major and a General Staff officer.[8]

9

Chief of the General Staff of Army Group Duke Albrecht of Württemberg

After my arrival in Strasbourg, I reported on 1 November 1918 directly to the commanding general. I had previously in peacetime served with Duke Albrecht when he was commanding general of the XIII Württemberg Army Corps. During the course of the war I ran into him several times at OHL meetings. The army group staff was very well established. I did not need to make changes. My Ia, Major von Stülpnagel, had also been in the 2nd Guards Regiment and we quickly worked well together.

The army group consisted of the Nineteenth Army on the right, Army Detachment A in the center, and Army Detachment B on the left. The army group's sector ran from Metz to the Swiss border, and it was very quiet. I thought it was possible, however, that after our withdrawal into the Meuse–Antwerp Position the enemy could try to break through south of Metz in order to threaten the Meuse–Antwerp Position in the flank and rear. On my recommendation, therefore, the commanding general ordered the Nineteenth Army to take all necessary precautionary measures to defend against such an attack. We strengthened the positions of the Nineteenth Army, the two army detachments, and the two Austrian divisions we had in reserve. The forces of the army group were primarily Landwehr and Landsturm divisions. During the long calm period on the southern end of the overall German line the army group's units had been able to reinforce strongly their forward fighting positions and their rearward positions.

The rear area of the battlefront was the German Homeland, and therefore socialist and communist propaganda, which was rampant throughout Germany, could strongly influence the operations of the army group. The propaganda targeted and exploited the yearnings of the elderly soldiers of our divisions to return to their families. The sedition advanced to the point where the troops were no longer willing to salute their officers. This was very difficult for the old soldier in me. But in such an aggravated climate, any violent reaction only would have increased the resistance of the troops. I therefore recommended to the commanding general that we abolish the military salute within the army group. Shortly after that directive made the rounds the old Landwehr and Landsturm soldiers started saluting their officers again on their own volition.

On 9 November 1918 the republic was proclaimed in Germany, and almost at the same time all German local rulers were deposed.[1] In the evening of 10 November we received the news from Spa that the Kaiser had departed for Holland. The events that preceded the Kaiser's decision are to my knowledge unclear to this day.[2] I am fully convinced that the Kaiser decided to leave the country because he believed it would be best for the country and the German people. Unfortunately, a considerable number of the soldiers whose minds had been poisoned by the propaganda of the leftist parties felt justified by the departure of the Kaiser. They now regarded the oath that they had sworn to the Kaiser as invalid, and therefore concluded they had every right to leave the army.

On 11 November at noon[3] the Armistice was signed with the condition that the German army would withdraw back across the Rhine. According to the orders issued by Field Marshal von Hindenburg, Army Group Duke Albrecht was to cross the Rhine only after the overall army front line tied in to the north had closed in on the line from Metz to Liège. Based on this, we organized in detail the transport of our army group and its deeply echeloned formations east of the Rhine. The army group headquarters remained with its operational staff in Strasbourg until the last day possible. In the meantime, we prepared our new headquarters in Freudenstadt in the Black Forest.

The soldiers' councils that already had been operating for a while were now legalized and now had the power to undermine publicly the morale and discipline of the German Army. Within our army group sector Strasbourg was the center of the sedition. From there the propaganda of the leftist parties targeted the front line with newspapers and leaflets. The leader of this hate propaganda machine was a clerk in the Strasbourg government. After legalization of the soldiers' councils he took over the chairmanship of the central soldiers' council in Alsace-Lorraine and called a meeting of the army group's soldier-councilmen at the city hall in Strasbourg. I drove to this meeting and was the first to speak, urging the rather unruly soldier-councilmen with very strong words not to forget their oath to the flag and to continue to protect our borders against a breakthrough by the enemy. Immediately after me a socialist member of the city parliament spoke, delivering an ugly hate speech against German officers. His comments were echoed by the leader of the soldiers' councils of Alsace-Lorraine. As the mood of the mob turned ugly, several especially rowdy soldiers started to come after me. I remained steadfast and calm and walked out of the room untouched.

Some soldiers waiting outside had been trying to influence my two drivers, but they remained loyal. I reached my staff car without further harassment and returned to my office. Shortly thereafter an enraged mob of soldiers tried to force its way into the offices of the army group headquarters. The leader of the gaggle, an ordnance artificer, stormed up the stairs leading to the reception room of the headquarters offices, wildly brandishing his rifle. I stepped in his way and yelled at him, "Your rifle is not on safe!" As he immediately looked down at the weapon, the clerks and orderlies grabbed him and dragged him back out into the street. After that, the mob of soldiers left the street in front of the headquarters building very quickly. On order of the commanding general, a company of a Württemberg Landwehr regiment that had always fought very bravely and had rejected the political propaganda was brought to Strasbourg to secure the army group headquarters. These brave Landwehr soldiers remained faithful to their German soldier's honor to the last day of the war.

Slowly the troops regained some of their sense as they realized that the imminent withdrawal of the army group across the Rhine as required by the Armistice could not be accomplished without proper leadership. The crossing of the Rhine went off without any friction, and the troops moved into quarters between the Rhine and the Black Forest. From our headquarters in Freudenstadt the commanding general and I made many inspection trips by car. One after the other the units of the army group were disbanded without any disruption, and then the troops were transported back to their home regions. The Austrian divisions also returned to their home country.

The republican government that was established in Stuttgart wanted to force Duke Albrecht of Württemberg to abdicate as the crown prince. I made it clear to a commission sent to Freudenstadt that Württemberg had abolished the throne, and the line of succession, therefore, had already lapsed. The members of the commission understood this. I drafted up an appropriate declaration of abdication, which then was published in the Stuttgart governmental newspaper. Duke Albrecht was very grateful to me for my assistance in this matter.

On 23 December 1918 the headquarters of Army Group Duke Albrecht of Württemberg was inactivated. Soon thereafter we received a telegram from Field Marshal von Hindenburg:

> For almost two years the armies of the Alsace-Lorraine front have been under the command of this army group. In the mountains as well as in the plains, the troops always distinguished themselves under the leadership of this army group in the attack as well as in the defense. Only the tenacious perseverance and the bitter struggle in the attacked operational sectors of this army group's positions made it possible for other army groups to conduct large-scale attacks. Upon the inactivation of

> this army group I therefore express my warmest gratitude to the well-seasoned staff.

I close my report on my activities during the World War with gratitude toward the many commanding generals at whose side I stood as chief of the General Staff, and who gave me their trust. Most of all, I wish to convey my faithful thoughts to all my comrades in arms in the World War.

10

After the War

Upon my arrival in Stuttgart virtually only red flags were flying. I could not help myself thinking that our military honor and the freedom of our German Fatherland had broken down. I nonetheless decided to devote my full strength to saving Germany.

After a short stay with my family I volunteered for the Border Security Force. On 10 January 1919, I was appointed chief of the General Staff of Army Border Security Command South. The commanding general was General of Infantry Kurt von dem Borne, who simultaneously commanded the VI Army Corps in Breslau.[1] In a separate building in that city I established the staff of the border protection headquarters.

Border Security Command South had the mission of defending the borders of all of Silesia, extending north up to approximately the area between Schneidmühle[2] and Bromberg.[3] It was on this very wide front that the newly formed Polish Army tried to break through. The command's mission of defending against the Poles was impossible to accomplish without reliable troops. I therefore telegraphed many of my faithful comrades from the World War, requesting their help in establishing the border security. My appeals were not in vain. Several hundred officers accompanied by their former subordinates rushed to Border Security Command South. With these troops I initially gained control of all the military uniform and weapons depots in the area and moved their stocks to the border regions, where I equipped the ever increasing stream of war veterans. I then organized them into complete units. A considerable number of reliable *Freikorps*[4] units were also formed, financially supported by local industry and agriculture. With this core of combat-experienced German troops it soon became possible to keep the attacking Poles at bay. At my specific recommendation, the War Ministry issued a decree that the border security units would remain without soldiers' councils. The fighting with the Poles in Upper Silesia and in the area of Rawitsch[5] was especially intense. It was at Rawitsch that I was forced to monitor with my fist in my pocket the transit of a French division to Poland.

At a meeting in Weimar in June, which was attended by a large number of members of our remaining army, I objected vigorously against acceptance of the peace conditions demanded by the Entente. But the disgraceful Versailles Peace Treaty was still signed. I submitted my resignation, but it was rejected. On 24 July 1919, I was appointed commander of the 26th Reichswehr Brigade, which largely consisted of troops from the former 2nd Guards Division. The new brigade's headquarters was in Fürstenwalde. Simultaneously, I was made chairman of the military commission in Berlin charged with rebuilding the army.[6]

On the last day of August 1919, I was assigned as chief of the General Staff of *Reichswehr-Gruppenkommando* II (II Corps) in Kassel, commanded by General of Infantry Roderich von Schoeler. From 18 May 1920 to 31 December 1924, I commanded the 6th Reichswehr Division, headquartered in Münster in Westphalia, and simultaneously commanded Area Command VI. I was promoted to lieutenant general on 1 October 1920.[7] Gritting my teeth, I was forced to endure the occupation of the *Ruhrgebiet* by Entente troops.[8] While in command of Area VI, I quietly laid the groundwork for the raising of several additional divisions to meet any necessary contingencies.

On 1 January 1925, I was assigned as commanding general of Reichswehr-Gruppenkommando I (I Corps) in Berlin, to which the 1st through 4th Reichswehr Divisions and the 1st and 2nd Cavalry Divisions were subordinated. On 1 October 1926, I was promoted to general of infantry.[9]

I retired from the army on 31 January 1927, after forty-one years of active service. I was given the honor of wearing the uniform of the 9th Reichswehr Infantry Regiment, which maintained the traditions of the 2nd Guards Regiment of Foot, in which I had entered the army as an officer candidate. It is my honest conviction that from officer candidate to general of infantry—in peacetime, during the World War, and during the postwar period—I always devoted my complete strength and abilities to the German Army, to which I will remain steadfastly faithful to the end of my life.[10]

Appendix A

Lossberg's Chronology

30 Apr. 1868	Born, Bad Homburg
13 Jan. 1886	Appointed *Fahnenjunker*, 2nd Foot Guards Regiment
13 Nov. 1886	Promoted to *Fähnrich*
17 Aug. 1887	Commissioned Lieutenant
1 Oct. 1894	Entered *Kriegsakademie*
17 Aug. 1895	Promoted to 1st Lieutenant
15 Mar. 1898	Candidate, Great General Staff
29 Mar. 1900	Promoted to Captain
18 Aug. 1900	Assigned to XIV Army Corps, General Staff
17 Feb. 1903	Assigned as Company Commander, 114th Infantry Regiment
22 Apr. 1905	Assigned to 19th Division as General Staff Officer Ia
27 Jan. 1907	Promoted to Major
1 Oct. 1907	Assigned as Instructor, *Kriegsakademie*
1 Oct. 1910	Assigned to XVII Army Corps, General Staff
1 Oct. 1912	Assigned as Battalion Commander, 2nd Battalion, 94th Infantry Regiment
16 June 1913	Promoted to Lieutenant Colonel
1 Oct. 1913	Assigned to XIII Army Corps, Chief of the General Staff
23 Jan. 1915	Assigned as Deputy Chief, Operations Division, OHL
24 July 1915	Promoted to Colonel
26 Sept. 1915	Assigned to Third Army, Chief of the General Staff
2 July 1916	Assigned to Second Army, Chief of the General Staff
19 July 1916	Assigned to First Army, Chief of the General Staff
21 Sept. 1916	Awarded *Orden Pour le Mérite*
11 Apr. 1917	Assigned to Sixth Army, Chief of the General Staff
24 Apr. 1917	Awarded the *Eichenlaub* to the *Pour le Mérite*
23 June 1917	Assigned to Fourth Army, Chief of the General Staff
3 Aug. 1917	Promoted to Major General
6 Aug. 1918	Assigned to Army Group Boehn, Chief of the General Staff
31 Oct. 1918	Assigned to Army Group Duke Albrecht of Württemberg, Chief of the General Staff
10 Jan. 1919	Assigned to Border Defense Army Corps South, Chief of the General Staff

24 July 1919	Assigned as Commander, 26th *Reichswehr* Brigade
31 Aug. 1919	Assigned to II General Command, Chief of the General Staff
18 May 1920	Assigned as Commander, 6th Division and Defense District VI
1 Oct. 1920	Promoted to Lieutenant General
1 Jan. 1925	Assigned as Commander, General Command I
1 Oct. 1926	Promoted to General of Infantry
31 Jan. 1927	Retired
14 May 1942	Died, Lübeck

Appendix B

Fritz von Lossberg's Medals and Decorations

- Iron Cross (*Eisernes Kreuz*), 2nd Class [German Reich]
- Iron Cross (*Eisernes Kreuz*), 1st Class [German Reich]
- Honor Cross of the World War 1914/1918 (*Ehrenkreuz des Weltkriegs 1914/1918*), with Swords [German Reich]
- Kaiser Wilhelm General Staff Officer Badge (*Kaiser-Wilhelm-Generalstabsoffizier Abzeichen*) [German Reich]
- *Pour le Mérite* [Prussia]
- *Pour le Mérite mit Eichenlaub* [Prussia]
- Order of the Red Eagle (*Roter Adlerorden*), 4th Class [Prussia]
- Order of the Crown (*Kronenorden*), 3rd Class [Prussia]
- Knight's Cross with Swords of the Royal House Order of Hohenzollern (*Königlicher Hausorden von Hohenzollern*) [Prussia]
- Honor Cross of the Princely House Order of Hohenzollern (*Fürstlicher Hausorden von Hohenzollern*), 2nd Class with Swords [Prussia]
- Knight's Cross of the Military Order of Max Joseph (*Militär-Max-Joseph-Orden*) [Bavaria]
- Military Service Order (*Militär-Verdienstorden*), 3rd Class with Swords and Crown [Bavaria]
- Commander's Cross of the Military Order of St. Henry (*Militär-St. Heinrichs-Orden*), 2nd Class [Saxony]
- Knight's Cross of the Albert Order (*Albrechts-Orden*), 2nd Class with Swords [Saxony]
- Commander of the Military Service Order (*Militärverdienstorden*) [Württemberg]
- Knight's Cross of the Order of the Crown (*Orden der Württembergischen Krone*) [Württemberg]
- Commander of the Order of the Lion of Zähringen (*Orden vom Zähringer Löwen*), 2nd Class [Baden]
- General Honor Decoration for Bravery (*Allgemeines Ehrenzeichen für Tapferkeit*) [Hesse]

- Military Service Cross (*Militärverdienstkreuz*), 2nd Class [Mecklenburg-Schwerin]
- Knight's Cross of the Order of Henry the Lion (*Hausorden Heinrichs des Löwen*), 1st Class [Brunswick]
- Knight's Cross of the House and Service Order of Peter Frederick Louis (*Haus und Verdienstorden von Herzog Peter Friedrich Ludwig*), 1st Class [Oldenburg]
- Commander of the Order of the White Falcon (*Hausorden vom Weissen Falken*) [Saxe-Weimar-Eisenach]
- Commander of the Saxe-Ernestine House Order (*Sachsen-Ernestinischer Hausorden*), 1st Class with Swords [Saxe-Coburg-Gotha]
- War Service Cross (*Kreuz für Verdienste im Kriege*) [Saxe-Meiningen]
- Hanseatic Cross (*Hanseatenkreuz*) [Hamburg, Bremen, Lübeck]

Appendix C

The Prussian/German Staff System, 1806–1918

During the Great War of 1914–1918 only the French Army had an organization remotely similar to the German General Staff.[1] Evolving from Frederick the Great's small Quartermaster General's Staff of the 1750s, the Prussian General Staff had become a distinct institution by about 1785. After Prussia was defeated decisively by Napoleon at Jena in 1806, the military reformer General David Gerhard von Scharnhorst reorganized the Prussian Army. The Prussian General Staff emerged from that process in the basic form that would characterize that organization up to the defeat of the Wehrmacht in 1945. The most positive of the foundational principles of the German General Staff are still present in the German Bundeswehr today. In contrast to the other great powers of the nineteenth century and the first half of the twentieth, the Germans always pursued a policy of building and maintaining the brain of their army before building its body.

The French established a General Staff in 1818, the Americans in 1903, and the British in 1904. But the Prussian/German General Staff was more than an organization. It was also a distinct branch of the army, with centralized management of the training and careers of the General Staff officers. The Americans and the British have never adopted such a system. During World War I an American or British officer was a General Staff officer only so long as he was assigned to a General Staff. Once he was assigned elsewhere, he reverted to his basic branch, be it infantry, artillery, cavalry, engineers, etc. The French used such an open system model for several years. In 1833 they adopted a closed General Staff Corps, but did not include the constant rotation between General Staff and field command assignments that the Germans used. The French system, in turn, resulted in the institutional inbreeding that led to their crushing defeat in 1870–1871.

In 1810 Scharnhorst established the *Allgemeine Kriegsschule* (General War School), the primary training institution for General Staff officers. From 1818 to 1830 the great Prussian military theorist Major General Carl von Clausewitz served as the school's director. During that period the future Field Marshal Helmuth von Moltke the Elder was a student there as a second lieutenant between 1823 and 1826. In 1859, the General War School was renamed the *Kriegsakademie* (War Academy).[2]

In 1815 the General Staff established its headquarters in Berlin. In 1821 the General Staff Corps came under the direct control of the chief of the General Staff and was organized into two primary divisions. The *Grosser Generalstab* (Great General Staff) was the national-level staff of the entire army; the *Truppengeneralstab* (General Staff with Troops) consisted of the trained General Staff officers serving with the field units at the army, corps, and division levels. The same body of General Staff officers rotated between both elements. The General Staff officers also rotated periodically to command assignments at various levels, to keep them in constant touch with the realities of service in the field units. But even during their periodic command assignments, those officers still remained under the direct control of the chief of the Great General Staff. Although many general officers in the Germany Army were themselves General Staff officers, that never was (and still is not) a basic qualification for promotion to the general officer ranks.

The Prussian/German General Staff did adapt and change over time. Throughout the nineteenth century the Prussian Army came under the direct command of the king. Initially, the chief of the Great General Staff had no actual command authority. He primarily was an advisor to the Prussian war minister, but not to the king. More often than not, the war minister himself was a serving or a retired officer. Further complicating things, the king's military cabinet controlled the army's personnel management system and exercised the ultimate authority over officers' commissioning, training, assignments, and awards. As the nineteenth century progressed, there was a constant political struggle for the king's ear among the three institutions. The military cabinet was responsible for personnel management, the War Ministry for organizing, training, and equipping the army, and the Great General Staff essentially was a planning and advisory body, with no operational control over Prussian forces in the field. In theory, the chain of command in wartime ran from the king (and later the Kaiser) directly to the senior commanders in the field.

The status and power of the Great General Staff began to change in 1857 with the appointment of Helmuth von Moltke the Elder as chief. Moltke immediately improved the military's inner relationships by establishing good working associations with the minister of war, General Albrecht von Roon, and the Prussian chancellor, Otto von Bismarck.

The General Staff built the operational plan for Prussia's 1864 war with Denmark, but right from the start it was obvious that the senior Prussian field commander, the octogenarian Field Marshal Friedrich von Wrangel, did not understand the war plan. King Wilhelm I of Prussia replaced Wrangel with the highly competent Prince Friedrich Karl and then took the unorthodox step of sending Moltke to the field as Friedrich Karl's chief of staff.

Following Germany's victory over Denmark six months later, Wilhelm granted Moltke the personal right of direct access (*Immediatrecht*) to the throne. Two years later, on 2 June 1866, Wilhelm delegated to Moltke the authority to issue orders in the name of the king during the Austro-Prussian War. That made Moltke the de facto commander in chief of the Prussian Army in the field. Prussia defeated its arch rivals Austria, Bavaria, and Saxony in only six weeks. During the 1870–1871 Franco-Prussian War, Moltke personally commanded the operations in the field, assisted by a staff of only thirteen General Staff officers. Moltke's successes in the Austro-Prussian and Franco-Prussian Wars solidified the position of the chief of the Great General Staff through the end of World War I. The *Kriegsakademie* was placed directly under the chief of the Great General Staff in 1872, and in 1883 Kaiser Wilhelm I extended the right of direct access to the throne to the office of the chief of the Great General Staff. And although the holder of that office was now on the same level as the war minister and the chief of the military cabinet, he now was really the "first among equals."

From the 1870s on, the chief of the Great General Staff directed the German Field Army in the name of the Kaiser in wartime. In peacetime he was responsible for war planning, intelligence, mobilization, deployment, and the training and management of the General Staff Corps. During peacetime, however, he had no power to command or to inspect the training and readiness of troops. The War Ministry retained the authority for training troops, weapons procurement, pay, administration, and issuing military regulations. The chief of the Great General Staff had no influence on the efficiency reports and career development of field commanders, unless they also happened to be General Staff officers. The military cabinet remained an independent agency that reported directly to the Kaiser.

Even after the establishment of the German empire in 1871 there technically was no such thing as a "German General Staff." The kingdoms of Prussia, Saxony, Bavaria, and Württemberg all maintained their own armies and each had a General Staff, but only the Prussian Great General Staff prepared war plans for the combined military forces of Germany. In time of peace there was a significant amount of cross-posting among the four armies, and all were organized, trained, and equipped based on common standards.

Bavaria had a separate General Staff, and its own *Kriegsakademie,* whose standards were on par with Prussia's. The king of Bavaria retained peacetime command authority over the Bavarian Army, although the German Kaiser had the right to inspect the troops and their training. Saxony maintained a separate officer corps and a war ministry to administer its army, but the German Kaiser exercised peacetime command. The officer corps of Württemberg's army was integrated with that of Prussia's, but the Württemberg War Ministry retained control over certain administrative functions. Hence, in the early part of Lossberg's memoirs he frequently mentions sending requests for support to Stuttgart, rather than to Berlin. On the eve of World War I, Bavaria deployed three of the German Army's twenty-five corps, Saxony fielded two, and Württemberg one. That was the XIII Army Corps, which Lossberg—although he was a Prussian officer—served in as the chief of staff from October 1913 to January 1915.

By 1914 the Prussian Great General Staff consisted of ten numbered departments and a series of named departments. They further were grouped under one of five *Oberquartiermeister* (deputy chiefs of the General Staff), under the chief of National Survey, or directly under the chief of the Great General Staff. The 2nd Department had the leading role, and the Railroad Department had the largest number of assigned personnel. The senior ranking *Oberquartiermeister* also had the courtesy title of *Generalquartiermeister* (vice chief of the General Staff), who substituted when necessary for the chief of the Great General Staff.

Chief of the Great General Staff
- Central Department: General Staff Personnel, Organization, and Administration
- 6th Department: Maneuvers
- Military History Department II: Older Wars

***Oberquartiermeister* I**
- 2nd Department: Germany, Operations, and Deployments
- Railroad Department: Movements
- 4th Department: Foreign Fortifications

***Oberquartiermeister* II**
- 3rd Department: France and Morocco; Britain and Egypt; Afghanistan
- 9th Department: Belgium, Netherlands, Switzerland, Italy, Spain, Portugal, America, and Germany's Colonies

***Oberquartiermeister* III**
- 5th Department: Operational Studies
- 8th Department: *Kriegsakademie*

***Oberquartiermeister* IV**
- 1st Department: Scandinavia, Russia, Persia, Turkey, and East Asia
- 10th Department: Austria-Hungary and the Balkans

***Oberquartiermeister* V**
- Military History Department I: Recent Wars

- Archives
- Library

Chief of National Survey

- Trigonometric Department
- Topographical Department
- Cartographic Department

Despite the *Truppengeneralstab* officers' being assigned to units in the field, the majority of the staff officers in those field units were not General Staff officers. The *Truppengeneralstab* officers reported directly to their respective commanders, but the chief of the Great General Staff remained their superior for "professional matters." The unit commander and the unit chief of staff (always a General Staff officer himself) wrote joint evaluation reports on those officers. For issues involving strict General Staff work, a *Truppengeneralstab* officer generally reported to the next higher General Staff officer. General Staff officers might oversee the routine staff work of a unit, but they seldom actually did it. General Staff officers were experts in operations and other areas, such as operational movements and ammunition supply, that directly supported operations. Technical experts often were assigned to work on the General Staff, but they were not actually members of the General Staff Corps.

At the start of World War I, the chief of staff of a field army supervised the assigned General Staff officers:

- Ia: Operations and Training
- Ib: Logistics and Operational Movements
- Ic: Intelligence
- Id: Artillery and Infantry Ammunition Resupply

Oberquartiermeister, who himself was a General Staff officer, supervised the rest of the field army staff, which included:

- II: Administrative and Personnel
- III: Judge Advocate General and Military Police
- IV: Medical and Veterinary

At the corps level, usually only the chief of staff, the Ia, and the Ib were General Staff officers. In some special cases a corps also might have a Ic. The division was the lowest echelon to which General Staff officers were assigned. The Ia was the only General Staff officer, and he performed the dual functions of operations officer and chief of staff. The divisional Ia typically was a senior captain or a junior major.

The key figure in the German staff system was the chief of staff. In the absence of the commander, the chief of staff had the authority to make decisions in the commander's name for all matters except legal proceedings. The commander had the final say, but he and his chief of staff discussed matters as almost equals until the final decision was made. It was almost, but not quite, a system of dual command. This peculiar relationship between the commander and his chief of staff was unique to the German Army. On purely operational matters, the chief of staff had the option of protesting to the next higher echelon chief of staff—for example, the corps chief of staff to the field army chief of staff—the decisions of his commander with which he did not agree. That right, however, was exercised only very rarely. In effect, then, the chief of staff was both a subordinate of his own commander and also the High Command's liaison to that commander. He was not, however, an all-encompassing chief of staff, as in the American or French armies.

A German chief of staff was more like a super operations officer and a de facto deputy commander. This comes out quite clearly in Lossberg's memoirs. During World War I the "Chief System" reached the peak of its power and influence. The *Oberste Heersleitung* (German High Command) increasingly held chiefs of staff rather than commanders responsible for tactical and operational failures. Many historians have argued that Ludendorff carried the Chief System to extremes, marginalizing many commanders, especially during the planning of the great German 1918 offensives. During Ludendorff's initial planning conference held on 11 November 1917, only chiefs of staff and other General Staff officers were present—no commanders.

The Germans had a virtually unique system for selecting and training General Staff officers. They entered the General Staff very early in their careers, as relatively junior officers. Lossberg, for one, started his General Staff training while he was still only a second lieutenant. Until about 1870 it was possible, although not at all usual, for an officer to become a qualified General Staff officer without attending the *Kriegsakademie*. Entrance to that majestic institution was based on a competitive examination that focused solely on military knowledge. A system of blind numbering on the exams was supposed to eliminate any bias the graders might have in favor of the aristocratic officers from the elite guards regiments. But the guards officers generally tended to score higher, because being stationed near Berlin most of the time gave them greater military training opportunities. If the entrance examination had been based on broader academic attainment, the officers from the middle class as a group would have done better, as they typically had a better general education than the aristocratic guards officers. Thus, noblemen were represented disproportionately in the General Staff through the end of World War I. Lossberg himself was one of those guards officers for eight years, prior to his entrance to the *Kriegsakademie*.

Nonetheless, in 1870 virtually none of the senior commanders in the Guards Corps had attended the *Kriegsakademie.*

Prior to World War I the course at the *Kriegsakademie* ran three years. Of the 140 to 160 officers who started the program each year, only about one hundred completed it three years later. The graduates then took another competitive examination for General Staff posting, with only about thirty being accepted. That group then underwent a two-year probationary period serving on the Great General Staff, followed by a final selection screening. Only about a half dozen officers per year made the final cut. Fully qualified General Staff officers between the ranks of lieutenant and colonel added the initials i.G. (for *im Generalstab*) immediately after their rank titles. Thus, Lossberg's official complete rank title as a colonel of the General Staff was *Oberst i.G.* They also wore distinctive double-wide carmine trouser stripes. General officers did not append the i.G. to their rank titles.[3]

Many of those officers who did not make the various cuts in the selection process, but who were still considered capable of good staff work, became *Adjuntantur,* working on the General Staff but not doing General Staff work proper. Others became instructors in officers' schools, and others returned to the line units. At one time officers who failed to make the final cuts still had a possibility of being admitted to the General Staff at some point in the future. That practice ended when Helmuth von Moltke the Younger was chief of the Great General Staff. At the start of World War I, the German officer corps had a total strength of 36,693. Of that number, only 625 were assigned to the General Staff—the *Grosser Generalstab* and the *Truppengeneralstab* combined. Only 352 of that number, however, were actually fully qualified members of the General Staff Corps. The others were *Adjuntantur* and specialist officers attached for specific duties.

The key to the German command system was the fact that the commanders and their staffs at all levels operated on the same set of principles and worked through the tactical decision-making process with the same set of intellectual tools. The General Staff officers at each echelon provided the common link in the process. Many critics over the years have dismissed this system as nothing more than "groupthink" on a huge scale, but such an assessment is far too simplistic and misses the main point. The system did not produce perfect solutions every time, but it almost always produced workable solutions. And it produced them quicker, which gave the Germans a huge tactical advantage over their opponents. The guiding principle was that a good plan now was better than a perfect plan tomorrow. Thus, in the *Kriegsakademie* there were no "school solutions" to the tactical problems. The only criterion for evaluation was whether the student's solution to the problem worked, or not.

Contrary to the rigid and hierarchical nature of militaries in general, and German society in particular, the German Army developed and practiced innovative and flexible command and staff techniques that many other armies tried to copy but almost none mastered. By the start of the twentieth century, *Weisungsführung* (leadership by directive) allowed great latitude to higher-level commanders at the army level and in some situations at the corps level. Rather than issuing explicit and detailed orders, the High Command issued generalized statements of its intent (*Absicht*), which then provided the framework for independent initiative by the subordinate commanders. This technique capitalized on the local commander's superior knowledge of the situation in his own area of operations, and also compensated for the slow and unreliable communication systems of the time. As World War I progressed, that freedom of initiative extended down as far as the battalion level. Such freedom of initiative at the lowest possible echelon was an essential component in the flexible defense tactics that Lossberg helped pioneer. Following the war, the military reforms of the Reichswehr extended the principle of initiative even farther down the chain of command, as the concept came to be known as *Auftragstaktik*, alternately translated into English as "Mission Command" or "Mission-Oriented Tactics."

The German General Staff was far from a flawless institution. Many historians have pointed out that General Staff training was more narrowing rather than broadening, and the General Staff Corps suffered from over-specialization. General Staff officers were trained to be experts in tactics and operations to the exclusion of all else. Before the Wars of German Unification, students at the *Kriegsakademie* studied leadership and the great military theorists. After the *Kriegsakademie* came under the direct control of the chief of the Great General Staff, the students focused almost exclusively on operations and tactics through the case study method.

The German General Staff system was never designed to produce officers with broad political and strategic vision, like Napoleon, Ulysses S. Grant, Ferdinand Foch, Alan F. Brooke, George Marshall, or Dwight D. Eisenhower. It did produce some of recent history's most talented operations officers at the tactical and operational levels, with Fritz von Lossberg being one of the most prominent examples. The irony, however, is that the Germans still lost two world wars while simultaneously setting tactical standards on the battlefield that remain unequalled to this day.

Notes

Translators' Introduction

1. Jonathan Bailey, *The First World War and the Birth of the Modern Style of Warfare,* The Occasional Number 22 (Camberly: Strategic and Combat Studies Institute, British Army Staff College, 1996).

2. David T. Zabecki, ed., *Chief of Staff: The Principal Officers Behind History's Great Commanders,* vol. 1, *Napoleonic Wars to World War I,* chapter 11, "Fritz von Lossberg" (Annapolis, Md.: U.S. Naval Institute Press, 2008), 174–186.

3. Timothy T. Lupfer, *The Dynamics of Doctrine: Changes in German Tactical Doctrine During the First World War,* Leavenworth Papers No. 4 (Ft. Leavenworth, Kans.: U.S. Army Combat Studies Institute, July 1981), 19.

4. Graeme Wynne, *If Germany Attacks: The Battle in Depth in the West* (London: Faber and Faber, 1940), 125–125, 160.

5. American and British usage of the term quartermaster notwithstanding, a Quartermaster General in the German Army of World War I was not a logistics officer. He was a deputy chief of staff, usually in charge of some specific function or group of functions. The first quartermaster general of the German Army was the equivalent of what we would today call the vice chief of staff of the army.

6. Erich Ludendorff, *My War Memoirs, 1914–1918* (London: Hutchenson, 1920), 386.

7. Wynne, *If Germany Attacks,* 131, 249; Lupfer, *The Dynamics of Doctrine,* 9–11.

8. Fritz von Lossberg, *Meine Tätigkeit im Weltkriege 1914–1918* (Berlin: Mittler und Sohn, 1939), 280–281.

9. Wynne, *If Germany Attacks,* 200.

10. Richard Holmes, *The Western Front* (London: BBC Books, 1999), 151.

11. Lupfer, *The Dynamics of Doctrine,* 30; Wynne, *If Germany Attacks,* 203, 206.

12. Lossberg, 283; Wynne, *If Germany Attacks,* 206.

13. Ludendorff, *My War Memoirs,* 422–427.

14. Wynne, *If Germany Attacks,* 213.

15. Army Group Crown Prince Rupprecht, *Operations Order Ia 8082,* 1 July 1918, Bayerisches Kriegsarchiv, Munich, Germany, File Hgr. Rupprecht, Bd. 112; David T. Zabecki, *The German 1918 Offensives: A Case Study in the Operational Level of War* (London: Routledge, 2006), 280–310.

16. Lossberg, *Meine Tätigkeit im Weltkriege 1914–1918,* 344.

17. Ibid., 345–349.

18. Wilhelm Ritter von Leeb, *Die Abwehr* (Berlin: E. S. Mittler und Sohn, 1938), 68–70.

19. Gerhard Gross, *The Myth and Reality of German Warfare: Operational Thinking from Moltke the Elder to Heusinger,* English translation edited by David T. Zabecki (Lexington: Univ. Press of Kentucky, 2016), 174–174.

20. Richard Simpkin, *Race to the Swift: Thoughts on Twenty-First Century Warfare* (London: Brassey's, 1985), 229.

Lossberg's 1939 Prologue

1. One can only speculate on what Lossberg's thoughts on the Third Reich were at the time of his death, three years after he wrote this.

1. Chief of Staff of the XIII Army Corps

1. General Staff officers rotated their assignments between the Great General Staff in Berlin and the General Staff with Troops, assigned to the units in the field. Periodically General Staff officers were given command assignments for career development. Upon completion of such assignments they always returned to a General Staff billet.

2. At the time this book was published in 1939, the issue of Germany's "War Guilt," as defined by the Versailles Treaty, was still a sensitive topic.

3. Thionville, France, was in 1914 known as Diedenhofen, in German Lothringen (Lorraine).

4. The General Staff officer Ia was the operations officer.

5. The General Staff officer Ib was the logistics and movements officer.

6. At the start of the war the Fifth Army was commanded by the Kaiser's son, Crown Prince Wilhelm, who was only a major general at the time.

7. Annexed by Germany in 1871 following the Franco-Prussian War, Elsass (Alsace) and Lothringen (Lorraine) were designated as Reichsländer (Imperial Territories) administered directly from Berlin. Alsace and Lorraine did not enjoy the same levels of local autonomy as all the other German kingdoms, dukedoms, and principalities that comprised the German Reich.

8. *Landwehr* brigades were territorial defense reserve units. Despite their Homeland defense mission, the Germans deployed several such brigades into the front lines during the early months of the war in 1914.

9. The *Nordmark* (Northern March) was roughly what is the modern state of Brandenburg, in northeastern Germany)

10. Now Charleville-Mézières, France.

11. Fabeck's nickname among the troops was "Southern Cross."

12. The preceding paragraph reflects the German experiences with *franc tireurs* (irregulars, or literally "free shooters") during the Franco-Prussian War of 1870–1871. At the start of World War I in 1914, German military leaders conceived of war as being conducted only between regularly constituted forces. Civilians had no business getting involved, and had no right to defend their country by force. Civilians who bore arms against the German Army, then, were regarded as war criminals, and thus subject to summary punishment and reprisals. When faced with such conduct by civilians, the Germans tended to act with surprise and outrage. The German interpretation of this point of international law was not shared by most of the other nations of the world. Herein lies the basis of the many German atrocity stories from the first months of World War I. See Barbara Tuchman, *The Guns of August* (London: Penguin Books, 2014), 347–348.

13. The word *Mörser* is often translated as mortar. In the German Army of World War I, however, a Mörser was not an infantry mortar or a trench mortar. Rather, it was a very heavy howitzer of the caliber 210mm and larger. A trench mortar was a *Minenwerfer*, and it was a weapon manned by crews from the pioneer infantry (combat engineers). It was a weapon similar in ballistic effect but significantly different in design from the British Stokes mortar, the prototype of all modern "stovepipe" infantry mortars. By World War II the Germans had adopted the almost universal mortar design and they reclassified it as a standard infantry weapon, They also changed the designation to *Granatwerfer*.

14. During the early years of World War I, German soldiers in the field wore the *Pickelhaube* leather helmets, which were largely useless against small arms fire. In the field, the helmet usually was worn with a cloth cover to protect the leather from the elements.

15. Now Charency-Vezin, France.

16. As mentioned in note 1.12, the German military at this point in the war saw this sort of thing differently than did most other countries. When Lossberg published his memoirs in 1939, he obviously still felt that international law was on Germany's side on this issue.

17. Ulans were light cavalry, traditionally armed with lances.

18. Dragoons were originally mounted infantrymen. By the twentieth century, however, dragoons were conventional light cavalry.

19. Now Fontaines-Saint-Clair, France.

20. *Jäger* were light infantry.

21. Ad hoc provisional units formed in the field were commonly designated by the name of their commander. Most such units never appeared in formal order of battle listings.

22. Now Gercourt-et-Drillancourt, France

23. Now Chatel-Chéhéry, France.

24. Lossberg spent most of World War I opposite the British.

25. Crown Prince Wilhelm, commanding general of the Fifth Army, made a similar recommendation to OHL on 2 September. Crown Prince Wilhelm, *My War Experiences* (New York: McBride, 1923), 64

26. The Fifth Army's subordinate units were the V, VI, XIII, and XVI Army Corps, V and VI Reserve Corps, IV Cavalry Corps, and Landwehr Division Francke.

27. Colonel (later Major General) Max Hoffmann was the operations officer of the Eighth Army after Hindenburg and Ludendorff took over. In his book, Hoffmann stated that when Ludendorff learned of the corps' being sent to the east, he told OHL "that we were positively not in need of these reinforcements." Max Hoffmann, *The War of Lost Opportunities* (1924; reprint, Nashville: Battery Press, 1999), 35.

28. Now Rembercourt-Sommaisne, France.

29. The French Third Army was commanded by General Maurice Sarrail.

30. Fleury-devant-Douaumont was one of several villages eventually destroyed during the fighting for Verdun in 1916.

31. The German Second Army was commanded by Colonel General (later Field Marshal) Karl von Bülow.

32. The Law of Action, or the Imperative of Action, is a principle of classical German military theory. By imposing that law on the enemy, that enemy becomes the object of and not the subject of events, and the number of his incalculable frictions increases accordingly.

33. This period of running skirmishes from 17 September to 19 October 1914, during which each side tried to outflank the other, has become known as "The Race to the Sea."

34. A hamlet north of Lachalade, Le Four de Paris was largely destroyed during the fighting in June and July 1915.

35. Reverse-slope defense is one of the basic defensive techniques to this day.

36. As a lieutenant general, the equivalent of a British or American major general, Falkenhayn was a very junior general officer to hold such a position, which gave him the authority to issue orders to commanders of far higher rank. The German Army was almost unique in its "function overrides rank" approach to military command.

37. Lossberg is referring to the German victories in the 26–30 September 1914 Battle of Tannenberg, and the 7–14 September First Battle of the Masurian Lakes.

38. Actually, modern warfighting experience contradicts Lossberg on this point. All modern logistics planning tables factor more ammunition for the defense than for the offense, while fuel expenditure factors are just the opposite.

39. As Lossberg notes later in his narrative, the German Seventh Army, which started the war on the extreme left flank in the south, had by mid-September been withdrawn, redeployed north, and inserted into the line between the First and Second Armies. The attacking right wing, as Lossberg described it, then, would have been the First and Seventh Armies. The strong defensive line, from the center to the left, would have been (north to south) the Second, Third, Fourth, Fifth, and Sixth Armies.

40. The Bavarian Cavalry Division did not have a numerical designation.

41. Lossberg obviously thought that despite the fact that Falkenhayn had the *de jure* authority of the position of chief of the General Staff, he somehow lacked the self-confidence because of his relatively junior rank. See note 1.36.

42. In his war memoirs, Crown Prince Wilhelm mentions visiting the forward command post of the XIII Army Corps on 22 September. Crown Prince of Germany Wilhelm, *My War Experiences*, 106.

43. It was commanded by Lieutenant General Adolf Francke.

44. Now Servon-Melzicourt, France.

45. In September 1918, Saint-Mihiel would be the focal point of the first large-scale offensive operation conducted by the American Expeditionary Force.

46. In 1920, Lüttwitz was the leader of the Kapp-Lüttwitz Putsch, an attempt to topple the democratic republic of Weimar Germany.

47. From 26 November 1918 until the Armistice on 11 November the American Expeditionary Force fought its costliest battle of World War I in the Argonne Forest.

48. Ersatz Divisions were Replacement Divisions.

49. During the Battle of Verdun in 1916, the 6 March–31 May fighting for the hill known as Mort Homme was some of the most horrific combat of World War I.

50. The foot artillery was the German Army's heavy artillery. It was called foot artillery because its gunners were not mounted and had to walk with the guns while they were being transported. The field artillery had lighter guns and all the gunners were mounted. Each time the heavy guns moved, horses had to be attached temporarily.

51. Konstantin Schmidt von Knobelsdorf had already been an officer for thirty-six years when in early 1914 he was assigned as Crown Prince Wilhelm's military tutor on the General Staff. When the Kaiser informed Crown Prince Wilhelm that he was being assigned command of the Fifth Army, he also selected Schmidt von Knobelsdorf as his chief of staff. The Kaiser told his son, "Whatever he advises, you must do." Later, during the Battle of Verdun in 1916, Wilhelm and Schmidt von Knobelsdorf had a falling out, and Colonel Friedrich Graf von der Schulenburg was assigned as the Fifth Army chief of staff. Crown Prince Wilhelm, *My War Experiences*, 206–208.

52. Crown Prince Wilhelm was only thirty-two years old when his father, Kaiser Wilhelm II, appointed him as commanding general of the Fifth Army. At the time he had never commanded anything more than a regiment of hussars.

53. During World War I, German divisions normally had only one fully qualified General Staff officer, who doubled as both the divisional chief of staff and the operations officer.

54. The commanding general of the Second Army was Colonel General Karl von Bülow, who was sixty-eight years old at the time.

55. Lieutenant Colonel Richard Hentsch was the chief of the *Nachrichten-Abteilung* (Intelligence Evaluation Branch) at OHL, and a member of Moltke's inner circle. Moltke sent Hentsch to the front with broad authority to make whatever adjustments in the German line that seemed appropriate. General Staff officers were not mere messengers. They were expected to know the intent of the chief of the General Staff and had the authority to issue orders in his name. On 8 September 1914, Hentsch met with a deeply pessimistic Bülow. The next day he met with First Army commander Colonel General Alexander von Kluck. Based on the precarious position of the First Army, Hentsch directed the First Army to withdraw behind the Marne. Military historians have been arguing about that decision ever since. Echoing Lossberg's criticism, General Max Hoffmann wrote in 1924: "What would have happened if Field Marshal von Kluck and General von Kuhl had refused to obey the order Lieutenant Colonel Hentsch had brought them, and had insisted on the attack by the First Army which they considered right and meant to execute? If they had done so, perhaps they would have become national heroes of the campaign." Hoffmann, *The War of Lost Opportunities*, 62.

56. Agreeing with Lossberg, Hoffmann wrote: "After the repulse on the Marne it was once more possible to try to make a rush forward instead of letting the front be strengthened for a trench war. This would have been possible if a decision had been taken to transport at least ten to twelve army corps from the left to the right wing, and with them to make a grand united attack on that side. That this plan, which was suggested by General [Wilhelm] Grüner, was not executed is the fault of the 2nd OHL," which was led by Falkenhayn. Hoffmann, *The War of Lost Opportunities*, 244–245.

57. This statement is technically correct insofar as the Allies never managed to

achieve a breakout and subsequent exploitation. However, the Allied counterattack at the Marne on 18 July 1918, and the series of concentric offensives following the British attack at Amiens on 8 August 1918, progressively pushed the German Army back until it was on the verge of collapse by the time of the Armistice on 11 November.

58. Now Charleville-Mézières, France.

59. Lossberg is referring to what the Germans to this day call *Der Kindermord bei Ypern* (The Massacre of the Innocents at Ypres). During the First Battle of Ypres (19 October–22 November), tens of thousands of only semi-trained young German volunteers and conscripts attacked in densely packed, linear formations. They were cut down in large numbers by the long-serving professional soldiers of the British Expeditionary Force. Many of those killed in that battle are buried in the German military cemetery at Langemarck, Belgium.

60. Now Beaucamps-Ligny, France.

61. Now Ligny-Saint-Flochel, France.

62. *Jäger* (literally hunter) units were elite light infantry.

63. Today this is a road called "Chaussée de la Garde de Dieu."

64. Those leaders were Hindenburg and Ludendorff.

65. These were the Battle of Tannenberg (26–30 August 1914) and the First Battle of the Masurian Lakes (7–14 September 1914).

66. The attack group was commanded by General Hermann Christian Wilhelm von Strantz.

67. This was the XIII Army Corps, commanded by General of Infantry Max von Fabeck.

68. Now Gdansk, Poland.

69. A combined (*gemischte*) brigade consisted of its own organic infantry, cavalry, and artillery elements and was capable of semi-autonomous operations for limited periods.

70. An army detachment (*Armee-Abteilung*) was a force detached from and operating independent of a field army. In essence, it was a small army. Armee-Abteilung Woyrsch was formed on 3 November 1914 under the command of Colonel General (later Field Marshal) Remus von Woyrsch. It was disbanded on 15 December 1917.

71. The German Army commonly used the term *Schwerpunkt* in the sense of a main effort, rather than the way Clausewitz used to term to mean center of gravity.

72. Now Stare Budy, Poland.

73. Each of the kingdoms of the German Reich—Prussia, Bavaria, Saxony, and Württemberg—maintained separate war ministries. In time of war the Prussian War Ministry served as the overall war ministry for the empire.

2. Division Chief of the General Staff of the Supreme Command of the Field Army (OHL)

1. Now Charleville-Mézières, France.

2. Now Gdansk, Poland.

3. The Prussian military cabinet exercised authority over all officer personnel matters in the Prussian Army, but not the Württemberg, Saxon, or Bavarian armies.

4. Britain's New Army, also referred to as Kitchener's Army, was an all-volunteer force formed in the United Kingdom following the outbreak of World War I. It was created on the recommendation of Field Marshal Lord Horatio Kitchener, who at the time was the secretary of state for war.

5. The standard French artillery at that time were 75mm, 105mm, and 155mm. American artillery, prior to America's entry into the war, were primarily 3-inch and 6-inch, with a few odd 4-inch and 5-inch pieces. Nonetheless, during the early part of the twentieth century several American factories were producing artillery projectiles in metric calibers, for export to the European arms market. According to Karl Rubis, historian at the U.S. Army Ordnance Corps and School, "Prior to American entry into WWI, there were an abundance of chemical/munition/industrial firms producing munitions and other war materiel under contract from the Allies (particularly Britain and France). Profits for the manufacturers was with the contracts to Allies, not the American Army. Du Pont actually was one of the leading manufacturers of powder for the allied effort. Other industries were producing a wide range of materiel. This abundance of production is why many of them got the nickname as 'merchants of death' due to their huge profits during World War I."

6. Commanded by General of Infantry Hermann von Strantz.

7. Hartmannswillerkopf is known to the French as Vieil Armand.

8. German divisions started the war in 1914 with two infantry brigades, each with two infantry regiments. Under the new divisional structure, a division had three infantry regiments, under a single infantry brigade.

9. The Germans finally attempted such a plan in 1918, when on 21 March they launched Operation MICHAEL, the first of the Ludendorff Offensives. Ludendorff, however, paid far less attention to the vulnerabilities in the Allies' lines of communication, and he planned to make the pivot north just to the west of Arras, a good forty miles from the coast. Operation MICHAEL failed.

10. In 1919 Seeckt became the last chief of the General Staff of the German Imperial Army. From 1919 to 1933 he was the chief of the Army Command (*Heeresleitung*) of the Reichswehr. He is credited with building the Reichswehr into a small but highly professional and innovative fighting force that after 1933 became the foundation for the rapid expansion of the World War II Wehrmacht.

11. At this point in the war gas attacks were conducted by releasing gas from the leading edge of one's own front lines and letting the wind carry it over the enemy's positions. This was a special handicap for the Germans, because the prevailing winds on the Western Front were usually west to east. As the war progressed, the ability to fire artillery gas projectiles directly into the enemy's lines reduced—but did not completely eliminate—the effects of the wind.

12. At this point in the war the Germans had not yet formed army groups.

13. Harnessed batteries had their own organic horses for mobility; unharnessed batteries did not, and had to schedule the temporary attachment of the horses necessary to make a move.

14. Later the XXXVIII Reserve Corps.

15. Liman von Sanders held the rank of field marshal in the Turkish Army.

16. As a Turkish field marshal, von der Goltz also bore the honorific title of Pasha.

17. Like almost everyone else in the German Army and Navy, Lossberg significantly overestimated the effect of submarine warfare. Nonetheless, the German submarine campaign did hurt Britain significantly, but not as badly as the British surface naval blockade hurt Germany.

18. Seeckt was Mackensen's chief of staff.

19. The Naval Corps consisted of two divisions of naval infantry, essentially the equivalent of the U.S. Marine Corps, or the British Royal Marines.

20. Now Pszczyna, Poland.

21. *Vollmacht,* which in the civilian context is translated as power of attorney, was a unique German military principle during World War I where a senior General Staff officer was given specific authority in emergency situations to issue direct orders to subordinate commanders in the name of the senior commander. It was used very sparingly, but as the war progressed Lossberg increasingly found himself entrusted with Vollmacht.

22. In December 1916, Tappen took command of the 5th Replacement Division, and in September 1917 he assumed command of the 15th Division. He retired from the Wehrmacht in August 1939 as a general of artillery.

23. An army task group (*Armeegruppe*) was somewhat larger than a field army, but not a full-fledged army group (*Heeresgruppe*). During World War I most army task groups were ad hoc and temporary organizations.

24. Now Neuville-Saint Rémy, France.

25. Despite its name, the Alpenkorps was a division-size unit.

26. Commanded by General of Infantry Ewald von Lochow.

27. Now Ablain-Saint Nazaire, France.

28. The nickname "Trench Devil" referred to his continual insistence on digging-in and constantly improving defensive positions.

29. A general of artillery (*General der Artillery*) was a rank title, equivalent to a lieutenant general in the British or American armies. At field army and above echelons, the general of the artillery (*General von der Artillery*) was the assigned duty position of the senior artillery officer, regardless of his actual rank. During Operation MICHAEL, for example, Georg Bruchmüller was the designated general of the artillery of the Eighteenth Army, although his actual rank was only colonel.

30. Commanded by Colonel General (later Field Marshal) August von Mackensen. Army Group Mackensen consisted of the German Ninth Army and the Danube Army, the Bulgarian Third Army, and the Ottoman VI Army Corps.

31. Commanded by General of Artillery Max von Gallwitz. Army Task Group Gallwitz was later designated the Twelfth Army.

32. The Germans considered Alsace part of Germany. They took Alsace and Lorraine from France during the Franco-Prussian War of 1870–1871. One of France's primary war aims during World War I was the recovery of both provinces. The French attacked into Alsace right at the beginning of the war in August 1914, but the Germans

quickly pushed them back into the Vosges Mountains, which were the western boundary of Alsace. The French dug in and until the end of the war held the crest ridge of the Vosges, which was just inside of Alsace.

33. The *Kaiserliches deutsches Generalgouvernement Belgien* was the military government of German-occupied Belgium during World War I.

34. Only the army headquarters, *Armeeoberkommando I* (A.O.K. I), was redeployed to the east to serve as a new command and control headquarters. The First Army's constituent corps remained in the west.

35. These units of the OHL reserve were not the same as the reserves of the individual armies. An army commander could commit his own reserves on his own authority, but he could not commit any of the OHL reserve units positioned to his rear without specific authority from OHL.

36. Now Sommepy-Tahure, France.

37. Now Souain-Perthes-lès Hurlus, France.

38. Officially, the Prussian and Bavarian Armies were separate organizations in peacetime, but they operated under a unified command structure in war. The Bavarian Army had its own General Staff and its own personnel management and officer promotion system.

39. During the remaining course of the war Lossberg changed his ideas on forward defense considerably, and he became one of the leading advocates of flexible defense.

40. The reason why it was such a high honor for a Bavarian general is that the 2nd Guards Division was a Prussian unit.

3. Chief of the General Staff of the Third Army (Champagne, 1915)

1. Only in the German Army did a chief of staff have such a degree of latitude and authority.

2. The 15th Reserve Division, commanded by General Eduard von Liebert.

3. The 16th Reserve Division, commanded by General Kurt von Ditfurth.

4. Commanded by General Carl Georg Wichura, commander of the 5th Reserve Division.

5. This was a destroyed village, now named Souain-Perthes-les-Hurlus, France.

6. Now Sommepy-Tahure, France.

7. At that point in the war, Prussia's Crown Prince Wilhelm was dual-hatted as the commander of both the Fifth Army and Army Group German Crown Prince. Later in the war Wilhelm and his staff were responsible for only the army group.

8. Now part of Vouziers and called Secteur de Blaise.

9. Such a situation was not at all unusual in the German Army, which practiced the principle that "position overrides rank." This approach was—and still is—unheard of in the British and American armies, and it is still practiced in today's Bundeswehr.

10. Now Souain-Perthes-lès-Hurlus, France.

11. This event is similar to another ammunition explosion in a rail tunnel shelter at Verdun on 4 September 1916.

12. Now Pontfaverger-Moronvilliers, France.

13. The gas was nonpersistent, which with careful timing allowed the attacking infantry to follow just as it dissipated.

14. In August 1914 the French XX Corps was commanded by General (later Marshal) Ferdinand Foch.

15. In twenty-first-century terms, this sounds like an appallingly high casualty rate, but for World War I it was quite moderate for a field army.

16. The primary purpose of a time fuze is to produce an air burst, as opposed to a point-detonating fuze, which produces a surface burst, or a delay fuze, which produces a subsurface burst.

17. During both World War I and World War II the Germans were masters of modifying captured enemy weapons and equipment and putting it back into service. During World War I, captured Russian guns with cut-down barrels were remounted on low-slung carriages with oversized wheels and assigned to infantry units down to the battalion level as individual infantry guns (*Infanterie-Geschütze*). These guns were not towed by horses. Rather, they were manhandled forward by their crews, following closely behind the second line of the first wave of the infantry attack.

18. In the cavalry, captains had the rank title of *Rittmeister*, rather than *Hauptmann* used by the other branches.

19. This is the first of the cycle of three Wallenstein plays by Friedrich Schiller.

20. The Battle of Skagerak is known to the Allies as Jutland. Despite Lossberg's enthusiastic comments, it was only a very thin tactical victory for the Germans. Simultaneously, it was a major strategic defeat. After Jutland, the German High Seas Fleet spent the rest of the war bottled up in its home ports.

21. The Fifth Army chief of staff was Lieutenant General Konstantin Schmidt von Knobelsdorf.

22. The ammunition was so called because of the green cross marking on the shell bodies. Green Cross shells were filled with either phosgene or chlorine. Both agents were lethal but nonpersistent.

23. The Battle of the Somme was a combined French-British operation, with the British carrying the main weight as the battle progressed. On 1 July alone, the British suffered almost sixty thousand casualties, approximately one-third of them dead.

4. Chief of the General Staff of the Second Army (The Somme, 1916)

1. The Germans at this point had not yet established army groups.

2. During World War I the Germans frequently formed ad hoc, temporary divisions in response to the tactical situation. Such units were named after their commanders. Division Frentz was commanded by Major General Emmerich Raitz von Frentz.

3. On 1 July 1916, the first day of the Allied Somme Offensive, the British attacked with thirteen divisions and the French with six divisions against the sector held by six divisions of the German Second Army. The day was a disaster for the Allies, especially the British. Despite putting the Second Army under severe pressure, the British alone suffered 57,470 casualties on that single day, including 19,240 who were either killed in action or later died of wounds. The French suffered approximately 7,000 total

casualties, and the Germans approximately 8,000 casualties, plus another 4,200 taken prisoner.

4. Falkenhayn was the chief of the German General Staff and de facto commander in chief on the Western Front.

5. The Ia was the operations officer.

6. The Ib was the logistics and movements officer.

7. German doctrine recognized two distinctly different types of counterattack: the *Gegenstoss* (hasty counterattack) and the *Gegenangriff* (deliberate counterattack).

8. One of the primary objectives of the Allied and especially British attack on the Somme in July 1916 was to provide relief to the French forces who had been defending Verdun against massive German attacks since February 1916. The Verdun operation had been Falkenhayn's plan to bleed the French Army dry. Ultimately it failed, leading to Falkenhayn's dismissal as chief of the General Staff in late August 1916.

9. *Ordonnanz* officers were administrative staff officers. They were not qualified General Staff officers, and almost always worked under the direct supervision of a General Staff officer. Only a very small percentage of the officers on any given staff were General Staff officers.

10. The General Staff officer IIa was the chief administrative and personnel officer.

11. Roughly less than half of the senior commanders in the German Army were qualified General Staff officers themselves. Attendance at the *Kriegsakademie* and qualification as a General Staff officer were not requirements for promotion to high command. Likewise, qualification as a General Staff officer was not in itself a guarantee for promotion to senior rank. In contrast, the U.S. Army today requires all officers to complete the Command and General Staff College to qualify for promotion to lieutenant colonel.

12. Division Liebert was a temporary division.

13. Hydrogen-filled observations balloons were dangerous to be in and around. They often exploded when shot. Near the end of the war some balloon observers had parachutes, but they were worthless if the balloon exploded. But balloons also were difficult and dangerous to shoot down. Because they were stationary, an aircraft pilot had to shoot the balloon from straight on, while flying directly at it. If he was too close when it exploded, the blast would bring him down, too.

14. A machine gun company was a regimental-level asset. A machine gun marksman battalion (*Maschinengewehr-Scharfschützen-Abteilung*) was part of the OHL Reserve, attached to frontline divisions as the situation required.

15. Division Dumrath was a temporary division commanded by Major General Konrad Dumrath.

16. The French North African colonial troops generally were respected by the Germans for their fighting ability.

17. Jäger were German light infantry.

18. At that time a typical German division had only one qualified General Staff officer assigned to the divisional headquarters. He functioned as a combined chief of staff and operations officer.

5. Chief of the General Staff of the First Army (The Somme, 1916)

1. After the war Manstein again served under Lossberg, when in 1919 the latter was the chief of staff of Command Group II, one of only two postwar army-level formations in the Reichwehr. Manstein served in World War II as a field marshal. Many historians consider him to have been the greatest German general of World War II.

2. Now Ferme de Maurepas, France, and Hem-Monacu, France, respectively.

3. Monacu Farm was known to the French as Ferme de Monacu.

4. The Battle of Cambrai, 20 November to 7 December 1917.

5. Mouquet Farm was known in French as Ferme du Mouquet.

6. Schleinitz retired as a lieutenant general in 1930.

7. As of the 14 August conference, the Battle of the Somme was still in progress. It lasted from 1 July to 18 November 1916.

8. Italy entered the war on the side of the Entente on 23 May 1915.

9. The German High Command was called OHL (*Oberste Heeresleitung*), while the Austrian High Command was called AOK (*Armeeoberkommando*). This can be confusing at times, because AOK in the German Army meant the headquarters of a field army.

10. The Sixth Battle of the Isonzo was fought between 6 and 17 August 1916.

11. This was the Russian Brusilov Offensive, 4 June to 20 September 1916.

12. By the end of 1917 there were two basic types of German divisions on the Western Front. The trench divisions (*Stellungsdivisionen*) were trained, organized, and equipped to hold the front lines. The attack divisions (*Angriffsdivisionen*) were trained, organized, and equipped for offensive operations. They were far more mobile than the trench divisions, and generally manned by younger men. The attack divisions were held in the rear and only moved into the front lines just prior to an attack. They also were the primary forces used for the deliberate counterattacks. During a major attack the trench divisions were capable of advancing in the follow-on echelons to provide support to the advancing attack divisions.

13. By 1918 Germany's premier artilleryman, Colonel Georg Bruchmüller, had perfected the system of integrating the light field artillery guns and the heavier foot artillery guns into effective fire support groups and subgroups. See David T. Zabecki, *Steel Wind: Colonel Georg Bruchmüller and the Birth of Modern Artillery* (Westport, Conn.: Praeger, 1994).

14. The pure defensive is a passive rather than an active defense.

15. The Kaiser was the titular commander in chief of the German Army. De facto command rested with the chief of the General Staff, who was now Hindenburg. Ludendorff as first quartermaster general was, in today's terms, the vice chief of the General Staff.

16. It was published in English translation as *General Headquarters 1914–1916 and Its Critical Decisions.*

17. OHL under Hindenburg and Ludendorff was called the "Third OHL." The "First OHL" was under Moltke the Younger, and the "Second OHL" was under Falkenhayn.

18. During the Battle of Verdun, the storm troop battalion commanded by Captain Willy Rohr had taken over as the Fifth Army's training unit for the newly emerging "storm troop tactics," also known more correctly as infiltration tactics.

19. Now Bouchavesnes-Bergen, France.

20. Commanded by General of Infantry Dedo von Schenck zu Schweinberg, commanding general of the XVIII Army Corps.

21. The Germans later designated that major defensive line as the Siegfried Position (*Siegfriedstellung*). The Allies called it the Hindenburg Line. Curiously, what the Allies in World War II called the Siegfried Line, the Germans themselves called the West Wall.

22. Lossberg calls them *Infanterie-Flieger*, but by 1918 close air support (ground attack) squadrons were called *Schlachtstaffeln*.

23. Instituted by Landgrave Friedrich II of Hesse in February 1769, the *Militär-Verdienstorden* (Order of Military Merit) was Hesse's highest military decoration. Originally called the *Pour la Vertu Militaire*, its design was almost identical to Prussia's *Pour le Mérite*.

24. 1770 *Füsilier-Regiment Lossberg*; 1780 *Füsilier-Regiment Alt-Lossberg*.

25. The 51st Reserve Division was commanded by Lieutenant General William Balck, father of the future General of Panzer Troops Hermann Balck, one of World War II's greatest Panzer commanders. See Hermann Balck, *Order in Chaos: The Memoirs of General of Panzer Troops Hermann Balck*, translated and edited by David T. Zabecki and Dieter Biedekarken (Lexington: Univ. Press of Kentucky, 2015).

26. Lossberg calls them *Schützengraben-Kanonen*, but by 1918 such guns were designated infantry guns (*Infantrie-Geschütz-Kanonen*).

27. Now Sailly-Saillisel, France.

28. During the German offensives in the spring of 1918 the Germans used several British tanks that they had captured and put back into service with German markings.

29. Literally, the Supreme War Lord.

30. Boelcke was flying his sixth sortie of the day with his two best pilots, Manfred von Richthofen and Erwin Böhme, and three others. During a dogfight with British aircraft, Böhme's landing gear hit Boelcke's upper wing.

31. The British Expeditionary Force started the war in 1914 with a regular army structure of only six divisions. By late 1916 the BEF had fifty-six divisions, but a large number of those were the "Kitchener's Army" divisions, hastily raised and trained starting at the end of 1914. For many of those units, the Battle of the Somme was their first real test of combat. On the other hand, Lossberg here is overstating the experience and training of the German Army in late 1916. The German regular army that started the war in 1914 also had been ground down by more than two years of war, and its ranks were starting to fill up with called-up older reservists and young conscripts.

32. France's Neville Offensive of April 1917 failed primarily because of a poor operations plan, poor security, and poor leadership on the part of the then-French commander in chief, General Robert Neville. The failure of the offensive led directly to the widespread French Army mutinies of that year.

33. Over the course of the war the designations of the various aviation units changed. By 1918 a fighter squadron was a *Jadgstaffel*, a bomber squadron was a *Kampfstaffel*, and a close air support (ground attack) squadron was a *Schlachtstaffel*.

34. By the time he was killed, Boelcke had forty air-to-air kills. But he also was the

first and most influential of the air combat tacticians. His combat rules, called *Boelcke Dicta,* were derived from the first systematic analysis of aerial combat.

35. Manfred von Richthofen, universally known as the Red Baron, was the highest-scoring ace of World War I, with eighty kills. His brother, Lothar, had forty kills. Lothar survived the war, Manfred did not.

36. Göring had twenty-two kills in World War I. After Manfred von Richthofen was shot down, Göring assumed command of his 1st Fighter Wing (*Jagdgeschwader* 1), popularly known as the Flying Circus.

37. German defensive positions were organized into three zones. The outpost zone (*Vorfeldzone*) was five hundred to one thousand meters in depth and manned with sparsely located early warning positions. The battle zone (*Kampffeld*) was up to two thousand meters deep. And the rearward zone (*Hinterzone*) was where the reserves and counterattack units were held, often in deep, reinforced bunkers. The leading edge of the battle zone was the main line of resistance (*Hauptwiderstandslinie*), with three or more successive trench lines. Between the battle zone and the rearward zone came another line of multiple trenches that served as the protective line for the artillery. The Germans held their forwardmost lines with minimal strength. While the French were putting two-thirds of their combat strength into the first two lines, the Germans put only 20 percent into the same positions.

38. Now Wrocław, Poland.

39. This was a significant turnaround for Ludendorff. Until they took over at OHL in July 1916, Hindenburg and Ludendorff had been at the forefront of Germany's "Easterners," arguing that the defeat of Russia would decide the outcome of the war. Once at OHL, they became staunch "Westerners."

40. Precision fire is directed against a point target. Normally, artillery fire is area fire, designed to bracket an entire area and everything in it.

41. Such soldiers were classified as "garrison service capable" (*garnisondienstfähig*).

42. The standard German heavy machine gun was the MG 08. The light machine gun variant was the MG 08/15, which was man-portable.

43. Germany conducted its first period of unrestricted submarine warfare from 28 February to 1 September 1915.

44. Wever was an early proponent of strategic bombing. When he was killed in an air crash in 1936, all German efforts to build a strategic bomber force died with him.

45. Now Bad Kreuznach, Germany.

46. An army detachment was somewhat less than a full field army, but significantly more than a single corps.

47. To this day, historians criticize the German Army for its harsh scorched-earth policy during Operation ALBERICH.

6. Chief of the General Staff of the Sixth Army (Arras, 1917)

1. Asking Ludendorff for Vollmacht over the heads of the army and army group commanders was an unprecedented action. The normal procedure for a General Staff officer was to request Vollmacht from his immediate commander. Yet, the situation was

so desperate that Lossberg believed he needed that authority immediately, which gave a mere colonel de facto command of the Sixth Army. When Kuhl learned about it he said, "If anyone can straighten out this tangle, he will." Such was Lossberg's reputation within the German Army at that point.

2. The creeping barrage was a technique used to support the infantry during the initial assault from their own line of departure to the enemy's lines. A wall of artillery fire moved forward slowly on a fixed schedule, with the infantry following behind as closely as possible. The intent was to keep the enemy defenders buttoned-up in their deep underground bunkers until the attacking friendly enemy was almost on top of them.

3. By this stage of the war the artillery preparations for major attacks could last up to two weeks. Such prolonged firing, of course, sacrificed surprise.

4. Now Ligny-Thilloy, France.

5. This is possibly an error. Geographically, Arleux does not fit into this line. It is too far east.

6. Otto von Below was the cousin of General of Infantry Fritz von Below.

7. Rather than a second award, the Oak Leaves represented the higher level of the Pour le Mérite. The Oak Leaves were awarded only 122 times during World War I.

8. The chief of the General Staff was Hindenburg.

9. Lossberg's memoirs were published in 1939. Von Below died in 1944.

10. Lossberg is describing the French Army's disastrous Nivelle Offensive of 16 April to 9 May 1917. Some of what he says in this paragraph is not correct. The mutinies did not start until 3 May. A total of forty-nine divisions were affected in some way, of which nine were completely combat ineffective and another twenty-five were seriously degraded. Despite what Lossberg writes about the mutinies being put down "with brutal force," Petain restored order within the French Army with a very light touch, and by improving significantly the conditions of the average soldier. Although courts-martial passed 629 death sentences on the leaders of the mutinies, only forty-three were carried out. On the other hand, the Germans seemed to have no knowledge of the condition of the French Army until it was well under way to being reconstituted. It was one of the biggest intelligence failures in the history of warfare.

11. Although the resumption of unrestricted submarine warfare imposed severe economic hardships on Great Britain, it also brought America into the war on the side of the Entente.

12. Both the 7.7cm *Feldkanone* 16 and the 10.5cm *leichte Feldhaubitze* 16 had approximately three thousand meters greater range than their respective late nineteenth-century predecessor models.

13. In the English language literature this is known as the Battle of Messines, during which the British took the Messines–Wytschaete Ridge. The Battle of Messines, from 7 to 14 June 1917, was a preliminary operation to the bloody Third Battle of Ypres, also known as the Battle of Passchendaele.

7. Chief of the General Staff of the Fourth Army (Flanders, 1917)

1. The artillery, engineer, and aviation advisors on a corps staff were the corps' senior officers in those specialty branches. They were seldom qualified General Staff offi-

cers. Although technically they were not the commanders of those functions, they nonetheless wielded extensive authority.

2. There is a distinct difference between the concepts of break-in (*einbrechen*) and break-through (*durchbrechen*). During World War I on the Western Front it was always possible to break into an enemy's position. Breaking through was almost impossible because of defense in depth and the limited mobility of the attacker.

3. What the Germans called the Battle of Flanders the Allies called the Third Battle of Ypres—more popularly known as Passchendaele.

4. Machine gun marksmen were assault machine gunners, specially trained for the attack. As Lossberg indicates, they were positioned well to the rear during the defensive and used only for special missions, such as air defense fire for artillery batteries.

5. Rather than the disintegrating link belts of machine gun ammunition used today, World War I machine gun belts were made of cotton web and were reused after the rounds were expended. When they became wet the belts tended to expand in thickness, jamming the guns.

6. At the height of a battle, telephone wires are very vulnerable to enemy artillery fire and other battlefield hazards.

7. The Germans called a very heavy howitzer larger than 240mm a Mörser. These were nothing like an infantry mortar or a trench mortar, which was a *Minenwerfer.*

8. Flat-trajectory (*Flachfeuer*) batteries were guns rather than howitzers. Guns had longer ranges than howitzers of the same caliber, but howitzers were more accurate.

9. As the war progressed, each division in the front line was supported by a six-aircraft *Fliegerabteilung* for aerial observation and liaison.

10. Originally the mission of the *Schutzstaffel* was to provide security for the *Fliegerabteilung,* especially from ground fire. By 1918 the *Schutzstaffel* had evolved into the *Schlachtstaffel,* whose mission was solely ground attack. Meanwhile, air superiority was the mission of the fighter squadron (*Jagdstaffel*).

11. In modern terminology this would be called reinforcing fires.

12. The mission of the fighter squadrons was air superiority.

13. In preparation for an assault, the attack divisions moved up into the front lines occupied by the trench divisions and then advanced from that line of departure. The trench divisions then followed and supported the attack divisions. When the attack reached culmination, the trench divisions then moved forward through the lines of attack divisions and established the new defensive line.

14. Lossberg's comment belies the stereotype of the German soldier as an unthinking automaton trained only to follow specific orders.

15. This was true at the time, but as the war progressed the Allies learned to commit tanks en masse, supported by artillery and covered by infantry. The first such coordinated use on a large scale was at Cambrai in November 1917.

16. The Naval Corps was a two-division corps of German marine infantry, operating in Flanders. Schröder was the corps commander.

17. Combat groups were ad hoc organizations assembled for specific missions. At a minimum they consisted of a standing corps, reinforced with additional combat assets.

18. After commanding the 11th Fighter Squadron (*Jagdstaffel* 11), Richthofen commanded the 1st Fighter Wing (*Jagdgeschwader* 1) from 24 June 1917 until his death on 21 April 1918. The 1st Fighter Wing became famous as "von Richthofen's Flying Circus." On 7 July 1918, Hermann Göring assumed command of the 1st Fighter Wing.

19. This is a reference to the physical massing of artillery, where the wheel hub of one gun is almost directly against the wheel hub of the adjacent gun.

20. Actually, the Allied artillery preparation started on 18 July and ran for thirteen days. During that period the British guns fired some 2 million rounds.

21. In the German armies of World Wars I and II, the rank of *Generalmajor* was the equivalent of a brigadier general in the U.S. Army.

22. The British intent was to exploit any break-in with the cavalry divisions and turn it into a breakthrough.

23. Now Langemark-Poelkapelle, Belgium.

24. During World Wars I and II, a German officer candidate (*Fähnrich*) served out his final period prior to commissioning as a probationary "third lieutenant" with a unit. Thus, unlike most other armies, German officer candidates often served in direct combat.

25. Bernhard von Lossberg served during World War II as a major general in the Wehrmacht's command staff.

26. The German Eighth Army's capture of the Baltic port of Riga on 3 September 1917 effectively neutralized Russia as a military force in World War I.

27. The resulting attack was the Caporetto Offensive (Twelfth Battle of the Isonzo, 24 October–12 November 1917).

28. The islands are now called Saaremaa, Muhu, and Hiiumaa, respectively. The German attack was designated Operation ALBION. It was the first fully coordinated attack ever conducted by the German Army and Navy.

29. *À la suite* promotions could mean various things in the German Army of the time. Essentially, such a promotion was honorary, with no increase in pay. Lossberg had been promoted from colonel to major general on 3 August 1917. His *à la suite* promotion to general directly under the Kaiser was the equivalent of an honorary appointment as one of the Kaiser's aides de camp.

30 Lyncker was the chief of the Kaiser's military cabinet, which controlled all officer personnel management in the German Army.

31. This peace accord was the harsh and draconian Treaty of Brest-Litovsk.

32. In fact, the U-boat campaign of World War I was a complete failure strategically, and the German surface fleet, the High Seas Fleet, was bottled up in its own ports by 1918.

33. Lossberg is absolutely correct in this assessment. By 1918 the Kaiser was an even less significant figurehead than he had been at the start of the war, and Hindenburg rarely interfered with Ludendorff or even interjected himself into the planning and decision-making processes.

34. In the event, Ludendorff came to the opposite conclusion on timing and ordered the start of the Operation MICHAEL offensive for 21 March 1918.

35. The Germans routinely organized Leaders' Reserves (*Führerreserven*) that moved

forward behind the leading echelons, prepared to assume command of units as officer casualties mounted.

36. Note Lossberg's critical distinction here between a tactical breakthrough and an operational breakthrough.

37. Lossberg frequently calls Operation MICHAEL, launched on 21 March 1918, the Great Battle of France.

38. Operation MARS, launched on 28 March 1918, was a failed attempt to restore operational momentum to the MICHAEL attack.

39. Lossberg's Fourth Army was north of the Operation MICHAEL sector. From north to south, the attack was conducted by the Seventeenth, Second, and Eighteenth Armies.

40. The Seventeenth Army in the north and the Second Army in the center were under Army Group Crown Prince Rupprecht of Bavaria. The Eighteenth Army in the south was under Army Group German Crown Prince.

41. At the start of Operation MICHAEL the mission of the Eighteenth Army in the south was to screen the attack of the main effort by the Second Army in the center, and block the movement northward of French reinforcements to support the British. Instead, the Eighteenth Army exceeded its objectives almost immediately and advanced farther and faster than either the Second Army or the Seventeenth Army in the north. Ludendorff, on the principle of reinforcing success, then shifted the main effort to the Eighteenth. But although reinforcing success is a sound principle at the tactical level, it is always far more difficult and not necessarily the correct course of action at the operational level.

42. Those forces were the bulk of the British Expeditionary Force, the destruction of which was the primary objective of Operation MICHAEL.

43. Originally planned as Operation GEORG, by the time Operation MICHAEL failed too few forces remained to execute the original plan. A reduced version of the plan then became Operation GEORGETTE.

44. That section is known as the Flanders Hills, north of Hazebrouck and south of Ypres.

45. The Fourth Army was to the north of the Sixth Army, which itself was north of the Seventeenth Army. The Seventeenth had participated in the MICHAEL Offensive.

46. Yellow Cross gas was commonly known as mustard gas. It was both persistent and lethal. Green Cross and Blue Cross gas were nonpersistent, meaning that they dissipated fairly rapidly. Green Cross was lethal, while Blue Cross was nonlethal but incapacitating.

47. The reason that the attacks started a day apart was that the German Army at that point did not have enough OHL-level heavy artillery to support both attacks simultaneously. After firing in support of the Fourth Army's initial assault, the heavy guns had to be shifted north rapidly to support the initial attack of the Fourth Army the following day. See Zabecki, *Steel Wind,* 78–80.

48. During the four 1918 offensives following the failure of Operation MICHAEL, the Germans increasingly were forced to commit trench divisions in the attack. This was a role for which the soldiers were neither trained nor equipped.

49. Now Mesen, Belgium.

50. The firing positions were predesignated and surveyed in. Ammunition was pre-stocked, and the positions were wired for communications. All the guns had to do was occupy their designated positions and they would be ready to fire. See Zabecki, *Steel Wind*, 78–80.

51. Now Nieuwkerke, Belgium.

52. Ludendorff at noon on 12 April actually issued the order to direct the main effort toward Bailleul and then Mont Kemmel. In doing so, however, he changed the entire operational scheme of maneuver for Operation GEORGETTE, condemning the attack to failure. The Germans were within five miles of Hazebrouck, which was one of the two most critical rail centers in the British logistics network. If Hazebrouck had fallen, it would have been disastrous for the BEF. But when Ludendorff shifted the attack to the northwest rather than the west, the German advance swung east of Hazebrouck, giving the British sufficient time to reinforce the units defending the town. In the end the Germans did capture Mont Kemmel, but GEORGETTE culminated as another tactical success and operational failure. See Zabecki, *The German 1918 Offensives*, 203.

53. In most of the German offensives of 1918, the attacking forces diverged rather than converged as they advanced, thus dissipating rather than concentrating their combat power. It was one of the most significant operational errors of the Ludendorff offensives.

54. Mont Noir (153 meters) is one of the Flanders Hills, immediately to the west of Mont Kimmel (156 meters).

55. The authorized strength of a German infantry regiment was 3,204 men and 193 officers.

56. As a young platoon leader in the Alpenkorps, the future General of Panzer Troops Hermann Balck took part in the seizure of Mont Kemmel. See Herman Balck, *Order in Chaos: The Memoirs of General of Panzer Troops Herman Balck*, translated and edited by David T. Zabecki and Dieter Biedekarken (Lexington: Univ. Press of Kentucky, 2015), 81–86.

57. Accompanying artillery (*Infantriebegleitartillerie*) were light field guns mounted on special carriages with oversized wheels. In the attack they were manhandled forward by their crews, keeping as close as possible to the advancing infantry. When assets were available, one four-gun accompanying battery was attached to each first echelon regiment in the main penetration sector. Such units usually were equipped with the older Model 1896 n/A 77mm field gun. Since everything was pushed forward by manpower, the accompanying guns could only carry very limited amounts of ammunition.

58. Controversy continues to this day over who or what brought down the Red Baron (known in Germany as *Der Rote Kampfflieger*). The Royal Air Force officially credited Canada's Captain Arthur Roy Brown with the kill. Historians today generally agree that Richthofen was killed by ground fire from a machine gun.

59. OHL, the German Army's senior command headquarters in the field, had no authority over the German Navy.

60. The ultimate objective of Operation HAGEN was to seize the BEF's channel

ports, and in the process drive the BEF off the Continent. The Germans would then turn south and defeat the French in detail before a critical mass of freshly arriving American divisions could tip the strategic balance. Planned and prepared in great detail, Operation HAGEN was never launched. See David T. Zabecki, *The German 1918 Offensives: A Case Study in the Operational Level of War* (London: Routledge, 2006), 280–310.

61. The Operation BLÜCHER (27 May–5 June 1918) diversionary attack was an impressive tactical success, but an operational failure. The follow-on Operation GNEISENAU (9–15 June 1918) diversionary attack failed both operationally and tactically. The failure of the further follow-on Operation MARNESCHUTZ-REIMS (15–18 July) diversionary attack was a complete strategic reversal for the Germans. Operation HAGEN was cancelled, and the Germans remained on the defensive for the remainder of the war.

62. Those heavy guns were shifted south to support the diversionary attacks designed to withdraw the French reinforcements from Flanders. The intent was to shift the guns back north to support Operation HAGEN when it was launched.

63. The force transfer system was called *Y-Transport*. For the details of the plan, see Zabecki, *The German 1918 Offensives*, 297–300.

64. The German attack culminated at that point. They had captured a huge sector of territory, but were then left defending an almost indefensible salient. They also failed to draw the French reinforcements away from Flanders.

65. This was Operation GNEISENAU.

66. The average American division in World War I was twice as large as the standard French, British, or German divisions. One of the main reasons for the large divisions is that the rapidly and greatly expanded U.S. Army did not have enough senior commanders and trained staff officers to command and control more divisions. However, the large American divisions proved to be very unwieldy in actual combat.

67. The worldwide influenza pandemic of 1918 infected some 500 million people and killed an estimated 50 to 100 million—3 to 5 percent of the world's population.

68. This was Operation MARNESCHUTZ-REIMS.

69. This intended attack by the Fourth and Sixth Armies was Operation HAGEN.

70. The main reason for the MARNESCHUTZ-REIMS attack was that there was only one rail line that ran across the northern base of the huge salient created by Operation BLÜCHER and the entrances on both ends of that rail line at Reims and Compiègne were in Allied-held territory. The German forces inside the salient could not be supplied properly. By capturing the key rail junction city of Reims through a double envelopment, the Germans would open up that line. MARNESCHUTZ-REIMS, however, was a complete operational failure from the first day.

71. This was the standard German excuse all throughout the post–World War I years for the failure of Operation MARNESCHUTZ-REIMS. And although information from German deserters and prisoners of war helped to fill in the details, as it does for any intelligence assessment, Allied intelligence and the senior Allied commanders, Petain and Foch, correctly assessed the situation and forecast the most probable German course of action. They then established the French defense for 15 July 1918 accordingly.

72. Lossberg's explanation of the French defenses is too simplistic and partially incor-

rect. Only the French Fifth Army, east of Reims, established a deep defense in depth. Because of the nature of the terrain, the French Ninth Army to the west of Reims established a forward defense along the Marne River. Also, Allied commander in chief Foch was not an advocate of defense in depth, but French Army commander in chief Pétain was.

73. The preparations were for Operation HAGEN, which by the morning of 18 July Ludendorff still intended to launch, despite the dismal failure of MARNESCHUTZ-REIMS.

74. Ludendorff finally fired Wetzell in September 1918, making him the scapegoat for his own failings. Nonetheless, Wetzell went on to a successful postwar career. From 1926 to 1927 he served as the chief of the Truppenamt (Troop Office), the interwar clandestine German General Staff. Wetzell retired as a general of infantry.

75. This was Operation MICHAEL.

76. Interestingly, Lossberg does not include the Sixth Army and his own Fourth Army.

77. This refers to Operation HAGEN.

78. The original plan for Operation HAGEN was based on twenty-six attack divisions, supported by thirteen trench divisions. On 19 July OHL withdrew four of those attack divisions from Army Group Crown Prince Rupprecht to support the Seventh Army in Champagne. On 20 July OHL withdrew another three attack divisions from Flanders, leaving only nineteen available for HAGEN. See Zabecki, *The German 1918 Offensives*, 280–295.

79. Lossberg is referring to Hindenburg.

80. Many historians have speculated that either Hermann von Kuhl or Hans von Seeckt would have made a far better first quartermaster general at this point.

81. In 1919 Reinhardt became the last Prussian minister of war, and later the first head of the army command (*Chef der Heeresleitung*) of the Weimar Republic. He was forced to resign after he supported the Kapp-Lüttwitz Putsch in 1920.

82. Blomberg later became a field marshal, minister of war under the Third Reich, and commander in chief of the German armed forces until January 1938. He was forced out of office in disgrace by Hitler during the Blomberg-Fritsch Affair, in which Blomberg was falsely accused of marrying a former prostitute. Hitler assumed personal command of the Wehrmacht after Blomberg's fall.

83. That is exactly what happened when the British attacked near Amiens on 8 August 1918.

84. Ludendorff called 8 August 1918 "The Black Day of the German Army" and believed that was the turning point of the war. Many British historians also refer to 8 August as "the day we won the war." Lossberg, however, is right. After the French attacked with American support on 18 July, the operational and strategic initiative passed into Allied hands, and the Germans never again came close to seizing it.

8. Chief of the General Staff of Army Group Boehn

1. In September 1918 Stülpnagel replaced Lieutenant Colonel Georg Wetzell as chief of the Operations Department at OHL. In 1931 Stülpnagel left active duty as a general of infantry. In the winter of 1932–1933 he served briefly as minister of war in the

Papen-Hitler government. In 1939 he was reactivated as the commander of the Replacement Army, but he was released within a matter of days after calling Hitler's war policy a disaster. In July 1944 Stülpnagel was implicated along with his cousin General of Infantry Carl-Heinrich von Stülpnagel in the plot to assassinate Hitler and was arrested. He was released after a short period of detention, but his cousin was executed at Plötzensee Prison in August 1944.

2. Now Hénin-Beaumont, France.

3. On 12 September 1918 the American Expeditionary Force, under General John J. Pershing, launched the Saint-Mihiel Offensive to clear the salient. It was the AEF's first major combat operation of the war. The Americans closed to the Michael Position by 15 September and considered the operation a great success. The Germans, however, had been conducting the evacuation for four days by the time the Americans struck.

4. On 26 September 1918, the U.S. First Army, supported by the French Fourth Army, launched the Meuse–Argonne Offensive. It was the largest battle fought by the U.S. Army to that time. The battle only ended with the armistice on 11 November 1918.

5. Lossberg misstates Ludendorff's role in his resignation. He, in fact, had little choice in the matter. On 24 October Ludendorff issued an army-wide memo saying that U.S. president Woodrow Wilson's Third Note to the German government was an unacceptable demand for unconditional surrender, and therefore a challenge to German soldiers to continue the resistance. The memo caused a political firestorm in Berlin, forcing the Kaiser to request Ludendorff's resignation.

6. Most military historians today would agree that Ludendorff was a gifted tactician and organizer. As a strategist, however, he was a total failure. Even as a commander on the operational level he had serious shortcomings.

7. After Ludendorff was forced to resign on 26 October, he and Hindenburg hardly ever spoke to one another again. Ludendorff always had a streak of religious mysticism. During the war he frequently looked into his Moravian Brethren prayer book for inspiration on the immediate military problem facing him. After the war he became anti-Christian, embracing worship of the ancient Nordic gods, and railed against Jews and Freemasons. During this last period of his life he shared many of the official ideologies of National Socialism, but in the end he even turned against the Nazis for not being Germanic enough.

8. Bernhard von Lossberg served during World War II as a major general, directly under Colonel General Alfred Jodel on the Wehrmacht Command Staff. Captured by the British at the end of the war, he was released from captivity in January 1947. He died in Wiesbaden, Germany, in March 1965, at the age of sixty-six.

9. Chief of the General Staff of Army Group Duke Albrecht of Württemberg

1. Germany up until the end of World War I was a confederation of four kingdoms (Prussia, Bavaria, Saxony, and Württemberg), several grand duchies, such as Baden, and numerous minor principalities, all with their hereditary ruling families. All those dynasties came to an end in November 1918.

2. It seems odd that Lossberg could have written this as late as 1939.

3. The armistice took effect at 1100 hours in the Paris time zone, which was 1200 hours in the Berlin time zone. Throughout the war the German Army on the Western Front operated on the Berlin time zone.

10. After the War

1. Now Wrocław, Poland.

2. Now Piła, Poland.

3. Now Bydgoszcz, Poland.

4. The *Freikorps* (Free Corps) were German volunteer right-wing paramilitary units formed immediately after World War I. Many such units served in border security roles under army control. Others, however, battled similar left-wing paramilitary groups inside Germany during the turbulent early years of the Weimar Republic.

5. Now Rawicz, Poland.

6. Lossberg's personal assistant as chairman of the commission was Captain (later Field Marshal) Erich von Manstein. In August 1916 Manstein had served under Lossberg as General Staff officer Ib (Supply) when Lossberg was chief of staff of the First Army during the Battle of the Somme. Mungo Melvin, *Manstein: Hitler's Greatest General* (London: Weidenfeld and Nicolson, 2010), 28, 40.

7. This was equivalent to a major general in the American and British armies.

8. After years of repeated German defaults on World War I reparation payments, which often were met with Allied threats of occupation, the German default of coal deliveries on 9 January 1923 proved to be the impetus for the French and Belgian military occupation of Germany's industrial Ruhr District on 11 January 1923. The occupation proved internationally controversial and divisive among the Allies. It lasted until 25 August 1925.

9. This was equivalent to a lieutenant general in the American and British armies.

10. Lossberg died in Lübeck, Germany, on 14 May 1942, at the age of seventy-four.

Appendix A: Lossberg's Chronology

This section is adapted from "Chronologies of German General Officers," Bundesarchiv/Militärarchiv, Freiburg, Germany, File MSg 109/10849.

Appendix C: The Prussian/German Staff System, 1806–1918

1. This section is adapted from David T. Zabecki, ed., *Chief of Staff: The Principle Officers Behind History's Great Commanders,* vol. 1, *Napoleonic Wars to World War I* (Annapolis, Md.: U.S. Naval Institute Press, 2008), 5–13.

2. The Bundeswehr's primary training school for General Staff officers is today called the *Führungsakademie* (Leadership Academy).

3. The Bundeswehr still uses the i.G. designation for its qualified General Staff officers.

Index of Military Units

Subject Index

www.ingramcontent.com/pod-product-compliance
Lightning Source LLC
LaVergne TN
LVHW050146080826
844660LV00002B/94

* 9 7 8 0 8 1 3 1 6 9 8 0 4 *